P9-CTQ-759

The
Human Personality

JEROME L. SINGER
Yale University

Under the General Editorship of
JEROME KAGAN
Harvard University

Harcourt Brace Jovanovich, Publishers
San Diego   New York   Chicago   Washington, D.C.   Atlanta
London   Sydney   Toronto

To Dorothy, Jon, Jeff, Bruce, Tarah, and Cory

Copyright © 1984 by Harcourt Brace Jovanovich, Inc.

ISBN: 0-15-540390-7
Library of Congress Catalog Card Number: 83-81890
Printed in the United States of America

Text and illustration credits appear on pages 468–469, which constitute a continuation of the copyright page.

Preface

The Human Personality is an introduction to one of the most exciting and challenging areas in the behavioral sciences. This book is designed to channel students' natural curiosity about their own and others' personalities into a consideration of how human variation can be systematically and rigorously investigated. Its chief objective is to convey to students my deep conviction that the humanity we all share is not only compatible with but essential to the scientific enterprise—the thrill of theory development, fact-finding, and hypothesis testing.

A fundamental premise of this textbook is that the study of personality is best understood as a natural outgrowth of basic psychology. Although important concepts have evolved from the clinical observations of early theorists such as Freud, Jung, and Sullivan, the current work in personality theory and research—including the study of physiological and motivational systems, the new research on emotion, the emergence of cognition as a central field, and the important work currently underway in developmental and social psychology—lies closer to the methods and findings of general psychology. Personality research is distinguished from general psychology at those points where individual variation in experience or expressive action reflects the functioning of the emotional and cognitive systems. This book thus pays considerable attention to issues of personal style—how we process and retrieve information, react to danger or threat, cope with interpersonal conflict, and demonstrate curiosity, excitement, joy, and love.

The text is organized around a distinction between the *private* personality of self-consciousness, memories, fantasies, and dreams, and the *public* personality of individual variation in our direct confrontations with our physical and social environment. The book places more emphasis on private experiences of emotions and dreams than most introductory texts, perhaps, but always in the context of their importance for objective research and measurement of inner life. Another special emphasis in this text is on the normal personality. While no one doubts the importance of the contributions that have emerged from clinical explorations with severely disturbed people, the early personality theorists created an imbalance in our perspective on human variation. In this text, most of the material is oriented toward personality patterns easily recognizable by students and toward research and quasi-clinical methods applicable to our daily lives rather than to the special settings of mental hospitals or psychoanalytic consulting rooms. Naturally, I have included references and case material from extreme situations, as well as a review of the clinical methods used to change personality, but I have made a considerable effort to differentiate personality research from the study of psychopathology.

Introducing students to the current complexity and sophistication of modern psychometrics and experimental or field-survey methods is a sensitive task. Even before reviewing the range of current research and assessment methods (Chapter 7), in the discussions of the early theorists I have alerted students to the necessity of hypothesis testing, objectivity, and replicability of research findings. While I have not highlighted personological study of the type associated with Henry A. Murray or Robert M. White, I have tried to show the value of such approaches within the broader framework. In examining the development of personality I have also tried to emphasize the importance of observation and experiment with children as an important alternative to retrospective accounts by adult patients, which still form a basis for so much theorizing by psychoanalytically oriented theorists. But I have also introduced students to the necessity of life-span approaches in the study of adult personality as a corrective for cross-sectional or time-limited experimental methods.

After an introduction to the general study of personality, Part 1 traces the shift in emphasis on the private personality from the work of Freud and Jung through the increasing concern with social-environmental influences of the Neo-Freudians, the social-learning theorists, and the existentialists—the humanistic "Third Force" of psychology—who sought to avoid reductionism and denigration of the constructive and self-creating capacities of the person. Finally, the emergence of a cognitive orientation and the new work on cognitive-affective relationships are represented by the early work of Kurt Lewin and Fritz Heider and the current emphases of Richard Lazarus, Silvan Tomkins, and Carroll Izard, among others. The text suggests the move toward an integration of earlier approaches, with social-learning theorists increasingly accepting cognitive and private-personality notions, and points the way toward operational definition and systematic research.

Part 2 examines the foundations of variation in the private personality— the emotional, motivational, and cognitive systems—and concludes with a description of the emergence of a concept of self that can be scientifically scrutinized. Part 3 moves to the public personality, with chapters reviewing the research on stress, anxiety, conflict, defenses, and coping mechanisms. These chapters also pay special attention to the emotions, including the available research on the positive and constructive human emotions of interest and joy, curiosity, creativity, altruism, and love. Part 4 concludes the book with a consideration of how personality develops and changes, with the final chapter devoted to the various psychotherapies and the problems of assessing their effectiveness.

Although an integrative thread runs through the text, with Chapters 8– 18 reexamining earlier theoretical notions in the light of new approaches, individual groups of chapters are designed for optional separate study. More than any other, Chapter 7 can be detached and read early in the course. Chapters 1–3 are best read together, with Chapters 4–6 in close proximity. Chapters 8– 11 form a closely related sequence, as do Chapters 12–13, 14–15, and 16–17.

Many other teaching suggestions are included in the Instructor's Manual that is available for this book.

I am indebted to the dozens of colleagues and patients and hundreds of students who have helped me try to make sense of the vast area of personality theory and research. The various drafts of the manuscript benefited from readings of specific chapters or of the full text by Rae Carlson, Kay Deaux, Bernard S. Gorman, Robert R. Holt, Jerome Kagan, Helen Block Lewis, Leon H. Rappoport, Joseph F. Rychlak, Dorothy G. Singer, Charles P. Smith, and Alden E. Wessman. Useful suggestions came from Michael Neale, Christopher Pino, and David Rollock, all of whom class-tested the manuscript at Yale.

I have had valuable help in bibliographic work from a series of research assistants, some by now full-fledged professionals. They include David Diamond, Michael Dineen, Jon Edelson, Susan Frank, Richard Gerrig, Andrew Gottlieb, Douglas Hammond, Mark Litt, Michael Ranis, Wanda Rapaczynski, Bruce Singer, Jeff Singer, Jon Singer, Helen G. Spencer, and Roni Beth Tower. And I much appreciate the manuscript typing and word-processing by Frances DeGrenier, Virginia Hurd, and Charlotte Shah.

This book was first commissioned by Judith Greissman, whose enthusiasm and astute criticism sustained me over the years. Valuable editorial assessments and aid came from Phyllis Fisher. My editor, Natalie Bowen, brought acute perception and a wonderful flair for English expression to my assistance. My greatest debt in completing the book is to Lorraine Bouthilet, who has worked closely with me for nearly three years in helping to edit and revise the earlier drafts and to prepare the summaries and glossary. Her fine psychological background and editorial gifts have been invaluable.

Jerome L. Singer

Contents

PART ONE
Theories of Personality

PART TWO

The Private Personality

Introduction: Exploring Personality

The Brothers Karamazov, a famous novel by the Russian novelist Feodor Dostoievsky, concerns the lives of the four sons of a well-to-do landowner. The oldest brother, Dmitri, is a dashing, handsome army officer, courageous and loyal but also extremely impulsive, emotional, and somewhat violence-prone. The second brother, Ivan, is much more reserved, rather cynical, highly intellectual, and full of guilt. Alyosha, the third brother, is almost unbelievably kind, innocent, religious, and determined to be helpful to others. And the fourth, Smerdyakov (actually Karamazov's illegitimate son by a mentally retarded peasant woman), is represented as servile, deeply bitter, and ultimately murderous.

Almost every reader can recognize some aspects of his or her own personality in one or another of the four Karamazov brothers. The personality psychologist is interested in the fact that four boys growing up in the same household with the same father and, for three of them, the same mother, should turn out to be so different from one another. At the same time, the brothers share certain characteristics, motivations, and goals because of the strong influence of their father.

One of the great theorists of personality, Sigmund Freud, attempted to understand what experiences in Dostoievsky's own life might have influenced the content of the novel. Freud pointed out that each of the brothers showed important characteristics that were a part of Dostoievsky's own personality. For example, Dostoievsky was at various times an impulsive gambler (just as he described Dmitri), who often lost all his money. He was also a gifted writer and intellectual, much like Ivan. After an early phase of revolutionary activity, which nearly led to his execution and resulted in his imprisonment by the government of the Russian czar, Dostoievsky became deeply religious and a strong supporter of the monarchy. In his religious zeal, he reflected aspects of Alyosha. Finally, like Smerdyakov, the sinister illegitimate son, Dostoievsky was an epileptic, suffering from convulsions and loss of consciousness followed by periods of depression.

The plot of Dostoievsky's novel hinges around the mysterious murder of the father and the trial of Dmitri for patricide. Freud suggested that some of the power and intensity of the novel come from the fact that Dostoievsky's own father had actually been murdered when the novelist was 18. But Freud went further. He suggested that the author's motivation to write the novel and the excitement that many people feel in reading it reflect a common human experience. According to Freud's personality theory, all children grow up with a mixture of love and hate toward their parents, sometimes even expressed, for boys, in a fantasy of killing their father. Freud pointed out that the three works often considered the pinnacles of literature in Western civilization— Sophocles' *Oedipus the King*, Shakespeare's *Hamlet*, and Dostoievsky's *The Brothers Karamazov*—all share the theme of a father's murder.

A scene from the MGM production of **The Brothers Karamazov.** *From the left: Lee J. Cobb as the father, Feodor; Yul Brynner as Dmitri; William Shatner as Alyosha; Richard Basehart as Ivan. Not shown is Albert Salmi, who played Smerdyakov.*

A SCIENTIFIC APPROACH TO PERSONALITY

The sketchy discussion above does justice neither to a complex and emotionally powerful novel nor to its implications for psychology. The discussion does suggest, however, the many kinds of questions that personality psychologists address in their research and in their theories, questions such as these:

1. Can we identify individual personality characteristics and styles that remain consistent in a particular personality across time?

2. Can we identify individual characteristics that make it possible to define one person as different from another? Ivan Karamazov is clearly different from Dmitri by being more inhibited, thoughtful, and involved with intellectual approaches to daily life. Dmitri, on the other hand, takes action again and again without advance thought but at the same time expresses his emotions openly; he shows warmth and tenderness where Ivan cannot. Are there a limited number of characteristics, or *traits*, that define the differences between these two brothers?

3. Can we discover how people develop differently, at least in their surface behavior patterns, even though they have the same parents and grow up in the same household and in the same culture? What kinds of childhood behavior might have been systematically rewarded or punished so that the Karamazov boys developed different styles of action and speech? To what extent do differences in behavior and daily life lead people, even in the same environment, to develop consistent differences in their beliefs, attitudes, fantasies, expectations, and interactions with others?

In this chapter, we shall look at some of the issues that attract personality researchers. Keep in mind that personality is not a physical entity or tangible thing, but an abstract pattern of consistent personal characteristics that psychologists try to identify. Like other scientists, psychologists group observed facts or data into hypothetical constructs—organizing principles or imaginary entities—that help them keep track of the complexities of natural phenomena. Just as an atom or an electron is hypothetical, personality traits or concepts like "self" or "personality" are useful hypothetical notions to organize complex observations.

The Public Personality and the Private Personality

Try this exercise on yourself. Look in the mirror as you do every morning. What is your face and figure like? Imagine that what you see has been videotaped and can also be seen by others. What do other people make of you? Are you tall or short, broad or slim, muscular or a bit flabby? Beyond these physical characteristics, how do you appear to others? Are you a fast talker or someone who takes a long time and mulls things over before saying what has to be said in a short sentence or two? Is your speech typical of the area you come from—whether a soft Southern drawl or staccato Brooklyn speech—or does it contain a trace of the foreign accent your parents or grandparents may still have?

But there are other features to consider besides the way you look and talk. You may be the kind of person who smiles a lot and laughs easily or, on the other hand, you may prefer to keep your feelings to yourself. If so, you may notice that you keep your lips rather tightly together and express good feelings only through a slight upward turn of the corners of your mouth. Do people think you are too emotional or do they regard you as rather distant and detached? Would people describe you as someone who is independent, self-contained, even selfish? If people were asked to describe you by listing your major personality characteristics, would they put *sociable, playful, cheerful,* and *altruistic* at the top of the list or would they start with qualities such as *ambitious, independent,* and *persistent*? And since the notion of personality implies some degree of regularity or predictability, you might also think about how *consistent* your behavior is. Are you the same way with everybody or do you find that with your closest friends you become quite a different person? Perhaps you put up a front of joking and laughing at parties, but when you are with people you're close to, perhaps you are often bitter and talk much more freely about the doubts you have about your future or life in general. If situations and different settings evoke different reactions from you, is there such a thing as "the real you"?

So far we have focused on your external appearance and behavior—the you that others see and listen to, the you that you present to the world. This is your *public personality.* It is the side of you that is visible to others and about which most people might agree, depending on how much time they have spent with you and in how many different situations they have seen you behave. Some psychologists, called *behaviorists,* attempt to restrict psychology to the public personality—to actions and words that can be observed and measured. They argue that the public personality is all that needs to be known for a scientific study of the human personality. They propose that information obtained about your behavior in a variety of situations is all that is necessary to be able to predict what you would do in new situations. From the behavioral standpoint, your personality is best defined through the consistencies of your speech patterns, your ways of walking and holding yourself, your reactions to situations of threat or intimacy, and the amount of talking, laughing, or frowning you do in social groups.

But is that public side of yourself the whole story of your personality? Aren't there many aspects of your experience on this earth that most people could not possibly know?

Suppose you grew up in a small apartment with three brothers and sisters and had to share a bedroom or wait your turn to get into the bathroom. Even in those crowded situations you might still find moments of privacy in which your thoughts followed paths different from anyone else's. There were times as you lay in bed before going to sleep when you had the most exciting day-

*Self-awareness—looking at yourself in a mirror or simply thinking about yourself—is a form of your **private** personality. How others appraise you—how you appear in a social setting, for example (below)—is a form of your **public** personality.*

dreams or imaginings that transported you to faraway countries and climes. It is not likely that you told your family or friends about many of these fantasies. But you remember them; indeed they are part of your most private self.

On a hike once in the woods you might have met someone else hiking along. You had an interesting conversation and this got you thinking about how strange and different some people really are. Perhaps you never shared this conversation with any of your friends or relatives. The memory of this encounter becomes part of your unique experience. We all have a vast store of such private memories that recur from time to time as we sit idly waiting for a bus or listening to a boring lecture. Sometimes such memories surprise us by emerging in dreams at night when we find ourselves involved with people we have not seen in years or whom we knew only casually.

These unique memories—truly yours alone in the whole world—are part of your *private personality*, which consists of all those aspects of your experience that are deliberately well hidden, as well as some you may not even be aware of. This is the side of yourself that others know the least about, and that you probably hope to understand more about from the study of personality.

In the past, many scientifically oriented psychologists preferred to put most of their effort into studying the public aspects of personality. Too often students have taken personality courses expecting to learn more about the full range of their experience, only to be disappointed when the course covered only the most easily researchable characteristics of their public behavior, but ignored the complex and elaborate private dimension. Many intelligent and sophisticated young people have criticized psychologists who paid so little attention to the private world of dreams and fantasies; they felt they could learn more by reading the works of great novelists and playwrights, such as Dostoievsky, Flaubert, Joyce, Ibsen, Hesse, or Strindberg. Today, in order to construct a fuller psychology of personality, psychologists increasingly feel that they must try to devise objective and scientific methods for describing our unique private experiences.

What Is Personality?

The human personality comprises public actions, gestures, statements, and nonverbal expressions as well as the private motives, wishes, beliefs, attitudes, day and night dreams, and styles of organizing information or experiencing emotion that delineate the unique individuality of each person within a given culture. While we may say casually that Joanna has an outgoing personality or Robert a shy one, a scientific orientation makes it essential that we take into account more complex possibilities. People within a given culture share many beliefs and motives and may often act and talk very similarly. Yet even individuals from the same family may react differently to the same situation. Individual lives develop over time, so that qualities shown in childhood may not be evident under the pressures of adult work demands or in new situations, such as an appointment to public office. The human personality is too broad to be pinned down to a limited set of traits or motives. Nevertheless, personality psychologists can define the following objectives:

1. to determine the major human motives that guide actions in individual directions
2. to determine the characteristic ways of experiencing emotions and of organizing new information that lead people to feel differently or to attribute different meanings to common situations

3. to determine the features of bodily constitution, whether inherited or acquired, which combine with social experience to predispose people to have specific ways of walking, talking, thinking, feeling, or relating to others.

In studying these common characteristics of human experience, the personality psychologist also examines the potentialities for differences among persons in motives, emotions, action tendencies, and modes of interpersonal relatedness, thus leading toward the delineation of unique lifestyles. The study of human personality involves ascertaining what people share in common, what different types of situations they confront regularly, and what different kinds of demands, expectations, and stresses may emerge during the course of a lifetime.

What Is Personality Psychology?

With the exception of pure mathematics, all sciences begin with the collection and recording of large amounts of observations about the phenomena under study. In astronomy, for example, it was only after the great Danish sky-watcher Tycho Brahe had gazed with naked eye at hundreds of stars and the five visible planets, and recorded their positions and movements, that other scientists such as Kepler, Galileo, and Newton could begin first to organize this mass of data into categories and then to propose theories about the nature of planetary motion.

Similarly, the psychology of personality began its evolution as a separate field when careful "person-watchers" began to describe regularities of human behavior and then to organize them into patterns or categories. At first such observations were carried out for literary reasons, as when the ancient Greek satirist Theophrastus described thirty "characters," or personality types. Or else they served medical purposes for ancient physicians such as Hippocrates or Galen, who delineated four personality types presumably related to four *humors*, or substances in the blood.

The medical objectives of identifying common and consistent behavior or thinking patterns, which might help in differentiating various mental illnesses, led to a further step in the collection of information that would influence the scientific development of the field of personality. In the first third of the twentieth century, the most extensive observations and descriptions of human behavior were found in psychiatric and neurological casebooks, such as those of Otto Kraepelin (types of mental illness) and Richard von Krafft-Ebing (varieties of sexual behavior). Detailed accounts of dreams, fantasies, distortions in communication, and childhood memories emerged from the reports of psychotherapy with emotionally disturbed adults carried out by physicians such as Sigmund Freud, Pierre Janet, Carl G. Jung, and Morton Prince. It is not surprising, therefore, that the first efforts to pull together clusters of similar behaviors into general classes or categories, and then to formulate a theory, were made by medical specialists, notably Freud and Jung, and an American psychiatrist, Harry Stack Sullivan.

The personality psychologist is, thus, first of all a *data collector*, a scientist who must find ways of making systematic observations of people. These observations should permit the identification of regularities—that is, similarities or differences that can be grouped into clusters, such as emotions or traits or, in the case of maladjusted behavior, symptoms. Once such regularities or patterns are identified, the psychologist can develop a theory about their origins, the factors that sustain such patterns in adult life, and the way these patterns help or hinder personal relationships, personal satisfaction, and adjustment to career and stress-producing situations.

Personality theories are abstract formulations designed to integrate large numbers of separate behaviors under a cause-effect relationship. The validity of a theory depends on the kinds of observations from which it is derived. If these observations are carelessly made or if they are not extensive, generalizations into theory, however attractive, cannot be sustained once further tests of the hypotheses derived from theories are done. For example, Freud's generalization that all little boys have erotic feelings toward their mothers and want to get rid of their fathers—the so-called Oedipus complex—is probably not a universal phenomenon. Research in other cultures, where family life is differently organized than it was in Freud's pre–World War I Vienna, suggests that he based his theory too much on the data he obtained from his own acute social observations and from his small group of emotionally disturbed middle-class patients. Even if Freud's theory is not comprehensive, its introduction served a useful scientific purpose: It encouraged investigators in psychology and anthropology to pay attention to the patterns of early childhood relations among fathers, mothers, and children and thus generated a wealth of new information and potential theory. In this sense, a theory can have *heuristic* (exploratory) value—that is, it can serve to provoke further careful research in relatively unexplored areas.

Because personality psychology is still a fairly new field for systematic study, and heavily dependent on collection of observations, personality psychologists do not yet function as "pure theorists," as do scientists in mathematics or physics. It was thus a major advance in personality research when Kurt Lewin, a brilliant German (and, later, American) psychologist, introduced experimental methods into the field in the 1920s. Lewin showed that information about human personality—on issues such as the nature of conflict, the effects of frustrated goal-seeking, the variations in the level of a person's aspirations—could be derived by setting up carefully controlled experiments. The experimental method can be used, as we shall see, to test theories or simply to collect systematic evidence from which new theories are formulated. It usually will lead to smaller-scale, more precise theories. Thus, the analyses by Lewin and by the learning psychologist Neal Miller of the different kinds of conflict between human wishes or motives led to carefully designed experiments with both humans and animals. These experiments revealed aspects of human conflict that had not been observed or well understood before. An important theory of conflict emerged from this work.

Personality psychologists attempt, then, to collect observations about human motives, wishes, and needs; about traits, beliefs, and action patterns, and then to formulate testable theories about relationships. They have pioneered the development of assessment methods to measure personality traits and to evaluate changes in various personality characteristics. They carry out experiments in relevant areas such as aggression, emotion, stress and danger, love and intimacy. They are concerned with whether there is true consistency in personality or whether new "personalities" emerge for an individual in the various stages of life. They are also interested in discovering whether the forces that determine personality are genetic or whether they are the result of experiences in the family or in the culture.

Some researchers collect information or test theories about general human issues or characteristics, such as stress or aggression. Others prefer to study individuals, usually through tests or interviews, and follow them up in different situations through the life cycle. Such investigators are often called *personologists* to distinguish them from the first group. Ideally, this emphasis on the individual is very valuable, but in practice, the personologist can rarely track enough people over a long enough time and obtain sufficient specific information to make the best use of this approach.

We have already identified some concerns of personality psychologists in the sketch of the Karamazov brothers. We shall see these concerns recurring again and again as we explore the major theories of personality, which attempt to provide comprehensive, integrated views of the complex phenomena of human uniqueness. They also emphasize the ways in which needs derive from some

Some Major Issues in Personality Psychology

combination of the basic physiology, or built-in structures, of our bodies and the specific experiences children encounter at different stages of life. Is there a limited number of human motives or needs? Is personality "fixed" by the age of 5? Or do people evolve gradually throughout life or even change considerably during the different stages of adulthood as new demands or social expectations come to the fore? Can we define a limited number of traits—such as assertiveness, independence, and desire for intimacy and closeness—that everyone has to some degree but which vary tremendously from person to person? Are there consistent patterns of information-processing and of interpreting the meaning of events?

Most theorizing and research in personality psychology have identified a limited number of key issues that influence the emergence of unique personalities. Psychologists want to know as much as possible about human motives and emotions. They also want to know about the *cognitive system*—the ways in which people organize information and attribute meaning to situations and to other people—and the way beliefs, fantasies, and dreams are formed. They want to understand how attitudes develop around a sense of self, how a person deals with real dangers, with conflicts between wishes that can create "inner dangers," with the nature of aggression and the potential for violence. Until recently, personality theorists tended to overlook some of the constructive, positive human emotions and inclinations. Today, they are much interested in feelings of joy and excitement, human enthusiasm, creative tendencies, and the capacity for love and intimacy.

In summary, personality psychology deals with (1) human motives and emotions, the presumed driving forces of personality; (2) questions of how personality is organized, and along what dimensions individuals vary to produce different patterns of traits or styles of thinking and experiencing that define uniqueness; and (3) the way in which personality develops and is modified by bodily structure, social situation, and the demands of the different stages of life in a given family or society. Theories attempting to integrate these questions into a comprehensive formulation have presented exciting challenges to researchers in personality and to psychologists in general. Let us now take a closer look at how personality psychology developed and then at some of the major types of personality theories.

A BRIEF HISTORY OF PERSONALITY PSYCHOLOGY

The Study of Human Traits   The history of personality psychology is necessarily brief because personality has been scientifically studied only since the early 1900s, when psychologists first constructed a number of different tests and procedures for measuring individual differences in psychological performance. Some of the earliest tests, such as those developed in the United States by James McKeen Cattell and in France by Alfred Binet, were designed pri-

THE PERSISTENCE OF AN
ANCIENT PERSONALITY TYPOLOGY

The ancient Greek physician Galen (c. 130–200 A.D.) proposed a theory that every human being manifested one of four *temperaments*, or personality styles, reflecting particular characteristics of the person's blood: *phlegmatic* (controlled and logical), *sanguine* (lively and easygoing), *choleric* (vigorous and prone to anger), or *melancholic* (sad or prone to somberness and worry). While we have no evidence for the physical characteristics associated with these temperaments, considerable research on relatively stable personality characteristics (traits) has suggested that Galen's classification may have merit.

Figure 1-1 depicts the relation between Galen's four temperaments and personality traits arranged in circular form to reflect the interaction of two basic dimensions that recur regularly in most statistical studies of personality traits: *emotional stability-emotional instability* (Eysenck) and *introversion-extraversion* (Jung). The notion of arranging the traits in a circle was first proposed by Wilhelm Wundt, one of the founders of modern psychology, and the statistical support for such a classification has been provided by the British psychologist Hans J. Eysenck (1981, p. 8).

FIGURE 1-1

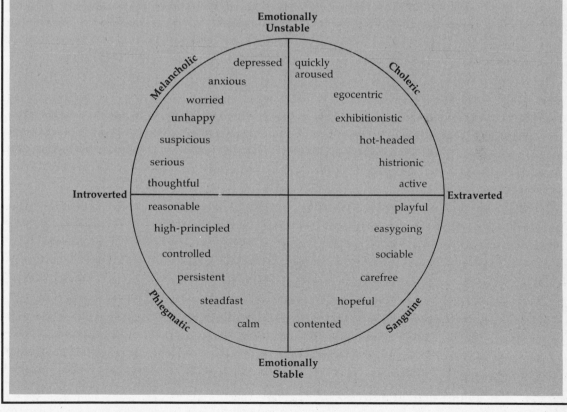

marily to measure intelligence as well as rapidity of movements, reaction time, and other perceptual or motor skills.

It was not long before psychologists perceived such tests as potentially able to measure more complex personality characteristics. In World War I, a team of American psychologists led by Robert S. Woodworth developed a questionnaire made up of such questions as "Do you daydream frequently?" The purpose of the questionnaire was to determine whether the respondent had fears, worries, self-doubts, or "nervous habits" that would make him unfit to undergo the rigors of military training or of actual combat. This type of questionnaire was extensively refined during the next thirty years. It became the basis for a long period of research on personality traits—characteristics such as introversion-extraversion, dominance-submission, or cheerfulness-sadness that everybody possesses to some degree.

A continuing issue in personality psychology relates to the question of whether or not there is a limited measurable number of traits or dimensions that define personality. Investigators such as J. P. Guilford, Raymond B. Cattell, and Hans Eysenck have devoted their careers to developing questionnaires and statistical procedures for studying large numbers of individuals in order to obtain evidence for the existence of basic personality factors.

The Clinical Method   Near the end of the nineteenth century, the Viennese neurologist Sigmund Freud evolved a method for the treatment of emotionally disturbed individuals that he called *psychoanalysis*. This procedure entailed regular daily interviews continuing for a year or more in which Freud's patients reported on their dreams, fantasies, and daily experiences as fully and frankly as possible. The psychoanalytic method provided a means for obtaining detailed accounts of a person's private behavior, thoughts, fantasies, and night dreams that previously had been relatively inaccessible. Thus the way was opened for learning a great many things about human personality of the kind that had formerly been the province only of great writers or of those who studied the peculiarities of mental patients.

Projective and Experimental Methods   During the middle years of the twentieth century, psychologists and psychiatrists began to combine the more formal measurement procedures of the questionnaire approaches with the more elaborate and personalized data obtainable from the clinical method. An outgrowth of this effort was the emergence of the so-called *projective* methods, such as the use of inkblots or ambiguous pictures. By reacting to the inkblots or pictures, people could indirectly express their private fantasies and ways of looking at situations in a shorter time than in the long, drawn-out psychoanalytic procedure. These techniques take advantage of the careful measurement procedures of psychological tests, but the ambiguous materials allow the respondents to reveal more private experiences and to express their own motives, defenses against fears, self-doubts, and fantasies without embarrassment or distress.

During the 1920s, particularly under the leadership of Kurt Lewin, psychologists also began to use experimental procedures to study important aspects of personality. Lewin and his students devised carefully controlled experiments to study problems such as frustration or the changes people make in their levels of aspiration—that is, the expectations they have about how well they will do in future situations. Lewin's research methods and theories opened the way for an extensive series of experiments on the nature of human conflicts and on the relative strengths of different motivations. More recently, the experimental studies of such investigators as Julian Rotter, Albert Bandura, and Walter Mischel have demonstrated the importance of social experience and learning in the development of personality.

In 1937, two textbooks on personality appeared, one by Ross Stagner, the other by Gordon Allport, that marked the birth of personality psychology as a separate field of investigation. During the 1940s, Allport and Henry Murray at Harvard University and Gardner Murphy at Columbia University and later at the City College of New York began to train dozens of young investigators in a variety of methods for studying personality.

During World War II, clinical psychology emerged as one of the most vigorous areas of the profession, giving another boost to the evolution of research methods. It encouraged extensive research on personality since many psychologists recognized that clinical work—that is, diagnosis and treatment of emotionally disturbed or maladjusted people—must rest on a sound knowledge of normal as well as deviant personality characteristics.

In more recent years, personality psychologists have elaborated the methods already mentioned—the questionnaires and projective tests and the clinical, psychoanalytic, and experimental approaches. As a part of the study of personality variation, they have also used systematic observations of individuals in their normal day-to-day situations. Researchers have moved increasingly toward studying the longer life course of an individual rather than relying on one test or observation in a single experiment.

THEORETICAL PERSPECTIVES

The field of personality psychology has evolved in two major ways. In addition to the emergence of methods of study, much of the excitement in the evolution of personality psychology as a unique discipline within psychology is due to the theoretical proposals of Sigmund Freud, Carl G. Jung, Alfred Adler, Harry Stack Sullivan, John Dollard and Neal Miller, Albert Bandura, Kurt Lewin, Gordon Allport, and Silvan Tomkins, among many others, which we shall consider in Chapters 2–6. It is important to remember that these theories themselves are derived from certain kinds of observations or data. Thus Freud, Jung, Adler, and Sullivan developed their theories from clinical work and personal introspection; Lewin, Allport, Bandura, and Dollard and Miller emphasized experimental methods; and Cattell and Eysenck drew mainly on questionnaire studies.

The complexity of the human personality has made it too vast an area to be encompassed by any single theory now available, though Freud's may have come closer than any other. As we examine the different personality theories, we shall see that each individual theorist or school comes at the problem from a slightly different perspective—views it from a slightly different vantage point. It is very much like the old fable about the blind men trying to describe an elephant: if one man has hold of its tail, another its trunk, and the third holds a leg, each man's description may be reasonably accurate for a sharply delimited area, but it is scarcely a satisfactory description of the whole animal. The major personality theorists often seem to be describing only limited portions of our complex public and private personalities. But this is the way science often progresses—through small-scale, delimited theories.

Theorists who study people intensively through the use of the clinical method, treating them for emotional disorders, emphasize the private personality and unconscious conflicts or other characteristics associated with maladjustment. Theorists who analyze questionnaire responses in their attempt to discover the basic dimensions of human personality have learned much more about the way the characteristics of the public personality are grouped and organized; their theories reflect little interest in the kinds of continuing inner experience or torments that clinicians hear about from their patients.

Psychologists who emphasize experimental methods as analogies for the day-to-day situations people face find out a good deal about how small groups of people react to frustrations or how they resist or yield to temptation. But these cross-sectional views of public behavior say little about how personality varies over a long life, about how intimate situations change and grow in complexity, or about how our memories, fears, and anticipations give us a sense of private continuity or separateness no matter how uniformly or apparently predictably we respond to the sometimes gimmicky manipulations of the experimenter.

To some extent, personality theories reflect major personality characteristics or life experiences of the personality psychologist. For example, Freud had an Oedipus complex; his devoted mother, much younger than his father, idolized him and believed a gypsy fortune-teller's account that he would someday be famous. She still referred to him as her "golden little Sigi" when he was a middle-aged man. And Harry Stack Sullivan's grandmother used to prevent him from climbing the stairs of their home when he was little by putting dead spiders on each step. Small wonder he developed a theory that placed great emphasis on the importance of mother-child interactions and on the child's early fantasies of a "good" versus a "bad" mother!

Whatever its background and personal origin, a personality theory must ultimately stand up under scientific scrutiny—that is, it must generate hypotheses that in some way can be tested by independent observers using the methods of science that permit repetition and reports to other scientists in professional journals, books, and meetings. While each individual theorist or school can contribute important insights, any comprehensive theory of personality should address a number of basic questions about human behavior and thought and about individual differences along certain major dimensions. In general, most of the personality theories adopt one or more of the following perspectives: (1) the *dynamic*, which involves a search for basic drives; (2) the *structural*, which identifies the "building blocks" of personality; (3) the *developmental*, which searches for the childhood roots of adult personality; and (4) the *adaptive*, which considers personality from the point of view of effective adjustment to the physical or social environment. Let us examine these perspectives more closely before considering the major personality theories.

The Dynamic Perspective

The term *dynamic* generally refers to a force impelling change. In psychology, the term usually refers more specifically to the motives or drives of human beings that lead them to engage in particular actions or to experience particular kinds of thoughts. What drove Dmitri Karamazov to compete violently with his father for the love of a young peasant girl when he was already virtually engaged to a rich and attractive aristocrat? Why was his brother Alyosha so strongly motivated to become a priest or a social worker despite the fact that he grew up in a family as materialistic as the Karamazovs?

Most personality theorists stress the importance of physiological needs in motivating more complex behaviors such as love, striving for political power, or scientific ambition. Some theorists attempt to reduce most human motives to a small number, as Freud did. Others, such as Henry A. Murray, prefer instead to identify a fairly large range of basic human motives or needs and then determine how individuals arrange these into hierarchies from least to most important as a basis for defining different personality types. But at least one theorist, George A. Kelly, felt that the attempt to describe human personality from the standpoint of motives or needs was not even useful. He preferred to emphasize the extent to which behavior is determined by the different ways in which people interpret situations and their expectations about what might happen in one situation as against another. Kelly's approach may seem a forerunner of what is today called the cognitive perspective, the emphasis on how people perceive and interpret situations as a key to the direction their beliefs and actions will take.

The Structural Perspective

Another perspective for looking at personality is to consider whether it can be described as having a *structure*—that is, whether it has different regions and functions. If so, are these areas organized in certain ways? Are some more differentiated (organized into components) than others? Are some more influential than others? The structural perspective deals with such questions.

The most famous structural system is Freud's division of the personality into ego, id, and superego. There are, however, other ways of viewing personality organization. One is the division, already mentioned, into *public* and *private* personalities. Another is Freud's and Jung's great emphasis on the *conscious* and *unconscious* aspects of behavior. Other psychologists organize *motives* into a hierarchical structure, with such physiological needs as food and shelter at the base of the system and social needs such as dominance or intimacy at the next level of organization. Psychologists who have emphasized the psychometric (measurement) approach to personality, such as Raymond B. Cattell, suggest that personality can be divided into surface traits, such as friendliness, and underlying, presumably more basic traits, such as introversion or extraversion. This kind of structural approach is also similar to Jung's rather complex notion that overt or conscious traits in the personality are at the same time represented unconsciously or privately in the personality by the opposite tendencies. Thus, a person who is sociable and friendly and likes lots of company may be, deep down, very shy, inhibited, and fearful of groups; this person is either not aware of this consciously or keeps such feelings private and avoids showing them to others.

The Developmental Perspective

Most theories of personality deal with the question of how personality traits and organization develop. This notion of an emerging and growing personality was a major contribution of Freud and his psychoanalytic theory. Freud felt that the main outlines of a personality structure had been formed by the age of 5 or 6 after passing through a regular sequence of experiences that all infants and toddlers share. While other theorists may disagree with the specifics of Freud's position, most do find it necessary to attend to the question of how personality characteristics do emerge in children as their cognitive and motor capacities develop and as they interact with parents and siblings or confront the demands of cleanliness, schoolwork, peer pressures, religion, sexuality, and so on. Related to this question of early evolution of personality is a critical issue: How much of the development of a child's personality and style of behavior is due to the specific experiences the child has had in the family or in the broader cultural environment and how much is due simply to the natural effects of heredity?

The Adaptive Perspective

Another way of looking at personality is the adaptive perspective—the extent to which individual variations or styles of behavior and thought serve a useful purpose in development and daily living. Are the personality differences we manifest simply idiosyncratic characteristics of our basic biological structure? Or have they evolved in part because certain types of thoughts or actions helped us function better within a particular family or within a particular subculture?

In his psychoanalytic theory, Freud paid little attention to the ways in which the individual related to the broader social and physical environment. His emphasis was primarily on a psychological conflict within the person. Theorists concerned with interpersonal relations, such as Sullivan, placed greater weight on the cultural influences in the development of children, but they too did not focus much on whether the children's personality characteristics really helped them survive or function effectively. Social-learning theorists, such as Walter Mischel and Albert Bandura, are more likely to emphasize the degree to which children develop differences because families and peer groups call their attention, through rewards and punishment, to particular kinds of responses. The learning process helps children adapt to a particular family or peer culture and later to modify earlier patterns as they move into a broader society.

THE MAJOR PERSONALITY THEORIES

In Chapters 2–6, we shall examine in some detail the theories of personality that continue to contribute to our current understanding of personality. Here, we shall just briefly mention them. The theories differ in comprehensiveness, in reliance on clinical observation in contrast to study of normal persons, and in the relative emphasis placed on experimental or other forms of systematic data collection as sources of information. They also differ in how closely they relate to the more general information about human beings obtained in the subareas of general psychology, such as physiological psychology, learning, perception, child development, and social psychology. The earlier theorists, such as Freud and Jung, were developing their views at a time when psychology was in its infancy, but many present-day psychoanalysts still discuss their theories without concern for the many significant contributions and technical advances in general psychology. As we shall see, however, with the exception of personality theories that are closely tied to specific schools of psychotherapy, there has been an increasing confluence of points of view among those theorists who emphasize behaviorist and social-learning approaches and those who emphasize the cognitive-affective orientation. This reconciliation reflects the fact that both groups rely on systematic data collection and experimentation and also draw more heavily on the scientific research emerging from the various subdisciplines of psychology.

In general, personality theorists fall into four major categories: *psychodynamic* theories, *behaviorist and social-learning* theories, *phenomenological and humanistic* theories, and, the most recent category, *cognitive-affective* theories. Some psychologists identify a fifth category—the *trait* theories—but these theories really represent systematic points of view about problems of measurement of human characteristics, and we shall consider these in Chapter 7.

Psychodynamic theories stem chiefly from the influence of Sigmund Freud. They emphasize efforts to understand human behavior and thought as a consequence of attempts to resolve the often unconscious conflicts between our basic drives, such as sex or aggression, and the limitations reality imposes on

Psychodynamic Theories

their satisfaction. Psychodynamic theories focus on the private personality—on the origins of wishes, fantasies, attitudes of love and hate, or particular kinds of sexual appetites. They derive their evidence chiefly from clinical observations, the study of emotionally distressed or psychotic persons through diagnostic assessments or psychoanalytic treatment. This evidence chiefly consists of verbal associations and dream reports, as well as the clinician's observations of individuals during interviews or treatment.

Behaviorist and Social-Learning Theories

Behaviorists aim to develop a psychology that meets the highest scientific standards of objectivity and reliable observation. To counteract the personal bias that often occurs when clinicians describe patients' behavior or when individuals give accounts of their own thoughts, behaviorists propose that psychology limit itself chiefly to directly observable behavior, movements, actions, and speech patterns that can be photographed or recorded with instruments and measured. They argue that human personality, to the extent that such a term is even useful, is nothing more than patterns of overt responses to different situations. Influenced by the precise studies of learning in animals and birds, behaviorists view personality differences as the result of differences in learning histories and in patterns of rewards and punishments (reinforcements) that increase the probability that certain responses will emerge under certain conditions.

The social-learning theories arose from the behaviorist orientation, but they emphasize observational learning in social situations as well as learning through specific response reinforcement. They focus primarily on the public personality and also stress the fact that specific situations evoke different reactions from people depending on their learning experiences. Social-learning theorists are dubious about the importance of underlying or unconscious motives in individuals. Their methods of research involve careful experiments in artificially created situations. Also, since learning approaches have proved effective in psychotherapy, social-learning theorists have increasingly utilized clinical information. This "school" generally remains closely tied to general psychology and, perhaps because of that experience, social-learning theorists have become interested in cognitive or information-processing issues in personality structure.

Phenomeno-logical and Humanistic Theories

Phenomenology is the study of private experience, and the phenomenological theories reflect, to some degree, a reaction against the emphasis on drive satisfaction and conflict of the psychodynamic approach and the narrow stimulus-response interpretations of the behaviorists. The phenomenologists argue that human experience is far too complex to be reduced to simple sequences of arousal and satisfaction of biological drives or to reinforcement of simple movements or verbal statements. They stress the breadth of human experience and the tremendous importance of the human need to find meaning in our experiences and to struggle for full expression of our capacities. To this approach, the humanists add the great importance of positive emotions, such as excitement and joy, and positive experiences, such as creativity and self-development, all of which were neglected in the earlier theories. While some of the phenomenologists drew on general psychological research and generated some formal studies themselves, most of the phenomenologists and humanists rely chiefly on observations drawn from clinical practice. In addition to their primary focus on the private personality, the humanists are also interested in public manifestations of creativity and personal fulfillment in the form of artistic or even political achievement.

The cognitive-affective orientation is so recent in psychology that it has not really taken shape as a distinct personality theory. It may be seen as an evolution that accepts the contributions of the other three theories but tries to relate them to important advances in the psychology of information-processing (cognition). Drawing on recent discoveries concerning the emotions, the cognitive-affective theory suggests that humans are motivated to reduce negative emotional reactions and to enhance positive ones, and to control emotions as well as possible but also to express them. Emotions themselves are chiefly evoked or controlled in the course of cognitive processes—that is, as people anticipate situations, assign meanings, and organize experiences. In this sense, the cognitive theorists accept some aspects of reinforcement and of the external environment as important for personality and also acknowledge the public personality, but they give greater weight to human thought, imagination, and planning and hence to the private personality. Cognitive-affective theorists are usually active research investigators as well, and more in the mainstream of general psychology than phenomenologists or humanists.

Cognitive-Affective Theory

EXPLORING THE HUMAN PERSONALITY

The psychology of personality is not only a highly intriguing area of psychology, it is also perhaps the most complex, because it takes as its dual problem both the overall ongoing pattern of relationships between people and the inner world of their private experiences as well. More than any other field of psychology, it pays attention to the uniqueness of each human being.

A good starting point for the study of personality psychology is to think of yourself as "the subject." Throughout this book, ask yourself whether or not the research described and the problems discussed apply to you. How would *you* answer the questions on an inventory of personality? How would *you* react if you were participating in a particular experiment? Of course, your own reaction may not be the last word, but there may be times when you find yourself saying, "This experiment is silly. I can't imagine that I would behave anything like that and I bet those subjects were just trying to fool the experimenter." Since one of the principles of this book is that we should be sensitive to the value of our own experience, perhaps psychologists should undergo many of the procedures in their experiments just to get the real feeling of what these may be like for their research subjects.

The psychology of personality should help us to understand something about the different kinds of emotions we experience in certain situations and how they relate to the novelty or strangeness we find in relationships with others. It should give us some clues as to why we feel lonely and isolated some of the time, and why some of us seem to feel that way all of the time. It should tell us about the motives we have, and how we respond to stress from the outside or conflict within. It should suggest some reasons why some of us are more persistently aggressive, fearful, creative, or ambitious than others.

The psychology of personality should also give us some clues about the more private aspects of our experience. It should tell us something about why some people have certain types of recurring dreams, why some people's fantasies are dark and foreboding, while others' are full of sunny vistas and happy adventures.

And the psychology of personality ought to consider to what extent the public and private personalities are related. Some behaviorists argue that the private personality is merely a by-product of underlying neural or bodily processes and that mental activities do not themselves have any causal influence on the course of our lives. Perhaps, as some behaviorists say, our dreams and fantasies *are* simply a function of the way our bodies work (like the spots that dance before our eyes when we shut them) and have very little to do with determining our behavior. Even if this were true—even if the private personality of our fantasies and dreams has no more importance than those phosphenes that flash on our retina—the novelty, richness, and elaborateness of our inner lives evoke our curiosity and cannot be ignored. Indeed it might even be argued that, forced as we often are into public uniformity by the conventions and economic pressures of our society or by the bombardment of the messages we receive from television, the uniqueness of our private personalities remains the last refuge for the true sense of individuality.

SUMMARY

1. The human personality involves the patterns of public actions, gestures, and statements or nonverbal expressions, as well as the private motives, wishes, beliefs, attitudes, day and night dreams, and styles of organizing information or experiencing emotions that delineate the unique individuality of each person within a given society. Personality is not a physical entity or a tangible thing, but rather an abstract pattern of consistent personal characteristics.

2. Personality may be viewed in two domains: the public personality and the private personality. The public personality consists of the external and overt appearances and behaviors that are visible to others. The private personality consists of the thoughts, feelings, and images that are part of each individual's experiences.

3. A comprehensive theory of personality should address a number of fundamental questions: What are the basic human motives? How is personality organized? How does personality develop? What aspects of personality lead to more effective adjustment to the environment? The various theories differ in which of these questions they seek to answer and which questions they emphasize. Four perspectives, or ways of looking at personality—the dynamic, the structural, the developmental, and the adaptive—represent the relative emphasis different theories place on these questions.

4. The dynamic perspective considers the motives or drives that lead human beings to engage in certain actions or to have certain kinds of thoughts. The question of whether there are basic physiological drives is often addressed by personality theorists. Some theories attempt to reduce most human motives to a small number of physiological needs. Others prefer to identify a large range of motives or needs and then determine how individuals arrange them into hierarchies as a basis for defining different personality types.

5. The structural perspective deals with the extent to which personality has special regions or organizing properties. The most famous structural system is Freud's division of the personality into the id, ego, and superego. Another way to organize behavior is in terms of the conscious and the unconscious aspects of behavior. Personality can also be organized according to its public and its private manifestations. Some psychologists consider a hierarchy of motives as a form of structure, with the physiological needs at the base of the system and the social needs at the next level of organization. Psychologists who emphasize the psychometric approach often describe personality in terms of surface traits and underlying basic traits.

6. Critical questions in the developmental perspective are: How much of the development of personality is a consequence of specific experiences in the family or the cultural environment, how much is the result of particular kinds of encouragement or identification with parental figures, and how much may be attributable to heredity?

7. The adaptive perspective considers the extent to which variations in behavior and thought serve a useful purpose in development and daily living. Have personality differences evolved in part because certain types of thoughts or actions help people function better in a particular family or subculture?

8. The four major categories of personality theories are the psychodynamic theories, the behaviorist and social-learning theories, the phenomenological and humanistic theories, and the cognitive-affective theory. Psychodynamic theories emphasize conflicts between basic drives or between a

physiological or unconscious need and the limitations on its satisfaction imposed by reality. They focus on the private personality and derive their evidence chiefly from clinical observation. The behaviorist theories emphasize objective and reliable measurement of observable behavior. They view personality differences as the result of learning and of rewards and punishments that increase the probabilities that certain responses will emerge under certain conditions. Social-learning theories arose from behaviorist theories, but they also use observational learning to explain personality development. The phenomenological and humanistic theories stress the importance of the human need to find meaning in experiences and to struggle for full self-expression. They give great importance to the emotions of excitement and joy as well as to self-developing experiences neglected by other theories. Their focus is mainly on the private personality. The cognitive-affective theory is a recent development that accepts the contributions of the other three major theories, but also relates them to advances in the psychology of cognition. It draws on discoveries concerning the emotions and their close tie to information-processing and to how human beings assign meanings and make sense of novel and complex environmental and social situations.

PART ONE

Theories of Personality

CHAPTER 2

The Psychoanalytic Theory
of Sigmund Freud

A woman in her middle forties sought psychotherapy because of recurring spells of mixed fearfulness and sadness. At one of her meetings with the therapist, she began by describing her annoyance at physicians who called her by her first name or even "Sweetie" or "Dear" but who expected her to address them as "Doctor." This led to thoughts of a dream in which, when she was preparing a meal, she suddenly seemed to be transformed into the Jolly Green Giant, a figure used in advertising a brand of vegetables.

Encouraged to comment on the dream, she found herself remembering an older brother—the "genius" of the family, the "apple of his parents' eyes," the woman remarked bitterly. "All the family resources went into getting him through college and medical school. When I finished high school I was sent straight off to work." Her thoughts then turned to a recent argument with her husband, a high-school principal, considerably older than herself. He objected to her plans to start school and perhaps to work toward a degree in nursing. "Just yesterday," she went on, "my kids were watching 'The Incredible Hulk' on television. I sat down with them and was so fascinated by the show that they started to laugh. That's the program about this scientist who because of radiation exposure has become a mutant. Whenever he's frustrated or angry he turns into a—huge green monster." Suddenly the woman shouted, "That's it, that's it! I want to be the Incredible Hulk!"

This excerpt from a therapy session exemplifies ways in which the psychoanalytic theory of Sigmund Freud has become a part of twentieth-century thought and culture. Even without formal study of the theory, most people see certain common themes underlying the woman's associations. She is resentful of her older brother's success, an example of "sibling rivalry." She feels suppressed by her husband in her aspirations to achieve a career. Her dream of the Jolly Green Giant and her fascination with the Incredible Hulk reflect the envy and rage that she has been holding back from awareness. Television programs like "The Incredible Hulk," "Superman," or "Wonder Woman," where ordinary people display superpowers, echo the fantasies of most people. Television writers draw on psychoanalytic ideas in order to design plots and characters that tap into human motives and will therefore appeal to a large audience. Psychoanalysis is not only a way to understand human motivation, it is also an influence on the culture it seeks to explain. In a sense, the psychoanalytic orientation created a whole new way of thinking—indeed, a new kind of literature and mythology.

Psychoanalysis represents a body of thought about our human wishes and how these wishes find expression through our dreams, reveries, beliefs, and actions. It is a theory that seeks to explain how individual personality differences are in part due to the experiences and conflicts of early childhood. Psychoanalysis is also a form of psychotherapy, a procedure for treating emotionally disturbed individuals, but it is important to remember that while psychoanalytic work with patients has uncovered interesting information about human behavior, psychoanalysis remains a set of loosely related assumptions and hypotheses rather than a proved body of scientific facts.

Freud's psychoanalytic theory of personality and its various offshoots influenced most of the scientific study of the human personality for the first half of this century. This influence was powerful despite the fact that these psychodynamic theories grew chiefly out of clinical work with emotionally disturbed individuals under less than scientifically rigorous conditions. The reasons for their attractiveness not only to psychologists but to much of the lay public is not hard to see. The theories address questions about our most private thoughts, fears, wishes, and fantasies; they deal with the private personality we recognize in our own dreams and memories. They explore everything from our deepest desires and irresistible passions to puzzling little rituals such as not stepping on cracks in the sidewalk. And, of course, they provide a way of making sense of the most flamboyant and bizarre forms of human behavior and the origins and causes of serious personality disorders such as psychoses.

Freud's emphasis was primarily on the theory as an explanation of the more private features of personality—the drives and conflicts of which we are often unaware, their expression in our dreams and fantasies or in the quirks and oddities of our behavior, the symptoms of neurosis or other severe emotional disturbances. He was less concerned with the public personality—why some people work harder at jobs than others, why some people enjoy classical music and fine art while others prefer popular music and comic strips, why some people seem sociable and others prefer intimate gatherings or solitary walks in the woods. Although Freud's followers began to pay more attention to the adaptive and behavioral implications of psychoanalysis—for example, how personality dynamics play a role in making some people more effective leaders or spouses or parents than others—Freud's emphasis remained largely on intrapsychic (within-the-mind) impulses and conflicts and how they shape personality.

FREUD'S INFLUENCE

Rarely in the history of science has an organized discipline been so dominated by the influence of a single individual as have personality and abnormal psychology by Sigmund Freud. Although psychoanalysis as a form of psychotherapy has lost some of its prestige and fashionableness in the past few

Sigmund Freud

SIGMUND FREUD

Sigmund Freud (1856–1939) was born in a Jewish family in Czechoslovakia but grew up in Vienna where he lived until forced to flee from the Nazis in 1938. His father was a modestly successful small businessman. His mother, much younger than her husband, doted on Sigmund, her first child; she believed in a gypsy's prediction that he would be a great man, and she undoubtedly stimulated his ambition and imagination. Freud was a gifted student, with unusual talent in writing and a scientific bent that initially led him into a medical and research career in neurology. But lack of advancement and financial pressures caused him to shift to private practice and treatment of neurotic patients.

Although Freud suffered from professional isolation, forced on him by his radical views of psychology, his personal life was for the most part free of serious difficulty or tragedy. After a five-year engagement (the fate of many impecunious young people in the Victorian era), he married Martha Bernays and they had six children. We can get a sense of the prudery of the period from the letters Freud exchanged with his fiancée during the late 1870s and early 1880s. In one, Freud criticized her because while they were out for a walk she stopped several times, bent over, and adjusted her stockings. Such actions were considered extremely provocative. It took Freud eighteen months before he could even bring himself to mention his distress at this behavior!

Freud's theories scandalized Europe and probably played a role in the greater sexual freedom that began in the 1920s and has characterized the latter half of this century. He continued his clinical work, informal teaching, and scholarly writing amid the necessity to support his family and confront the changing political conditions in Austria. After many years of working in relative isolation, in 1900 his book *The Interpretation of Dreams* and his psychoanalytic method of treatment began to attract attention and more and more followers.

In the last fifteen years of his life, Freud suffered from an excruciatingly painful cancer of the mouth and jaw. He struggled against this severe illness with remarkable bravery, continuing his practice, writing, and other intellectual work unabated. In his last two years Freud and his family faced the dangers of Hitler and Nazism. When the Germans occupied Vienna in 1938, Freud narrowly escaped prison through the good offices of his British disciple, Ernest Jones. Jones and Marie Bonaparte, a Greek princess who had been a patient of Freud's and had gone on to become a well-known psychoanalyst herself, arranged for him and his family to leave for England. Freud lived there peacefully, still busily working on a further systematic statement of psychoanalytic theory until he died in 1939.

decades, the general theoretical approach developed by Freud continues to have a vigorous impact on intellectual discussion in philosophy, anthropology, literature, and the humanities, as well as in psychology. According to polls in the 1970s, Freud's name is one of the most widely recognized by people all over the world along with Mao, Churchill, Marx, Einstein, Roosevelt, and de Gaulle. Freud's theories, whether they are scientifically valid or not, have become part of our culture and day-to-day life, as we talk about "inhibitions," "defensiveness," "wishful thinking," "ego trips," "Oedipus complex," or "sibling rivalry"—all Freudian terms.

Within the broader sphere of intellectual thought, the influence of Freud can be seen in the literary works of James Joyce, William Faulkner, and Saul Bellow, among many others; in the paintings of the surrealists; in the plays of Eugene O'Neill, Arthur Miller, and Tennessee Williams; and in dozens of motion pictures, such as Alfred Hitchcock's *Spellbound* and *Psycho* or Orson Welles' *Citizen Kane*. Literary critics such as Edmund Wilson, Lionel Trilling, Leslie Fiedler, and Harold Bloom show Freud's influence; anthropologists such as Margaret Mead and Gregory Bateson, sociologists like Talcott Parsons, and political scientists like Harold Lasswell were greatly influenced by the psychoanalytic perspective.

Within psychology itself, prominent theoreticians of personality such as John Dollard and Neal Miller, Kurt Lewin, Abraham Maslow, Henry A. Murray, Robert W. White, and Silvan S. Tomkins all acknowledge their exposure to psychoanalytic theory. And Erik Erikson, the founder of the new field of *psychohistory*, developed his theories out of a solid grounding in psychoanalysis.

PERSPECTIVES FOR UNDERSTANDING PSYCHOANALYTIC THEORY

Any comprehensive account of psychoanalytic theory is complicated by the fact that Freud never produced a final, large-scale formal statement that integrated all the details of his system. David Rapaport, the greatest of psychoanalytic scholars, began such a synthesis, but it was terminated prematurely by his death in 1960 (Rapaport, 1960a, 1960b). Rapaport proposed that psychoanalytic theory could be best understood by examining it from five perspectives, the *dynamic*, the *economic*, the *structural*, the *developmental*, and the *adaptive*. We shall briefly discuss each of these.

The Dynamic Perspective What motivates human action and thought? On the basis of his clinical findings and interpretations, Freud theorized that motives grow out of (1) biologically rooted *drives* or needs and (2) the transformation or displacement of those drives. The transformation of a drive takes place under circumstances in which directly expressing the drive would arouse terrible and diffuse *fear* or anxiety, or would expose the individual to real danger. Humans act in certain ways or experience certain thoughts because they are, in effect "programmed" to satisfy fundamental drives or urges: hunger, thirst, sex, aggression. But there are times when direct expression of a drive is unacceptable or dangerous—a man in church cannot make obvious sexual overtures to an attractive woman across the aisle. Even the conscious thought of doing so in such a setting is likely to arouse anxiety and is considered by many to be sinful. Some people might transform such a drive by displacing the sexual thought with thoughts of spirituality and religious intensity. Others might transform the drive into self-recrimination and guilt, thus avoiding conscious awareness of their lustful thoughts.

Freud believed that drives are like a set of internal appetites continuously demanding to be appeased. The individual can neither ignore nor permanently fulfill the basic drives because in cyclical fashion they build up and press for discharge, are satisfied, and then build up again. Drives have specific goals, but if a goal is not available, other related goals can be substituted. The substitution of acceptable goals from those that are not acceptable is termed *displacement*.

According to Rapaport, the psychoanalytic model of motivation was characterized by Freud in the following way: Periodically an infant gets hungry, and therefore becomes extremely restless; the mother appears and offers a bottle or her breast. Sucking the breast, the infant gradually sinks into a peaceful sleep. Suppose, however, the mother does not arrive immediately, so that the infant becomes more and more overwhelmed by hunger. Then comes a period of extensive motor restlessness followed by crying. The baby shakes all over and screams. It is an intolerable experience. Moreover, it is the prototype for what Freud termed *diffuse anxiety*, a horrible, "free-floating," uncontrollable fear produced by the naked discharge of unacceptable drives or the coming to consciousness of desires that conflict with other strong desires.

If the mother has been regular and prompt in coming to her child, then when the infant becomes restless, it begins to *imagine* the mother. This "hallucination," as Freud called it, of the mother or the breast or bottle temporarily gratifies the drive and prevents it from becoming too overwhelming. This *imaginary gratification* helps the child to delay the flooding of drive excitation and also becomes the basis for the development of what Freud called the *ego*, a term for the processes of thought and self-control that permit a more effective adaptation to reality. In this way, the theory sets the stage for the great importance of imagination, fantasy, and private experience in human self-regulation.

The woman fascinated by the Incredible Hulk was very likely angry at her husband for his lack of sympathy with her aspirations for personal development. This anger was multiplied by its tie to her envy of her older brother, who had so much parental adulation and so many opportunities denied to her. Too "civilized" to express her aggressive impulses by attacking her husband physically or yelling at him, or perhaps even to think about doing so, she dreams of being a giant or fantasizes about the power of the Hulk. Such vicarious experiences, according to psychoanalytic theory, may temporarily reduce her aggression, but the sense of impotent rage returns again and again and may account for her periods of depression. Indeed psychoanalysts have often described certain types of depression as self-directed rage. Suicide has been called the ultimate form of an aggressive impulse displaced onto the self rather than directed at family members or other frustrating persons or situations.

The Economic Perspective Classical psychoanalytic theory assumes that the expression of a drive always results in expenditure of energy. What kind of energy? Freud never defined it more precisely than to indicate that it was physiological in origin. But his theory required the notion of some kind of energy in order to provide quantitative underpinnings for ideas like drive build-up, storage, pressure for discharge, blocking, and displacement. Theorists of psychoanalysis have been critical of Freud's use of energy, and the economic perspective is now less emphasized.

Psychoanalysis places great stress on *objects*, a term referring to all the people or bodily parts or psychological situations that a growing child persistently associates with gratification of her or his impulses. Certain desirable objects recur so regularly that they become invested with a great deal of energy, or *cathected*, to use the common psychoanalytic term. Our own body or sense of self is generally highly cathected. Next are those persons with whom we grew up—mother, father, family. Psychoanalysts regard certain abstract symbols as displaced representations of highly cathected parents, a displacement we see in terms such as "mother tongue" or "fatherland." And a nation's flag is a highly cathected symbol, as Vietnam war protesters found when they were attacked by "hard hat" construction workers for burning the American flag. Our personalities are formed in part around the objects we cathect.

The Structural Perspective In the early 1920s Freud introduced the concepts of the *id*, the *ego*, and the *superego* to describe the way he thought the human mind was structured and organized. What part of the personality represents the purest expression of our drives and what parts seek to organize and control these drives? Although Freud had a dynamic view of personality that conceived of active forces (drives) and counterforces (inhibitions) within the individual that determine behavior, he began to conceive of hypothetical agents within the individual that could either be in conflict or operate in relative harmony. These agents he termed the id, the ego, and the superego.

The Id The *id* is the personality's key link to the biological drives. It is the source of the mental energy whose ebbs, flows, investments, and attachments determine the economy of the personality. Until recently in the development of psychoanalytic theory it was considered to be the source of all energy for the ego and superego. The id is, in effect, a chaotic reservoir of energies that are constantly being pressed by the drives toward immediate discharge. It operates on the *pleasure principle*—"I want what I want when I want it"—and does not take reality constraints into account. Id energies are mobile and can attach themselves to almost any object. The id's basic representation can be seen in an infant's somewhat disorganized grasping and sucking and the way the infant quickly becomes overwhelmed and cries at any delay in gratification. According to psychoanalysis, we are unlikely to experience the id directly except perhaps in sexual climax or in the gusto of biting into a juicy steak.

Freud after 1920 placed his greatest emphasis upon the sexual drive, *eros*, and on the aggressive drive, *thanatos*, which is sometimes called the *death instinct*. According to psychoanalytic theory, most of our desires, wishes, and behavior can be shown to be psychological representations of these two drives. Even in moments of greatest tenderness, as in love-making, the aggressive drive can manifest itself as well. How many times do lovers say things like "I could eat you all up," sometimes even punctuating their words with an actual nip? Is our fascination with vampires and the Dracula story a symbolic representation of this mixture of sex and aggression?

The Ego   The *ego* represents the *executive* branch of the mental apparatus—the structure of the mind that gets things done, thus enabling the drives to attain their objects and discharge their energies. In the first few months of life, the infant is practically all id and attains satisfaction primarily by sucking on anything within sight or touch. These first observations and movements become more and more refined, and the infant's actions begin to adjust to the way things move and look in the "real," outside world. Thus, the ego gradually emerges, beginning, as Freud suggested, with the child's imagining or "hallucinating" the absent mother and thus partially discharging the drive through fantasy. The ego becomes the system for delaying gratification—a vital function, because if wishes cannot be fulfilled, the child will be overcome by massive distress or anxiety that can endanger the organism. The ego serves the organism by warding off anxiety, while still seeking for ways to satisfy the drive when a more propitious moment occurs for discharge. The notions of timeliness, delay, and planning are important to the ego's function, and its motto might well be "There's a time and place for everything."

Defense Mechanisms   The adult ego operates through *defense mechanisms*, which prevent the raw emergence of unacceptable or embarrassing drive demands into consciousness. Such eruptions can create acute anxiety, an overwhelming and painful experience of utter terror that few people can stand for very long. The two most basic forms of defense are *denial*, in which a person tries to act as if the threat or conflict does not exist at all, and *repression*, forgetting or expelling from consciousness the memory or images of the desired object or the conflicting situations that pose a threat.

Another major defense is *projection*, whereby a person avoids facing unacceptable desires by attributing them to someone else. Freud noted that paranoid schizophrenics (mental patients with delusions of persecution) often claim that many of the people "whispering behind their backs" or conspiring against them are homosexuals. He proposed from a study of such individuals' fantasies and thought processes that the patients themselves were often attracted to persons of the same sex; they could not consciously accept such desires without anxiety, however, because of their upbringing and the social disapproval of homosexuality. To defend themselves against this homosexual impulse they attributed it to others. They sacrificed reality, in effect, in order to avoid confronting their own "shameful" desires.

SCIENTIFIC EVIDENCE OF REPRESSION

An analysis of how forgetting occurs in an actual psychoanalytic session supports some of Freud's views of repression. Figure 2-1 shows the averaged relationship for ten patients between their speech patterns, sudden forgetting of thought or other material, and subsequent flow of speech following the episode of forgetfulness. By examining the tape-recorded transcripts of actual therapy sessions, Luborsky (1977) was able to show that as patients touched on difficult topics—usually their relationship with the therapist (the transference)—there was an increase in hesitations, exclamations of uncertainty, and other signs of cognitive disturbance (see left half of graph). After the instance of forgetting, the speech disturbances are reduced (right half of graph), suggesting that the defense of repression has served temporarily to reduce anxiety. Studies of this type provide some of the best evidence so far available to back up Freud's original observations of how defenses worked in the psychoanalytic session.

FIGURE 2-1

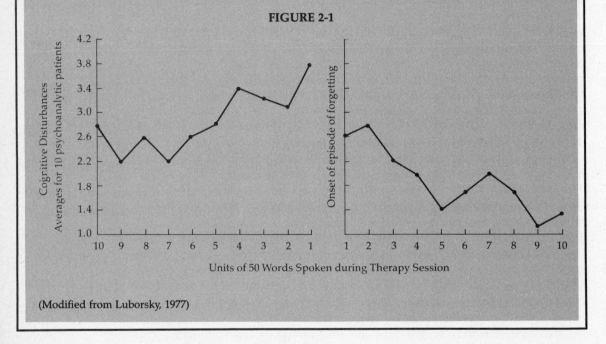

Units of 50 Words Spoken during Therapy Session

(Modified from Luborsky, 1977)

Two defenses, *rationalization* and *intellectualization* call upon the higher powers of intellect to avoid confronting more "primitive" desires. If you are on a diet and succumb to the temptation of a rich dessert, you may rationalize your behavior by telling yourself, "Actually, I need more energy. I've been feeling tired lately." Or if you reluctantly accompanied your friends to a bullfight or boxing match, you might defend yourself against feelings of excitement by intellectualizing, saying to yourself, "This whole scene is sociologically fascinating. Who would believe adults could behave so primitively! I'm going to write a paper on this."

A defense that can often be detected when someone is too polite or too humble is *reaction formation*, which is an effort to trick oneself (and others) about one's impulses by pretending the opposite. Employees who have been frequently humiliated by the boss may act in a humble and polite fashion or even convince themselves that the boss is right, lest angry impulses come to the surface and lead to words or actions that could endanger their jobs.

The ego defense that Freud felt was most significant for maturity, social structure, and creativity is *sublimation*. Here the primitive impulse becomes displaced or transmuted into a form of thought or behavior that is socially valued. In psychoanalytic terms, a child who is curious about parents' sexuality would fear peeking into their bedroom and risking humiliation or punishment. The child then might displace or sublimate that sexual curiosity into scientific curiosity and become interested at an early age in studying nature through a microscope or telescope. Such a socially respected hobby might lead to a valuable career in science. Freud offered the hypothesis that the principal structures of society—such as religion, architecture, the arts, and law—may all be sublimations of humanity's sexual and aggressive impulses.

The Superego The *superego* is the component of the mind that sums up the moral commands, values, and prohibitions incorporated from parents or from representatives of religion and society. Freud stressed the superego's prohibitive and punitive aspects, but other psychoanalysts have emphasized its idealism and potential for noble aspirations—a quality called the *ego ideal*. The ego's task, as we have seen, is to restrain drives from unrealistic expression, but it seeks "practical" ways to allow sexual or aggressive impulses to emerge. Freud recognized however, that as we grow up in the reality of our families and cultures, in which we face the clear-cut danger of being arrested or reprimanded for overt expression of sexual or aggressive drives, we also create an additional "reality"—the pain and guilt of our conscience, which attacks, denounces, or shames us for even *thinking* violent or lustful thoughts. The superego is the advocate of the strict rules or taboos we have learned from parents, teachers, and clergy. The ego's task, therefore, is not just to modify the drives lest they clash with reality but also to avoid conflict with the ideals or punishing prohibitions of the superego. Indeed it is more often the case that the ego's task for a child past age 6 and for the adult is to defend against expression of drives so as to avoid the anxiety produced by conflict between the id and the superego. It is in this sense that psychoanalytic theory is intrapsychic, primarily a theory of the *private* personality.

Often, people who are not conscious of conflicts between id, ego, and superego may experience symptoms such as headaches, various other physical reactions, or periods of severe depression. In Shakespeare's *Macbeth*, Lady Macbeth goads her husband into killing Duncan, the old king of Scotland. During the murder scene, she says that she would have killed the king herself had he not reminded her of her father as he lay sleeping. Later in the play,

In "The Incredible Hulk," a recent television series, a greenish giant emerges whenever David Banner, a mild-mannered physicist, gets angry. The Hulk, who occasioned the dream that opened this chapter, is a TV writer's fantasy of how id impulses of aggression burst through the controls of ego and superego. The popularity of this series attests to an important need of many child (and adult) viewers, who long to be free to express rage when society's rules call for restraint.

Lady Macbeth develops the hysterical reaction of somnambulism (sleepwalking). She keeps trying in her sleep to wash her hands and rid herself of the murdered man's blood. Of course, one interpreter might say that her guilt is based on an actual crime. But a Freudian might argue that we have already

THE INTERPLAY OF PERSONALITY AGENTS: AN ALLEGORY

One way to understand how Freud proposed that the id, ego, and superego interact is to think of them as three rulers of a "country," the human being. The id is king (or queen), the ego his prime minister, the superego the high priest (or priestess) of the realm. The id is an absolute hereditary monarch. He is owed complete obedience, but he is spoiled, willful, and completely self-centered. He wants what he wants when he wants it. The ego is the prime minister. He (or she) doesn't care at all about whether what the monarch wants is good or evil. The amoral ego's job is to get things done, avoid revolution or disruption of the monarchy, and prevent destruction of the organism (anxiety).

The ego may get an order from the monarch such as "I want that man's money and I also want his land." The ego, operating on the reality principle, must remonstrate with the id, pointing out that just taking things could make an enemy of the rich man and encourage him to attempt to assassinate the king or to form a conspiracy against him. There is also the possibility of a conflict between the king's decrees. Hadn't the monarch recently also given the man money as a reward for siding with him against his enemies? Here, too, the high priest (the superego) has to be considered. He will condemn the king for greed and argue that kings should have nobler purposes.

The crafty ego tries to find a way around all this. He devises a plan for setting up an elaborate cultural festival in honor of the king. Naturally, the rich man will want to contribute heavily to show his loyalty. The high-priest superego can be appeased because the festival is a worthwhile enterprise, brings support for the religion, and perhaps becomes a permanent celebration in which the masses can take part so that it fulfills the "nobler" ambitions of a king.

The monarch is temporarily calmed down by the arrangements the ego has worked out. Soon, however, he reverts to his claim for more of the man's money and property. And so the crafty ego must go to work again trying to satisfy the king's wishes without risking revolution or denunciation by the high priest or superego.

The ego is the perfect civil servant or Machiavellian statesman for a greedy prince. He tries to get things done without endangering the kingdom. His only aim is to keep the monarch in power (or, in effect, avoid danger to the individual).

The prime minister has a host of underlings—the ego functions and the defense mechanisms—to help him. The ego functions scout out the terrain, organize the festival, and encourage the participation of the wealthy. The defenses try to sustain the ego's power by avoiding too heavy a demand or irrational and conflicting orders from the practically insane, selfish king. They remonstrate with the king or try to deceive him. "I never heard what you said"; or "I can't remember what order you gave me" (repression); or "That man's not rich at all—he's really poor" (denial); or "Be careful and don't get involved with that man at all—I know for a fact he's conspiring against you" (projection); or "I'm sure, keeping in mind your best interests and avoiding the criticism of the high priest, what you really meant to say is that you respect the man so much you want to reward him further with more money and present him with some public honor" (reaction formation).

had a clue that Lady Macbeth linked Duncan with her own father. The intensity of her feeling is occasioned by her longstanding ambivalent feelings of love and hate toward her father as well as her involvement in Duncan's death. In her normal waking state, she shows no signs of being guilty; but her punitive superego operates at the unconscious level and causes her somnambulism and ritualistic handwashing.

The structural perspective in psychoanalysis thus shows how our mental processes are constantly engaged in a kind of power struggle between three elements: the id, which represents a blind, timeless thrust toward the gratification of our most basic needs or wishes; the ego, which strives to find realistic ways for expressing such needs or wishes without endangering the organism; and the superego, which tries to restrict such gratifications by calling on the moral, religious, or ethical codes and strictures we have incorporated from our parents or from society. Our private personality is continuously involved in intrigues and maneuvers between these three components of the *psyche* (another word for mind). The relative strength of these three components produces different personalities. People characterized by impulsivity, headstrong action, and abrasive directness may have a stronger balance of id over ego and superego; such persons often get into difficulties with their families, neighbors, or the law. People with a well-developed ego but an undeveloped superego may be crafty and clever about getting what they want; such persons may become successful "con artists" and swindlers; they may attain political power, and then abuse it; they may even end up as criminals. And people with an overdeveloped superego may become straitlaced conformists, tormented by guilt for the slightest thoughts about sexuality. Of course, such a person could also become a religious leader or a crusading district attorney or a writer who adopts a high moral tone, such as John Milton, the author of *Paradise Lost*.

The Developmental Perspective

A basic tenet of psychoanalysis, which persists even in modifications of the theory, is that early childhood experiences are the determinants both of adult personality and of any emotional disturbances that appear in later life. According to psychoanalysis, personality is formed by the ways in which a child deals with a series of phases, or stages, that all children must pass through in the first five years of life. These stages are called the *oral* stage, the *anal* stage, and the *phallic* stage. Freud's biological emphasis led him to propose that children experience sexual and aggressive drives right from the start, and that they are focused on a different bodily orifice in each of the three stages.

For Freud, the view expressed in Wordsworth's statement that "the child is the father of the man" was central to psychoanalytic theory. Freud believed that childhood experiences are stored in the brain, that many childhood desires are built into adult bodily mechanisms as drives seeking gratification around specific areas of the body—the mouth, the anus, or the genitals—and that these drives continue to demand satisfaction. At least, their mental representations from childhood are never completely lost. In Freud's words, "None of the infantile mental formulations perish. All the wishes, instinctual impulses, modes of reaction and attitudes of childhood are demonstrably present in maturity and in appropriate circumstances can emerge once more" (Freud, 1962, Vol. 13, p. 184).

2 • THE PSYCHOANALYTIC THEORY OF SIGMUND FREUD

The Oral Stage   In infancy and babyhood a child is totally dependent, and is focused on the need to obtain milk by sucking a breast or bottle and later by biting and chewing food. The infant's psychosexual gratifications are built around dependency and oral activities. If for some physical reason the infant has unusually strong sucking needs, it may experience greater than usual frustration during this period. Or more likely, if the mother or other nurturant figure is careless or overanxious, the infant may have sucking difficulties and develop a *fixation* (psychological overemphasis) on oral intake, sucking, or angry biting. An orally fixated child may develop hard-to-break habits such as thumb-sucking, nail biting, or overeating, and in adult life become a heavy drinker or smoker. Orally fixated adults may chew their food noisily, pick their teeth conspicuously, or have other nervous mouth mannerisms. This oral tendency might be transformed into caustic humor of the kind known as "biting remarks."

The Anal Stage   By age 2 or 3, a child must begin to control urination and defecation, activities that parents—and indeed most societies—find unpleasant unless carried out in appropriate locations. The child usually enjoys urinating and defecating and the buildup and release of the tension around the excretory orifices. Such pleasurable release is soon met by disgusted looks, angry comments, and often spankings from the child's caretakers. A necessity for delay and self-control is thus introduced, and the child may react with anger or aggression. The efforts at control over bowel habits become associated with experiences of humiliation, shame, disgust, and contempt. The child must cope with this situation by learning self-control, and there often ensues a battle of wills between a mother who tries to get a child to the proper receptacle in time and a child who resists producing what is demanded and then does so later in his or her pants, only to provoke a reaction of dismay.

The capacity for self-control and inhibition comes out of this phase, according to psychoanalytic theory. Overemphasis on toilet training and overfocusing on this phase of parent-child relations may lead to a fixation in the anal stage so that it persists as a prominent feature of the adult personality.

Since every child passes through this phase, a normal continuation can be seen in "dirty" jokes, in using "foul" language, and in derogatory words for the human backside. Someone with a greater fixation is, on the one hand, overly upset by bad smells or, on the other, someone who delights in bathroom humor. Children forced to have excessive concern with toilet training often become neat, finicky, self-controlled, indeed miserly and rigid adults, as a reaction formation against recurrent pressure for anal gratification. There may be elements of anal sadism—the aggressive component that emerges amid all this neatness—such as the joy of playing "dirty tricks" on people. In Herman Wouk's novel *The Caine Mutiny*, the ship's captain, Mr. Queeg, is depicted as a person overly concerned about petty details in the day-to-day operation of the ship. He also has the curious habit of rolling little balls around in his hands and other signs suggesting that, despite all his neatness and control, the anal desire to play with feces is still being expressed.

The Phallic Stage   Between the ages of 3 and 5, Freud proposed, all children enter the phallic stage of preoccupation with urination and their genital organs. Here the theory begins to differentiate the experiences of boys and girls, in accord with Freud's dictum that "anatomy is destiny." Today, the phallic stage is one of the most controversial and questionable aspects of Freudian theory and may well be a product of his own upbringing in his central European, male-dominated culture. Sometimes boys will line up by the curb or near a stream or lake to see who can urinate the farthest. Obviously such competition is impossible for girls. Therefore, Freud said, while both boys and girls obtain sexual pleasure by playing with their genitals, girls experience a sense of something missing, a feeling he called *penis envy*. This lack, he felt, becomes a key feature of the psychic structure of women, and is reflected in women's persisting need to overcome this loss. Girls grow up, Freud believed, resigned to the fact that they can never equal men except by incorporating a man's penis during sexual relations or, symbolically, by carrying a child in the womb. Some boys (and indeed some girls) try to account for girls' lack of a penis with a fantasy that their parents have cut it off as a punishment; this is the origin of *castration fear*. Some parents, disturbed about childhood masturbation, do threaten their sons that "it will fall off" and in this way may further these fantasies.

Today, of course, with the women's movement, this aspect of Freud's theory, in which women are perceived as "crippled males," is the subject of tremendous controversy. Freud probably viewed himself as a radical in his position on women in the sense that he was making sexuality more explicit and freeing women from their neurotic inhibitions about sexual pleasure. Today many consider him a prejudiced and unscientific observer, who held women back by attributing their status to an anatomical difference. There probably are women with "penis envy," but undoubtedly Freud grossly oversimplified the many complicated differences in social experiences between men and women and ignored most of the constructive aspects of women's experience.

During the phallic stage, the child begins to experience a sexual attraction for the parent of the opposite sex. Freud named this the *Oedipus complex* (for boys) and the *Electra complex* (for girls), using the names of Sophocles' characters in dramas portraying incest and father-son, mother-daughter rivalries. Freud believed this was an inevitable stage of development, the son envious of the father's intimate moments with the mother and yearning for continuing closeness with her without the father's interference. The boy's resentment of the father can produce conflict, since a little boy's desire to get rid of "Big Daddy" might arouse father's wrath and evoke the punishment of castration. Girls at first might also feel a rivalry with the father (since for both sexes the mother is the nurturing figure in the oral stage); they might also, Freud implied, accept "castration" (their lack of a penis) as punishment for these feelings. Ultimately, the conflict over incestuous wishes in boys and girls is resolved by identification with the parent of their own sex. Boys incorporate the father's strength, potential aggression, and assertive sexuality as part of the masculine

THE RAT MAN:
A PSYCHOANALYTIC CASE STUDY

One of Freud's most famous cases is the "Rat Man," a man of 29 who was suffering from a severe obsessional neurosis (Freud, 1962, Vol. 10). He reported a series of recurrent thoughts and doubts which were so overwhelming and repulsive that he could not concentrate effectively on his work; indeed, he had been almost completely disabled for some time. The precipitating cause of his coming for treatment was a recurring tormenting thought, a picture in his mind of rats nibbling at the backside of his sweetheart. He also had similar thoughts of rats feeding on his father's anus.

Freud treated this young man almost daily for about a year. He subsequently prepared a lengthy report and theoretical discussion of the case, which reads in many ways like a detective story. Little by little, Freud made more sense of the strange obsessional thoughts. Early childhood experiences relating to toilet training and anal erotic feelings helped explain the rat image, as well as childhood feelings of fear and resentment after being punished by his father for masturbating and for biting someone. As a child, the patient had seen a rat near his father's grave and fantasized that it had been nibbling on the corpse. The neurosis was precipitated shortly after the man's army captain, an authority he resented, had told him the story of an Asiatic punishment involving live burial of a prisoner who was then attacked from behind by rats. It seemed almost inevitable that these obsessive thoughts occurred at a point of maximum conflict—when the man was faced with the necessity of giving up the mistress he loved in order to marry a more socially acceptable, attractive, and wealthy young woman. Freud was able to show that the occurrence of the obsessive thoughts provided a temporary escape from the conflict, because the neurotic symptoms prevented him from completing his education and therefore having to take the step of marrying and abandoning his beloved mistress.

Although Freud does not give details on the actual nature of his patient's personality change, the treatment seems to have been successful, with the young man restored to effective functioning (although he was later killed in World War I).

identity, while girls identify with the mother's receptivity, nurturant qualities, and capacity for childbearing.

Freud believed that only by incorporating these parental attitudes and ways of thinking can a child be prepared for more advanced forms of abstract thought and moral maturity. A child who fails to resolve the dilemmas of the Oedipal stage and who does not develop an internalized adult perspective—the superego—grows up a moral cripple, a psychopathic personality, a person without conscience or capacity for guilt. Conflict may remain even after the parent has been incorporated as superego. Some children cannot resolve their problems with parents and remain fixated in the Oedipal stage, with consequences that are widely recognized. The boy who grows up attracted only to older women, the inhibited man who still shares a two-room apartment with his widowed mother, the woman who scorns all suitors and grows into virginal old age taking care of her beloved father—all are instances of Oedipal fixation. Some of Freud's classic cases of hysterical neurosis involved women with unconscious love-hate fixations on their fathers.

The Genital Stage   Freud believed that the groundwork for the formation of personality was essentially complete after the child had passed through the Oedipal phase between ages 5 and 6. During the next six years the child represses sexual interests and allies himself or herself to same-sex groups. This "latency period" ends with the bodily changes that signal adolescence, such as growth of body hair, menstruation and breast development in girls, spontaneous emissions and voice change in boys. Next comes a move toward the final or *genital* stage of adolescent and adult sexual interest.

The Adaptive Perspective   There are a few hints that Freud was somewhat interested in the way in which the structure of the mind is related to adaptation to the environment rather than to organization of instinctual drives. But it was not until after Freud's death that the emphasis in psychoanalysis shifted to *ego psychology* (Chapter 3). Freud himself seemed to feel that his greatest contribution as a psychologist was to help us understand the little-known aspects of human behavior—the complex scenarios of the unconscious drives, their displacements of energy, and their transformations. The vast unconscious realm of the mind, of which human waking awareness is only the tip of the iceberg, is what he sought to comprehend.

MANIFESTATIONS OF THE UNCONSCIOUS

The Meaning of Dreams   Freud's theory of dreams was a revelation to most people who were puzzled by the confusing, sometimes downright bizarre sequences of images in their dreams. His method of analysis involves having patients recount their mental associations to each segment of a dream. Usually such associations lead to the realization that a dream is an attempt at wish fulfillment, an expression in consciousness of instinctual drives transformed by the *censorship* that the ego uses to hide the naked impulses of the id. What emerges as the dream is disguised so that the *manifest content* of the dream—its plot or story line—is less threatening than the underlying message, or *latent content*, which contains unacceptable and frightening wishes.

For example, a man undergoing psychoanalysis dreamed of having to grapple with a dark-haired, pimply-faced intruder who kept bursting into his hotel room while his new bride stood nearby in terror. The young man nearly killed the dark intruder but then released him. The man's associations led him to remember that long ago he burst in on his parents while they were making love during a stay at a resort hotel. He also recalled that his domineering father had been urging him and his new wife to spend some weeks sharing a vacation

Gregory Peck and Ingrid Bergman in Alfred Hitchcock's Spellbound. *Psychoanalysis has inspired many books, plays, and films; in* Spellbound, *a man's repressed memory of his brother's accidental death leads to later confusion of self-identity and unwarranted guilt. Robert Redford's recent film* Ordinary People *has a similar theme.*

cottage with the parents, a demand the young couple felt to be intrusive on their privacy. And, finally, the man realized the significance of the intruder's dark hair and pimples—the family name was Schwartzkopf, German for "blackhead"! Clearly, the dream revealed a longstanding Oedipal rivalry with his father, revived by the recent threat of the father's intrusion on the dreamer's privacy with his new wife. The latent content reflected the pressure of hostile wishes and sexual rivalry that the younger man could not accept consciously.

Freud and hundreds of other psychoanalysts subsequently showed how daydreams and fantasies could often be similarly explained. One woman's recurrent fantasy (often associated with sexual arousal) that she was being held captive in a sultan's harem was shown to be linked to her attraction to older, powerful men and ultimately to her father. By disguising the father's identity as a powerful but exotic figure and making herself a prisoner who had no choice but to submit, the woman's ego was permitting her to express her childhood attachment to her father without evoking the wrath of her superego.

Similarly, Freud showed that tongue slips are often an eruption of unconscious feelings into speech. A psychoanalyst in training who had been struggling with resentments against his father and, more recently, against authorities in his school, concluded his presentation of a paper by saying, "As Fraud once wrote. . . ." When everyone laughed, he apologized and reread the sentence, but once again he mispronounced the name of the "father" of psychoanalysis as "Fraud"!

The Concept of Transference
Another manifestation of the unconscious and one of Freud's most important discoveries was the concept of *transference*, the tendency for patients to develop strong feelings toward the psychoanalyst—sometimes of affection and love (positive transference) and sometimes of anger and hostility (negative transference). By studying these intense emotions, which were much stronger than the "neutral," noncommittal attitude of the therapist warranted, Freud came to recognize that most people carry around with them elaborate but unconscious sets of expectations and wishes with regard to authority figures or others who remind them of their early childhood experiences with parents. Such feelings erupt not only in psychoanalytic sessions, where they can be closely studied, but in ordinary social relationships where they can account for irrational love attachments "at first sight" or for sudden outbursts of hostility at bosses or supervisors who justifiably criticize an employee in the course of a routine work situation.

The concept of transference was extended by subsequent psychoanalysts as a key concept not only in therapy but in many situations of daily life. We have all grown up with wishes or fantasies about how situations or relationships in our lives will develop. When we find ourselves in situations that are ambiguous or that partially resemble significant periods of our childhood, we draw on these fantasies. Often such fantasies are distortions, and we are puzzled or upset by why things do not work out as we unconsciously expected. The transference phenomenon is thus a representation of the private plans or "scripts" we bring to social situations. This notion is important in cognitive theories of personality as well as in psychoanalysis, as we shall see in Chapter 6.

EVALUATION OF PSYCHOANALYTIC THEORY

Freud's theory continues to be a kind of general framework against which other personality theories are judged, not because it is "correct" but because it was the first major effort in modern times and still remains the most com-

TABLE 2-1

Freud's Career and Contributions

	Personal Life	Professional Career	Discoveries and Contributions
1882–1897	Early medical research career; brief study of hypnosis and psychopathology in France; marriage and private practice.	Collaboration with Joseph Breuer using hypnosis to treat neurosis; development of free association as basic technique.	Catharsis; sexual conflict and defenses against disturbing wishes as bases for neurotic symptoms.
1897–1902	Self-analysis.	Professional isolation because of his emphasis on sexuality as a basis for complexes; publication of *The Interpretation of Dreams* (1900).	Theory of dreams as wish fulfillments; concepts of two types of thought—primary and secondary; the Oedipus complex; relationship of dreams, slips of the tongue, and humor to neurotic symptoms.
1902–1918	Development of psychoanalytic school and followers; defections of Adler and Jung; crystallization of psychoanalysis as an organized body of theory and clinical practice.	Extensive clinical practice; visit to the United States; university appointment and growing fame.	Development of theories of childhood sexuality, libido theory, and energy concepts; theories of paranoia, depression, cultural "totems and taboos"; concept of transference.
1918–1926	Increasing world fame and influence.	Revision of theory of anxiety; introduction of concept of the death instinct and greater emphasis on aggression as well as on sexual repression.	Theory of eros and thanatos (drives toward sexuality and aggression); structural theory (id, ego, superego); anxiety as the core experience and defense mechanisms as bases for personality differences and symptom patterns.
1926–1939	Heroic struggle against cancer of jaw; flight from Nazis in Vienna to settle in England; death.	Emphasis on social and cultural implications of psychoanalytic theory.	Theory of religion as a form of defense or "illusion"; group behavior and culture as defenses against eros-thanatos conflicts.

prehensive of personality systems. Eighty years after the formulation of the theory, scholars and critics continue to examine its implications and apply it to fields as diverse as historical analysis and the critical examination of literary texts. Psychodynamic concepts, derived both from the theory and from modifications of psychoanalytic treatment, continue to be used by psychiatrists, clinical psychologists, and social workers in a variety of mental-health settings. The recognition of the importance of early childhood experiences and of the way in which fantasies from childhood color adult thinking, the potential meaningfulness of dreams, the importance of anxiety and of the defense mechanisms in personality structure, the possibility of making sense of "odd" behavior or neurotic symptoms—all these things are an integral part of psychological thinking. The theory, whether or not correct in details, has thus had an enduring and pervasive influence on thought in Western civilization.

Limitations of the Psychoanalytic Method

Freud's method of free association made it possible to study the complex working of the private personality over a long period. The extent to which people do their thinking at an apparently unconscious level emerged from this procedure. But the method in itself is a private one. We must depend on the account of what happened as reported by a particular psychoanalyst. The theory itself calls attention to the many ways in which our early wishes, fears, and attitudes may bias our interpretations; even well-trained psychoanalysts are not free of such potentially distorting views. The psychoanalytic method is therefore best regarded as a *hypothesis-engendering procedure*. Its observations and conclusions, indeed all elements of the theory, must be tested by more objective procedures. Extensive scholarship has also called attention to inconsistencies in Freud's concepts, shifts in his definitions of terms, and to many vague areas in the structure of the theory (Gill and Holzman, 1976).

Although Freud was dubious of experimental tests for his theory, a huge body of research has developed in the past forty years aimed at testing various concepts in psychoanalysis. A compendium of such studies published by Fisher and Greenberg (1977) indicates that many specific predictions derived from psychoanalysis have been verified. The clusters of traits relating to "oral" and "anal" personalities seem to emerge again and again, although the origin of these characteristics in actual childhood experiences of feeding and toilet training are less well established. Also supported are concepts such as castration anxiety in males, homosexual fear in paranoid schizophrenics, and various aspects of the Oedipus complex in some (but certainly not all) men. In later chapters, as we review specific issues in personality such as aggression and anxiety, we shall examine more specific research stimulated by psychoanalysis.

Many concepts of Freud have an appealing poetic flavor, but for a personality theory they defy normal scientific evaluation. Eros and thanatos, the life and death drives; the id, ego, and superego; the broad use of sexuality to refer to many kinds of bodily pleasures; the concept of cathexis—all turn out to be too vague to be proved or disproved and thus fail to meet critical tests of scientific value. A whole body of recent research on the psychophysiology of the sleep cycles (Chapter 10) suggests that Freud's insistence on the drive-related, wish-fulfilling function of all dreaming was too sweeping and incorrect, except in some instances.

Freud overemphasized the private personality, as we have noted, perhaps because he realized that many of the childhood experiences recounted by his patients could never have occurred and were probably childhood fantasies. He overlooked the extent to which adult behavior actually does play a part in shaping a child's thoughts and actions. And we might wonder to what extent his own Oedipus complex was stimulated not only by his childhood thoughts but also by the almost seductive overprotectiveness of a mother much younger than his father, a mother who aroused his fantasies with tales of a gypsy's predictions about her "golden boy." As we shall see in Chapter 3, subsequent developments in ego psychology and neo-Freudian theories have placed more emphasis than Freud did on the pattern of interaction among parents or other adults, siblings, and the growing child. As Fisher and Greenberg (1977) point out, the research evidence suggests that boys develop a masculine identification and incorporate a father's moral standards more often when the father is a positive nurturant figure rather than the distant and frightening one suggested by Freud. And, of course, many of Freud's views of how women develop their sex-role attitudes and personality orientation have been discredited on both theoretical and empirical grounds.

Finally, Freud limited his theory to elaborating the transformations and dynamics of drives. Although he wrote that the goals of human existence were "loving and working," he virtually ignored the ways in which people go about their daily work, enjoy adventure or leisure, or how adults develop long-term friendships quite apart from sexual gratification. As we shall see, other personality theories do address these questions. Despite all these limitations, we cannot easily dismiss Freud. The sweep of his imagination and scope of his views are too vast to be ignored even if many of the details of his theory have been disproved or supplanted.

Freud held a tragic view of human nature. He believed that human beings could never completely overcome the power of their basic drives. He believed that civilization and culture were products created by humans at great psychic expense in an attempt to resist the continuing pressure of their biological drives. Progress could come only at the cost of continued repression. This was a brave if tragic view, since Freud refused to ignore the reality of evil in the world. He felt that humans could make only small gains at best against the forces of their instinctual drives. To use his comparison, we are all like the people of Holland and the Lowlands, who erect stronger and stronger dikes but are never free from struggle against the incursion of the raging seas.

SUMMARY

1. Psychoanalysis is a theory about relationships between human wishes and the way these wishes find expression through dreams, reveries, beliefs, and actions. It seeks to explain how personality develops from the experiences and conflicts of early childhood. Psychoanalysis is also a form of psychotherapy.

2. Psychoanalysis was originated by Sigmund Freud, a Viennese physician and neurologist. Freud theorized that motives grow out of biologically rooted drives and the *transformation* of these drives, which takes place when expressing the drives would arouse terrible fear or anxiety. Drives have specific goals, but if a goal is not available, other related goals can be substituted; this substitution is called *displacement*.

3. Psychoanalysis stresses the concept of *objects*, a term referring to all the people, bodily parts, or psychological situations that a child relates to gratification of its impulses. Some objects recur so regularly that they become invested with a great deal of energy. Freud used the term *cathexis* for this investment of energy.

4. Freud introduced the concepts of the *id*, the *ego*, and the *superego* to describe the way he thought the mind was structured and organized. The id is the key link in the personality to the biological drives. The ego is the part of the mind that gets things done, thus enabling drives to attain their objects. The ego operates through *defense mechanisms*, the most basic of which are denial and repression. Other defenses are projection, rationalization, intellectualization, reaction formation, and sublimation. The superego focuses on the moral commands, values, and prohibitions incorporated from parents or from representatives of religion and society.

5. According to psychoanalysis, personality is formed by the ways in which a child deals with a series of stages that all children pass through in the first five years of life. First is the *oral* stage in which psychosexual gratifications are built around dependency and oral activities. Next, at age 2 or 3, is the *anal* stage, when a child must begin to control urination and defecation. The capacity for self-control and inhibition comes out of this stage. The third stage is the *phallic* stage, at ages 3 to 5, when children pass through a phase of preoccupation with urination and their genital organs. Here Freud's theory differentiates the experiences of boys and girls. During the phallic stage, a child begins to have a sexual attraction for the parent of the opposite sex, called the Oedipus complex (for boys) and the Electra complex (for girls). After passage through the phallic stage at about ages 5 to 6, the groundwork for the formation of personality is essentially complete.

6. Freud's method of dream analysis in which patients recount their mental associations to each segment of a dream led to the realization that a dream is an attempt at wish fulfillment. What emerges as the dream is disguised so that the manifest content of the dream is less threatening than the latent content, which contains unacceptable and frightening wishes. Freud showed how daydreams, fantasies, and slips of the tongue can be similarly explained.

7. One of Freud's discoveries was the concept of *transference*, the tendency for patients to develop strong feelings of affection and love (positive tranference) or of anger and hostility (negative transference) toward the psychoanalyst. By studying these intense emotions Freud recognized that most people carry around with them an unconscious set of expectations and wishes

with regard to authority figures or other people who remind them of their early childhood experiences with parents.

8. Psychoanalytic concepts and methods continue to be used by psychiatrists, clinical psychologists, and social workers. Psychoanalysis, however, is best regarded as a hypothesis-engendering procedure with observations and conclusions that must be tested by objective methods.

CHAPTER
3

The Evolution
of Psychoanalytic Theory

In 1909 Sigmund Freud received the first international recognition of his work when he was invited to lecture on psychoanalysis at Clark University in Worcester, Massachusetts. Accompanying Freud to the United States was his young colleague, the Swiss psychiatrist Carl G. Jung. Writing of this trip, Jung (1963) described how he and Freud daily interpreted each other's dreams although, as Jung discovered, Freud refused to be completely candid with the younger man lest he lose his "authority."

Jung had a dream in which he was in a place that seemed to be his home, with a first floor furnished in eighteenth-century style. He went downstairs and found a dark, paneled room decorated in sixteenth-century style. Then he went farther down into the cellar, and there was a room with stone walls of Roman origin. He became increasingly excited in the dream, opened a slab on the floor and went even deeper, finding a prehistoric tomb with skulls, bones, and broken pottery.

As he thought about his dream, Jung was convinced that it symbolized the story of his life and intellectual development. Jung had grown up in a 200-year-old house with much of the furniture dating from the seventeenth century. He had studied the German philosophers, such as Kant and Schopenhauer, and later he had been drawn to scientific discoveries in archaeology and anthropology and to Darwin's theory of evolution. All of this contrasted with the "medieval" religious beliefs of his parents. Jung decided that his dream represented in symbolic form his own profound curiosity and desire to trace deeper and deeper into human consciousness the ways in which human history and evolution were reflected in dreams and fantasies. He was sure, however, that Freud would not accept such an interpretation, since it did not fit neatly into the psychoanalytic concept of the Oedipus complex. So Jung faked some associations, relating the bones in the subcellar to his desire to kill off members of his family. Here is how he describes what happened and his feelings about it:

While I was trying to find a suitable answer to Freud's questions, I was suddenly confused by an intuition about the role that the subjective factor plays in psychological understanding. My intuition was so overwhelming that I thought only of how to get out of this impossible snarl, and I took the easy way out by a lie. This was neither elegant nor morally defensible, but otherwise I should have risked a fatal row with Freud—and I did not feel up to that for many reasons.

My intuition consisted of the sudden and most unexpected insight into the fact that my dream meant myself, my *life and* my *world, my whole reality against a theoretical structure erected by another, strange mind for reasons and purposes of its own. It was not Freud's dream, it was mine. . . .* (Jung, 1964, p. 44).

CHANGES WITHIN CLASSICAL PSYCHOANALYSIS

The preceding anecdote indicates some of the directions psychoanalytic theory was to take after Freud. Within the orthodox theory, many changes occurred, but these were assimilated into the theory because their proponents—primarily Heinz Hartmann, David Rapaport, and Erik Erikson—were less critical than Jung was and sought to show how consistent their views were with Freud's. An example of the changes is Hartmann's emphasis on the fact that many ego functions, such as abstract thought and language development, emerge naturally in the human mind, not just in response to conflict or drive deprivation. The view that the ego is in part autonomous, independent of the id, suggests that many experiences and actions evolve because they help the organism adapt to the realities of survival in the physical and social environment. Thus, *ego psychology* opened the way for psychoanalysts to pay increasing attention to the public personality, the ways we communicate with others, and the ways we learn to conform to society's demands.

A further extension of ego psychology appears in Erikson's proposal that development in childhood is more than just a passage from oral to anal to phallic stages. Erikson showed how cultural experiences and social expectations impinge on the child to generate feelings of trust during the oral stage, autonomy and independence in the anal stage, and exploratory behavior and initiative in the phallic stage. More than this, development does not cease with the passage through the Oedipal period but continues throughout life.

Another movement within the classical wing, the *object-relations school*, broadened the view of the private personality. Initiated in part by the British psychoanalyst Melanie Klein, proponents of the object-relations school question the emphasis on specific drives and the economic and structural perspectives of the classical theory. They propose that early childhood motivation is not so much the pursuit of pleasure—that is, gratifying a sexual drive—as it is attachment to *objects*. These objects are generally the people in the child's environment or parts of their bodies, particularly the mother's breast. The object-relations school emphasizes the way in which the "pictures" or "concepts" of parents become central to all thinking; it thus reflects an extension of the private personality. At the same time, by emphasizing that motivation is oriented toward people rather than toward gratification of biological drives, the theory resembles Sullivan's view, to be discussed later in the chapter, which stresses interpersonal relationships. Hence, it also opened the way for analysts to explore the public personality. The observations of infants and children by psychoanalysts such as Anna Freud, René Spitz, and Margaret Mahler were also important in the shift in focus from sexual gratification toward object relations. They all came to see the significance for infants of the people around them, a contrast with the emphasis on drive satisfaction.

JUNG'S EXPANSION OF THE PRIVATE PERSONALITY

The first two major breaks from Freud were initiated by Carl Jung and by Alfred Adler, each of whom developed different theories. Jung's emphasis was on the working of the unconscious mind and the private personality, while Adler focused on the public personality and social influences on private wishes. Moreover, the effects of their theories have been quite different. Jung's elaborate theory exists independently of most psychodynamic approaches, but Adler's concepts, to be discussed later in the chapter, have been so subtly and unobtrusively integrated into other psychodynamic theories and, even more, into psychotherapeutic practice that he often receives no credit as a theorist. Jung's theory, which he called *analytic psychology*, calls for more detailed presentation because it proposes a far-reaching expansion of the unconscious processes that psychoanalysts introduced as a basis for personality organization.

Jung's Approach to Dreams Jung relied on a modified form of psychoanalytic treatment of patients as his means of acquiring what he viewed as scientific information. He believed that interpretation of dreams should not be based on free association to elements of a dream. Rather, he used a dream as the starting point for exploring the imagery sequences that a patient could produce, a method he called *active imagination*. If a man recalls a dream in which he is walking through the narrow aisles of a law library with piles of books stacked up on each side, Jung might ask him to picture the dream again and then to produce a continuing series of images. The patient might imagine a book on constitutional law and then see himself "walking" through the pages of the book and reading about a First Amendment case. This might next lead to images related to this case, and so on. Jung preferred to encourage these images to unfold and to study their

CARL G. JUNG

Carl G. Jung (1875–1961) was a Swiss psychiatrist who came from a family with a long tradition of involvement in the Protestant ministry. He had an extraordinarily broad education in classics, history, and anthropology before choosing a career in medicine and psychiatry. Jung's tremendous intellectual curiosity and his special interest in the unusual aspects of human experience made him dissatisfied with the way psychiatry was being practiced.

In the early 1900s, when he was working at a mental hospital in Zurich, Jung was among the first psychiatrists to examine in detail the complex life of schizophrenic patients. He developed the technique known now as the word-association test in which patients are asked to give their first association to a list of words such as *table, bed, father, brother.* Studying the language and associations of schizophrenics and influenced by his study of Freud, he suggested that schizophrenics are in many ways waking dreamers. Their thought processes are expressed in the symbolic forms and transformations of basic drives that Freud had discovered in the night dream. This insight by Jung continues to be helpful to persons working with psychotic individuals.

One of Freud's earliest and most respected collaborators, Jung eventually parted company with Freud's circle in 1913 and established himself independently as a practitioner and theorist after some years of personal trial and self-doubt. Remaining in Switzerland, he became world famous as a psychotherapist who worked mainly with mature and relatively successful people, including many distinguished artists and writers. Throughout his long life, he published many books and articles. His influence waned during the 1920s through the 1950s, but it has increasingly been revived, perhaps because of the emphasis contemporary students and intellectuals placed on spiritual and even mystical experiences.

In exploring the complexity of the human mind, Jung delved into alchemy, Oriental religions, and the myths and legends of many cultures, and he even investigated the beliefs in flying saucers and parapsychology that began to emerge in the early 1950s. His influence continues to grow—particularly among literary and philosophical people—because of the sweeping mythological power of his theorizing and his great emphasis on how much can be found in dreams and even in the pictures people draw.

properties instead of concentrating on how the details of the dream could be traced to childhood experiences or to particular interpersonal situations. Jung also encouraged patients to draw pictures of their dream images or to invent on. Jung preferred to encourage these images to unfold and to study their fantasies on the spot and expand them into sequences of images. This method—the use of mental imagery and daydreams to overcome neurotic problems—has become part of a growing psychotherapy movement in Europe (Singer, 1974).

Jung's View of Human Motivation

Although Jung accepted Freud's identification of the significance of sexuality as a human motive and used some of Freud's notions of psychic energy as well, he believed that there were other important human motives. He thought that everyone should try to become more thoroughly fulfilled, to find a place in their society, and to gain some kind of spiritual understanding or serenity. Freud and other psychodynamic theorists reduced religious beliefs to the incorporation into the psyche of attitudes about parents (God the Father); Jung, on the other hand, showed more respect for the intrinsic value of spiritual interests; he felt that such beliefs were often reflections of an inherent human need to transcend the limitations of daily experience.

Jung accepted the hypothesis that there is always a tendency of the organism to gratify drives and to return to a state of relative equilibrium. But, in an important contrast to Freud, Jung introduced a fundamental concept called the *principle of opposites* in which he stated that for every wish there is an alternative wish. A person who expresses one side of a drive or wish will repress its opposite. The repressed drive, since its energy is undischarged, seeks expression in the unconscious or in the private personality generally and influences dreams and fantasies. For example, a little girl may heed her mother's admonition, "Be good to your new baby brother" and will consciously try to be nurturing and kind. But the very notion of "kindness" implies the mind's awareness of "meanness," and so as she grows up, the girl may have dreams or fantasies of tormenting little boys, despite her overtly "good" behavior to her brother.

Structural Characteristics of Personality

In contrast to Freud's emphasis on the conflict between id, ego, and superego, Jung stressed the balance between conscious and unconscious thoughts. The structure of the mind, according to Jung, has three levels. The first level, an extensive area, is the *conscious*. Next is a middle layer of unconscious content that derives in part from actual experiences of growing up in a family and in part from individual desires; Jung called this level—the unique, individualized portion of the mind— the *personal unconscious*.

The third layer, also unconscious, is one that human beings grow up with and share. This layer, the *collective unconscious*, represents one of Jung's most original, controversial, and provocative notions. Essentially he proposed that just as arms and legs and other parts of the human body have evolved through the centuries to function in specific ways, so too the mind itself has inherited a set of capacities that are representative of the actual experiences of earlier generations. The collective unconscious unites all human thought around common experiences from human evolution—our fear of wild animals or of the dark, our association of water with birth and cleansing or refreshment, our image of the sun as life giving and energizing.

Stored in every human being's mind are images that reflect the person's cultural and even racial characteristics (Jung, 1959, Vol. 9). These images are called *archetypes*, the inherited symbols that crop up in dreams, legends, and artifacts, however diverse on the surface cultures or nationalities may be. Familiar archetypes include *Mother Earth* or *Mother Nature*, transformed by different cultures into the Egyptian goddess Isis and her son, the infant god Horus, or the Virgin Mary and her infant, Jesus; *the sun* as a symbol of masculinity and energy; *the moon* as a symbol of femininity and receptivity; *the hero*, endowed by many legends in all nations with superpowers, who must prevail over huge monsters and the forces of evil. Such a hero was the Roman Hercules, and for us nowadays there are Superman, James Bond, and the ruggedly virtuous cowboy hero typified by John Wayne.

Another archetype is *the trickster*, a sly, conniving character, sometimes evil but sometimes simply mischievous. In Norse legends, the trickster is represented by Loki, the God of Fire; in German folklore by Til Eulenspiegel, the merry prankster; in Shakespeare's *A Midsummer Night's Dream* by the fairy jester, Puck; by the Joker or Jack in the playing-card deck; and by such cartoon figures as Bugs Bunny and Woody Woodpecker. From his principle of opposites, Jung seems to be suggesting that while many of us try consciously to conform to society's demands—to obey laws, to be helpful to others—unconsciously we may want to be mischievous, tricky, or disrespectful. That is why we often find ourselves admiring clever rogues—why Satan in Milton's poem *Paradise Lost* is more interesting than the Archangels, why we enjoy watching Bugs Bunny's tricks, or the slippery rebelliousness of Charlie Chaplin.

Jung's hypotheses of archetypes and of the collective unconscious are largely speculative and probably untestable scientifically. Still, his emphasis on common symbols and recurring themes across cultures as well as within cultures adds a further dimension to our understanding of the private personality. For Freud, most symbols are reducible to childhood fantasies related to the oral, anal, or phallic stages. For Jung, human experience goes beyond this body-centered emphasis and involves a broader spectrum of yearning and curiosity. Our fascination with nature and the mystery of birth and the life cycle, our search for transcendence from the physical toward a spiritual relationship with God or some cosmic force are as real and basic to human evolution and the human personality as are hunger, thirst, and the sexual drive.

Ego, Self, Persona, and Shadow   Jung thought of the ego as a directive structure within the personality, more or less as Freud did. Freud, however, did not emphasize the experience of *self* or of an image of oneself. Jung put

Charlie Chaplin in **Modern Times.** *As here, Chaplin often embodied the Trickster, a Jungian archetype found in many cultures. The Trickster represents the side of the personality that yearns to defy the law, rules, convention, and propriety.*

the sense of self—its intactness, inherent value, and possibilities for further development—at the core of his system. What a person presents to the public is not the entire self but only a limited side of it—the *persona*, a term based on the masks that ancient Greek actors wore to portray the comic and tragic elements of human experience. If we are fortunate, our persona will be in harmony with our own inner image of self. More often, however, we feign cheerfulness when we are feeling sad or good health when we are uncomfortable, perhaps out of fear of offending or disturbing others or of admitting weakness. Or we may act politely or humbly with our supervisors or teachers, while feeling angry or rebellious inside. If there is a persisting gap between our persona and our self-image, we may find our dreams or fantasies containing characters or situations that are very different from our public presentation. This underside of our personality, the suppressed opposite often at the fringe of consciousness, is represented by what Jung called the *shadow*. If our persona is that of a noble, virtuous person, our resentments of envy may be reflected in dreams of violence, revenge, or in archetypes of a hostile kind. A little girl or boy who tries so hard to be good may dream about Dracula or other vampires, werewolves, or monsters, those archetypes that represent images of hostile forces.

Jung's theory of the psyche is quite speculative but, like a work of art, it creates a new kind of mythology about people. Unfortunately, despite its esthetic attractiveness, it is not always useful in forging a precise, testable set of propositions about the workings of the human personality.

Jung's Personality Typology   An influential feature of Jung's theory stems from his work on psychological types. Jung felt that personality patterns emerge from continuous growth and the interplay in the mind of four basic functions. The four functions are *sensation*, the direct, realistic perception of the environment; *intuition* (which even Jung found difficult to define), the subliminal, unconscious perception of meaning; *thinking*, the appraisal of information in an orderly, rational sequence; and *feeling*, the experience of positive or negative emotions about an object or person. A sensation-oriented person is acutely aware of the taste, smell, and feel of things and of all surrounding sights and sounds, but does not care much about the implications or significance of experiences. An intuition-oriented person seeks to understand reality by using guesses and glimmerings about the meaning and mystery of daily experiences. A thinking-oriented person is characterized by care and logic and precision in mental activity, and a feeling-oriented person emphasizes the emotional qualities or inherent values of an experience. For a poet, feeling and intuition might predominate; a scientist like Einstein might show more thinking and intuition.

In addition to these four functions, Jung distinguished two fundamental attitudes—*extraversion* and *introversion* (Jung, 1971, Vol. 6). Extraverted people are oriented toward the external environment, toward practical matters, simple and clear details, and the people and objects around them. They are not much given to theoretical or imaginative thought, but plunge actively into the social stream, living in the immediate present and relatively unconcerned about either the past or the long-term future. Extraverts tend to readily accept the clichés and conventional morality of their surroundings.

By contrast, introverts are oriented toward their own private experiences—their thoughts and ideas, images and memories, and their own sense of self. Introverts like to reason things out and work with abstractions, and their focus is more on personal self-development than in trying to meet the expectations of society. Jung felt that these differences in orientation are pretty well born with us and cannot be changed. Each function—thinking, feeling, sensation, intuition—is expressed with an introverted or an extraverted attitude.

Jung differed from Freud by showing little interest in the earliest years of life. He did not reject the notion of an Oedipus complex, but believed that it was not inevitable, that it would occur only in families in which parents fostered their children's sexual interests or encouraged rivalries for their affections. Jung stressed the psychological importance of age 10 or 11; by that age the

Jung's Influence and Contributions

RESEARCH SUPPORT
FOR JUNG'S PERSONALITY TYPOLOGY

Rae Carlson attempted to make an empirical test of the validity of Jung's personality types of introversion-extraversion and thinking-feeling or sensing-intuiting by relating these types to the recall of personal memories (1980). Subjects were classified as Jungian types on the basis of a questionnaire, the Myers-Briggs Type Indicator (Myers, 1962), and were then asked to describe their most vivid personal experiences of several emotions, such as joy, anger, and shame.

Carlson found that introverted-thinking types differed from extraverted-feeling types in the content of these memories. The former were more effective in the recall of emotionally neutral, factual details while the latter recalled and recreated the emotional, or affective, tone of their experiences. For example, here are the memories of joy reported by two women. The first is an introverted-thinking type, the second an extraverted-feeling type:

> I was 22. I awoke in the hospital after giving birth to my only son. It was Mother's Day. My first conscious move was to see if my stomach was flat, and the next to find out whether I had had a boy or a girl. When the nurse told me that it was a healthy boy, I felt a wave of elation to know that we had both come through safely, and when my son was given to me to hold, I felt pride, protectiveness, and happiness. Physically, I felt calm and able to undertake anything.

> One day we were visiting in our daughter's home. As I sat watching my husband playing with our granddaughter, I experienced a sense of tremendous joy. I had a lump in my throat

and tears in my eyes, and I thought, "This is really living!" I didn't say anything to anyone.

Do the introversion-extraversion and thinking-feeling components of the personality independently affect personal recollection? Yes. Carlson found that memories of subjects classified as feeling types were more emotionally intense than those of thinking types while introverts and extraverts did not differ in emotional vividness. Extraverts, either thinking or feeling, referred more frequently to interpersonal and social situations as the source of their emotions than did introverts.

To demonstrate the validity of the intuiting-sensing dimension of Jung's theory, Carlson also had her subjects write a letter introducing themselves to an imaginary overseas pen pal, whom they were told they would get to know well. Most intuitive types made some reference to possible common interests with the unknown correspondent even if only through a reference to an international news item. Sensing types, on the other hand, began their letters with physical self-descriptions and generally included no reference to the pen pal. Thus, intuitive personalities "invented" details about the unreal pen pal while sensing types focused on their own experiences. Neither extraverts and introverts nor thinking and feeling types differed significantly from one another on this task.

In sum, Carlson found some support for the construct validity of Jungian typology, demonstrating that different psychological types predictably differ in their performance on laboratory tasks that are analogous to meaningful real-world situations.

child's mental life and intellectual capacities are more developed, and a sense of direction and group identity are more critical than for the infant or young child. Moreover, in his practice and theory he focused on the problems of adult life and on some of the periods of middle age when adults begin to question the meaning and direction of the life they have chosen. His work was a forerunner of research and interest in "passages" and "midlife crises."

Jung was much more optimistic than Freud. He saw human beings as striving constantly to fulfill their creative capacities. Later in his career he put great emphasis on the notion that even our dreams may present future possibilities that stir us to new directions of growth and development if we will only pay attention to them. Dreams do indeed have the quality of predicting the future—not in any magical sense, but in indicating directions in which we want, and perhaps are beginning, to move. This certainly was the case in Jung's own dream, cited at the beginning of the chapter. He made his life work one of probing deeper and deeper into the inner regions of the mind and relating individual thought to human evolution.

In contrast to Freud's consistent stress on the "animal" nature of humanity, Jung's view of personality placed a great importance on esthetic and spiritual tendencies. Yearnings for beauty and cosmic understanding have evolved for countless centuries and are inherent in the human species; they are not reducible, as Freud seemed to suggest, to infantile sexual or aggressive drives. Here Jung's view is closer, as we shall see, to that of personality theorists like Gordon Allport, Carl Rogers, and Abraham Maslow, who emphasized growth and self-fulfillment, not just conflict resolution.

Many of Jung's concepts, such as the collective unconscious, archetypes, and the relationship of persona to self, ego, and shadow, are difficult to define precisely and to test through research. Personality psychologists, however, have found his concepts of introversion and extraversion extremely useful, and many research studies have been carried out examining the possibility that they provide a fruitful way of looking at normal personality. As we shall see, the study of introversion-extraversion crops up again and again in research on personality traits or styles of thinking and behaving.

ADLER'S EMPHASIS ON THE PUBLIC PERSONALITY

After World War I, two major trends, one European and one American, merged to push personality theory toward the public personality—toward a concern with what goes on between people rather than what goes on inside one person's mind. The first trend was socialism in Europe, and the second was the spirit of trial-and-error empiricism that was a part of America's frontier heritage.

Some psychoanalysts, beginning with Alfred Adler and later Karen Horney and Erich Fromm, were influenced by the socialist idea that proclaimed the preeminence of the environment over heredity. They began to pay more attention to the ways in which the personality of children is affected by how their parents treat them and also by the social surroundings of the family itself. Alfred Adler (1870–1937), one of Freud's earliest and closest adherents, was the first to move personality theory in this social or interpersonal direction.

ALFRED ADLER

Alfred Adler, like Freud, was Jewish and lived most of his life in Vienna. As the second son in his family, he found himself continually striving to match the accomplishments of his older brother. This experience combined with early physical illness from which he recovered with strenuous efforts, undoubtedly influenced his later theoretical emphasis on compensatory strivings, the will to power, and the role of inferiority feelings or sibling rivalry in personality development. Adler's medical practice was located in a neighborhood where many athletes and acrobats lived or worked. From treating them, he learned how their special skills developed as a compensatory effort to overcome early physical handicaps and feelings of inferiority.

Following his medical training, Adler came in contact with Freud soon after the publication of *The Interpretation of Dreams*. He emerged quickly as one of the dominant figures in Freud's small circle during that first decade of the twentieth century, and Freud highly praised and respected his early work on inferiority and compensation. Just as Freud was crystallizing the importance of the drive theory with its focus on childhood sexuality, Adler was becoming critical of the narrowness of this view. He began to feel more and more that the social patterning of the family was more important than the sexual drives in leading to a phenomenon such as the Oedipus complex. A bitter struggle ensued within the small circle of Viennese psychoanalysts, which even-

tually led to an unfriendly parting between Freud and Adler.

Adler gradually formed a new group and because of his extraverted personal style and his socialist political orientation, he attained a certain amount of influence in Viennese academic and political circles in the period after World War I. In the 1920s, Adler established child-guidance clinics in the Austrian state schools, and his work with children and families laid the foundation for many current practices in school psychology and family therapy.

When a more right-wing group seized power in Vienna in the early 1930s, Adler left Austria and moved to New York. He lectured widely, often to workers' groups. He did not write as much as Freud and Jung, but instead tried to reach the general public through lectures on child care. Although small groups of Adlerian-oriented psychotherapists formed in New York and Chicago, Adler's influence on American psychiatrists never approached that of Freud. Eventually, however, the positions he had taken—his emphasis on the human being's social experience as a critical and constructive feature of life and his emphasis on family organization—all became incorporated into the clinical practice of many mental-health workers. His orientation also influenced the deviations from classical Freudian theory introduced by Karen Horney and Erich Fromm, among others, and contributed to the establishment of social psychology.

Adler's Individual Psychology

Adler called his approach *individual psychology* to emphasize the unique development of each person. He also wished to stress the fact that the highest stage of individual development comes when people can experience and express concern for their fellow human beings and take action to help them.

Adler believed that all human thought and action necessarily involve some kind of goal, and that eventually two major goals are discernible in the development of every child. The first is the striving to overcome *inferiority* and to attain *superiority*. Feelings of inferiority may result from a sense of being weak and small in relation to adults or from some actual physical defect from disease or accident. This striving can be turned to creative use, but it can of course also lead to excesses and self-defeating behavior. The short stature of Napoleon and the congenital withered arm of the Emperor Wilhelm II of Germany are often cited as examples of physical inferiorities that these men strove to overcome by power and conquest.

The second major goal that Adler defined is the motive of *social interest*—the striving to be useful to others, to feel a significant part of the larger whole. This concept, which Adler emphasized more and more toward the end of his life, is in sharp contrast to Freud's emphasis on drives, defenses, and intrapsychic conflicts as the focus of personality theory.

Adler proposed that a great deal of human experience is built around subjective "fictions"—sets of mental pictures or internal propositions we develop about what kind of life we want to lead. They become signposts that guide us in the directions we wish to take. Adler perceived that while such fictions are pervasive in human experience, they can lead to serious distortions of reality. These encapsulated or organized guiding images eventually have to be tested against the reality of social experience and are useful and adaptive only to the extent that they foster genuinely useful human encounters. Such fictional goals or mental guideposts should not deter the fullest development of the individual's potential. If compensation for actual or believed inferiority is overemphasized, social interest and expressing concern for others may be impeded.

Adler also proposed that mankind has evolved into a "social animal" through a Darwinian natural selection—that is, certain subspecies or types of early human being survived to reproduce because they learned how to subdue their individuality at crucial times in the interest of the group. This view is a foreshadowing of sociobiological theories of altruism. Adler was quite aware, however, of the inevitable tension between individual development and the needs of the group.

Adler was especially interested in the effect of *birth order* on personality development—on the child's perception of himself or herself within the family and the impact of parental expectations on the child. For example, the oldest child may be called on to look after younger brothers and sisters; this child's personality may therefore take on some aspects of parental authority. Some later-born children feel rivalrous with older siblings and become overly ambitious and competitive. Others feel overwhelmed by the older children and give up the fight almost completely. Adler believed that an only child is in danger of developing a fantasy of omnipotence, which may prevent the child from working hard to attain specific ends. This fantasy can also make a first child a vulnerable individualist, self-centered but unprepared to expend effort to attain goals.

Adler lectured frequently to public groups, because he placed a great deal of emphasis on educating parents about their potential for influencing their children. He emphasized childhood as a period of trials of different possibilities for action, possibilities that would gradually become crystallized as useful

Adler's View of Personality Development

directions for the three problems of life: *occupational*, *sexual*, and *social*. He felt that the Oedipus complex was an unnatural development and not inevitable as Freud believed. Every child might try out in its play the possibility of being a father or mother, and this was perfectly normal in the course of make-believe play. The parent-child relationship would become sexualized (Oedipal) only if the parent pampered and petted the child to excess.

In keeping with Adler's emphasis on parental or adult influences on the growing child, he devoted much attention to the educational process. Education is one of the aspects of human experience that Freud largely ignored. In Adler's view, teachers must regard children as individuals, reinforcing their unique qualities whenever possible so that children are encouraged to maximize their strengths. He was especially concerned about finding ways for working-class children to obtain the same educational opportunities as middle-class children. He also believed that education should incorporate practical and vocational training opportunities to motivate and encourage those children who are not inclined toward the more traditional academic subjects.

Adler paid much more attention to adolescents than did Freud or other psychodynamic theorists. He felt that early occupational choice actually helped integrate one's life. He would approve today's early decisions, bringing college freshmen into pre-med, pre-law, or pre-engineering curricula. He believed that by crystallizing goals early and working on them steadily, a young person is less prone to develop unrealistic fantasies or unattainable life-styles that can only provoke frustration and bitterness.

Adler never developed a thoroughly integrated view of personality structure or individual differences. Instead he described a great variety of *life-styles*, a person's consistent pattern of relating to others or to society, many of which are based on fictions that people seek to sustain even against great odds. His descriptions of the "life-lies" that he saw neurotics acting out sound similar to the current "games people play."

| Implications of Adler's Approach | Adler's interest in family relationships and life experiences provides a transition from the private personality that predominates in the theories of Jung and Freud to an awareness of the role of social interaction as a part of normal development. His theory thus directly influenced the neo-Freudian psychoanalysts such as Horney, Fromm, and Sullivan and foreshadowed the strong environmental emphasis of the social-learning theorists (Chapter 4). Adler's view of the guiding fictions of the individual also is a precursor of the cognitive personality theorists' emphasis on personal ideas or constructs (see George Kelly's work in Chapter 6). Adler's emphasis on life-styles points toward the current work on cognitive or affective styles as major personality dimensions. His attention to birth order has generated a good deal of research, much of which does support his view that important psychological implications follow from the sequence of a child's placement in the order of siblings and also from the overall size of the family (Sutton-Smith and Rosenberg, 1965; Zajonc, 1976). |

Considering the fact that Adler's writings and theories lack the elegance, detail, and scholarliness of Freud's, a surprising number of Adler's practical suggestions about child-rearing, parent-training groups, child mental-health clinics, early prevention, uses of direct confrontation or challenging by the therapist in adult treatment, and the focus on current rather than early childhood issues have all become part of education and mental-health work. It is ironic that while Adler is less known or respected, his approach has probably been more influential in what teachers and therapists do in their work than the more prestigious, intellectually challenging theories of Freud and Jung.

THE NEO-FREUDIANS' SOCIAL PERSPECTIVE

Toward the end of the 1930s a group of dissidents known as *neo-Freudians* developed within the rigidly controlled society of classical psychoanalysts. Led by Karen Horney, Erich Fromm, and Clara Thompson, a respected circle of young psychoanalysts had come to question Freud's emphasis on infantile sexuality and his neglect of the interpersonal experiences of the growing child and of the adult.

Horney's Emphasis on Security

Karen Horney (1885–1952) achieved considerable prominence in the late 1930s and 1940s with books addressed to the general public, such as *The Neurotic Personality of Our Time, New Ways in Psychoanalysis,* and *Self-Analysis.* Closest to Adler in her approach, she did, however, place greater emphasis on intrapsychic and unconscious phenomena than he did. Even more than Adler she viewed human beings as social from the start, not as biological creatures who acquire social interests. To Horney, the basic insecurity of the child is a more critical factor than the pressures of biological drives; therefore, defenses and neurotic trends are efforts to provide individuals with a sense of "safety" in their relationships. Neurotic trends can characterize not only a child who grew up in a particular family but also the so-called normal population, whose members come from particular cultures or social groups with special stresses, such as ethnic minorities subjected to prejudice or women striving for equality in an antifeminist culture. She felt consequently that a whole society could be sick, a point of view in keeping with the social reformist views of the neo-Freudians.

Personality variations develop from the way parents treat their child. If parents are themselves insecure or angry, they cannot provide a child with a sense of security. Helpless children growing up in families that are not attuned to the children's needs may suffer *basic anxiety*. If the children try to handle anxiety by repression—that is, by trying unconsciously to avoid thinking about or noticing the threats, they may develop a sense of emptiness and hopelessness since they have not practiced alternative skills for coping with such threats.

The anxious adult may try to *rationalize* problems by focusing on sheer logic (much as Dr. Spock does in *Star Trek*) or to *externalize* them, attributing causes of behavior to the actions of others. The inner sense of helplessness is always close to the surface, even with such defenses.

Horney's theoretical orientation was essentially an outgrowth of her clinical experience and interests. She never developed a comprehensive view that included the issues of the normal personality. Her major contribution was to shift attention away from intrapsychic conflicts toward a greater recognition that the way parents behave toward each other and toward their children may create insecurities and fears. From the efforts to overcome anxieties of early childhood within particular family constellations, specific personality differences emerge. This was a change from Freud's emphasis on the inevitable progression through oral, anal, phallic, and Oedipal stages. Horney also rejected the penis-envy theory of femininity and was one of the first psychodynamic theorists to move toward a view of women freed of the male perspective that dominated earlier theories.

Fromm's Cultural Emphasis

Erich Fromm (1900–1980) extended even further Horney's views on the development of personality styles and "neurotic" societies or subgroups in a society (1947). Fromm, like Horney, was trained as a Freudian psychoanalyst, but he had a background in social research rather than medicine.

Fromm was especially influential, particularly in the 1950s and 1960s, as a social critic writing from a neo-Freudian psychoanalytic perspective, rather than as a personality theorist. Like Adler, he emphasized the basic dilemma that although humans develop as unique individuals, at the same time they feel alone and insignificant unless they can feel a part of a larger group. Because freedom of individuality carries with it the terror of isolation, human beings often long to *Escape from Freedom*, as one of Fromm's books was titled, and to merge with an authoritarian or dogmatic group that relieves its members of the necessity for thinking or acting independently.

Fromm broke most sharply with psychoanalytic drive theory in his belief that it is not biological motives, such as sexuality, but social relationships that serve as primary incentives. In a productive life a person accepts the challenge of freedom, develops skills and constructive personality traits, and offers them to other individuals or to society in love and service.

Fromm prepared a list of traits, such as loyalty and tenderness, that reflect productive living. Under stress, these traits can become exaggerated, so that loyalty would become possessiveness and tenderness would become sentimentality. He grouped these traits into personality styles that we can all recognize in ourselves or others. One style he called a *receptive* personality, someone who is taking all the time, and who desperately needs support from parents, relatives, friends, the government, or God. Another style is the *hoarding* personality, characterized by saving and owning possessions as a concrete sign of security. Socially such persons thrive in cultures such as American Puritanism, with its thrift, hard work, and its emphasis on righteousness. The

CLARA THOMPSON:
THE PSYCHOLOGY OF WOMEN

Clara Thompson, an American physician trained in psychoanalysis in Budapest and Vienna during the 1920s, was a leader of the neo-Freudian group. Closely associated with Karen Horney and influenced also by Harry Stack Sullivan (she was his analyst), she pioneered in promoting a more balanced view of the psychology of women. While she accepted more than did Horney the role of biological differences between the sexes, she used her clinical experience and careful analysis of historical and cultural factors to demonstrate the limitations of Freud's view that "woman has a lasting feeling of inferiority because she has no penis." She called attention to the persistence of this view in Freud, since in one of his last major papers, written in 1937, he expressed pessimism about a psychoanalytic cure for female neuroses. He proposed that a woman's strongest motive when coming for therapy was that somehow she could obtain a male organ. Thompson wrote, "It seems to me when such a wish is expressed the woman is but demanding in this symbolic way some form of equality with men." She noted that her clinical experience failed to confirm Freud's view, as did the early memories of many women about their anatomy and their physical differences from men. She called attention also to the following possibilities:

1. Freud took a male's view in assuming that women are as preoccupied with their genitals as men, but he did not recognize that women could take equal pride in their reproductive capacity and sexuality.
2. Freud saw women primarily in the context of nineteenth-century Viennese culture and paid little attention to vast differences in the cultural and social roles of women in other societies around the world.

Thompson suggested that the pervasive view of women's presumed inferiority (accepted by women as well as men), not only physical but mental, was a consequence of attitudes fostered in a male-dominated society, in part to bolster the male's ego. "Women . . . have had difficulty in freeing themselves from an idea which was part of their life training. Thus. . . .even when a woman has become consciously convinced of her value she still has to contend with the unconscious effects of training, discrimination against her, and traumatic experiences which keep alive the attitude of inferiority" (Thompson, 1942/1964, p. 233).

Thompson also called attention to woman's economic dependence on men, fostered by a society that offered less education and vocational training to women. She analyzed certain personality traits, such as narcissism, passivity, and masochism, "which are generally considered typically feminine and which have even been described in the psychoanalytic literature as the outcome of women's biological makeup" (ibid., pp. 235–36). She showed that they could arise not from a sense of organ inferiority but from recurring and pervasive experiences of powerlessness and of the necessity to define personal value, economic security, and intellectual or emotional fulfillment only through means defined by male attitudes—for example, marriage, childbearing, homemaking, and sexual attractiveness.

Thompson's views on the psychology of women, published in 1942, long predate the analyses and assertions of the feminist movement and illustrate the greater sensitivity of the neo-Freudians to cultural factors in personality development.

exploitative personality is forever seeking to possess what others own, willing to use any force or guile to achieve both power and possessions.

Finally, Fromm also called attention to a new style that has emerged in America, the *marketing* personality. This is the person to whom image is all. The salesperson, the TV game-show host, the person whose orientation is selling a service or product or himself or herself no matter what the quality of the service or product, the politician with charisma, a broad smile, and no program—these are all representatives of the marketing orientation.

Fromm's theory focuses more on the public personality than the theories of other psychoanalysts, and his writing often adopts a moralistic and social-reformist tone. A major drawback of his theorizing is that it is not organized into a scientifically testable form.

SULLIVAN'S INTERPERSONAL THEORY

Harry Stack Sullivan (1892–1949) is generally considered the most original thinker in American psychiatry. He came closer than anyone since Freud or Jung to developing a comprehensive theory of personality—one that can encompass both normal and deviant behavior. Sullivan's life-style, however, was one of much action and restless change; as a result he wrote less than the other major figures in the field. And he died suddenly at a much younger age than the other personality theorists. Sullivan's books, including *The Psychiatric Interview* (1954), *Clinical Studies in Psychiatry* (1956), and *The Interpersonal Theory of Psychiatry* (1953), are largely transcripts of lecture series he gave and lack the polish, thoroughness, and scholarship of written books.

Unlike the other major psychoanalytic theorists, Sullivan was American-born. The only child of an Irish-American farm family, he grew up in rural New York in great loneliness and isolation. Sullivan never had the stable, traditional life-style of Freud, Jung, or Adler. He never married, he drank heavily, he was painfully shy and awkward, and yet he forced himself again and again into situations that demanded public speaking and social action.

Trained in medicine and psychiatry, Sullivan was attracted to psycho-analysis in 1916, when it was little known in America, and practiced it for many years in mental hospitals. Sullivan was one of the first to carry on systematic psychotherapy with schizophrenics, mentally ill persons whose symptoms involve extreme social withdrawal and distortions of thinking. Although many psychiatrists believed schizophrenia to be the result of some kind of brain damage or disease, Sullivan and others he trained showed that schizophrenic patients could often be helped through modified psychoanalytic procedures. Sullivan also pioneered in broadening the treatment of schizo-phrenics to include what is called milieu therapy, or use of the environment in treatment, such as enlisting the whole staff of the ward to assist a patient

Influences on Sullivan's Thought

Harry Stack Sullivan

to change self-defeating patterns. Sullivan was remarkably effective in dealing with shy, disorganized young schizophrenic men. His sensitivity to their difficulties in making themselves understood gradually led him to shift from a study of intrapsychic processes to interpersonal attitudes and the more public characteristics of communication.

In addition to his psychoanalytic training and extensive mental-hospital experience, Sullivan was also exposed to the thinking of the American social scientists John Dewey, George Herbert Mead, and Edward Sapir, who examined the impact of language, gestures, communication by shared symbols, and the entire social environment on personal development. Mead, for example, proposed that our sense of self depends in large part on definitions provided by those around us. Sullivan came to believe that Freud's concepts of unconscious drive transformations were too vague, and he put more stress on behavior that can be directly observed, such as patterns of communication between people. He sought to "operationalize" the concepts of psychoanalysis—that is, to define them in terms of acts or events subject to outside observation or "consensual validation," the agreed-on definitions of a group. For Sullivan the interview of the two-person group (the *dyad*) and the words and gestures that pass between people became the fundamental units of analysis, not simply the thoughts or fantasies in a person's mind. In this sense Sullivan moved even more radically than Adler, Fromm, or Horney toward the public personality. His position forms a bridge between the psychodynamic theories of personality and the experimentally oriented social-learning theories that we shall examine in Chapter 4.

Sullivan's Approach   Sullivan sought to explain intrapsychic mechanisms in a form related to the way we process information or communicate it to others. A person who has had unpleasant sexual experiences may talk on and on about the dangers of fluoridation or the threat of radioactive contamination posed by nuclear reactors. As long as this communication pattern succeeds, the person does not have to think about personal sexual fears. These fears have been *dissociated*, in Sullivan's terminology, but they are not lost in the limbo of the unconscious mind. If the therapist steers the conversation to sex, the sexual material will come out. Sullivan tried not to think of the unconscious and conscious as places, as if they were some sort of lost-and-found departments. Similarly, he tried to avoid the term *repression*, which implies a complex, unconscious process of blocking or forgetting ideas and feelings. Instead he proposed the term *selective inattention*, implying an active process that could be more or less functionally defined; a person may seem to have forgotten an unpleasant experience because to some extent he or she failed to notice it in the first place.

Sullivan's View of Motivation   **Satisfactions and Security**   Sullivan proposed two major forms of motivation: *satisfactions* and *security*. Satisfactions are similar to the basic drives central to classical psychoanalytic theory. Sullivan believed, however, that security is more important in personality development than drive satisfaction. Like Horney, he viewed early childhood experiences within an interpersonal context. The dependency of children makes them vulnerable to the inconsistency of their parents. Sullivan carried this notion a step further. Not only may the mother be late with breast or bottle, thus alarming the hungry child; she may also, because of her own early background, be anxious or disorganized. Through a host of subtle gestures, remarks, fumblings, or facial expressions, she will communicate her own insecurities to her child. Thus, in Sullivan's view, anxiety can be transmitted to the child through interpersonal transactions. These facial expressions and remarks of parents or other adults, whether negative or positive, are incorporated in the child as *personifications* (internalized mental pictures) of acceptable or unacceptable attitudes or behavior—the good mother or the bad mother, the good me or the bad me. Here Sullivan's position anticipated the acceptance among orthodox Freudians of the notion of object-relations and object-representations, as described earlier in this chapter.

Dealing with Insecurity   Growing up relatively helpless, the child is inevitably exposed to some situations in which the mother (or other adult caretaker) is insecure or anxious. In order to survive, a child must develop a way to avoid the anxiety provoked by insecurity and uncertainty. Here Sullivan introduced the notion of *security operations*, which steer a child's thoughts, communications, and actions away from situations likely to be reminders of the areas in which parental anxieties, failures, or confusions were communicated to the child. One way for the child to maintain security is to define a limited, well-known region of experience called the *self-concept*. In effect, the child establishes a "secure island," the known "me," and clings to that rather than risk the dangers and ambiguity of the "not me." We all cling to such an image of self, shaped in part by how our parents treated us, even if that image is not entirely flattering.

Another security operation is *dissociation* or obsessional substitution. In this operation, a person engages in all kinds of irrelevant concerns or talk in order to avoid a problematic area from childhood—for example, the pain of maternal rejection, revived by the possibility that a person to whom one is attracted will likewise be rejecting. Also, Sullivan translated such Freudian defense mechanisms as reaction formation and projection into security operations. For example, a man might shift attention away from his confusion about his sexual identity by talk that is full of bluster and macho sentiment (reaction formation) or by excessive blaming of others (projection). In neither case will anyone be likely to bring up the issue of sexual problems or doubts.

Sullivan's emphasis on security and anxiety dominates his motivational perspective and his theory of personality. While this emphasis is not so rigid as the straitjacket of Freud's drives, it implies that all the complex human personality characteristics derive from distress and conflict. As a psychiatrist he probably focused too much on an effort to understand deviant behaviors, thus neglecting the more constructive aspects of growth stressed by later theorists.

Modes of Thought and Communication

Sullivan suggested that human thought and communication occurred in three modes: the *prototaxic*, the *parataxic*, and the *syntaxic*. The *prototaxic* mode represents something close to the experience of infants or preverbal children, who have not yet learned to separate self from others, or their own sensations and vocalizations from the noises and movements of the world around them. Insecurities and anxieties arising in this preverbal stage may persist into adult life but will probably never be identified because there are literally no words to describe them. The feeling of spookiness we get in strange situations, the sense of the uncanny on a dark night in foreign surroundings or even at home when the wind rustles the curtains on a moonless night—such experiences come closest to reproducing the anxieties of the prototaxic mode.

It is in the *parataxic* mode that most early development occurs. Here children operate through those accidental associations of events with words that form the basis for their memories. Although children can now differentiate "self" and "other," "me" and "not me," they do not yet know the rules of causality, or logical sequence, or the difference between accident and determinism. A young woman in psychotherapy remembered bouncing a ball against the side of her house when she was 4. Her grandmother came out and reprimanded her: "Rosemarie, stop that noise! Do you want to be the death of your sick brother?" The next day the boy died and Rosemarie grew up believing herself responsible. For years afterward she tried to dissociate the whole episode by telling people there were two brothers in their family, "forgetting" that there had been three.

The mature and most socially effective mode of experience is the *syntaxic*, which involves logical thought, awareness of causality, and the ability to communicate in a form that is consensually valid—that is, in keeping with the agreed-on language structure and rules of understanding in the society. Freud had distinguished between id-dominated thought (primary-process thinking) and ego-dominated thought (secondary-process thinking). Sullivan's syntaxic mode is comparable to secondary-process thought, but it always implies an interpersonal transaction—a communication (even if only mental) to someone else.

The Developmental Perspective

Sullivan paid much more attention than did Freud to the full range of the infant and preschooler's experiences. He called attention to the *empathy* between mother and child, the mutual and reciprocal exchange of emotion. Research has shown that mothers differ greatly in how they hold their infants, how often they talk to or smile at them—indeed, whether they cuddle them or beat and shake them in anger.

While Sullivan accepted Freud's notion of oral, anal, and phallic stages, he called them "zones of interaction" to suggest that the most important thing was how mother and child interacted in connection with toilet-training, weaning, and other activities related to drives.

Sullivan placed great emphasis on the period from ages 6 to 10, the "juvenile" period. He pointed out that associations with other children in school force a child to decide what aspects of self and parents are especially "me." Such experiences lead further to a self-identity and to an internal "critic," similar to Freud's superego, that develops not out of the Oedipal phase but out of a variety of real interactions with the outside world. At this age, children also develop a feeling of the norms and expectations of their peer group and can incorporate them more or less as part of their self-system.

Sullivan was especially effective in his concept of *chumship*, or the same-sex "best friend" intimacies that develop in the juvenile and early adolescent period. It is a key period in the formation of the capacity for interpersonal intimacy, a major source of adult human security. Many people remain fixated at juvenile relationships, however, and cannot develop heterosexual intimacy in which sexual desire is linked to feelings of tenderness. Sullivan suggested that chumship remains for many people an important form of intimacy and enjoyment. Men and women sleep with their spouses and share certain common pleasures of child-rearing and householding, but the real "fun" of life comes for some men in hunting or bowling with other men and for some women in shopping, talking, card-playing, or sharing traditional domestic chores with other women.

Sullivan came to insist that "personality" is evident only in interactions between two or more people. Even when we are ruminating alone, we have an audience in mind: our parents, siblings, friends, or perhaps famous politicians or actresses. Sullivan regarded the notion of the self—the private concept of who one is—as essentially a defensive or conservative maneuver designed to hold the organism together and maintain a sense of security. Sullivan's theory remains, like Freud's, a pessimistic one; human personality is constructed out of childhood conflict and defensiveness, not out of adaptive and "healthy" growth in the personality.

Implications of Sullivan's Approach

Much of what Sullivan accomplished was to show the extent to which Freud's ideas could be expanded to the public manifestations of personality and especially to social communication and nonverbal interactions between people. He opened the way to the extensive research on how language and gestures express personality. His work carried to its extreme the emphasis of the neo-Freudians on the extent to which children's evolving personalities are influenced not only by intrapsychic pressures and fantasies but also by the ways that parents, siblings, and other adults talk to and treat them. Sullivan put more emphasis than Freud on subtle mother-child interactions and stressed the idea that personality patterns develop well into adolescence. He opened the way for psychoanalytic concepts to become a part of a more general behavioral science of interpersonal behavior and human communication.

ERIKSON'S EXTENSION OF THE PSYCHODYNAMIC THEORY OF DEVELOPMENT

Erik Erikson, working somewhat more closely within the classical psychoanalytic tradition than Sullivan, proposed a broader and far more elaborate conception of development over the entire life span. His insightful observations of children's play and of the behavior of children in different cultures led him to recognize that human issues beyond the problems of feeding or toilet-training were crucial in development. In some societies mothers are, by custom or necessity, less regularly available to infants. They may arrange for babies to be fed but not be present for cuddling, for providing consistent security, for helping with the child's first steps, and for all the other important happenings in a child's life. Thus a key element that enters into the experience of children in early infancy is not just oral gratification but whether or not they can *trust* their parents or other adults.

Erikson went on to propose a series of psychosocial stages, each of which has distinctive basic problems or "crises" that must be resolved if the personality is to develop adequate or effective coping structures. Children who pass through each stage satisfactorily will acquire a positive sense of themselves from their accomplishments and capacities that can serve them effectively over the life course. But children who must adopt less adequate solutions will encounter difficulties—characterized by a life of mistrust, for example, or of shame or doubt, or of role confusion.

Erikson's eight psychosocial states and their solutions are described briefly below. Because of the possibility of testing them in research form, we shall return to them again in Chapter 16 when we examine personality over the life course.

The Eight Psychosocial Stages

1. **Early Infancy: Basic Trust vs. Mistrust**   The first stage of development is one of utter powerlessness in the infant. Without the consistent and dependable attention of an adult, the child is completely helpless and insecure. Regularity and familiarity are key experiences on which a child builds a sense of basic trust as a secure foundation for later growth, and, as suggested above, far more is involved than just regular feeding. The mother who wanders out of sight, who in uninterested in playing with the child, who is too easily angered by the natural restlessness, crying, or soiling of the infant conveys her consistent rejection to the child, who experiences a sense of abandonment and mistrust that can blight later human relationships.

2. **Later Infancy: Autonomy vs. Shame and Doubt**   Although Erikson linked the second stage (ages 2 to 3) to toilet-training, many other aspects of growth during these years are important. Now the child learns "to stand on its own two feet"—to walk, to climb, and to talk, all of which establish autonomy and independence. A mother who hovers too close, who shames the child over

ERIK ERIKSON:
EXPLORER OF THE LIFE CYCLE

Erik Erikson (b.1902) was born to Danish parents living in Germany. In his early childhood his parents were divorced, and his mother married a German-Jewish physician named Homburger. An early history of wandering through Europe, studying art and being uncertain about "where he belonged" undoubtedly sensitized the young man to the importance of the concept of a personal identity, a notion that he made a central theme of his work. He himself for a time used his stepfather's name, then combined it with a new surname he coined from his first name, so that some of his early writings are signed as Erik Homburger Erikson. In his mid-twenties Erikson obtained a position as a teacher and child-care worker in a Viennese nursery school associated with psychoanalysts and with the Freud family. He was psychoanalyzed by Freud's daughter Anna and then received formal psychoanalytic training at the Vienna Institute. During these years Erikson was one of the first psychoanalysts to systematically observe children's spontaneous behavior, their play and games and fantasy activities. Later he went on to explorations of children's play and of parents' child-rearing behavior in other cultures, including several American Indian tribes. His exposure to this research and to the ideas of cultural anthropologists like Margaret Mead and Gregory Bateson also influenced Erikson to broaden his views of the complex ways in which children's development reflects not only their passage through oral, anal, phallic, and genital stages but the impact of the culture in which they were reared.

Erikson came to the United States in the early 1930s. As one of the few child psychoanalysts in the country and one who had the backing of the Freud family, he was invited to teach and do research at centers of interdisciplinary personality study, such as the Yale Institute of Human Relations and the Harvard Psychological Clinic. He also was closely associated with David Rapaport, a founder of the ego-psychology movement within psychoanalysis, at the Austen Riggs Foundation, a private mental hospital in Massachusetts.

In 1950 Erikson published *Childhood and Society* (revised in 1963), a book in which he used his observational studies of children to outline an extension of the psychoanalytic theory of development. In pointing the way toward a more extensive role for culture in the formation of personality, Erikson was led to recognize that later stages of "crisis" in life, such as those relating to identity formation in adolescence, inevitably play a role in shaping personality. His writings on identity captured the imagination of many young people in the 1960s. Erikson turned his attention to examining the psychological development of important figures in history, and his books on Martin Luther and Gandhi initiated the exciting new field of psychohistorical research.

"accidents," who gasps at every stumble, may create an inner sense of shame or doubt in the child about his or her ability to function independently. Erikson felt that successful experiences in this stage help a child develop a secure sense of personal worth or self-esteem. Added to the capacity to trust others, this sense prepares the child to feel confidence, enjoyment, and optimism in the face of new crises.

3. Early Childhood: Initiative vs. Guilt Erikson saw this third stage (ages 3 to 5) as roughly overlapping the phallic period, but he extended its implications. Although an Oedipal conflict might emerge, the increased mobility and imaginative capacity of this stage encourage exploratory play and attempts at self-assertion or aggression. If the child's parents are critical of such self-initiated activities, the child may incorporate a pervasive sense of guilt. Soon not only acts but even thoughts of self-assertion will be subject to guilt. But if the family atmosphere encourages exploratory and imaginative play, the child may develop spontaneity and assertiveness as a lifetime personality trait.

4. Early School Years: Industry vs. Inferiority   Erikson, like Jung, emphasized the fact that from ages 6 to 11, the child learns many intellectual and motor skills, including reading, writing, and athletic skills. As mastery of these skills is attained, a stronger sense of the child's self and capacities emerges. If there are failures, then poignant feelings of being "incompetent" or "inferior" emerge to haunt the child through life. Social relations are also part of this skill development, although Erikson placed less emphasis than Sullivan on chumship and interpersonal intimacy during this phase.

5. Adolescence: Identity vs. Role Confusion   In this period, Erikson believed, the major crisis the adolescent faces is the establishment of a satisfying sense of personal identity and meaningful goals. Adolescents should develop a clear sense of their masculinity or femininity, sexual orientation, and their general direction in life—for example, as "jock" or scholar or both, as fun-loving or a hard worker, as career-oriented or a drifter. In their efforts to identify, young people often seek romance quickly or become enthralled by rock stars, movie stars, or athletes. Crushes and early romantic attachments also give a sense of identity through being someone's "steady" or "best friend." Successful experiences of these kinds are necessary or else an adolescent may move into adult life without a clear sense of identity and personal direction. Erikson is a particularly sensitive and insightful writer on the problems many contemporary adolescents have in finding themselves in their complex and changing societies.

6. Early Adulthood: Intimacy vs. Isolation   In their twenties, young adults confront the crisis of whether to live alone or to establish an intimate, long-term relationship with another person. For most people this means love and marriage. Merging one's life with another's through sexuality and shared goals, housekeeping, and mutual support is a critical step. This is the stage in which one must decide to "commit" oneself, to establish a life line intertwined with another. Of course, some individuals commit themselves to a religious institution or choose a life of celibacy, isolated sexually perhaps but not socially. Those who do not achieve an intimate relationship, perhaps because of a history of mistrust or self-doubt, must find other compensations and commitments or else confront isolation and loneliness as the years go on.

7. Middle Adulthood: Generativity vs. Stagnation   In the long middle phase of life between the late twenties and sixties most adults face issues of child-rearing and watching their young develop and move into their own spheres of activity. Generativity represents more than child-rearing, however. It also involves productive work and the experience of being socially useful and effective in society. Someone who fails to be reasonably contributory as a parent, a worker, or a citizen may have a sense of emptiness and of life as meaningless.

8. Late Adulthood: Ego Integrity vs. Despair   Erikson maintained that personality change and organization are still evident in old age. People who pass reasonably well through the earlier stages—who have a sense of identity, who have experienced reasonable periods of intimacy and generativity—look forward to old age with courage and optimism. They can look back on their accomplishments, whether in child-rearing, work, care for others, or service to the community, and feel satisfaction and a sense of being an integrated individual. Persons who avoid closeness or fail in intimate situations, who do not serve their families or society, who survive by irresponsible means or by extreme dependency, may be flooded with a sense of despair and a terror of old age, illness, and death. In a famous short novel, Leo Tolstoy described the agonizing, lonely death of Ivan Ilyich, a superficially successful government official who had never truly loved anyone or allowed himself to care deeply about his work or about his relationship to others. By pointing out that we can change and grow as we reach our later years, Erikson moved far beyond the scope of other psychodynamic theorists.

With his emphasis on the changing patterns and expectations of society, on the crises of different age periods, on the total life cycle as a series of periods requiring personality development and change, Erikson freed the psychodynamic theories from their limited emphasis on the first five years of life and on simple drive satisfaction and anxiety reduction as accounting for personality development. Erikson stayed within the fold of the psychoanalytic movement by accepting the importance of sexuality, the nature of unconscious conflicts, and the persistence of childhood attitudes in adult thought and behavior. And, in his stress on life crises, he retained the central role of conflict as a determinant of personality formation. On the other hand, given Erikson's attention to the lifetime growth potential of the adult and his stress on the great role of cultural patterns and social change, his view of personality development is so broad that he seems to have moved beyond the more restricted "child is the father of the man" emphasis of most psychodynamic theories.

Implications of Erikson's Approach

PSYCHODYNAMIC THEORIES TODAY

We have charted a long course in examining the changes, variations, and evolution of psychoanalytically derived theories of personality. Freud stressed the private personality and intrapsychic conflict, the pressure of biological drives for discharge, and the organization of personality around the relative strengths of the id, ego, and superego. Jung elaborated the structural properties of the unconscious, emphasized the importance of more constructive or spiritually oriented motives, but except for his discussion of introversion-extraversion, placed less emphasis on the public personality or social experience. The object-relations and ego-psychology movements in psychoanalysis focused on the child's adaptation to its parents and to the demands of outside reality. Adler and the neo-Freudians emphasized even more the cultural contributions to a child's development, including the influence on children of the ways their parents related to them. Sullivan's focus on the interpersonal and Erikson's focus on the psychosocial crises within each developmental period moved psychodymanic theory even further toward the public as well as the private personality and also, to a considerable degree, closer to theories of personality that rely on systematic research, such as the social-learning and cognitive-affective approaches (Chapters 4 and 6).

All the psychodynamic theories share an emphasis on unconscious motives, on earlier life experience influencing adult attitudes, and on personality as emerging out of crisis or an effort to obtain security, to reduce anxiety, or to deal with conflicting wishes. As we shall soon see, other views suggest that growth and development are instead natural processes that are bound to occur unless environmental obstacles interfere. The contemporary psychodynamic orientation seems so close to these other points of view that we may wonder why psychodynamic theory or psychoanalysis needs a special status. Most current personality theorists accept the insights provided by psychoanalytic views of the defense mechanisms, of transference phenomena, and of parent-child interaction in the developmental cycle; few psychoanalytic thinkers argue strongly for the strict formulations of Freud's drive theory, his energy theory, or even the id-ego-superego structure of personality. It may be that the great stream of psychoanalysis will soon merge and become diffused in the general flow of scientific psychology.

SUMMARY

1. Many changes occurred in post-Freudian classical psychoanalysis. *Ego psychology* opened the way for psychoanalysts to pay attention to the public personality. The *object-relations* school broadened the view of the private personality by proposing that early childhood motivation is built around attachment to objects and people.

2. Jung's theory, called *analytic psychology*, proposes a far-reaching expansion of the unconscious processes. According to Jung, the structure of the mind has three parts: a conscious level; a middle level of unconscious content derived from actual experiences and from individual desires, called the

personal unconscious; and a third level, the *collective unconscious*, in which are stored the images that reflect the cultural and racial heritage of all human beings. The collective unconscious is detected through recurring images, called *archetypes*. Jung put the experience of self, or of an image of oneself, at the core of his system. The part of the self we present to others is called the *persona*, and the part we suppress is called the *shadow*.

3. Jung felt that personality patterns emerge from the interplay of four basic functions: *sensation, intuition, thinking*, and *feeling*. Jung also distinguished two fundamental attitudes: *extraversion* and *introversion*. Extraverted people are more oriented toward the external environment and objects around them; introverted people are oriented toward their own experiences, thoughts, images, and sense of self.

4. Jung stressed the period of age 10 or 11, when mental life and capacities are more developed, and also stressed the importance of adult life. He was more optimistic than Freud, believing that human beings strive to fulfill their creative capacities.

5. Adler called his approach *individual psychology* to emphasize the unique development of each person. He believed that the highest stage of development is represented by people's concern for their fellow human beings. Adler stated that all human thoughts and actions involve one of two major goals—the striving to overcome inferiority and to attain superiority and the striving to be useful to others. He proposed that human experience is built around subjective "fictions"—mental pictures—about the kind of life a person wants to lead.

6. Adler was especially interested in the effect of birth order on children. He emphasized childhood as a time of various possibilities for action that affects the three problems of life: occupational, sexual, and social. Adler did not have an integrated view of personality structure, but instead described a variety of "life-styles," or patterns of relating to others and to society. Many of Adler's suggestions about child-rearing, parent-training groups, child mental-health clinics, and early prevention have become part of education and mental-health work.

7. In the 1930s a group of neo-Freudians, led by Karen Horney, Erich Fromm, and Clara Thompson, questioned Freud's emphasis on infantile sexuality and his neglect of the interpersonal experiences of the child or adult. Horney viewed human beings as social from the start of life, not as biological creatures who became social. The basic insecurity of the child is more critical than pressure from biological drives, and therefore defenses and neurotic tendencies are efforts to find security in human relationships. Horney rejected the psychoanalytic theory of femininity and was one of the first psychodynamic theorists to move toward a view free of the male perspective.

8. Erich Fromm was more influential as a social critic writing from a neo-Freudian psychoanalytic standpoint than as a theorist. He emphasized

that although humans develop as unique individuals, they feel alone and insignificant unless they can identify themselves as a part of a larger group. Fromm believed that social motives are the primary incentives and was concerned with the ways people achieve a productive life.

9. Harry Stack Sullivan explained intrapsychic mechanisms as related to the way people process information and communicate it to others. Sullivan proposed two forms of motivation: satisfactions, which are similar to biological drives, and security, which is more important to development than drive satisfactions. Security operations include development of a self-concept, selective inattention, and dissociation, or obsessional substitution.

10. Thinking, according to Sullivan, occurs in three modes: *prototaxic, parataxic*, and *syntaxic*. The prototaxic mode is close to the experience of children before they can talk and before they can separate self from others or their own sensations and sounds from the noises or movements around them. In the parataxic mode, the self and others are differentiated, but the child does not know the rules of causality, logical sequence of events, or the difference between accident and determinism. The syntaxic, the mature and socially effective mode, involves logical thought, awareness of causality, and ability to communicate in a consensually valid form.

11. Sullivan called attention to the empathy between a mother and child, the mutual and reciprocal exchange of emotions. He placed great emphasis on ages 6 to 12 and believed that chumships, or same-sex intimacies, are a key to the formation of the capacity for interpersonal intimacy and a source of adult human security.

12. Sullivan showed how Freud's ideas could be expanded to the public manifestations of personality and to social communication and nonverbal interactions between people. He opened the way for research on how language and gestures express personality, and for psychoanalytic concepts to become part of a general behavioral science of interpersonal behavior and human communication.

13. Erik Erikson proposed a broad conception of development over the entire life span. He outlined a series of eight psychosocial life stages, each of which has distinctive problems that must be solved if the personality is to develop effective coping strategies. These stages and problems are: (1) early infancy and basic trust vs. mistrust; (2) later infancy and autonomy vs. shame and doubt; (3) early childhood and initiative vs. guilt; (4) early school years and industry vs. inferiority; (5) adolescence and identity vs. role confusion; (6) early adulthood and intimacy vs. isolation; (7) middle adulthood and generativity vs. stagnation; and (8) late adulthood and ego integrity vs. despair. Erikson freed the psychodynamic theories from their concentration on the first five years of life and on drive satisfactions and anxiety reduction.

CHAPTER 4

Behaviorist and Social-Learning Theories

The personality theories discussed so far arose mainly out of European clinical treatment; only Sullivan was trained in the United States. We have already noted that his translation of psychoanalysis into the interpersonal transactions probably stemmed from his exposure to the American functionalist and behaviorist schools of social science. For most of this century, the United States has been the wellspring for personality research that requires scientific rigor and objectivity and that focuses primarily on publicly observable behavior. The terms *functionalism* and *behaviorism* reflect the efforts of psychologists in the first several decades of this century to stress actions, movement, and the adaptive responses of animals and humans as a basis for building a scientific psychology.

This functionalist spirit clearly underlies the research of Edward Lee Thorndike, who worked in the early part of this century. He believed that to understand such behavior as learning and intelligent activity, one should begin by studying animals to find out whether there are consistent principles that explain all learning. In the course of his research, Thorndike proposed a series of laws of learning, the most influential of which has been the *law of effect*. This law states that animals acquire new responses if a random response they make results in circumstances that are satisfying to the organism. Repetition or practice, he further proposed, strengthens a habit only when some kind of internal confirmation occurs along with the response. This confirmation must be tied to an inner feeling of physical satisfaction (such as getting food when hungry) or to the satisfaction of gaining control over new situations. In his proposal, Thorndike was formulating an early form of what has become the important principle of *reinforcement*. His emphasis on the inner emotional experience of satisfaction is also suggestive of the cognitive-affective theory (Chapter 6).

At about the time Thorndike was carrying on his research, the Russian physiologist, Ivan Pavlov was making his world-renowned discovery of the *conditioned reflex*. Working with dogs, Pavlov and his students showed that when food was placed in a dog's mouth, a salivation response followed. If a bell was rung at or shortly before the time food was put in its mouth, eventually the dog salivated just to the ringing of the bell. Here Pavlov seemed to be describing a fundamental law of how organisms acquire responses to new stimuli. The pairing of new stimuli with stimuli that have already produced well-established responses is the heart of conditioning.

Pavlov opened the way for a more systematic and objective study of learning. No longer did psychologists need to ask people what they were thinking or whether events were satisfying or not. By studying animals they could determine what behavior leads to more or less rapid *acquisition* of new responses and also to more or less rapid *extinction*, or disappearance, of newly conditioned responses.

THE EMERGENCE OF BEHAVIORISM

One of the first psychologists to perceive the implications of Pavlov's discovery was John B. Watson (1878–1958). Between 1910 and 1920 Watson brought about a revolution in American psychology by introducing the concept of *behaviorism*. For most practical purposes, Watson said, it is not necessary to be concerned with thinking or internal mental processes since most human behavior can be observed directly in relation to external events. Conditioning is the clue to how people acquire the responses that make up their personalities. The behaviorist orientation swept through American psychology in the 1920s and 1930s. Three theorists and researchers emerged in the 1930s to dominate psychological thinking, especially in the area of learning and its implications for the study of personality. They were Clark L. Hull (1884–1952), Edward C. Tolman (1886–1959), and B. F. Skinner (b. 1904).

Hull's Drive-Reduction Model

Hull's theoretical position drew heavily on Pavlovian conditioning and the study of lower animals to set up *paradigms*, or styles of experimental design for studying what might ultimately be the basic laws of learning. Hull believed that such laws would apply not only to other animals but to adult human behavior as well. In keeping with this theoretical position, he made extensive use of drive-reduction theories of learning. That is, new responses are acquired or learned systematically when they occur at almost the same time as the satisfaction or reduction of a basic drive (hunger, thirst, or sex) in the organism. Thus, he combined Thorndike's law of effect, objectified as a reduction of a biological drive, with Pavlov's conditioning experiments or pairing of stimuli. The recognition of biological drives as motives of behavior and of the reduction of drives as a key feature of learning opened the way for a bridge between psychoanalytic dynamics and experimental psychology.

Throughout the 1930s and 1940s Edward C. Tolman rivaled Hull in his influence on learning theories. Tolman, however, was more interested in discovering how animals and people develop purposive, goal-directed behavior. His theory focuses on the *stimulus characteristics* of the organism's environment—how the animal organizes what Tolman called a "cognitive map" of its environment in order to guide itself efficiently to a goal. Thus Tolman's theory has a strong *cognitive* quality. Learning depends not only on what responses the animal makes but on how simple or complex the environment looks. Tolman conducted a good deal of research to show that even without drive reduction, animals organize information about their environments for later use as directional guides to reach a goal.

Tolman's Purposive-Behavior Orientation

The third quarter of this century witnessed the potent influence of B. F. Skinner, whose work exemplified the objective behaviorism Watson envisioned. Skinner insists that concepts about what is presumably happening inside the organism are unnecessary. We need only to study the responses an organism produces and the patterns in reinforcing circumstances that lead to an increase in the number of responses of a particular type. If a pigeon pecks at a white square and food follows, it will peck at that square more often. Under what circumstances or *schedules of reinforcement* will it continue to peck at white squares or eventually give up making that response?

Skinner's Objective Behaviorism

All human behavior and personality (in itself a superfluous concept in Skinner's view) are explicable in terms of stimulus and response. For Skinner, the task of psychology is to learn how responses can be systematically controlled or *shaped*. Skinner does not deny that people think they think and that people remember dreams when they wake up in the morning. He simply claims that such private phenomena do not make any difference in the way behavior comes under stimulus control. Variations in personality can be explained as a consequence of different reinforcement histories and the different ways people respond to an identical stimulus.

DOLLARD AND MILLER'S PERSONALITY THEORY

The first major personality theory with roots in behaviorism, American learning theory, and experimental research with animals was formulated by John Dollard (1900–1980) and Neal Miller (b. 1906), colleagues at Yale. Dollard was trained as a sociologist and also worked in anthropology. In addition, he was one of the first American social scientists to obtain training in psychoanalysis in Germany.

Neal Miller is one of the outstanding experimentalists of this century with contributions to learning theory, the theory of conflict, the neurophysiology of the self-rewarding centers of the brain, and, most recently, in autonomic control, biofeedback, and behavioral medicine. Miller also underwent psychoanalysis in Vienna, so that both he and Dollard brought "inside" knowledge to their attempt to develop a new personality theory that would recast Freud's insights into a form amenable to systematic experimental study. In their book *Personality and Psychotherapy* (1950), their aim was to bring together three traditions: psychoanalysis; the learning theories of Pavlov, Thorndike, and Hull; and the findings of anthropology and sociology, as well as psychology.

Four Basic Principles of Learning

Dollard and Miller proposed that four factors are necessary for learning in animals and humans: *drive* (motivation), *cue* (the stimulus or context), *response* (an act or thought), and *reinforcement* (the reward or drive-reducing object). If we are to learn, we must want, notice, do, and get something.

Dollard and Miller were working at a time when one of the most exciting implications of psychoanalysis was its motivational emphasis on drives, which seemed to connect biology with overt behavior. The concept of drives also lent itself relatively easily to systematic examination in the animal laboratory. Dollard and Miller centered their theory on drives, which they define as "strong stimuli which impel action. . . . Any stimulus can become a drive if it is made strong enough. The stronger the stimulus, the more of the drive function it possesses" (Dollard and Miller, 1950, p. 30). This broad notion of drive is modified somewhat by their emphasis on "primary or innate drives," in an attempt to link their concept with the Freudian notion of drive.

Under most circumstances in our society, as Dollard and Miller point out, people are not driven by hunger or thirst since famine is relatively rare nowadays. Therefore, what we respond to most of the time are *secondary* or *learned drives*, which are acquired versions of the original primary drive. We dress up to look as attractive as possible before important social engagements not to lure an immediate sexual partner but to win praise or admiration, the need for which is presumably a secondary drive derived from sexuality.

Cues represent the informational aspect of the learning process. Cues determine when or where we will respond and also to some extent which response we will make. If the telephone rings we rise from the chair and move toward the phone. Any stimulus in the environment may have drive or cue functions. Stimuli vary in strength, and the stronger stimuli have more drive strength and cue value. Very weak sounds ordinarily will not have much drive strength, while extremely loud noises may propel us into action. Weak sounds may, however, have an important *cue-value* and elicit a distinctive response. Whether a telephone rings softly or loudly will ordinarily not make a difference as to whether we answer it. On the other hand, we may ignore the faint whimpering of a sleeping baby, whereas a shift to lusty crying may impel a response since it signifies an urgent need. We learn to pay attention to cues. Thus, learning includes acquisition of a response of *attentiveness* under particular circumstances. A sailor quickly notices dark clouds on the horizon because he has learned to pay attention to weather conditions.

The *response* is an essential feature of the learning process because it must be produced before it can be rewarded. Dollard and Miller write: "A good part of the trick of animal training, clinical therapy, and school teaching is to arrange the situation so that the learner will somehow make the first correct response. A bashful boy at his first dance cannot begin to learn either that girls will not bite him or how to make the correct dance step until he begins responding by trying to dance" (Dollard and Miller, 1950, p. 35).

They next demonstrate the importance of hierarchies of responses. Some responses are much more frequent because they have been better established than others as habits. Responses can be described in terms of their *probability of occurrence*, with the most likely response called the dominant response in the initial hierarchy and the least likely response called the weakest response. Learning *reorders* the responses in a hierarchy. A weaker response, if rewarded, moves up into a higher level of probable occurrence. This makes possible the development of a new hierarchy. Such hierarchies are usually learned, but Dollard and Miller are careful to point out that crying, an unlearned response, is developmentally more probable for the very young child than saying "no," a learned response. Indeed we can imagine the developmental sequence: first crying, then turning the head away, and then saying "no." At a later age, the child's responses are reordered and the "no" comes before crying.

Reinforcement is also a critical part of the learning process. Once you determine that a particular act, such as giving candy to a hungry child, can be used as a reinforcement to strengthen a given stimulus-response connection, you can use the same act as a reinforcement for any other stimulus-response connection.

A key concept in Dollard and Miller's theory is that *reinforcement is impossible when there is no drive present*. A drive must be at least partially reduced after reinforcement; otherwise the individual would continue endlessly to perform certain acts under drive pressure. Presumably the drive ultimately reaches a zero point before it goes up again.

Dollard and Miller acknowledge that it is hard to trace the specific features of reinforcement when drives are internal. Their drive-reduction theory seems to operate reasonably well for hunger and thirst, but they run into a problem with the sexual drive, for they cannot avoid the fact that sexual activities *increase pleasure*. In fact, it is hard to show that the drive has been reduced at all (except after an orgasm); Dollard and Miller move rather hastily away from this tricky problem.

Dollard and Miller also call attention to the *learning dilemma* as a leading factor in helping individuals learn new behavior. This is a confrontation with a difficult situation in which a learned response is not reinforced and other trial responses are necessary. They cite the example of a mother who was concerned because her child was slow in learning to talk. After questioning, it turned out that she had become so adept at picking up her son's every need through his gestures that he really did not have to talk. She smothered him with so much attention that words were unnecessary for the boy to get what he wanted. On the advice of a psychologist, the mother pretended not to understand the child's gestures. In this new and more difficult set of circumstances, the little boy had to try some new responses, including trying to talk, and before long he was speaking normally.

Characteristics of the Learning Process

As suggested above, reinforcement is not only important to acquiring a new habit, it is also essential if the habit is to be maintained—that is, neither forgotten nor extinguished. It is important to distinguish the two: Forgetting occurs when a response is not practiced; extinction occurs when a practice response *has not been reinforced*. Extinction is produced under circumstances in which (1) there is relatively little drive strength, (2) it takes a great deal of effort to produce the response, or (3) there are strong alternative responses. Children who are "bribed" to stop whining by getting a piece of candy may persist in whining for a while, but if no candy is ever given or the whining is ignored, the response will eventually die out. Many parents don't recognize this simple principle. They reinforce children off and on when the children "make pests of themselves." Then they wonder why their children seem so obnoxious so much of the time.

Another critical factor in learning is *generalization*. Learning transfers from one situation to another depending on how similar the two situations are. If a specific response to a given pattern of cues is reinforced the likelihood increases not only for that pattern of cues to elicit the specific response but also for other *similar patterns of cues* to evoke the same response. Generalization then depends on the greater or lesser similarity of the characteristics of a cue: its color, shape, or social context. A child whose mother worked had a number of baby-sitters, most of whom didn't show much interest in the child. Then Grandma came, bringing with her cookies, toys, and much smiling. Thereafter, the mother notices that the child behaves well with other *elderly* sitters but not when teenagers are called in. The principle of generalization is also a key to the psychoanalytic phenomemon of tranference.

Conflict and Motivation

Dollard and Miller tried to translate the complexity of psychoanalytic theory into the principles of drive, cue, response, and reinforcement, derived from their analysis of the learning process. They are not much concerned with demonstrating the specific properties of the sexual drive and the changes that instincts undergo. They focus instead on how drives come into conflict with one another and produce responses that seem unusual and inexplicable on the surface, but which make sense if the underlying conflict is analyzed.

From studies with rats, Miller (1944) derived the now well-established finding that an animal's motiviation to *avoid* an unpleasant goal increases sharply as the animal approaches the goal. In other words, approach movements or effort expended decrease more and more as the goal is neared. When the animal is moving *away* from an unpleasant situation, the intensity of effort or speed also falls off quite rapidly. This situation contrasts with behavior when an animal is approaching a *desired* goal. Effort increases considerably as it gets closer but the effort does not decrease nearly so rapidly even when the animal moves fairly far away from the goal. In graph form, approaching and leaving a desired goal produces a *flatter* curve (or *gradient*) than is the case with an unpleasant goal (see Figure 4-1). Dollard and Miller distinguished four types of conflicts in motivation, each with a different *approach* and *avoidance* gradient: (1) approach-approach conflict, (2) avoidance-avoidance conflict, (3) approach-avoidance conflict, and (4) double approach-avoidance conflict.

Approach-Approach Conflict   An *approach-approach* conflict involves two equally desirable goals. A student walking down the street realizes that he is in the neighborhood where two of his friends live, each of whom he likes

FIGURE 4-1
An Approach-Avoidance Conflict

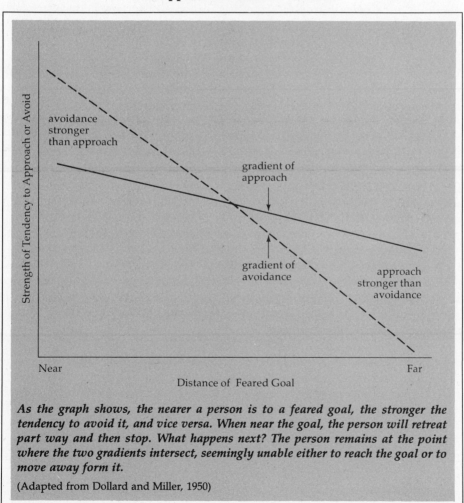

As the graph shows, the nearer a person is to a feared goal, the stronger the tendency to avoid it, and vice versa. When near the goal, the person will retreat part way and then stop. What happens next? The person remains at the point where the two gradients intersect, seemingly unable either to reach the goal or to move away form it.

(Adapted from Dollard and Miller, 1950)

equally well. He does not have time to visit them both, so he hesitates momentarily. Judy or Marcia? Then he sees a motorcycle in the window of a store across the street, and he crosses to look at it. Once across the street, it is no problem to decide whom to visit since Judy's house is now closer than Marcia's. He heads off toward the nearer goal. Since the *gradient* is flatter, a chance movement in one or another direction quickly resolves such a pleasant conflict. This situation is reminiscent of the old story about the donkey that starved to death when it stood between two equidistant piles of hay and could not decide which way to go. According to Lewin's and to Dollard and Miller's analysis (as well as the experimental findings), such a paralysis is unlikely in a simple approach-approach situation.

Avoidance-Avoidance Conflict   Unfortunately, life does not present us with many easily resolved conflicts between equally desirable alternatives. More common are *avoidance-avoidance* conflicts, in which we must choose between two equally *un*desirable alternatives. Consider a boy who has been doing badly at school and is being pushed around every day by a gang of older boys in the schoolyard. He complains to his parents, but they are unsympathetic. When he tries to get them to let him stay home, they call him a coward and threaten to punish him if he turns up at the house before school lets out. As he leaves for school, he feels a sense of relief once he is a block or so away from home and from his parents' threats. But then he realizes he is just one block from school and he remembers the frustration and pain that await him there. Each step he takes toward the school frightens him and he starts back toward home until he *really* is caught in the middle.

Such conflicts can be resolved only by drastic means. The boy might play truant and lie to his parents about being in school; this ploy works until he is caught and labeled a delinquent. Or he might develop a psychosomatic illness—an actual physical disease (such as an asthma attack) brought on by the severe stress he is under. In the most pathological instance, he might literally be unable to move and stand stock still, showing the symptoms of catatonic schizophrenia. In Truffaut's film *The Four Hundred Blows*, a young boy is so torn between two unpleasant possibilities that at the end he seems to be running right into the sea. The director stops the film there, with a final still shot of the boy's anguished face.

Approach-Avoidance Conflict   The *approach-avoidance* conflict, with one desirable and one undesirable goal, is also common. Barbara, who stutters, hates to have personal interviews with strangers because her stutter is then at its worst and she is often horribly embarrassed. But she desperately needs a job. One day a friend tells her that he has lined up a really first-rate computer programming job for her—exactly what she wanted. All she needs to do is have a personal interview with her prospective employer and it will be arranged. Barbara knows that this situation will present a problem. Still, she wants this job and the interview is several weeks away, so she has no trouble writing away for an appointment. Approach motivation is stronger and avoidance motivation is weaker when she is far away from the goal.

When the day of the appointment comes, she is aware of some fear but she gets into her car and sets off. The nearer she gets to her appointment, the more painfully aware she is of the confrontation ahead of her. How such an approach-avoidance conflict is resolved depends on the relative balance of forces. Many people have missed out on jobs because they could not face interviews, so Barbara may turn her car around and go home. Others have plunged ahead even with terrible discomfort because they felt the work was so important, so perhaps Barbara will get the job after all.

Double Approach-Avoidance Conflict   Most of our major dilemmas in life are more complicated than the straightforward approach-avoidance conflict just described. They involve *double approach-avoidance* conflicts. Consider a woman who loves her husband but who has begun a passionate affair with a man who works in her office. Her husband is attractive, good-hearted, and a fine companion but not very sexually stimulating. As she sets out to meet her lover, she realizes again that she may hurt her husband and perhaps ruin her marriage by visiting the other man. She turns and heads home looking forward to her husband's welcome. Suddenly she begins to worry that her new lover will end the affair if she breaks another date with him. This thought is unbearable, so she whirls around again and heads for her rendezvous.

Double approach-avoidance conflicts can be even more difficult if the issues are not clearly understood or if they are repressed. Suppose the young woman's problem stems from the fact that her husband is a nice fellow, from a good family; he's a man who has dark hair like her own father. She may, without conscious awareness, have difficulty making passionate love to him because it evokes incestuous fantasies or memories of her father. The man at the office may be fair-haired and from a lower socioeconomic background, freer in his language and body movements. Such a man represents the *cue*, a generalization from her own adolescent fantasies, of sexual abandon. Confronted by a double approach-avoidance conflict based on repressed childhood fantasies, the young woman may develop neurotic symptoms and recognize the origin of her dilemma only after extended psychotherapy.

In their theory of conflict, Dollard and Miller took a tremendous stride in demonstrating how conflicts can determine behavior and personality patterns. Although their motivational perspective is close to Freud's in its emphasis on drive-reduction and conflict, it differs in being deliberately more vague about specific drives but more precise in describing different specific patterns of conflict and their resolution and the role of reinforcement in the acquisition or extinction of habits.

The developmental approach of Dollard and Miller follows in outline Freud's psychosexual levels without, however, insisting on the inevitability of the oral, anal, phallic, and Oedipal stages. Instead, they are concerned with the way they are *socialized* through parental reinforcements of preferred responses in the areas of feeding, cleanliness, and sex training. In this respect, their learning approach is closer to the neo-Freudians' emphasis on parent-child inter-

How Personality Develops

actions. Dollard and Miller interpret the predominance of sexuality as a human drive from a social standpoint. It is not inherently as strong or pervasive a drive as Freud claimed, but it is definitely the drive that is systematically suppressed and surrounded by taboos from early childhood through adulthood. Remember, of course, that they were writing in 1950, when there was little sexual freedom in speech or practice, and sexual depictions in literature and movies were banned. Children who in the course of ordinary self-exploration fondle their genitals in the same way as any other bodily part often evoke parental wrath or anxiety. This may lead the children to associate the genital area with anxiety. At the same time, the genitals may take on a special important or mysterious quality because they evoke such an intense reaction from adults.

Later in life, a young adult may reexperience some of that earlier terror and conflict in normal adolescent sexual responsiveness. Here the theory reveals a major difference from Freud; Dollard and Miller, like Sullivan, emphasize the interpersonal context of the psychosexual learning process. The same approach appears in their treatment of the Oedipus complex, which they felt was stimulated by a particular family constellation in which a father becomes jealous of his son's dependent interest in the mother.

Two of Dollard and Miller's findings have been especially influential. They called attention to *sex-typing* and *social-role* acquisition through systematic differential reinforcement of boys and girls by parents. A boy who comes back from play beaten and weeping is often told to "stop crying, go back and fight like a man." A girl's weeping is more acceptable and she will not be urged to fight. Such differential social reinforcement leads to crystallization of the sex differences in personality that many have assumed to be biologically "given."

Different orientations to self and others grow from attitudes reinforced by parents. Dollard and Miller also were among the first to describe parental reinforcement of anger and aggression. Indeed, their analysis of the way in which anger is socialized is a decided advance over Freud, who neglected the child's expression of anger and early control over aggressiveness. Dollard and Miller described the *anger-anxiety conflict* of a child who has been frustrated and never succeeds in getting any useful results from expressing anger but rather is punished for such expression. The child then becomes anxious every time his or her anger is aroused and soon may repress even awareness of anger. An adult with such an anger-anxiety conflict may develop so much distress after minor criticism by a spouse or a boss that all he or she experiences is a need for a drink or for more food rather than an awareness of normal anger.

Implications of the Theory

Perhaps the best compliment that can be paid to the work of Dollard and Miller is that it did not result in a separate school with adherents and opponents, but was smoothly incorporated into the mainstream of psychological research in personality and psychotherapy. Here are some implications of Dollard and Miller's theory as they presented it in 1950:

1. They showed that psychodynamic formulations can be translated into the language of learning theory in such a way that specific hypotheses about the theory can be tested in laboratory research with animals or humans.

2. They introduced concepts such as *cue-producing responses*, described methods for putting *anxiety* into operational terms, pointed to the importance of labeling and of the deficit aspect of neurosis (lack of social experience), as well as its conflictual aspect.

3. They emphasized the significance of imitative learning as a part of the way a child develops.

4. Their work on the ways in which attachments and dependency in childhood lead to specific learning possibilities and limitations opened the way for extensive child-development research to test psychoanalytic theories.

5. Their work represents an important link between the intrapsychic emphasis and the study of public representations of personality. Their approach involves social learning, taking into account the context in which the learning takes place and also emphasizing observable behaviors as much as possible. They also stress the ways in which reinforcement occurs through interaction with other people.

By emphasizing drive reduction, Dollard and Miller committed themselves to a view of the organism as inactive whenever biological drives were satisfied. They left little room for curiosity or activity that might be intrinsically rewarding in itself. Perhaps the major limitation of their theory is its "neatness." Subsequent theorists have shown that concepts likes drives and cues, while fairly easily defined for animals in the laboratory, turn out to be far more difficult to define for human beings in complex social situations.

ROTTER'S EXPECTANCY THEORY OF SOCIAL LEARNING

Julian Rotter (b. 1916) is one of the most distinguished clinical psychologists in America. For many years he pioneered in the construction of the diagnostic procedures and psychological tests now used by every clinician. In 1954 he published *Social Learning and Clinical Psychology*, in which he proposed an approach to personality influenced by the cognitive psychology of Kurt Lewin and Edward C. Tolman. Rotter's theory was still cast in the framework of behaviorism, with an emphasis on precise definitions of observable actions; it also relied heavily on learning-theory notions of reinforcement. Rotter attempted, however, to provide a more purely psychological theory, in contrast to the theories with biological needs as motivators and drive reduction as the key principle for learning. His book set up principles of a personality theory tied to human research and a systematic formulation of how the practice of clinical psychology could be derived from a *social-learning* model. Rotter believes that most human behavior is learned in social situations and that interaction with, and the influence of, other people is crucial to the way behavior is organized. Rotter has devoted much of his professional career to methods for presenting his personality theory and related clinical practice in researchable form.

Reinforcement and Expectancy

Rotter took the important step of formulating reinforcement more broadly than Dollard and Miller or any other learning theorist except Skinner. For Rotter, reinforcement is not only drive reduction; it is any action, condition, or state that affects movement toward a previously established goal. Positive reinforcement facilitates movement toward a particular goal; negative reinforcement inhibits or blocks movement toward a goal.

Reinforcement is produced by a *reinforcer*—any of a wide range of reactive behaviors made by others after a person has made a response. We can identify reinforcers by observing what responses a person produces again in the same setting. If, for example, a response evokes a smile or a friendly laugh from someone, we can then predict that the person will try that same response again. And, we can now identify a smile as a reinforcer for this individual.

Rotter's theory liberates motivation from the restricted emphasis on biological drive or anxiety reduction that prevails in both the psychoanalytic approach and Dollard and Miller's approach. His position is nearer to Skinner's in examining characteristics of the environment (including others' reactions) that gradually *shape* specific response patterns. Unlike Skinner, however, Rotter believes that one consequence of reinforcement in human beings is that they will begin to develop mental images, attitudes, or self-communications in their private personality about what circumstances will be positively or negatively reinforcing—that is, they will develop the attitude of *expectancy*.

The notion of expectancy is a concept that underlies Rotter's system. He wrote:

> *The occurrence of the behavior of a person is determined not only by the nature of importance of goals or reinforcements, but also by the person's anticipation or expectancy that these goals will occur. Such expectations are determined by previous experience and can be quantified (Rotter, 1954, pp. 102–3).*

Rotter's concept of expectancy has been a major contribution to psychology. Of course, this notion is implicit in many theories of motivation from Freud's stress on the transference phenomenon to Adler's fictive goals, and it is evident in George Kelly's emphasis on personal constructs (Chapter 6). Rotter's contribution lies in the fact that he worked to develop methods for measuring expectancy in specific situations.

Rotter's theory leads to the postulation of *sets* of generalized expectancies. He proposed that our expectations about what circumstances will specifically

MEASURING GENERALIZED EXPECTANCY

A rather complicated experiment demonstrates that Rotter's concept of generalized expectancy can be measured (Chance, 1952). In the experiment two psychological tests were used, a word-association test and an inkblot test. There were four experimental conditions: (1) the subjects were told that both tests measured heterosexual adjustment; (2) the subjects were told that both tests measured leadership capacity; (3) the subjects were told that the word-association test measured heterosexual adjustment while the inkblot test measured leadership capacity; (4) the subjects were told that the word-association test measured leadership capacity while the inkblot test measured heterosexual adjustment. If expectancy is generalized it should show up more in conditions 1 and 2, where the tests are presumably measuring comparable traits, than in conditions 3 and 4, where the tests are presumably measuring different traits.

In all four conditions, the subjects first estimated what scores they expected to receive on both tests. Then they took only one of the tests, the inkblot test. Next the subjects were told their scores on the inkblot test; these scores had actually been set by the experimenter, and were either seven points or fourteen points higher than the scores the subjects had estimated they would make on the test. After receiving this information, the subjects reestimated their *expected* scores on the word-association test and then took the test.

What were the results? Did generalized expectancy occur? When the subjects thought that both tests measured the same thing, generalized expectancy occurred. In other words, the subjects' scores on the first test, as told to them by the experimenter, influenced their estimate of scores on the second test. But in conditions 3 and 4, when the subjects thought that the tests did not measure the same thing, the scores on the first test did *not* influence their estimates of scores on the second test. Moreover, those subjects who were told that their scores were fourteen points higher than their estimates, rather than only seven points higher, showed *more* generalized expectancy. From studies like this Rotter concluded that expectancy generalization could be demonstrated and that the extent of such generalization depends on the amount of change that occurred in the original set of expectancies (the greater the discrepancy in scores from one's estimate, the more the generalization to another related situation).

reinforce us can gradually be extended to cover a number of comparable situations. Thus, some people who expect reinforcement because they work hard at school gradually come to expect hard work in many situations to yield good results. One of the constructs he emphasizes is the expectation that reinforcement will be provided either from the external environment or from a person's *own* evaluations of the environment. This led to the development of the famous locus-of-control questionnaire which is today one of the most widely used instruments in psychological research (Chapter 12). Another generalized expectancy that becomes a kind of trait is interpersonal trust, which has been the focus of Rotter's recent work. His test of interpersonal trust measures the extent to which a person's reinforcement history has led to a generalized expectancy that other people's statements and actions can or cannot be trusted.

How Expectancies Develop

Rotter did not suggest a specific sequence of development. He indicated that parental interaction with a child will inevitably reinforce certain kinds of behaviors and not others. In the process of these experiences, a child will begin to organize his or her personality around expectations for positive reinforcement and to avoid situations in which negative reinforcement has occurred. Behaviors for which no reinforcement occurs will naturally drop out also. If reinforcement is intermittent—when the child receives positive reactions only about a third or half the time—then the extinction of a particular expectancy will take a longer time (as Skinner's research on partial reinforcement also shows).

Rotter proposed that there can be self-reinforcement by the things we say to ourselves verbally. In this way he put considerable emphasis on private internal communication as a part of what maintains expectancy levels. Some externally derived reinforcement is occasionally necessary, however, to sustain such self-generated expectancies.

It is interesting to note that, in keeping with his social-learning point of view, Rotter defines two positions with respect to maladjusted behavior that reflect a particular value judgment. The first, which he ascribes to psychoanalysis and to Rogers' self-theory (Chapter 5), he calls the *self-centered* point of view. This approach emphasizes an individual's personal feelings of happiness, well-being, and harmony, and freedom from pain as the criteria for good adjustment. The second, which he calls the *social-centered* point of view, emphasizes the extent to which a person is making an effective contribution to others or to society as a whole and is fulfilling some useful role in the society. As Rotter had noted, this position is similar to Adler's emphasis on social interests. Rotter prefers to see this social criterion employed in any decisions about what is maladaptive. He assumes that people who contribute to the welfare of others are ultimately likely to be rewarded, liked, and praised so that their own private feelings of happiness and well-being will also eventually increase.

BANDURA'S SOCIAL-BEHAVIOR THEORY

Observational Learning

An important advance in social-behavior approaches to personality has come from the work of Albert Bandura (b. 1925). Of special importance was his concept of *observational learning*, in which children and adults initiate new responses by observing what others are doing or even by reading about certain actions. Reinforcement and drive-reduction theories cannot explain this common occurrence. The numerous experiments stimulated or directed by Bandura (1971) make it clear that many different kinds of responses can be learned without any actual reinforcement. Thus, the way is open for a more truly *social*

4 • BEHAVIORIST AND SOCIAL-LEARNING THEORIES

view of personality development, for children can learn behavior simply by watching how parents or older siblings react to different situations. They can also profit from vicarious (indirect) experiences; if a little girl's older brother gets punished before her eyes for stealing cookies, she will think twice before she tries it herself.

Bandura (1971) made a useful distinction between *acquiring* response possibilities and *performing* such responses. We learn many kinds of *potential* styles of response from imitating (modeling) our parents' or other adults' behavior or from movies, television, or reading. The kinds of responses that become habitual, however—the kind we make on a regular basis—depend on the extent to which we were systematically rewarded or punished for such responses.

This seemingly simple distinction, which is similar to Skinner's concept of schedules of reinforcements, is really more powerful than it might appear, because it helps us understand some of the complexity and contradictions in human behavior. A person may have many more potential responses in his or her repertoire than are manifested in any specific situation. Also, part of what has been acquired is a set of *expectations* about the relationship between a certain response and the likelihood of being reinforced for that response in a particular situation. This can explain why many people show such contrary patterns of responses in different settings.

Other key notions of Bandura's are *generalization* and *discrimination*, which explain not only how many similar behaviors can be acquired without trial and error in each individual case (generalization) but also how specific distinctions between situations are acquired (discrimination). Bandura and Walters (1963) were especially astute in showing how in our society boys have had to learn that while mild aggression toward other boys is acceptable as a sign of "masculinity," such behavior toward sisters, girls in general, and parents or older relatives is definitely not acceptable. Thus, effective learning requires *discrimination*. In contrast to the psychoanalytic view, which places aggression "inside" the person, social-learning theory looks to a person's specific reinforcement history and the capacity or incapacity to *discriminate* among appropriate behaviors as clues to impulsive behaviors.

Another contribution of social-learning theory is its analysis of the implications of a person's prior learning and of the predispositions the person brings to situations as a result. For example, Bandura and Walters (1959, 1963) found that children who already have strong tendencies to be dependent on others are more likely to be influenced by social reinforcements for their dependent behavior. Highly dependent children are also more likely to imitate the behavior of others than are children who are not inclined to be dependent. This approach opens the way for extensive study of personality traits. Bandura and Walters also pointed the way toward integrating theories of emotion with learning when they wrote that social learning occurs especially when people are emotionally aroused; moderate emotional arousal leads to more focused attention in the acquisition stage of the learning process (1963).

A

B

C

D

Training children as warriors in the Dani tribe of New Guinea involves (A) pretend play-fights with seeds representing militia; (B) practice on inanimate moving targets; (C) simulated battles with harmless grass spears; (D) observational learning by watching actual battles from above.

BANDURA'S MODEL
OF OBSERVATIONAL LEARNING

Figure 4-2 traces the sequence that occurs in observational learning. Column 1 lists the characteristics of the stimuli—including emotional attraction and implications for practical use—and the characteristics of the observer, such as the predisposition to notice certain stimuli. Column 2 lists the activities that are necessary for the stimulus, once noticed, to be retained in memory. In column 3 the observed activities, now firmly established in memory, are replayed mentally to see if imitation is possible. (Watch-ing an Olympic athlete perform may lead the observer to think of imitation, but he or she may not be physically capable of actually doing so.) Finally, in column 4, if the actual or imagined imitation was reinforced, the observer will try to reproduce it overtly. Notice the increased emphasis in this theory on information-process-ing, imagination, and cognition—a sharp contrast with the overt response-reinforcement emphasis of earlier behaviorists.

FIGURE 4-2
The Observational-Learning Sequence

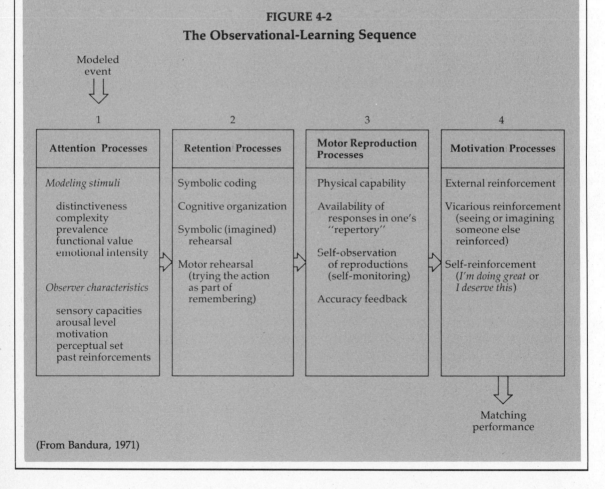

(From Bandura, 1971)

In a sense, the social-learning approach to personality is somewhat more like a "how to" manual of personality than a comprehensive description. That is, the social-learning position argues that each one of us must be studied in terms of our idiosyncratic reinforcement history as far as it can be ascertained and also in terms of our responses to specific situations. To discover why a young boy is aggressive, we would need to find out whether he was often frustrated and whether his parents had a punitive attitude. In addition, in order to predict what he would do in a given situation, we would also have to know more about which frustrations were more upsetting or distressing to him. Furthermore, we would need to know how his parents behaved in every situation the boy might have observed: their behavior toward strangers, toward authority figures such as the police, and toward each other in conditions of sobriety or drunkenness.

Social-learning analysis moved the study of personality much further into an examination of social settings and their special characteristics than any other personality theory. The advantage of this *situational* approach has been to encourage more imaginative research on precisely how people interact with the demands of the situation and how their previous experiences with socializing agents are related to this behavior. This emphasis on settings led some social-learning theorists to be especially skeptical of the notion of personality traits (Mischel, 1968).

Another methodological influence of social-learning theories is the examination of how to produce new responses. Social-learning theories have become a background for systematic work on behavior modification and on improved methods of training children for effective social experience. Children can learn to use their observational powers to generate new responses they have not had in their repertoire; these new responses are then systematically reinforced in situations that involve cooperative or helping behavior instead of aggressive or self-damaging behavior. Thus, the social-learning model carries exciting possibilities for producing favorable behavioral changes and healthy attitudinal development in children not only through psychotherapy but through training procedures that can become part of nursery school or elementary education.

Social-learning theory is an exciting and viable position. Work by Bandura (1971) and Mischel (1973) shows an increasing interest in the information-processing pattern of individuals and recognition of self-reinforcing tendencies. Indeed, Bandura (1978) has been elaborating a theory of self-efficacy (Chapter 12) that is moving social-learning theory closer to the intrapsychic or cognitive points of view, with their greater emphasis on private personality. The difference is that Bandura, in the best social-behavior tradition, has developed some specific experimental methods for studying self-efficacy and expectations of self-competent behavior.

The Social-Learning Approach as a Method

SUMMARY

1. For most of this century American psychologists have emphasized personality research that requires scientific rigor and objectivity and that focuses on publicly observable behavior. Edward Lee Thorndike proposed several laws of learning, the most influential of which was the law of effect. This law states that animals acquire new responses if a random response they make results in circumstances that are satisfying. The Russian physiologist Ivan Pavlov discovered the conditioned reflex, in which new responses are acquired when a new stimulus is paired with a stimulus that already produces a response. Both of these discoveries were important in the development of personality theories.

2. John B. Watson revolutionized American psychology and introduced behaviorism. Beginning in the 1930s three psychologists dominated psychological thinking in the area of learning and its implications for personality: Clark L. Hull, Edward C. Tolman, and B. F. Skinner. Hull made extensive use of drive-reduction theories; Tolman showed more concern with the way animals and people develop purposive goal-directed behavior; Skinner's emphasis was on the responses an organism produces and the patterns of reinforcing circumstances that lead to an increase in number of responses of a certain type. Hull's drive-reduction theories led to incorporation of psychodynamic views of motivation into a learning-theory framework. Tolman's approach led theorists to consider patterns of expectancy or purpose, while Skinner's showed how to identify environmental factors that may determine persisting personality styles.

3. The first major personality theory based on behaviorism was formulated by John Dollard and Neal Miller. They proposed that four factors are necessary for learning: drive, cue, response, and reinforcement, with drive at the center of their theory. Reinforcement, which is also critical, is impossible if there is no drive present. Reinforcement is necessary to maintain a habit, as extinction occurs when a habit is not reinforced. Another critical factor is generalization. Dollard and Miller focused on the way drives come into conflict with one another and produce responses that seem unusual but which make sense if the underlying conflict is analyzed. They identified four types of conflict in motivation, each with a different approach and avoidance gradient. The developmental approach of Dollard and Miller emphasized socialization through parental reinforcement of preferred responses in feeding, cleanliness, and sex training. Dollard and Miller carried personality and learning theory forward in several ways, but subsequent theorists have shown that concepts like drive and cues, while fairly easily defined for laboratory animals, are difficult to define for human beings in complex social situations.

4. Julian Rotter's theory was influenced by the cognitive psychology of Kurt Lewin and Edward C. Tolman. Reinforcement, according to Rotter, is any

action, condition, or state that affects movement toward a previously established goal. Rotter believes that as a consequence of reinforcement, human beings develop expectations, mental images, attitudes, or self-communications about what circumstances will be positively or negatively reinforcing. A concept that underlies Rotter's system is expectancy, and he worked to develop methods for measuring expectancy in specific situations. Rotter does not propose a specific sequence of development, but does state that parental interaction with a child inevitably reinforces certain behaviors and not others.

5. Social-learning analysis moved the study of personality into an examination of social settings and their characteristics, and this situational approach encouraged research on precisely how a person interacts with the demands of a situation. Another methodological influence was the examination of how to produce new responses. Social-learning theory thus became important in systematic work in behavior modification and in ways to train children for effective social functioning.

6. An advance in social-behavior approaches to personality came from the work of Albert Bandura. Of special importance was the concept of *observational learning*—and social learning through *modeling*. Bandura distinguished between *acquisition* of response possibilities and the *performance* of such responses. Two other key notions in the theory are *generalization* and *discrimination*. Another contribution of social-learning theory is the analysis of an individual's prior learning and the predispositions brought to a situation as a result of such learning.

CHAPTER 5

Psychology's "Third Force": Humanistic Theories

During the 1960s a point of view labeled *humanism* emerged in psychology and other behavioral sciences. This term conveyed deep concern with making the whole person—the total organism—the center of study and encouraging the fullest development of our potentialities as human beings. Humanism, a loose coalition of several schools of thought, was clearly a revolt against the analytic and reductionist trends of the psychodyamic theories with their concepts of id, ego, superego, cathexis, object-relations, and so forth. It also opposed "rat psychology"—the learning theories of the behaviorists, who all too often took conditioning of rats, dogs, or pigeons as models for personal experience.

To dramatize these approaches, which stress self, personal experience, evolving potentiality, and wholeness, the humanists are often described as the "Third Force" in psychology (the other two forces being psychoanalysis and behaviorism). From today's perspective, however, such arbitrary classifications seem less useful. Nevertheless, the personality theories we shall review in this chapter represent a useful corrective to some of the reductionism of the earlier theories. They point to the importance of attending to the experience of self, a concept now increasingly being incorporated into both psychoanalytic and social-learning theories. They also focus more on how we *perceive* the world, not just on what responses we make, thus indicating the importance of cognition and information-processing in motivation. And they direct attention to issues neglected by earlier theories: human curiosity, exploration, and self-development.

ORGANISMIC (GESTALT) PERSONALITY PSYCHOLOGY

Organismic, or Gestalt, psychology provided a source of stimulation for much of the Third Force movement. "Gestalt" is a German word that refers, in general, to the idea of a configuration or unified whole that cannot be divided into its parts without losing something. Terms such as *organismic* and *holistic*, as used in personality research and medicine, reflect an emphasis on understanding the whole person, on integrating body and mind, and on avoiding excessive analysis or reductionism. Many of the concepts in Gestalt psychology can be traced back to the nineteenth-century philospher-psychologists Franz Brentano and Edmund Husserl. Husserl advanced the theory of *phenomenology*, the study of direct experience. He argued that we can never really know the outside world since everything is filtered through our own private experience. Along with Brentano, he maintained that consciousness is always directional or intentional; it is the consciousness of *something*—not just the consciousness of redness, for example, but of the redness of an apple.

During the pre-World War I years and the 1920s the Gestalt psychologists, led by Max Wertheimer, Kurt Koffka, and Wolfgang Köhler, devised experiments to study how we experience the world. Wertheimer's famous studies of the phi phenomenon showed that when two lights flash on and off near each other, they look as though they are moving back and forth. The movement does not "exist," but our brain and perceptual apparatus experience it. Another Gestalt concept is the principle of *Prägnanz*, which states that we always try to structure our perceptions into the most symmetrical, regular, simple, and pure form; if we look at a circle that is not quite closed we tend to see it as closed. Another important notion is that of *figure and ground*. If we look at a homogeneous scene, we separate out parts of it to focus on and leave the rest as background. We do the same with ambiguous figures. These concepts about inherent human tendencies to organize an unstructured field into a unified whole are fundamental to most of the organismic views of personality.

Kurt Goldstein (1878–1965) was one of the outstanding specialists in brain disease and brain damage in the first half of this century. He made contributions to the understanding of many behavioral disorders that follow when the human brain is injured. Following World War I, Goldstein was director of a hospital in Germany for soldiers whose head wounds had caused brain damage. In running this hospital, Goldstein was able to learn how human beings manage to rebuild their lives when the most critical organ of the body has been badly hurt. He and his colleagues also carried out detailed case studies to pinpoint precisely the nature of the behavioral defects brought about by damage to particular areas of the brain.

Goldstein was struck by the fact that massive brain damage cuts off the most complex and delicate of human functions, the ability for *abstract thinking*, or as Goldstein put it, the ability "to take an attitude toward the possible." This, he believed, was the greatest intellectual capacity of the human being. Abstraction involves the ability to play out in one's mind a whole set of various possibilities and integrate them into more general classes. Thus, a patient sorting different-colored wool might be asked to sort them into four categories. Most people would quickly divide them into red, yellow, green, and blue even though the wool reflected slightly different shades of the four colors. But the

Goldstein's Studies of Brain Injury

brain-injured patient might not be able to recognize these four categories; instead, he might divide the wool into nine or ten. He could not make the abstraction of redness, as in red versus blue, but had to deal with each different shade of red as if it were a unique color and not part of a general category.

Goldstein was impressed by the clever ways in which his patients managed to overcome their defects. Often they would appear to be solving the problems very readily. When they were tested more carefully, however, it turned out that they had employed a kind of roundabout method to compensate for their actual limitations. One man had suffered damage to areas of the brain that control vision. Because of gaps in his visual field he could not see some of the words in a sentence, but he managed to make up for these gaps by moving his head. By tracing the words with his head movements he got the "feeling" of the different words much as he might have if he had written them. In this way, he could read despite the deficiencies in his visual perception.

Goldstein also saw that many patients tried to avoid confronting their intellectual limitations by leading meticulously controlled lives. They kept their rooms well organized, with their shoes neatly lined up under the bed, and they arranged their day-to-day movements around the hospital according to a strict schedule. He discovered that they did so because they lacked the ability for abstraction that would permit them to generalize easily from one situation to the next. Even minor changes in the daily schedule could produce what Goldstein called a "catastrophic reaction," an overwhelming experience of anxiety. In other words, the patients were aware of their defects; they were striving to maximize the capacities they did have and to minimize the consequences of the severe injury to their intellectual functioning.

Goldstein went on to develop a theory of anxiety based on a fear of the unknown—in a sense, the fear of fear itself. He proposed that all human beings aim to actualize their potentialities as fully as possible, and this means that they must be able to structure their lives in such a way as to avoid situations of extreme ambiguity.

Goldstein's purpose was to encourage physicians and psychologists to change their general conception of human beings. Although he never developed a comprehensive theory, he attempted to convey the importance of viewing people as functioning within a total organismic structure in which the principles of Gestalt organization could be used to define not only maladaptive behavior but normal and effective functioning.

Angyal's Holistic Theory

Andras Angyal (1902–1960) was a psychiatrist who made important contributions to the understanding of schizophrenia in the 1930s and 1940s. He was especially adept at using interviews of patients and observation of their behavior on the ward to show the relation between their symptoms and their striving for understanding and meaningfulness. This striving, he felt, is an essential part of the total personality even in severely disturbed individuals.

Angyal went even further than Goldstein in his analysis of the psychological importance of efforts to complete incompleted tasks and to "fill in the circle" that characterize human behavior. He was intrigued with this human tendency to achieve symmetry and structural organization. In this respect he is closer to the Gestalt psychologists than any other personality theorist.

Autonomy and Homonomy For Angyal, all human behavior involves tension caused by the simultaneous struggle for *autonomy* and for *homonomy*. We all seek to stand out against our environmental backgrounds as individuals— that is, we all want to be *autonomous figures* who can bring our experience under our own control. At the same time, in the desire for *homonomy*, we all strive to become an organic part of something that is larger and broader than ourselves. At the physiological level, we strive to be united with another person or to procreate ourselves. At the cultural level, we strive to be part of a larger unit such as a family or an ethnic, religious, or national group.

Levels of Existence Angyal describes three levels of existence toward which we must all strive—satisfying drives, achieving one's potentialities, and finding meaning in relation to others. The satisfaction of drives, such as hunger and thirst, and the necessity of avoiding pain and death are fairly clear-cut and easily definable. Angyal believed, however, that the other levels or motives were of equal or greater significance.

In describing the second level, Angyal said that the struggle for self-expression involves the need "to discover ways of living in accordance with one's potentiality" (Angyal, 1965, p. 18). But achieving one's potentialities is not easy. Adolescents have many problems because they see the tremendous range of possibilities that seem open to them, and they must decide what commitments to make. Determining the roles we will play as members of a society is a crucial motive for existence.

It is at the third level of existence that a person confronts the most complex of aspirations, the heights and depths of emotions, fears and failures, as well as fulfillments. This is the struggle to exist at a level in which we can *"mean something to someone else"* (Angyal, 1965, p. 18).

Angyal believed in the importance of a sense of meaningfulness at each stage of human development. He was unusually eloquent in describing how elderly people, even though retired and physically cared for, are often not happy because "they suffer from the diminution of their usefulness, from the feeling that they cannot be a help to anybody anymore" (Angyal, 1965, p. 20).

Duality Angyal proposed that the distinctive quality of a human personality emerges not only from autonomy, homonomy, and meaningfulness but also from duality—the struggle between each person's healthy and neurotic sides. For Angyal, personality is like one of those ambiguous Gestalt configurations of figure and ground, with a constant shifting between the more childish and distorted features of the personality and the more healthy, well-organized, and balanced functions. Defense mechanisms not only hide a person's specific neurotic trends, but if the neurotic organization is dominant, they often blot out the healthier aspects of personality. People beset with feelings of deep shame and lack of self-esteem will not be aware that they have other characteristics that are attractive and socially useful. Although concepts such as the id and the ego are not important in Angyal's system, he was interested in the notion of the superego. He emphasized that there is a *healthy* conscience, which is a part of all human experience; there is also the conscience emphasized in classical psychoanalysis, based on an irrational fear of reprisal.

For Angyal, anxiety is an inevitable feature of growth and development. *Differentiation*, which is basic to growth, requires giving up earlier patterns and trying out newer ones. The ambiguities of confronting the unknown—the first day at school, the beginning of a new job or marriage, parenthood—all evoke anxiety. Angyal wrote, "The human fear of death is identical with the fear of not being able to live humanly, and the anxiety inherent in growth must be viewed in the same light" (Angyal, 1965, p. 12).

The Development of Personality Styles As a psychiatrist, Angyal often approached personality differences through his descriptions of the various types of neuroses and psychoses. Angyal was close to Adler in proposing that each person has a *dominant style* of coping with the problems of life although each may use different methods of coping.

The dominant style in the neurosis of hysteria is the method of *vicarious living*. This approach is found in people who deny some of their own basic characteristics and try to live as if they were someone else. Children whose family experience has convinced them that they are insignificant or unimportant or who have actually been ignored may not recognize some of their own important qualities and personality characteristics. Such children may strive to play the role of another person or may imitate someone they are close to.

In the case of the obsessive-compulsive personality, such as the son in the Box on page 103, Angyal suggested that someone who grew up in a family of extreme inconsistency would be afraid to make a genuine commitment of emotion and involvement with another person. The result, therefore, is a pattern of choosing unimportant issues so as to simulate such commitment. The compulsive person may engage in petty, irrelevant acts such as an excessive involvement with minor details of a job or with preparations for a trip rather than attending to important issues, for example, how the job or trip will affect the lives of other persons.

Maslow's Humanistic Orientation Abraham Maslow (1908–1970), who was strongly influenced by Goldstein, made a significant advance in extending organismic theories to the description of the normal personality and human experiences such as curiosity, creativity, and joy. Unlike many other organismic theorists, Maslow was an American academic psychologist who had done research on primate learning and social dominance. He began reexamining concepts of human motivation related to Goldstein's proposal that people strive to fulfill their intellectual and physical capacities even when faced with handicaps. Maslow's term for this fulfillment was *self-actualization*, by which he meant developing our capacities to become

ANGYAL'S CASE OF THE DOMINEERING FATHER

Angyal described the case of a man with a domineering father who showed extreme swings of mood in relation to his son. At times, he was affectionate, played with the child, and told him interesting and imaginative stories. At other times, he showed violent outbursts of rage and would beat his son so badly that the child thought he would be killed. The boy had numerous fantasies, including one in which his father was killed by a cunning bandit who came to the house cleverly disguised as the father. As Angyal put it, the fantasy dramatized the child's confusion as to whether he was living in a loving house or in a cruel, alien world that merely masqueraded as benign. The fantasy was aimed at dispelling his confusion about the father, whose behavior made him both God and devil.

But this daydream, implying the murder and loss of the underlying good father, was unac-ceptable to the boy and failed to alleviate his doubts. He began to behave compulsively, such as making sure when out walking to step only on stones and never to walk on the bare earth—a magical hope of resolving his confusion. Once as he walked in the backyard he ran out of stones to step on and suddenly stood stock still on the last stone between the yard and his rear steps. He stayed there for an hour until finally his father came and picked him up, thus freeing him from his immobility. Once the boy overheard his father saying "I live only for the family," only to hear his grandfather say "No, you only live for yourself!" All of these seeming contradictions made the boy grow into a man endlessly shifting back and forth between positions, unable to take a stand except on irrelevant and unimportant issues in daily life.

a fine artist or athlete or scientist, or a conscientious worker in our trade, science, or art. The human capacity to experience and appreciate beauty, whether in nature, literature, music, or art, is also an expression of self-actualization. We shall discuss this key concept of Maslow's in more detail shortly.

Motivation versus Expression   Maslow believed that psychoanalysis and the learning theories overemphasized deficiency motives, such as hunger, thirst, and sex. Curiosity, self-actualization, and love of beauty are at least equally important for the human personality. He made an important distinction between *motivative* behavior, which he called *striving* (coping and achieving), and *expressive* behavior, which includes *existing*, *growing*, and *self-actualizing*.

Maslow was one of the first psychologists to talk about experiences of joy and intense excitement. Indeed, Maslow chose as one of his research areas the study of people who had reached a high point of self-actualization—creative people such as Albert Einstein and Eleanor Roosevelt—in an effort to determine how they managed to attain such high states of achievement in their development. Maslow also wanted to understand what he called *peak experiences*—moments of great happiness or experiences of enlightenment and wonder, during which we suddenly feel an ecstatic sense of oneness with the universe. Standing at the seashore and watching the sunrise, we may suddenly be transported into a sense of awe in relation to the vast cosmic force.

Patty Duke as Helen Keller and Anne Bancroft as Annie Sullivan, her teacher, in **The Miracle Worker.** *Photo A shows the moment when the deaf, mute, and blind Helen Keller realized that the pattern of her teacher's taps on her hand meant "water" and that communication was possible. This breakthrough in human contact was a peak experience for them both, as is clear from photo B.*

Two Forms of Love   Maslow was also interested in the concept of love and made a distinction between what he called *B-love* ("being-love") and *D-love* ("deficit-love"). He believed that people are often attracted to each other because they are trying to satisfy states of deprivation (D-love). They feel unlovable; and if someone seems to like them, they may become attached to the other person even though the other person may really be quite unattractive. In this way, there may develop a symbiotic relationship between two people who cling to each other out of their own personal needs rather than out of any real concern about the other person.

By contrast, *B-love* is characterized by a deep feeling for a person because that person has shown self-fulfilling qualities, characteristics of self-development that are inherently attractive. These qualities bring about the desire to help the person carry these self-fulfilling experiences even further. Thus *B-love* is an attraction that involves a fuller mutuality and an attempt on the part of both partners to help each other develop to their highest potentialities.

Self-actualization.   As we noted earlier, the overarching theme of Maslow's theory is his notion of *self-actualization*. His listing of the manifestations of self-actualization throws down a sort of challenge to personality psychologists to confront more fully the issues that psychoanalysts and social-learning theorists have neglected:

1. Self-actualization involves a full, selfless approach to experience with complete concentration and absorption in the experience itself.

2. Self-actualization is a continuous process. Each choice of whether to be honest or dishonest becomes a part of the growth process.

3. Self-actualization involves the development of a sense of self. This means that one relies on one's own personal, direct experiences as a starting point. Maslow gave the example of a man asked to give his opinion of a glass a wine. If he needs to look at the label beforehand, then he is depending on external sources to help him decide whether or not he approves. It would be more appropriate to adopt an attitude of what Maslow called "making a hush"—to close his eyes, fully experience the savor, and then muse on how the wine really strikes him.

4. Self-actualization calls for directness and honesty in as many situations as possible. It requires acceptance of the responsibility for one's own actions. Here Maslow's position is close to the existentialist orientation, to be discussed shortly.

5. Self-actualization means working "to do well the thing that one wants to do." If we study to become an accountant or physician or psychologist, we should try to master the necessary skills and carry out our work as competently as possible. If we are confronted by a challenge to which we respond with our utmost skill and effort, we may have a peak experience, a moment of ecstatic wonder and joy.

6. Peak experiences are the high points of self-actualization. One kind of peak experience is helping others recognize their own special qualities and their

own capacities for peak experience—Maslow's *B*-love. Such striking experiences can scarcely be reduced to Freudian or learning-theory drive-satisfaction models.

7. Finally, self-actualization means becoming aware of one's own prejudices, limitations, and neurotic trends, and struggling to deal with them.

In his later years, Maslow became more a "guru" or spiritual teacher than a scientist. Unfortunately, we are left with a sense of vagueness, even of banality, about much of Maslow's writing. Who, after all, will not agree that living life to the fullest is desirable or that human experience is heightened not just by satisfying basic needs or coping with adversity but also by experiencing beauty or by the thrill of using our skills and serving others? The task of a personality theorist is to take concepts like curiosity, joy, excitement, and love and then to demonstrate systematically how they are related to a variety of human functions such as development, perception, learning, and memory.

SELF-THEORIES

The self, as a concept of psychology, has had a long and stormy history. Wilhelm Wundt, the founder of experimental psychology, rejected it as unnecessary, and many psychologists have gone along with his view. They say that the concept of the self is too vague and undefinable to be useful in scientific psychology. But many other psychologists maintain that the concept of the self is essential to an understanding of personality. Their research and theorizing has led them to believe that there is a sense of self in all human beings. It is our personal identity, the real "me," the part of us that is ours and ours alone, or, as William James put it, that which is "peculiarly ours."

The phenomenological and organismic theorists not only accept this concept, they insist that more attention must be paid to the experience of self. Differentiation of the organism involves the development of a feeling of self and of others. Remember that Freud rarely talked of self and that the social-learning theories are just beginning to introduce the concept of "self-efficacy." It remained for psychologists like Gordon Allport and Carl Rogers to carry out research on, and to theorize about, this most central aspect of personality.

Allport's Emphasis on Individuality   Gordon Allport (1897–1967) was a professor at Harvard University for 37 years and, with Gardner Murphy, one of the founders of personality psychology as a subdiscipline within psychology. Unlike most other organismic or phenomenological theorists, Allport was not a clinician and therefore focused most of his attention on normal personality.

Although basically a *phenomenologist*—that is, someone who stresses the immediacy and uniqueness of human experience—Allport was also concerned about asking researchable questions. He contributed to the quest for flexible yet rigorous methods for the systematic, scientific study of personality. His earliest work introduced the study of *expressive behavior*, the physical movements, gestures, and speaking mannerisms that define the public personality. He stimulated the development of research methods for comparing samples of behavior from the same individual taken on different occasions to test the possibility that the *uniqueness* of personality could be systematically pinned down. He also pioneered in the scientific analysis of personal documents, such as letters and diaries, produced over a person's lifetime, to see if they yielded consistent traits and styles that could be measured quantitatively. Allport also was one of the first psychologists to develop a questionnaire that measured basic values people have that may guide their actions. Such values include the entrepreneurial emphasis of the business executive, the theoretical emphasis of the scientist, and the human-welfare emphasis of the social worker.

Allport was one of a group of psychologists who emphasized the importance of identifying and measuring a basic, presumably limited, number of human traits. In contrast to Cattell or Eysenck (Chapter 7), however, he did not believe that a person could be described simply by his or her scores on a series of trait scales—for example, high on ambitiousness or achievement, low on emotional stability, moderate on affiliativeness, low on conformity, and so on. Rather, Allport believed that each individual, while sharing certain traits with all other humans, shows a unique *patterning* of traits. A psychology of personality should develop methods for studying the uniqueness of a person (the *idiographic* approach) as well as for discovering general principles applicable to many people (the *nomothetic* approach).

Allport identified three dispositions, or aspects of personality. *Cardinal* dispositions, such as Napoleon's lust for power, color someone's entire lifestyle. Most people lack such master motives or ruling passions, which underlie almost every choice made or action taken. Instead, they can be identified by their *central* dispositions, or consistent tendencies—the kinds of qualities that would be mentioned in a letter of recommendation, such as trustworthiness, seriousness, thoroughness. Finally, Allport identified *secondary* dispositions, which may emerge in specific situations but which are not generally characteristic of a person's behavior. After a few beers, someone may giggle a lot and make silly puns who ordinarily would be rather serious and quiet in public.

The Self   Gradually Allport shifted his interest in measuring traits to developing a notion of the *self* as the central concept for a psychology of personality. Indeed, in Allport's theory, even more important than biological survival is the full expression of a person's traits as public manifestations of the self. In this respect, his theory is close to an existentialist point of view and also to Carl Rogers' position, as we shall see later in this chapter.

Allport was dissatisfied with the term "self" because he felt it had too many popular meanings. He coined a new term, "proprium," which has not, however, been adopted by other theorists. The proprium has seven manifestations or forms in which it develops and becomes integrated eventually into a mature sense of self-identification—the sense of "me" or "I":

1. the sense of bodily self
2. the sense of self-identity
3. the sense of self-esteem
4. the sense of self-extension
5. the sense of self-image
6. the self as rational
7. the striving toward long-range purposes or distant goals

A mature adult has the ability to be sensitive to the needs of others, to become deeply involved in society, to relate warmly and intimately to others, to show passion and compassion. Maturity for Allport also includes the ability to be objective about oneself and to approach oneself with the kind of humorous lightness that can deflate any inclination toward vanity or pomposity. Allport was one of the first personality theorists to emphasize humor as an important ingredient of personality—not just for defensive purposes, as Freud said, but as a constructive aspect of growth.

Values An integrated set of values—a philosophy of life—was for Allport a primary requisite of maturity and an area in which he carried out major research. He did not imply that any particular organization of values was the best one, but he did believe that persons with a unifying philosophy live fuller, more satisfying lives and can give more meaning to each daily event and each pattern of their human relationships.

Implications As can be seen, Allport placed relatively little emphasis on human development, preferring instead to describe the personality of the mature adult. He introduced the concept of *functional autonomy* to indicate that for whatever specific reason a motive might have originated in childhood, it later might serve more general adult purposes. Adult motives such as scientific curiosity or hobbies such as jogging generate their own rewards irrespective of any links to earlier childhood conflicts. Neither love nor curiosity can be reduced to attempts to resolve Oedipal or psychosexual conflicts. Allport viewed human beings as persons striving for new experiences, trying to organize such experiences into concepts, and always working to find order and rationality even with limitation that may have been the result of childhood experiences.

For Allport, most normal individuals are not dominated by unconscious strivings. He felt that the emphasis Freud and Jung placed on such unconscious material was too much a consequence of their contact with severely disturbed or neurotic people. In a healthy person the flow from desire to thought to action is natural and effortless.

Allport, while recognizing the significance of the private person, does not attribute to the private aspects of personality the great range and complexity that the organismic and the psychoanalytic theorists do. He was also aware of the extent to which external relationships between people are an important facet of personality. This led him to his emphasis on human traits or characteristics that can be observed by others and measured. In this respect, he played a leading role as a founder of the experimental study of the psychology of personality.

Carl Rogers (b. 1902) is perhaps the most famous clinical psychologist in America. Client-centered, or nondirective, psychotherapy, which he introduced in his book *Counseling and Psychotherapy* in 1942, has become one of the main forms of therapeutic practice used by psychologists, college and high school counselors, pastoral counselors, and other mental-health professionals all over the world. As a psychologist, Rogers also made an important contribution to the scientific study of psychotherapy. By the simple expedient of tape-recording the therapeutic sessions, he introduced a practical method for analyzing the pattern of interchange between therapist and patient; for the first time researchers could evaluate what communication patterns seem to be most helpful in producing "movement" in therapy and growth and self-awareness in the patient.

Roger's Emphasis on Self-Awareness and Growth

Motivational Perspective Rogers came to the conclusion that what really counts in human life is personal or private experience. He takes a clear stand against Freud's view that people carry within themselves a primitive set of instincts that, if unchecked, will be expressed in acts of unrestricted sexuality or aggression. Of course, Rogers does not deny that people do engage in actions that are hateful, harmful to others, and that involve direct physical gratification without concern for the effects. He argues that such actions reflect distortions in human experience brought about by difficulties and failure in self-development. Rather than the expression of unbridled instincts, they are the symptoms of the *suppression* of the full capacity to be human and individual.

In keeping with this position, Rogers proposed, as had other organismic theorists, that the major motive for behavior is *actualizing* of human potentialities. All other human motives—such as hunger, thirst, and sex, as well as strivings for achievement or artistic expression—can be seen as manifestations of the basic attempts of human beings constantly to fulfill their inborn capacities. Of the actualizing tendencies, *self-differentiation* is the most critical feature. It is the movement of the person toward becoming a fuller, richer, and more self-sufficient individual that gives the main thrust in a person's life. According to Rogers' phenomenological position, everyone is constructing an individual reality. The most valued experiences are those that help a person become more fully actualized, and the experiences that are avoided or that create difficulties are those that minimize self-development.

Rogers defines the self as the organized, consistent, conceptual Gestalt composed with perceptions of the characteristics of the I, or me, to other and to various aspects of life, together with the values attached to these perceptions. It is the Gestalt which is available to awareness, though not necessarily *in* awareness (Rogers, 1959, p. 2). The self eventually becomes differentiated into the self of the *self-concept*, a person's current perception of his or her characteristics and qualities, and the *ideal self*, the person he or she hopes to become. This notion bears obvious resemblance to the ego-ideal component of Freud's concept of the the superego, as well to important notions of other personality theorists.

The Developing Self   The growing child, Rogers believed, needs *unconditional positive regard*, a spontaneous, warm love without any restrictions or demands, in order to develop naturally and to feel fully alive. Since most children can experience such unconditional affection only occasionally or inconsistently from parents, they may engage in almost desperate efforts at times to obtain positive regard from others. Often such attempts may lead to denying their own negative feelings or simulating attitudes such as "helplessness" to win some attention from adults. Growing children may gradually come to believe that affection from others is possible only "on condition" that they behave in a particular manner or suppress contradictory impulses. Our self-concept is gradually crystallized around a set of beliefs about how we should feel, think, or act in order to experience positive regard from others and the sense of self-esteem that follows from winning others' affection. When we confront circumstances or become aware of thoughts or emotions that are not congruent with that self-concept, the sudden experience of the emotion of anxiety signals a threat to the stability of the self.

Rogers believes it is inherently human for us to experience contradictory desires, to be resentful as well as generous. Problems develop when we have come to believe that we can maintain self-esteem only by denying a significant portion of our feelings. Such a problem is evident in the case of a man with a self-concept of being a poor but honest civil servant, who is given an opportunity to make a sizable amount of money by granting a license for a building renovation that has legal-code defects. He might not have been tempted at one point in his life, but if he has a teenager about to enter college, he may find himself in conflict. While he may reject the offer, he may also try to repress awareness of conflict by *distorting* the situation. ("It was a trick to trap me") or by denying it ("I'm above temptation"). He may find himself troubled as the years go on by periods of anxiety or tension that represent his attempt to deny his feelings of hostility about his lot in life, an honest but underpaid bureaucrat. In his earlier development, he was reared on strict *conditional* regard rather than unconditional *positive* regard, so that he could not allow himself to accept openly his *natural* mixed emotions or temptations. Thus he suppressed a whole side of himself, and therefore was a troubled human being.

Experiencing and Expressing the Self   A critical feature of full living is openness to experience. For Rogers, in our private personality no emotion or thought should be alien. We should not be threatened by awareness of a sudden sense of terrible rage at a member of our family or a deep attraction to someone sitting nearby on the bus. Actions based on these feelings would be self-defeating and harmful to others, but the feelings themselves are expressions of our genuine selves. We can think through the implications of our thoughts and their associated emotions rather than act impulsively upon them. Too often, because people have denied themselves a wide range of awareness, they are totally confused and may find themselves suddenly engaged in actions without any sense of control.

In his later work, Rogers wrote about trusting oneself fully and taking chances, and he increasingly stressed the importance of creativity as a part of satisfactory living. Nevertheless, his theory remains one built around private, conscious experience, the thoughts and emotions of the individual, and he paid little attention to overt action.

Implications   With his emphasis on the self-concept, Rogers gave a more central focus to the phenomenological, humanistic, and organismic theories. He led the way in developing operational measures for testing hypotheses about the self-concept, its relation to the ideal self, and the importance of emotional rapport in human relationships. Rogers' approach can scarcely be termed a comprehensive or detailed theory of personality, but it has served to keep the notion of self "alive" and to indicate its possible value for personality research.

THE EXISTENTIAL ORIENTATION

Existentialism as a philosophical movement in European intellectual history can be traced to the work of Soren Kierkegaard (1813–1855), a Danish philosopher and theologian. Kierkegaard focused on the basic dilemmas of the human condition—our realization that we are essentially alone in the world, that life is full of uncertainties and ambiguities that can never really be resolved, and that we cannot know if there is a God or if we stand in his grace. The challenge of living comes in confronting these ambiguities honestly. Rather than letting custom, convention, dogma, or blind obedience to authority dictate our actions, we must learn to choose a course at each crossroad that is honestly based on our own imagination and the fullest exploration of our values.

May's Existential View of Anxiety

The existential personality theorists amplify and extend Angyal's emphasis on *meaningfulness* as the essential motive in human thought and behavior. The clinical psychologist Rollo May (b. 1909) is a well-known exponent of this position. May carried out research on anxiety that brought him into contact with Goldstein. Later he studied psychoanalysis and was influenced by neo-

Anxiety, by Edvard Munch. *This famous painting seeks to capture the sense of dread, loneliness, and terror that the Danish philosopher Søren Kierkegaard described as characterizing all human experience.*

Freudians such as Sullivan, Fromm, and Thompson. His thinking was also affected by the writings of the Protestant theologian Paul Tillich.

A chief concern of existentialism is the issue of free will. For May, such freedom is more than an escape from traditions, dogmas, and bureaucratic rules and regulations. To be free one must expand one's self-awareness and find ways to take *responsible* individual actions. To be free is to be aware of all the possibilities in life—the choices between satisfying basic needs, adhering to conventions, or committing oneself to others and to significant social values. But such awareness also leads to the "dizziness" of many possibilities. Anxiety, as in organismic theories, is a normal phase of human growth and individuation. Children may feel anxiety simply because they lack sufficient experience and knowledge of society's conventions and so cannot interpret many cues. An adult has evolved to the point of a *reflective* self-awareness; the choices available in life are clearer, but this means one must sometimes take a stand against others or against traditions or conventions. Sometimes an adult confronts not only choices from ignorance but must face conflicts of *values*, which give rise to anxiety.

To illustrate the importance of values, May cites the example of Tom, a laboratory worker whose bodily reactions were being monitored in a famous study on gastric functions and emotions. Tom lay awake one night talking over with his wife what might happen if he lost his job and had to go on welfare. The next morning his physiological indices of stress were the highest ever encountered by the doctors. The key remark he made was, "If I couldn't support my family, I'd as soon jump off the end of the dock." What caused this overriding anxiety was not the fear of physical deprivation—he and his family could have sought public assistance—but rather the threat to a status that Tom, like so many parents in our society, held even dearer than life: the ability to fulfill his role as a provider for his family. The loss of this status would be tantamount to not existing as a person (May, 1967, pp. 72–73).

From the existentialist perspective, the willingness to confront and to make choices, to act with awareness, is what makes life meaningful and exciting. Guilt and neurotic anxiety stem from failures to live authentically, the times we took the easy or conventionally safe road even when our deepest values suggested otherwise—the "cop-outs" of our experience.

One of the most memorable and moving passages in American literature occurs in Mark Twain's *Huckleberry Finn*. Huck and his friend, the fugitive black slave, Jim, are floating down the Mississippi on a raft. While Jim hides, some men on the lookout for runaway slaves interrogate Huck about where Jim can be found. Huck confronts a terrible conflict for he believes that slavery is legal and that as a Christian to lie about Jim will doom him to Hell for eternity. Yet a deeper sense of humanity prevents him from surrendering his friend. He ends his inner struggle with the thought, "I'll go to Hell, then!" and lies to Jim's pursuers to save his friend. At this moment, Huck exemplifies what the existentialists mean by an *authentic* or meaningful existence—a commitment through action and responsibility for a fellow human being. Huck is as free as a human can be, because he can confront what appears to be a dreadful fate and yet act in a manner responsive to his deepest values.

KAFKA'S *THE CASTLE*: HOW DO WE KNOW WHERE WE STAND?

Franz Kafka's novel *The Castle* is a compelling metaphor of the human existential dilemma. A civil engineer named K. receives an order to come to an Austrian village dominated by a castle, the seat of government, to do some technical work. When he arrives, it turns out that no one expected him and he cannot get a clear answer as to what his duties are and when he is to begin. His efforts to obtain definite instructions from the complicated bureaucracy of petty officials in the town only involve him in further ambiguities. When he tries to get an appointment with higher officials in the Castle itself or even to talk to the Castle by telephone, he meets further obstacles and bad connections. K. never gives up his quest, however; he stays on and on at the village seeking some way of getting through to the Castle and finding out where he stands. Reading the novel, we are made aware as in a nightmare of the tragic dilemma of our essentially solitary existence. We also admire K.'s courage, as he refuses to yield in his determination to define his status and chooses again and again to persist in his inquiries rather than just go away or settle into some humdrum conventional routine.

Existentialism as "Conscience"

It would be hard to demonstrate that there is anything like a broad existential theory of personality, especially since the leaders of this philosophical movement are critical of formalized, analytical, logical structures in science. Existentialism is best regarded not as a full-blown personality theory but as the "conscience" among them. It goes beyond the naturally evolving self-actualization views of the organismic-humanistic theories to propose a set of ideals for human existence. Where Freudian or humanistic psychotherapists seek to alleviate anxiety or view it as a sign of unfulfilled development, the existentialist tries to *amplify* the experience of guilt to help the individual recognize life's possibilities most fully (Maddi, 1976). The existential approach, thus, focuses heavily upon consciousness and the private personality, but always in the framework of the ultimate necessity for *choice, commitment,* and *action* if life is to be more than an empty charade.

To sum up, although the "Third Force" in psychology does not encompass a well-developed personality theory, it does serve as a corrective for the heavy concentration on drive reduction, conflict resolution, and reinforcement that characterize the psychodynamic and learning-theory orientations. By emphasizing self-actualization, positive experiences of joy, wonder, curiosity, and the key roles of *self* and *meaning* in personality development, the organismic theories establish a basis for a comprehensive view of the normal, mature personality. The insistence on the significance of meaning and private experiences of knowing also serves as a bridge between psychodynamic and social-learning theories and the cognitive-affective personality theories. The human personality is formed and motivated not only by drives or rewards and punishment but by the search to understand, to appreciate, and to organize our experiential world.

1. In the 1960s humanism emerged in psychology and other behavioral sciences as a revolt against the analytic and reductionist trends of the psychodynamic and learning theories. To dramatize the approach, humanism is sometimes called psychology's "Third Force." The humanist theories point to the importance of the self—how people perceive the world, not just the responses they make—and of curiosity, creativity, exploration, self-development, and self-fulfillment. Humanism includes the organismic, existential, and phenomenological perspectives.

2. Gestalt psychology was a source of stimulation for much of the Third Force movement. Kurt Goldstein, a neurologist, found that massive brain damage eliminates the capacity for abstract thinking. Yet his patients managed to get around their defects in many clever ways and maximized the abilities they did have. Goldstein believed that human beings, even with brain damage, strive toward an equilibrium, a sense of wholeness.

3. Andras Angyal was a psychiatrist who went even further than Goldstein in basing his theories on Gestalt psychology. For Angyal, all human behavior involves tension in the struggle between *autonomy* and *homonomy*. Angyal describes three levels of existence: satisfying drives, achieving one's potential, and finding meaning in relation to others.

4. Abraham Maslow extended organismic theories to the description of the normal personality and human experience such as curiosity, creativity, and joy. He made an important distinction between *motivative* behavior (striving) and *expressive* behavior (existing, growing, and self-actualizing). The overarching theme of Maslow's theory is self-actualization, which involves a fully selfless approach to experience—a development of the sense of self, directness and honesty, doing well what one wants to do, having peak experiences, and becoming aware of one's prejudices and neuroses and struggling to give them up.

5. The concept of self is controversial. Some psychologists say it is too vague and undefinable to be useful. Others maintain that it is essential to an understanding of personality, and that there is a sense of self in all human beings. Phenomenological and organismic theorists insist that more attention should be paid to the experience of self.

6. Gordon Allport, one of the founders of personality psychology, was interested in bodily expressive behavior—that is, the movements, gestures, and mannerisms that define a person's public personality. He tried to find methods to systematically measure uniqueness of personality, he pioneered in the study of personal documents to see if consistent traits or styles could be measured from them, and he did questionnaire studies of values. Allport emphasized the importance of human traits, especially the unique patterning of traits of each individual. He identified three dispositions, or aspects of personality: *cardinal*, *central*, and *secondary*. Allport came to believe that

the self was the central concept for a psychology of personality. He introduced the concept of functional autonomy to indicate that however a motive might have originated, it might serve adult purposes more generally.

7. Carl Rogers is perhaps the most famous clinical psychologist in America. He believes that what really counts in human life is the personal or private experience of an individual. Rogers proposed that the major motive for behavior is *actualization* of the human personality. Of the actualizing tendencies, self-differentiation is the most critical. It is the movement of a person toward becoming a fuller, richer, more self-sufficient individual. The self becomes differentiated into the self of the self-concept and the ideal self. According to Rogers, the growing child needs unconditional positive regard, a spontaneous warm love without any restrictions or demands. An essential feature of full living is openness to experience.

8. The existential personality theorists emphasize *meaningfulness* as the essential motive in human thought and behavior. Rollo May is a well-known exponent of this position. A chief concern of existentialism is the issue of free will. To be truly free we must expand our self-awareness and find ways to take responsible individual actions. Anxiety is a normal phase of human growth and individuation. The willingness to confront and to make choices, to act with awareness, is what makes life meaningful. Guilt and anxiety stem from failure to live authentically.

9. The humanistic theories serve as a corrective for the psychodynamic and social-learning theories, concentration on drive reduction, conflict resolution, and reinforcement. The insistence on the significance of meaning and private experiences of knowing also serves as a bridge between psychodynamic and social-learning theories and the cognitive-affective theories.

CHAPTER 6

Cognitive-Affective Theory

Each of the personality theories reviewed thus far exemplifies a special view of humanity. The psychoanalytic model shows the ego endlessly seeking to control and redirect id-derived impulses; indeed Freud used the image of a rider (the ego) on a wild horse (the id). The neo-Freudian view reflects more the sense of a defensive, frightened, or insecure child striving for security. The behaviorist and social-learning position in its earlier forms summons up images of a rat in a maze or a pigeon being reinforced for pecking on a certain square. And the organismic theories at times seem to be inspirational glorifications of authenticity and self-actualization.

The cognitive-affective approach, which has emerged since the 1960s as a major way in which psychologists look at human behavior, presents a view of a person striving to deal with ambiguities in the "real world," processing sensory information, curious about novelty, and thinking about plans for the future or decisions to be made. Finding meaning in the world, reducing incongruities between our expectations and the new information presented in a situation, pursuing with some zest situations that are moderately novel but not fraught with unknown possibilities—these are the touchstones of the vision of the human being as exemplified in the cognitive movement.

FORERUNNERS OF THE COGNITIVE-AFFECTIVE APPROACH

We have already mentioned Kurt Lewin (1890–1947), one of psychology's true geniuses, and his development of experimental research methods for studying personality and motivation or conflict. Lewin stressed the interplay of forces in a *psychological field*—the organized mental "map" or "picture" of our life situations, our goals, and the steps necessary to achieve them and to avoid the obstacles in our path. He thus emphasized not just actions that were reinforced (as in a social-learning view) but *appraisal*, a mental process. Two students may have the same goal—for example, getting an A in biology—but very different mental pictures of that goal. For one, the goal is simply to feel

Lewin's and Heider's Contributions

successful and to gain the approval of his classmates. For another the A is one more hurdle on the long road to her distant goal—admission to medical school and practice as a physician. Lewin constructed diagrams based on topological principles from physics and mathematics that would lead to a systematic way of translating human experience into a theoretical system comparable to such formulations in the "hard" sciences. One of these diagrams is shown in Figure 6-1. His emphasis was on *cognitive processes*—that is, on the ways in which we organize information and think about ways of carrying out our intentions.

Fritz Heider (b. 1896), used many of Lewin's field-theoretical concepts, but he believed that Lewin was premature in trying to translate an appraisal of the psychological field into terms derived from physics or mathematics. The first step of a science of interpersonal relations should involve an attempt to capture more directly how people look at situations, how they try to organize new information into mental categories, try to assign meaning to random events, and try to determine the causes of their own or others' actions. He called attention, therefore, to our tendency to make attributions and also to try cognitively to *balance* our experiences, fitting new information as well as possible into our well-established knowledge and beliefs.

Heider and a colleague, Marianne Simmel, made a film in which three abstract shapes bounce up and down, approach or move away from one another, and touch or not touch one another. Viewers invariably interpret these movements in human, interpersonal terms, attributing meanings such as desire, anger, jealousy, or affection to the locomotions of these geometric figures. The

FIGURE 6-1

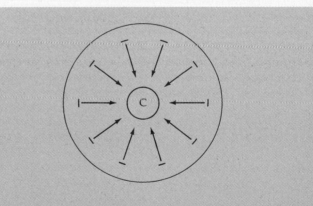

This diagram and photograph illustrate Lewin's description of a child confronted with an array of unpleasant choices or threats. The child experiences hopelessness and, in Lewin's words, "contracts physically and psychically under the vectors coming from all sides," striving to build a wall or shell, an "encysting of the self: the child becomes obdurate."

(Adapted from Lewin, 1935)

6 • COGNITIVE-AFFECTIVE THEORY

importance of balancing new information with previous beliefs, of making things fit in human terms, of attributing events to "causes" such as effort and luck, have all influenced the cognitive movement in social psychology, especially attribution theory, as well as personality psychology (Weiner, 1972).

The experimental studies stimulated by Lewin and the increased importance Heider placed on people's attributions and interpretations of interpersonal events have been tremendously influential in modern social psychology. The focus of much of this work remains on social processes and group responses, however, rather than on ongoing individual experience and the organization of personality. It was a distinguished clinical psychologist, George A. Kelly, who first studied individual personality from a cognitive-appraisal orientation.

George A. Kelly (1905–1967) proposed an image of the human being as a "scientist," constantly arranging the complicated information of experience into *personal constructs*, organized systems of beliefs and expectations about how human relations "work," about how some people are alike and others different (Kelly, 1955). For Kelly, the world "out there" is real. The constructs we form are private "successive approximations" of what is happening in our physical and social environments. Some of these approximations are not useful, however, because they do not incorporate enough of the available information that would help us relate to the environment. Therefore, to function effectively in the world, we must be prepared to continuously *reexamine* and modify our constructs. In addition, if people are to get along with one another, they must first of all recognize that they may be viewing the same set of events from different vantage points. They may be organizing what they perceive into different personal constructs. Once they recognize this difference in perceptions, they can begin to share their assumptions and eventually find some reasonably common ground for communicating and interacting.

Characteristics of Constructs   Constructs inevitably entail the association of previous experiences into formulas, such as "most college jocks are lamebrains." A professor who had formed such a construct based on a few earlier experiences might approach some athletes in a history class with a condescending manner, only to find that they were genuinely curious and eager to learn.

Each of us eventually builds up a *hierarchy of constructs*, an organized grouping of beliefs around a central theme, with some components general and enduring, others specific and more easily changed or modified. The intense loyalty some people feel toward their families may also be included in the construct of patriotism or allegiance to their nation, as symbolized by the flag. Other constructs of patriotism may extend not just to reverence for the flag but a commitment to all decent citizens and to the fundamental constitutional principles of the nation of which the flag is only a relatively minor symbol.

Behavior follows a cycle that Kelly termed *circumspection, preemption,* and *control* (the CPC cycle). An individual faced with a new situation strives to organize it in some meaningful fashion. This takes reflection and consideration of alternatives (*circumspection*). The individual then makes a decision (not always at a conscious level) and settles on one organized construct. This is *preemption*. The behavior that follows this sifting and selecting will then to some extent be determined or *controlled* by the construct system.

The nature of the construct system is open to the possibility of either relatively narrow or relatively flexible interpretations. The CPC cycle has the potential of being too controlled a sequence. But there is also the possibility of a *creative* cycle. Here the individual tries out many constructs and holds back before making commitments. This allows for review of a wide range of possible actions and also, in other respects, allows for enjoyment of various esthetic and sensuous possibilities. A person wandering through a field of flowers may notice only that they are a familiar kind and that there are a lot of them. Wordsworth, the poet, wanders through such a field. He knows very well that these are just flowers but he "plays" creatively with alternative constructs. Although he feels as "lonely as a cloud," the lively movement of the flowers in the breeze soon encourages him in his mind to "dance with the daffodils" and to brighten his mood.

Kelly, perhaps more than any other theorist, argued that personality psychologists do not need to resort to notions about motivation. He felt that the critical step in assessing personality is to ascertain the nature of the construct system. Often abnormal behavior grows out of a construct system that is too narrow; some individuals fail to develop alternatives in the form of more complex or more flexible constructs so as to deal with new information by changing their established and rigid beliefs.

Constructs and Emotions   Kelly was especially ingenious at translating terms such as threat and anxiety into construct language. *Threat* occurs when someone faces the possibility of a drastic change in a central core of constructs (an athlete proud of his skills learns that because of injuries he cannot play any longer) or when constructs of the most fearful or frightening situations actually seem about to be fulfilled (a woman brought up to fear violence in men discovers that her husband gets physically abusive when drunk).

Anxiety, on the other hand, is the terrifying experience that emerges when one's organized anticipations or constructs do not seem appropriate to the events that are taking place (as in the classic dream in which the dreamer is walking naked down a busy street). Kelly wrote of a person about to try a new and unaccustomed course of action:

> There are times when a person hesitates to experiment because he dreads the outcome. He may fear that the conclusions of the experiment will place him in an ambiguous position where he will no longer be able to predict and control. He does not want to be caught with his constructs down (Kelly 1955, p. 14).

How do people go about finding solutions? Kelly used the term *aggression* in a somewhat unusual way to describe active efforts by an individual to attain a fuller picture of the perceptual field or to modify the construct system drastically. When we push actively into the world in order to find out more about it and to increase the complexity of our construct system, we are likely to interfere with other people and *their* construct systems. It is, perhaps, unfortunate that Kelly used the term *aggression* for what might better have been termed *self-assertion* or *exploration*.

Hostility is a more serious problem in Kelly's system. People who constantly attempt to verify predictions made from narrowly established constructs are hostile. They keep trying to verify these constructs even in the face of the fact that there is contradictory information present. The hostile individual does not examine other possibilities but doggedly seeks to confirm preconceived constructs and, thus, inevitably is likely to hurt others by ignoring what they have said or implied or by forcing a one-sided view upon them.

Within Kelly's system, *guilt* is a product of situations in which people feel that they have violated their central core of personal constructs. For the individual whose construct about self includes integrity and deep concern for others as a basic human value, the act of having lied to a friend or even just the impulse to lie evokes guilt. Guilt in this system, thus, could be the result of actual behavior. Or it could be the result of intended behaviors or even fantasies, especially if the core of the construct system is so rigid that it does not permit the distinction between a fantasized intention and an action.

Individual Differences, Pathology, and Psychotherapy   We can now see the ways in which the more complex notions of individual difference and psychopathology found, say, in psychoanalytic theory can be translated into Kelly's construct terminology. Individual differences appear in part because individuals have different hierarchies of constructs. These constructs differ not only in their content but also in dimensions such as *flexibility-rigidity* or *narrowness-breadth*. They also differ in relation to the roles or situations in which people find themselves.

Psychopathology is evident when someone persists in using the same set of constructs again and again in the face of failure of expectations. Many of us have placed bets on the wrong team or horse. The emotionally troubled person often is one who never wins but keeps on betting. The problem may be that abnormal persons tend to attribute the difficulties they experience not to their own faulty construct systems but to a cruel fate or to the malevolence of others. In this sense, such individuals further confound the possibility of changing their behavior in an effective direction.

Changing Personality   Kelly was especially interested in the therapeutic approach to changing constructs. Therapy obviously requires, first of all, an atmosphere in which a patient is willing to examine the range of his or her constructs. Then begins the working out with the therapist a way to modify the constructs that are ineffective or invalid in relation to the life situation of the patient. Kelly advocated a directive and active role for the therapist. By this he did not mean that the therapist should be authoritarian or dictatorial toward the patient. On the contrary, therapy cannot occur unless patients actively take responsibility for self-change. The therapist must, however, provide a new repertory of constructs and behaviors to help patients examine their current assumptions and also help them validate assumptions as they change.

Kelly valued role-playing and actively playing out novel situations in the therapist's interaction with the patient. He also developed an instrument for psychological assessment, the Role Repertory Test, that can be used to help clients recognize the pattern of their constructs and identify those that are too rigid, too flexible, too narrow, or too broad (see Figure 6-2). The test results encourage clients to try practicing new ways of construing situations or new approaches to people.

FIGURE 6-2

No.	1	2	3	4	5	6	7	8	9	10	11	12	13	14	15	Construct
	Self	Mother	Father	Brother	Sister	Spouse	Pal	Ex-pal	Rejecting person	Pitied person	Threatening person	Attractive person	Accepted teacher	Rejected teacher	Happy person	
1																Related—Unrelated
2																Contented—Discontented
3																Nervous—Calm
4																Friendly—Unfriendly
5																Self-confident—Insecure
6																Cold—Warm
7																Easygoing—Driven
8																Hypercritical—Accepting
9																Dependent—Independent
10																Intelligent—Dull-witted
11																Impulsive—Slow-moving
12																Kind—Cruel
13																Handsome—Ugly
14																Quiet—Talkative
15																Dependable—Unreliable

In Kelly's Role Construct Repertory Test (REP), respondents list the names of people in their lives who correspond to the vertical-column categories (such as pal, rejecting person). They then match these people with the constructs in the horizontal column (such as friendly-unfriendly). By statistical analysis, the respondents can determine the narrowness or breadth of specific constructs and how they relate to their families, friends, and selves.

(Adapted from Kelly, 1955)

Implications   Kelly's view, like Rotter's somewhat similar expectancy theory (see Chapter 4), has been criticized because it does not state clearly why a person should *do* anything, that is, why constructs should inevitably lead to actions. His notion of aggression is, perhaps, the only suggestion along this line but it is not spelled out sufficiently. Yet Kelly's approach has been fruitful in stimulating research on cognitive complexity as a personality characteristic; it also forms an important bridge to the new developments in cognitive theories of personality. While Rogers and others may have overstressed feelings and dealt too little with conscious thought, Kelly seems to have minimized the range of excitements and despairs people feel. We need both cognitions and emotions to capture fully the complexity of the human personality.

CURRENT TRENDS IN THE COGNITIVE-AFFECTIVE APPROACH

The cognitive orientation in psychology began about 25 years ago as a result of new developments in computer simulations of human thought and scientific concepts of feedback systems.

Plans and Images as Key Concepts

In 1960 George A. Miller, a specialist in the psychology of language and information-processing, joined with Eugene Galanter, who had worked on psychophysics and sensory processes, and Karl Pribram, a leading researcher on the physiology of the brain, to produce a slim but influential book, *Plans and the Structure of Behavior* (1960). These investigators sought a new set of scientific concepts or "metaphors" to help explain the continuous flow of behavior, taking into account what was then known about computers and other information-processing systems. They also depended heavily on an understanding of *cybernetic* phenomena, or events in the natural world that maintain an equilibrium and adjust to discrepancies between actual and desired conditions in the environment. An example is a thermostat that will switch on a furnace whenever the temperature drops below the degree to which it is set.

Miller and his colleagues first pointed out that human beings are continuously engaged in using their previous experiences to *anticipate* each new situation. If the situation does not match this anticipation, they go into action and explore the incongruity until an adequate match can be made. The general background of information with which people come to a new situation, added to their values and preferences, makes up an *image*. Like linked segments of a computer program, which provide alternative routes to be followed, these images are organized into *plans of action* that individuals set up in relation to specific environmental circumstances confronting them.

As shown in Figure 6-3, a sequence of behavior involves the following steps:

1. The person tests to determine whether a situation conforms to the original plan.

2. If no unexpected behavior by others occurs and the situation is not changed in any way, the plan is unnecessary and it simply "exits."

3. If the situation is not *congruent*—that is, if it does not conform with expectations—then the person "operates" in an attempt to change either the situation or his or her behavior.

FIGURE 6-3
The Test–Operate–Test–Exit Sequence (TOTE)

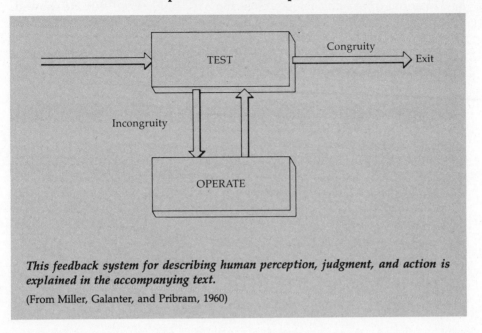

This feedback system for describing human perception, judgment, and action is explained in the accompanying text.

(From Miller, Galanter, and Pribram, 1960)

4. The above activity ordinarily persists until the person makes some match between environmental information, behavior, and the original plan.

So far, you may be inclined to feel that something is missing from the cognitive approaches described to this point. You may agree that how we organize our experiences and how we match new experiences against old ones is an important part of human behavior. But is a human being really so much like an electronic computer running through its programs? Where is the excitement when an outfielder makes a sensational catch of a ball that looked as if it was sailing into the stands? Where is the thrill of recognition when in the midst of a mass of strange faces in a crowd we suddenly spot someone we love? Fortunately, not all cognitive theorists have been insensitive to life's pains and delights. At about the same time as the work described above came an important turning point in the development of personality theories, with the 1959 publication of Ernst Schachtel's book *Metamorphosis* and the 1959 journal article by Robert W. White, "Motivation Reconsidered: The Concept of Competence." These works by two distinguished scholars with outstanding backgrounds in psychoanalytical theory as well as psychology reflected a shift in the dynamic theories away from the concept of drive, which had so dominated personality and learning theories, toward a greater emphasis on emotions and cognition.

White's Concepts of Effectance and Competence

In a remarkable analysis of the theoretical and research literature, Robert W. White (b. 1904) raised questions about the concept of drive and pointed out its limitations from a physiological standpoint (White, 1959, 1960). He showed, by citing the relevant experimental literature, that drives like hunger, thirst, or sex do not function as described by Freud and other psychoanalysts. Drives are not simply tensions that build up and then are discharged by consumption or consummation.

White also called into question the emphasis on drives as determiners of all complicated behavior. He pointed to the extensive research and theorizing of Jean Piaget (1896–1980), the great Swiss student of child development. White was struck by Piaget's careful observations of the behavior of very young children. Even infants are responsive to external movements and show a curiosity, an interest in the environment that cannot be explained by any known drive theory.

White suggested that a source of human motivation quite apart from the satisfaction of biological drives is a need to satisfy curiosity and to learn more about the environment. He postulated needs he called *effectance* and *competence*—the tendency to develop physical and cognitive capacities to their fullest as part of normal growth. This concept is similar to the notion of self-actualization originally proposed by Goldstein and also emphasized by Rogers and Maslow.

Schachtel's Linkage of Sensory Information, Emotion and Memory

Ernst Schachtel (1903–1975) was a psychoanalyst closely associated with the neo-Freudian school. In his beautifully written *Metamorphosis*, he proposed a more thoroughly "humanistic" psychoanalysis, free of the narrow and abstract concepts of classical Freudian theory. Schachtel asserted that *affect* or *emotion*, rather than cyclical biological drives, ought to be viewed as the primary motivational process. He also emphasized the importance of curiosity, environmental stimulation, exploratory activity, and competence as key factors of the human behavioral repertory.

Schachtel suggested that there are two types of affective experience: *embeddedness affect* and *activity affect*. The first is closely related to security; it is what we feel when wanting to be a part of a larger whole, of wanting to be satisfied, to withdraw into states of quiescence or sleep, to rid ourselves of irritating pressures. Activity affect is related to joy and excitement. We seek stimulation and novelty and try as much as possible to enliven our experiences.

Schachtel also examined our sensory experiences. He described how we can distinguish the senses in terms of how close to or far away from the body the information we process is. For humans *taste*, *smell*, and *touch* are body-oriented. But we can hear noises from quite far away and, of course, vision is the sense we rely on most of all in organizing our experiences of distant objects.

Schachtel proposed that our sensory experiences can be viewed along what he called an *autocentric-allocentric* continuum—meaning nearest to–farthest from the self—with the more "primitive" senses (taste, smell, and touch) at the

THE AUTOCENTRIC-ALLOCENTRIC
MODALITIES AND DOGMATISM

Schachtel proposed that people who lose close-ness to the autocentric modalities—taste, touch, smell—may become increasingly cold and detached in adult life. Such people, who rely heavily on dogma, verbal clichés, and standard-ized abstractions, are likely to have lost touch with the kind of differentiated experiences rep-resenting all of the senses that characterize childhood.

An interesting test of this notion was car-ried out by Kaplan and Singer (1963). Measur-ing simple sensory discriminations of a group of adults, they found, as expected, that most people could make much finer distinctions between visual or auditory stimuli than they could between stimuli of taste, touch, or smell. They then compared subjects who had fairly good ability to detect the difference between two smells, or two cloths of differing texture, or two closely related foods with subjects who showed much less ability to make these autocentric dis-criminations but who showed equal ability to discriminate in the allocentric modalities of hearing and vision. They then examined the responses of the same two sets of subjects to a questionnaire developed by Rokeach (1960) that measures the tendency to hold dogmatic beliefs. Those subjects who had difficulty making dis-tinctions between differing tastes, touches, and smells were also more likely to score high on *dogmatism*—that is, they tended to make gen-eralized statements, such as those showing gross ethnic or political prejudice.

Schachtel's approach helps us understand why certain works of art have special appeal. A fine poet not only describes a scene in visual terms but somehow captures the quality of taste and touch and smell that we have ourselves only dimly recalled from a similar experience. When the poet Keats writes of a freshly poured glass of wine with "beaded bubbles winking at the brim" we can practically taste the wine. Shake-speare is full of imagery that recaptures tastes and smells as well as sights and sounds. When Hamlet has killed Polonius by accident and is asked where he has hidden the body in the Dan-ish King's castle he replies: "Indeed if you find him not within this month, you shall *nose* him as you go up the stairs into the lobby." Schachtel moved the cognitive position closer to emo-tional experience and to what we privately feel as part of our most intimate sensations. His position therefore represents a deepening of the implications of the cognitive orientations beyond Kelly's "human as scientist" model or Miller, Galanter, and Pribram's computer analogy.

autocentric pole and the distance senses at the allocentric pole. All normal perception demands both autocentric and allocentric modalities, but there is a difference in the way we organize our thoughts or encode sensory experi-ences in our memories. The autocentric experiences of taste, touch, and smell are harder to communicate to other people. They are far more a part of our private personality than what we hear or what we see. When it comes to remembering experiences and then communicating these memories to others, we are likely to have many more words and descriptive systems for charac-terizing visual and auditory experiences than experiences of taste, touch, and smell. Because the child's experience is so much related to body-centered sen-sory modalities, many of the child's memories cannot really be recaptured in adult life. Here Schachtel was presenting a very important alternative to explain

Freud's notions about repression and Sullivan's concept of the prototaxic mode. Schachtel's position is that many events of early childhood cannot be recalled not because they are full of conflict but because they were experienced in sensory modalities not as susceptible to verbal abstraction; therefore they are less likely to be stored in a way that is convenient for recall.

TOMKINS' COGNITIVE-AFFECTIVE THEORY

Perhaps the most comprehensive and original theory of personality to emerge in the past twenty years is the cognitive-affective theory of Silvan S. Tomkins (b. 1911). Tomkins pointed out that both psychoanalysis and behaviorism seriously neglected conscious experience in the human condition. On the basis of empirical and philosophical evidence he developed a carefully reasoned and detailed criticism of the drive and wish-fulfillment theories. He then proposed a more general view which sought to show how information-processing and emotion are closely intertwined systems that motivate thought and action and are more important than drives in the organization of personality.

Tomkins emphasized both the influence of information and computer theory on personality psychology and the research findings of central brain mechanisms that evoke emotions of "joy" and "distress." He proposed that a theory must deal with the great flexibility of human behavior, the great range

Silvan S. Tomkins

of potential goals and objectives that characterize human experience, and also take into account the highly differentiated and specialized emotional structure which characterizes our species.

Tomkins' theory is elaborate and extensive, full of new concepts. It proposes that human behavior and thought arise from the operation of five bodily systems: the *homeostatic* or autonomic mechanisms, the *drives*, the *affects* or emotions, the *motoric* system, and the *cognitive* or information-processing network. The human being has evolved with a highly specialized and differentiated system of emotions, and these serve as the major motivational system. The emotions amplify drive signals to alert us to the danger of physiological deficits such as hunger. But even in the absence of drive pressures, the emotions react differently to the *rate, persistence,* and *complexity* of new information that the organism must process. The emotions thus motivate behavior by responding not only to internal drives but also to the ongoing information-processing characteristics of experience and behavior.

Tomkins hypothesized that we are "wired" through evolution to experience the negative emotions of startle or distress when we confront a sudden novel situation that we have not anticipated in our images or plans (see Figure 6-4). Information received at a more moderate pace can arouse interest or surprise, which are positive emotions. Although there are only a limited number of emotions, they interact in numerous and intricate ways. The *primary affects* are interest, enjoyment, surprise, anger, distress, sadness, fear, shame, contempt, and disgust. These serve to clarify the complex information-processing we carry out as we steer ourselves through the physical and social environment. We seek (1) to *maximize* positive emotions such as joy, surprise, or interest and (2) to *minimize* negative emotions such as anger or fear. At the same time, we seek (3) to *express* emotions as fully as possible and also (4) to *control* them. Thus these four possibilities of emotional experience and expression are central to all motivation.

Since we seek to maximize positive affects such as interest or joy we look for situations in life that are novel but not too novel. We also strive to anticipate events so that we can experience joy when we recognize a match between the events and our private images. If we are confronted with a persisting incongruity or frustration—for example, our inability to find a job or to resolve a conflict with a lover—we first may be enraged. As the situation persists and active efforts to resolve it fail, we may become sad or depressed. Notice that this theory provides flexibility for dealing with a wide range of potential human conflicts, including neuroses of childhood origin as well as current existential dilemmas.

Tomkins stresses the importance of the face as the major communicator of information about affect and hence of information about motivation. The human face is structurally developed to produce different reactions to available information in the environment. Through evolution these facial expressions have been useful, because humans have been socially oriented in order to

The Central Role of Emotions

FIGURE 6-4

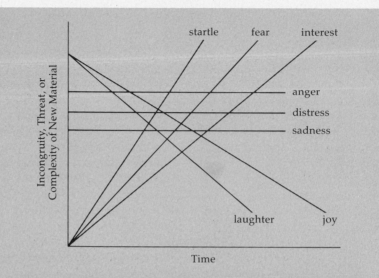

As the graph shows, a person's emotional reaction to a stimulus depends on the suddenness and incongruity of new information and the time it takes for incongruity to be reduced. Note that laughter and the positive emotion of joy are aroused when incongruity or threat is relatively quickly reduced, but that if high levels of incongruity persist, the negative emotions of anger, distress, or sadness may emerge.

(Based on Tomkins, 1962)

survive. Much of Tomkins' research was devoted to studying the subtle changes in the human face as expressive of affect. He concluded that there are indeed relatively few expressions: fear-distress, anger, sadness (the weeping response), joy or laughter (the smiling response), and shame-humiliation or contempt (see the photographs in Chapter 8, page 191).

Personality Styles and Development

As we have seen, for Tomkins the cognitive and affective systems are closely intertwined and essentially inseparable. While innate tendencies cause particular affects to occur, as suggested above, people can also learn patterns that emphasize certain affects more than others, such as the British "stiff upper lip," the tight control of any show of distress in the face of hardship or defeat.

Socialization experiences in family settings or cultural groups may lead to more or less emphasis on the anticipation of positive or negative events. In this way they influence the expression of positive or negative affect, and stylistic patterns of expressing affect emerge. Among scientists Tomkins studied, he discerned a continuum or *affective polarity*. At one extreme is a group of

AN EXAMPLE OF TOMKINS' AFFECT DYNAMICS

Let us suppose you happen to be home alone early one autumn evening. The doorbell rings. As you move to answer the door the possibilities about who might be there quickly flit through your consciousness. It could be a friend or relative who occasionally drops in on an evening. A more remote possibility might be a magazine salesman, because you have heard from others that one has been around recently in the evening. In effect, then, even as you move toward the door you are already drawing on your own background of memories—what Miller, Galanter, and Pribram as well as Tomkins would call your *image*; you are establishing some anticipation which can then be verified when you actually open the door.

There before your open door stands a gorilla! Your immediate reaction almost certainly would be to show the *startle reflex*. Your eyes blink, your arms are thrust up and back, your body is bent forward. Within a split second you open your eyes and again see the gorilla and become overwhelmed with fear. In effect, you are confronting a stimulus that cannot be *matched* to any of your anticipated plans; this produces a high level of incongruity or cognitively unassimilable material with an associated high level of density of neural firing within a very short time. The emotion of fear or terror is thus evoked by the situation.

Suddenly the gorilla says in a rather child-like voice: "Trick or treat!" Now you remember that this is Halloween and in an instant you can make a mental match with a well-established national custom although not one you had been prepared for just at this moment. There is a sudden reduction in the novelty and complexity of the situation and you show the affect of joy, in a burst of relieved laughter.

Let us suppose for a moment that it was a real gorilla! The incongruity and threat of the situation persist at a high level and you cannot make any sense of it. The animal starts to advance into the house and you experience terror, then rage and anger at this intrusion. It forces its way in and you retreat back into the house and try to stem its advance, angrily throwing things at it while trying to find a source of escape. You are now a prisoner of the gorilla. It clomps around the house, knocking over furniture, breaking glasses, eating the fruit you had in a bowl, and you find yourself alternating between anger and despair. You experience a little more familiarity with the situation but still are helpless. With familiarity you are more likely to experience a somewhat lower level of persisting incongruity. This will lead to the affect of distress and sadness.

Although this is hardly a realistic example, it does illustrate the point that our information capacities are indeed closely related to the particular kinds of emotions we can experience—a critical feature of Tomkins' theory.

---

individuals who feel that there is an "ultimate truth." They approach facts with a determined skepticism, constantly examining them to remove all the errors they expect to find. Such an approach Tomkins linked with early socialization experiences of humiliation and contempt. At the other extreme lie individuals who grew up in settings that encouraged positive affect and playfulness. Scientists socialized around the anticipation of positive affect might be less concerned with whether there is an ultimate truth and more likely to carry out research and speculation for the sheer fun of it. Such individuals might show more smiles, more laughing responses, and also much more surprise and interest as if each new finding in an experiment were a delightful revelation.

In this World War II photo, a French citizen watches in anguish as the last French troops leave his city after France's surrender to Germany in June, 1940. Note how he seems to struggle to keep himself from bursting into tears—an unmanly act in his culture.

Tomkins does not suggest that these affective polarities represent discrete types but rather a continuum along which we all vary. The ideal is a healthy balance between the two extremes.

Script Theory   A novel feature of Tomkins' work is his use of *script theory*. We have already discussed the importance of anticipatory plans, images, and constructs in the framework of cognitive theory. Research in cognition and in artificial intelligence (the study of how to program computers to "think" and solve problems) has adapted the notion of a script to explain how we deal with a situation when we are presented with limited information. For example, suppose we are told, "John went to a restaurant, ate lunch, and left." Most of us can fill in additional details from our own well-established scripts: John must have taken a seat, looked at the menu, decided on what to have, told the waiter, waited for his order, eaten, paid his check, and tipped the waiter. For some situations we have elaborate and detailed scripts and for others very sketchy ones. We all carry around thousands of well-learned scripts relevant to a variety of social situations (Schank and Abelson, 1977.) Many scripts are socially shared. But the scripts crucial for personality differences are those we have "written, directed and continuously act in" (Tomkins, 1979), based on certain significant experiences in our lives, often in early childhood. How we use these scripts when we confront new situations in our daily lives depends on whether they are linked to positive or to negative emotions.

Implications

Tomkins' theory presents a large-scale alternative to psychodynamic theories that focus on drives and stages of psychosexual development. He argues that the interaction of information-processing with the various emotions is the major determiner of motivation and personality differences.

Tomkins' emphasis on the four principles of maximizing positive emotions, minimizing negative emotions, and both expressing and controlling emotions is not in opposition to the social-learning view of reinforcement. It represents an effort to include the notion of different emotions within a precise formulation of what circumstances are more or less likely to be reinforcing. A situation with an incongruity gradient that rises at a moderate rate (novelty) will be reinforcing (positive affect of surprise-interest) just as much as a situation leading to a sharp reduction of incongruity (positive affect of joy). By its emphasis on information-processing, however, Tomkins' theory has moved away from the social- learning theories and further toward the importance of the private personality and of consciousness as a critical feature of the reinforcement process.

AN OVERVIEW OF COGNITIVE-AFFECTIVE THEORY

In this chapter we have traced the emergence of the modern cognitive-affective theory of personality. It represents a coalescence of the contributions of Lewin, Heider, White, Schachtel, the cognitive-experimental researchers, and, particularly, the emphases of Kelly's construct theory and Tomkins' integration of information-processing with the differentiated emotional system. Let us now examine in more detail some of the specific implications of the cognitive-affective approach for personality psychology.

Motivational Perspective

Human behavior is perhaps best viewed in terms of an information-processing system. People are continuously drawing on their memories and expectations to develop plans for dealing with each new situation they encounter. Ultimately, however, the response they make depends on their *interpretation* of that environment, an interpretation that reflects their previous experience and anticipations. The degree of differentiation and flexibility in past experiences and anticipations may interact with the relative clarity or ambiguity of a particular physical or social situation. Thus, the cognitive position does not minimize the importance of the physical environment. Indeed, the special characteristics of the environment and the need for varied and complex environmental information are critical in a cognitive theory.

Within given cultures or social settings certain types of external situations or events are well understood by practically any person who encounters them. In most Western European and American societies, red lights at street corners mean "Stop!" and imply dangerous consequences if one drives or walks past them. There are, however, many social situations in which there are sharp conflicts between what at first seem like clear-cut expectations and what emerge as the "actual" expectations of the environment. For example, young police officers are trained to adhere to the laws and ethical codes of their society. But suppose they find that a sizable number of the police on the job accept small "gifts" from shopkeepers to overlook minor violations such as parking near the shops. If the newcomers on the squad stick strictly to the law and to the formal ethical code, they will arrest individuals who offer them bribes. But

Video games teach young people a variety of skills that may have value in the market-place, but they do not provide the experience in social interaction that teaches people how to read others' emotions and communicate their own.

then they will find that they have evoked the anger of many of their older colleagues. Thus the social situation provides these young police officers with a set of imbalances that are not as easily resolved or classified as a red traffic light. Similarly, in the early developmental experience of a child there may be contradictions between what parents say and do or between what parents say and what peers say.

The daily task of each of us is to organize and assimilate all the complex information in each new environment and then bring it into congruity with our anticipations and plans. If we fail to do this, we must learn to act upon the environment either to increase the available information or to modify the environment so as to bring it into line with our anticipations. Thus a cognitive point of view implies that there is a constant feedback system between information-gathering and environmental action. In this respect it presents a theoretical advance over the more purely phenomenal orientation that does not explain why people should *act* at all.

Motivation involves the reduction of incongruities and the exploration of novel environments to enhance the positive affects of interest or curiosity. In cognitive-affective theory, then, circumstances that increase positive affect, such as opportunities to explore novel environments with some degree of control over the complexity and difficulty of assimilation of the new information, are reinforcing. The matching of novel material or seemingly incongruous events with previously established plans or images also produces the affect of joy or happiness and consequent positive reinforcement. Negative affects arise primarily in circumstances that suddenly present masses of unassimilable materials. They also appear when anticipations and previously established cognitive structures continue to fail to integrate new material over long periods of time (as in confronting the reality of the death of a beloved person). Circumstances that permit *expression* of affect are likely to be positively reinforcing. Similarly, situations in which an individual can *control* expression of affect are also positively reinforcing, especially where expression might be dangerous, embarrassing, or harmful to others.

Central Mechanisms and the Self

Most cognitive theories emphasize an "executive" or "central matching station" as part of the cognitive system. Such a central system establishes "rules" for selecting new information, storing it, and matching it against previous anticipations and plans in a particular environment. These rules allow only the most relevant information to be stored, thus increasing the likelihood that it will be remembered and potentially modify earlier experience. In addition, cognitive theories often make the assumption that private experiences such as conscious thoughts, fantasies, or images provide an *alternative* environment to the external world (Singer, 1974). Such thoughts may be reshaped and reorganized and further acted upon by thought itself in much the same way as new inputs from the physical or social environment. Thus there is a constant restructuring of material in the memory system; memory is never simply a process of passive storage.

Most cognitive theories also assume that some attitudes, beliefs, or patterns of information are more *central* or *self-oriented* than others and therefore are more likely to evoke complex affective responses. Cognitive theories tend to view the self as an *object* of cognition or a part of perceived experience rather than as an agent. Because our most personal feelings are associated both with a long background of memories from childhood and our most frequent experiences, they have the most complex network of related images, memories, and anticipations. Novel material that does not fit in with expectations about the self will generate a sense of incongruity. In the face of persisting incongruity, experiences relating to the self will evoke greater intensity of distress or anger.

How Cognitive Styles Influence Personality Variation

In contrast to social-learning theorists who deemphasized individual differences or personality traits, cognitive theorists have been intrigued by consistencies in personal styles of information-processing and how these styles affect behavior. The term *cognitive style* reflects the findings that people differ systematically in the kinds of strategies or approaches they take when confronted with the task of organizing or integrating new information. Shown a series of pictures or of written descriptions of different people, some subjects in an experiment may try to keep in mind only the separate details of each stimulus (concrete style) while other subjects may immediately try to find some common principle or category that links them all together (abstract style). Such variations in a concreteness-abstraction approach to information-processing can have widespread implications for how people put together experiences to form the kind of personal constructs described by Kelly (Harvey, Hunt, and Schroeder, 1961). Other styles reflect how much emphasis people place on cues from the physical or social environment in interpreting events rather than relying on their own more personal memories or bodily sensations (field dependence versus field independence). The field dependence-independence cognitive style has been shown to be linked to a wide variety of personality differences ranging from patterns of social interaction to career choices (Witkin and Goodenough, 1981, Chapter 9).

Developmental Sequences and Capacities

A major thrust of the cognitive approach has come from the research on child development by Heinz Werner, Jean Piaget, and Kurt Lewin. Werner showed in numerous studies of children's perception, language, and symbol development that growth involves sequences of movement from gradual differentiation of perceptions or skills through integration of newly differentiated capacities into more organized abilities. He talked of *spiral* types of development because in the shift from differential movements to smoothly organized, effortless locomotion there may be periods of fumbling, or even regression, until a new structure evolves. The beginning toddler who gets up on two feet after becoming an expert on her hands and knees will for a while be less smooth and less efficient at walking than she was at crawling. After a while, once this new level is practiced, walking becomes effortless and graceful, clearly superior to crawling.

Piaget emphasized various stages in the growth of children's mental capacities from birth to about age 12, when they become capable of abstract thought. Lewin, in a famous film made in the 1920s, showed that for a child aged about 2, sitting down on a chair is extremely difficult, since one must turn away from a chair to lower oneself into it. For a young child "out of sight is out of mind"; since the chair does not "exist," the child is afraid of falling. Research of this type points up the importance of the cognitive capacities of the child in development.

While social-learning theory has on the whole minimized the importance of stages or sequences of development in favor of specific patterns of reinforcing experiences, the cognitive and social-learning theories are not completely irreconcilable. Zigler and Child (1973) reviewed the literature on socialization of the child and argued in favor of what they called a cognitive-developmental position. They proposed that while for certain periods of development children are incapable of dealing with particular kinds of information-processing, the speed or complexity of the mental structures they form within a stage or in moving from one stage to another can be influenced extensively by *social experience*. This position is congruent with Werner's (1957) emphasis on *spiral* types of development, in which children may reach a particular point and stay at a plateau of development for a period of time until they are either structurally ready or are encouraged through social learning to move to the next level.

Some cognitive-affective theorists call attention to the emotional training of children in families that emphasize autocentric in contrast to allocentric processing, or vice versa. Other theorists discuss socialization of particular types of affective expression and differentiation. From the cognitive-affective standpoint there is no need to assume that there are *specific* psychosexual phases that a child must pass through. Rather, a child who has limited motor and cognitive abilities may obviously be more focused on close-to-body experiences, and these experiences are less easily labeled and less easily stored in memory in a form accessible to the adult (Schachtel, 1959).

Some families minimize the child's experience of negative affect; other families make extensive use of negative affective responses in an effort to control behavior. From the cognitive standpoint, conflicts can develop if a child's natural curiosity is inhibited, if serious misinformation is presented, or if the child is exposed to conflicting words and actions or conflicting sets of beliefs. A child may grow up in a family in which there is a strict requirement of attention to Biblical teachings and emphasis on memorizing material such as the Ten Commandments; at the same time the child may hear the parents openly advocate physical violence or the killing of members of other nations or cultural or racial groups. The child must somehow reconcile these discrepancies.

Emotions and Socialization

The growing child must also master information about others' experiences or emotional expression, and at early ages this may be more difficult than at later ages. A child under 3 or 4 who is teased by being threatened with the possibility of seeing ghosts may be terrified. A somewhat older child may be intrigued by ghosts, but may not immediately accept their reality, while not completely disregarding the possibility. This ambivalence can lead to the kind of fluctuation between interest and fear that characterizes the way that children between 7 and 11 watch horror movies. For younger children such films may be so frightening that they burst into tears or hide under the seat. The older child may be frightened but has had sufficient previous experiences to know that it is "only a movie."

Cognitive theories also are inclined to accept the notion that there may be basic groupings of cognitive structures integrated around major themes. These groupings may be more or less differentiated. A sense of "self" may be more differentiated for some than for others; one consequence of this may be heightened inner awareness and separation of self from the pressures of social demand (Chapter 11).

Development of Deviant Behaviors

Cognitive and social-learning positions do not differ dramatically with respect to the origins of grossly deviant personality characteristics or psychopathology. Cognitive theorists perhaps place somewhat more emphasis on developmental failures, produced occasionally by actual physical handicaps, so that some young people fail to develop the conceptualization skills needed for performing many of the informational and social tasks of society. Cognitive theories also give more weight to the elaborate private processing that goes on in the growing child in the form of fantasies and make-believe. They recognize, of course, the import and impact of reward and punishment to which a child is exposed in social interaction. Particular deviant behaviors can therefore be attributed to failures of differentiation within certain regions of the overall cognitive structure of an individual.

For example, a child who develops a great deal of ability to play by himself or herself, reads well, and has technical skills with chemistry sets, chess, or ham radios may have been sheltered from day-to-day interactions with other children. Thus, he or she may possess a highly differentiated set of cognitive skills and subtle affective reactions available in relation to *private* behaviors (or with the ham radio, communications at a distance). But this more seclusive child may not know the subtle details of how to "read" other peoples' faces, or how to tell when other children are teasing or are serious, or how to adapt to the give and take of a group of peers.

Quite recently an extensive body of research has developed around the notion that many developmental difficulties and many personality problems can be explained by the ways in which people assign causality. *Attribution* theory (Weiner, 1972) suggests that a person may attribute relative success or failure in performance either to *external* forces (luck, or the presumed difficulty of the task) or to *internal* or private events (one's own efforts or abilities). A child who has a strong motive for achievement may be more likely to take all the credit for any successes in a school task or a social situation. This system of attribution helps to maintain the child's self-esteem. Others may regularly attribute the causes of behavior to chance, a kind of *que será será* ("whatever will be, will be") mentality. Such persons may give up easily in the face of frustrations or difficulties on the assumption that luck is against them anyway.

The evolution of an adequate theory of personality has involved the sharpening of many concepts and the gradual discarding of other concepts, such as psychic energy or cathexis, that are untestable or inaccurate. Especially important has been a remarkable growth of sophistication about the questions that need to be asked and the research methods that can be employed to answer these questions.

The cognitive and cognitive-affective approaches to personality have attempted to redress the imbalance produced by the neglect of the private person and of conscious experience as well as of the complexities of information-processing. The cognitive movement has taken into account the fact that humans are thinking organisms who reason consciously about possibilities and also anticipate events or project private images that need to be matched against new events. Thus, reinforcement in the social-learning sense depends heavily upon the cognitive appraisal of the situation and the expectations brought to the situation by an individual. Expectations or plans may, however, be illusory or misguided in relation to specific situations and this accounts for individual variations in emotional response, perceived threat, or the necessity for action to reduce incongruities.

Most present-day investigators and theorists take seriously the contributions of cognitive theorists who stress information-processing, attribution of meaning, and attention to private experiences as human functions that need to be related more effectively to overt behavior. At the same time the important contributions of social-learning theorists and the increased emphasis of the psychoanalysts upon public interaction behaviors have opened the way for many challenging kinds of systematic research possibilities.

This chapter began with a brief summary of the view of human beings implied by the different personality theorists. The cognitive-affective approach seeks to represent human beings as forever curious, seeking to attach meaning to the events around them, anticipating and preparing for the future, but also passionate and intense. In the very act of reducing ambiguity or establishing meaning we can range from terror and despair to excitement, surprise, and joy. Clearly, human experience has an emotional excitement that goes well beyond the information-processing routines of the computer.

SUMMARY

1. The cognitive-affective approach to personality presents the view of a person striving to deal with ambiguities in the "real world," processing sensory information, curious about novelty, and thinking about plans for the future or decisions to be made.

2. George A. Kelly described the human being as a "scientist," constantly arranging complicated information into constructs. To function effectively people must constantly examine and modify their constructs and build them up into a hierarchy, an organized grouping of beliefs around a central theme. Behavior follows a cycle of circumspection, preemption, and control, the *CPC cycle*. Kelly argued that notions about motivation are unnecessary to explain behavior, and he translated many ideas such as threat and anxiety into construct language. Individual differences appear because people have different hierarchies of constructs, and psychopathology is evident when someone persists in using the same set of constructs in the face of failure of expectations. Kelly was interested in the therapeutic approach to changing constructs and emphasized that there must be an atmosphere in which clients are willing to examine their constructs and, with the help of the therapist, begin to modify them.

3. In 1960 George A. Miller, Eugene Galanter, and Karl Pribram explained behavior with concepts based on what was known about computers, information-processing systems, and cybernetics. Human beings use their past experience to anticipate each new situation. If the new situation is incongruous with anticipations, people explore the incongruity until a match is made. The information that people bring to a situation is called an *image*, which is similar to a computer program in providing plans of action.

4. Robert W. White wrote a famous article in which he questioned the emphasis on drives as determiners of complex behavior. He cited research by Piaget showing that children are interested in the environment in a way that cannot be explained by drive theory. He postulated a need called *effectance*—the tendency to develop physical and cognitive capacities to their fullest as a part of normal growth.

5. Ernst Schachtel tried to construct a "humanistic" psychoanalysis. He asserted that *affect* or emotion should be viewed as the primary motivational process. He also emphasized curiosity and competence. He proposed two types of affect: embeddedness affect, wanting to be part of a large whole, and activity affect, related to joy and excitement. Schachtel suggested that sensory experience can be viewed along an autocentric-allocentric continuum, with taste, smell, and touch at the autocentric pole and hearing and vision at the allocentric pole. Many events of childhood are not recalled because they were experienced in sensory modalities not susceptible to verbal abstraction.

6. Silvan Tomkins' theory of personality is perhaps the most comprehensive and original of the past twenty years. It proposes that behavior and thought arise from the operation of five systems: the homeostatic system, drives, affects or emotions, the motoric system, and the cognitive or information-processing system. Human beings have specialized and differentiated emotions that serve as the major motivational system by responding to internal drives and also to the information-processing characteristics of experience and behavior. The primary affects are interest, joy, surprise,

anger, distress, sadness, fear, shame, contempt, and disgust. People seek to maximize positive emotions and minimize negative emotions, and they also try to express and to control emotions. They look for situations that are novel, but not too much so, and try to anticipate events so that they can experience joy when they have a match between events and their own images. The theory provides flexibility for dealing with many potential human conflicts. A novel feature of Tomkins' work is his use of script theory to explain how people deal with a situation when they have limited information. The scripts crucial for personality development are those based on significant experiences in life, especially early childhood.

7. In cognitive-affective theory, motivation involves the reduction of incongruities in the environment and exploration of new environments to enhance positive affects. Negative affects arise with masses of new material that anticipation cannot integrate. There is no agreement about the structural characteristics of personality, but most theorists emphasize the interrelation and interactions of the personal and environmental systems.

8. Most cognitive theorists emphasize a central "executive" as part of the cognitive system, which establishes rules for selecting new information, for storing it, and for matching it against anticipations and plans. Some of the major cognitive styles are field dependence versus field independence and concreteness versus abstraction.

9. The cognitive-affective approach to development comes from research showing that growth involves sequences from gradual differentiation of perceptions and skills to integration into more organized abilities.

10. Cognitive and social-learning theories are similar with respect to origins of deviant personality characteristics and psychopathology. Many cognitive theorists emphasize developmental failures of conceptualization skills needed for informational and social tasks. They also give more weight to private processing of information in the form of fantasies and make-believe.

CHAPTER
7

Research Methods and Personality Assessment

CAESAR: Let me have men about me that are fat;
Sleek-headed men and such as sleep a-nights:
Yond Cassius has a lean and hungry look;
He thinks too much; such men are dangerous. . . .
Would he were fatter! . . . He reads much;
He is a great observer, and he looks
Quite through the deeds of men: He loves no plays,
As thou dost, Antony; he hears no music;
Seldom he smiles; and smiles in such a sort
As if he mock'd himself, and scorn'd his spirit
That could be mov'd to smile at anything.
Such men as he be never at heart's ease
Whiles they behold a greater than themselves;
And therefore are they very dangerous.

This speech from Shakespeare's *Julius Caesar* sketches a set of assumptions about personality that continues to be made by many of us, including personality theorists and researchers. Shakespeare puts into Caesar's mouth a theory of personality traits that was widely held in medieval and Renaissance Europe. Caesar's theory implies, first of all, that personality traits are consistent over time and in different situations. Second, Caesar's judgment is based to some extent on physical characteristics: Cassius has "a lean and hungry look." He also implies that there is a relationship between physical characteristics and personality styles. Caesar's description of Cassius extends next to his habits and facial expressions. Note that Caesar mentions how rarely Cassius smiles, and that his smile is sardonic. Habits such as reading, not going to plays, and not enjoying music all suggest that Cassius is too thoughtful and serious. Finally, like a modern psychodynamic theorist, Caesar puts together the pattern of physical characteristics, emotion as shown in facial expression, and behavior to infer Cassius' underlying motivational structure—envy of his superiors.

A great writer like Shakespeare can portray a character succinctly and make him come alive for us. But unlike a scientist, a creative artist like Shakespeare has no need to *prove* that Caesar's personality assessment of Cassius—the presumed link between body type (leanness), habits (sleeplessness, reading), tastes (dislike for music, careful thinking, and observation), emotional patterns (infrequent and sardonic smiling) and an underlying motive of envy of the powerful—is correct. The artist creates an imaginary world, the value of which is tested only by the appreciation and pleasure of an audience. The personality theorist starts out in much the same way, formulating an imagined or hypothesized set of relationships. But this is only the first step of a scientific analysis. The scientist has an obligation to find ways of defining all the relevant terms and making the generalizations concrete and tangible so that they can be subjected to systematic observation, experiment, and measurement. Theories as far reaching as those of Freud and Jung are intriguing examples of scientific myth making, but they must also stand the test of systematic research and evaluation.

So far, this book has described broad general theories of personality. We turn now from theory to research and begin to examine the extensive research enterprise that must lay the empirical foundation for sophisticated and precisely formulated theories of personality. To do so we must first take a closer look at the methods employed by personality researchers. These methods are designed

1. to *assess* personality—that is, to find ways of studying the unique characteristics of individuals in an objective manner, as free as possible of the observer's bias

2. to develop systematic procedures for collecting information that will *test* or *elaborate on* theories

3. to *describe* or *discover* new relationships in the field

4. to *predict* specific patterns of thought, attitudes, or behavior from personality descriptions

5. to *evaluate* the possibilities of *changing* personality.

THE OBJECTIVES OF PERSONALITY RESEARCH

To study personality scientifically a researcher must (1) make as explicit as possible the concepts being studied and the methods used to study them and (2) attempt to communicate the findings in a form that can be verified by other scientists in any part of the world. The second requirement is especially difficult in the psychology of personality because the way that information is collected depends to a great extent on patterns of customs, traditions, and language in the researcher's cultural setting.

Verification or Clarification of Theory

From a scientific standpoint, a theory of personality that does not make sufficiently concrete assertions so that it can be proved or disproved through research is much less interesting and valuable than one that lends itself to testing by objective methods. For example, concepts such as the death instinct in Freud's theory or the persona or shadow in Jung's theory (Chapters 2 and 3) are difficult if not impossible to test. Some of Freud's proposals, however, are amenable to testing; for example, his linkage of a preoccupation with toilet habits and defecation (anal orientation) and personality traits such as stinginess, orderliness, and obstinacy has been tested in many studies. In Jung's case his proposal that human traits can be arranged along an introversion-extraversion continuum is reasonably testable and has consistently been supported in questionnaire studies (Carrigan, 1960) and in studies using projective methods (Singer and Brown, 1977). Indeed, the theory implicit in Shakespeare's description of Cassius—that lean men are serious, tense, and thoughtful while fat men are more amiable—has been elaborated upon and tested in the research on body types of William Sheldon (1942) and Hans J. Eysenck (1953).

It is important to remember that research rarely tests a vast comprehensive theory. Rather, attention is paid to components of the theory that can be singled out and examined. Sometimes research does attempt to test hypotheses derived from the basic general assumptions of a theory. For example, Freud's theory of aggression as an inherent human drive constantly pressing for discharge and partially satisfied by vicarious experiences of violence, such as watching a prizefight or a televised gun battle, has been subjected to rather careful research study (Chapter 14).

Usually personality formulations are not sufficiently precise to allow the elegant research condition of what is called a *critical test*, a specific experiment or other form of data collection that can clearly disprove a theory or indicate the relative power of two or three competing theories to explain particular research findings. Occasionally it is possible to set up an experiment that almost amounts to a critical test. For example, as we shall see later in this chapter, there are at least two different formulations of why people become depressed and how this depression influences their behavior; efforts to test these theories with various research methods come about as close as possible in providing critical tests of theory in personality psychology.

Another important objective of personality research is the identification, description, or discovery of new relationships between variables relevant to understanding individuality. For example, the experimental psychologists Solomon Asch and Herman Witkin began a series of studies in the area of perception. They were interested in knowing how people in a dark room decide when a tilted rod in front of them is actually perfectly vertical—in other words, at a right angle to the earth. In the course of the studies, Witkin became impressed with the striking difference in how people decided when the bar was actually upright. Some of them used information from their own body experiences (the self) and others from the external environment (the *field*). Witkin spent more than 25 years exploring the many different relationships in a host of personality variables between persons who rely on the visual field and those who rely on the self in forming judgments about a variety of situations.

Description and Discovery of Relationships

Part of the researcher's job is to define variables as precisely as possible. One way to do so is to spell out a set of defining operations—that is, a series of measurement procedures that permit others to repeat the observations of the variable. Sometimes this simply means a carefully prepared paper-and-pencil questionnaire measuring a personality dimension such as introversion-extraversion or achievement motivation.

A variable may be defined through a set of experimental procedures. The great pioneer of experimental personality research, Kurt Lewin, developed with his students a variable that he called *level of aspiration*. He had people play a pinball-like game and state what score they believed they could attain. If they reached that score, would they maintain the same level of aspiration for the next turn or raise it higher? Suppose they failed to get the score and fell well below. Would they lower it for the next turn, or would they stick to their high goals? This procedure opens the way for a variety of interesting ways to study how people set goals for themselves in many life situations, how they adjust to adverse information or failure, how rigidly they cling to unrealistic hopes. Literally hundreds of experiments were generated once the possibility of objectively studying aspiration patterns was available to investigators.

A challenge for personality research is to ascertain whether personality variables can predict the ways in which an individual, or group of persons with common characteristics, will respond in a new but theoretically relevant situation. After all, if personality measurement procedures do not predict future behavior or thought patterns, then we might well question whether personality is a useful concept for scientific purposes.

Behavior Prediction

For a period during the late 1960s and early 1970s there was serious concern among personality researchers and social psychologists because personality tests did not seem useful in predicting individual differences in performance in psychological experiments. An illustration of this failure in prediction is a series of experiments designed to see what would lead passers-by to help a person who fell on the street. It turned out that such things as the presence or absence of other witnesses or the age of the fallen person were often more significant than the personality of the passer-by. Subsequently, in an important paper Carlson (1971), reviewing the literature on personality research, called attention to the fact that predictions were often made from single tests. She noted that when more extensive personality measurements were carried out and when such measurements were reliable and were based on more than one variable or one test taken on one occasion, it was possible to make adequate predictions. As we shall see, much of modern personality research is designed to develop groups of tests and methods of studying people on several occasions so that the predictive potential of personality variables can be more effectively assessed.

Personality Change A final goal of research is to determine whether psychological or social influence or intervention can lead to personality change. Going back to Caesar's theory (Shakespeare's, really), we might ask whether a fat Roman who lost weight might turn into an envious, plotting Cassius. Or we might ask what forces come together to lead a person to give up ambition and settle for simple pleasures, or why a docile, devout child should grow into a selfish and ruthless tyrant, as apparently happened with many historical kings. To what extent is personality malleable and, if it is, what does personality research tell us about the ways to produce consistent change?

This question is, of course, vitally important to people whose personality characteristics have led them into serious personal difficulties. People who are habitually impulsive often get into fights, accumulate debts, and bring distress on themselves and their families. Others who show consistent patterns of fear or shame may not be able to use their talents or intellectual gifts effectively. Alice James, the sister of two of America's geniuses in psychology and literature, the brothers William and Henry James, was probably close to them in intelligence and imagination. Throughout most of her life, unfortunately, she suffered from imagined illnesses, fears, and doubts, and only rarely could she muster the energy to display hints of her talents.

Today most people believe they can change their personalities. They enroll in the Dale Carnegie Institute, they take courses in assertiveness training, they seek psychotherapy, or they embark on meditation or transactional-therapy weekends. The task for the personality researcher is to set up scientific procedures to study the possibilities of personality change in normal and disturbed persons and the aspects of a personality most susceptible to modification. Researchers also need to consider how much emphasis to place on changing the public personality and how much on modifying thoughts, fantasies, beliefs, cognitive styles, and levels of consciousness that characterize the private personality.

HOW IS INFORMATION ABOUT PERSONALITY OBTAINED?

As in other fields of psychology, research on personality generates hypotheses and accumulates data from many sources and by many methods. It includes clinical case studies and other interview methods; psychological tests, questionnaires, and projective techniques; and various types of experimental research. In the remainder of this chapter we shall look at some of these methods.

The most extensive information and most interesting concepts and hypotheses in the psychology of personality have come from the acute observations by gifted clinicians of a few people whose lives they studied during psychotherapy or diagnosis. The case method remains a major window to the study of the complexities of human personality over a period of time. **Clinical Case Studies**

In psychoanalysis, Sigmund Freud believed he had found an approach that was not only valuable as a treatment of emotional disturbance but was also a valid scientific method for accumulating information about the human personality, particularly the private personality and unconscious processes. The psychoanalytic method calls for the patient to lie on a couch with the analyst sitting to the side just out of the patient's view. The patient is encouraged to engage in free association—that is, to say whatever words or phrases come into his or her head and to continue this activity throughout a 45 or 50 minute period. The analyst usually remains silent except to intervene when it appears that the patient is blocked in producing free associations or is showing other signs of *resistance*—for example, reporting only the most trivial kinds of material, such as menus or baseball scores. The analyst's comments or interpretations are intended primarily to increase the free flow of associations.

Our concern here is not with the therapeutic effectiveness of psychoanalysis but with its collection of data or information. Essentially the method provides therapists with frequent sessions with a patient over several years and with an opportunity to explore the most personal details of a patient's life, particularly the patient's fantasies and dreams. Psychoanalysts and other psychotherapists have been able to elicit detailed knowledge about the human personality over a period of time that was never available before to anyone in human history. Within the psychotherapeutic method the clinician is constantly formulating hypotheses about incidents from the patient's past and predictions about the patient's reactions to future situations. Because of the private nature of psychotherapy, however, it is necessary to rely on the clinician's account of whether or not these hypotheses or predictions are verified.

The limitations of the clinical case-study methods are fairly obvious:

1. They depend on the observations of the therapist or interviewer who may be biased and who—consciously or unwittingly—may omit facts that do not conform to a preferred theoretical position.

2. The subjects of case studies are often extremely disturbed individuals who come seeking help and who may not be willing or able to present a fully rounded picture of their life situation.

3. The pattern of interaction between patient and therapist may generate special conditions that are not characteristic of the patient's other life situations, thus yielding a distorted picture.

Even with these limitations, the clinical methods can yield worthwhile information. Researchers have been ingenious in examining individual sessions between therapists and clients to test various hypotheses about the therapeutic process. Using written transcripts of tape-recorded sessions, researchers have also been able to develop reasonably objective methods to make predictions about the emergence of defenses or about personality patterns that lead to discussion of particular themes or references to particular emotions.

Research using actual clinical sessions is difficult and tedious because several trained raters must usually read over the long transcripts of therapy sessions. Nevertheless, this procedure is valuable in helping personality researchers gain more precise and objective information from the rich mine of information hitherto available only to the individual clinician.

Individual Interviews

A more limited source of the same kind of information obtainable from extended clinical treatment is the individual interview, which may last anywhere from thirty minutes to several hours. After all, if we want to know something about an individual's personality, why not ask that individual directly to talk about his or her life, social experiences, and interpretation of events? Psychiatrists rely heavily on the interview to determine sanity or insanity and to make diagnoses of mental illness that may result in hospitalization or treatment recommendations, or may even yield evidence to be used in criminal cases. The so-called mental-status interview attempts to elicit evidence mainly about the public personality but also to gain some clues about private experiences. Typically, it is conducted somewhat informally and is designed to cover areas such as personal mannerisms and appearance; speech patterns; emotional quality, such as sadness or inappropriate laughter; general orientation to time and place and ability to identify oneself or others; the main content of thoughts; and the subject's awareness or insight into his or her peculiarities, limitations, or problems.

Although the interview continues to be a major source of information for clinical purposes, its value for learning about personality is questionable. Only the most flagrant forms of disorientation resulting from brain injury and mental illness or of severe depression as often shown by "suicidal threats" can be reliably ascertained. Analyses of how well interviewers agreed with one another about psychiatric diagnoses, about personality functioning, or even about the simple facts of a person's life have shown that there is not much consistency

THE MENTAL-STATUS EXAMINATION

A regular form of interview designed for evaluation of personality and assessment of mental competence for legal and psychiatric purposes is the *Mental-Status Examination*. It calls for a series of semistructured questions designed to evoke answers and other evidence of the clarity of the interviewee's thought processes, emotional variability, specific preoccupations or worries, and awareness about personal problems or motives (insight). Table 7-1 presents a psychiatrist's sample report on a patient being considered for possible commitment to a mental hospital. Mental-status reports of this type, along with psychological tests such as the Minnesota Multiphasic Personality Inventory and the Rorschach inkblots, formed the basis for the testimony that convinced the jury in the case of John Hinckley, the would-be assassin of President Reagan, that the young man was legally insane.

TABLE 7-1
A Mental-Status Report

Category	Report
General appearance, attitude, and behavior	He is friendly and cooperative and has made no complaints about ward restrictions. He smiles in a somewhat exaggerated and grotesque manner.
Discourse	He answers in a deep, loud voice, speaking in a slow, precise, and somewhat condescending manner. His responses are relevant but vague.
Mood and affective fluctuations	His facial expressions, although not totally inappropriate, are poorly correlated with subject of discourse or events in his environment.
Sensorium and intellect	The patient's orientation for place, person, and time is normal. His remote and recent memory also is normal. Two brief intelligence measures indicate about-average intelligence.
Mental content and specific preoccupations	He readily discusses what he calls his "nervous trouble." He complains of "bad thoughts" and a "conspiracy." He reports hearing voices saying, "Hello, Bill, you're a dirty dog."
Insight	The patient readily accepts the idea that he should be in the hospital. He feels that hospitalization will help him get rid of these "bad thoughts." He is not in the least defensive about admitting to auditory and visual hallucinations or to the idea that everyone on earth is his enemy.

(Modified from Kleinmuntz, 1982)

(Korchin, 1976; Matarazzo and Weins, 1972). Generally speaking, as suggested above, interviewers agree better about the more obvious classifications, such as the brain-injured or psychotic person, but when it comes to detailed descriptions of personality traits, agreement is quite poor.

In summary, interview data—whether derived from a series of psychotherapy sessions or from a single somewhat structured or organized life-history review—can provide extremely interesting material for the personality researcher. Special efforts are needed to avoid the bias that may be introduced by an interviewer or by the special purpose of a psychotherapy session. Interview material is necessary to provide a kind of basic background and richness of detail against which other sources of personality data can be set. Specific methods for scoring the written transcriptions of taped interview data can be especially useful to test research hypotheses.

PSYCHOLOGICAL TESTING: QUESTIONNAIRES AND PROJECTIVE METHODS

A major contribution to personality assessment has been the development of *personality questionnaires* and a variety of *projective methods*. These organized and systematic approaches can yield scores that lend themselves more easily to quantitative, statistical analyses and to research exploration, avoiding many of the hazards of personal bias possible in the case study or interview.

Some Principles of Test Construction and Evaluation

Personality questionnaires originated during World War I primarily to substitute paper-and-pencil self-reports for psychiatric interviews, since thousands of recruits and draftees had to be screened for signs of emotional disturbance that would make them unfit for duty. During the 1920s and 1930s psychologists developed many personality questionnaires designed not only for screening the emotionally disturbed but also for such purposes as selecting the best-qualified workers for business and industry. In the course of these efforts psychologists developed many important new statistical and procedural concepts. Since the technology of personality test construction is one of the major scientific advances in personality research, we shall review some of the key terms and procedures employed in this field of mental measurement (psychometrics).

Personality questionnaire studies and a great deal of other research rely on the statistical concept of *correlation*. A correlation is a measure of the relationship between two sets of variables. Suppose we wanted to test Julius Caesar's assertion that thin men are envious and fat men are not; we could weigh 100 men and also give each one a personality questionnaire designed to elicit indications of envy (jealousy, resentment of superiors, for example).

We would then look at the distribution of weights from lowest to highest and of envy scores. If the heaviest man was highest in envy, the next heaviest a bit lower in envy, and so on, until, finally, the thinnest man had the lowest envy score, we would be looking at a perfect *positive* correlation—that is, a correlation coefficient of 1.0. If it were the other way around—if the scores showed that the heaviest men were the least envious and the thinnest men the most—the result would be −1.0, a perfect *negative* correlation. This would support Caesar's hypothesis. If there were no relationship whatever, with some fat men being envious and some thin men being unenvious, and no consistency at all between the variables, the correlation coefficient would be 0.

Because the methods of personality measurement are not perfect, the theories not precise, and the ability to collect full information limited, the correlations psychologists obtain are practically never perfect. A correlation of .50 between two variables is quite a respectable one, provided the correlation is *statistically significant*—that is, if the same correlation would probably be obtained in at least 95 out of 100 retests.

Often psychologists recognize that a single measure of a variable may not give a full enough picture. They might want to include several measures of a particular variable such as introversion-extraversion, and correlate each one with all the others. They would then arrange the correlations into what is called a *correlation matrix*, a table showing all the correlations—Test 1 vs. Test 2, Test 1 vs. Test 3, Test 1 vs. Test 4, Test 2 vs. Test 3, and so forth. Using a complex statistical procedure called *factor analysis*, psychologists can then determine whether all these tests of introversion-extraversion measure one common dimension even though no two of them are correlated very highly with each other. Since psychologists often use as many as a dozen or more different tests or methods of observation with large numbers of subjects, thus yielding a very large correlation matrix, factor analysis is a powerful tool for determining the minimum number of common factors that may define a large number of tests or combinations of tests, ratings, observation scores, and other measures.

In constructing a personality questionnaire, a psychometrician must meet certain standards of procedure. A test should first of all be *reliable*. This means that a good test should yield consistent results on repeated administration to the same subjects. Like a watch, a test is an instrument, and an instrument that lacks reliability is worthless. One way of ensuring such reliability is to develop questionnaire items that are clearly phrased, and to repeat the questions in slightly different ways and in forms that hang together statistically.

Of course, a test that is reliable but *wrong* is of little value. For example, your watch may never lose or gain a minute, but if it has been set at the wrong time to start with, the fact that it is *consistently* fast or slow does not help you to know the correct time. In other words, your watch does not provide you with a valid measure of the time. The crucial requirement for a personality test is its *validity*, the accuracy with which it measures what it is supposed to measure. Establishing validity for personality tests is a persisting challenge. Suppose we want to find the validity of a test of *dominance*. One way would

ESTABLISHING THE VALIDITY
OF A PERSONALITY SCALE

As part of his effort to establish objective materials for estimating generalized expectancies, Julian Rotter (Chapter 4) developed a scale to measure interpersonal trust (1967). The scale involves a series of statements such as "Most elected public officials are really sincere in their campaign promises" and "Parents can usually be relied on to keep their promises." Persons who consistently agree with statements like these would score high in interpersonal trust, while low scorers could be assumed to generally mistrust what people say.

As one way of estimating the validity of the questionnaire Rotter administered the scale to fraternity and sorority members who would know their housemates reasonably well. The subjects were also asked to nominate housemates especially high and low on a series of traits presumably related to trust—dependency, gullibility, and trustworthiness—as well as to a series of control variables—humor, popularity, and friendship—not especially related to trust. (Such ratings by a group of peers are called *sociometric*

scores. The control variables were included as a check for the "halo effect" a tendency to characterize people in an indiscriminately positive or negative fashion.) As a further check subjects rated their *own* trust and also answered a questionnaire measuring social desirability (the tendency for subjects to give the answers they believe are expected of them rather than answers that express their actual attitudes.)

Table 7-2 presents some of the resulting correlations. The participants' own responses on the interpersonal-trust scale correlated + .38 with the housemates' (sociometric) ratings of trust while they correlated negligibly with most of the other scales and showed practically no correlation with social desirability.

These results suggest that each subject's own test responses about trust of others' statements are more or less confirmed by the observations of friends. The correlation of .38, while only moderately high, is statistically significant. Keep in mind that many of the fraternity or sorority members could not have known each other that

be to measure dominating behavior in a series of other situations and show that our test correlates highly with these other ways of measuring it. Or we might ask friends who know a group of persons to rate each one on dominance. If the raters agreed with one another and then if the test showed at least a moderately high correlation with the average of those ratings, we would have reasonable evidence of the validity of the test. Since personality researchers often try to measure broad tendencies such as introversion or achievement motivation or sociability, it is difficult to find ways of establishing test validities. Frequently a group of tests all developed somewhat differently but designed to measure essentially the same behavior, trait, or attitude are used together to ensure greater validity.

Because of the care taken in the construction of questionnaires and the availability of *norms*—that is, tables of responses from large numbers of respondents broken down by age, education, social or ethnic status, and other characteristics—paper-and-pencil measures of personality are often described as *objective* methods. This is in contrast to *projective* methods, such as inkblot well or that long, so that there might have been no correlation at all between a subject's self-report on a trust scale and the others' appraisal of the subject's attitude. Ideally, other evidence such as observing a person in various settings—for example, in a discussion group or in a game—would be desirable to clarify the validity of a scale.

TABLE 7-2

Measuring Interpersonal Trust

Combined Intercorrelations of Sociometric and Test Scores
Combined Groups (N–156)

Variable	2	3	4	5	6	7	8	9	10*
1. Interpersonal-trust scale	−.23	.38	.09	−.03	.31	.20	.19	.29	.13
2. Sociometric dependency		−07	−.36	.78	−.45	−.46	−.53	−.06	−.05
3. Sociometric trust			.34	.13	.62	.43	.42	.39	.02
4. Sociometric humor				−.33	.26	.61	.66	.14	−.08
5. Sociometric gullibility					−.24	−.43	−.60	.01	.01
6. Sociometric trustworthiness						.57	.50	.24	.01
7. Sociometric popularity							.83	.05	−.11
8. Sociometric friendship								.09	−.15
9. Self-rating of trust									.31
10. Social- desirability scale*									

*N = 114 for all correlations involving this scale

(Modified from Rotter, 1967)

or story-telling procedures (which we shall consider shortly), where the examiner's judgment often enters into scoring and interpretation.

The Minnesota Multiphasic Personality Inventory (MMPI)   The Minnesota Multiphasic Personality Inventory has been the most widely used and thoroughly studied questionnaire for the past forty years. Its development is the result of a collaboration in the late 1930s between a psychologist, Starke Hathaway, and a psychiatrist, J. C. McKinley. They sought to combine the kinds of questions that are asked in a lengthy psychiatric interview with the objectivity and efficiency of a paper-and-pencil test. The MMPI contains 550 statements such as "I am happy most of the time," "I enjoy social gatherings just to be with people," "I have never had a fainting spell," "I believe I am a condemned person," to which the respondent answers "yes," "no," or "?" (uncertain). When the test was developed, those items that discriminated between specific types of neurotic or mentally ill persons and a "normal" group of persons

Questionnaires

(generally hospital visitors or relatives of patients) were formed into statistically related groups of questions (*scales*). The depression scale was so named because the items that make it up were best able to discriminate persons with the clinical illness of depression from the normal sample; similarly, the items forming the schizophrenia scale differentiated those mental patients who showed hallucinations, social withdrawal, and other symptoms of schizophrenia from the normals. The critical feature of this questionnaire is that it is *empirically derived;* items were included only if they proved to be more often selected by a specific psychiatric group than by the normals and even if the cluster of items that form a scale did not always make "theoretical" sense.

The MMPI items are grouped into ten scales: hypochondriasis, depression, hysteria, psychopathic-deviancy, masculinity-feminity, paranoia, psychasthenia, schizophrenia, hypomania, and social introversion (see Table 7-3). Since the items of the test to which those labels have been assigned reflect particular dimensions or variations of personality, it is possible to identify *patterns* of personality—to develop a "personality profile"—of an individual by finding those scales in which his or her scores exceed the normal range.

An important innovation in the MMPI was the introduction of scales to detect biased or careless answers. People who want to "fake" the test and appear normal might be inclined to answer many items as "?" or to deny ordinary human failings, such as unwillingness to sneak into a movie free if they could get away with it. By totaling the "?" responses, it is possible to estimate how extensive the evasions may be. A special lie scale (L) includes ordinary human foibles. A person who denies too many such common failings would receive a high L score and the results would be taken with a grain of salt. A more elaborate validity check is found in the K score, a statistically derived procedure that measures the extent to which respondents may be generally hiding bad habits or symptoms. Finally, since the test is long and sometimes boring and confusing, some people might answer questions almost at random. This pattern can be detected by the F scale. The MMPI is therefore not easy to outguess or fake.

Despite the MMPI's popularity and continued wide use, it has limitations. The items are too full of references to pathology and often seem downright funny, if not insulting, to normal groups of respondents. The MMPI has been parodied by the humorist Art Buchwald, who made up a series of items such as "My eyes are always cold," "A wide necktie is a sign of disease," "When I was younger, I used to tease vegetables," and "I use shoe polish to excess" (*American Psychologist*, 1965, *20*, p. 990).

The original samples of psychiatric patients whose responses formed the basis of the scales were extremely small (sometimes fewer than 20) and the original diagnoses may not have been well established. In the forty years since the test was developed, psychiatric classifications have changed. For example, more people now describe themselves as depressed. The individual scales themselves have low reliabilities, and there are other psychometric limitations to the instrument. Still, the MMPI opened the way for many improvements

TABLE 7-3
The Validity and Clinical Scales of the MMPI

Scale	Sample Item	Interpretation
?	No sample. It is merely the number of items marked in the "cannot say" category.	This is one of four validity scales, and a high score indicates evasiveness.
L	I get angry sometimes (False).*	This is the second validity scale. Persons trying to present themselves in a favorable light (e.g., good, wholesome, honest) obtain high L scale elevations.
F	Everything tastes the same (True).	F is the third validity scale. High scores suggest carelessness, confusion, or "fake bad."
K	I have very few fears compared to my friends (False).	An elevation on the last validity scale, K, suggests a defensive test taking attitude. Exceedingly low scores may indicate a lack of ability to deny symptomatology.
Hs	I wake up fresh and rested most mornings (False).	High scorers have been described as cynical, defeatist, and crabbed.
D	At times I am full of energy (False).	High scorers usually are shy, despondent and distressed.
Hy	I have never had a fainting spell (False).	High scorers tend to complain of multiple symptoms.
Pd	I liked school (False).	Adjectives used to describe some high scorers are adventurous, courageous, and generous.
Mf	I like mechanics magazines (False).	Among males, high scorers have been described as esthetic and sensitive. High-scoring women have been described as rebellious, unrealistic, and indecisive.
Pa	I am happy most of the time (False).	High scorers on this scale were characterized as shrewd, guarded, and worrisome.
Pt	I am certainly lacking in self-confidence (True).	Fearful, rigid, anxious, and worrisome are some of the adjectives used to describe high Pt scorers.
Sc	I believe I am a condemned person (True).	Adjectives such as withdrawn and unusual describe Sc high scorers.
Ma	I am an important person (True).	High scorers are called sociable, energetic, and impulsive.
Si	I enjoy social gatherings just to be with people (False).	High scorers: modest, shy, and self-effacing. Low scorers: sociable, colorful, and ambitious.

*True or False responses within parentheses indicate the scored direction of each item.

(from Kleinmuntz, 1982)

in test construction, and most personality tests reflect the lessons learned from the extensive research it engendered.

The California Psychological Inventory (CPI)   The California Psychological Inventory is the result of efforts to capitalize on the research derived from the MMPI and to produce a personality questionnaire designed for use with normal populations. Developed by Harrison Gough, the CPI was administered to thousands of normal individuals, resulting in a pool of 480 items responded to as "true" or "false." These items are grouped into eighteen scales, three of which are checks to measure the "validity" of the individual's responses. The other fifteen scales measure such personality variables as dominance, sense of acceptance, achievement via conformity, achievement via independence, self-control, and tolerance. Great care was taken to have a large, well-described, and fairly representative sample of subjects on which to base the norms. Retests to establish the reliability of the scales have correlation coefficients of .80 to .90, which are quite satisfactory by psychometric standards. Validity was established in two ways: ratings by friends and self-reports. Other validity checks were also made such as a correlation of the CPI self-report of intellectual efficiency with actual academic achievement.

The CPI has been widely tested and is a major tool for personality research with normal groups. Its chief limitations are the somewhat atheoretical or loose combination of scales which make it up and the fact that many of the scales overlap with one another statistically—that is, they correlate more than .50. Therefore, it is often not clear that unique dimensions are really being measured (Thorndike, 1959).

The 16 Personality-Factor Inventory (16 PF)   Raymond B. Cattell has been by far the most active and productive investigator into the nature of personality traits. More than any other specialist in psychometrics, he has sought to develop a general personality theory. Cattell has made extensive use of the technique of factor-analyzing questionnaires and other types of data, such as ratings or observations of individuals, autobiographical data, and actual behavior in specific situations. He has used factor analysis to distinguish *surface* traits, or public manifestations of personality, from *source* traits, which resemble psychoanalytic drives or complexes in representing basic private tendencies for thought as well as for action.

One outgrowth of Cattell's efforts was the development of a questionnaire designed to measure the full range of human surface traits (Cattell, 1956). Cattell repeatedly found evidence that sixteen scales were enough to measure these dimensions; his manual for the 16 PF questionnaire asserts that "these are the main dimensions that have been found necessary and adequate to cover all kinds of individual differences of personality found in common speech and psychological literature. They leave out no important aspect of total personality" (Cattell and Stice, 1957).

The 16 PF is made up of four alternate forms of 187 items each, designed to measure each of the sixteen personality factors. Because the original factors were derived statistically from pools of items that clustered together in sometimes puzzling ways, Cattell first made up Latin or Greek names for each of the surface traits they presumably measured. In the current manual, however, the traits are listed as (1) warmth; (2) abstract thinking; (3) calmness, stability; (4) dominance; (5) enthusiastic or impulsive; (6) conscientious; (7) venturesome; (8) sensitive; (9) suspicious; (10) imaginative; (11) shrewd; (12) self-doubting; (13) experimenting; (14) self-sufficient; (15) self-disciplined; (16) tense or driven.

When further factor analysis is carried out on Cattell's scales, they tend to cluster into two major dimensions: *adjustment-anxiety* and *introversion-extraversion*, which are similar to the two dimensions in the shorter Maudsley Personality Inventory, developed by the British psychologist Hans J. Eysenck. Eysenck has proposed that most human beings vary along two dimensions, *neuroticism* (anxiety and emotional overresponsiveness versus emotional stability) and *introversion-extraversion* (quiet, retiring, and introspective versus outgoing, impulsive, and sociable). As we shall see, the theme of introversion-extraversion as a fundamental human orientation emerges again and again in personality studies. Unlike Eysenck, Cattell continues to believe that it is important to examine the surface traits and to look at personality as reflecting different patternings of the sixteen personality factors described in his test. Both Cattell and Eysenck stress the fact that questionnaire results must be checked against other sources of data. Eysenck has been especially ingenious in making predictions of how people will differ in experimental situations on the basis of their scores on introversion-extraversion and neuroticism (Eysenck, 1965, 1981). He has also presented some evidence in support of the linkage of personality patterns to body type—that introverts do tend to be taller or leaner, as Shakespeare suggested.

The Personality Research Form (PRF)   A frequent criticism of the questionnaire approach is that people have certain attitudes (response sets) in taking tests that are important in how they respond to the items. For example, some people like to answer "yes" or rate themselves high on almost every kind of trait that comes along in a questionnaire; others say "no" or use low ratings. Another attitude that can affect test results is a concern for social desirability, the tendency for people to answer items not as they apply to themselves but according to what they think is "normal" (Edwards, 1959). Recent questionnaires have been carefully developed to rule out the influence of yea- or nay-saying and also to rule out the influence of social-desirability attitudes.

One of the most advanced questionnaires in terms of its methodology of development, its sophisticated use of factor analysis, and its careful validation of each subscale is the Personality Research Form (PRF) constructed by Douglas N. Jackson in 1967, some sample items and definitions from which are shown in Figure 7-1. Jackson selected a list of needs or human motives (for example, dominance, aggression, achievement) originally developed by Henry A. Murray and organized items measuring these needs into a format that would minimize the chances of answers determined by social desirability.

FIGURE 7-1
Sample Items and Scale Definitions from Jackson's Personality Research Form (PRF)

Achievement: Strives to get things done; is goal-oriented; sets high standards

Affiliation: Likes associating with people; wants friends; maintains friendships

Aggression: Is argumentative, vindictive, and assertive to the point of hurting those who get in the way

Dominance: Seeks leadership; is self-expressive and controlling

Harm-avoidance: Avoids risks and dangerous situations; seeks to avoid personal injury

Nurturance: Is considerate and empathetic toward others; provides assistance

Understanding: Values knowledge; has intellectual orientation and curiosity

(Modified from Jackson, 1967)

Using statistical procedures, he also constructed the scales measuring each need in such a way that they were relatively independent of the scales for the other needs in the questionnaire. Consequently, there is much less overlap between the separate scales than in the CPI or the 16 PF questionnaires. Each need was validated by an independent procedure involving judgments of friends or relatives concerning the importance of these needs for the individuals who took the initial form of the test. The PRF has proved useful in showing the patterns of relationships that link public personality characteristics both with private personality patterns, such as daydreaming, and with forms of overt behavior, such as drug or alcohol use by young adults (Segal, Huba, and Singer, 1980).

Evaluation of the Questionnaire Method   Some personality researchers have raised serious doubts about questionnaires. For example, Mischel (1968) and Fiske (1973) asked whether people really show much consistency in traits from situation to situation and whether the questionnaires, checklists, and observational reports show the same *patternings* of traits or merely reflect the characteristics of the measurement device itself (method effects). Questionnaires often correlate with one another while behavior ratings correlate with other behavior ratings irrespective of what is being measured. On the other hand, recent work by Block (1971, 1975) and numerous subsequent studies have shown that people are relatively consistent in trait behaviors particularly if the traits are measured not just once or twice but on numerous occasions (Chapter 17). Many questionnaires do reveal consistent factor patternings; "method effects" have been shown to be less important than was believed (Huba and Hamilton, 1976).

In Shakespeare's *Hamlet* the young hero teases the pompous courtier, Polonius:

> HAMLET: *Do you see yonder cloud that's almost in shape of a camel?*
> POLONIUS: *By th' mass and 'tis, like a camel indeed.*
> HAMLET: *Methinks it is like a weasel.*
> POLONIUS: *It is back'd like a weasel.*
> HAMLET: *Or like a whale.*
> POLONIUS: *Very like a whale.*

The projective methods in psychology are based on the principle that attempts by human beings to give form and meaning to ambiguous shapes like clouds will reveal their private personality—their inner feelings, wishes, daydreams, and deep-lying motives. Clouds were in fact involved in the Cloud Pictures test, an early effort to study personality devised by the German psychologist, William Stern. Other techniques using ambiguous stimuli for people to react to include drawing human figures or other pictures (Draw-a-Person, House-Tree-Person methods), listening to vague sounds (Skinner's Verbal Summator), rearranging abstract shapes and designs (Lowenfeld's Mosaics, Kahn's Symbol Arrangement Test), selecting paper-doll cutout figures (for example, policemen, adults, witches) from an array and telling stories about them (Make-a-Picture Story Test), completing incomplete sentences, and choosing most liked and disliked faces from a series of photographs of mental patients (Szondi Test). The two projective techniques with the greatest staying power and the most extensive use in both clinical and research assessment are the Rorschach inkblots and the Thematic Apperception Test.

Rorschach Inkblots   In the period between 1912 and his premature death in 1922 the Swiss psychiatrist Hermann Rorschach experimented with a method for studying personality and diagnosing mental illness by having persons look at inkblots and answer the question, "What might this be?" He called this method "psychodiagnostics" and this was the name of his thoughtful, original book, published after his death (1942).

In the form most widely used for the past sixty years the Rorschach method is based on presentation of a set of ten inkblots printed on stiff white cardboard (see Figure 7-2). Five of the blots are black-gray (achromatic) and five have colored ink mixed with black (chromatic). A respondent is shown the blots one at a time with Rorschach's instructions. Most people give three or four responses for each card; for example, "a bat," a "wishbone," "two people playing patty-cake." The examiner goes over the cards again with the subject at the conclusion of the presentation of all ten to ask *where* on the card each response was located—whether it was the whole blot, or a large segment, or some small or unusual detail. This inquiry also determines what features of the blot seemed to evoke the response—whether it was the *form* primarily (a response such as "a butterfly"), scored F, or the *color* (such as "a bloody smear"). A color response is scored C if form is absent, CF if color dominates form, or FC if form and color are well integrated ("a red bow tie"). Responses involving

FIGURE 7-2
An Inkblot Similar to a Rorschach Inkblot

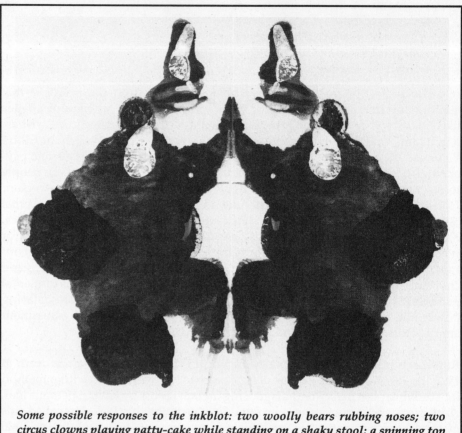

Some possible responses to the inkblot: two woolly bears rubbing noses; two circus clowns playing patty-cake while standing on a shaky stool; a spinning top (in the inner white space, with the card held upside down). Note that no single response is greatly significant—it is the pattern of responses to all ten cards that is necessary for interpretation.

textures or shades of gray are scored separately from color. Rorschach's deepest interest was in responses that mentioned human movement—people in action, such as "two footmen bowing," "a ballet dancer twirling fans," "two ladies waving goodbye." The actual content of responses (for example, human, animal, objects, anatomy, sex references), the degree of ordinariness or originality, and the degree to which the response matches the shape of the blot are also scored.

Rorschach's method was far ahead of its time in emphasizing the fact that human beings place a stamp of originality or uniqueness in the way they process information and organize experiences. An emphasis on wholes in a person's choice of responses to the inkblots, if consistent throughout the cards, may reflect extreme casualness or even incapacity, especially if the person gives a vague whole reaction like "clouds," "a bat," or "a butterfly" to each card. But such an emphasis can reflect ambition and striving for intellectual power if the person attempts to integrate the material into a clear, well-organized percept that reasonably matches the shape of the blot, as in the second response in Figure 7-2. In interpretation, therefore, much attention is paid to organization, structure, clarity, precision, and originality, on the one hand, or to the downright bizarre nature of a response, on the other (calling a blot a "slithery, menacing rattlesnake" when most people agree that it looks like a butterfly or a bow tie).

Of special interest are color and human movement. Rorschach proposed that response to color reflects the emotional tendencies of an individual. Someone who gives many color responses, especially of the C or CF variety, would likely be emotionally responsive and impulsive with great fluctuations of feelings and a rather self-centered orientation. A person who gives more form-dominated color responses would be "appropriately" emotionally responsive, warm, empathic, and concerned for others. In Rorschach lore, high FC people buy their friends presents they think the friends want; high CF people buy presents that they have always wanted themselves.

The human-movement response, Rorschach thought, was the key to the inner life—the world of fantasy, imagination, and creativity of the private personality. He seems to have based this insight on his accumulated statistics, which suggested that M responses were more commonly given by imaginative persons with rich fantasy lives. It is certainly conceivable that people who are attentive to their inner thoughts and wishes—those "movements in the mind's eye" that so often concern human relationships—are also more likely to report seeing humans in action on the inkblots. Rorschach also thought that persons who see movement on the blots may actually be more restrained or controlled in their own overt movements, perhaps inhibited or cautious in muscular activity.

While Rorschach interpretations often have the flavor of astrological readings (and unfortunately may, in poor hands, have no more validity than diagnoses based on the movements of the stars), there is ample evidence that some features of the Rorschach method do relate to behavior. Literally thousands of research studies (of which certainly some fair proportion meet good scientific standards) have supported many of Rorschach's interpretations. The Holtzman Inkblots, a more recent development with alternate forms and a standardized format, permit effective research use of the procedure (Holtzman, Thorpe, Swartz, and Herron, 1961).

More impressive is the evidence that variables like movement and color responses do indeed relate to overt behavior or to imaginative capacities. A series of reasonably well-controlled investigations with normal adults and children as well as schizophrenic patients has shown that persons with more M than C responses are actually more likely to sit quietly in a waiting room, are more systematic in approaches to problem solving, are more likely to tell imaginative stories, and are rated by interviewers and observers as more thoughtful. People who respond with few M and more C responses are more likely to use physical gestures when defining verbs like "to twist," "to tangle," "to squeeze"; they are also more impulsive, more restless, more likely to get into fights and to show strong emotions (Singer and Brown, 1977). The limited effectiveness of the Rorschach as a predictor of behavior in situations as diverse as pilot training and performance in industrial situations has led some investigators to decry its value. On the other hand, the many relationships between responses to the inkblots and particular personality dimensions such as extraversion-introversion, defensiveness, anxiety, aggressive behavior, and imagination all attest to the originality and value of Rorschach's original insight that our ways of organizing ambiguous information may reveal something about our public and private personality characteristics (Rickers-Ovsiankina, 1977; Singer, 1981; Singer and Brown, 1977).

The Thematic Apperception Test (TAT)   In the course of his pioneering efforts to find methods for intensive study of the individual personality over a long time period, the Harvard psychologist Henry A. Murray developed a procedure in which he hoped to use recurrent fantasy as a way of exploring and measuring human motives or needs (Murray, 1938). With a colleague, Christiana Morgan, Murray prepared a series of ambiguous pictures about which respondents were asked to tell a story. They were to relate the events leading up to and following the situation in the picture—what was happening, and what the characters were feeling and thinking. Eventually published as a series of twenty cards, the Thematic Apperception Test (TAT) has become one of the most widely employed projection techniques. It is an instrument that, with appropriate variations, has been used almost as extensively for research on personality and motivation as it has for clinical evaluation.

The premise underlying the TAT is derived from Freud's view that human motives are expressed as fantasies, daydreams, and fleeting mental images of "possible" or "impossible" situations. If people tell stories about a series of pictures, their fantasies or daydreams are likely to surface in the stories they think of. The stories of a person who is especially motivated by a need for achievement and accomplishment are likely to involve themes of successful effort, working toward practical goals, and striving to finish an important task, as in the following possible response to the sample TAT card in Figure 7-3:

> *This young woman comes from a poor but hard-working Minnesota farm family. She is the oldest of six children and her mother expects a good deal of help from her. Right now she's very torn in conflict between her feeling of obligation to the family and her desire to get more education. She's a top student in a two-year college and has won a scholarship to the University of Minnesota. She knows her mother will need help with the younger children but she's determined to go on for advanced education. She wants to be able to develop a career in business or social service. She decides to work summers and save up a great deal of money so she can help the family that way but goes off to school anyway.*

FIGURE 7-3

A Sample Thematic Apperception Test (TAT) Card

See the accompanying text for two possible responses to this picture.

A story like the one above suggests *autonomy* and *achievement* as well as a practical awareness of steps needed to reach a goal. If someone consistently produced stories like this in response to a series of TAT pictures, the scoring would suggest a person full of achievement fantasies, who might strive actively to bring such thoughts to reality. Another person whose underlying pattern of motives involves the need for close relationships, interpersonal intimacy, and warmth might interpret the same picture in terms of a romantic conflict. The younger woman is torn between obligation to her aging mother and her love for a soldier who wants her to marry him and join him overseas.

Murray believed that people caught up in their storytelling would not recognize the themes in their stories. Thus the TAT should yield results different from those obtained if he simply asked someone a question such as, "How important is achievement in your life?"

A TAT is usually scored by breaking each story down into the major need expressed (such as achievement, power, affiliation, nurturing others, aggression, sex) and the major environmental force, or *press*, on the hero or heroine (such as others' aggression, dominance, or rejection). It is assumed that the hero or heroine of the story is a representation of the storyteller; research has confirmed that characteristics of TAT-story heroes do resemble those of the storyteller (Lindzey and Kalnins, 1958). By evaluating the relative importance of need and press on the basis of how often and with what significance they recur in the stories, it is possible to construct a list of the major needs or motives of the storyteller.

The TAT is a rather complex and cumbersome instrument to score and to use in clinical practice. It yields almost too much information if a person tells detailed stories to each card (Tomkins, 1947); at the other extreme, with disturbed adolescents or mental patients, the story content is sometimes so sparse that there is almost nothing to score. Some critics say that the reliability of the scores is not very high, but Atkinson (1981) did a profound theoretical analysis of TAT-like measures to demonstrate that even though a person's *need for achievement* score or *affiliation* score may vary widely from story to story (just as the stream of thought fluctuates) the accumulated effect of such motives across a large number of stories can be quite a reliable and valid indicator of actual behavior or of an actual trait.

The extensive research of McClelland (1961, 1975) and Atkinson (1981) has provided a vast amount of evidence from the TAT and similar storytelling techniques concerning the motives of *achievement*, *power*, and *affiliation*. They have shown that the technique has good predictive power. A long-term follow-up study by McAdams and Vaillant (1982) compared the TAT scores on intimacy motivation for 57 men who had taken the test in 1952 with their reports obtained fifteen years later about such things as income, work enjoyment, marital enjoyment, and vacation patterns. The intimacy motive was defined as a continuing predisposition toward close, warm, and communicative interpersonal exchanges, and it was scored from TAT stories by persons unfamiliar with the later status of the participants. Results indicated that 1952 intimacy scores were significantly correlated with later evidence of a sustained, mutually reported happy marriage and also with reports of enjoyment of work.

The TAT complements the Rorschach because it emphasizes the *content* of fantasy—the themes and preoccupations of the private personality. The Rorschach tells more about the *structure* of personality—the nature and type of imaginative or emotional tendencies—and the *style* of thought rather than the individual's specific motives. Taken together, both instruments are useful not only for clinicians but also for researchers who are interested in exploring in more systematic ways the relationship between the manifestations of public and private personality (Singer, 1981).

CASE STUDIES AND LIFE HISTORIES

We have now reviewed some of the major techniques used by psychologists for measuring personality traits and motivational trends. Let us next consider how these approaches are combined with other assessment tools in carrying out systematic research on the theoretical issues in the field of personality.

During the 1930s at the Harvard Psychological Clinic, Henry A. Murray and a brilliant group around him began to do intensive case studies of normal individuals. These case studies required not only extended interviews but also psychological testing with both questionnaires and projective tests. In addition, assessment of these normal individuals involved putting them into small-scale experiments, such as stress interviews, where they were forced to answer highly embarrassing questions or were challenged to justify some of their most heartfelt values. Individuals were not only studied alone but in group settings so that observers could ascertain their patterns of social interaction and the more public manifestations of their personality.

Case Studies with Normal Individuals

Sometimes it has been possible to study normal individuals over many years and to examine whether early patterns of behavior or of thoughts and beliefs can predict career and marital choices, accomplishments, and capacities to cope with the inevitable stresses of life. Robert W. White's *Lives in Progress* (1966) is such an approach to studying individuals over a period of time, while the work of Bernice Eiduson (1974), who followed up forty male research scientists over a decade of their adult life, applies this approach to a group of individuals with similar careers.

Since most people grow up in families, it is important to learn how the entire family group influences the development of personality patterns. Such studies have been possible chiefly with families of abnormal individuals because they are more readily accessible for investigation.

Family Case Studies

A group led by Theodore Lidz (1965) at the Yale Psychiatric Institute carried out an important family study. Seventeen families of hospitalized schizophrenic patients were studied for a period of up to five years by means of extensive interviews, projective tests, and other methods. The purpose was to obtain information about the personalities of the family members and their interactions, as well as the overall atmosphere in the family. One question raised was whether the pattern of pathology—that is, the peculiarities of thought and action of the schizophrenic patient—could be shown to be a reflection of the mannerisms and interaction patterns of the parents. In this research it was possible to show that out of the total mass of material an investigator could take the test and interview records of patients and match them perfectly with the records obtained from their parents. It was also possible to show that the written personality descriptions of the patients based on the test materials alone coincided with the biographical material even though the original test analyses were carried out by a diagnostician who did not know what individuals were involved. Studies like this with "normal" families remain to be done.

Life Histories of Abnormal Individuals	In the files of many clinics and hospitals are large numbers of case histories of individuals who received treatment in their youth or early childhood and on whom extensive records are available. Because of this store of information, a fruitful approach to tracking down the patterns of personality characteristics over long periods of time has developed. Many of these same individuals currently show severe disturbances such as schizophrenia or impulse disorders (tendencies to be excessively violent or involved easily in criminal acts). Researchers can therefore compare the childhood records and current records to try to determine what characteristics these patients had in childhood that might be relevant for the later manifestations of severe disturbance.

Ricks and Berry (1970) tracked down about a hundred individuals who as adults showed severe disturbance and who had also been seen in a child-guidance clinic where research data were available. As a comparison group these investigators located one hundred other individuals who had also come to that clinic as children, but who as adults had no serious emotional disturbance and were functioning adequately. This group provided a control; comparing the two sets of records, the researchers could discern the patterns of family relationships for those subjects who later became severely disturbed.

Naturalistic Case History Approaches	Studies of naturally occurring behaviors of children and adults over a period of time have the advantage of showing how people respond in their day-to-day situations amid friends or families without the artificial atmosphere of a laboratory or clinic interview.

Csikszentmihalyi (1974) carried out a series of investigations of individuals who reported on all of their behavior for a period of several days or weeks by keeping a daily log. They were encouraged to record their casual behavior such as the amount of time spent chewing gum, smoking, engaging in idle conversations, daydreaming and listening to music. These studies give a better feeling of the continuing quality of behavior. Specific recurring actions or recorded thoughts then can be grouped into particular personality manifestations. Recent studies of mood variation in people as an indicator of their personality patterns have also used this log-keeping approach. People periodically write down their moods or emotions at various points in a normal day and also record the situation they were in (Linville, 1982; Wessman, 1979).

THE EXPERIMENTAL METHOD IN PERSONALITY RESEARCH

Since the 1920s when Kurt Lewin developed experimental approaches to test theoretical hypotheses about personality, the laboratory approach has been in some respects the most prestigious way of investigating personality. Some of the excitement and challenge of experimental approaches to personality comes from the fact that the researcher establishes conditions that permit control and observation of behavior in "miniature" life situations. Laboratory situations are well suited to look at events simulating real life in which the researcher can test different theoretical interpretations that cannot be resolved with other methods. A good experiment in personality psychology usually has the following characteristics:

1. Theory-derived hypotheses and operational formulations. Suppose an experimenter wishes to compare how 10-year-old boys and girls react to being left alone with someone of the same or opposite sex while trying to solve a puzzle. The hypothesis, derived from Sullivan's theory of "chumship" at this age, is that if two boys or two girls are together they will cooperate to solve the puzzle. But a boy and a girl will not work together. The operations to be measured are the amount of time the two children work together on the puzzle, the time it takes them to solve the puzzle, and the accuracy of the solution (Berndt, 1981).

2. Careful definition of the subjects and their representation in general child or adult population of the culture. The above experiment might be done with white middle-class children attending a small suburban school. Or it might be done in an inner-city school with mostly deprived non–English speaking chidren who recently arrived from another country. In either case the results would be applicable only to similar children in a similar setting.

3. Careful specification of the *independent* variable (the factor being systematically controlled or varied) and *dependent* variables (those yielding the evidence of the effects of the experimental manipulation). The independent variable in this experiment is "sex of subject." The dependent variables might be number of errors made, time taken to produce the correct solution, and amount of time the children worked together.

4. Quantitative and statistical analysis. The boys and girls might show an average score of three errors with little variation when same-sex pairs are together and an average score of five errors when opposite-sex pairs are together. Is a difference of two errors enough to warrant a conclusion that confirms or does not confirm the hypothesis? Statistical analyses can show whether or not differences of this size can be relied on to show up again and again if the experiment were repeated.

Some Major Experimental Approaches

Of the many different ways to do experimental research on personality, we shall discuss only a few of the main approaches. An experiment may test a general theoretical proposition—for example, that there is such a phenomenon as *repression*. Freud's psychoanalytic theory places great importance on repression. But is it possible to demonstrate its existence without simply relying on the report of a psychoanalyst? A test of the demonstrability of repression was carried out by Glucksberg and King (1967). Lists of words were flashed on a screen, and subjects were asked to memorize them. Some words on the first list (*dog*, for example) were conceptually linked to some on the second list (*cat*—another animal). As certain words on the first list appeared on the screen the participants received an electric shock, while no shock was given for other words. Later, when the subjects' memory was tested, not only had the "shocked" words on the first list been forgotten but also the *unshocked* words on the second list that were conceptually linked to them. This was true even though the words had been learned equally well. The important thing to note here is that the nature of the subjects, individual differences between them, and other factors were not considered in this research. Rather, the focus was to provide a precise and direct test of a general process in human personality, specifically the reality of the repressive mechanism.

Another kind of experiment may test alternative possibilities derived from two opposing theories. A study by Rizley (1978) examined two theories of depression, Seligman's theory of *learned helplessness* and Beck's theory of *cognitive appraisal*. Rizley carried out two experiments to test which of these theories seemed better able to predict how severely depressed college students would behave compared to students who were not depressed. In the experiments each student was assigned a task with an outcome that could be measured objectively. In the first study, although the results of the task were really determined by chance (unknown to the subjects), the depressed students were more likely to say that good results stemmed from luck but that unpleasant outcomes were the result of their own effort or ability. This supported Beck's view that the attitude of the depressed person is self-disparaging rather than Seligman's hypothesis that depression stems from actual ineffective behavior. In the second experiment Seligman's learned-helplessness theory was again not supported. It was found that nondepressed ("normal") students overemphasized their ability to produce "good" results while depressed individuals overemphasized their influence on "bad" results. The depressed students were actually more "accurate" in their recognition that the good results could be occurring because of chance! The data seem to support Beck's theory more than Seligman's, but neither theory is fully supported. So Rizley proposed a new theory, *cognitive helplessness*, suggesting that people prone to depression have failed to learn to attend carefully to, or to make effective use of, available information and so they often cannot determine what effects on others are really their own doing and what effects are sheer chance. This is a good example of the fact that research often leads to new theories.

The Rizley experiment makes use of individual differences in degrees of depression, but it really seeks to test a *general* proposition, not the specific nature of the individual differences. Experiments like these have a clarity and elegance; still they do not resolve all of the issues raised by either of the theories nor do they address more profound questions as to the nature of human depression in the face of the long-term life experience.

An attempt to increase the subtlety of experiments in personality has come through the introduction of the concept of a *moderator variable*. Such a study was carried out by Shapiro and Alexander (1969), who were interested in the differences between introverts and extraverts, which they predicted would be seen more clearly if the participants were in situations differing in degrees of stress or anxiety. Thus, *anxiety* was a moderator variable that they assumed would make introverts and extraverts behave differently. By exposing subjects to different levels of threat about receiving a shock they showed that the differences in behavior between introverts and extraverts who were *not* anxious were very slight, while the differences in the behavior of those threatened with shock were greater. Their findings suggest that a personality predisposition as measured by a questionnaire of introversion-extraversion is especially apparent *only* when there is already some degree of intense emotional arousal, anxiety or the fear of a painful shock. Under more neutral or less threatening conditions personality differences may be less apparent.

Investigators are designing more and more experiments with moderator variables in which at least two factors, such as predispositional tendency and immediate state of emotional arousal or stress, are taken into account before predicting certain behaviors as outcomes. Ultimately, meaningful experiments in psychology should take account of the following factors, all of which have an effect on an individual's behavior:

1. Attention to the physical characteristics of environments and the symbolic or specialized meaning they may have for subjects

2. The particular experimental demands made upon subjects and their interpretation of these demands

3. The immediate emotional state or set of expectations subjects bring to the experiment, for example, whether something has just angered them or whether or not they approach the experiment trustingly or suspiciously

4. The subjects' longstanding predispositions—such as cognitive styles, personality traits, or generalized sets of expectancies—that they bring to the experiment

This brief survey of methods shows that even though psychologists have developed an important technology and guidelines for personality research, a sense of incompleteness remains. Careful scrutiny of the methods suggests that some of them are oversimplified, gimmicky, and artificial, often failing to capture the richness and complexity of a human life. In Part II, as we explore the ways in which personality research deals with cognition, emotion, aggression, stress, and love and intimacy, we shall see that the field is still evolving. Such continuous change is the touchstone of the scientific enterprise.

SUMMARY

1. Research methods in the study of personality are designed (1) to assess or measure personality; (2) to systematically collect information that will verify or clarify theories about personality; (3) to describe or discover new rela-

tionships about personality; (4) to predict specific patterns of personality; and (5) to evaluate the possibility of changing personality.

2. Information about personality is obtained from many sources and in many ways. These include (1) clinical and interview methods; (2) psychological questionnaires and projective techniques; (3) case studies and life histories; and (4) various types of experimental research.

3. The case studies of psychoanalysts and other psychotherapists yield extensive information and interesting hypotheses. Clinical methods can yield worthwhile information, especially when researchers use reasonably objective methods such as tape recordings and transcriptions of clinical sessions. The individual interview provides a source of information similar to that found in clinical treatment. In interviews, usually, people are asked directly to tell about their lives. The interview method is much used for clinical purposes, but it is not of much value for research on personality.

4. Psychological tests and questionnaires are a major tool in the study of personality because they yield organized and systematic data that can be statistically and objectively analyzed. A good psychological test should be reliable and valid, and carefully prepared norms should be available. Examples of personality questionnaires are the Minnesota Multiphasic Personality Inventory (MMPI), the California Psychological Inventory (CPI), the 16 Personality Factor Inventory (16 PF), the Maudsley Personality Inventory, and the Personality Research Form (PRF).

5. Projective methods are based on the principle that when people try to give form and meaning to ambiguous stimuli, they will reveal their inner feelings, wishes, and underlying motives. The two best-known projective techniques are the Rorschach inkblots and the Thematic Apperception Test (TAT). Unlike personality tests and questionnaires, with projective methods the examiner's judgment often enters into the scoring and interpretation of the responses.

6. Personality research sometimes uses case studies and life histories. Some case studies require extended interviews and psychological testing. Sometimes it is possible to study normal individuals over many years and to examine whether early behavior or thought can predict later career and marital choices and accomplishments. Case studies of families, especially families of mentally disturbed patients, have also been made. A way to track down patterns of personality characteristics over long periods of time is now available because clinics and hospitals have case records that can be used for research purposes. There is now more emphasis on naturally occurring behavior of children and adults. This has the advantage of studying how people act in ordinary day-to-day situations rather than in the artificial setting of a laboratory.

7. The laboratory or experimental approach to personality research is in some respects the most prestigious. A good experiment usually has the following characteristics: (1) theory-derived hypotheses and operational formula-

tions; (2) careful description of the subjects; (3) careful specifications of the independent variables (the variables being controlled or varied) and the dependent variables (variables yielding evidence of the experimental manipulation); and (4) quantitative and statistical analysis.

8. Experiments in personality should include: (1) attention to the environment and its meaning to the subject; (2) experimental demands made on the subject and interpretation of these demands; (3) emotional state or expectations of the subject; and (4) the longstanding predispositions of the subject.

PART TWO

The Private Personality

CHAPTER
8

Motivation and the Emotional System

In the spring of 1981 a group of young men in Northern Ireland began a hunger strike designed to force the British government to treat them as political rather than as criminal prisoners. One after another, they starved to death. By midsummer nine had died and several more were dying. What were the motives that impelled such behavior? Idealism in the cause of the Northern Irish Catholic minority? A sense of failure and hopelessness for their cause? The fear of possible public shame if they were to survive once others had died? From the reports of their families and others it seems unlikely that they all wanted to die but rather that they had a series of different but converging sets of anticipations and expectations. Once they were well along the road toward starvation, their weakened physical state may have made it more difficult for them to rethink their situation or to energize themselves sufficiently to give up the struggle and take nourishment.

THE COMPLEX DETERMINANTS OF MOTIVATION

Extreme examples like that of the Irish prisoners point up some of the crucial questions all personality theorists must face. What factors in our bodies, brains, and social environments come together to give thought and behavior *direction* and *intensity*? How important are the needs we share with all animals for food, water, sexuality, reduction of pain, and survival in the face of attack—*drives*, as learning-theory psychologists and psychoanalysts call them—in shaping human behavior? Consider some of the many different desires, intentions, hopes, and actions of human beings: political ambitions, attempts at composing beautiful music, repeated efforts to climb Mount Everest, the "simple" yearning of grandparents to see their grandchildren. Are all of these ultimately reducible to modifications and variations of the biological drives?

Motives are those features of bodily responses and thoughts that lend a specific direction and intensity to our actions. A hunger pang may make you vaguely aware of your stomach, but usually it takes the specific taste sensation or mental picture of melting cheese and sausage, for example, to lead to action (*direction*) and to the strong emotional experience (*intensity*) that makes you say, "I'd really go for pizza right now!" Indeed, you may not necessarily be hungry—that is, food deprived— to act on this motivated direction and intensity. A pizza commercial with a full-color close-up of sizzling mozzarella and pepperoni or just the shout of your roommate, "Hey, let's all go down for a pizza!" can arouse the motivated thoughts and actions. Perhaps even reading these words may motivate you to thoughts about food or even to quit reading and head out for a snack.

Of course, the likelihood of the "pizza motive" being activated may depend on other factors. If you have just finished a huge dinner or gobbled up a whole pizza, your roommate's call or the TV commercial may be less compelling. Or you may be suffering from a stomach virus and mention of a pizza may just make you feel sicker. Personality predispositions may also come into play. Someone who has chosen an ascetic life and renounced all pleasures or someone with a tremendous achievement motive who refuses to interrupt study time may not respond even to a hunger pang or to the imagined taste or image of a pizza. Such considerations indicate the complexity of motivated behavior; they also indicate how various body systems, social experiences, and situational demands must be considered together to define human motivation.

In the late 1950s researchers in physiological psychology, on the one hand, and in information-processing and cognition, on the other, began to question the adequacy of drive-reduction theories of motivation. Physiological studies, for example, provided evidence that factors related to the hormones or to the pathways (neural tracts) in the brain play a role in quieting or in activating the organism, quite apart from the extent to which drives like hunger, thirst, or sex had been satisfied. The so-called "pleasure" and "punishment" centers of the brain were discovered; these areas, if stimulated electrically, led an animal to act as if it had been rewarded or punished (Delgado, Roberts, and Miller, 1954; Olds and Milner, 1954) (see Figure 8-1). Consequently, reinforcement could no longer be explained solely in terms of hunger, thirst, or sexual satisfaction, or feelings in the mouth, belly, or genitals. Brain areas that involve information-processing, perception, and thought were found to be near these reinforcement centers, so that an animal's appraisal of situations might be more reinforcing (rewarding or punishing) than food intake or sexual activity (Hunt, 1965; Pribram, 1963; Pribram, Spinelli, and Kamback, 1967).

Drive Reduction versus Intrinsic Motivation

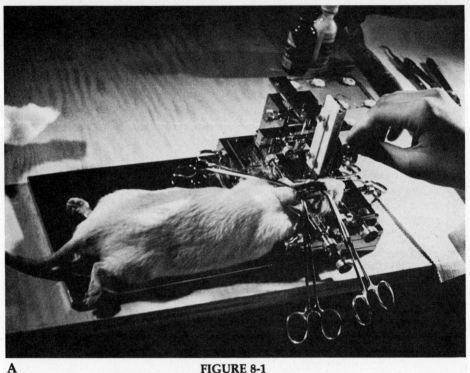

A
FIGURE 8-1
Studying the Brain's "Pleasure Center"

In photo A, a microelectrode is implanted in the so-called pleasure center of the brain of an anesthetized rat. In B, the wired rat is conscious and free to move about. By pressing a lever, the rat can stimulate that area of its brain with a mild electric shock. The rat's tendency to continue to press the lever suggests that the animal receives pleasure or positive reinforcement from this stimulation, without any reduction of a drive such as hunger or thirst.

The Interaction of Body and Mind

> *Tell me where is fancy bred,*
> *Or in the heart or in the head?*
> *How begot, how nourished?*
> *Reply, reply.*
> *It is engend'red in the eyes,*
> *with gazing fed . . . .*

In this little song from *The Merchant of Venice*, Shakespeare succinctly poses a key question, one that is the starting point for most theories of personality. In those days, the word "fancy" meant attraction, desire, or love. Shakespeare asks, What is the source of human motivation and what sustains it—does it arise in emotion (the heart) or thought (the head)? And Shakespeare answers, "It is engend'red in the eyes," that is, in the information-processing or the

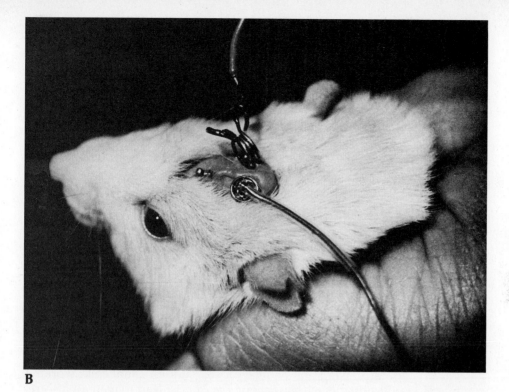

B

cognitive system, with stimulation initially derived from the environment. Shakespeare's insight about the role of external stimulation in initiating interest and in providing the first "nourishment" for human motivation has certainly been sustained by research such as that of Piaget and J. McV. Hunt.

In addition, however, it is now apparent that emotions are critical features of motivation, and that complex thought processes, reflections about past experiences, and mental explorations of future possibilities also play an important part in directing actions. The "heart" and the "head" as well as the "eye" must all be considered in answering Shakespeare's query, "Where is fancy bred?" Let us look first at the body mechanisms, glands, neurochemical transmissions, and brain structures that underlie the motivating effects of drives and emotions, as well as such specifically human motives as power, nurturance, affiliation, achievement, and play.

BODY-REGULATORY SYSTEMS

Recent research in the past two decades has made it clear that a series of basic bodily processes provide the organism with a foundation on which more specific motives are based. These processes are silent in the sense that they operate without any awareness on our part. We cannot identify the instant when a hormone like adrenalin pours into our bloodstreams, when certain chemical substances known as neurotransmitters are secreted at the nerve endings in our brains, or when activity along the network of brain fibers called the ascending reticular system leads to a sense of arousal or great alertness. Nevertheless, the operation of these processes as part of the machinery of the body determines our general levels of excitement or wakefulness, our capacity for clear attention and concentration or controlled thought, and also our general sense of sadness or vitality.

Hormones and Neurotransmitters During periods of stress the adrenal glands release hormones called *epinephrine* and *norepinephrine* into the bloodstream. These hormones are also secreted by the nerve endings at the connections between neurons in the sympathetic nervous system. Recently, precise methods for measuring the secretion rate of these hormones have documented the role such substances play in the behavior of animals and humans. Moreover, it is now known that not only are electrical impulses transmitted across the synapse (the gap between the adjacent nerves) but also that chemical substances called *neurotransmitters* are secreted at the nerve endings.

The evidence is fairly clear that traumatic, stressful situations such as parachute jumping, boxing, automobile racing, sudden changes in working conditions, or viewing movies like *Jaws* or *The Exorcist* lead to increased secretions of epinephrine and norepinephrine. There is, however, litle evidence that secretion of these substances is related to the occurrence of specific emotions, but rather it seems likely that they are related to general levels of *arousal*, in which the organism is in an excited state that may reflect a variety of emotions.

Recently, much greater attention is being paid to the evidence that these chemical substances are found in the brain. Norepinephrine, for example, is found in high concentrations near the hypothalamus and other areas of the limbic system, which suggests that it is important for emotion and emotional expressiveness. All of the new "mood drugs" have fairly definite effects on the amount of norepinephrine in the brain. If a drug reduces the norepinephrine level, it tends to lead to depressive feelings and behavior. If a drug increases the release of norepinephrine at the nerve endings or its accumulation at receptor areas of the brain, the result usually is diminished depression and more positive emotions or a good deal of overt activity.

Other neurotransmitters, such as serotonin and dopamine, are also being studied for their possible effects. Research on well-known drugs such as reserpine or chlorpromazine has found that these drugs are related to the naturally secreted enzymes and neurotransmitters at nerve endings. A great deal of attention is being paid to *serotonin* because its action is related to the actions of well-known drugs. The data suggest that many of the drugs used for medication as well as drugs used for producing altered states of consciousness, such as marijuana, morphine, and LSD, are chemically related to substances naturally secreted in the nervous system.

Nevertheless, there is little reason to believe that the buildup or depletion of a particular amine in the brain has specific motivational properties. Essentially, the chemical substances in the body seem to be related to gross changes in feelings of excitement or fatigue, alertness or drowsiness. In an exciting situation, the psychological meaning of the situation is more important than chemical changes in the body in determining whether specific emotions or motivated actions will occur, according to most investigators working at the behavioral end of the research in this area. The chemical activities in our bodies seem primarily to give a "feeling tone" to our thoughts or behavior. We may get excited or interested or active, but *about what* depends less on chemicals than on our longstanding patterns of social and emotional experience.

While the neurochemistry of the body sets a foundation for general moods, there are other influences of a more cyclical or rhythmic nature that influence our wakefulness, alertness, or sense of liveliness. If you think about your own patterns or those of family members or friends, you can identify some people as morning folks, those who get up early and are vigorous and active early. Others tend to sleep late and are more lively and attentive in the afternoon or evening. Clearly, aspects of our sleep-wakefulness pattern may serve as another basic groundwork influencing the *intensity*, if not necessarily the direction, of our motivational structure.

The Possible Functions of Sleep

Most human beings spend about one-third of their lives sleeping. A great deal of research has examined the function served by sleep and the special role of the two major kinds of sleep: *S sleep*, characterized by synchronous (simultaneous) brain waves—the EEG stages 2, 3, and 4, with no rapid eye movements (REM)—and *D sleep*, characterized by desynchronous brainwaves and REMs—the EEG Stage 1 sleep in which dreaming occurs (see Figure 8-2). Anyone who has been awakened in the middle of the night or who has tried to waken someone else at such times is well aware that under such circumstances human beings can be at their worst in terms of irritability and rage. It is also obvious that people who have not slept for long periods of time can become extremely upset and disorganized. In other words, we have all seen evidence of the potential for gross emotional arousal produced by insufficient sleep.

Careful research carried out under fairly controlled laboratory conditions has not, however, provided really clear-cut evidence of the more general functions of sleep. Indeed, after summarizing the research, Wilse B. Webb (1971), one of the major sleep researchers, says "the effect of sleep deprivation is to make the subject fall asleep."

Hartmann (1973) reported on research attempting to pin down some of the cognitive and personality factors relating to the functions of sleep. Reports by subjects on their sleep patterns were obtained and subsequently checked

FIGURE 8-2
The Functions of Sleep

Data Base	Functions of S Sleep	
Hints from physiology-chemistry of sleep	Anabolism: macromolecule (RNA or protein) synthesis	Anabolism and synthesis of macromolecules to be used partially in the functions of D
Sleep deprivation	Prevent lethargy or physical tiredness	
Sleep as a response	Restoration after exercise, pain or injury, or excessive catabolism	
Psychology of tiredness	Restoration after "physical" tiredness	

	Functions of D Sleep	
Hints from physiology	Repatterning	Repair, reorganization, formation of new connections in cortex and the catecholamine systems ascending to cortex required for optimal attention mechanisms, secondary process, and self-guidance during waking
Sleep deprivation	Focus attention and keep out extraneous stimuli; maintain ego integrity; restore ability for new learning; repattern or consolidate memories	
Long and short sleepers Variable sleepers	Restoration after new learning and "psychic strain" including anxiety and depression	
Age changes and pathological states	Restoration at times of new learning and at times of irritability and depression	
Sleep as a response	Restoration of catecholamine systems; restoration after reticular stimulation or hyper-vigilance; restoration after new learning	
Psychology of tiredness	Restore recent, subtle ego mechanisms and secondary process	
The dream	Shunting out for repair (during D) of certain brain systems necessary for flexible attention, subtle feedback regulated emotion, continuing sense of self	

This diagram lists many potentially significant factors in the third of our lives we spend sleeping that may produce variations in our waking emotions, our cognitive structures, and even our personality patterns.

(From Hartmann, 1973)

by laboratory investigation. In the laboratory the subjects were divided into *long-sleepers* (an average of 9.7 hours per night) and *short-sleepers* (an average of 5.6 hours per night). Hartmann and his collaborators found that almost all the subjects had about the same amount of S or non-REM sleep in their cycles, but for the long-sleepers the amount of D or REM sleep was much greater. The long-sleepers showed approximately twice as much D time and three times as many rapid eye movement periods within these D periods as did the short-sleepers.

Psychological tests were administered to the subjects, and they were also interviewed at length. Long-sleepers showed more nervousness, anxiety and depression, and less energy, aggression, and ambition than the short-sleepers, who showed more social presence, more ability, and a much higher energy level. The short-sleepers presented themselves as "all-American"—that is, normal, extraverted, unworried, not inclined to spend much time thinking about problems, and more likely to be active in the issues that confronted them.

Hartmann characterized the long-sleepers as people who "spent considerable time worrying over . . . problems . . . . The long-sleepers could be seen as constantly 'reprogramming' themselves as opposed to the relatively 'preprogrammed' short-sleepers" (Hartmann, 1973, p. 65). Hartmann proposed that the special need for D sleep seems related to an attempt on the part of the body to restore the balance of the neurotransmitters in the brain. He believes that these chemicals are particularly drawn upon when daytime activities involve introspection, worry, self-examination, and other intense mental activity.

While Hartmann's conclusions are far from proved, they do have interesting implications for grosser patterns of motivation. The relative quantity and quality of sleep and arousal may be more important than most motivational theorists have emphasized. It is possible that some persons who are habitually given to deep thought, worry, or intense concentration may really need more sleep. If they do not get it they may be irritable, angry, or impulsive the next day and fail to recognize why they are in such a mood.

Conscious Biological States: The Drives

The biological states discussed so far—neurotransmitter balances, states of arousal, and deprivations of Stage 1 REM sleep—ordinarily do not attain representation in consciousness. In other words, we are not usually aware of all the chemical reactions and electrical activities constantly going on in our bodies. Biologically related drives such as hunger, thirst, sex, and pain reduction, however, do appear in consciousness in a rather specific form. If you regularly eat three meals a day, you usually notice near noon that no matter what activity you are engaged in your thoughts drift to the important question of what to have for lunch.

The motivational significance of hunger, thirst, and sex is obvious; still, we cannot deny the fact that human values and emotions can override the pressures to gratify biological drives. The Irish prisoners' refusal of food in protest against British rule of Northern Ireland, or the ability of the entertainer Dick Gregory to endure long periods of fasting to publicize socially significant causes—such examples point up potentialities in all humans. A conflict of values between lovers can lead to a loss of interest in sexuality in one or both of them despite many earlier experiences of great passion together. A young artist caused difficulties for himself on several occasions when in the midst of a passionate embrace a new approach to a painting flashed across his mind and he abruptly interrupted his lovemaking to go back to his easel!

THE EMOTIONAL OR AFFECTIVE SYSTEM

The terms *emotion* and *affect* have come to be used relatively interchangeably in psychology. "Emotion" refers to the experience of passion or feeling, but more precisely psychologists have used it to mean any basic organismic response. Emotions are a person's reactions to the rate and complexity of new information that needs to be processed; these reactions are manifested along three dimensions: (1) facial expression and bodily gesture; (2) physiological reaction, including heart rate, blood pressure, skin temperature, brain rhythms, and muscular tension, especially in the face and limbs; and (3) personal awareness, such as "I feel happy!" or "I'm angry!" This awareness can occur in private thought or can be communicated to others by speech or by responding to a checklist of adjectives. "Affect" used to refer primarily to the facial-expression component of emotion. Psychiatrists would describe mental patients who smiled when they recounted sad events as showing "inappropriate affect." Today affect is still used to refer to the overt expressive feature of emotion, but it is also often simply a synonym for emotion, and "affective responses" imply all three of the preceding components.

When people are willing to pour millions of dollars into the box offices so that Richard Pryor or Woody Allen can make them laugh or so a movie like *Jaws* can terrify them, it seems obvious that emotional expression is a motivating principle. Why then have psychologists and other scholars of human nature tended, on the whole, to play down the significance of emotion as a motivational system and to view it more often as an "epiphenomenon" or side effect? Scientific or high-level intellectual work itself requires considerable self-discipline and avoidance of distraction. Is it for this reason perhaps that scientists who have written about human emotions have tended to minimize their significance or to view them as disruptive forces? This may have been the case, especially because so much clinical work and research has emphasized the unpleasant emotions of anger, anxiety, and depression. Indeed, Freud himself—whose very name means "joy" and whose work called attention to the tremendous role of emotion in human experience—practically never discussed the constructive or positive side of affective experiences.

More recently, however, there has been a recognition in psychology that emotions have integrating and constructive value in human experience as well as being sources of difficulty for effective living (Izard, 1971, 1977; Leeper, 1965; Mowrer, 1961; Tomkins 1962, 1963). It is becoming apparent that emotions are more than generalized states of arousal (Duffy, 1962; Lindsley, 1957). Indeed, human beings could not sustain the intellectual and physical effort of artistic and scientific activities were it not for the excitement accompanying scientific discovery or the creation of an artistic masterpiece.

One of the major thrusts of personality research in the past fifteen years has involved the exploration by investigators such as Silvan Tomkins (1981), Carroll Izard (1977), Paul Ekman (1972), and Gary Schwartz (Schwartz, Weinberger, and Singer, 1981) of the possibility that there may be a limited, clearly differentiated group of basic emotions. Their theoretical analyses and studies of facial expression, self-report, and psychophysiological patterns have led to the *differential-emotions theory*. This theory proposes that a small but discrete number of emotions can be regularly identified and that more complex experiences such as love, jealousy, anxiety, or depression represent combinations of these basic affects.

THE FACE AND EMOTION

More than a century ago, Charles Darwin (1872) proposed that facial expressions in animals and humans are related to adaptive functions. Facial expressions of anger may be remnants of the baring of teeth as part of a threatening act in earlier days. Similarly the down-turned mouth and drooping expression associated with sadness in an adult seem a toned-down form of the distress response and weeping of an infant.

Recent research by Izard (1971, 1972, 1977) and by Ekman, Friesen, and Ellsworth (1972) demonstrated that there are indeed fundamental emotions that yield the same facial expressions and experiential qualities (see Figure 8-3). Moreover, these emotions are identifiable in widely different cultures from all over the world. As Table 8-1 shows, when subjects from twelve different countries were shown photographs selected to represent fundamental emotions, the percentage of agreement on the whole was quite high. It is interesting to note, however, that in the Japanese culture there was less agreement on some of the emotions, particularly shame-humiliation.

There seems little doubt that we are "wired" to *experience* a limited number of different emotions and to *express* them on our faces. There also seems to be good reason to believe that we have evolved with particular facial expressions for showing particular emotions: happiness and joy by the smile; surprise and interest by raised eyes and a focused head-forward stance; sadness by a drooping mouth and slackening jaw muscles; disgust by tightened muscles beneath

FIGURE 8-3

The Facial Expression of Emotion

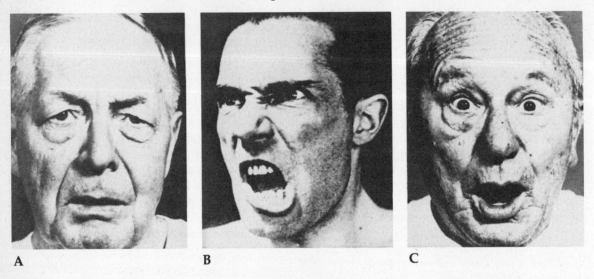

A   B   C

In literate cultures, the expressions in these photos have been judged to be sadness (A), anger (B), and surprise (C). When 189 New Guinea adults were shown these photos and asked to choose the one in which "his child died and he felt sad," 79 percent chose photo A, convincing evidence that the facial expression of emotion is the same in literate and preliterate cultures.

the nose and wrinkling of the nose; anger by clenched and exposed teeth; and fear by widened eyes. In fact, all facial expressions are signs of emotions.

Evidence of emotions can also be obtained through the study of brain reactions (Deglin, 1973; MacLean, 1970; Papez, 1951; Pribram, 1970; Simonov, 1975). The limbic system of the brain as well as the left and right hemispheres of the brain seem to be differentially related to the positive and negative emotions (Delgado, Roberts, and Miller, 1954; Olds and Milner, 1954; Schwartz and others, 1974). A recent very careful study (Ahern, 1981) showed that when persons imagined different scenes and rated these for emotions like happiness, sadness, fear, and anger, the positive emotions were associated with greater brain-wave activity in the left hemisphere of the brain while negative emotions were tied to right-hemisphere activity.

Even when there is no obvious change in facial expression, the occurrence of positive or negative emotions can be shown by measuring electrical activity

TABLE 8-1

Cultural Agreement on the Emotions Represented by Facial Expressions

| | Cultural (national) group | | | | | |
	American[a]	English[a]	German[a]	Swedish[a]	French[a]	Swiss[a]
N=	89	62	158	41	67	36
Interest-excitment	84.5	79.2	82.0	83.0	77.5	77.2
Enjoyment-joy	96.8	96.2	98.2	96.5	94.5	97.0
Surprise- startle	90.5	81.0	85.5	81.0	84.2	85.5
Distress-anguish	74.0	74.5	67.2	71.5	70.5	70.0
Disgust-contempt	83.2	84.5	73.0	88.0	78.5	78.2
Anger-rage	89.2	81.5	83.2	82.2	91.5	91.8
Shame-humiliation	73.2	59.5	71.8	76.2	77.2	70.0
Fear-terror	76.0	67.0	84.0	88.8	83.5	67.5
Average	83.4	77.9	80.6	83.4	82.2	79.6

| | Cultural (national) group | | | | | |
	Greek[a]	Japanese[a] (Tokyo)	Mexican[b]	Brazilian[c]	Chilean[c]	Argentinian[c]
N=	50	60	616	82	90	168
Interest-excitement	66.0	71.2				
Enjoyment-startle	93.5	93.8	97	97	90	94
Surprise- startle	80.2	79.2	54	82	88	93
Distress-anguish	54.5	66.8	61	83	90	85
Disgust-contempt	87.5	55.8	61	86	85	79
Anger-rage	80.0	56.8	86	82	76	72
Shame-humiliation	71.0	41.2				
Fear-terror	67.8	58.2	71	77	78	68
Average	75.1	65.4				

[a] From Izard, 1977.

[b] The Mexican data were obtained by Dickey and Knower (1941).

[c] The data from Brazil, Chile, and Argentina were obtained by Ekman and Friesen (1972). Ekman and Friesen also obtained data from a Japanese sample on the same six emotions they studied in South America, and they obtained somewhat higher percentages of agreement than those obtained by Izard.

(Ekman, Friesen, and Ellsworth, 1978).

in the face and brain (Schwartz and others, 1974). Schwartz and his collaborators discovered that when an individual imagines pleasant—or unpleasant—scenes, there are changes in the electrical muscular impulses in the face. This electrical activity is the same as that occurring when a facial expression is manifested. In other words, during happy thoughts the same muscles that produce a smile show electrical activity even though the facial expression appears blank.

Also, Izard (1972) proposed that the many biochemical changes associated with states of anxiety and depression may play an important role in sustaining a mood, just as the feedback from our facial muscles seems to do. Work by Schwartz, Weinberger, and Singer (1981) has indicated that persons who imagine "happy" scenes while exercising—for example, jogging—show reduced blood pressure afterwards. Persons imagining "angry" or "sad" scenes do not show such reductions after exercise. Thus, exercise may not be useful in reducing blood pressure if one is experiencing unpleasant emotions. There are also differences in blood pressure after "angry" or "sad" imagery when people are not exercising. This supports the differential-emotions theory of physiological patterns associated with specific emotions. The mounting evidence suggests, then, that emotions are real—that is, that they constitute a major system of organismic function with clear differences between positive and negative emotions and, very likely, between specific emotions. In the 1970s there was a dramatic breakthrough in psychological research with respect to the relationships between specific affects and facial expression.

Given that emotions constitute a basic organismic system, what does this imply for our understanding of human motivation and personality variation? Let us take a closer look at some research on the significance of facial expressions for interpersonal relations and styles of interaction.

The Social
Importance of
Facial
Expressions

According to the differential-emotions theory (Izard, 1977; Tomkins, 1962, 1963), the face has a critical role not only in the expression of emotion but also in providing emotional information to other people that may, in turn, influence their motives or emotions. For example, if I am lecturing in class and notice that all my listeners have wrinkled up their noses and look as if they were detecting a bad smell—that is, if they seem to be showing the affect of *disgust*— I would be so thoroughly disconcerted that I would not be able to continue my lecture. Did a bad smell drift into the room or is it what I was saying that created these looks? Are my students trying to tell me something? In any case, my message has not been evoking the interest, surprise, and joy that I had hoped for from my audience.

The human face is the single most meaningful stimulus we confront in our environment. Extensive work, such as that by Wolff (1963), has indicated that as early as 3 weeks of age an infant will focus on the eyes of a care-giver. Compared with many other stimuli, such as photographs of pandas, bottles, checkerboards, or bull's-eyes' targets, the face evokes more visual attention

CULTURAL INFLUENCES
ON BASIC FACIAL EXPRESSIONS

Specific cultural patterns on the display of emotions in different social settings may often mask the underlying similarities across cultures in facial expression of emotion. Paul Ekman and Wallace Friesen filmed the facial expressions of Japanese and American students while they were watching a gruesome movie of tribal circumcision rites, one often used to arouse distress by Lazarus (1966) in his studies of cognitive control of emotions. When viewing the film with fellow students, both Japanese and Americans showed very similar facial expressions of terror and distress. When viewing the film in the presence of an "authority figure"—a professor in a white coat—the Japanese showed much more smiling behavior. Thus, even though the "natural" reactions to frightening or disturbing situations may be similar in both cultures, the Japanese often mask experiences of fear or uncertainty by smiling when in a situation they view as judgmental (Ekman and Friesen, 1975; Friesen, 1972).

and quieting of motor activity, including reduction in heart rate, in 6-month-old infants (Kagan and Lewis, 1965; McCall and Kagan, 1967).

The importance of the face in establishing patterns of "attachment" or closeness between infant and an adult is increasingly evident. Similarly, the manifestations of needs and positive emotion in an infant and its fear that an adult will leave are more directly linked to vision and hearing than classical psychoanalytic theory would suggest. Studies by Kistiakovskaia (1965) and by Shaffer and Emerson (1964), as well as the analyses of Walters and Parke (1965), suggest that it is the face and voice of the parent that play the critical role in forming strong human attachments. After all, the infant needs to recognize only a limited number of facial expressions, and these are fairly stable across cultures. The signaling function of a smile or a frown is one of the earliest consistencies in an infant's experience.

Eye contact is another important social signal. Extensive research in social psychology emphasizes the importance of eye contact in maintaining feelings of trust and cooperation in two-person conversation (Exline, Gray, and Schuette, 1965). There is also evidence that people in a face-to-face situation find the face of the other person so compelling that it is hard for them to think unless they shift their eyes away from the other person's face or shut their eyes. In one study (Meskin and Singer, 1974) subjects were asked to think about situations that required them to imagine scenes from childhood or other incidents requiring long-term memory. When they were face to face with the interviewer, they showed a much greater tendency to shift their eyes to the side of the room than when they were being interviewed through a loudspeaker with no one else present. In another study (Rodin and Singer, 1977) subjects found it especially difficult to engage in thinking that involved visual imagery when they were facing another person. They responded by either looking up at the ceiling or shutting their eyes.

How well can people "read" others' facial expressions? We make judgments all the time on the basis of facial expressions. A woman smiles at a man and he thinks, "She likes me." Or she frowns and he decides, "She doesn't like me." Is he correct in interpreting her feelings from her expressions?

Lanzetta and Kleck (1970) carried out an experiment in which the subjects watched the flashing of red and green lights, with the red lights always followed by electric shocks and the green lights never associated with shock. Subjects who saw a red light knew they were about to receive a shock and tensed up; the red light therefore became a signal of emotional arousal. Subsequently the subjects were shown videotapes of their own faces as they watched the lights. They also saw videotapes of the faces of the other subjects. The subject's task was to report whether the face on the screen was reacting to a red or a green light prior to actually receiving a shock. It turned out that the subjects could tell significantly better than chance whether someone was seeing a red or green light and showing fear or relief. Indeed the subjects were as good at judging the facial expressions of others as of their own expressions.

Of particular interest was the finding that the subjects who were especially good at detecting whether others were responding emotionally (that is, reacting to the red light) were themselves more difficult to read by others. Those subjects who were *least* accurate in making judgments about others' faces were themselves more facially expressive. The people who actually had the greatest *physiological* response to the shock (as measured by galvanic skin response—GSR) turned out to be the best judges of others' expressive behaviors even though their own facial expressions were by no means so clear.

Lanzetta and Kleck intepret their results in the following way: Many children are punished for showing their emotions too strongly. Therefore they try to learn to control crying or loud laughing, which leads to a good deal of conflict around the whole area of emotional expressiveness. The conflict between expression and control leads, in turn, to a high level of internal physiological responsiveness that is not manifested by overt facial expression. This early preoccupation with facial expression of emotions may account for the greater sensitivity of such individuals to the facial expression of others.

A study by Buck, Miller, and Caul (1974) used a somewhat similar approach but in this case subjects were videotaped while they were watching slides that varied from extremely pleasant to unpleasant content. Here the task was to guess from videotapes of the subjects' faces whether they were watching a pleasant or unpleasant scene. Women turned out, on the whole, to express their emotions more fully in facial expression and therefore to be more easily judged than men. Like Lanzetta and Kleck, Buck and his collaborators found that the more easily judged the facial expression of an individual was, the less likely he or she was to show internal or physiological reactivity as measured by skin resistance and heart rate. In other words, the emotion showed in the face but not in the physiological indicators.

These investigators went a step further into examining some personality characteristics of "internalizers" and "externalizers." They found that the internalizers—persons who showed more inner reactivity but not much overt facial expression—were likely to have lower self-esteem, to be more socially introverted, and more impersonal in the way they described their emotional experiences. An extreme example of this kind of person was a well-known psychologist who practically never laughed out loud or even smiled broadly. If he heard someone tell a joke or describe a humorous incident, he responded with a barely perceptible smile and the spoken words, "ho, ho" or "laugh, laugh." His was a case of extreme control over spontaneous emotional expressiveness.

Reading Facial Expressions

All of us learn to some extent to control our emotional expressiveness. Children who cry a lot often hear their parents say, "Don't be a crybaby!" Indeed few things can be as withering to a child as a look of contempt or anger on a parent's face, and such looks are likely to come when a child whines and cries. In some families even loud shouts of excitement and joy are severely criticized.

Gradually as we grow up, our facial expressions become less vivid and communicative. A "poker face" is widely esteemed by businessmen and diplomats, as well as poker players. An exception was Nikita Khrushchev, the former premier of the Soviet Union, who during his visit to the United Nations, shocked the delegates and many observers by his open expressions of joy as well as anger or contempt. Of course, in Russian culture such emotional expressiveness is more widely tolerated. When the cosmonaut Yuri Gagarin returned from the first human orbit of earth, he was greeted in front of the Kremlin by Khrushchev with a kiss on the lips before a crowd of hundreds of thousands. Imagine what Americans would have said if President Kennedy had kissed John Glenn on the lips when Glenn returned from the first American earth-orbiting flight!

Because of our general control of emotions, then, it becomes a special skill to become sensitive to others' facial nuances, and often we are not adequately trained for this. Since the psychology of emotions and facial expressions is a new research area, even highly skilled clinicians have not received much exposure to the possibilities of understanding facial expressions. Ekman and Friesen (1975) have engaged in an extensive research project attempting to pinpoint the subtle and rapid changes that occur on peoples' faces as they experience a range of emotions. In the course of this work, they have used photographic techniques that permit them to detect microchanges in facial expression by "freezing" the camera at various points and also by focusing on particular areas of the face. They are able to show fleeting patterns of facial expression, such as fear or anger, which flash quickly across an individual's face as he or she discusses important events, but which would often go undetected in a complex social interaction.

Ekman and his collaborators have been using the photographic records they have developed to train psychotherapists and other mental-health workers in how to detect signs of emotional distress and depression that might otherwise be missed in the course of standard psychiatric interviews. Some of these photographs are shown in Figure 8-4.

The subtlety of changes of affect has been demonstrated in an intriguing experiment by Schwartz and others (1974). They measured the electrical activity of facial muscles when people were thinking about a happy situation, a sad one, a situation likely to induce anger, or a neutral situation. They predicted that four muscles of the face would show different electrical patterns in relation to the thoughts and the images of the individuals. Specifically, the frontalis, corrugator, masseter, and depressor muscles were each expected to show—and, in fact, did show—different patterns for the three affective situations and the neutral situation. Images of a happy event were accompanied by very different muscular activity than the other three situations, while danger and sadness differed from each other and strikingly from the neutral situation in pattern.

A technique for helping people identify the nonverbal cues by which emotions and intentions are expressed has been developed by Robert Rosenthal of Harvard University. The technique, called the Profile of Nonverbal Sensitivity (PONS), is designed to teach people how to recognize the subtler cues in their social environment. Rosenthal's approach is not directed primarily at training mental-health workers, but rather toward demonstrating that reading of others' emotions is a cognitive skill that can be taught to anyone.

Frank (1978) developed a rather elaborate experiment to see if college students could be trained to increase their general sensitivity to the nuances of interpersonal situations and to heighten their social sensitivity. After meeting for about ten weeks in a small group to review one another's dreams and daydreams, without attempts at interpretation, and to empathize with these imaginary experiences, the students showed a significant improvement in their ability to discriminate the complex emotions in the photographs of Rosenthal's PONS procedure.

EMOTIONS AS MOTIVES

The shift of emphasis in personality theory from the biological drive-reduction model toward a broader conception of human motivation opens the way for

FIGURE 8-4
Four Basic Emotions

These four photos show the result when the subject was asked to demonstrate (A) disgust, (B) anger, (C) joy, and (D) fear.

(From Ekman and Friesen, 1975)

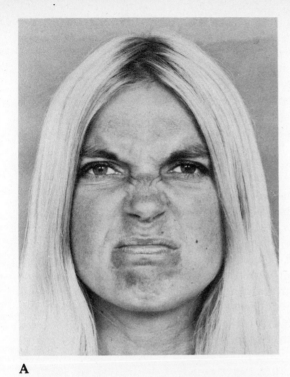

A

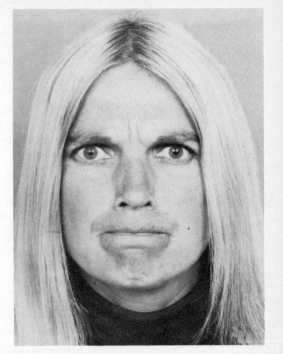

B

C

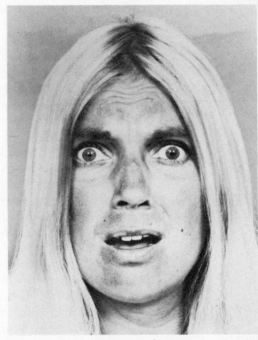

D

a consideration of the motivating role of the emotions. As Tomkins (1962, 1963) has proposed, the affects are a more flexible system than drive reduction for providing direction and intensity to behavior because emotions can be aroused by a great variety of situations, environmental events, others' actions or facial expressions, as well as by our own memories or anticipations. Emotions can be linked to a vast range of experiences—from the fearful ones of early childhood that psychoanalysts have emphasized to the excitement and joy engendered by activities as diverse as surfing, chess playing, or gazing at Michelangelo's *David* in Florence.

Early Socialization of Emotions

Even if it is agreed that emotions play a role in "coloring" our experiences or lending an intensity to our actions, how do they serve as motives? Pribram's research on the brain (Pribram, 1963; Pribram and others, 1967) led him to suggest that those areas of the brain consistently linked with positive or negative emotional expression in animals are also anatomically and physiologically related to areas of the brain associated with self-rewarding or self-punishing experiences—in other words, with reinforcement. Tomkins' theory of emotions (Chapter 6, page 129) contains a similar view in its four principles that underlie all motivated behavior.

Situations consistently evoking positive emotions gradually become organized into *schemas* (sets of expectations) that lead us to seek out these situations again and again. Situations evoking anger and fear or distress we learn to avoid. For any given individual growing up in a particular family, certain sets of experiences become linked consistently with positive or negative emotions. Thus, the psychoanalytic emphases on feeding and toilet training can be understood in terms of a child's joy and interest or terror and distress, depending on parental attitudes. But there are many other experiences of early development that take on special emotional coloring as well. An active, exploring girl may be punished or humiliated in one family (where parents are fearful that she will damage the furniture or bric-a-brac) and encouraged by parental enthusiasm and laughter in another. A somewhat clumsy or inept boy may be greeted with contempt or derision from his family or schoolmates, while another may find that little mistakes of movement or speech elicit nothing but good-humored laughter.

Family experiences may systematically emphasize expression of some emotions and suppression or control of others. Tomkins' research on *affective polarities* identified individuals or groups who, through early family experience, were encouraged to express and to value positive emotions such as joy and laughter or surprise and interest. Such individuals approach their work, their social lives, and the world as if it were all a game or an intriguing mystery. At the other extreme are persons socialized to inhibit gaiety and intense curiosity, often as a consequence of being humiliated and carped at by parents. Such individuals often show intense suspicion; they appear "down in the mouth," with noses wrinkled up as if anticipating a bad smell. Even when they are greatly gifted intellectually, they may be specialists in criticism of others, showing undue attention to detail and great skepticism of the more wild or romantic flights of fellow scientists, artists, or political leaders (Tomkins, 1965). While research support for Tomkins' theory of affective styles is still sparse, there is increasing research interest in exploring how emotions are socialized and become crystallized into regular motivational patterns.

In keeping with Tomkins' proposal that we seek to experience and express our emotions and yet also to control them, most human societies have developed rituals or cultural institutions in which strong emotional reactivity is acceptable. Hearing footsteps while walking through a strange, deserted neighborhood late at night is an experience likely to cause terror in most people, one we don't actively seek out on a regular basis. Yet millions of persons go to horror movies like *Friday the 13th* or *Halloween* and can express their fears publicly because they know the situations are controlled and "safe." But not everyone reacts in the same way to such movies. Persons who have experienced severe terror in their lives—victims of senseless violence or survivors of World War II mass extermination camps, for example—find it much harder to "enjoy" opportunities to express negative emotions.

Some people have crystallized well-organized desires to reach higher and higher levels of emotional arousal through novelty or threat. Zuckerman (1978) has developed a series of questionnaires measuring sensation-seeking. His research documents the fact that we all vary in the extent to which we are experience sensation-seekers, thrill sensation-seekers, or disinhibition sensation-seekers. Experience sensation-seekers are constantly on the lookout for novelty, for some different kind of circumstance that can arouse their emotions. Young adults who score high on the experience sensation-seeking scales are also likely to be heavy users of hard drugs (Segal, Huba, and Singer, 1980; Zuckerman, 1978). Persons who score high on thrill sensation-seeking often court danger as rock-climbers, hang-gliders, or scuba-divers. Persons seeking disinhibition often turn out to be emotionally overcontrolled or caught up with guilty, power-hungry, or fearful daydreams. They seek to show their emotions more openly through the effects of heavy alcohol use (McClelland, 1975; Segal, Huba and Singer, 1980; Zuckerman, 1978). Activities stemming from the sensation-seeking motives, in which individuals seek newer and newer "highs" of experience and expression, sometimes have self-defeating consequences for their daily lives or their bodies.

The emotional system is more differentiated and less diffuse than other bodily functions, such as the hormonal and sleep-wakefulness systems. Emotions are linked to specific patterns of cognitive processing and serve as general positive or negative reinforcers. But humans also develop highly specific, recurring motivational trends, such as needs for power, achievement, affiliation, or scientific understanding. The personality-assessment procedures described in Chapter 7 make it clear that people differ systematically in which of these many motives predominate in their lives or in their work or social situations. We shall look more closely in later chapters at how some of these

Emotions and Specific Motives

motives, the conflicts between motives, and the defenses develop and function in the adult personality. For the present it is important to recognize that the emotional system and the principles of enhancing positive emotions, reducing negative ones, controlling and yet also expressing emotions serve as a framework for understanding the close tie between bodily systems, cognition, and directed action. We can see this possible link by examining the list of human motives in Table 8-2. This listing encompasses the psychoanalytic and learning-theory emphasis on biological drives, the neo-Freudians' views on security as well as survival or satisfaction, and the humanists' concern with self-actualization and personal growth. The Survival and Security column of

TABLE 8-2

The Human Motives

Motives	Survival and Security (deficiency motivation)	Satisfaction and Stimulation (abundancy motivation)
Motives pertaining primarily to body functions	Avoiding hunger, thirst, lack of oxygen, excessive heat or cold, pain, overfull bladder and colon, fatigue, overtense muscles, illness, and other disagreeable body states.	Attaining pleasurable sensory experiences of tastes, smells, sounds; sexual pleasure; bodily comfort, exercise of muscles; rhythmic body movements.
Motives pertaining primarily to relations with the environment	Avoiding dangerous objects and horrible, ugly, and disgusting situations; seeking objects necessary to future survival and security (e.g., shelter); maintaining a stable, clear, certain environment.	Attaining enjoyable possessions; constructing or inventing objects; understanding the environment; solving problems; playing games; seeking environmental novelty.
Motives pertaining primarily to relationships with other people	Avoiding interpersonal conflict and hostility; maintaining group membership, prestige, and status; being cared for by others; conforming to group standards and values; gaining power and dominance over others.	Attaining love and positive identifications with people and groups; enjoying other people's company; helping and understanding other people; being independent of others.
Motives pertaining primarily to the self	Avoiding feelings of inferiority and failure in comparing self with others or with one's ideal self; avoiding loss of a sense of identity (one's place in society or the world); avoiding feelings of shame, guilt, fear, anxiety, or sadness.	Attaining feelings of self-respect and self-confidence; expressing oneself; feeling a sense of achievement; feeling challenged; establishing moral and other values; discovering a meaningful place of self in the universe.

(Modified from Krech, Crutchfield, and Livson, 1974)

the table mostly reflects attempts either to avoid negative affect or to exert control over our emotions. The motives pertaining to body deficiencies, dangers, or discomforts all involve emotions of fear or terror; the motives dealing with the physical environment involve negative affects of fear, anxiety, or disgust. Those pertaining to interpersonal situations involve avoiding negative emotions of anger, fear, or humiliation, while the motives pertaining to self in this column reflect not only avoidance of terror, anxiety, depression, and shame or guilt, but experiences of good control over emotions that may avert feelings of inferiority and failure.

The Satisfaction and Stimulation column suggests a fuller expression of emotions as well as the effort to enhance positive emotions. Most situations are those in which actualities confirm our anticipations or in which the positive emotions of surprise and interest are evoked by moderate but manageable degrees of novelty. The cognitive aspects of reducing incongruity or possessing the skills to cope with moderate ambiguities and challenges are a key feature. Self-respect or feelings of self-worth are closely tied to appropriate levels of emotional control and also to expressions of joy and excitement. Think of the extreme emotional control displayed by star tennis players like Bjorn Borg or Chris Evert Lloyd during the match itself and then the ecstatic leap into the air when the final point is won. However different our specific motives may be, whether athletic success and achievement, attaining power over others, feeling a close sense of intimacy with a spouse or family, it is the avoidance of negative feelings, the enhancement of positive feelings, the control of emotions, and the fullest expression of emotion that underlie these motivated actions.

Since specific emotions depend heavily on our pattern of information-processing, we must now turn to a consideration of the cognitive system to construct a fuller picture of the personality. Our discussion of emotions and motivation has stressed the determinants that characterize all humans—the physiological functions of glands, neural structures, arousal, and sleep, biological drives, and the emotions. Whether or not emotions are as central to personality as has been suggested, there is no doubt that they add a flavor or element of color to human experience. We are all caught in the continuing dilemma of wishing to control our emotions completely, as does Mr. Spock in *Star Trek*, but we also identify with the expressiveness, impetuosity, and warmth of Captain Kirk. The interplay between emotional expression and emotional control is one of the central factors that forms the human personality.

SUMMARY

1. A crucial question in the study of personality is: What motivates behavior? What factors or *motives* in our bodies, brains, or social environments come together to give thought and behavior a direction and an intensity?

2. Certain body-regulating systems that operate without our awareness provide the foundation for specific motives. During stress the adrenal glands secrete hormones called epinephrine and norepinephrine; these hormones are also released by nerve endings in the sympathetic nervous system. In addition, chemical substances called neurotransmitters are secreted at nerve endings. In stressful situations, the secretion of epinephrine and norepinephrine increases. This secretion seems to lead not to any specific emotion but to an increase in the general level of arousal.

3. Sleep-wakefulness patterns may influence the intensity of the motivational systems. The brain stem reticular formation seems to be critical for waking and sleeping. Research also points up the likelihood that arousal is determined both by the outside world and by central brain mechanisms. Indeed, meaningfulness of the situation is more important than amount of external stimulation. The sleep cycle is relevant to human motivation. Using the electroencephalograph (EEG) to measure brain waves throughout the night, investigators found a cyclical consistent pattern of brain-wave activity and rapid eye movements (REM). A high frequency of dreaming occurs during the Stage 1 EEG-REM stage. There has been a good deal of research to examine the function of sleep and the functions of the two major kinds of sleep—S (non-REM) sleep and D (REM) sleep. People deprived of sleep can become upset and disorganized, but the general functions of sleep are still not known.

4. Emotions are an individual's reactions to the rate and complexity of new information to be processed. These reactions are shown in (1) facial expression and bodily gestures; (2) physiological changes, such as heart rate, blood pressure, and muscular tension; and (3) awareness of the emotions ("I feel happy," "I am angry"), which can occur in thought and be communicated to others.

5. Theoretical analyses and studies of facial expression, self-reports, and psychophysiological patterns suggest that a small but discrete number of emotions can be identified and that the more complex experiences, such as love, jealousy, anxiety, and depression, are combinations of these basic emotions. All facial expressions are signs of emotions.

6. According to the differential-emotions theory, the face has a critical role not only in the expression of emotions but as a signaling system—that is, in providing emotional information to other people. Eye contact, another social signal, is important in maintaining feelings of trust and cooperation in two-person conversations. Research has shown that people can accurately "read" the facial expressions of others. Everyone learns to some extent to control emotional expressiveness, and as we grow up our facial expressions become less vivid and communicative. It is therefore a special skill to be sensitive to the facial nuances of others.

7. Emotions can be motivating in several ways. Pribram proposed that areas of the brain linked with positive or negative emotional expression are ana-

tomically and physiologically related to areas associated with self-rewarding or self-punishing experiences. Tomkins' theory of emotions is similar. He proposed four principles that underly all motivated behavior: (1) the need to increase positive emotions, (2) the need to avoid negative emotions, (3) the need to express emotions as fully as possible, and (4) the need to control emotional expression.

8. The emotional system is more differentiated and less diffuse than other systems. Emotions are linked to specific patterns of cognitive processing and serve as general positive or negative reinforcers. The emotional system serves as a framework for understanding the close tie between bodily systems, cognition, and direct action.

CHAPTER 9

Information-Processing
and Cognitive Style

Next time you are in a bus terminal or any public waiting room try the following experiment on your own cognitive behavior. Interrupt your thoughts every few minutes to ask:

What is happening just now? Was I paying attention to the other people in the bus terminal or to the loudspeaker announcements? Or was I thinking about the people around me? Have my thoughts drifted to memories of previous vacations, parties, or athletic events? Or was I thinking of the future, plans for the next week's activities, getting a summer job, my life beyond college? Was I daydreaming about being a famous rock star or meeting a world-famous scientist who would offer me a job as an assistant? How much of my mental activity was just processing material from the physical and social setting—the shabby seats of the terminal, the smell of stale popcorn and cigarette smoke, the rumbling of buses starting their engines, the voices of people saying their goodbyes? Or was I oblivious to all that and immersed in faraway thoughts? Was my reverie triggered by a face in the crowd that reminded me of an old friend and the good times we had in high school?

If you try conscientiously to pursue this line of self-observation, you will be aware of the extent to which your cognitive system is continuously processing information from both external and internal environments. In his classic work *The Principles of Psychology*, published first in 1890, William James (1950) described this phenomenon called the *stream of thought*. Human consciousness, James wrote, is continuous, responding to external stimulation and reshaping it, responding to memories and reshaping them, always with a sense of "these are *my* thoughts, *my* experiences."

THE COGNITIVE SYSTEM

In Chapter 8 we discussed the "running machinery" of the body—the glands, neural networks, synapses, and emotions—that determines the underlying direction, intensity, and flavor of our experience, but not any specific *content*. It is the *cognitive system* that provides the content of our experiences and the ways we learn about our environment. It is thus the system that moves beyond our innermost feelings to form a link with the physical and social milieus in which we move and from which we incorporate our memories, wishes, plans, and intentions.

Cognition is a series of processes through which the light waves, sound waves, smells, textures, and tastes of the world outside us are "transformed, reduced, elaborated, stored, recovered, and used. It is concerned with these processes even when they operate in the absence of relevant stimulation, as in images and hallucinations. Such terms as *sensation, perception, imagery, retention, recall, problem-solving* and *thinking*, among many others refer to hypothetical stages or aspects of cognition" (Neisser, 1967, p. 4).

A major task of cognitive psychology has been to develop models of the cognitive sequence, beginning with sensory input through storage and retrieval of information. What is now known is that there is a series of *choice* points even in the rapid processing of simple information—for example, buffer periods, when material is held in short-term memory, or searches of long-term memory. At each of these choice points, individual differences in processing styles or skill come into play and open the way for variation not only in what gets attended to, perceived, stored, or recalled later but also in the way in which such processing activities are carried out. Think of two witnesses to a common event—for example, two children who see their parents quarreling. Each child may recall the event differently; that is, they may have *processed* the event in different ways. One child focuses on specific details: "Mom was crying while Dad paced up and down trying to be very careful in what he said but then all of a sudden he threw a cup against the wall!" The other child may not remember anything specific, but attends only to the overall event with overwhelming emotional force: "It was terrible!" From such processing differences psychologists can delineate what are called *cognitive styles*, a major area for personality research, as we shall see later in this chapter.

The Cognitive Sequence

Let us look at the sequence of events involved in the way a person explores an environment and processes the information. Suppose you go to a party at your friend Judy's. You have been there many times so her place is familiar. And you thought you knew all her friends, but as you enter you see an unfamiliar person sitting on the sofa. This stranger and everything in the room within the range of your vision make up the *stimulus input*. This input now becomes a part of your *sensory register*, but even at this near-instantaneous phase of the cognitive sequence you are already exercising some selectivity and control—you are temporarily ignoring the general hubbub of conversation and the lyrics of a song being played on the stereo. The immediate visual representation of the person on the sofa—called the *icon* by some cognitive psychologists (Neisser, 1967)—is then transferred to a temporary "buffer zone," the *short-term memory system* (STM). There a series of complicated control operations must occur or else the material fades away and can never be retrieved. This fading of new material is what happens when you are introduced to a lot of strangers at a party. If you do not concentrate on their names and repeat them to yourself, you find ten minutes later that you cannot remember a single name even though the faces are familiar. For material to be transferred from short-term to long-term memory, it is necessary for a whole sequence of information-processing events to occur (see Figure 9-1).

Processing over Time Let us return to the party to discover how this sequence works. You entered the room with some anticipations, a rough "plan" based on your previous familiarity with Judy's friends. The stranger was not expected, however, and you experience the emotion of surprise at the same time as you rapidly explore your store of long-term memories to determine if you can "place" this new face. Within split seconds you are aware he looks a little like your cousin Bill, who was killed in an accident a few years ago, and there is a faint twinge of recognition-pleasure and then sadness about Bill. You cannot place the person

FIGURE 9-1
The Cognitive Sequence

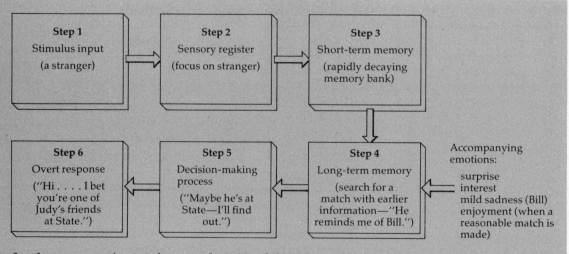

See the accompanying text for an explanation of the steps in this diagram.

---

after all. So you try a quick mental hypothesis of who he could be. You know that Judy has recently transferred to another school and since you have not met any of her new classmates, you figure he might be one of them. You experience some mild interest and curiosity and so you now move to an *overt response*: "Hi. My name's Ben. I bet you're one of Judy's friends at State." He answers, "You're right. I'm Joe McLane and Judy is in my biology class." You experience a twinge of mild pleasure now that you have fit things together, and you store his face in long-term memory as an image; you also attach some semantic or meaningful label to the face, such as "Judy's friend at State."

Cognitive psychology is concerned with elucidating the many complex elements of very rapid information-processing sequences of the kind just described. What rules determine which things or persons we notice and which we ignore? How do we selectively tune out some stimuli and focus on others? How important are the senses of vision, hearing, and smell? How many times does material have to be replayed or rehearsed in short-term memory to get into long-term memory? How do we search long-term memory to match up incoming stimuli with what is already stored there?

The concept of short-term and long-term memory is only one of a number of distinctions needed to understand how we store and then retrieve information on demand. Tulving (1972) has distinguished between *episodic* memory (the storing of concrete events, such as faces and nature scenes) and semantic memory (the storing of meanings such as verbal labels or abstract concepts). Cognitive psychologists are also interested in continuous rehearsal processes, such as talking silently to oneself, reminiscing about particular experiences, or daydreaming about future events. All these processes provide increased complexity to the memory store even when they are self-generated rather than in response to external situations. Moreover, these processes have an effect on the control operations we exercise on input from the environment that passes from the sensory register into the short-term memory system. The concomitant role of emotions, not recognized until recently by cognitive researchers, is likely to be a prominent issue in future research (Bower, 1981; Rychlak, 1976; Tomkins, 1962; Zajonc, 1980).

PERSONALITY DIFFERENCES AND THE COGNITIVE SEQUENCE

Processing new material takes place over time—very rapidly, but not instantaneously—and, as we have seen, it involves several key steps or choice points. Each of these points offers opportunities for considerable variation in how individuals acquire and retain information, and they also allow for the development of habitual *styles* of individual differences that may form the basis for more pervasive personality orientations. Let us now examine some key areas in which personal patterns of information-processing have been identified.

Attentional Strategies   Personality differences can be seen in the ways people focus their attention in cognitive sequences. Some people can filter out extraneous information, while others cannot sort out the essentials and become confused (Broadbent, 1958; Treisman, 1969; Moray, 1970). In any room we enter there are hundreds of large and small objects, corners, edges, depths, heights, noises, faces, smells confronting us; we must therefore have some preliminary *attentional strategies*—advance instructions we give ourselves on what to attend to—so that we can limit ourselves to the most important or relevant information. These strategies work remarkably well, as can be seen from the following experiment: A subject wears special earphones through which a different verbal message is coming into each ear (a *dichotic*, or dual, sensory experience). The subject is instructed to listen only to the words coming into the right ear and to repeat, or *shadow*, those words softly. Under such conditions the material presented to the left ear is usually not even "heard" and is certainly not stored in memory for later retrieval, as memory tests demonstrate. Yet people usually have an overriding attentional strategy that comes into play despite specific instructions from the experimenter. They are especially responsive to and on the alert for any material in the environment that is personal and touches on themselves or their values. Although subjects who are shadowing speech messages to their right ear are normally oblivious to what is said into their left ear, if their name is suddenly spoken into the left ear they hear it at once. Even when people are sound asleep, they show responses like fist-clenching if told in advance to do so whenever hearing their own name in a list of irrelevant words (Oswald, Taylor, and Treisman, 1960). Hoelscher, Klinger, and Barta (1981) have shown that words spoken near a sleeper were worked into dream content during Stage 1 EEG-REM sleep, especially when these words touched on important current concerns. When subjects reported their dreams they incorporated these words into the plot of the dream, but they did not include words that were unrelated to their current worries or motives.

There is a story, perhaps apocryphal, that Julius Caesar could carry on a conversation, read a book, and dictate a letter all at the same time, a feat requiring rare attentional strategies. Neisser (1976) demonstrated that with extensive practice people can indeed learn to do more than one complex task at the same time. He described an experiment in which the subjects read stories while at the same time writing lists of words dictated by the experimenter. After practice and an initial slowing down of reading speed, the participants were able to read rapidly and accurately while also writing the dictated words accurately. They could also identify the common thread in a series of dictated words—for example, words concerned with travel or transportation. Thus, attentional strategies can be viewed as *learned skills*. In addition, many individuals enter each new situation not only with strategies of single or dual attention but also with a kind of running commentary to themselves or an orientation on how material should be stored. A writer or humorist may "case" a room, noticing everything and everybody in it, and almost automatically storing away clever or humorous associations and possibilities for future use.

Severely emotionally disturbed individuals, such as schizophrenics, have difficulties with attentional strategies. They often cannot maintain a fixed attentional set toward completion of a task; in a reaction-time experiment they are likely to miss the cue if there is a long gap between the initial "ready" signal and the flashing of a light that is the cue to press a button (Shakow, 1963). They also have trouble sorting out relevant from irrelevant details and cannot persist with an attentional strategy they have been instructed to follow (Chapman and McGhie, 1962). Blatt and Wild (1976) cite a letter from a schizophrenic patient to his mother that begins with mention of their personal relations, then suddenly shifts into describing the pen he is using to write and then to the country where the pen was made, the patient's love for geography, and the eye color of his first geography teacher. Although there is little evidence about the causes or "cures" of these peculiarities of attentional strategies in chronic schizophrenics, it is possible that their information-processing deviations may lead to difficulties in thinking and communication that could make them seem "crazy" (Holzman, Levy, and Proctor, 1976).

The British psychologist Donald E. Broadbent (1958), a pioneer in cognitive research, proposed an ingenious theory of stylistic differences in information-processing and attention. He used the analogy of two translating machines. One machine might translate each word as it came in and thus produce a rapid output. A second machine might wait until an entire message had been received and then translate all of it. A French phase such as "Je viens de lui voir" would be translated very rapidly by the first machine as "I come of to him to see." The second machine would take longer to present its output but it might give the proper idiomatic translation, "I have just seen him." There are advantages in each approach depending on the need—speed or accuracy.

Processing Strategies: Short and Long Sampling

Broadbent suggested that human variation in constitution, brain structure, or early socialization may bring about two different styles of responding to new information that are similar to the styles of the machines in his analogy. He called these styles *short sampling* and *long sampling*. Short samplers may react immediately to each new stimulus by choosing the most immediate match from long-term memory. Long samplers may wait to respond either until the information is complete within a context or against an array of previous information. Broadbent reviewed some of the important findings of Eysenck and other investigators on introversion-extraversion. Extraverts, according to Broadbent, may well be individuals who make a rapid overt response based on information as it comes in, with only a minimal attempt to take into account previous experience or fuller context. By contrast, introverts constantly take into account their previous experiences and review the total situation with the result that they take much longer to make responses. In such situations the introverts seem hesitant, awkward, and bumbling while the extraverts seem lively and sharp. In situations where there is no premium on time but where accuracy is emphasized rather than speed, the extraverts seem overeager, awkward, and less efficient while the introverts seem careful and reasonable.

Selective Inattention and Defenses

You may recall that Sullivan (Chapter 3) preferred the term *selective inattention* to Freud's term *repression* in describing a major defense mechanism. The cognitive sequence provides a number of choice points where a particular attentional or processing strategy may be used to avoid conflictual material. We shall examine in more detail the defenses and their relation to information-processing in Chapter 13, but it may be helpful here to discuss how a style or regular way of approaching information may give the appearance that something has been repressed when in actuality the information may never have been stored in the first place.

Luborsky, Blinder, and Mackworth (1963) photographed the eye fixations of subjects who were viewing pictures with neutral images intermingled with embarrassing or provocative images. One composite picture, for example, included a man reading a newspaper—a relatively neutral subject—with a naked woman standing nearby. Luborsky and his co-workers showed that the visual scanning strategies of some individuals reflected the nude's embarrassing, taboo presence. Persons with a pattern of repression or conscious avoidance of conflictual material (as determined by other personality measures) tended systematically not to spend much time looking at the nude figure. In other words, they showed selective inattention, making it unlikely that they would store the taboo material in the brain by allowing it to shift from short- to long-term memory. Such an approach may also characterize the extravert or short sampler. People who have been frightened about certain sexual material may develop a short-sampling processing style, continuously scanning new inputs quickly but rarely sticking with something potentially threatening lest it provoke embarrassing thoughts, desires, or memories. Whether such processing styles reflect basic tendencies or are the results of socialization experiences is an intriguing area for research.

Encoding, Storage, and Retrieval

The moment we perceive something we are already acting on it. And we act on it in relation to what we recall from previous perceptions of similar stimuli. In this sense, later retrieval of new information depends in part on the way we first *encode* it—that is, how we translate the complex patterns of sound or light into structures susceptible to brain storage. Psychologists increasingly believe that we encode information in one of two ways. We can store it in verbal labels that identify abstract concepts or categories, such as "hat, a form of headgear," or we can store it as a kind of image or representation, a mental picture of a hat on a chair. Tulving (1972) calls these two systems *semantic* memory and *episodic* memory, respectively. Both systems, verbal-semantic and visual-episodic, seem to be valuable methods of storage, each with special advantages. Obviously if we wish to retrieve information quickly, storing words in semantically related categories—our mental dictionary—has advantages. To recall "table" we can quickly explore "furniture" associations. If, however, we have to describe exactly what a table looks like and what objects are on it, as a trial witness might, we would have to rely more on whatever image we encoded. Seamon (1973) demonstrated that the most efficient retrieval of material comes if one encodes both words and images, and Craik (1977) has shown that encoding by meaning leads to much more efficient retrieval than encoding by pronunciation or mental pictures. Meaning usually involves some combination of verbal and visual or auditory encoding.

Some people prefer to encode material in verbal form while others favor visual representations. Persons who score at the extremes on a verbalizer-visualizer dimension have been identified through questionnaires. They differ on physiological measures, such as breathing patterns and brain waves, and also in psychological response patterns. Visualizers, for example, are more likely to be excitable, hyperactive, and hypersensitive, and to favor esthetic, social, and religious values. Verbalizers are more controlled and prefer theoretical, economic, and political values (Hiscock, 1978; Richardson, 1977).

Left-Right Brain Differences

There are reasons to believe that the brain is organized to deal separately with verbal and imagery processes (see Figure 9-2). The left hemisphere of the cerebrum seems tied to expressive communication and verbal, logical, sequential thought while the right hemisphere seems more closely associated with global or image-oriented thought and receptive, rather than expressive, functions (Gazzaniga and Ledoux, 1978; Ornstein, 1977).

FIGURE 9-2
Left-Right Brain Differences

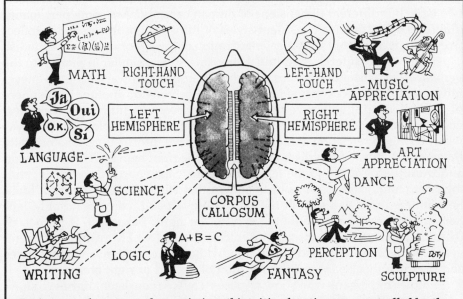

Brain research suggests that artistic and intuitive functions are controlled by the right side of the brain, while logical, rational processes are controlled by the left side. (The functions shown in the drawing are speculative, and not definitely established by research.)

Does the evidence that the left and right sides of the brain differ somewhat in function have implications for personality differences? There is research indicating that the right hemisphere is linked to negative emotions, to spatial or imagery processing, and to thinking of pure melodies, while the left hemisphere is linked to verbal and mathematical thought and positive emotions (Ahern, 1981; Rosenberg, 1980). Is it possible that each half of the brain reflects two basic but different dimensions of human capacity? Are some personality differences that involve consistent styles of information processing or reflective thought correlated with greater activation of the left or right hemispheres?

Adults who differ in their initial encoding styles, similar in pattern to the verbalizer-visualizer differences, also demonstrate brain-wave patterns or eye-movement differences that suggest they "favor" one or another hemisphere of the brain during reflective thought. An approach to studying such differences has emerged by examining the direction in which people shift their eyes when trying to reflect on a question or to retrieve information. Anatomically the neural pathway from the left eye goes to the right hemisphere of the brain and from the right eye to the left hemisphere. Since our eyes normally shift together (conjugately), it has been shown that stimulation of the right-brain hemisphere leads to a shift of the eyes to the left and, correspondingly, left-hemisphere stimulation shifts the eyes to the right. Bakan (1971) proposed, therefore, that eye-shift direction, which he called CLEM (conjugate lateral eye movement), can be used to detect individual differences in encoding styles and presumably also in relative excitation of the left or right brain.

Studies of persons who show consistent left- or consistent right-eye shifts when engaged in reflective thought do offer some support for Bakan's views. Right shifters (that is, those whose left brains are most active) are more analytic in perceptual performance and score higher on measures of verbal-concept formation, mathematics scores, and measures of mathematical, scientific, or theoretical interests. Left-shifters are more imagery oriented, more hypnotically susceptible, more inclined to daydream, more creative and esthetically oriented (Bakan, 1978; Gur and Reyher, 1973; Meskin and Singer, 1974; Rodin and Singer, 1977). Left- and right-shifters even differ in where they prefer to sit in college lecture halls, with left-shifters sitting on the right side and right-shifters to the left of center.

Memory

Once material has been stored in the brain, at least temporarily, some complex processes must go on to assure longer-term storage and then subsequent efficient retrieval. The research on memorization suggests that material is best recaptured when it is set in contexts that are themselves easily retrieved and also when there is continuous rehearsal or private mental practice. If you want to study for an examination, reading rapidly through a chapter is not an efficient method for learning purposes. For later retrieval on the examination, it is preferable to take a more active approach to the material, organizing it into categories, then mentally playing out these categories and attempting in your mind's eye to go through them and, in effect, preparing a set of potential questions and answers from the chapter.

Here we see the merging of perceptual process not only with memory but also with the whole structure of ongoing thought and fantasy. A person who spends a good deal of time thinking and rethinking about events will be more likely to establish a great variety of contexts and associative cues to this material so that it can be more easily recalled. By contrast, someone who spends little time actively replaying material but instead is busily working on processing a tremendous variety of new material will have only the vaguest patterns stored in memory. The result of these two strategies will be different when people are asked to reproduce material that has been presented to them. Extensive evidence supporting processing-style differences of this kind has been summarized by Eysenck (1976) for introverts and extraverts. Here again, what looks like repression may be failure by extraverts to engage in active mental rehearsal of material and to generate complex cognitive structures.

A series of experiments carried out by Paul (1959) explored *memory styles*. Adults listened to a story, usually a legend from a foreign culture that was unfamiliar and therefore completely new material. Paul found fairly clear-cut stylistic patterns in the way that people recalled this material. His subjects could be classified as *importers* or *nonimporters*; the former tended to introduce additional material not initially in the story in order to clarify or elaborate what had been presented and also to make the story more coherent. Nonimporters gave only the sketchiest kind of story and stuck closely to the initial presentation.

Another, similar distinction between the two kinds of style emerged quite strikingly in a study by Lazarus, Eriksen, and Fonda (1951). They interviewed clinical patients and also gave them psychological tests designed to find out how they coped with anxiety. Some patients (called *sensitizers*) showed a pattern of responding to anxiety or threat by means of defenses such as *intellectualization*—that is, by attempts to reason and explain their reactions at a conscious level. Others (*repressers*) reacted to anxiety by *forgetfulness* or *denial*, avoiding conscious thought and denying awareness of conflict. The stylistic differences of *repression-sensitization* bear considerable similarity to the *short-sampling* versus *long-sampling* or the *importing* versus *nonimporting* trends in the way people approach information-processing situations.

Implications Once we recognize that information-processing involves a sequence across time, we can see many sources of individual variations at each step of the process. Some of these variations may be a function of a momentary situation, the amount of light or distracting noises, the pressures to react quickly or accurately, our previous familiarity with the situation. Our review of just some of the research suggests, however, that there are consistent patterns or response styles, some involving the ability to sustain attention or to select a particular stimulus and to ignore extraneous material. Some consistencies are related to the *form* in which information is transferred from the short-term to the long-term memory store. The way we think about material once it is stored may also reflect a style variation leading to differences in what we retrieve when asked for our memories. So far, however, no investigators have pulled all of these variations together to see if they are the result of one fundamental underlying style or are simply variations within each step of the cognitive sequence. Nor is there much information about the origins of these specific styles. There is, however, an extensive body of research that links a more general cognitive style, called field dependence-independence, to a host of personality variations. In the next section we shall examine this cognitive style in detail.

FIELD DEPENDENCE-INDEPENDENCE: A COGNITIVE STYLE

In the 1940s Solomon Asch and Herman A. Witkin began studying a basic perceptual process—how people decide whether an object is perpendicular to the ground or whether it is tilted to some degree. They were interested in learning whether people use cues from the background of the object (the field), or whether they rely on their own bodily posture to provide information about verticality. In the course of this research, they began to notice interesting individual differences in the way people solve this apparently simply perceptual task.

Asch soon shifted his interest to social psychology. But Witkin became more and more intrigued by the individual differences in how people deal with the perceptual situation of determining whether an object is vertical. From these observations grew a long-term and complex program of research that Witkin directed for thirty years. Over 3,000 experimental studies have been carried out, examining all aspects of perception of the vertical especially as related to individual styles. Witkin and his collaborators, notably Donald

Goodenough and Helen Lewis, broadened their research on correlates of the style to include not only other perceptual or cognitive performances but also a great range of personality measures. They studied phenomena as diverse as shame or guilt in the course of psychoanalytic treatment, the use of language in social interaction, variations in cultural patterns, and the development of different types of psychopathology.

The original procedures from which Witkin and his collaborators derived their observations of individual differences in information-processing styles all involve perceptual performance (see Figure 9-3). In the Rod and Frame Test (RFT), subjects are seated in a dark room facing an illuminated rod that can be tilted at different angles from a perpendicular position with the earth. The subject's

**Measuring
Field
Dependence-
Independence**

FIGURE 9-3
Testing Field Dependence and Field Independence

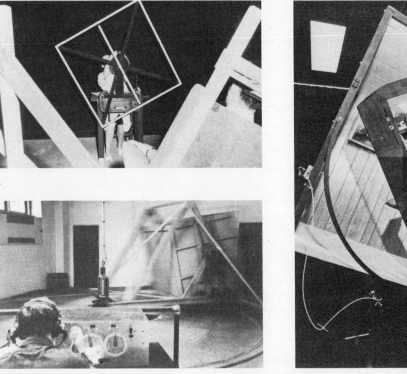

A

C

B

(A) Rod and Frame test, (B) Body Adjustment test, (C) Rotating Room test. These three tests are described in the accompanying text.

(From Witkin and Goodenough, 1981)

task is to indicate when the rod is truly vertical. Many people have difficulty with this task when they have no environmental cues and so accept the rod as vertical when it is actually at a 10–20° angle from the earth. This would be equivalent to someone looking at the famous Leaning Tower of Pisa and saying that it is standing straight.

In a second situation—the Body-Adjustment Test (BAT)—a person is seated in a tiltable chair in a small, unlit, tiltable room. The room may be tilted, for example, at an angle of 25° on the left from the vertical, and the observer's chair may also be tilted to the left about 15°. The person is asked to report when his or her chair is vertical with the earth. Obviously to decide whether one is truly vertical in this tilted room, one must ignore the tilt of the room and base the judgment on the pull of gravity on one's own body. Witkin (1977) described a man who was tilted 22° to the left in his chair while the room was tilted 35°, also to the left. Asked which direction his chair should be moved to bring him back to being straight, he insisted that he be shifted *left*. Try tilting a chair at 35° from the vertical! It is clear that he was completely ignoring his own body's sense of balance and depending on the environmental cues—the field—instead.

Still a third situation involves a fixed chair in a room that slowly rotates on a circular track. In this Rotating Room Test (RRT), the field around the person remains vertical but body cues are altered by rotation. In this situation individuals who perform more accurately in the RFT and BAT by relying on body cues for verticality become more confused and do not do as well as individuals who rely on the external framework for determining verticality.

Extensive research has indicated that performance in these artificial environments varies along a continuum from heavy reliance on the body-centered, or vestibular, cues of balance at one pole to extreme dependence on the cues provided by the visual field at the other pole. Since these differences do not affect overall adequacy of performance, they are regarded as styles, not skills or abilities. Dependence on the visual environment is called *field dependence* while reliance on bodily cues and resistance to environmental cues is called *field independence*. Field dependence-independence is not a typology. It is based on scores in a normal distribution, and most people lie somewhere in between the extremes.

Witkin and Goodenough (1977a) emphasized that specific abilities are related to each pole of the field dependence-independence continuum. Field-independent persons are better at skills of discerning material in a complex environment as in the Embedded Figures Test (EFT) (see Figure 9-4). They are also more capable of carrying out tasks that involve delineating the details of body parts when asked to draw a human figure or restructuring shapes to form new patterns. Persons who score high in field dependence are better at skills requiring use of environmental cues and situations that involve remembering faces or details of interpersonal situations. Field-dependent persons show more incidental learning of social stimuli (Goodenough, 1976). For example, field-dependent persons, asked later to describe things that went on in a roomful of people, may remember more about incidental events than field-indepen-

FIGURE 9-4
The Embedded Figures Test

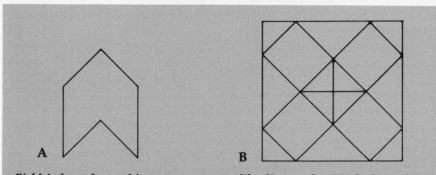

Field-independent subjects can more readily discern the simple figure (A) embedded in the complex diagram (B) than field-dependent subjects—that is, they are more capable of cognitive restructuring.

(From Witkin and others, 1977)

dent persons. Some psychologists have pointed out that since the EFT correlates with measures of intelligence or social maturity, personality differences related to this test may be simply differences of ability, not of style (Zigler, 1963). They say that if the EFT is to be used as a measure of cognitive style, the experimenter must use some statistical procedures to eliminate differences attributable to general intelligence.

There is an impressive body of evidence that field dependence-independence is a reliable and consistent style of adult and childhood behavior. Followup studies have also demonstrated that it is persistent over many years. While no definitive full-scale multi-trait multi-method study has demonstrated the "trait purity" of field dependence-independence, a large network of studies leads to the strong conclusion that when several measures are used together, individuals who are consistently field dependent or field independent can be identified and that such differences in cognitive processing appear in a whole variety of other settings.

Self-Nonself Differentiation

As a consequence of sorting and categorizing the literally hundreds of studies involving perceptual and personality correlates of field dependence-independence, Witkin and Goodenough (1977b) proposed that they reflected an underlying style of *self-nonself* differentiation, which is manifested in two kinds of situations or tasks: cognitive restructuring and interpersonal skills. Field independence is demonstrated by skill in cognitive restructuring—that is, by reshaping information, matching previous experience with new inputs, and by relying more on private thoughts, imagery, or plans. The field-dependent person may show greater interest in social situations and more skill in relating to other people or remembering details about people. The field-independent person is more differentiated or complex in dealing with self-generated experiences, such as memories or plans, while the field-dependent person shows more differentiation in respect to nonself-originated stimulation.

Some researchers have implied that field independence is "better"—that is, more adaptive—than field dependence. However, many of their experiments do not show this. For example, Nebelkopf and Dreyer (1973) studied the way in which individuals learn concepts. They presented a series of shapes and forms one after another until a gradual pattern emerges that allows a person to decide what the basic unifying concept is. Both the field independents and the field dependents require the same number of trials to learn a concept. But the field-independent individuals develop hypotheses in advance, looking for methods of testing the hypotheses as new information is presented, throwing out one hypothesis after another until finally they have one that gives them, all at once, the proper solution. The field-dependent people do not seem to start out with any hypotheses. Rather, they look for clear-cut clues in the information that is being presented to them and leap on any striking evidence to match it with what has previously appeared. Thus they gradually accumulate information that eventually leads them to the appropriate concept. Both styles of concept formation produce equally satisfactory solutions.

Field Dependence and Personality Differences

A surprising range of differences in relation to major personality systems exists between individuals who score high or low on field dependence as measured by the Rod and Frame Test or the Embedded Figures Test.

Emotional Differences   A thoughtful monograph by Helen Lewis (1971) was designed to show that field dependence is related to proneness to experience *shame* as a predominant emotion and also as a basis for social interaction. Field independence is more likely to be associated with experiences of *guilt* and related behaviors. Shame often involves a sense of personal humiliation in relation to others, the expectation of mockery, derision, or contempt from real or imagined persons in the environment. By contrast, guilt is an emotion derived from action or perhaps intended actions; therefore the experience is related more to personal evaluation of such actions. In guilt the self provides punishment, while in shame the expectation is of punitive or mocking responses from others.

Patients who had come for psychotherapy were tested for field dependence and field independence. Subsequently, excerpts from their therapeutic interviews were recorded. Independent judges rated the interview transcripts for the number of times in a session that patients referred to anxiety or stress related either to shame or to guilt. In addition, a measure was developed of "spurts of feeling" to look for periods of fluctuation of affective state during sessions. When results of the ratings were compared, clear-cut reliable differences did emerge. Figure 9-5 shows the differences in the relative occurrence

FIGURE 9-5
Shame and Guilt in Psychotherapy

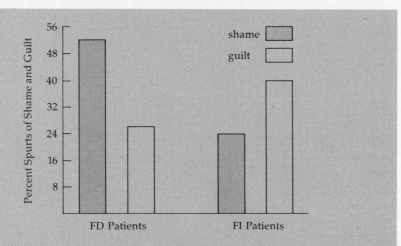

Note that expressions of shame are more characteristic of field-dependent patients than of field-independent patients, who are more likely to express guilt. The reason is described in the text.

(From Lewis, 1971)

of statements involving shame and guilt and also in "spurts of emotion" associated with shame and guilt for field-dependent and field-independent patients. As field-dependent persons describe their life situations they constantly refer to what others might be thinking of them, or how others will react to their appearance or actions. The field-independent persons are more likely to describe actions they have taken and then to express feelings of guilt and self-recrimination for these acts rather than to emphasize the response of other people to their behavior. Thus, the findings from actual therapy sessions, objectively rated, support the hypothesis that field dependence is linked to more frequent experience of the emotion of shame while field independence is more frequently linked to the emotion of guilt.

Witkin and Goodenough (1977a) reviewed about twenty studies with self-ratings and ratings by others of people who were classified as field dependent or field independent. The field-dependent subject, in their description,

> *likes being with others, [is] sociable, gregarious, affiliation-oriented, socially outgoing, prefers interpersonal and group to intrapersonal circumstances, seeks relations with others, shows participativeness, shows need for friendship, [is] interested in people, wants to help others, has a concern for people, has wide acquaintanceship, knows many people and is known to many people* (Witkin and Goodenough, 1977a, p. 672).

In contrast, the field-independent subject

prefers solitary activities, [is] individualistic, cold and distant in relations with others, aloof, never feels like embracing the whole world, [is] not interested in humanitarian activities, highly interested in intellectual activities, values cognitive pursuits, [is] concerned with philosophical problems, concerned with ideas and principles rather than people, task-oriented, has work-oriented values such as efficiency, control, competence, excelling (Witkin and Goodenough, 1977a, p. 672).

There are also indications that field dependents attribute more benign attitudes and intentions to other people. That is, they see other people as friendlier, more likable, warmer, more open-minded, and kind. In one fascinating study that should be a guide to college students in choosing instructors, DiStefano (1970) reported that field-dependent teachers are likely not only to rate their students more highly on positive emotions, but actually to give students higher grades.

Field independents tend to use more negative terms in describing interactions with other people (Gates, 1971) and, in general, are more able to express hostility toward others (Witkin and Goodenough, 1977b). There is even a suggestion from a study by Mones (1975) that field dependents are more likely to smile in social interactions with others than field independents.

Interpersonal Differences   Greene (1973) identified by statistical analysis a group of nonverbal behaviors that seemed to represent "dependency." These included such activities as licking the lips, movements of the tongue and other mouth-oriented activities, touching the mouth with one's hands, or gesturing with palms up, all presumably reflecting an "intake" or receptive orientation. A group of subjects were observed in interview situations when they were either two feet or five feet away from the interviewer. Greene found that when the distance was changed from two to five feet, field independents did not differ in their reliance on such dependency gestures. But the field dependents increased significantly in the amounts of such dependent nonverbal behaviors when they were seated further away from the interviewer.

Another study (Trego, 1972) called for subjects to walk along a corridor toward someone until they reached the distance they usually liked to maintain in normal social interaction. As might be expected, field dependents oriented themselves *toward* the position of the other person, irrespective of the characteristics of the physical environment. The field independents were more likely to relate to the physical characteristics of the environment in determining how close or distantly they placed themselves in a conversation.

A series of studies also indicates that field independents have a more impersonal orientation—they relate to objects, structures, or abstract implications of the environment—while field dependents relate specifically to the human being with whom they are interacting (Birnbaum, 1975; Witkin and Goodenough, 1977b).

Cognitive styles are manifested early in life. In research carried out with children in naturally occurring real-life situations (Coates, Lord and Jakabovics, 1975), field-dependent children spent more time engaging in social play—that is, in interactions and games involving other children. Field-independent children were more likely to engage in solitary games.

Even adult forms of play show cognitive-style differences. Schreiber (1972) compared the field-dependence scores of college athletes who were primarily in team sports, such as baseball, hockey or football, with the scores of athletes who were in individualized activities, such as track, swimming, gymnastics, or wrestling. As might be expected, the team players were significantly more field dependent than the individual-skill–oriented players.

Career-Choice Differences Field-dependent and field-independent individuals express different interests on vocational questionnaires and differ remarkably in their hobbies and choice of occupations. Field-independents are interested in professions that emphasize cognitive restructuring more than interpersonal sensitivity, such as science, mathematics, management, and mechanics, while field dependents are more likely to be interested in humanitarian and social-welfare areas—careers in the ministry, social work, teaching young children, the social sciences, or selling or advertising (Witkin and others, 1977).

Does cognitive style play a role in a student's college career? A long-term study of college students carried out by Witkin and others (1977) suggests that it does. Freshmen were given the Embedded Figures Test. When the investigators traced their subsequent college careers, they found that the students shifted their majors quite consistently in the direction implied by their field-dependent or field-independent status. In other words, field-dependent students who at first majored in mathematics or science tended to shift toward social welfare or teaching careers. It is important to note that this result was predicted by the Embedded Figures Test even when general intelligence differences as measured by the SAT scores were statistically controlled. The data from these studies suggest that when intelligence is ruled out, cognitive style is a predictor of ultimate career choice.

Psychopathological Differences Some of the most striking differences came from studies of emotionally disturbed groups. In an important paper, Witkin (1965) summarized the evidence that field dependents show a different pattern of psychological defense mechanisms than field independents. The studies point up again and again that field dependents make more use of mechanisms such as repression or "primitive" denial. That is, they blot out completely or apparently fail to notice or remember events that have important psychological implications. By contrast, field independents describe distressing conflicts, but accompany these descriptions with elaborate rationalizations or explanations. The field independents seem more like the long-sampling introverts, sensitizers, and importers we discussed earlier in the chapter, but research has yet to forge specific links.

There is also evidence that field dependents show hysterical neurotic symptoms and personality characteristics, and formulate their complaints around bodily ailments or physical conditions. Field-independent individuals are more likely to show obsessive-compulsive personality traits or to report their problems in terms of inner torments and conflicts rather than physical symptoms.

Cultural Differences   Some of the most intriguing differences were discovered in the many studies of the cognitive styles of various cultural groups around the world. In a fascinating monograph, Witkin and Berry (1975) described the consistent evidence that tribes or cultures engaged in subsistence-level agriculture are more likely to be field dependent, while tribes or cultures that depend primarily on migratory hunting turn out to be more field independent. The cognitive restructuring abilities and the sense of personal autonomy have special adaptive value in a bleak or harsh physical setting. Eskimos must differentiate their hunting cues and landmarks from a uniform landscape of

A member of an agrarian society. Because agrarian societies stay put for long periods, their members build up an elaborate system of social interaction. As a result, research has shown that they are commonly found to be field-dependent and to score low on cognitive-restructuring measures such as the Embedded Figures test. By contrast, migratory hunters, such as the Eskimos, are more autonomous. As a result, they are likely to score higher on measures of field independence and cognitive restructuring (Witkin and Goodenough, 1981).

snow. Members of the Arunta tribe must subsist in a monotonous desert ecology. By contrast, organized farming cultures that group together in tightly packed villages must learn interpersonal skills; their members need to communicate and cooperate with other people.

Witkin's concept of field dependence-independence constitutes perhaps the strongest body of evidence available for any trait or style in personality psychology. Many questions remain unanswered, of course. Although perceptual measures like the Rod and Frame Test do not correlate appreciably with intelligence, the widely-used Embedded Figure and Figure-Drawing tests do. Many investigators have not statistically corrected for intelligence differences between groups, and their results may reflect these differences, not differences in cognitive styles.

Appraisal

The studies demonstrate that women are more field dependent than men. It may well be, however, that such sex differences are a product of the kinds of tests employed and that in other situations women may score higher in field independence. In general, the sex differences pose ambiguities for the theory since there is little constitutional evidence to account for them. Lewis (1971, 1976) suggested that differences in rearing patterns for the sexes, with parents' or other adults' differential treatment of children emphasizing shame and guilt, may be relevant.

The research, accumulated over almost thirty years, has seen changes in terminology and emphasis. Perhaps the newer formulations of field dependence-independence as a *style* and interpersonal sensitivity and cognitive restructuring as *skills* will help avoid difficulty in the future.

Finally, not enough work has been done to demonstrate similarities or differences between field dependence-independence and traits measured by other procedures such as Cattell's independence versus subduedness (Cattell, 1969); Rotter's locus of control (Chapter 11); and the various measures of introversion-extraversion or sensation-seeking (Zuckerman, 1979).

Much remains to be done, but Herman Witkin, who died in 1979, must be honored for pursuing with amazing energy the implications for personality of the individual differences that emerged in his laboratory when studying so seemingly basic a response as perception of the vertical.

SUMMARY

1. The cognitive system provides the content of our experience and the ways in which we learn about the environment. In the sequence of events involved in the way a person explores the environment and processes information, individual differences exist in attention patterns, processing strategies,

emotional reactions, details of material stored in the memory, efficiency of retrieval, and in the type of storage. The first step in the sequence is the *sensory input*. This is transferred to the *short-term memory*. For material to be transferred from short-term to *long-term memory*, a whole sequence of information-processing events must occur.

2. Attentional strategies, which can be viewed as learned skills, differ. Some people can restrict their attention to essentials, while others cannot seem to. Severely emotionally disturbed individuals often have difficulties with attentional strategies.

3. Information-processing strategies also seem to differ. Broadbent suggested that some people are *short-samplers*—they may react to each new stimulus by choosing the most immediate match from long-term memory. Others are *long-samplers*—they may wait until the information is complete within a context or match the information against an array of previous information before making a response.

4. There is evidence that people store, or *encode*, information in one of two ways: (1) in verbal labels or abstract concepts or (2) in representations or images. Some people prefer to encode materials into verbal forms and others favor visual representations, although retrieval is most efficient if both words and images are encoded. Encoding preferences are related to various personality differences.

5. The left hemisphere of the brain seems to be linked to expressive communication and to logical sequential thought, and the right hemisphere with more global or image-oriented thought and to receptive functions. People who differ in their initial encoding styles also demonstrate differences in brain-wave patterns or eye movements that suggest they "favor" one hemisphere.

6. Once material has been stored in the brain, complex processes must go on to ensure longer-term storage and subsequent retrieval. Here there is a merging of perceptual processes with memory and with the structure of ongoing thought and fantasy. A person who thinks and rethinks about events will be more likely to establish a variety of contexts and associative cues. There is evidence that introverts and extraverts have different memory-processing styles. A series of experiments found different patterns in the way people recall material. Some are *importers* who tend to introduce material not originally in a story, and other are *non-importers* who give sketchy stories and stick closely to the originals. Other research with clinical patients differentiates *sensitizers* (those who respond to anxiety or threat by attempts to reason and explain their reactions) and *repressors* (those who react by forgetfulness or denial).

7. The cognitive style of field dependence-independence or self-nonself differentiation is one of the major discoveries in personality psychology emerging from laboratory research. The procedures for measuring field

dependence-independence involve perceptual performance, specifically perception of verticality. People who score high in field dependence are better at skills requiring use of environmental cues.

8. Field dependence-independence is related to many personality variables, including the emotions, interpersonal behavior, career choices, psychopathology, and cultural patterns.

CHAPTER

10

Dreams, Hypnosis, and the Stream of Consciousness

"Woodshadows floated silently by through the morning peace from the stairhead seaward where he gazed. Inshore and farther out the mirror of water whitened, spurned by lightshod hurrying feet. White breast of the dim sea. The twining stresses, two by two. A hand plucking the harpstrings merging their twining chords. Wavewhite wedded words shimmering on the dim tide.

"A cloud began to cover the sun slowly, shadowing the bay in deeper green. It lay behind him, a bowl of bitter waters. Fergus' song: I sang it alone in the house, holding down the long dark chords. Her door was open: she wanted to hear my music. Silent with awe and pity I went to her bedside. She was crying in her wretched bed. For those words, Stephen: love's bitter mystery. . . .

"Memories beset his brooding brain. Her glass of water from the kitchen tap when she had approached the sacrament. A cored apple, filled with brown sugar, roasting for her at the hob on a dark autumn evening. Her shapely fingernails reddened by the blood of squashed lice from the children's shirts.

"In a dream, silently, she had come to him, her wasted body within its loose graveclothes giving off an odour of wax and rosewood, her breath bent over him with mute secret words, a faint odour of wetted ashes.

"Her glazing eyes, staring out of death, to shake and bend my soul. On me alone. The ghostcandle to light her agony. Ghostly light on the tortured face. Her hoarse loud breath rattling in horror, while all prayed on their knees. Her eyes on me to strike me down. . . .

"Ghoul! Chewer of corpses!"

"No, mother. Let me be and let me live."

This passage from James Joyce's novel *Ulysses* captures through words of exceptional beauty the experience of ongoing consciousness. The young teacher, Stephen Dedalus, gazes out of his apartment window at the nearby sea. An image from the waves recalls a song he was singing at home while his mother lay dying in the next room. This evokes painful memories of her deathbed pleadings for him to pray for her. Having turned away from Catholicism, Stephen stubbornly refused. He remembers a dream in which her ghostly corpse returns to haunt him and he struggles in his thoughts between guilt and self-assertion. Notice how Joyce traces the sequence of thought from the perception of external events to remembered scenes and sounds and then, eventually, to a flood of poignant inner memories of dreams; the outside world is ignored and images of a most private nature predominate.

In this chapter we shall look at the continuous flow of conscious thought. Just as the cognitive system involves processing information from external sources, it also involves attending to, organizing, and reacting to material drawn from long-term memory. Differences in personality styles are seen not only in how we deal with external information but how we attend to our *images*, or mental reproductions of external events, and to those elaborations of memories or creations of possible future events we call *daydreams*. We shall also examine the role of states of consciousness in personality organization. These states range from extreme alertness or vigilance through the intriguing phenomenon of sharply restricted consciousness called *hypnosis* and the states of drowsiness or sleep when we experience reveries and nocturnal dreams.

IMAGERY

Memory provides the content from which we construct the plans, daydreams, fantasies, and nightdreams that are the special features of private experience. But human memory itself is derived from at least two kinds of information stored in our brains: (1) the words or concepts into which we organize what we see and hear and (2) the images or more concrete representations of those visual and auditory experiences. *Imagery* is the remarkable capacity we have for duplicating, in some roughly analogous form, the sights, sounds, smells, touches, tastes, and even body movements we experience through our sense organs. If you look intently at a chair and then quickly look away at a blank wall, you can usually "reproduce" that chair when it is not in sight, even though your image of it may be fuzzier and less easy to hold in your mind's eye than a photographic reproduction. A few people do have what is called *eidetic* imagery, which enables them to "see" images with photographic clarity, but most people vary in the vividness and controllability of their imagery.

You will recall from Chapter 9 that our eyes move as we scan an object. When we try to imagine an object or a picture, photographic studies demonstrate that we also try to duplicate our eye-movement patterns (see Figure 10-1). Since the chances are very small that two people would scan a scene with identical eye-movement patterns, it is unlikely that their efforts to imagine the scene later would yield exactly the same images. Thus, as we move from direct perception to imagery we open up many possibilities for human variation in private experience.

The Nature of Imagery

There is considerable controversy among cognitive psychologists about whether images are like photographs or audiotape recordings or whether they are vague mental concepts or wordlike representations. The evidence indicates that images do have a special sensory quality; that is, auditory images are processed by the ear mechanisms and brain areas that process externally generated sounds, and visual images use the brain pathways of the ocular system. Nevertheless, images are rather different from what the camera or tape recorder produces.

Great modern artists portray not just the literal details of a scene that most people will agree are there, but the *quality* of the experience, the imagery of it that remains after we look away or that returns later on when we try to remember what we saw.

Paintings such as Picasso's *Guernica* (see Figure 10-2) may be more accurate representations of imagery than the realistic paintings that we all find so much easier to understand. Compare the eye movements in Figure 10-1 with *Guer-*

FIGURE 10-1
Three Ways of Looking at a Face

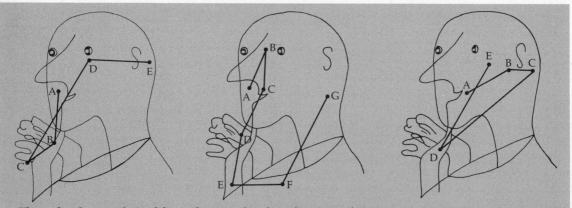

These sketches are derived from photographs of eye fixations of three persons inspecting the same line drawing of a face. Note that the eye-fixation path starting with A follows a different course for each. Studies of imagery suggest that mental reproductions show a similar path. Clearly, we all take in very different features of a stimulus right from the start, a fact that allows for great variation in our recall and imagination processes.

(Modified from Noton and Stark, 1971)

10 • DREAMS, HYPNOSIS, AND THE STREAM OF CONSCIOUSNESS

FIGURE 10-2
Guernica (1937), by Pablo Picasso

In this painting, Picasso sought to capture the experience of the bombing of the town of Guernica during the Spanish Civil War. The painting is not photographically literal. Picasso has reproduced the way someone who was there might remember the scene, with the fragmented details and the emotional horror that are part of the imagery of the event. In a sense, the painting is more "realistic" than any photograph because it is closer to what we would see in our mind's eye and what we would feel.

nica. You can see that Picasso caught the way in which your eyes might have traveled in witnessing that terrible bombing of a peaceful village. In thinking back on this incident, you would not recall it with the kind of literal detail of a photograph but rather in terms of scattered eye movements that had scanned the scene rapidly. Your thoughts would also revive the *emotional impact* of the bombing. Suppose you were trying to recall the bombing in the daytime with your eyes open. Then there would be competition between new material in your physical environment impinging on the retina and the "old" material from long-term memory. Consequently, your daytime imagery would probably have a paler, less vivid, and less representational quality than a photograph of the bombing. Your imagery would probably be more like *Guernica*, a representation of the experiences of that event rather than a cinematic reproduction of it, images of partial figures, distorted and twisted, all conveying a sense of horror and fear.

The Usefulness of Imagery

Even if images are fuzzier and less controllable than audio- or video-tape recordings, at times they do have distinct advantages over words in helping us retrieve past events. We have already noted that visualizing an event may

---

IMAGERY

recapture the emotional component of the experience. Simply thinking the words "I saw the bombing of the city of Guernica" does not convey the emotional punch of a visual image. There is considerable evidence from clinical work that patients express stronger positive or negative emotions when they imagine scenes than when they verbally sum them up (Singer, 1974). Thus, the imagery system is useful in recapturing the feel or flavor of our experience, and our most efficient learning occurs when we combine verbal encoding with imagery encoding.

Research by Peter Sheehan (1972) supports the view that imagery encoding helps the learning process. He conducted studies of *incidental learning*—that is, absorbing information without trying to *learn* and not expecting to need it later. Sheehan showed that when people are exposed to stimuli with instructions either just to name them or else to generate images of them, without realizing they would later be tested, the stimuli dealt with through imagery were better recalled.

Of special interest from the standpoint of personality is the evidence that persons who believe their imagery is vivid do better on such tests of unexpected recall of events. Sheehan used a questionnaire designed to determine how people differ in their self-ratings of vividness of visual, auditory, or olfactory imagery. High raters in vividness scored better in experiments on incidental learning. Exposed to a series of words, for example, some of which they expected to have to learn while others were not supposed to be learned, they apparently used imagery in mentally processing all the words they saw and scored higher on the incidental items than those who reported less vivid imagery. Although not much is yet known about how people develop the tendency for vividly imagining things or why some people cultivate this tendency more than others, it is known that imagery can be useful in producing effective and emotionally intense memories.

Imagery and "Reality" When we are producing imagery, our attention to this internal world may interfere with our ability to detect external stimuli. How we process information from the environment may, in part, be influenced by the fact that we enter new situations with anticipations that themselves involve pictures or sounds drawn from long-term memory. Here we come close to the ticklish philosophical question of how we know what is "real" and how we separate our expectations from the realities "out there." Sydney Segal and her collaborators (1972) carried out an important series of experiments, adapted from a method developed by Perky (1910). Segal's experiments call for the subject to look into a white plastic cone, which produces the effect of a homogeneous visual field and minimizes extraneous visual stimulation (see Figure 10-3). At the point of the cone, where the subject's eyes are focused, the subject is asked to imagine as vividly as possible a picture, such as a red tomato or a yellow banana. Unknown to the subject, a slide projector flashes a picture at the same fixation point. Sometimes the photograph is of the same object that the subject is trying to visualize and sometimes it is a picture of a geometric shape, such

FIGURE 10-3
Studying the Perky Phenomenon

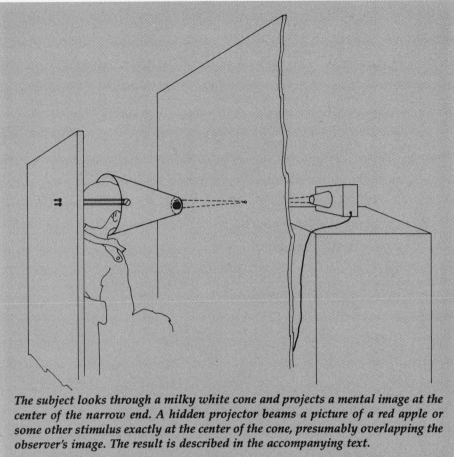

The subject looks through a milky white cone and projects a mental image at the center of the narrow end. A hidden projector beams a picture of a red apple or some other stimulus exactly at the center of the cone, presumably overlapping the observer's image. The result is described in the accompanying text.

(From Segal, 1972)

as a triangle. Surprisingly often, observers do not notice that an externally generated signal has been flashed at the same point that they are imagining the red tomato or yellow banana. When we imagine an object, we may be literally interfering with our ability to perceive what is "really there" in front of us.

Segal carried out numerous experiments to find the conditions under which this blocking of external signals by personal imagery is most effective. Lying on one's back yields a stronger effect than sitting up, for example (a result that supports the psychoanalytic use of the couch to encourage patients to produce strong imagery). Segal also explored the ways in which external signals, even though not consciously noticed, can influence an image. A woman instructed to imagine the New York City skyline, while unknown to her a red tomato was flashed on the fixation point, reported that she imagined the skyline at sunset against a fiery red sky.

Reality, Segal proposed, is essentially a probability decision. Largely from circumstantial clues, a central "operator" in our cognitive system makes an initial guess or decision as to the reality of an experience.

> *On the basis of this decision, further data may be processed; but the data are probably processed more rapidly and effectively if they confirm the initial guess. . . . Thus, if the experience is inferred to be internal, one may decide to disregard it totally (especially if in a situation of danger) or one may decide to follow it through (if one is more relaxed or if an experimenter has urged one to describe her experiences). If the experience is inferred to be external, one usually reacts to it behaviorally by defining it more fully or by some approach or avoidance response* (Segal, 1972, p. 96).

Some people, on the basis of factors as yet little understood, are inclined to pay attention to their own imagery more than other people and to value it more highly. Fusella (1972) used Segal's procedure to study individual differences in separation of one's own imagery from externally generated pictures. He found, first of all, that subjects who rated their imagery to be especially vivid as they were imagining scenes against the fixation point of the cone were significantly less likely to detect any external cues. He had already measured the subject's inner attentiveness (their involvement with their own thoughts) and their proclivity for vivid and enjoyable daydreaming. Individuals who scored high on both these dimensions were more likely to report vivid visual imagery. They also were more likely not to detect the external signal, the picture flashed while they were producing imagery. It thus seems likely that some people prefer to concentrate on private images rather than on the external world. Fusella's results imply that they are willing to risk losing information from the external environment in order to concentrate on this process of elaborating their inner experiences.

To sum up, imagery is a fundamental human capacity. While imagery is rarely as vivid as direct perception, it can help with certain types of learning and memory tasks and with the revival or arousal of strong emotional experiences. As in other aspects of the cognitive system, individual styles play a role in the vividness of imagery and in how much importance people assign to their images as against the information coming from the outside world.

DAYDREAMS AND THE STREAM OF CONSCIOUSNESS

Imagery refers to the reproduction of specific scenes or events—a chair or a friend's face. Terms like *imagination, fantasy, daydream,* and *stream of consciousness* refer to the ongoing flow of sequences of images and thoughts. In the excerpt from *Ulysses* we note perceptions (the sea, the waves), auditory images (the song), visual images (the mother's glass), sequences of self-talk or interior monologue ("No, mother. Let me be and let me live."), and sequences of images forming a fantasy, memory, or recalled dream (such as the mother's corpse). Although William James wrote of the psychological importance of the flow of thought nearly a hundred years ago, systematic research on this process dates only from the late 1950s (Singer, 1966, 1975a, 1975b). Some of this work grew from efforts to study daydreams and fantasies. In popular usage, daydreaming was wishful, somewhat fanciful thought of future events or of make-believe settings. When investigators began collecting samples of fantasies and daydreams, it became clear that such phenomena were better defined as *shifts of attention* away from an immediate physical or mental task toward material derived from long-term memory—that is, they were regular features of the stream of consciousness (Freud, 1907/1962; Klinger, 1971; Pope and Singer, 1978a; Singer, 1966, 1975a, 1975b).

Between 1910 and 1960, when behaviorism dominated American psychology, ongoing thought and fantasy were scarcely studied because psychologists could not find objective, measurable ways to capture these phenomena of the private personality. True, Freud and Jung had made such experiences more accessible with their techniques of free association and active imagination, but researchers still had to depend on the possibly biased report of a therapist about a patient's fantasies. With the development of the projective methods of personality assessment (Chapter 7), psychologists began to study waking fantasy more actively, because they could score and analyze responses to inkblots or to ambiguous pictures.

Methods for Studying Daydreams and Fantasies

Projective Techniques   As indicated in Chapter 7, the Thematic Apperception Test (TAT) lent itself especially well to studies of recurrent fantasies that seemed to have motivational importance. A person who told stories that emphasized achievement or aggression could be studied in other situations to determine if such fantasies were related to overt behavior or if, as a Jungian might suggest, the fantasies reflected the opposite trend from the way the person acted overtly. Extensive research (Klinger, 1971) has made it clear that the relationship is a direct one; the more fantasy themes expressing a certain motive, the greater the tendency for a person to engage in direct action in keeping with those themes. McClelland and his collaborators have pointed up the predictive value of *achievement* fantasies in studies of enterprising behavior (McClelland, 1961; McClelland and others, 1972). They found that people who consistently responded to TAT-like materials with stories about striving to succeed at tasks or to pursue careers do indeed show similar tendencies in their daily lives. They also found that men who tell TAT stories with themes involving power motivation or fear of domination by others are likely to be heavy drinkers.

When Hermann Rorschach developed his psychodiagnostic projective method, he found that persons who saw more human figures, especially active figures, in the ambiguous shapes of the inkblots were likely to be imaginative in thought but inhibited in action. Subsequently, extensive research has demonstrated that persons whose Rorschach responses include several of these human movement (M) responses tend to be more deliberate or controlled in the way they move and also to be more reflective, fanciful, purposeful, and creative in their thought processes (Singer and Brown, 1977). These results are found in groups as diverse as mentally retarded children and adults; normal children, adolescents, and adults; and schizophrenic patients in hospitals. Frequent M-responders also recall more dreams and experience more frequent daydreams. Persons who give few human-movement responses are more likely to be physically aggressive and impulsive in motor activity (Singer and Brown, 1977).

Such differences are exemplified in a "fun" study carried out by Meltzoff and Litwin (1956). They asked people to listen to a Spike Jones laughing record in which there is continuous laughter that leads most listeners eventually to crack up with laughter. When subjects were encouraged to listen silently without reacting, those who had showed few M responses in their Rorschach scores were much more likely to break down and start laughing sooner than those who showed a frequent pattern of M responses. The Rorschach "introversives" thus did indeed seem better able to control their overt emotions and motor reactions.

TAT stories can also be scored for general imaginative tendencies, not just motivational themes. For example, in response to a card showing a boy looking at a violin, one person might describe only the visible details of the picture: "A boy sitting near a table staring at a violin." Another person might mention the boy's thoughts, his parents, his violin teacher, thus *transcending* what is actually shown in the picture. By scoring transcendance in the TAT cards, psychologists can obtain an estimate of the imaginative tendency of an individual, the inclination to invent a plot for a static scene. TAT transcendance scores correlate with other measures of imagination, such as the projection of human movement ("two men dueling") onto the Rorschach inkblots or scores from questionnaires and self-reports of daydreaming and imaginative attitudes.

Questionnaires: Styles of Daydreaming   Several investigators have begun asking persons to describe their daydreams and to answer direct questions about their inner lives. These responses can be organized into questionnaires so that large numbers of persons can be studied and their responses analyzed statistically. In this way psychologists can gain an indication of the range, frequency, and patterning of daydreaming or related inner experiences in the normal population. An example of such a questionnaire is the Imaginal Processes Inventory (IPI) in which persons indicate the relative frequency of occurrence of a daydream or a pattern of behavior related to daydreaming (Singer and

Antrobus, 1963, 1972; Huba, Aneshensel, and Singer, 1981). Responses to this questionnaire, along with other measures of personality or attitude and behavior sampling approaches, will eventually provide better information about the structural relationships between frequency of daydreaming and between patterns of daydreams and other personality characteristics. Generally, three major forms of daydreaming emerge from these questionnaires: positive- constructive fantasies, guilty-dysphoric (hostile or fearful) fantasies, and poor attentional control (difficulty in sustaining a stream of fantasies) (Segal, Huba, and Singer, 1980).

Administration of the questionnaires, sometimes supplemented by interviews, to thousands of people show that practically everybody reports that they daydream every day. Daydreams such as "I am held in the arms of a warm and loving person who satisfies all my needs" are reported as relatively frequent by more than ninety percent of respondents. Daydreaming is essentially a normal phenomenon in the sense that it is commonly reported by people once they think about it.

Sex differences in daydreaming are not great with respect to frequency, but they do show up in relation to content and some structural characteristics. Women are somewhat more likely to report daydreaming about personal appearance, grooming, and clothes or desire for affiliation and ties to others. Women are also more willing to admit to fanciful types of daydreaming, those more removed from day-to-day reality. Men are more likely to report heroic or athletic-achievement daydreams; they also show a pattern of hostile-aggressive fantasies, or of daydreams associated with feelings of guilt and self-recrimination. Daydreaming is at its peak in adolescence but does not really drop off sharply through the years; research by Giambra (1974) shows that the elderly have a good deal of positive fantasy.

Segal, Huba, and Singer (1980) administered the IPI to college students from Yale University and Murray State University to examine the relationship of drug and alcohol use to daydreaming. They found that those who used considerable amounts of alcohol, marijuana, or multiple drugs, showed no differences in the factor patterns from those who did not. In other words, drug use did not, in itself, restructure the private cognitive experience that individuals reported. Contrary to popular stereotypes, students who used *hard* drugs—heroine, cocaine, and LSD—were not interested in enhancing and elaborating their private experience. Rather they seemed to be externalizers or *sensation-seekers* (Chapter 8), individuals looking for new experiences from the environment, not for elaborations of their own inner thoughts (Zuckerman, 1979).

Rodin and Singer (1977) measured daydreaming in their study of overweight young men as compared with normal-weight men. The study is relevant to an assumption that some people gain weight because they cannot resist food when it is put in front of them; they are not responding to internally derived hunger signals but to external cues and their inability to resist visual stimulation. The overweight subjects did not differ from normal-weight subjects in scores on positive daydreaming or future planning. The overweight subjects did, however, report less visual imagery in their daydreaming than did the normal-weight individuals. They thus had less experience in privately visualizing incidents and seemed more vulnerable to external visual cues. This result was supported when it was found that overweight subjects more frequently shifted their eyes or shut them completely if asked a thought-provoking question when they were facing an interviewer. Without skills in private visualization and dependent on external cues, the overweight men had difficulty in thinking, and the difficulty was compounded if they had to search their memory while confronted with the powerful attraction of the interviewer's face.

Thought-Sampling Methods   While questionnaires are useful, they primarily measure traitlike, long-term predispositional tendencies to daydream. Psychologists have become increasingly interested in tapping into the ongoing flow of consciousness, much as James Joyce and others have done in literary works. Two approaches have been devised that capture spontaneous thought sequences in a way that permits hypothesis-testing and quantitative analysis. One is a laboratory procedure in which the experimenter controls all forms of environmental input by putting the subjects in a sound- and lightproof room, where they are asked to detect signals, such as rapidly presented tones. The subjects are interrupted periodically to determine if they are experiencing any thoughts unrelated to the task of detecting the signals. The second procedure keeps subjects in a more natural situation, sitting or walking about in a room. A beeper, the kind that physicians often carry to signal them to call their answering service, is attached to the subject and goes off at random intervals. The subjects then record whatever they are doing and thinking, and they may be asked to rate such thoughts for vividness of imagery, personal importance, and other characteristics.

Findings from several laboratory studies demonstrate that even when people are processing auditory signals at the rate of one per second and are performing accurately, they still show a great deal of daydreaming and other thinking. The experimenter can decrease such stimulus-independent and task-irrelevant thoughts by increasing the complexity of the task or imposing a financial penalty for missed signals. Task-irrelevant thought can be increased by allowing more time between signals or by exposing subjects to frightening or emotionally arousing radio broadcasts or films before the task (Antrobus, Singer and Greenberg, 1966; Antrobus and others, 1970; Horowitz and Wilner, 1976). Initially high-daydream oriented subjects do not differ from subjects with low-daydream scores in the accuracy of their signal detection. As time goes on, however, the high-scoring daydreamers seem to find the simple-minded task less interesting than their own thoughts, and they show not only an increase in stimulus-independent thoughts but also a gradual decrease in the accuracy of their detections. This is the case despite the fact that they are motivated by financial rewards to perform effectively. The subjects predisposed to daydreaming prefer their own thought world even at the cost of losing some money (Antrobus, Coleman and Singer, 1967).

Some subjects assign a high priority to their own private thoughts and use them as a means of distraction or self-entertainment. Pope (1978) found that subjects who report frequent daydreaming on the Singer-Antrobus IPI scales (1972) engage in longer private sequences of thought unrelated to the physical environment. He also found that persons who are field independent in their cognitive style (Chapter 9) are less likely to focus their thoughts on the immediate present. They also unreel longer skeins of fantasy before changing a mental sequence.

Methods for sampling thoughts in naturally occurring situations lack the precision and control of laboratory procedures, but they have the advantage of greater "realism." They also permit more extensive sampling of fantasies from a person's life than is possible in a signal-detection booth (Hurlburt, 1976; Klinger, 1978, 1980; Pope, 1978). According to Csikszentmihalyi (1975) surgeons spend at least one-third of their time during actual operations in daydreaming about "wine, women, and song"—not unlike the doctors in the TV series "M*A*S*H." Pope (1978) found that persons who are reclining or sitting still, or who are alone have longer thought sequences and more thoughts relating to past or future than do persons moving around the room, sitting upright, or—especially for men—in the company of another person.

Determinants of Thought

Since our private personality is manifested to us primarily through our awareness of our daydreams and stream of consciousness, it is worthwhile trying to ascertain what factors produce our continuous flow of images and interior conversations. Exploring the determinants of this continuously changing stream is a new challenge for psychologists.

Variation and Novelty　Psychoanalytic theory emphasizes that daydreaming and, indeed, a good deal of conscious thought reflects either unfulfilled sexual and aggressive drives or the attempt to inhibit awareness of these drives through intellectualization, rationalization, or other defense mechanisms. But research evidence suggests that ongoing thought plays a broader role in human experience. For one thing, there is reason to believe that the human brain is continuously generating stimulation. When we are awake, we have to learn to ignore this inner environment in order to pay attention to our physical environment, to avoid missing steps on a staircase or to notice an oncoming automobile. If, however, we are in a waiting room with nothing to do or if, like Stephen Dedalus, we are gazing idly out on a familiar scene, we become more aware of the spontaneous activity of our brain.

Current Concerns　Eric Klinger (1978, 1980) explored the role of *current concerns* as a determiner of the stream of consciousness during waking as well as the sleeping thought of dreams. Where Freud emphasized unresolved unconscious conflict as a determiner of thought, Klinger's questionnaires showed that tasks undertaken but not completed and conscious intentions not yet carried out popped up consistently in spontaneous thoughts or nightdreams. While some of the current concerns reflected serious conflicts—for example, worries about sexual potency—most were simply unfinished business, such as bills to be paid, exams to be studied for, arrangements to be made about dates.

Klinger (1978) also carried out a study in which the subjects were fed two different messages, one into the left ear and one into the right ear (dichotic listening). The subjects were instructed to attend only to material coming into the right ear. When material presented to the left ear touched on what Klinger had previously established as each subject's major current concerns, the subjects switched to processing only the material from the left ear or else they allowed it to intrude and mix with the material coming into the right ear. They did not do this if material presented to the left was unrelated to current concerns.

Prior Stress and Recurring Thought   If someone is in a confusing or ambiguous situation or in one that is emotionally arousing, thoughts about those situations will recur later in consciousness (Horowitz and Wilner, 1976; Zachary, 1978). A complex experiment by Klos and Singer (1981) with college freshmen examined how longstanding conflicts and more immediate or recently occurring situations combined to determine the ongoing contents of consciousness. The hypothesis was that if young adults relive in imagery an unpleasant struggle with their parents, especially one that is unresolved, such an event would be likely to stay in their thoughts. The researchers proposed that when uncompleted situations cropped up in the subject's thoughts, they would most likely be accompanied by unpleasant and high levels of emotional arousal. In addition, it was proposed that those students who had conflict with their parents would be most susceptible to remembering unresolved, nonconstructive conflicts simulated in a laboratory setting.

In the experiments, the college freshmen answered questionnaires about relationships with their parents and were also interviewed about their current concerns. They were then assigned to one of six experimental conditions in which they vividly imagined and acted out either a problem-solving situation with a parent (for example, how to arrange to help someone) or a *confrontation* with a parent (for example, a conflict over use of the car). The confrontations were either *constructive*, with the parent showing understanding and concern, or *nonconstructive*, with the parent being critical, suspicious, and not allowing full expression of the son's or daughter's position. The situations were also *resolved* or *unresolved*; that is, half of the problem-solving and half of the two types of confrontation ended up with some clear outcome, while the other half ended with the issue unsettled. After simulating the appropriate imagery and rating the different emotions they felt, each participant sat quietly for a while. For the next twenty minutes each was interrupted about every 45 seconds to report on spontaneous thoughts. These thought-samples were tape recorded and later rated by judges, who were unfamiliar with the hypotheses or experimental conditions, for similarity to the particular conflict situation in which the subject had participated (see Figure 10-4).

FIGURE 10-4
Adolescent Stress and Parental Confrontation

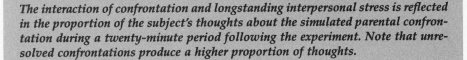

The interaction of confrontation and longstanding interpersonal stress is reflected in the proportion of the subject's thoughts about the simulated parental confrontation during a twenty-minute period following the experiment. Note that unresolved confrontations produce a higher proportion of thoughts.

(From Klos and Singer, 1981)

The results point up how these various factors come together to increase the likelihood that thoughts about a recent experience (the simulated mutual problem-solving or the constructive-nonconstructive confrontation) will recur later. The unresolved situation in the problem-solving simulation is more likely to be thought about than a resolved one (a confirmation of the "unfinished business" effect). Notice, however, that *nonconstructive* confrontation with parents is *most* likely to come back into thoughts, resolved or unresolved. Ratings of emotions during the subsequent thought stream of the subjects in the two confrontation situations, especially those that were nonconstructive, also reflected their *anger* at parents. Current concerns also composed a significant part of the ongoing thoughts of the subjects. The major determinant of whether thoughts about the confrontation recurred was the longstanding parental relationship; those students who had numerous problems with their parents were

most likely to show recurrent thoughts about the simulations whether or not they were resolved, but especially if it had been a nonconstructive confrontation. Imagine then how painful Stephen's conflict with his dying mother must have been and how often it must have flashed back in his thoughts.

Constructive Possibilities of Daydreaming

On the basis of recent research, daydreams are seen as having adaptive possibilities. At least, they add a spice and interest to our lives as we go about our routine business or as we find quiet moments of solitude. More than that, however, they offer valuable clues to the unfinished business of our lives, not only immediate day-to-day tasks but also our major goals and value systems. We try, in the press of affairs, to avoid thinking about these goals and trends, pay too much attention to new external stimuli, or "lose ourselves" in television programs. But somehow our brains keep processing and reprocessing material. If we learn to "tune in" on the images in our free-floating consciousness, we will see important elements of the major interests and desires that characterize our lives. In addition, attention to such processes may heighten our sensitivity and empathy for the feelings of others (Frank, 1978). Daydreams may also give us a novel or humorous perspective that can reduce some of the distress we all feel in the natural course of living (Singer and Switzer, 1980).

ALTERNATE STATES OF CONSCIOUSNESS: HYPNOSIS AND DREAMING

Daydreams are facets of daily conscious experience. Other states in which we process information are seemingly more mysterious or intriguing because they appear to involve alternate states of consciousness. In particular, *hypnosis* and *nocturnal dreaming* have been relatively well studied scientifically and have important implications for understanding personality variation.

Think for a moment of some of the states of consciousness in your life. You can easily identify the extreme variations in alertness—the hypervigilance when taking a tough exam or playing for the winning point in a tennis game to the vague, confused, drifting quality of attention and thought when you are drowsy and about to fall asleep.

Perhaps you can identify other states of consciousness. Many young adults have drunk enough alcohol to be aware that their motor coordination is poor, their speech is slurred, and their thinking and communication confused. Being high on marijuana produces other effects, but there certainly is a sense of being in a different state of consciousness from ordinary waking life.

Have you ever been hypnotized? If not, perhaps you have become so intensely absorbed in a book or music that you have lost touch with your surroundings, forgotten to turn off the kettle on the stove, or believed that you were the character in the book or the song. That absorption is very close to a hypnotic state. Many people take up meditation, and once "into it" feel as if their consciousness has been altered. Or perhaps one day walking alone in the woods or by the seashore, you felt a profound excitement, a closeness to God or nature.

These variations in consciousness have often been believed to have mystical overtones, but psychologists are now studying them with the same tools of scientific analysis they use for investigating perception or conscious problem-solving.

Hypnosis

Hypnosis is one of the most mysterious of all human phenomena. It was discovered in the latter half of the eighteenth century by the Austrian physician Franz Anton Mesmer (1734–1815). Mesmer, whose name became a synonym for hypnosis (*mesmerism*), believed that he could cure persons with various ailments by drawing impurities from them with magnets. He found that people under his suggestions became seemingly paralyzed and compliant with his directions as he went over their bodies with magnets. Mesmer's emphasis on electricity was soon disproved by French scientists, but after more than a century and a half during which hypnosis was mainly regarded as a trick of traveling charlatans or mystics, hypnosis became a subject for careful and scientific research. Dozens of well-conducted studies have demystified hypnosis and defined its relationship to the cognitive and affective systems.

What are the characteristics of hypnosis? After instructions by a hypnotist—who doesn't need the old-fashioned paraphernalia of wands, mirrors, or waving hands; actually, hypnosis can even be self-administered—subjects show the following behavior:

1. *Focused attention.* Hypnotized persons focus solely on the hypnotist's voice or on a part of their own bodies, or on an image, as suggested by the hypnotist.
2. *Passivity.* Hypnotized persons do not initiate any activity without the hypnotist's suggestion.

3. *Acceptance of unreality and suggestibility.* Hypnotized persons act as if they believe the hypnotist's improbable statements and do not ask for verification. Under hypnosis, people often act in ways that seem outlandish, such as imitating an animal or attempting to swat an imaginary buzzing fly. Although under extremely complex circumstances hypnotized persons may be led to act in ways that could be illegal or harmful, they almost always resist such suggestions (Levitt and Chapman, 1979).

4. *Amnesia.* Hypnotized persons often forget their hypnotic experience after they emerge from the state, especially if the hypnotist suggests posthypnotic amnesia.

Most of us are familiar with hypnotic demonstrations of individuals being unable to unclasp their hands or holding their arms out rigidly. Careful research shows that almost all these demonstrations, once considered evidence of the superpowers or mysterious qualities of the hypnotic trance, can be duplicated by individuals who are simulating hypnosis—in other words, by persons playacting the part or merely by people who are encouraged to perform these strange and seemingly "superhuman" acts without reference to hypnosis (Barber, 1979). In general, most investigators of hypnosis no longer view it as a distinct state; they prefer to consider it as part of a continuum with other forms of intense absorption, concentrated thought, vividness of imagery (Barber, 1979; Sheehan, 1979), memory patterns (Cooper, 1979), or role enactment (Sarbin, 1972).

A major issue in personality psychology involves the ease with which some persons enter into hypnosis, while others seem resistant or "unsuggestible." Until Hilgard's contributions (1965), many people believed that hypnotically susceptible people were weak personalities—hysterical types who were naturally suggestible and who could be swayed by the strong personality of a more dominant individual. Hilgard and his collaborators demonstrated that under comfortable circumstances almost anyone, if cooperative, can attain some degree of hypnosis.

Once hypnosis was viewed as normal, attitudes shifted. "Good" hypnotic subjects are now described not as being weak-willed but as having special abilities such as vivid imagery (Hilgard, 1979; Sheehan, 1979). It is quite possible that at a time when being hypnotized was seen as a sign of *weakness* or *subservience*—as it was represented in movies or in fictional characters like the sinister Dr. Svengali—many imaginative persons resisted hypnotic suggestions by using their imagery to distance themselves from the voice of the hypnotist. Once hypnotic susceptibility was regarded as a skill, such individuals may have used these same capacities to enter into the state.

Hypnotic susceptibility does show some characteristics of a persisting trait. A correlation of .60 between scores for hypnotic susceptibility was obtained when college students were followed up ten years after the initial testing (Morgan, Johnson, and Hilgard, 1974). Persons who become deeply absorbed in a book, generate vivid fantasies about the characters, or show more daydreaming and imagery tendencies, including having imaginary playmates in childhood, are likely to be good hypnotic subjects (Barber and Glass, 1962; Crawford, 1982; Sarbin and Coe, 1972; Sheehan, 1979). Josephine Hilgard (1979) interviewed hundreds of individuals in depth about their life experiences and then related the interview data to measures of hypnosis on the Stanford Group Hypnotic Susceptibility Scale. She found that persons with an intense capacity for appreciating or becoming absorbed in nature or in reading or art are good subjects (See Table 10-1).

Little is yet known of how hypnotic susceptibility develops. Morgan, Johnson, and Hilgard (1974) did find that identical twins show greater similarities in hypnotic susceptibility than fraternal twins. This indicates a possible constitutional basis for hypnotizability. Evidence that hypnotic susceptibility is related to greater preference for activities related to the right hemisphere of the brain also suggests some biological predisposition (Bakan, 1969; Bowers, 1979; Sackeim and Gur, 1978).

The ability to lose oneself in a book or movie is often positively correlated with the ability to undergo hypnosis.

TABLE 10-1

Ratings of Involvement in Samples of High
and Low Hypnotizable Subjects (Ss)

	Percent of Ss with high involvement	
Involvement areas	High susceptible (N-42)	Low susceptible[a] (N-15)
Savoring of sensory experiences	93	20
Drama	79[b]	20[c]
Reading	76[b]	13[c]
Daydreams-child	74	13
Daydreams- adult	36	7
Mental space travelers	45	0
Physical space travelers	33	0
Creativity	26	13
Religion	19	13

[a]High involvement was defined as a rating of six or seven on a seven-point scale.
[b]Of Ss showing reading and/or drama, which are closely related areas, thirty-nine of forty-two, or 93%, showed one or both; two showed reading only, three drama only. Only one case was low in both areas. On one case the information was missing.
[c]Of Ss showing reading and/or drama, which are closely related areas, four of fifteen, or 27%, showed one or both; one showed reading only, two showed drama only, and one showed both areas.

(From J. R. Hilgard, 1979)

Childhood experiences of persons differing in hypnotic susceptibility may play a significant role. Josephine Hilgard (1979) found evidence that a determinant of adult hypnotizability is a pattern of early childhood fantasy (see Table 10-1). Sometimes such fantasy helps a child cope—by tuning out a punitive parent, for example—but the child often daydreams or plays with imaginary companions for their own sake. Also, parents who themselves are imaginative or esthetically inclined seem to stimulate such fantasy in their children (Chapter 16).

To sum up, hypnosis is possible for all human beings. Because it was discovered by Mesmer in a medical framework, it has been regarded too much as a clinical or abnormal phenomenon. In actuality, however, the capacity for intense absorption and for temporarily shifting attention from external cues to one's own images or the voice of a hypnotist and the images that a hypnotist suggests may be a cognitive skill or simply a preferred information-processing style. The ability to use imagery intensely or to enact a role may account for the value of hypnosis in helping people withstand pain or to engage in behavior requiring remarkable self-control or even control of autonomic or "involuntary" bodily actions. Barber (1979; Barber and Wilson, 1979) demonstrated that conscious imagery can produce many of the effects usually associated with hypnosis, including physiological changes. Hypnosis and imagery have both been helpful to many people in coping with pain, changing moods, or shifting attitudes. The day is past when we need to fear hypnosis or view it as evil or sinister.

Dreams have long been the most glamorous, mysterious, and intriguing of the phenomena that characterize the private personality. We can take a step toward demystifying them by setting them into the framework of the cognitive system. At one extreme, the cognitive system is designed to process information coming in through our senses from the external environment. The imagery function of the system duplicates this external material, but it also draws on material from long-term memory. Daydreams or fantasies derive chiefly from this inner environment. Hypnosis drastically restricts both external and internal stimulation by focusing all the subject's attention on the words of the hypnotist. The subject then elaborates on these instructions through private imagery. Dreams are at the other extreme of the continuum—external cues are shut out to a great degree and the stream of consciousness reflects only the activity of the brain's long-term memories. The great developments following the discovery of Kleitman, Aserinsky, and Dement of the sleep cycle and of the association of vivid dream recall with the Stage 1 EEG-REM phase of sleep highlighted the fact that dreaming may be a form of information-processing during a time when chemical changes in the nervous system are establishing a basis for long-term storage of the new learning gleaned during the day.

Dreams and Dreaming

The Relation of Nightdreams to Daydreams   Our nightdreams do indeed have a good deal of continuity with daytime thought (Hall and Nordby, 1972; Klinger, 1971; Singer, 1966). Calvin S. Hall (1956) pioneered in the systematic examination of continuities between waking fantasies and personality characteristics of individuals and the themes that could be identified as occurring regularly in the nightdreams they reported. Persons who are characterized by considerable involvement with their fathers or who score high on measures of authoritarian tendencies are likely to have dreams in which their father figures or kings appear with some regularity (Meer, 1952), and persons who remember a great many dreams are also likely to report a great many daydreams (Singer, 1975a, 1975b). In general, the structural properties and emotions occurring in nightdreams are similar to the characteristics of daydreams as measured by questionnaires (Starker, 1974; Foulkes and Fleisher, 1975).

Styles in Dreaming and Dream Recall   The evidence by now is pretty conclusive that we all carry on some kind of mental activity throughout the night (Arkin, Antrobus, and Ellmann, 1978). Why some people remember dreams more frequently than others is not well understood (Goodenough, 1976). One explanation may relate to how we awaken in the morning. Often our tendency is to shut off the alarm, leap out of bed, and rush to the bathroom. But if we

THE RELATION OF DREAM CONTENT TO RECENT CONSCIOUS THOUGHT

The following dream was reported by a man whose daydreams and daytime thoughts had been studied by a thought-sampling method for several days before the dream:

I am in Canada visiting Bill, a younger former associate of mine. We are on an extremely steep mountain. There are dozens of skiers who are coming down this incline with great speed, often taking long leaps before coming back down to earth. Bill points upwards and says, "Let's keep walking up there and we can get some skis and ski down." I find myself appalled as I see the steepness of the mountain. As we climb higher I become more and more aware that I am not a good enough skier to come down at the rate of other skiers.

I put on some skis and am trying in my slow fashion to cut slowly sideways across the mountain face rather than schussing straight downhill. I notice my friend Bill whizzing by with great confidence. Suddenly, however, he takes a very bad fall and lies in the snow obviously having hurt his leg.

Later I am visiting Bill and another even younger man who now shares an apartment with him. I realize that both Bill and his new roommate have recently had marital problems and are living bachelor lives. I say to them that while I appreciate some of the advantages of bachelorhood I am really quite happy with my own wife after 20 years of marriage.

A surprising number of details from this man's recent waking thoughts turned up in the dream. The dreamer was a middle-aged man who was an executive in a well-established engineering company. He seriously questioned his ability to master the required technology (*to schuss downhill*) as the firm moved into new areas of engineering. He had also been examining in his thoughts the value of his intensive work for the company. He wondered whether he could keep

lie quietly, we are likely to remember our dream and to replay it several times. This replay increases the chances that the dream will be recalled spontaneously later in the day and then perhaps thought about further. People who are inclined not to dwell on their private experiences—the extraverts, field-dependents, short-samplers, and repressors—may be less prone to report dreams simply because they have taken less time to relax and replay their thoughts.

Evidence from sleep-cycle research is quite conclusive in showing that vivid dream material occurs in the Stage 1 EEG-REM phase, beginning at least half an hour after a person has fallen asleep. It was first assumed that the rapid eye movements and dreaming are associated because the dreamer is "looking" at the dream, but this assumption does not hold up on closer scrutiny. Rather, there is evidence (Singer, 1966; Foulkes, Spear and Symonds 1966) that persons who are inclined to be introspective have vivid dreams immediately upon falling asleep without any signs of eye movements. Foulkes reported that persons who are more emotionally stable and psychologically minded—that is, self-examining and curious about interpersonal motivation—produced vivid dreams early in the night, shortly after falling asleep, while persons with emotional disturbance and neurotic tendencies showed their most vivid dreams up the pace, considering his apparently diminishing physical strength and skill.

Several events in recent days had triggered some of these thoughts. In one of them he and his wife had set out on a quiet walk on a marked trail in the woods. They took the wrong path and ended up climbing a mountain; they then had to retrace their steps down a steep incline. Despite what seemed at times an impossible climb, they both emerged none the worse. He had also been watching the Olympic games on television, with many thoughts and conversations about the intensity and determination required for the athletes to reach the levels of skill necessary for international competition.

The man's dreams can be understood as a representation in visual form of a whole series of questions and thoughts that had been going on in his conscious mind. These included intense emotions as well as unfinished business and current concerns. There were fears and doubts associated with the difficulty of maintaining his standards of scientific work as his company moved toward more technological development. This thought brought to mind his former colleague, Bill. Though younger, Bill had always seemed more technically competent, but in recent years he had suffered setbacks at work and in his personal life. A new younger colleague also seems likely to have greater professional skills, but again (and here the dream fades over in a wish, perhaps) the older man can say, "Well, I can still climb that mountain, and I can also say that I have a more fulfilled personal life."

Thus, the symbolism of the dream was probably not created completely within the dream but was already anticipated in the man's daytime thoughts. Usually psychologists do not have daytime records and samples of ongoing thought as in this case. And in a psychotherapy session a patient's associations to a dream are after the fact. The likelihood is that many of our daytime thoughts contain symbolic or allegorical associations, which we may store together and think about further during the day. But the press of daily affairs may prevent us from noticing how much time we spend in self-reflection, and we are therefore surprised by the symbolism and imagery of our dreams.

later in the night during the peak of the rapid-eye-movement phases. This research suggests that personality differences do play some role in the degree of vividness of dream content and in other features of sleep.

Unfinished Business and Current Concerns   Klinger (1977) emphasized the importance of current concerns for understanding both day- and nightdreams. We finish up every day with a whole series of completed tasks and fulfilled anticipations or wishes. But we also have many experiences of incongruities and discrepancies or of unfinished business. Some of these continuing concerns relate to our intentions for that specific day and many more to goals and motives of our lives that can rarely be achieved on any single day. Thus the day's events become part of a broader context. Often in our daytime thoughts we begin to make connections between present events and previous experiences, even though in our concentration on current tasks we do not notice these new associations of thoughts.

Nightdreaming may be a continuation of this daytime mental activity, but it takes place under circumstances in which we are not steering ourselves through a physical and social environment and processing new information through our senses. In our dreams, without the pressure of new information from the external environment, we can elaborate on the unfinished business of the past day and sketch out in more detail the connections we began to see between our day's activities and our more general scheme of goals and motives.

The Visual Language of Dreams   The vivid quality of dreams and their seeming distortions, transformations, and symbolic or metaphoric properties are probably a consequence of the fact that this activity is taking place when only the dreamer's visual or imagery capacities are involved. Freud recognized this in his distinction between two modes of thinking, the *primary* and *secondary* processes. The primary process he related to the primitive, childlike aspects of brain functioning; it is therefore concrete and pictorial in quality. The secondary process is related to abstraction and the higher thinking processes that involve the use of language. This distinction had also been made by the neurologist Hughlings Jackson, whom Freud admired. Jackson (1878) had suggested that the two strains of thought are more like receptive and expressive systems related to right- and left-hemisphere functions of the brain. (Chapter 9).

Research on the dual coding system (Paivio, 1971) and on the distinctions between the adaptive functions of the left and right hemispheres for processing verbal-sequential information, on the one hand, and imagery and emotional content, on the other, suggests that it is not useful to look on the material of a dream as more regressed or primitive. Among the sensory receptors, only the eyes are really shut off from processing external material during sleep. Perhaps this is why the visual medium predominates in almost all dreams. But thinking in "pictures" imposes limitations on the complexity of mental activity that can occur during our sleeping thought.

Presleep Stress and Dream Content   A useful study by Breger, Hunter, and Lane (1971) was an important advance in helping us understand how dreams are formed from the current fears or stresses and daily pressures of life. They studied college students in a sleep laboratory for several nights. By awakening them during the Stage 1 EEG-REM phases of the sleep cycle throughout the night, they obtained sequences of dreams and thus had available much more material, closer to the actual dream period, than is ever available to a psychoanalyst.

In the first two studies, Breger and his co-workers organized a psychotherapy group made up of volunteer students, whose dreams were elicited during sleep periods prior to the therapy sessions. Then, after a participant had been the focus of attention in a session, his or her dreams were obtained on two successive nights and compared with those of the control group, who were going about their day-to-day lives. The therapy sessions proved to be quite stressful, and the participants reported dreams that night and the next night that were characterized by less pleasant interactions, less adequate roles of the dreamers, and unhappier outcomes than occurred in the dreams of the control group.

PERSONALITY AND REM-SLEEP DEPRIVATION

William Dement's important discovery about the sleep cycle indicates that if subjects are awakened whenever they enter Stage 1-REM sleep, they end up deprived of REM sleep for the night. On the nights subsequent to several REM-deprived periods, "rebound" effects appear—that is, during the sleep cycle, subjects will spend more time in Stage 1-REM sleep as if making up for the loss. But personality differences are evident in how strong these rebound effects are. Young adults who showed more tendency to make up for lost "dream time" after REM deprivation were found to be more extraverted, less imaginative, less effective in spatial tasks related to right-hemisphere functioning than subjects equated for IQ who did not show the rebound effect. Presumably those persons whose daily lives are characterized by more fantasy and imagery can continue this process into sleep without necessarily undergoing a special REM period. For the less imaginative person, the REM cycle seems to be more needed to help maintain a psychological balance (Cartwright, 1977).

Breger, Hunter, and Lane went on to study five individuals who were about to undergo major surgery. These individuals were observed in the sleep laboratory on four consecutive nights before the operation and then on three separate nights from a week to five weeks after the operation during a period of good recovery. Personality test data and psychophysiological data were also obtained. The investigators sought to ascertain the meaning of the surgery for the five subjects, its import not only as a generalized stress but how specifically stressful it was for them and what it seemed to imply, such as "helplessness in the hands of others." The dreams of the surgery group were then compared with the dreams of two control subjects who did not undergo surgery.

Statistical analyses were carried out on the content of dreams with great attention paid to issues such as *body image, hostility,* and *castration fears.* This study was somewhat limited because the control group was younger and in good health compared to the surgical group, therefore less preoccupied with physical concerns. Nevertheless, the results indicate that themes related to surgery were incorporated into nightdreams in ways relevant to the meaning of the surgery for each individual. The dreams of the two groups in the post-surgery period were more similar than in the presurgery period, thus supporting the hypothesis that prior stress and current fears do influence dreams directly. Although Freud proposed that dreams are "the royal road to the unconscious," the studies by Breger and his co-workers suggest that dreams also reflect people's conscious daytime worries, fears, and hopes as well as their longstanding psychodynamic trends.

We began this chapter with a sample of stream-of-consciousness writing depicting the ongoing thought of a highly intelligent, sensitive, and poetic young man. Thought samples from many people show the same complex interweaving of perception, imagery, memory, and dream recall that characterize Stephen Dedalus's interior monologue. True, there are stylistic differences in the literary associations, metaphors, and poetic allusions. Two other characters in *Ulysses*, Leopold and Molly Bloom, can be differentiated from each other and from Stephen in their styles of stream of consciousness (Steinberg, 1979). What research and theory in personality show, however, is the inherent continuity for each of us between the various phenomena of our private personalities. The ways we process information from the outside world, reduplicate what we see and hear through imagery, replay memories, or set up potential future acts in our daydreams—these ways are tied to our capacities for intense concentration, even hypnotic susceptibility, and to the mysterious visitations of our nocturnal dreams.

SUMMARY

1. Human memory is derived from at least two kinds of information stored in the brain: (1) words or concepts, and (2) images or concrete representations of what we see or hear. *Imagery* is the capacity for duplicating the sights, sounds, smells, touches, tastes, and body movements we experience through our sense organs. The imagery system is useful in recapturing experiences, especially their feel or flavor, and the most efficient learning occurs with combined verbal and imagery coding.

2. Terms like *imagination, fantasy, daydream,* or *stream of consciousness* refer to the ongoing flow of sequences of images and thoughts. With the development of projective methods, psychologists had a useful technique for studying imagination and daydreams. Recently, investigators have asked people to describe their daydreams, to answer questions about their inner life, and to respond to questionnaires about daydreaming. Almost everyone daydreams every day. Daydreaming often occurs in calm and quiet situations, but it can occur in many others. Men and women do about the same amount of daydreaming, but women's daydreams are more likely to be about personal appearance and desires for affiliation, whereas men's daydreams are about achievement and feelings of guilt, hostility, and aggression. Daydreaming reaches a peak in adolescence, and it does not decrease much in later years.

3. Ongoing thought, or the stream of consciousness, has been measured in the laboratory by having subjects in a light- and soundproof room, requiring them to detect signals, and then interrupting them to ask about their thoughts. Or subjects may be in a natural situation but interrupted randomly by a beeper and at that time asked to record their thoughts. Even when people are rapidly processing auditory signals they daydream a good deal.

4. Because the private personality is evident primarily in daydreams and stream of consciousness, it is important to ascertain what factors produce this continuous flow of images and thoughts. There is reason to believe that the human brain is continuously generating stimulation. Usually we ignore this stimulation in order to attend to the outside world, but especially if we are in a quiet or monotonous situation, we become aware of our thoughts. Current concerns and unfinished business consistently surface in our thoughts.

5. Daydreams can have adaptive value. They are a resource for planning the future and for considering possible courses of action. Thinking of make-believe possibilities stimulates new ideas in work and social relationships.

6. In recent years psychologists have been interested in studying alternate states of consciousness, especially *hypnosis* and *nightdreaming*. Hypnosis is characterized by (1) focused attention, (2) passivity, (3) acceptance of unreality and suggestibility, and (4) amnesia. Most investigators no longer view hypnosis as a distinct state, but rather as a form of intense absorption, concentrated thought, vividness of imagery, and role enactment.

7. Hypnotic susceptibility has some characteristics of a persisting trait. Persons who can become absorbed in books, nature, or art, who daydream and have vivid fantasies are usually good hypnotic subjects. Little is known about how hypnotic susceptibility arises, but it is possible that there is a biological predisposition, and that childhood experiences may foster it. Hypnosis is a possibility for all human beings, and can be considered a cognitive skill or information-processing style.

8. Dreams have long been considered the most glamorous, mysterious, and intriguing of human phenomena. Research during the past several years suggests that dreaming may be a form of information-processing at a time when chemical changes in the nervous system are establishing long-term memories. Nightdreams have a good deal of continuity with daydreams and waking fantasies, and persons who remember many of their dreams also report many daydreams. Also, the structural properties and emotions occurring during nightdreams are similar to the characteristics of daydreams.

9. The vivid symbols of dreams and their seeming distortions, transformations, and symbolic properties probably result from the fact that the visual modality which does not convey abstract information is most active. Like daydreams, nightdreams are often related to current concerns, unfinished business of the day and stressful experiences. Although Freud proposed that dreams are "the royal road to the unconscious," research now indicates that dreams reflect conscious daytime worries, fears, and hopes of people as well as their underlying psychodynamic tendencies.

CHAPTER
11

Belief Systems and the Concept of Self

Que sera, sera.
The future's not ours to see.
Whatever will be, will be.
Que sera, sera.

—from Livingston and Edwards, "Que Sera, Sera"

It matters not how strait the gate,
How charged with punishments the scroll,
I am the master of my fate;
I am the captain of my soul.

—from W. E. Henley, "Invictus"

A fascinating contrast in organized beliefs about the self and the world emerges from the two verse excerpts above, the first a popular song, the second a famous poem. The song accepts fate and external circumstances as the prime causes of whatever happens to us, and it implicitly advises us to flow along acceptingly. The Henley stanza describes the opposite orientation: Our lives are determined by our own personal characteristics, not by chance, or fate, or accidents or nature, or the activities of other persons.

Of special significance for personality psychology are the beliefs we hold about ourselves. The concept of a "self" has long intrigued personality theorists. A self, of course, is not an object, a visible structure like a heart or a brain. It is a construct, a hypothesized feature of personality that can be useful in psychology because people hold many different beliefs about their "inner selves," or about the boundaries between self and others, or about the power or vulnerability of the self. The self is, to a great extent, a creation of human beings in their effort to assign differentiated meaning to experiences. People say things like "I'm sorry I have to let you go from this job. It's not personal; we just need to reduce our costs." The "it's not personal" reflects a widespread belief that there is indeed an inner self.

In our efforts to make sense of the world we attribute causality or blame to events or to others' actions. We may develop *styles* of attribution that reflect systems of belief about how things work in the world. Our belief systems form both anticipations of what may happen in the future and explanations for what happened in the past. From the standpoint of personality, then, variations in behavior may reflect consistent patterns of belief systems. In this chapter, we shall first look at one style of belief, the attribution of causality to our own actions versus attribution to influences over which we have no control. This style of belief—called *locus of control*—was proposed by Julian Rotter (Chapter 4), and it has been a topic of considerable research. We shall then look at how belief systems interact not only to produce interpretations of events but also to serve as guides for action.

LOCUS OF CONTROL: WHAT DO WE RELY ON?

In his research, Rotter (1966) proposed that individuals differ systematically in the degree to which they believe that their actions are self-determined rather than influenced by external circumstances. He developed a set of inventory items to measure what he named locus of control, or source of reinforcement. Suppose a person consistently attributes success or failure (positive or negative reinforcing circumstances) to luck, fate, chance, or the influence of powerful people. Or suppose the person believes that success or failure cannot be predicted because the environment is so complex. Such an individual would score on Rotter's inventory as someone whose locus of control is *external*. On the other hand, someone whose answers indicate a belief that successful or unsuccessful outcomes are determined by one's *own* actions or by one's own personal characteristics (such as intelligence, persistence, wisdom) would obtain a score favoring an *internal* locus of control.

Rotter's questionnaire, known as the Internal-External (I-E) Locus of Control scale, has emerged in the last twenty years as one of the most widely used of all personality measurement instruments.

Do subjects scoring at different ends of the I-E scale differ in their achievement orientation—that is, in the efforts students are willing to put forth to get high grades for example? Messer (1972) found that elementary school boys who scored as Internals in locus of control, particularly because they took credit

Internals and Externals

for successful outcomes, were more likely to get higher school grades and higher scores on achievement tests. Girls, however, who assumed responsibility for their own poor performances were likely to get higher grades and higher achievement scores as well. In other words, for boys Internal locus of control was based on success and spurred them on to achievement, but for girls the feeling of responsibility for failure seemed to lead them to push harder.

An interesting example of how questionnaire responses about beliefs correlate with emotional reactions and actual behavior is presented in a study by Karabenick (1972). Subjects who had been rated as Internal or External had to perform a series of tasks, some of which were difficult and some easy. Subjects rated as Internals reported more satisfaction than Externals especially when they solved the difficult tasks. They also reported more dissatisfaction when they failed easy tasks. On the other hand, Externals reported more satisfaction when they solved easy tasks. The results suggest that Internals have a clearer sense of goal direction and are more achievement-oriented.

The relationships between the assignment of causality and achievement have been studied by the so-called attribution theorists, such as Weiner, Nierenberg, and Goldstein (1976). The emotions that people experience after successes or failures in achievement are determined in part by the reasons they ascribe to the results. For example, persons who attribute success to their own *abilities* or *efforts*—an important new distinction not made in most of the earlier research on the I-E scale—are likely to experience positive emotions and pride, but if they fail, they are likely to experience shame. Those who attribute outcomes of their actions to external causes are less likely to show such a wide range of emotional responsiveness. A person who attributes success to effort is equally likely to attribute failure to a lack of effort. People who emphasize luck rather than personal effort are less likely to try harder after a poor performance.

Belief about causality can influence not only achievement but the style of performance in a variety of tasks. Placed in a situation in which they confront a dilemma, Internals seek out information that can help them do something about their circumstances, while Externals rely on others (Seeman and Evans, 1962). Internals are also more likely to try to acquire information relevant to the problem they face (Davis and Phares, 1967). Thus, the relative emphasis on one's own effort as a determinant of outcomes leads to an active approach to acquiring information, rather than a dependence upon others' aid.

Sims and Baumann (1972) carried out a study of victims of severe tornadoes in the South. Subjects who scored higher on measures of externalization reacted to the tornado warnings or threats with fatalism and inactivity rather than seeking information or trying to protect themselves. Similarly, Seeman and Evans (1962) reported that among hospitalized TB patients, the Internals knew more about their illness and asked many more questions of the doctors than did Externals. A similar result was obtained for men imprisoned for crimes; Internal locus-of-control prisoners sought and obtained more information about parole than Externals.

Generally speaking, Externals display more *learned-helplessness* effects—that is, the tendency to give up in difficult situations and to show either withdrawal or marked dependency reactions (Hiroto, 1974). When Internals and Externals are confronted with situations in which reinforcements for their activities are occurring randomly, they both respond with poor performance. Only the Externals, however, show the helplessness effect (Lefcourt, 1976).

Internals are more likely than Externals to be defensive and to avoid risks or challenges. The Externals are able to attribute their failures to bad luck or to the environment, but since Internals are more likely to attribute failures to their own limitations, they are less willing to risk themselves in extreme situations (Lefcourt, 1976).

Rotter (1975) urged researchers to keep in mind that the three determinants of a behavior potential, according to his theory, are: (1) the expectancy of the individual, (2) the value of a reinforcement, and (3) the psychological situation itself. He felt that too many investigators using his scale failed to take into account the reinforcement value of a situation—that is, how intensely a person cares about the result. Rotter also cautioned against a tendency to use the locus-of-control inventory in specific situations, when the test was designed for estimating a general behavioral tendency.

Limitations and Implications

Recent analyses have made it clear that some people who score as Internals on the Rotter scales do so because they believe in a "just world," one in which efforts, integrity, or honor can be rewarded. At the opposite pole are those who respond with external attributions of control because they feel that our fates are often controlled by vast, often hostile forces—for example, bankers, capitalists, multinational cartels, power-hungry communist bureaucrats, or the military-industrial complex. One can also obtain a score on the Rotter scale through an organized set of beliefs about a "predictable world" (Collins, 1974). Internals basically believe that the world is predictable because one really *can* make sense of events and anticipate them; Externals are more likely to emphasize the random nature of the world. Rotter (1971) has shown that Externals who also have a basic general expectation that they can trust others will emphasize luck and randomness, but Externals who have a persisting lack of trust as one of their belief systems will attribute outcomes to powerful groups or economic structures that influence our lives.

BELIEF SYSTEMS, PERSONALITY TRAITS, AND OVERT BEHAVIOR

Research on locus of control highlights a dilemma that has challenged social psychologists as well as personality researchers for several decades: What is the relation between attitudes and actions? Psychologists are now convinced that attitudes or organized groups of beliefs—about such things as school achievement, racial prejudice, social issues—are key features that define human experience. Yet it often turns out that scores on attitude questionnaires do not predict actual behavior in real-life situations (Wicker, 1969). Bickman (1972), for example, reported that of a large group of persons who were interviewed, 94 percent expressed strong feelings about the importance of picking up litter or rubbish. But of this group only about 2 percent actually bent down and picked up some conspicuously placed rubbish as they left the interview room.

From the standpoint of personality research the discrepancy between attitudes and actual behavior presents a challenge for better sampling of (1) people's beliefs and attitudes about themselves and their characteristic behavior as well as their views about life events, and (2) people's interpretations of the meaning of different situations. If psychological instruments are to predict people's characteristic reactions, psychologists will have to do more than administer a questionnaire like Rotter's scale. They must also study a series of behavioral reactions in related situations and look for uniformities in people's interpretations of the situations as well.

Recent solutions to the problem of proper measurement of beliefs or attitudes do point up the key role that belief systems play in defining personality patterns and overt actions. One approach is to sample a person's attitude toward a specific situation, such as premarital sex, to learn whether it is positive or negative. Once this is established, the following steps can be taken:

1. Determine what *consequences* the person anticipates and also how important these consequences are (*intensity* or *value*).
2. Sample the person's beliefs about the *social norms* for this behavior (for devoutly religious persons, the social norms dictate more severe objections to premarital sex than the norms of agnostic or liberal subcultures).
3. Ascertain how strongly the person feels the need to *comply* with the norms of his or her subculture.
4. Multiply the scores for expectation of outcome by personal value or intensity of the consequences and compare this score with the understanding of social norms multiplied by personal commitment to those norms.

This procedure will define an intention to act that does predict overt behavior (Fishbein and Azjen, 1975).

Cognitive Orientation and Prediction	An approach to measurement of beliefs with relevance to personality patterns was developed by Hans Kreitler and Shulamith Kreitler (1976). They defined four cognitive orientations around which beliefs cluster and suggest specific actions. According to the Kreitlers, simply looking for consistencies in behavior across situations may be a futile and irrelevant exercise, considering the great range of our thoughts and interpretations of different settings. More important is to show that behavior is predictable when the predictions are

based on accurate assessment of the meaning of situations, on the one hand, and the concordance of four cognitive orientations or belief systems, on the other. Therefore, in doing a study, they first sample the meanings people assign to specific situations and then predict behavior in only those situations on which there is high agreement about the meaning. They then assess the four belief systems that make up a cognitive-orientation cluster (CO). These four belief systems are:

1. *Beliefs about personal goals.* These are the beliefs that begin with "I" and assert a desired relationship, either positive (wanted) or negative (rejected). A goal belief may be expressed generally ("I want fame") or specifically ("I want to win an Academy Award"); it may be longstanding ("I want to recover my health") or it may be temporary ("I want to take a nap").

2. *Beliefs about self.* Here the beliefs also begin with "I," but describe self, habits, feelings, and abilities: "I believe I'm a lucky person," "I think I can get ahead by my own efforts," "I'm inclined to be cautious about outdoor activities," "I don't pay much attention to religious rules."

3. *Beliefs about norms and rules.* Here the emphasis is on values, ethics, social norms, and standards, and therefore the beliefs do not involve an "I" assertion but are stated impersonally: "People should be charitable to the poor," "Using make-up is phony and demeaning," "It's important to resist authoritarian actions by the government."

4. *General beliefs.* These are beliefs people report about the world around them or their summated expressions of what life situations involve. Such beliefs may or may not be true—that is, they may be demonstrably in error ("The world is flat") or they may be exaggerated or reflect what Freud called *transference* ("Older people are always trying to dominate younger ones," "Blondes are sexier than brunettes").

Specially designed questionnaires are geared to tap the four types of beliefs as they are expressed in specific situations—such as tasks providing opportunities to display curiosity or tasks that demonstrate school achievement—on which people have shown agreement as to their meaning. If, for example, scores on personal goals ("I want to explore the sources of the Nile"), beliefs about self ("I'm intrigued by puzzles,"), normative beliefs ("People respect explorers and scientists"), and general beliefs ("Nothing ventured, nothing gained") all point in the same direction, the Kreitlers can predict the extent of curiosity that will be shown in several different situations, all involving exploration (see Figure 11-1). From studies of reaction to pain, use of defense mechanisms, achievement, speed or slowness of performance, and many other situations, lawful relationships can be demonstrated between private beliefs and overt action.

For personality traits, the Kreitlers show that organized self-beliefs and goals correlate with other measures such as questionnaires of introversion-extraversion or locus of control, as do individual conceptions of what society

FIGURE 11-1

Belief Systems and Behavior

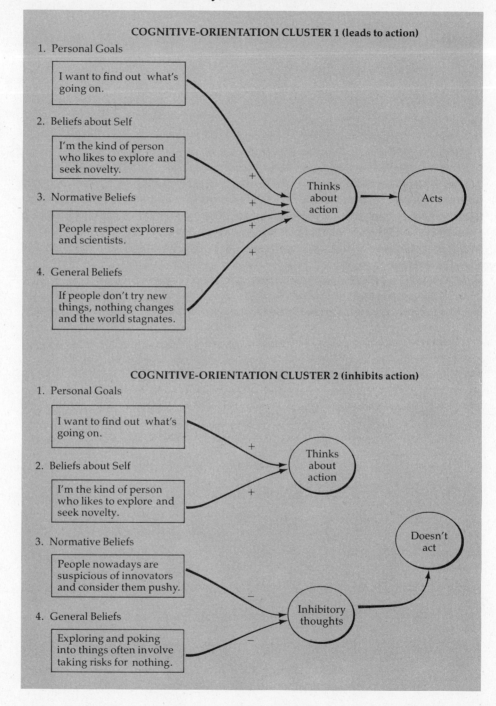

COGNITIVE-ORIENTATION CLUSTER 1 (leads to action)

1. Personal Goals

> I want to find out what's going on.

2. Beliefs about Self

> I'm the kind of person who likes to explore and seek novelty.

3. Normative Beliefs

> People respect explorers and scientists.

4. General Beliefs

> If people don't try new things, nothing changes and the world stagnates.

Thinks about action → Acts

COGNITIVE-ORIENTATION CLUSTER 2 (inhibits action)

1. Personal Goals

> I want to find out what's going on.

2. Beliefs about Self

> I'm the kind of person who likes to explore and seek novelty.

3. Normative Beliefs

> People nowadays are suspicious of innovators and consider them pushy.

4. General Beliefs

> Exploring and poking into things often involve taking risks for nothing.

Thinks about action

Inhibitory thoughts → Doesn't act

expects or how things work in the world. They propose that traits are general, tightly clustered sets of beliefs arrayed along the four cognitive orientations and that they reflect self-attitudes and goals mixed with already "filtered" clusters of beliefs about cultural ethics and the "facts of life" (Kreitler and Kreitler, 1976, 1982).

A major role in the cognitive system and its function in human personality must be assigned to the organized, conscious belief systems of an individual if, as the work of Fishbein and Azjen (1975) and the Kreitlers suggests, these belief systems predict behavior and even what defense mechanisms people will manifest under pressure. The importance of belief systems does not preclude the possibility, so emphasized by psychodynamic theorists, that some behavior is unconsciously motivated. People may be deceived about their own goals or habitual behavior or even their own personal characteristics (Sackeim and Gur, 1979). They may have rehearsed mentally or behaviorally certain attitudes so often that the thoughts have become automatic in the way they unroll in a real situation. For example, a white person who grew up in a racially prejudiced environment may intellectually have no antagonism toward blacks but may still find conversation awkward if seated next to a black at a small dinner party. An interesting topic for research would be to examine conscious beliefs in the four orientations proposed by the Kreitlers and, in cases where there are discrepancies between categories, to explore whether childhood attitudes are still present. By taking contradictory attitudes into account, prediction of conflictual behavior in certain situations might be quite accurate.

Another implication of the studies of locus of control and of cognitive orientation is that psychologists must take conscious beliefs about self quite seriously as a component of personality structure. Freud, and most psychodynamic theorists until recently, placed little emphasis on conscious beliefs about self; the ego is an agent or executive component of personality but not something people are aware of or think about as "I" or "me." Increasingly, however, it is recognized that a major way in which we organize ever-present ambiguous information has to do with whether or not it relates to our sense of self or presents a threat to our self-esteem or to our sense of individuality. Personality researchers and theorists as well as psychoanalysts are therefore paying more attention to issues of how beliefs about the self develop and the forms they take.

How the four belief systems of a cognitive-orientation cluster work in predicting overt behavior from questionnaire responses. Only if at least three of the four beliefs point in the same direction does action result.

(Based on Kreitler and Kreitler, 1976)

THE STUDY OF SELF

The concept of self is no longer regarded as mystical, fuzzy, and unscientific by responsible personality researchers. If researchers accept the evidence that people's beliefs about themselves can actually direct their courses of action then their task becomes one of finding ways of *measuring* self-beliefs and their implications for personality variation. Let us look at some recent advances in research on the self-system in personality.

The Self as Object or Agent

It is important to identify the two forms in which psychologists use the concept of self (Smith, 1950). Some investigators focus on *self as object*—that is, the self as a state of awareness of our own experience or as the object of others' interests or attentions. Other investigators place more emphasis on *self as agent* or *self as process*—that is, the extent to which our self-awareness or self-esteem makes a real difference in how we behave with others or in what kind of actions we take in the real world.

The concept of *self as object* is in many ways easier to handle and phenomenologically more obvious. Even chimpanzees seem to have a concept of self. In one experiment a red spot is put on a chimpanzee's head, and the animal then looks at its reflection in a mirror. The chimp reaches up and touches the red spot on its *own* head, not the one in the mirror (Gallup, 1977). Human infants between 18 and 24 months also begin to demonstrate such self-recognition (Amsterdam, 1972; Lewis, 1979).

Self-recognition and self-awareness—identification of our thoughts, fantasies, and emotions as our own experiences, different from those of others—form a basis for a private self. We may also recognize a public self, the way we appear to others, our overt actions and verbal or gestural expressions. Arnold Buss (1980) has put special emphasis on the differences in how much weight people place on the private versus the public self.

Buss also proposed a distinction between the *sensory self* and the *cognitive self*. The former is a direct, concrete, perhaps inherently more primitive reaction of identification or discrimination as manifested in mirror recognition, location of a pain or twitch, or identification of our own picture. The cognitive self involves identification of our own thoughts and images, praise or blame of ourselves in the same way that we praise or blame others, and, finally, recognition that others have thoughts and feelings not identical with our own. Methods are available for the systematic study of the cognitive self, going beyond mere speculations about self as object.

Studies by McGuire (1984) exemplify the research on the self-concept as a function of perceived differences. McGuire and Padawer-Singer initiated systematic research into how young people describe themselves. They decided to begin at the beginning—to make two simple requests of a group of sixth-graders: "Tell us about yourself" and then "Describe what you look like." The first responses are called a *general self-concept* and the second a *physical self-concept*. Working from a cognitive point of view, McGuire and Padawer-Singer proposed that the most salient items would be characteristics in which the children perceived themselves as different or *unique*.

With regard to the first question, 25 percent of the responses concerned habitual activities, such as recreation or daily routines. Another 20 percent referred to important people in the children's lives, such as parents, siblings, and friends. Interestingly, pets made up a good portion of this category, indeed, dogs were mentioned more frequently than teachers despite the fact that every child had a teacher and only a minority actually had a pet. Another category was made up of specific likes and dislikes and, to a lesser extent, hopes and desires. It is interesting that 18 percent of these 12-year-olds mentioned career aspirations.

Seventy percent of the children had been born in the metropolitan area where the study was done, but only 6 percent of these children mentioned their birthplace, while 22 percent of the remainder, who had been born elsewhere, spontaneously mentioned this fact. This highly significant result is even more clearly pointed up by the fact that 44 percent of the children born in foreign countries mentioned their birthplace, while only 7 percent of those born in the United States did so.

Most of the children had black or brown hair. Again, in responding to the second question, a significantly higher percentage of children with red or blond hair mentioned this characteristic spontaneously. Similar results were obtained with respect to eye color—children with blue or green eyes (the atypical pattern) more often mentioned this fact than did children whose eyes were brown. A similar trend emerged with respect to weight; those children who were above or below average weight were more likely to refer to this characteristic.

In effect, therefore, the critical feature in self-description for these children turns out to be, as the investigators proposed, the *uniqueness* of their experience, their background or their physical characteristics. Labeling specialness as part of self runs counter to what might be called defensiveness or the tendency to suppress aspects of our personality about which we might feel strange or uncomfortable.

Self-awareness and Self-consciousness

Consciousness can run from complete absorption in an external stimulus— exploding fireworks in the night sky—through awareness of bodily pains, twitches, or emotions to complete absorption in fantasies or memories (Singer, 1966; Waterbor, 1972). *Self*-consciousness involves a shift of attention toward ongoing inner experience, along with the recognition that these are "my" thoughts or "my" aches, or even, when confronting a vivid external stimulus, "I really love to watch fireworks! I'll never forget the ones we had on July 4th in the Bicentennial Year!"

Buss (1980) proposed a theory that integrates various approaches to studying self-consciousness and self-awareness. He suggested that a distinction be

How context or setting influences self-awareness. The child who is clearly different in appearance from his or her playmates is more likely to include the special characteristic—such as weight, glasses, or skin color—as part of a self-description.

made along two dimensions: (1) private self versus public self and (2) disposition of style versus a transient situational influence. There may be momentary circumstances that heighten *private self-awareness*, such as looking into a mirror, or *public self-awareness*, such as talking in front of an audience. Each of these circumstances affects our experience and actions differently. Parallel to these transitory situations, which affect all of us, are longstanding habits or styles of *private self-consciousness*—for example, a continuing sensitivity to dreams or fantasies—or *public self-consciousness*—for example, a habitual preoccupation with how we appear to others. Presumably we all vary in the extent to which we emphasize private or public self-consciousness in our belief systems. Using this theory, investigators can hypothesize what can happen to people in situations that highlight either private or public self-awareness. Or they can make predictions about different patterns of behavior for individuals who score high or low on measures of public and private self-consciousness.

Fenigstein, Scheier, and Buss (1975) constructed a questionnaire to measure self-consciousness (see Figure 11-2). It includes statements concerned with:

FIGURE 11-2

A Questionnaire Assessing Private and Public Self-consciousness

Private Self-consciousness Statements
  I reflect about myself a lot.
  I'm generally attentive to my inner feelings.
  I'm always trying to figure myself out.
  I'm constantly examining my motives.
  I'm alert to changes in my mood.
  I tend to scrutinize myself.
  Generally, I'm aware of myself.
  I'm aware of the way my mind works when I work through a problem.
  I'm often the subject of my own fantasies.
  I sometimes have the feeling that I'm off somewhere watching myself.

Public Self-Consciousness Statements
  I'm concerned about what other people think of me.
  I usually worry about making a good impression.
  I'm concerned about the way I present myself.
  I'm self-conscious about the way I look.
  I'm usually aware of my appearance.
  One of the last things I do before leaving my house is look in the mirror.
  I'm concerned about my style of doing things.

(Adapted from Fenigstein, Scheier, and Buss, 1975)

preoccupation with past, present, and future behaviors
sensitivity to inner feelings
recognition of positive and negative attributes
introspective behavior
the tendency to picture or imagine oneself
awareness of physical appearance and presentation
concern over the appraisal of others

After administering the questionnaire to about 200 college students, they carried out a factor analysis that yielded three factors. One factor they called *private self-consciousness*; it is concerned primarily with self-awareness of one's own thoughts and dreams. The second factor is related to awareness of the self as a *public object*. The third factor they called *social anxiety*; it reflects distress or discomfort about a series of situations in which one is being scrutinized by others, or being required to speak before a group. Fenigstein, Scheier, and Buss concluded that public and private self-consciousness represent a particular process of attention focused on the self, whereas social anxiety is a *reaction* to this particular process. According to Buss's theory, private self-consciousness involves extended private rehearsal, continuity in imagery, and antici-

SELF-CONSCIOUSNESS AND IDENTIFICATION WITH PARENTS

Do people develop styles that lead them to be especially conscious of their inner experiences—their private selves? If so, what is the origin of such styles? Singer and Schonbar (1961) attempted to answer these questions by asking a group of adult women to keep a record of their nightdreams for a month and to answer a questionnaire on the frequency of their daydreams. They found that the woman reporting more daydreams recalled more nightdreams and also showed other indications of greater self-awareness in other kinds of reporting, such as the stories they told.

Singer and Schonbar hypothesized that the origin of such a predisposition toward self-awareness might stem from childhood identification patterns in the family that continued into adulthood. The sociologist Talcott Parsons (1963) found that in most American families, the mother emphasizes storytelling, fantasy, and spiritual values whereas the father represents work and the outside world. Singer and Schonbar, therefore, hypothesized that the more self-aware women would be those who identified more with

their mothers, and that women more allied in attitudes with their fathers would be less attentive to inner experiences. They administered scales of attitudes and typical behaviors. Each subject filled out the questionnaire three times: first, as she would normally respond; then, as she thought her father would respond; and finally, as she thought her mother would respond. The experimenters could then identify how close the "self" responses were to the way the women believed that their father and mother would answer the same items. The results indicated that more self-aware women were more likely to give similar responses for themselves and their mothers; the women who showed less interest in or awareness of their own thoughts, dreams, and emotions had less discrepancy between their self-attitudes and their father's. Similar results have been found for men (Singer, 1975a). These preliminary findings suggest that identification patterns in the family may indeed be linked to styles emphasizing an awareness of one's own thoughts and dreams.

pation of heightened intensity of experience. It should, therefore, lead people to greater knowledge of the domain of their own thoughts, feelings, and opinions. Adults across a wide age spectrum who score high on private self-consciousness are also high scorers on the positive-constructive daydreaming scale of the Imaginal Processes Inventory (Barrios and Singer, 1981).

Private self-consciousness should also lead to more intense emotional responses since preoccupation with an experience should heighten its importance. Tesser and Conlee (1975), for example, found that persons who think about an already liked friend later show a greater liking for the friend. And those who initially dislike someone show a relative increase in disliking if they think more about the person.

Recurrent tendencies toward self-awareness in public or private situations can become crystallized into traits or styles (see Figures 11-3 and 11-4). The Fenigstein, Scheier, and Buss scales have been used to delineate persons high or low in public or private self-consciousness and to examine their behavior under controlled conditions. Persons scoring low and high in private self-

FIGURE 11-3

Private Self-consciousness

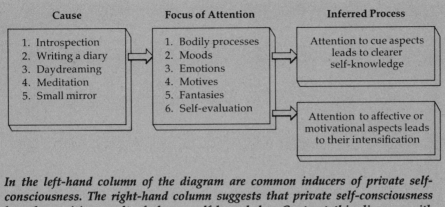

Cause	Focus of Attention	Inferred Process
1. Introspection 2. Writing a diary 3. Daydreaming 4. Meditation 5. Small mirror	1. Bodily processes 2. Moods 3. Emotions 4. Motives 5. Fantasies 6. Self-evaluation	Attention to cue aspects leads to clearer self-knowledge
		Attention to affective or motivational aspects leads to their intensification

In the left-hand column of the diagram are common inducers of private self-consciousness. The right-hand column suggests that private self-consciousness has the positive result of clearer self-knowledge. Contrast this diagram with Figure 11-4.

(From Buss, 1980)

consciousness tasted a peppermint drink on two occasions, rating the strength of the flavor each time. When given the second drink, they were told it was stronger than the first drink. The subjects with high private self-consciousness did not change their ratings, but the low scorers increased their ratings even though the drink was actually the same. Persons scoring high on the private self-consciousness scale also resist political propaganda.

What about persons who score high on the scale of public self-consciousness? Fenigstein (1974) found that such individuals are sensitive to group rejection. Following an experience of being shunned or ignored, people who score high on public self-consciousness are far less attracted to the group and state they would be less willing to join a group in the future. Other experiments indicate that high scorers on public self-consciousness are more likely to change attitudes in public situations and are much less consistent or accurate in their behavior when social situations change.

So far we have emphasized the measurement of beliefs about self. But isn't it possible that some people do not really "know themselves" or that they brush aside their desires, wishes, and prejudices as if they were nonexistent?

Self-awareness and Self-deception

Even if most people can rationalize or reorganize their perceptions to bring them into congruence with their public behavior, recognition of contradictory inner tendencies may emerge. Some of the great moments of literature hinge on crises in which individuals pierce through the veil of self-deception into an awareness of their guilts, failures, and unfulfilled potential. In Tolstoy's

THE STUDY OF SELF

FIGURE 11-4
Public Self-consciousness

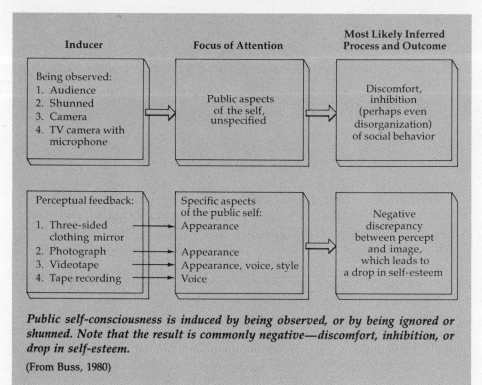

Public self-consciousness is induced by being observed, or by being ignored or shunned. Note that the result is commonly negative—discomfort, inhibition, or drop in self-esteem.

(From Buss, 1980)

The Death of Ivan Ilyich, a rather ordinary, proper, middle-aged man is dying of an illness. As he reviews his life, he realizes how much of his past behavior, while respectable by most public standards, somehow did not reflect all he was capable of. He had entered a loveless marriage merely for economic advantage and social status. He had plunged into government work not out of genuine commitment to his duties but to avoid thinking of all the aspects of life that he had not experienced. In the agony of this great awareness of how much of his own potential had indeed been wasted, Ivan Ilyich suffers more than from the physical pain of his disease.

In long-term intensive psychotherapy, a patient often experiences something like the peeling of layers off an onion—down indeed, as one patient put it, to the very "stink" itself—the self-centeredness, the failures, the real or imagined guilt. In stripping away layers of self-representation and self-deception, people may also encounter a more positive nature. Kindness, esthetic sensitivity and love, suppressed in favor of a "tough" or "cool" front, may recur in their thoughts. Psychotherapists like Carl Rogers and Rollo May believe that once this deepened awareness has been revealed, the individual reaches a highly exciting moment of human experience, a point of decision that involves a conscious determination to act differently—to struggle against previous symptoms, conflicts, and failures.

Can systematic studies of self-deception go beyond clinical anecdote? Research indicates that individuals who say they are prone to depression are more likely to overestimate their failures and therefore to experience a kind of "learned helplessness." At the same time, interestingly enough, individuals who are "normal"—that is, less likely to experience depressive reactions—overestimate the degree of their success or their personal control over events. Perhaps a certain amount of self-deception plays a valuable defensive role in preventing us from experiencing sadness and depression (Alloy and Abramson, 1979; Rizley, 1978). Since there is certainly a strong element of chance in life, believing that successes are of your own making can help you avoid crippling doubts.

Sackeim and Gur (1978) prepared audiotapes of experimental subjects' voices and mixed these up with tapes of others' voices. The subjects often either did not recognize their own voices (false negatives) or called other people's voices their own (false positives). When subjects were presented with their actual voices, they took longer to respond with a "Mine" or "Another's" than for other's voices. Under those circumstances there was also a strong physiological response as measured by changes in the galvanic skin response (GSR) taken at the same time; this was the case whether or not the subjects correctly stated, "That's my voice." The delayed reaction time and the GSR arousal were both indications that at some level a subject "knew" it was his or her own voice even though reporting that it was not! Sackeim and Gur also showed that persons who gave false negatives or false positives to the audiotapes of their voices scored higher on a questionnaire that measured self-deception and denial. Therefore, they established evidence for self-deception as a psychological phenomenon.

Freud suggested that a person's self-deception or defensiveness varies as a function of recent experiences of pleasure or distress. Sackeim and Gur examined Freud's suggestion by asking subjects to take some vocabulary tests. Half were assigned the hardest items, half the easiest. Those who experienced success because they had easy items subsequently recognized their own voices more rapidly or else made more "false positive" judgments, taking another's voice for their own. Those who experienced failures subsequently were more likely to make "false negative" responses, failing to identify their own voices.

Sex Differences and Sex Roles as Beliefs about Self

Among the developmentally earliest and psychologically most significant forms of organized beliefs about self are those dealing with sexual identity. With rare exceptions, we are all born either male or female; there are distinct differences between the sexes in genetic structure, hormonal activity, and anatomical structure. Women, for example, have two X chromosomes, men only one; women are anatomically and physiologically constructed to produce reproductive eggs and to bear children, and men are specialized to produce sperm and impregnate women. On the average, from birth males are taller and heav-

A group of coal miners. One result of the women's movement is the discovery that many jobs traditionally regarded as for men only can be performed just as effectively by women—and vice versa.

ier than females, and as adults as well as children they are stronger physically (Maccoby, 1980). Throughout recorded history and in many different cultures and tribes in the world, men are more likely to be warriors and hunters while women serve in the nurturant role as the child-rearers, gardeners, and homemakers. In most societies these differences have been reinforced by religious, traditional, and legal customs. It is hard to disentangle the extent to which "anatomy is destiny," as Freud wrote—that is, to determine whether some of the personality differences between men and women are the product of cultural expectations and socialization patterns rather than inborn predispositions. In other words, to what extent does our awareness of the physical characteristics that define us as male or female generate a complex series of beliefs about our personal goals, personality traits, or about what society expects and what the world is like?

Constitutional Factors   In recent years significant progress has been made in clarifying the nature of sex differences. Despite boys' greater physical size at birth and their greater vulnerability to illness, there are few if any behavioral differences between the sexes in the early years. Girls, perhaps because their brain hemispheres are less specialized (the right for imagery and the left for language), seem to mature more rapidly in speech and language use and show fewer difficulties in communication (Witelson, 1976).

Although it has been suggested that boys have more energy and play more vigorously than girls from their earliest years, careful observations fail to support this supposed constitutional difference. Given encouragement and comparable playthings, girls can be as rambunctious and lively as boys during the first three years. Individual children, however, irrespective of sex, show great variation in activity levels (Maccoby, 1980).

Early Socialization and Play   Consistent sex differences in play styles have been observed in a wide range of social classes and cultures. In the play of preschool boys and girls, boys are more aggressive and more likely to play games involving adventure and danger, while girls play games of nurturance and practical daily life ("house," "school") as well as adventure. Boys rarely play "girls' games" like "cooking" or "taking baby to the doctor," but girls are increasingly willing to play what were once "boys' games" like "cowboys" or "monsters" (Maccoby, 1980; Singer and Singer, 1981; Sutton-Smith, 1971).

There is reason to believe that sex differences in overt aggressive behavior and in play styles reflect extremely early differences in socialization of boys and girls. Children generally grow up in families in which women (mothers, grandmothers, aunts, older sisters) clean or dress a child, while men are more likely to be playful, tossing a child up into the air and tickling (Maccoby, 1980). Adults also treat boys differently from girls. Mothers often interact with girl babies with pretend games of nurturance. By 18 to 24 months, girls are showing the first signs of make-believe play involving "feeding dolly" or putting it to sleep and boys are imitating cars, airplanes, or animals (Fein and others, 1975).

The amount of male chauvinism and macho behavior that pervades a culture and the amount of homophobia (fear of homosexuality) influences how parents respond to children's spontaneous games. While it is now acceptable for girls to play "boys' games," most parents in America feel uncomfortable when a 3-year-old boy plays with dolls, pretends to be baking pies, or likes to play house with the girls. Try imagining your reaction if you had a son who always wanted to be dressed up nicely, who did not want to get dirty, who enjoyed playing with a large dollhouse rather than a toy space station or garage. Suppose he preferred playing jacks or jumping rope to playing ball and wrestling. While our society indulges tomboys, it humiliates "sissies." Massive cultural forces urge both mothers and fathers to treat the sexes differently. Even with the feminist movement, parents may be subtly influenced to discourage boys from showing the nurturant, rules-making, and orderly styles that characterize girls' play. A television commercial recently depicted a father visiting the hospital nursery to see his newborn son. He proudly carried his first present, a baseball glove!

Sex Identity and Sex Role   When and how do boys and girls develop a sense of sex identity, a belief system that one is male or female and that such an identity is constant? Evidence from a number of studies shows that children develop a clear sense of their biological sex between the ages of 3 and 4 (Maccoby, 1980). The most dramatic evidence in support of the social-learning position on sex identity comes from the work of Money, Hampson, and Hampson (1957), who reported on those very rare cases in which sex at birth is ambiguous because of a failure in development of distinct genital structures. At the time those cases were studied, chromosomal analyses indicating genetic sex structure were not possible and so sex was assigned arbitrarily. Parents simply decided to rear the children as boys or as girls. If the decison was made by age 3, the children identified themselves throughout life as the sex assigned and had no special problems. Hence, sex role is largely a matter of personal belief.

On the whole, sex identity is a powerful influence on the way in which children organize the complex information about their environment and their selves. The notion that "I am a boy" or "I am a girl" becomes a central scheme for grouping all kinds of new information. By age 4, children are aware of the continuity of sex identity, they look to their own sex more than the opposite sex when exploring a new social setting, and they rely on hair style or dress to establish the sex of another person (Maccoby, 1980). They begin to incorporate social expectations about "boyness" and "girlness" into their own views and show the beginnings of *sex-role stereotyping*—that is, expectations that boys grow up to be policemen, firemen, soldiers, cowboys, and pilots while girls become mothers, nurses, teachers, or secretaries. Although we now know that women can and do hold almost any job formerly thought to be masculine, parental attitudes and cultural orientation can cause children to express such stereotypic notions.

A group of 4-year-olds was asked to choose toys and occupations that were "boys'," "girls'," or both. Children whose choices reflected a strong tendency to assign toys or occupations to a specific male or female category came from homes where the parents themselves scored higher on traditional sex roles in a personality inventory. These sex-stereotyping children also had watched more commercial television in which sex stereotyping is common, while the other children had watched more public-television shows such as *Mister Rogers' Neighborhood* and *Sesame Street* in which an effort is made to break away from traditional role models (Repetti, 1980).

Cultural Expectations   We have seen how boys and girls are launched from the start on different paths in terms of adult expectations. A girl who comes home messy and in tears after a fight may be soothed by her mother, cleaned up, and kept indoors lest she mingle with bad company. A boy returning in the same condition is often encouraged to go out and fight back or praised for putting up a good fight. Tears are acceptable for girls, but boys are encouraged to "be a man and stop crying." Boys are reinforced by both parents, by the myths of a culture (Hercules, Superman), by books, movies, and—especially now—by television, for being athletic, physically aggressive, fearless, emotionally controlled, and professionally competent. Girls are reinforced for physical attractiveness, neatness, nurturant and caretaking behavior, sociability, and family responsibility.

Such differences lead to striking average adult differences. In a study of over one thousand freshmen at two different colleges (one a northeastern Ivy League school and one a rural Kentucky state university), clear-cut differences between the sexes emerged (Segal, Huba, and Singer, 1980). Men described themselves as aggressive, achievement-oriented, dominant, relatively fearless, and autonomous. Women reported themselves as nurturant, desirous of intimacy and friendships, fearful, and less ambitious. But the influence of feminism and attitudes about sexual equality was apparent in the fact that the differences between men and women at the Ivy League college (presumably reflecting more up-to-date trends), while statistically significant, were relatively small. The differences between the rural college students were huge; the men were far more aggressive and achievement-oriented, the women far more nurturant and affiliative. Apparently the 1970s message of a new mix of masculine and feminine traits had not reached the border-state area where both men and women still saw themselves in traditional roles.

Androgyny   A major thrust of the women's movement has been to encourage women to become more assertive. In the consciousness-raising groups that formed during the late 1960s, they were encouraged to learn to defend themselves, if necessary, and build up physical prowess. As affirmative-action programs made opportunities available, it became clear that women could function as well as men as bus drivers or police officers or business executives. Television now features women as superheroes or detectives (*Wonder Woman* and *Charlie's Angels*)—although it should be noted that the Angels are always at the beck and call of an unseen man.

Unfortunately, in the rush toward "masculinizing" women, there has been little effort to help men modify their patterns or expectations. If men grow up expecting princesses (who are also good cooks and homemakers), where will they find them? We can foresee a great many unhappy pairings unless men begin to learn some of the nurturant, tender characteristics that women were socialized into. Sandra Bem (1975) developed a series of measures and studies emphasizing the adaptive importance of *androgyny*, a personality style resulting in high scores on both masculine and feminine traits. An androgynous person is optimally assertive *and* nurturant, ambitious *and* tender, for example. Our world, however, is not yet ready for "feminine" males. When measures of personal adjustment are used as criteria, high scores for women on the scales for *both* masculine and feminine traits are good predictors of adjustment. But for men only high scores on masculine traits predict good adjustment (Flaherty and Dusek, 1980; Golding and Singer, 1983).

Industrialized societies no longer require that men be primarily warriors and hunters. Even modern warfare requires less and less the tough aggressive impulsive male; a female finger can push missile-launching buttons just as well as a male's. The rambunctiousness encouraged in boys may often make it harder for them to adjust to school and get the education that is necessary. At some point if we are to have a better balanced, adaptive society, serious efforts will have to be made to help parents overcome their fears and allow boys to develop some of the feminine skills and nurturant traits. Beliefs about self based on sex may help us organize and clarify many ambiguities, but they may also lead to distortions and difficulties in a changing world.

Self-Esteem Some of the most crucial beliefs we have are those that deal with self-esteem, the importance or value we place on ourselves. People often refer to "inferiority complexes" or to feeling "small" or worthless. One of the important contributions of Carl Rogers was his identification of the clinical importance of self-esteem. He and his colleagues developed approaches to measuring that construct so that one could determine whether psychotherapeutic efforts were actually enhancing a client's self-esteem. Let us examine next some measurement approaches and personality implications of our beliefs about self-worth or self-esteem.

By far the most extensive studies of the self have emerged in work on self-esteem. Here the focus turns from self as object to self as agent, because it is assumed that persons with high self-esteem will function more effectively in society, achieve more, take more reasonable risks, and be more willing to share or to care for others. The first problem, again, is for psychologists to demonstrate that there is a reasonable basis for identifying self-esteem as a human characteristic and then to devise reasonably objective methods for measuring it.

The work of Michael Rosenberg (1965) will be used as an example of this research. Rosenberg developed a questionnaire with such items as "On the whole I am satisfied with myself," "I certainly feel useless at times," "At times I think I am no good at all." The use of the multitrait-multimethod approach (Chapter 7; Hamilton, 1971) with the Rosenberg Self-Esteem scale suggests that a construct called self-esteem is measurable and that it does have unique characteristics. Indeed, when the scale is examined in relation to other measures, it turns out that persons who show a good deal of self-derogation or low self-esteem on the Rosenberg scale report feelings of gloominess or disappointment in interviews. They also show evidence of depressive emotionality as measured on still another scale. Similarly, low self-esteem turns out to be associated with psychosomatic symptoms, greater interpersonal insecurity, greater difficulty in making friends, greater feelings of being hurt by criticism, and greater indications of shyness. Other data reported by Rosenberg (1965) indicate that persons who report low self-esteem also report that they experienced less parental interest in them or rejection by their families. They were also less likely to be active in extracurricular affairs or to show leadership tendencies.

Implications There is considerable evidence that differences in beliefs about self-esteem lead to striking differences in attitude and behaviors. Elementary school children characterized as high in self-esteem are more active, more expressive, and more confident than children scoring at either low or moderate levels. They are better at assessing their own or others' abilities, more successful in schoolwork, social, and athletic activities; more creative and less willing to be influenced in their judgments by pressure from authorities. They also show more curiosity and exploratory behavior. By contrast, children who score low on a measure of self-esteem are more socially isolated, physically weaker and incapable of defending themselves, more fearful in interpersonal encounters, and more preoccupied with "inner" problems (Coopersmith, 1967; Lesser and Abelson, 1959; Maw and Maw, 1970).

Children who have proven records of success in schoolwork or in social relations are more sensitive to what is needed to accomplish tasks and to reach their goals. They are likely, therefore, to adopt a more realistic attitude when asked to compare the beliefs about their *actual* and *ideal* self-images. Bauer and Achenbach (1976) found that students who showed more discrepancies between self and ideal self also were more likely to score higher on Byrne's Sensitization scale (Chapter 9) and on a measure of introversion. Thus, they were more likely to use such defenses as intellectualization rather than repression and to be more attuned to inner experience. Bauer and Achenbach suggest that, since introverts work harder to outperform extraverts on measures of perception and learning (Eysenck, 1979), the discrepancy between actual and ideal self serves to motivate them toward higher achievement. This is especially likely if self-esteem level is already fairly high. On the other hand, immature and maladjusted children may not have as much disparity between actual self and ideal self because they rate themselves low on both (Katz, Zigler, and Zalk, 1975).

Self-Efficacy   In the late 1970s Bandura (1977, 1978) focused much of the work in social-learning theory on *self-efficacy* and its implication for changing behavior. Self-efficacy, a form of self-esteem, reflects beliefs about how well we can organize and carry out "courses of action required to deal with prospective situations containing many ambiguous, unpredictable, and often stressful elements" (Bandura and Schunk, 1981, p. 587). Bandura proposed that self-directed behavior comes about through the operation of a self-system that "comprises cognitive structures and subfunctions for perceiving, evaluating, motivating, and regulating behavior" (Bandura and Schunk, 1981). He stressed that self-satisfaction often depends on the mental comparisons we make between our standards and our actual accomplishments. Research indicates that our beliefs about our self-efficacy lead to whether we undertake particular activities, the amount of effort we put into them, and the length of time we persist in difficult situations (Bandura, 1977; Bandura and Schunk, 1981).

An experiment by Bandura and Schunk (1981) examined the conditions of approaching a new task that were most conducive to rapid progress in self-directed learning, mastery, and the sense of self-efficacy. They studied different ways of motivating 8-year-olds to undertake self-directed learning of arithmetic skills and problem-solving. A crucial factor in producing effective effort, accomplishment, and subsequent feelings of self-efficacy was whether the child set up short-term (*proximal*) or long-term (*distal*) goals (see Figure 11-5).

FIGURE 11-5
Self-efficacy, Intrinsic Interest, and Goal-Setting

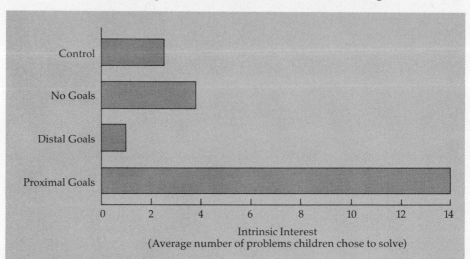

Intrinsic Interest
(Average number of problems children chose to solve)

The children in this experiment were assigned to one of four conditions: (1) the experimenter suggested that they set a goal of at least six pages of problems (close or proximal goal); (2) the experimenter suggested a goal of 42 pages (far or distal goal); (3) the experimenter made no reference to goals; (4) the children were in a control group with no exposure to instructional materials. As the graph shows, the children who set a proximal goal later developed greater intrinsic interest, as measured by the number of problems they actually chose to solve.

(Adapted from Bandura and Schunk, 1981)

If the children tried to finish six pages of arithmetic problems they worked harder, learned more, and felt better about themselves than when their goal was to finish 42 pages. Children who worked to reach proximal goals attacked a new set of problems with more enthusiasm. Realistic goal-setting is thus a valuable way to help people develop an interest, to accomplish something, and then to feel more self-esteem and self-efficacy which, in turn, can motivate later effective performance.

Bandura's research on self-efficacy thus supports an increasing recognition that organized cognitions or beliefs about the self are critical features in personality organization. His work, along with the other recent studies of self-esteem, make it clear that this once-elusive area of the self is susceptible to systematic research exploration.

How Does Self-Esteem Develop?   A study of 12-year-old children (Sears, 1970) indicated that for both boys and girls, high self-esteem is associated with good achievement in reading and arithmetic. Children who come from smaller families, who are born earlier in the family series, and whose family shows considerable warmth within the family unit, all are more likely to have high self-esteem. For boys, high self-esteem is also associated with less dominance by the father in the husband-wife relationship. If the father shares dominance with the mother, he may help his sons achieve self-esteem by, in a sense, leaving room for them to achieve some successes and demonstrate effectiveness. In a family with an extremely powerful father, there may be an almost inherent competitiveness in which the father not only dominates his wife and the other members of the family, but may subtly undercut a boy's small signs of effectiveness, thus contributing to his low self-esteem.

In general, self-esteem comes about in part through the comments and attitudes of others. At the same time, for most normal individuals actual achievement and successes in school athletics, work, or social interchange are important in developing self-worth. Excessive praise or warmth from a parent without sufficient and clear instances of actual achievement is less likely to generate an accurate and effective sense of self-worth. Bandura's work on self-efficacy points up the subtle interplay between actual accomplishment, motivation, and the development of an organized belief system of self-esteem.

The Reality of Self

In many ways, the notion of self lies at the core of all theories of personality. It is no longer useful to call it a myth, although it is probably a mistake to say there is one true personality or one basic self. Psychologists have made progress in measuring the self-concept, self-consciousness, self-deception, and self-esteem. Research is still needed to examine self as object and as agency in a variety of settings or environments and in various subcultures or age groups. Also still necessary is research linking beliefs about the self to other cognitive processes and to emotional experiences and expression. In our exploration of the cognitive system and personality we have learned that belief systems are important determinants and predictors of overt behavior or personality variation. Beliefs about the self seem especially critical. We can now look forward to a new era when study of the hitherto elusive concept of self presents an exciting and challenging reality.

SUMMARY

1. In an effort to make sense of the world, people attribute causality to events and to actions of individuals. They develop styles of attribution that reflect systems of belief about the world. These belief systems form both anticipations of the future and explanations of the past.

2. One style of belief—called *locus of control*—is concerned with the attribution of causality to our own actions versus attribution to influences over which we have no control. Julian Rotter developed a set of inventory items, known as the I-E scale, to measure locus of control. If a person believes that success

or failure depends on luck, fate, or powerful people or that success and failure cannot be predicted, that person would score as a locus-of-control External. But if a person believes that outcomes are determined by one's own actions or personal characteristics, then that person is a locus-of-control Internal. Rotter has urged researchers to keep in mind that according to his theory the three determinants of behavior are: (1) the expectancy of the individual, (2) the value of the reinforcement, and (3) the psychological situation itself.

3. A question that has challenged psychologists is: What is the relation between attitudes and actions? Psychologists are now convinced that attitudes or organized sets of beliefs are key features of human experience. Yet scores on attitude tests often do not predict actual behavior. This discrepancy shows that researchers must take account of (1) people's beliefs and attitudes about themselves and their characteristic behavior as well as their views about life events, and (2) people's interpretations of the meaning of different situations. Kreitler and Kreitler have defined four cognitive orientations around which belief systems cluster and point toward specific actions. These four orientations are: (1) beliefs about personal goals, (2) beliefs about self, (3) beliefs about norms and rules, and (4) general beliefs.

4. Psychologists use the concept of the self in two ways: self as *object* and self as *agent* or *process*. The former refers to the self as a state of awareness of our own experience or as the object of other persons' attention or interest. The self as agent or process focuses on the extent to which our personal identity or degree of self-awareness or self-esteem makes a difference in how we behave.

5. Buss proposed a distinction between the *sensory* self and the *cognitive* self. The former is direct and concrete, as when we react to our own picture or to a pain or twitch. The cognitive self involves identification of our thoughts and images, praise or blame of ourselves, and recognition that others have thoughts and feelings different from our own.

6. Self-consciousness or self-awareness involves a shift of attention to ongoing inner experience with the recognition that these are "my" thoughts. Buss suggested that a distinction be made between (1) private self versus public self and (2) disposition or style versus a transient situational influence. Buss and his co-workers constructed a questionnaire to measure self-consciousness, which, when factor analyzed, yielded three factors: (1) private self-consciousness—concern with self-awareness or one's own thoughts and dreams, (2) self as public object, and (3) social anxiety or distress about situations in which one is being scrutinized by others.

7. Sexual identity is one of the most significant forms of organized beliefs about the self. Research on constitutional factors in sex differences shows that there are few differences in energy and vigor between the sexes in the early years. However, consistent differences in play styles have been observed in a wide range of social classes and cultures. There is reason to believe that these sex differences reflect very early socialization. Children develop

a sense of biological sex between the ages of 3 and 4. Gender role seems to be determined by social factors, and by the sex role assigned to the child. The differential treatment and expectations of boys and girls can lead to striking adult differences.

8. Some of the most crucial beliefs are concerned with the importance or value we place upon ourselves—our *self-esteem*. Use of the multitrait-multi-method approach with Rosenberg's self-esteem scales suggests that the characteristic is measurable and that it does have unique features. Differences in self-esteem lead to striking differences in attitudes and behavior. Elementary school children rated as high in self-esteem are more active, expressive, confident, successful at school work and athletics, creative, curious, and less willing to be influenced by authorities. Research on *self-efficacy*, a form of self-esteem, indicates that beliefs about self-efficacy are related to our willingness to undertake certain activities, the amount of effort we put into them, and the length of time we persist in difficult situations.

9. In general, self-esteem develops as a result of the comments, verbalizations, and attitudes of others. At the same time, actual achievement and success in schoolwork and athletics and in social interchanges are important. Bandura's research on self-efficacy points up the subtle interplay between accomplishment, motivation, and the development of an organized belief system of self-esteem.

PART THREE

The Public Personality

CHAPTER
12

Stress I: Frustration and Danger

One quiet weekend morning in 1972, a West Virginia dam burst. The dam had held a huge quantity of sludge, the waste from strip-mining operations, and millions of tons of this liquefied material poured into a narrow valley of linked communities. As the great ugly mass slipped at crazy angles through the valley of Buffalo Creek, it wiped out dozens of houses in its path, drowning those people who did not have sufficient warning of the onrushing waters to run up the sides of the steep hills behind their homes. The flood missed some houses and hit others in its unpredictable course. As the survivors watched, the black tide destroyed the homes of their neighbors and dragged screaming children, parents, and animals to their deaths. Those persons whose homes the flood had missed as well as those who had been injured or who had lost family or possessions in this horrible disaster were in a state of shock for months afterward. A team of mental-health specialists carried out extensive studies of the survivors. Working closely with legal help, they were able to convince the courts that the company responsible for the inadequate safety precautions owed compensation not only to those persons who had been physically injured or lost property, but also to the many survivors who had sustained severe emotional trauma as a consequence of this totally unexpected disaster (Erikson, 1976).

On a spring day in 1977, a band of black Muslims of the Hanafi sect took over three buildings in Washington, D.C., and terrorized their many hostages by brandishing guns and swords and threatening to behead them if their demands were not met. One of the buildings seized was the headquarters of the Jewish charitable agency B'nai B'rith. One hundred people were forced to huddle together in a small space, bodies nearly piled on one another while for 39 hours their captors, apparently unaware that most of the hostages were not Jewish and many were not even associated with the agency, spewed forth anti-Semitic remarks. There was bloodshed before the eventual surrender of the Muslims. During their three days of captivity the hostages experienced constant terror for their lives and suffered from physical and psychological stress including profound feelings of helplessness and powerlessness. The hostages' immediate reaction on release was naturally one of joy. Although they had suffered some pains during their captivity, most were found to be medically fit and were released to go home. Almost at once they began to suffer from psychological symptoms—recurring images of bodies piled up, blood, knives, threatening faces; fears of taxis (because some of their captors had been taxi drivers), fears of elevators, staircases, and loud noises. They suffered from bad dreams, difficulties in concentration, and recurrent preoccupation with being captured again (Belz and others, 1977).

Fortunately most people in our country do not have to confront such dangerous and stressful experiences as the two preceding examples. Yet the reality of our daily lives forces us to confront thousands of lesser frustrations and dangers—a near-miss in an auto accident, failure in a job interview, rejection by a lover, the continuing awareness of the possibility of another accident to a nuclear power station like that at Three Mile Island in Pennsylvania or of a nuclear war. Personality ultimately is shaped by a range of stressful situations—from the simple frustrations of our intentions, such as getting to a rock concert too late to buy a ticket, to confrontations with serious illness, financial loss, and life-menacing situations—"the heartaches and the thousand natural shocks that flesh is heir to," as Hamlet puts it.

From this point on, our study of personality will increasingly concentrate on the *public* personality—on the ways in which the outside world with its physical and social characteristics impinges on the individual and how humans act upon their environments and express their personality styles in relationship to people around them. The distinction between private and public personalities is only a convenient fiction, but it helps us think systematically about this complex area.

In this chapter we shall consider how human beings face frustrations and deprivation, how they respond to externally derived danger. Frustration, danger, and conflict in childhood may help shape the coping capacities of the adult personality and therefore may play an important role in normal adaptation. In addition, prolonged periods of frustration, danger, or conflict—or, in some cases, brief but very extreme periods of danger—may lead to longer-term psychological effects, modifying personality and also causing significant changes in bodily functioning and indeed serious disease processes.

FRUSTRATION

Can you envision a human being growing up in an environment in which every desire is immediately granted, every intention fulfilled? Even the children of kings and queens or of the richest parents find that servants forget to bring food they've asked for, other siblings demand priority for toys or treats, or custom and protocol impose restrictions on their ceaseless search for pleasure. Fairy tales recount instances of people who exhaust their supply of magic wishes and revert to a humbler condition in the end. Our consciousness is made up of a continuing series of wishes and intentions only a few of which can be acted upon at all and even fewer fulfilled. In a sense, much of life is characterized by the obstacles that confront us as we try to achieve our goals. Freud built his psychodynamic theory around what he called the "vicissitudes of the instincts," by which he meant the ways in which our wishes are frustrated, persist though we will in seeking to fulfill them. Lewin attempted to develop a mathematical description of the personality by diagramming patterns of human needs as forces impelling persons toward goals in the face of barriers and obstacles.

Since blocked intentions are characteristic of everyone's experience, a major source of variation in personality lies in how we react to such frustration, either when we first encounter such a block or when we experience persisting difficulty in moving toward a goal. Let us examine how psychologists have been systematically conducting research on patterns of frustration and the consequences of persisting blockage of movement toward a goal.

Frustration refers to the blocking of an individual's efforts to satisfy a bodily need, such as hunger or thirst, or, more generally, to the blocking of attainment of a psychological goal. People suffer all kinds of frustrations daily since their needs and goals are so varied and extensive. Two ways in which they differ in dealing with frustration are:

1. how they establish goals—whether few or many with correspondingly low or high odds of frustration (some people may minimize the chances of experiencing much frustration because they limit their goals drastically)
2. how they respond to frustration—with aggression or violence; childish whining, tantrums, or self-pity; helplessness or depression; or active and effective coping and "substitution reactions"—that is, accepting alternative but related satisfactions for the originally desired object or activity.

Frustration, then, is a general description of failure of goal attainment, either temporary or chronic. Only if it is chronic is it likely to lead to stressful circumstances. We sometimes speak of frustration as if it were an emotion in itself, but ever since the careful analyses of goal behavior carried out by Kurt Lewin (1935), it seems best to limit the term frustration to an actual or perceived blockage of efforts to reach a particular goal. Some particular emotions may be the *consequence* of frustration, as well as behavior ranging from effective coping strategies to violence, disorganization, or apathy.

Table 12-1 presents a method based on research data for scoring the severity of the consequences of various frustrating circumstances or changes in a person's life. Such scores are often used to estimate the degree of life stress someone is experiencing. Bereavement, the loss through death or prolonged

TABLE 12-1
Social Readjustment Rating Scale

Life change	Life-change units
Death of spouse	100
Divorce	73
Marital separation	65
Jail term	63
Death of close family member	63
Personal injury or illness	53
Marriage	50
Fired at work	47
Marital reconciliation	45
Retirement	45
Change in health of family member	44
Pregnancy	40
Sex difficulties	39
Gain of new family member	39
Business readjustment	39
Change in financial state	38
Death of close friend	37
Change to different line of work	36
Change in number of arguments with spouse	35
Mortgage or loan for major purchase (e.g., home)	31
Foreclosure of mortgage or loan	30
Change in responsibilities at work	29
Son or daughter leaving home	29
Trouble with in-laws	29
Outstanding personal achievement	28
Wife begins or stops work	26
Begin or end school	26
Change in living conditions	25
Revision of personal habits	24
Trouble with boss	23
Change in work hours or conditions	20
Change in residence	20
Change in schools	20
Change in recreation	19
Change in church activities	19
Change in social activities	18
Mortgage or loan for lesser purchase (e.g., car, TV)	17
Change in sleeping habits	16
Change in number of family get-togethers	15
Change in eating habits	15
Vacation	13
Minor violations of the law	11

(Adapted from Holmes and Rahe, 1967)

separation of a loved or needed person, is the form of frustration that evokes the greatest stress for most people in normal life situations (Holmes and Rahe, 1967).

Frustration and Physiological Deprivation

Until the 1960s, psychologists emphasized straightforward studies of the frustration of basic needs, such as hunger or thirst. Conditions could easily be set up to starve or dehydrate animals in the laboratory and then to measure the strength of their motivation by studying how many times they dashed toward a food or water dish, or how much weight they would pull to reach such a goal. Important findings emerged from such work with respect to the relative importance of drives such as thirst, hunger, and sex in the motivation of rats. Animal studies led to work on the role of aggression as a consequence of frustration, on the generalization or displacement of aggression following frustration, on the nature of conflict behavior, and more recently, in research by Seligman and his associates at the University of Pennsylvania, on studies of "learned helplessness" following frustration (Seligman, 1975).

Efforts to measure drive through systematic deprivation of food, water, or sex turn out to be far more complex than had been anticipated (Bolles, 1967). Indeed, many factors besides sheer deprivation of food or water or sexual expression lead to hunger, thirst, or sexual behaviors. The limitations of a pure deprivational view of sexual drive, for example, were demonstrated in a study by Fisher (1962). He noted that male rats had a series of rapid intromissions and climaxes with a female in heat, but the refractory or delay periods immediately after ejaculations became longer and longer until interest in the female terminated. If, however, a new female in heat was introduced into the presence of the male, he immediately initiated sexual activity.

In a curious way, this result echoes Lewin's classic demonstration of satiation in a far simpler situation: He required subjects to write their names over and over again on a piece of paper until each person finally complained of complete fatigue and inability to go on. Lewin then asked the subjects to turn over the sheet and sign their names. People simply went ahead and signed despite their claims of complete exhaustion. Thus, behavior that may appear to be motivated by a physiological drive may be psychologically determined and strongly influenced by external information such as novelty.

In effect, then, frustration, even when involving fairly basic bodily processes, does not depend on the arousal of a need from "within." Extrinsic factors are obviously important in stimulating movement toward a goal. This raises questions about psychoanalytic views of behavior as motivated by inner drives and also points up the limitations of simple analyses of frustration behavior. Research on children initiated by Lewin and various collaborators (Barker, Dembo, and Lewin, 1943) indicated that if children are in a room with several toys and see a preferred toy behind a barrier, they will want to play with that toy. If movement toward the preferred toy is blocked, the child will show regressive behavior characterized by disorganization, more undifferen-

SURVIVAL MOTIVATION
AND THE STRENGTH OF HUMAN TABOOS

In October 1972, an airplane crashed in the remote Andes mountains. Some thirty passengers survived the impact, among them members of a Uruguayan high school rugby team. Of these thirty, only sixteen (mostly rugby players) lived to be rescued more than ten weeks later. Piers Paul Read's *Alive* (1974) is the story of these survivors, their determination to live, and their decision to break one of the most deeply ingrained of human taboos: feeding off the bodies of those who had died.

At first the team captain, informal leader of the stranded players, rationed the available food. Each person received one chocolate square and a deodorant cap full of wine per meal. But such nourishment could not sustain the vigorous climb necessary to scout the region and even that little food could not last.

As early as the fourth day, one boy had referred to eating human flesh, saying "I'll cut meat from one of the pilots. After all, they got us into this mess." At the time, his statement was not taken seriously. By the tenth day, several boys realized they must eat the flesh of their dead friends if they themselves were to survive. Said one, "It is meat, that's all it is. The souls have left their bodies and are in heaven with God. All that is left are the carcasses which are no more human beings than the dead flesh of the cattle we eat at home." A meeting was called to discuss the question.

The boys made a pact that if any more were to die, their bodies were to be consumed. But they were still unwilling to eat the bodies of those who had not made such a decision. Discussion dragged on throughout the day until four rose and went out into the snow to cut and dry the meat. Later one of these same young men overcame his revulsion and forced down a sliver of the flesh.

Others followed but still not all would eat. The analogy one boy made led several more to consent: "It's like the Holy Communion. When Christ died he gave his body so that we could have spiritual life. My friend has given us his body so that we can have physical life."

tiated movements, banging things up and down—desultory play lacking organized and constructive goals.

When goal-directed behavior is blocked, the reaction of a child or an adult depends also on the person's own experiences with frustration—the available coping skills used in the past, specific knowledge about this blockage of the goal and ways of coping with such a block, and previous successes and failures in the specific situation and in more general frustration situations. In addition, the actual nature of different contexts in which frustration takes place is being increasingly explored. Thus, an individual who has been frustrated is more likely to be aggressive if the obstacle to goal attainment itself involves some aggressive act or the threat of force than if the barrier involves no direct threat but merely difficulty or ambiguity (Baron, 1977).

Human beings are at times subjected to extreme forms of physiological deprivation. Whole nations may be the victims of severe food shortages, as were the Irish in the 1840s with the failure of the potato crop or as millions of

LABORATORY STUDIES OF LEARNED HELPLESSNESS

Seligman's hypothesis that depression results from learning of one's inability to control one's environment stemmed from observations he made while investigating the relationship between fear conditioning and operant learning in dogs (Seligman, 1975).

Seligman and his colleagues classically conditioned a number of dogs using electric shock as the unconditioned stimulus. Dogs were restrained in a hammock and subjected to unavoidable shocks that they could do nothing to lessen.

These dogs were later compared to control animals on a signalled escape-avoidance task using a shuttle box. This device consisted of two chambers separated by a partial barrier across which all the dogs were physically capable of jumping. Dogs had to jump this barrier to avoid shock. On every trial, a tone would sound and ten seconds later an electric shock spread along the floor of whichever compartment the dogs were in when the tone was presented. When a dog jumped the barrier, the shock was terminated. By jumping within ten seconds of hearing the tone, a dog avoided a shock altogether. If the dog did not jump, shock continued for sixty seconds.

Normal dogs easily learned to escape shock by fleeing to the other side when they heard the warning tone. Dogs who had previously been subjected to unavoidable shock in the classical-conditioning experiment responded differently. They ran agitatedly around the shocked chamber during the beginning of the initial trial then sat down and whined, passively accepting the shock. On subsequent trials the dogs resigned themselves more quickly, never learning to escape.

By 1975, Seligman had tested 150 dogs who had previously experienced the unavoidable shock. One hundred of these (67 percent) showed the helplessness effect and failed to avoid shocks. Of the several hundred control animals used, only about five percent were helpless ("naturally depressed") even though they had received no inescapable shock, perhaps because of their history before reaching the laboratory.

people in parts of Africa, India, and Haiti still are. What is significant for personality study in these tragic human situations is that behavior is governed not by direct and obvious methods of satisfying hunger but by a whole variety of human symbolic meanings and variations in response styles. It is a grisly thought, but one that follows from a simple-minded drive theory of action, that starving people ought simply to become cannibals. Yet such acts are rare even in the most extreme circumstances; whole tribes starve quietly without killing their children or the feebler members. Human values, inhibitions against violence, religious taboos continue to operate to a remarkable degree. Survival motivation in the face of severe hunger can break some taboos, but only under unusual circumstances in which meanings are reinterpreted.

Studies of prolonged states of frustration or of basic need deprivation point up the possibility that apathy and regressive behaviors are more common than aggressive reactions. Increasingly, this has forced psychologists' attention to the question of possible control over a situation or, at least, its predictability. Again, we see the importance of a cognitive appraisal of the situation. When human beings—and many animal species—learn that a desired outcome (attaining food, attaining freedom, reducing the likelihood of pain, or attaining some psychological or social goal) depends on circumstances that cannot be predicted or controlled the only feasible response is passive yielding.

Seligman (1975) carried out a series of studies on what he termed *learned helplessness*, analyzing a variety of situations in terms of the extent to which an organism, because of severely frustrating or painful circumstances that were clearly beyond its control, developed a specific state of apathy. After chronic frustration the animal behaves as if it has learned to be helpless, to act dependently, and not to show appropriate self-serving actions. This helplessness not only prevents it from dealing with the problem it faces but may generalize to other circumstances that it confronts. Tomkins' affect theory also suggests that the persistence of information that cannot be incorporated into earlier schema or integrated into a new concept will first arouse anger and then distress or despair (Tomkins, 1962, 1963).

Learned Helplessness

Predictability, Hope, and Helplessness   The fact that animals learn complex response contingencies, which implies that they have a sense of *possibility*, has been an important advance for the understanding of animal learning. Humans also possess this capacity and rely heavily on it. Indeed, the tremendous significance of *hope* as a critical factor in human adjustment comes into play here (Stotland, 1969). In one experiment (Glass and Singer, 1972), individuals were deluded into thinking that they had control over a situation when they really had none, and they functioned more effectively than when they believed themselves to be utterly powerless.

Although helplessness and apathy in the face of frustration have been most extensively demonstrated in animal experiments, they do appear in studies with normal adults and children as well. Roth and Bootzin (1974) presented two groups of young adults with a series of problems. One group was given problems that could easily be solved. The other group confronted problems that were simply not possible to solve. The subjects were then taken into another room and presented with more problems that were projected on a TV screen. In this case, all the problems were solvable but varied in difficulty. When the tenth new problem was presented, the screen blurred suddenly, so that the problem was difficult to read. Which group of subjects took action to deal with the situation?

Those who had worked on the unsolvable problems were quicker to ask the experimenter to fix the screen. Nevertheless, even with this attempt at coping, these subjects performed more poorly than subjects who had experienced successful problem-solving. It seems likely, therefore, that the initial effects of failure may be to arouse a certain amount of general distress, but as failure persists, then despair or depression emerges and fosters helplessness and inadequate performance.

COPING WITH FRUSTRATION

David C. Glass and Jerome E. Singer (1972) found that one's ability to cope with frustration after exposure to unpleasant noise was affected by psychological as well as physical parameters of noise presentation.

Unpredictable, irregular noise leads to poorer ability to tolerate frustration afterward than noise with a predictable onset. After exposure to unpleasant noise that came on either regularly or unpredictably, participants were presented with four line-tracing problems, two of which were impossible. Subjects who had heard loud predictable noise proved more persistent on this frustrating task than those who had heard loud unpredictable noise.

Hypothesizing that unpredictable noise was more aversive because it led subjects to believe they could not control their environment, Glass and Singer next explicitly manipulated perceived *control* over noise. In this experiment, all subjects listened to the same loud unpredictable noise previously found to cause aversive aftereffects. Subjects in the "perceived-control" condition were instructed that they could stop the noise at any time by flicking a switch beneath their seat but that the experimenter preferred them not to. Few of these subjects used the switch, even though they could have terminated the noise by doing so. The subject's tolerance for post-noise frustration (again using pencil tracings) and accuracy in proofreading, a new task, were assessed after the noise ceased. Subjects in the "no-perceived-control" condition were treated identically but were not told of any way of terminating the noise.

During noise presentation, subjects in both conditions eventually adapted to the noise. But the aftereffects of stimulation were much more pronounced for those who felt they had no control over the situation. Subjects who believed they could have stopped the noise tolerated later frustration better and proofread more accurately (see Figure 12-1).

Thus, a psychological state such as helplessness, arising from uncontrollable stress, may affect our reaction to subsequent environmental stressors. Similar results are obtained whether the stress beyond the subject's perceived control is noise or bureaucratic inflexibility (Glass and Singer, 1972) or uncontingent, unavoidable electric shock (Seligman, 1975; see the Box on page 280).

In a study with children, Dweck and Reppucci (1973) arranged for a teacher to present a group of children with problems that they could not solve at all. After such a history of failure, the pupils were unable to solve a new group of problems, which were easily solvable, when they were presented by the same teacher. But notice that cognitive processes are important: When the children were given identical problems by a different teacher, one with whom they had not had an experience of failure, they were able to solve them. They made a clear distinction between the two situations. In the case of humans, the effects of continued frustration are influenced by a wider range of associations and complex thought processes than is found in animals, where helplessness generalizes more easily.

Helplessness and Depression   Seligman's conception of apathy and self-defeating attitudes has been useful in forcing psychologists and psychiatrists

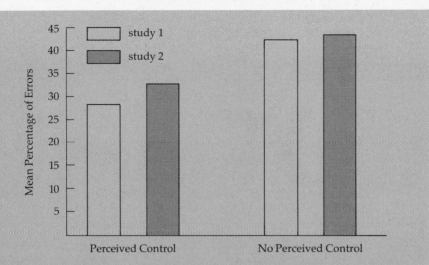

FIGURE 12-1

The Aftereffects of Perceived Control

While being subjected to an unpleasant noise, two groups of subjects were given a proofreading task. One group believed they could stop the noise whenever they wished; the other group believed they had no such control over the noise. The graph shows the resulting percentage of proofreading errors in two separate (replicated) tests.

(Derived from Glass and Singer, 1972)

to look at the nature of persisting failure or frustration. Because of the implications of this work for understanding and treatment of depression, an intense research effort has emerged to pin down the basis of helplessness.

An important question for personality psychology has arisen from two points of view about depression, those of Seligman and of Beck (1967). Seligman's orientation has been situational—people become apathetic or depressed when they confront a series of noncontingent (unpredictable or inexplicable) failures. Beck, who has a more personalistic and cognitive orientation, proposed that some individuals, because of constitutional factors, early experiences, or both, develop an attitude of appraising events from a negative or hopeless point of view. For Beck, the depressed person is someone whose self-communication—that is, ongoing thought—reflects an expectation of failure and a belief that chance, rather one's own abilities or efforts, influences a situation. While Seligman might argue that such an orientation already reflects helplessness, there is little evidence that people who are chronically depressed have experienced the specific patterns of failure that Seligman would posit. Indeed, Seligman's "depressed" subjects were college students whose scores on inventories like the Beck Depressive Index (Beck, 1967) were far lower than those of hospitalized depressed patients. Seligman's position may have overemphasized the objective situation of the individual (perhaps because so much of the work was done with animals where "objective" success or failure—avoiding or receiving a shock—can be easily controlled). If it is just the discovery that one's behavior cannot affect outcomes that determines depression, then animals or people who have experienced 100 percent reinforcement without contingency—that is, without any connection with their own actions or efforts—should certainly show apathy or depression.

The study by Rizley (1978, described in Chapter 7) points up some of the problems for the helplessness theory, especially as it applies to depression. As we noted, Rizley found that nondepressed people may erroneously overemphasize their control over situations—a kind of defensive optimism. Findings of this type also occur when self-esteem is the personality variable rather than depression. Individuals with high self-esteem scores continue to expect to perform successfully on a future task even though they experienced some failures; persons with low self-esteem are more likely to anticipate failure irrespective of feedback from actual performance (McFarlin and Blascovich, 1981).

Abramson, Seligman, and Teasdale (1978) proposed a revision of the helplessness theory to include the subjective interpretation of a situation. In this revision, an objective noncontingency—that is, a random outcome of some performance that is unconnected with one's effectiveness—may lead a person to review present and past noncontingencies and then attempt to explain the extent. If this explanation leads to a conclusion that one cannot control the situation in the future, the symptoms of helplessness may follow. It remains to be seen whether this new fusion of actual experience and cognitive appraisal will better explain the occurrence of helplessness following prolonged frustration. Several studies make it clear that a characteristic of "normality" is what has been termed an "illusory warm glow," that is, a tendency to evaluate circumstances in a slightly unrealistic but hopeful fashion (Lewinsohn and others, 1980). Alloy and Abramson (1979) have pointed out that depressed persons are "sadder but wiser"; they are more accurate in identifying failure and in detecting the operation of chance factors than the more hopeful, nondepressed individuals.

Learned helplessness in human beings appears to be a measurable, readily identified characteristic with important consequences for persisting inadequacy in performance and chronic depressed affect. A history of past failures that either suggests a lack of basic abilities or that one cannot predict or anticipate future events may contribute to a feeling of helpless despair. Often, however, origins of helplessness cannot be traced to specific noncontingent failures. Rather, some people consistently notice and remember their experiences of chronic frustration or failure and seem to exaggerate them. Thus, their helplessness arises from a cognitive-affective style that leads them to anticipate failure and not to try hard enough to cope with the inevitable frustrations of daily life.

Ethical considerations prohibit laboratory studies of extreme frustration in human beings. Our understanding of how people cope with powerful limitations on their freedom or threats to their survival must depend on careful study of the accounts of survivors of harrowing experiences. Unfortunately, examples of humans exposed to enslavement, to imprisonment in concentration camps or, more recently, to the risk of massacre as hostages to terrorism are numerous enough. Behavioral scientists have recently been able to obtain detailed accounts of such experiences and have also been able to follow up survivors to evaluate longer-term effects of severe forms of frustration. Let us take a closer look at some issues that have emerged from studies in which people were exposed to great danger and experienced intense fear.

The Limits of Sheer Survival

While frustration is a daily occurrence for all of us, danger is far less common. When danger does occur, it has consequences that influence personality dramatically. Generally speaking, the word "danger" is best applied to situations that directly threaten our physical freedom, our safety, or our lives. There are, of course, situations in which we are confronted with loss of job or the esteem of our friends and relatives, or our sense of personal value and identity. Such situations, however, are generally treated as threats to the ego or to self-esteem and probably are best separated from situations that present what might be called "clear and present danger," situations that inevitably evoke an initial response of fear followed by some efforts at escape or other coping reactions. The nature of the human personality is so complex and so tied to symbolic meanings and personal fantasies about the self and self-identity that danger to life may conflict with the sense of threat to personal integrity. Some of the instances of great human courage reflect the willingness of individuals to risk or give their lives to preserve their beliefs or to save others.

In the Nazi concentration camp at Auschwitz in September 1944, a group of Jews assigned to work in the crematoria decided, in the face of certain death, that the least they could do was to slow down the cremation process. Working together extremely well, they managed to accumulate weapons and explosives and blow up two of the four ovens before they themselves were all killed (Kren and Rappoport, 1980). And of course we also know of individuals who risk their own lives to save others. During a terrible fire a distinguished psychologist, Sydney Segal, having managed to save her two daughters, rushed into a flaming room in an attempt to rescue her son and died with him there.

Confronting Physical Danger

There are, of course, many times when danger is not compounded by complex values, and when escape and survival are the most natural of human responses. An important issue in personality study has to do with how effectively individuals cope with the dangers they confront. The normal response to awareness of danger is the emotion of fear. Without fear, human beings would be incredibly vulnerable to genuine dangers. Thus, a first step in dealing with danger is to recognize that a situation presents a genuine risk to life. What follows then is the normal fear response, or what Janis (1971) has termed *reflective fear*, which is distinguished from neurotic fear or anxiety for the following reasons:

1. Reflective fear is highly responsive to specific cues in the environment that indicate danger, and such fear rises or decreases more or less proportionately with the actual danger.
2. It causes an increase in alertness and attentiveness, with an effort to look for escape routes or to determine the exact nature of the danger.
3. It leads to an attempt to gain any available help or reassurance from others.
4. It requires a compromise between extreme alertness to risk and an effort to assimilate the awareness of threat into previously prepared cognitive structures—a sense of hope, reassurance from others, a plan of help.

If persons experiencing fear do not make some effort to reduce its level through hope, a plan, or some reassurance, their judgment may be impaired and they may behave ineffectively.

Our capacity to cope with genuine danger depends in part on the effective working of the different organismic systems—our emotions, our cognitive capacities, and our communication skills and motor abilities. Of course, some dangers we survive only by sheer luck. In the Buffalo Creek disaster, the erratic course of the sludge flood was unpredictable; it passed some houses and left them unscathed, while descending without warning on others and completely destroying them and their inhabitants. Obviously, a first step in coping with danger is the amount of time we have to appraise the danger cognitively. Here previous experience may be critical. Highly skilled drivers have a much better chance of survival than novice drivers if their cars suddenly skid on ice. Both will experience fear, but the experienced driver will respond appropriately, noticing more quickly the direction of the skid and the possibilities for turning into it without risk from oncoming vehicles. The inexperienced driver may simply panic and engage in random jamming of the brakes or turning of the wheel, only to worsen the skid.

Not only is cognitive appraisal of the danger important, but the availability of previously rehearsed motor responses is also critical, as the preceding example shows. The "survival training" of people who are expected to risk their lives—soldiers, police, firefighters, movie stunt experts, mountaineers—exposes them again and again to simulations of situations that they may encounter. Once these persons are well trained, they should reach the point where, confronted with the real situation, they immediately appraise the extent and immediacy of the danger and automatically react by hitting the ground, or crawling toward protective obstructions, or whatever activity is appropriate. "Programmed" to perform such actions, they do not need to concentrate on physical acts, so they are free to carry on more elaborate cognitive appraisals of sources of aid or alternative steps to reduce the danger.

If the cognitive and motor systems are working properly, there still remains the possibility that some persons are more prone to excessive fear and its disruptive effects than others under some circumstances. On the other hand, some persons may be overly daring and, because of overconfidence, put themselves at risk. In a case study by Janis (1971), a young man named Don went swimming in a dangerous surf despite the fact that it was obvious to anyone with his background how dangerous it was. He had just learned that the football team on which he played had been selected to play in the Rose Bowl. His tremendous excitement about this news led him to plunge into the surf, with the result that he was swept far out into a treacherous current. After hours of struggle—during which time he was believed to have drowned—he managed to survive and regain the shore, chiefly because he was so experienced a swimmer that he had a remarkable store of information and physical coping capacities. From the standpoint of personality, it is also important to note that Don was naturally optimistic and positive, and it may be that his freedom from hopelessness and from negative self-attitude helped him to survive.

Don's case is especially instructive because after he got back to shore and was hospitalized, his delirious talk was transcribed verbatim, which permitted a reconstruction of his stream of consciousness during the long hours in the water. One can trace his initial terror followed by the institution of pre-established coping responses. As an experienced swimmer, Don had planned what he would do if he ever was dragged out to sea. He struck out for the open sea beyond the waves and then drifted to conserve energy until the tide eventually turned. His first reactions reflected positive, constructive thought rather than self-reproach. As he fought to stay adrift, he found himself reviewing his life with his family and examining his feelings about the beautiful but artificial young woman he was attracted to. Eventually some deeply despairing notes crept into his thoughts, but generally he struggled to think again of hopeful possibilities. Periods of confusion followed, so that even after he had made it back to shore safely he dragged himself much farther onto the beach than was necessary. For almost two days in the hospital he suffered from loss of memory and impaired sense of personal identity, but he soon recovered complete awareness. Nightmares and other troubling thoughts persisted for months afterward, and it was apparent that his sense of personal invulnerability, which had led him to take his foolish swim in the first place—but which had also sustained him with positive thoughts during the ordeal—was now lost.

We know how danger has been dealt with chiefly from accounts of survivors. It seems that prior coping plans, the necessary motor skills, a positive self-attitude, and even a sense of humor are important in sustaining an individual. An orientation that includes positive self-communications, a form of "the power of positive thinking," with a history of some life success and of previous coping experiences all seem necessary. An established self-efficacy orientation (Bandura, 1977) may be critical as a predisposition the individual brings to a dangerous situation.

Survival training enables these mountaineers to quickly assess and react to any danger they encounter, without being disabled by fear.

The Consequences of Exposure to Danger

Despite the fact of survival, the exposure to extreme danger exacts a price. Twenty years after World War II, Archibald and Tuddenham (1965) found continuing signs of depression, irritability, jumpiness, fatigability, sweaty palms, or dizziness in World War II veterans who had suffered extreme combat conditions with consequent combat fatigue. Similar results have emerged for veterans of the Korean War. Even for men who seemed to have recovered completely from war neurosis, the exposure to combatlike noises from tape recordings produced marked reversions to their earlier symptomatology (Dobbs and Wilson, 1960).

Dor-Shav (1978) followed up 42 survivors of Nazi concentration camps and compared them to 20 individuals of comparable age, background, and education who had not been incarcerated. She administered a battery of tests, intelligence measures, projective techniques, and personality questionnaires to both groups. Her data suggest that the concentration-camp victims are less imaginative and creative, more constricted, more persevering and shrewd, but also more global and less subtle in their thinking. The evidence of personality constriction and of persisting anxiety was greatest in those who suffered imprisonment at earlier ages. As Dor-Shav notes, "the price is still being paid" (Dor-Shav, 1978, p. 11).

Too little is known of what part brushes with danger or death play in the formation of personality in "ordinary" life situations. It seems likely, however, that the realistic dangers, the regular exposure to violence, and the injuries or deaths in the family that characterize the lives of the urban poor must take their toll. The so-called "street-sense" of youths from city ghetto areas may represent a hypervigilant alertness that aids them to survive. This jumpy superalertness may create a long-lasting tension and a readiness for fight and flight that may be counterproductive in school or job situations requiring quiet persistence and entirely different kinds of concentrated attention.

In the course of an attempt to develop a questionnaire that would identify individuals who might have difficulties in sticking it out during a prolonged sensory-deprivation experiment, Marvin Zuckerman (1979) constructed a scale called Thrill and Adventure Seeking (TAS), which is made up of items that indicate a preference for activities like waterskiing, flying, scuba diving, riding in open convertibles, and sky diving. Although people who respond positively to many items of this scale may not have done any parachute jumping or scuba diving, an examination of their life-styles shows that they have indeed engaged in some fairly risky activities. Zuckerman believes that adventure-seeking is just one manifestation of a general personality trait of sensation-seeking, a continuous desire to raise one's level of excitation, to encounter novel situations, and to try new settings for experiences (see Chapter 8).

Seekers after Danger

Hymbaugh and Garret (1974) found that 21 sky divers scored higher on sensation-seeking than did 21 control individuals matched with them for age, sex, occupational, and socioeconomic status. Other studies cited by Zuckerman (1979) indicate that risk-takers like firemen, riot-squad police, racing-car drivers, and parachutists scored significantly higher on both thrill and adventure seeking and on general sensation-seeking scales than did otherwise matched civil servants and college students. A group of volunteer divers who did underwater rescues without monetary reward scored higher on thrill-and-adventure–seeking scales as well as on general sensation-seeking scales than did engineering students of the same age. Among professionals, Irey (1974)

As might be expected, people who score high on sensation-seeking scales tend to prefer sports like hang gliding and other activities with a high level of risk, excitement, and novelty.

found that psychologists and paraprofessionals who worked in "crisis intervention units" scored higher on all of the sensation-seeking scales than physicians or clinical or academic psychologists.

To support his view that sensation-seeking or the desire for increased tension is a basic trait, Zuckerman (1978) showed that sensation-seekers have stronger physiological responses to novel stimuli of only moderate intensity. He also cited his work with Monte Buchsbaum at the National Institute of Mental Health, which indicates that sensation-seekers respond to increasingly stronger levels of stimulation, such as flashing lights, with higher electrical responses of the brain, while those who score lower on these scales show involuntary reductions of evoked potentials to stimulations at high intensities. There also are suggestions that sensation-seekers show lower levels of monoamine oxidase (MAO), a chemical which in the brain appears to control the neurotransmitters that produce rapid swings of emotion or mood. Sensation-seekers among college students show higher levels of both androgens and estrogens, male and female hormones, than do students scoring at average or lower levels on these scales. Some researchers believe that sex hormones activate norepinephrine by limiting the effects of MAO.

Clearly, then, while danger is something most people avoid, some subgroups of our species look more actively for new challenges, new adventures. Anecdotal accounts suggest that when such thrill-seeking does result in injury or near loss of life, even these daring souls have nightmares and traumatic neuroses. They differ from most of us, however, in the fact that as soon as possible, they are off again seeking new risks and adventures.

TRAUMATIC STRESS

The power of processes of memory, self-consistency, and anticipation are nowhere more evident than in the long-term consequences of relatively brief periods of severe stress. Although there may be significant physical discomfort or damage, as in the case of the B'nai B'rith hostages, the body recovers relatively quickly once medical care is provided. But at this point, psychological consequences often emerge. There are recurrent thoughts about the severity of the danger, feelings of helplessness or of failure to take action, images of revenge, memories of those who died, anticipation of future dangers. Such thoughts are experienced as recurring mental images or regularly repeated bad dreams. These create in miniature a renewed situation of stress that unquestionably influences the gross psychophysiological structure of the organism, leading to hypervigilance, to extreme sensitivity to noises or potential dangers, and in the case of organically vulnerable individuals, to psychosomatic illnesses. The very power of our imagination to take us backward in time or to move us forward into the realm of possibility apparently makes us all the more vulnerable once we have been exposed to truly terrifying real-life circumstances.

A good deal about personality has been learned from the psychotherapy offered individuals who developed long-term neurotic reactions. Psychologists now, it is sad to say, have opportunities to learn about personality from treatment of individuals who have undergone grave physical danger or who have been victims of terrorism, such as the Iranian hostages in 1980–81. Belz and others (1977) have described how the victims of the Hanafi Muslim takeover in Washington responded during the terror and then how prolonged their reactions were. As part of a team of therapists at the University Health Service of George Washington University, Belz and his colleagues were close to the site of the takeovers and had begun to plan in advance for the possibility of a treatment program for hostages, even while the siege was still on. By examining in some detail the procedures used and their effectiveness, we can gain some insight into the impact of danger on personality and identify those

A HOSTAGE REMEMBERS

In May 1980, when the American hostages were still being held in Iran, Diana Cole, who had been a hostage of the Hanafi Muslims three years earlier, wrote about her experiences and the aftermath. Here are some excerpts from her account (from *Newsweek*, May 19, 1980):

I was one of the 134 men and women seized by the Hanafi Muslims in their armed takeover of three Washington, D.C., buildings in March 1977, and as each new ordeal unfolds [in Iran], I relive my own experience as a hostage.

At times I marvel that I am alive to tell the tale. "Nobody promised you tomorrow," said Hamaas Abdul Khaalis, the leader of the group that held me hostage. That refrain spins round and round within me. It's easy to take life for granted—until you lie on a bare concrete floor while strangers who brandish rifles and machetes strut above you, and your ears ring with the chant of your captors. . . .

"Be strong, be strong, and let us strengthen one another," a Hebrew saying goes. As I repeated those words, I found the strength to accept my fate. Then, after 39 hours of captivity, we were released—the result of negotiation about which we hostages had known little. I left unharmed, but not unchanged. I found I possessed a new and different vision of the world—one more urgent and at the same time more resigned. I married the man I loved and settled old quarrels with my family and with myself. . . .

As a hostage, I remembered the successful Israeli rescue mission at Entebbe. Successful—though one hostage, an elderly woman, was left behind, several hostages died and the leader of the Israeli commandos perished with them. Then I recalled the fatal shoot-out at the Munich airport that followed the seizure of Israeli athletes by Black September terrorists at the 1972 Olympics. . . .

Another thought disturbed me. At Munich, the Olympic Games had continued after the briefest of intervals. If we were slaughtered—whether by our captors or by the cross fire of our rescuers—how many hours would the world mourn?. . . . Isolated from the world, you wonder if the world cares. You remain a hostage, and so you decide that it does not. Thus tormented, surrounded by armed guards, alarmed by every sound, you wait in your prison and continue to wait.

Therefore, never say to a former hostage, "I understand that you were treated well." "Yes," he may reply. "I certainly am grateful to have come out alive." But to be held a prisoner, to live from moment to endless moment at gunpoint—the constant and palpable threat of death—hardly constitutes good treatment. Call it by its proper name, terror—a terror that affects both mind and body, and whose lingering effects, including nightmares, anxiety and a certain jumpiness, may never disappear.

conditions under which the psychologically damaged individual can be helped toward normal functioning.

Within 24 hours after the victims of the building seizure in Washington were released as medically fit, they began to experience a considerable range of distressing symptoms. An important first step to help them was simply to bring them together in a group. Many of the individuals had whole series of fearful thoughts and various grueling experiences during their imprisonment, but they had had surprisingly little opportunity to share them with one another at the time. Thus, an initial step in helping them reestablish some degree of control over their lives was to have them describe their experiences, so that in a sense the actual dimensions of the event could be spelled out.

It was also very important for the former hostages to learn that during their worst terrors, several of them had had the same odd thoughts, such as a secret desire that the Muslims would be proficient in the use of their swords. "If I am to be beheaded, let it be done neatly, without pain," was a common inner reaction of several of them. It was important for them to recognize that their inner terrors and fantasies were not signs of insanity, vulnerability, or cowardice, but were natural human expressions under conditions of deep danger.

A next step was providing the former hostages with some practical techniques for dealing with persisting tension, including some that were developed in behavior-modification training. For example, the subjects were trained in the Jacobson progressive relaxation method, in which muscles are alternately tensed and then relaxed starting in the feet and working up through the body. This experience helps to identify the relaxed state and also often moves a person relatively quickly into a state of deeper relaxation. The group also learned techniques for identifying sequences of thoughts that became cyclic and self-tormenting. They were shown how to break these thought cycles, either by the use of self-injunctions such as "Stop!" or by substituting distracting positive images, such as scenes associated with nature, faraway places, or moments of joy from the past.

Many individuals in the group were prone to guilt reactions or to other forms of self-recrimination. While undoubtedly some of these responses were carry-overs of longstanding personality styles, an attempt was made to present useful alternatives that might help them cope with their specific problems. Here the guilty thoughts were examined for their actual implications. How realistic were they? What would be the most likely outcome had the individuals taken other courses of action? The situations were put into perspective in relation to other significant experiences, such as loss of loved ones through death or separation.

The group also needed help in learning to assert their rights with friends, relatives, and strangers. Often friends were oversolicitous, and strangers came up to them out of the blue and asked them to describe what had happened. Reassurance in how to say "No" and some rehearsal of techniques for dealing with strangers were helpful. Such training restored their natural ability to express their feelings clearly to others.

A final step, desensitization, was to make sure that the former hostages gradually but systematically began to take part in activities about which they had grown excessively fearful. They were encouraged to begin by imagining and then by actually taking short and then longer taxi rides, first by taking friends along, and then eventually taking longer rides alone. Ultimately, the entire group returned to the scene of their victimization and spent almost half an hour in the room going through the experience.

The treatment approach described above shows again the importance of viewing personality effects in terms of interacting systems. The psychophysiological component of the experience required treatment through relaxation and related muscular feedback. The cognitive aspects, involving so much ambiguity and confusion, needed clarification through the sharing of memories. The private affective reactions benefited from a sharing of experience so that the group recognized that terror or seeming cowardice is not a unique response or inherent moral weakness. Longer-term dynamic attitudes, such as proneness to guilt, needed to be approached through some form of personality self-examination. And, finally, the group needed actual practice of new responses and gradual motor and fantasy rehearsal to counteract newly developed phobic reactions.

So potent is the human memory, however, that even addressing all of these systems in a systematic fashion cannot completely eliminate all the thoughts and psychophysiological-feedback effects in cases of trauma. It may be that long-term predisposing trends in the personality make some individuals unusually vulnerable to persistent traumatic reactions or make them less capable of responding effectively to treatment. Thus, though many people have similar short-term reactions to trauma, long-term reactions may differ because of variation in individual personality structure.

Stress-Response Syndromes

A useful way to clarify how personality patterns intersect with stress situations and thus lead to different symptoms and treatment possibilities has been presented by a psychiatrist, Mardi Horowitz (1976). During a five-year period in which Horowitz studied more than 50 individuals who had undergone several periods of extreme stress or trauma, he identified three major neurotic styles—or, more broadly, general personality orientations—that show somewhat distinctive responses to a severe stress: the *hysterical*, the *obsessional*, and the *narcissistic* styles. Horowitz noted for each of the three personality styles the major "defects" that would lead to the persistence of the traumatic reaction and its deleterious influence on the personality. For each he provided a table indicating how the defect can be "countered" through particular patterns of therapy (Tables 12-2, 12-3, 12-4).

While much of what Horowitz proposed has yet to be borne out of systematic research, his orientation seems valuable in tying together the complex issues raised in looking at the personality under stress. Horowitz's approach shows that people throughout life are developing a systematic series of strategies for dealing with new information, for organizing emotions and expressing them, for defending themselves against frightening thoughts or events, and for dealing with memories or anticipating the future. In this sense, the sudden occurrence of intense frustration or severe trauma comes into play in relation to an established complex set of personality characteristics. We may ask, for example, if the therapy team at George Washington University might not have had even better success in helping the victims of the Hanafi Muslims

TABLE 12-2
The Hysterical Style

Function	Style as "defect"	Therapeutic counter or approach
Perception	Global or selective inattention	Ask for details again and again; encourage concrete imagery
Representation	Impressionistic rather than accurate	Have person reconstruct and relive the experience with full emotional expression
Translation of images into words	Limited	Encourage talk; provide verbal labels
Associations	Limited by inhibitions Misinterpretations based on schematic stereotypes, deflected from reality to wishes and fears	Encourage production Repeat and clarify
Problem-solving	Short circuit to rapid but often erroneous conclusions Avoidance of topic; emotions are unbearable	Keep subject open; interpret Support

(Modified from Horowitz, 1976, p. 25)

TABLE 12-3
The Obsessional Style

Function	Style as "defect"	Therapeutic counter or approach
Perception	Detailed or factual	Ask for overall impressions and statements about emotional experiences
Representation	Isolation of ideas from emotions	Link emotional meanings back to ideational meanings
Translation of images into words	Emotional meaning missed in a rapid transition to partial word meanings	Focus attention on images and reactions to them
Associations	Sets of meanings shifted back and forth	Keep patient focused on major problems (holding operation); interpret defenses and "warded-off" meanings
Problem-solving	Endless rumination without reaching decisions	Interpret reasons for warding off clear decisions

(Modified from Horowitz, 1976, p. 31)

TABLE 12-4
The Narcissistic Style

Function	Style as "defect"	Therapeutic counter or approach
Perception	Focus on praise and blame rather than objective events Denial of "wounding" information; vulnerable to self-related criticism	Avoid being provoked into either praising or blaming Counteract denials with tactful timing and wording
Representation	Uncertainty of attribution as to self or another person	Clarify who is who in terms of acts, motives, beliefs, and sensations
Translation of images into words	Meanings of words and events shifted in a confusing way	Consistently define meanings; encourage decisions as to most relevant meanings or weightings
Associations	Overbalanced in terms of finding routes to self-enhancement rather than clear descriptions	Hold to other meanings; cautiously deflate grandiose meanings
Problem-solving	Reality distorted to maintain self-esteem, obtain illusory gratifications, and forgive self too easily for actual errors or failures	Point out corruptions (tactfully); encourage and reward fidelity to reality; support self-esteem during period of surrender or illusory gratification; help develop appropriate sense of responsibility; discourage unrealistic gratification from therapy

(Modified from Horowitz, 1976, p. 46)

had they taken these systematic personality differences into account in developing their treatment orientation.

Implications In many ways, this chapter has been much like a horror story. If we are to understand the human personality in its fullest range, we must be prepared to examine not only its inner systems—the passing fantasies and memories, wishes and dreams—but its pattern of total systemic response to extreme frustration, helplessness, and mortal danger. The inner or private personality of our thoughts and fantasies reflects again and again the consequences of exposures to frustrations or danger, even if somehow or other we manage to put up a good front. Even with such bravado in our public presentation, the evidence in this chapter shows that trauma ultimately does take its toll. Despite efforts at repression, even the hysterical personality described by Horowitz eventually begins to experience traumatic dreams. Many survivors of the World

War II concentration camps who have forced themselves back into the real world, using their sharpened vigilance to make a way for themselves, still reflect in a variety of psychological tests the persistence of those terrible years. Our personalities are inevitably shaped not only in the nursery or in interactions with our parents, siblings, or friends, but also by those often almost random occurrences of severe frustration, helplessness, and danger that are part of life on this planet. By considering the kinds of psychological preparation people have for coping with stress not only when it occurs but after it has passed, we may eventually understand more fully the nature of personality functioning in its broadest sense.

SUMMARY

1. Frustration refers to the blocking of an individual's effort to satisfy a bodily need or, more generally, to the blocking of attainment of a psychological goal. A way of looking at personality differences is to consider (1) the small or large number of goals a person establishes, with correspondingly low or high chances of frustration, and (2) how people respond to frustration.

2. Until the 1960s psychologists emphasized laboratory studies, usually with animals, of the frustration of basic needs, such as hunger or thirst. Research showed that behavior appearing to be motivated through a physiological drive may actually be psychologically determined and influenced by external information, such as novelty. When goal-directed behavior is blocked, the reaction depends on a person's past experiences with frustration. Studies of prolonged states of basic-need deprivation suggest that apathy and regressive behavior are more common than aggression.

3. Seligman carried out studies on *learned helplessness* in which, after chronic frustration, an animal behaves as if it has learned to be helpless. Such helplessness may generalize to other circumstances. Helplessness and apathy in the face of frustration have been shown to appear in human beings as well as in animals.

4. An important question for personality psychology has arisen from two points of view about depression, Seligman's and Beck's. Seligman's view is that people become depressed when they confront unpredictable or inexplicable failures. Beck's view is that some people, because of constitutional factors, early experiences, or both, develop an attitude of appraising events from a negative or hopeless standpoint.

5. The term danger is applied to situations that directly threaten life, bodily integrity, or physical freedom. Although danger occurs far less frequently than frustration, it does influence personality dramatically. An important issue in personality study is how people cope with danger. The normal response to awareness of danger is *reflective* fear. Reflective fear is different

from *neurotic* fear or anxiety because (1) it is responsive to cues in the environment that indicate danger, (2) it causes increased alertness and an effort to escape or determine the exact nature of the danger, (3) it leads to an attempt to obtain help, and (4) it requires an effort to assimilate the awareness of threat into previously prepared cognitive structures.

6. "Survival training" involves repeated simulations of dangerous situations to the extent that in the real situation the well-trained person immediately sets in motion a rapid appraisal of the danger and automatically institutes the appropriate motor activities. An orientation that includes positive self-communication and a history of some life successes and of previous coping experiences all seem necessary.

7. Survivors of extreme danger show reactions for many years. Men who have suffered extreme combat conditions continue to have signs of depression, irritability, dizziness, and other signs of personality difficulties. Concentration-camp survivors also show persisting anxiety and other personality constrictions.

8. Some people seek out danger. Zuckerman constructed a scale to measure thrill and adventure–seeking attitudes and behavior. Zuckerman believes that adventure-seeking is one manifestation of a general personality trait of sensation-seeking, a desire to raise one's level of excitation and to encounter novel situations.

9. After conditions of extreme stress, the body usually recovers reasonably rapidly once medical care is provided, but then psychological consequences often emerge. A good deal has been learned about personality from the psychotherapy offered to people who develop these psychological problems. The therapy usually involves (1) sharing thoughts and experiences with others, (2) training in relaxation and thought-stopping, (3) rational-emotive approaches to dealing with guilt and other forms of self-recrimination, (4) self-assertiveness training, and (5) desensitization.

10. A way to clarify how personality patterns are related to reactions to stress situations and to development of different symptoms requiring different treatment has been outlined by Horowitz. He identified three major personality orientations that show somewhat distinctive responses to severe stress. He called these orientations or styles the hysterical, the obsessional, and the narcissistic, and described a therapeutic approach for each style. Although Horowitz's notions need systematic research, they show that people throughout life develop strategies for dealing with new information, for organizing emotions and expressing them, for defending themselves against frightening thoughts or events, and for dealing with memories and for anticipating the future.

CHAPTER 13

Stress II: Anxiety and Defense

Millicent Lee was on her way by car with her two young children for a visit to her parents, with whom since childhood she had had many disagreements. As she drove into the Holland Tunnel between New Jersey and New York City, Millicent suddenly was aware of a terrible sense of horror and dread. She found herself shaking so that she could barely control the steering wheel and could almost see the sides of the long tunnel crashing down upon her. With utmost effort, she managed to reach the other end of the tunnel but then had to pull over. She felt her heart beating rapidly and loudly, her face and palms sweating. After a few minutes she calmed down enough to turn the car around and drive back home, but not long after, she found that it was difficult for her to drive the children anywhere. She had to abandon her carpool arrangements and to depend on her husband to take the children to school. Soon she found she could not drive alone at all and was relying more and more on neighbors and friends to help her. As soon as she thought of traveling by car, especially in tunnels or across bridges, she experienced terror, her palms sweating and her heart beating fast. She also experienced a dreadful fluttering in her stomach. (clinical case record of the onset of a phobia following an anxiety attack)

THE PSYCHOLOGICAL IMPORTANCE OF ANXIETY

Anxiety and conflict have been considered by most personality theorists in this century as the core issues around which human personality develops. *Anxiety* is the term used to describe our emotions in situations in which we experience a high level of fear that is not appropriate to the situation (as in the case of Millicent Lee) or when the fear is without a clear object. Anxiety also reflects an intense inner conflict in which some of the elements of the conflict may not be consciously accessible. Millicent Lee's mixed feelings about visiting her parents, whom she felt had always disapproved of her and had rejected her in her youth, undoubtedly played a role in her anxiety attack.

Anxiety, then, is a feeling of fear and dread when there is no obvious reason for the fear and is a result of extreme, usually unconscious, inner conflict. Anxiety feelings may range from mild vague uneasiness to almost paralyzing terror. Research by Izard has shown that fear is best regarded as a basic emotion while anxiety usually involves a mixture of fear and other emotions such as anger, sadness, or distress (Izard, 1977). Freud in his book *Inhibitions, Symptoms and Anxiety* first formulated the central role of anxiety in personality and in the development of symptoms and neuroses (Freud, 1926). Other theories of anxiety emerged in the latter part of the 1940s and during the 1950s.

Most clinicians agree that many of the differences in human behavior reflect the varying ways we cope with irrational fears or the direct, "free-floating" experience of anxiety and also the ways in which we defend ourselves against the awareness of serious conflict and seek to avoid the conscious experience of anxiety. As Freud pointed out, we scarcely need to define anxiety, for who among us has not experienced, seemingly from nowhere, the sudden feeling of "butterflies in the stomach," of chilling terror that we cannot explain?

Theories of Anxiety

Our review of personality theories in Chapters 2 through 6 has already indicated the central role of anxiety in personality development and patterning. In classical psychoanalysis, anxiety brought about by the conflict between the drives of the id and the attempted suppression of these drives by the superego and ego is the core problem of existence. Personality is formed initially by efforts to defend ourselves against the eruption of anxiety. Sullivan's interpersonal theory makes a distinction between satisfactions and securities. It differs from classical analysis in proposing that anxiety is not occasioned by drive frustrations but rather by fears of loss of love or rejection by significant adults. Learning theories, especially in the Dollard-Miller period, focused upon anxiety as a drive that stimulates learning under certain conditions and interferes with it under others.

Goldstein's approach to anxiety is intrinsically cognitive; he maintained that we experience anxiety because we continually confront new situations that must be organized and integrated. This point of view broadens the scope of the concept without ignoring the importance of the parent-child relationship and calls attention to the tie between anxiety and growth or self-actualization. Maslow and May, whose humanistic and existential positions we discussed earlier, were both strongly influenced by Goldstein's orientation and they, too, emphasized the growth-related nature of anxiety as well as its more pathological implications. From the existential point of view, anxiety is closely related to the fear of a sterile life and of the meaninglessness of death.

The writings of Franz Kafka have highlighted the far-reaching and awesome implications of the existential approach to anxiety. In Kafka's *Metamorphosis*, a young man who has been leading a narrow, unimaginative, protected life, avoiding choices again and again, wakes up one morning to find that he has turned into a giant beetle. His attempt to understand his new condition and to relate in these strange circumstances to his utterly confused parents exemplifies something of the sense of loneliness that we face in the world. If you imagine yourself awakening to find you've been transformed into a huge, loathsome vermin, you can experience something of the sense of an eruption of anxiety into consciousness.

The technical problems for psychologists studying anxiety have proved to be very complicated. Consider the case of someone who prefers to stay indoors when others are outdoors, who prefers reading to parties. Such an individual might be considered to be anxious about social situations by relatives and friends or by mental-health professionals. But if asked directly, this individual might deny any fear or anxiety and state that seclusion is a form of life that is personally convenient and congenial.

Defining Anxiety in Scientific Research

Many psychodynamically oriented mental-health professionals would say that such a person is avoiding situations likely to arouse anxiety and that the seclusive behaviors betray an unconscious terror. Some behaviorists, on the other hand, argue that we do not need a construct such as fear or anxiety to explain behavior. We merely accept the fact that some people avoid certain situations and define their behavior from that standpoint without assuming that they avoid a situation because of an underlying emotion. While that explanation may suffice in some instances, research with animals suggests that avoidance behaviors may reflect an underlying fear response (Rescorla and Solomon, 1967).

The Experience of Anxiety　Practically all investigators agree that the personal report of anxiety is the single most important feature in establishing the properties of this emotional response. Generally speaking, when people claim to be anxious, they report that they are aware of a sense of terror, of agitation, of specific or vague fears; they also describe the kinds of discomfort that can be identified physiologically, such as rapid heart rate, sweating palms, butterflies in the stomach.

Izard (1972) developed the Differential Emotions Scale (DES) to study the way in which different experiences of affect cluster together to define a unique emotion or complex blends of emotions (see Figure 13-1). This scale requires individuals to rate on a scale from 1 to 5 the extent to which they experience particular emotions during a specific situation. In one instance, Izard administered the scale to black college students just after the National Guard and local policemen had invaded their campus and opened fire, killing two students and injuring several others. The students were asked to recall the scene as vividly as possible and then to describe the feelings by completing the DES. What emerged were especially high scores for fear, distress, shame, anger, and interest. Thus, what most people would regard as an extreme anxiety

FIGURE 13-1
Instructions and Sample Items for the Differential Emotions Scale

This scale consists of a number of words that describe different emotions or feelings. Please indicate the extent to which each word describes the way you feel at the present time.

Record your answers by circling the appropriate number on the five-point scale following each word. Presented below is the scale for indicating the degree to which each word describes the way you feel.

1	2	3	4	5
very slightly or not at all	slightly	moderately	considerably	very strongly

In deciding on your answer to a given item or word, consider the feeling connoted or defined by that word. Then, if at the present moment you feel that way very slightly or not at all, you would circle the number 1 on the scale; if you feel that way to a moderate degree, you would circle 3; if you feel that way very strongly, you would circle 5, and so forth.

Remember, you are requested to make your responses on the basis of the way you feel at this time. Work at a good pace. It is not necessary to ponder; the first answer you decide on for a given word is probably the most valid. You should be able to finish in about 5 minutes.

1. downhearted	1 2 3 4 5	26. guilty	1 2 3 4 5
6. astonished	1 2 3 4 5	35. afraid	1 2 3 4 5
18. attentive	1 2 3 4 5	44. joyful	1 2 3 4 5
20. ashamed	1 2 3 4 5	61. angry	1 2 3 4 5

(From Izard, 1972)

reaction following the trauma clearly reflected not only fear and other emotions, but the more positive affect of interest as well.

In another study Bartlett and Izard (1972) first divided 160 college students into high- and low-anxiety groups based on their scores on the State-Trait Anxiety Inventory (Spielberger, Gorsuch, and Lushene, 1970). The students filled out the DES in their own dormitory rooms under quiet conditions. They were asked to imagine a situation that made them anxious and then while keeping it in mind, to check off the adjectives on the scale. In a second situation, they were administered the same tests but this time when actually confronting an anxiety-provoking situation, their midterm examinations. The emotional profiles for these students under the real and under the imaginary conditions are about the same (see Figure 13-2). The students who reported themselves as consistently high in anxiety levels also report very high scores

FIGURE 13-2
High- and Low-Anxious Emotional Patterns

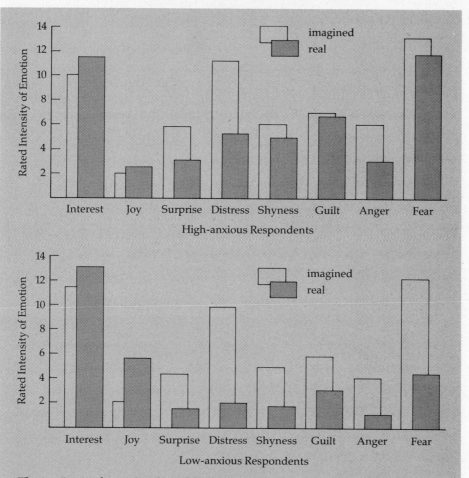

The patterns of emotions rated by high- and low-anxious student respondents (based on the State-Trait Anxiety Inventory) when they imagined an anxiety-provoking situation and just before they actually encountered such a situation—their midterm exams. Note that the profiles are roughly similar, with interest, distress, and fear highest, but that intensities are higher for the high-anxious subjects in the imagined situations, perhaps because midterms represent a **real** fear and not the unknown threat that often occasions anxiety.

(Adapted from Izard, 1977)

on interest, and high scores on distress, shame, guilt, and, of course, fear. The imaginary anxiety situation resembles the real anticipation of a test. Note that the imagined results, reflecting objectless anxiety, produce more intense emotion ratings than the more focused (real) test situation. Anxiety thus appears

---

THE PSYCHOLOGICAL IMPORTANCE OF ANXIETY

to be a blend of fear with at least one other emotion when we measure its occurrence in conscious experience.

The Facial Representation of Anxiety   Ekman and Friesen (1975) have delineated the facial expressions that characterize a person who is experiencing extreme fear or anxiety (see Figure 13-3). If shown pictures of these expressions, most people, not only in our society but in a number of others, identify them correctly. Ekman and Friesen demonstrated the differences between surprise and fear. In anxiety or fear, the lower lip is generally more taut than in a surprise reaction. Generally, the mouth is open, and the lips are drawn back and are extremely tight. The muscle tension around the eyes, the lower forehead, and the mouth during extreme fear can be measured electrically.

Autonomic Nervous System Reactions   Anxiety is accompanied by rapid and sometimes almost audible heartbeats, feelings of dizziness, and increased blood pressure. People also feel that they cannot breathe or they may be almost completely out of breath. There sometimes seems to be a lump or tightness

FIGURE 13-3

The expression of fear or extreme anxiety.
(From Izard, 1977)

in the upper chest; there may also be nausea and sometimes diarrhea. Gell-horn (1967) analyzed the pattern of relationships between heart rate, blood pressure, and sympathetic and parasympathetic systems of the body to demonstrate that a breakdown in adequate blood circulation can follow acute fear and can lead to death. He showed how the phenomenon of so-called "voodoo death" can be explained by bodily reactions to terror. If a person from a culture where magic is taken very seriously is placed under a curse and genuinely believes in the power of witchcraft, he or she may die without any known disease except a sense of hopelessness and terror.

The Neurochemistry of Anxiety   Research has indicated that the transmission of the chemical substance norepinephrine at nerve endings (see Chapter 8) is especially prominent in the experience of extreme fear. Most research on animals does not adequately differentiate extreme fear from the anxiety that we speak of in humans. Still, as we shall see shortly, differentiation is possible in terms of private experience, if not physiologically.

Gray (1976, 1978) carried out studies to pinpoint the consequence on the brain and on behavior of the many anxiety-reducing drugs developed in the last 25 years. He called attention to the fact that alcohol has been used for hundreds of years because it seems to reduce anxiety. More recently, millions of people have become dependent on anti-anxiety drugs such as those sold under the names of Librium and Valium. The interference with the transmission of norepinephrine that characterizes these drugs and alcohol may have other important effects. Gray proposed that there are serious costs, as well as benefits, of the neurochemical blocking effect of anti-anxiety drugs. He writes:

> A person who fails to give up behavior that is repeatedly punished may be courageous or inflexible, depending on the circumstances and on one's value judgments. But two other effects of the anti-anxiety drugs are obviously harmful. They reduce the person's capacity to react to changes in the environment; and, what is more important, they keep a person from developing persistence in the face of unpredictable adversity. Since unpredictable adversity is one of the most predictable ingredients of life, this effect may make the price of the anti-anxiety drugs too high (Gray, 1978, p. 45).

MEASURING ANXIETY AND STUDYING ITS CONSEQUENCES

From the standpoint of personality, the most extensive research has been concerned with identifying individuals who consistently differ in their levels of anxiety and with determining the extent to which such persisting characteristics make an important difference in behavior patterns. This method of identifying high or low anxiety patterns is also employed for testing hypotheses, such as the so-called drive hypothesis related to learning-theory models.

Test Anxiety: A Special Form of Disorganizing Fear

It was natural for psychologists working in universities to focus their attention on the question of test anxiety. Here were obvious examples all around them of their students' extreme reactions during midterm or final-exam periods. Counseling services were besieged by distressed students; there were reports of sharp increases in physical illness during pre-exam periods. It is not an accident that student outbreaks and riots peak during spring final exams. The examination is a fairly clear-cut, well-defined situation in which psychologists can study the manifestations of the dreadful emotion of anxiety.

The most extensive and systematic work on test anxiety has been done by two brothers working independently, Seymour and Irwin Sarason. Seymour Sarason led a team of investigators in studies of the testing situation in elementary schools (Sarason and others, 1960). These studies of elementary school children provide evidence that those who score higher on questionnaires measuring their fears and concerns about tests have consistently inferior performance on ability tests. This result is not attributable to the fact that high scorers on anxiety have lower intellectual ability; naturally, if someone has less capacity, then tests would be more frightening. The data suggest that it is not intellectual difficulty that leads to test anxiety, but rather that students who show a great deal of fear about upcoming tests exaggerate and overemphasize the personal threat they see in the testing situations (Sarason, 1960).

Irwin Sarason's work emphasized the significance of test anxiety for college students. In a typical experiment (1971), he administered a test anxiety scale (TAS) to a group of college students. Those who scored high on this scale typically answered "true" to items like "I get to feel very panicky when I have to take a surprise exam," and "false" to items like "If I knew I was going to take an intelligence test, I would feel confident and relaxed beforehand."

He divided the subjects into those who scored above and those who scored below average. In each group, he assigned half of the subjects to a "neutral condition" and the other half to a condition of intellectual threat. Under the neutral condition, subjects were simply instructed to respond to a word-learning task; there were no other explanations or implications. The other subjects were led to believe that the task measured intelligence and that their ability to learn the words would give a good indication of their ability.

The subjects with high test anxiety performed slightly better than the low test-anxious subjects when there was no implication that the test measured intelligence, but they performed more poorly when the instructions emphasized achievement and intellectual ability. It is not basic ability that separates high and low test-anxious subjects, since under neutral instructions the former scored slightly better. What makes a difference is motivation. The high test-anxious subjects became more disorganized when they believed that there was a threat to their sense of personal identity. Few people are ready to admit that they are not intelligent. Under such threat, high test-anxious individuals fall apart more than low test-anxious subjects. These differences are specific to the test situation. Subjects who score high on a measure of general anxiety do not show the disorganized response to the testing situation.

Several studies indicate that what goes wrong for the test-anxious subjects may be actual physiological changes, such as rapid heart rate and sweating or physical restlessness (Berry and Martin, 1957). Highly anxious subjects also keep saying things to themselves like "What's coming up next? I really am going to have trouble with this one! What's going to happen if I don't pass the exam?" (Phares, 1968). Thus, the feedback from emotional distress and its physical consequences create further disorganization. In addition, the interior monologue may prevent the kind of thinking that ought to be devoted to answering the questions.

Irwin Sarason (1971) summarized the evidence from a number of experiments, which demonstrated that test-anxious individuals are constantly on the lookout for signs in the environment that can be interpreted as useful in helping them perform more effectively. Moderate anxiety, therefore, can generate vigilance and alertness, but high anxiety provokes disorganization (Korchin, 1976).

Assuming test-anxious subjects misread the cues in their environment and overload their internal channels so that they devote less attention to focusing on the exam questions and their answers, how can this tendency be modified? If subjects watch someone fail a test they are about to take, what follows is a worse performance by high test-anxious subjects than on previous similar tests, but a better performance by low test-anxious subjects than in previous tests. The low test-anxious group actually seems to be motivated to do better by seeing the failure of another. Observing a successful performance by someone else does not, however, improve the performance of the high test-anxious subjects.

Again and again, the data compiled by Irwin Sarason and others (Allen, 1971; Wine, 1971a, 1971b) point out the important role of attention in test anxiety. Wine found that simply explaining to high-anxious subjects the importance of focusing on the task does not work. A systematic training program, however, does improve their performance. One training program gives specific practice on how to take tests by focusing on the task and ignoring other thoughts and fantasies during the test. The subjects also observe effective test-taking behavior by another person on videotape and learn relaxation techniques. More extended training involves control of attention, opportunity to observe how others managed to do this, and also training in self-relaxation. After such sequential training, high test-anxious subjects report less conscious anxiety just prior to and during the test, and they actually improve their performance. Providing anxious persons with specific concrete cognitive techniques or skills can thus moderate the deleterious effects of test anxiety.

Test anxiety is a specific and relatively focused fear pattern. A person may perform well in a wide variety of other stress situations and still have difficulties in the testing situation. It is this type of person who has been particularly likely to benefit from the special treatment employed for test anxiety (Sarason, 1971). Thus, to some extent, we are dealing with a special type of exaggerated fear reaction. What can we say about more general patterns of anxiety?

The Manifest Anxiety Scale

We have already mentioned that learning theory defines anxiety as a drive rather than as an emotion. A series of studies was generated by the development of a scale—the Manifest Anxiety Scale (MAS)—designed to test this hypothesis. Janet Taylor first constructed this scale to identify individuals in terms of their self-reports of the extent to which they experience anxiety. Her hypothesis was that if anxiety is a drive, then it should lead to more rapid conditioning of highly anxious subjects. Studies conducted by Taylor (1951) and later by Taylor and Kenneth Spence (1952) did indeed find that persons rated as high-anxious subjects on the MAS showed faster eyelid-conditioning than subjects who scored low on the scale. For verbal-learning tasks, however, which involve long-established habits—or associated meanings for words—high-anxious subjects perform less well because they are more likely to experience interference effects from old habits. That is, if someone is trying to learn to associate two words such as "table" and "eggs" under high-anxiety conditions, the old habits of associating "ham" or "bacon" with "eggs" would interfere with learning the new connection of "table" with "eggs."

An important step in helping psychologists to understand the nature of the differences between high- and low-anxious individuals in response to scale items like the MAS was made by Saltz (1970). In an analysis of all the studies, Saltz argued that high scorers on the MAS are particularly susceptible to the stress induced by potential failure. That is, they have a greater ego investment in demonstrating intellectual competence and satisfactory performance. On the other hand, individuals who score low on these scales are susceptible to the stress induced by physical pain. Thus, in the case of the conditioned-eyelid response to which high-anxious subjects condition more rapidly, the slightly painful puff of air that produces the conditioning reaction is more disruptive to low-anxious subjects. But in the case of verbal learning, in which the performance of the highly anxious is more likely to be disrupted, the situation involves intellectual performance and the likelihood of socially evaluated failure.

Clearly, this interpretation moves away from an emphasis on anxiety as a drive toward a more information-processing point of view. In other words, an individual's appraisal of the situation and the expectation of what kinds of situations are likely to be distressing—failure in intellectual tasks or the experience of physical pain—may determine whether performance will be enhanced or disrupted under conditions of stress. Support for Saltz's position came in an experiment by Glover and Cravens (1974) on word-list learning by subjects rated as high and low in anxiety. Subjects received either (1) no stress, (2) stress of possible failure, or (3) stress of pain (electric shock). The results did not support the Taylor and Spence theory that anxiety functions primarily as a drive, but it did support Saltz's differential hypothesis. High-anxious subjects were more likely to be concerned about the social implications of failure, responding with poor learning in condition 2, while the low-anxious subjects performed more poorly under threat of pain.

One important direction of the research on anxiety has been to examine the differences between (1) anxiety as it occurs under a specific stress situation and (2) anxiety as a chronic or continuing characteristic of individuals. Spielberger (1971) has been a leading advocate of the importance of developing two measures of anxiety—the *A-State*, to estimate how anxious a person feels in a specific situation, and the *A-Trait*, to measure how anxious a person feels generally over a period of time. He proposed that situations involving threat generate a *state* of anxiety in almost anyone, depending on the intensity and persistence of the threat. There are people, however, who consistently perceive potential failures or risks to self-esteem as very threatening. They would score high on anxiety as a *trait*.

Anxiety as a State and as a Trait

A study by Edmunson and Nelson (1976) provides a useful example of the value of separating out state and trait anxiety. They studied high-anxious and low-anxious individuals in their performance on verbal learning tasks. First, they proposed that words can be characterized along a number of dimensions, such as their written quality, their sound, their meaning, and also the image that they are likely to evoke. Thus, a word like "elephant" has a certain length and patterning of letters, it has a three-syllable sound, it has a special meaning that is part of a general class of animal labels, and it also for most people evokes a rather specific image of a large grayish animal with a long trunk, large floppy ears, huge feet, and a little wiggly tail.

Edmunson and Nelson considered the possibility that one consequence of anxiety is that it leads people to focus too much on the external or more superficial characteristics of a situation. Therefore, anxious subjects might overemphasize the sound or appearance of the word rather than taking into account its broader meaning (a type of animal) or being able to generate a pictorial representation of the word. The study showed that high levels of anxiety (as measured by the A-Trait scores) did indeed impair performance on the verbal-learning task. Sometimes, however, subjects who had scored low on the A-Trait scale became quite anxious because of the stress of the task. Thus it was necessary to measure their A-State. When the investigators considered the combination of trait-anxiety and state-anxiety scores, they improved the clarity of their findings. High anxiety was associated with noticing surface characteristics of words, such as appearance or sound, and with disruption of attention to meaning and imagery that could have aided retention.

A persistent problem in personality measurement has to do with the extent to which traits are evident in different situations. One approach to determining the generality of a predisposition to anxiety is to analyze a variety of possible situations that might be stressful and find out if they cluster into a smaller number of categories (Endler, 1973). When statistical analyses of such situations are carried out, they define three general fairly independent classes of stressful situations. These are (1) *interpersonal* situations (usually involving some threat to self-esteem), (2) situations that are *inherently ambiguous*, and (3) situations of *physical danger*. From the perspective of the theories of anxiety, the interpersonal situations or threats to self-esteem are linked to the psychoanalytic emphasis on loss of love or experiences of shame and humiliation, while the situations involving ambiguity tie more closely to the organismic and existential orientations. The situations of physical danger, of course, are the real-life stressors.

Shedletsky and Endler (1974) pointed out that some individuals show anxiety in all situations, but that there are few such people. They proposed that better measurement and understanding of the role of anxiety must come by taking into account more systematically the special types of situations or stressors to which individuals respond differentially. This position was supported in a study by Lamb (1973), who found that persons scoring high on public-speaking anxiety, a specific A-Trait, did indeed react with anxiety when asked to simulate a public-performance situation. But they did not show any greater stress than subjects with low public-speaking anxiety when the simulated stress was physical discomfort. It is clear that psychologists need to be more precise in defining the situations in which individuals may show A-Trait anxiety.

DEFENSE MECHANISMS AND COPING STRATEGIES

Most personality researchers and clinical practitioners agree that one of Freud's greatest contributions was his identification of the defense mechanisms and his demonstration that many personality differences in adults reflect the repeated use of particular defenses to ward off anxiety. As White (1972) suggested, followers of Freud, such as Wilhelm Reich (1945) and Karen Horney (1945), elaborated on Freud's use of defenses to propose that repeated use of defenses may become crystallized into a "character armor" or protective organization around which an entire life-style may be built. White's own studies of ongoing life patterns point to individuals who formed a whole series of choices around particular defenses. In addition, as White has written, the defense mechanisms as adaptive devices may impede a person from obtaining over the long run important information that could be useful for effective coping responses or a more fulfilled life-style.

In the example of phobic anxiety at the outset of this chapter, Millicent Lee's fears prevented her from visiting her parents and finding out that, once with them, she could manage without being humiliated by them. Actually, in that instance, psychotherapy did allay her fears and she was soon able to visit her family. She found that while she never could be really close to them, it was pleasant to share their enjoyment of the grandchildren and the children's delight in the contact with their grandparents.

Defenses are specific methods of coping with anxiety, but they may also be part of broader adaptive strategies for organizing complex information and for dealing with a variety of adverse or demanding situations (Haan, 1969; Kroeber, 1963). As we noted in Chapters 9 and 10, some of the defensive patterns such as repression or denial may be special cases of the necessary selectivity of cognitive processing when we are confronted with the massive and varied stimulation that surrounds us. Particular cognitive styles such as field dependence-independence may reflect longstanding patterns of pre- ferred emphases on the use of self versus external sources of information in making judgments. Both methods are adaptive and useful although one or another may be more effective in a specific situation (Witkin and Goodenough, 1981). Confronted with potential anxiety, the field-dependent person may emphasize repressive defenses, while the field-independent person may be inclined to manifest defenses such as rationalization, intellectualization, or projection (Chapter 9). When defenses are used repeatedly, however, to avoid awareness of anxiety they are, as White suggested, maladaptive and can become the basis for unhappy or neurotic life-styles (Shapiro, 1965; Sullivan, 1956).

Maladaptive and Constructive Aspects of Defenses

In the rest of this chapter we shall examine how particular defense mecha- nisms against anxiety may lead to the development of personality structures or traits. We shall note how the defenses vary both in anxiety reduction and in distortion of reality and also consider how they may be aspects of an adap- tive or coping stategy that can have constructive possibilities for effective living.

Types of Defenses

Repression   Repression, or motivated forgetting, is considered the basic defense mechanism since it essentially is an attempt to avoid direct awareness of threatening conflictual material that might evoke such powerful anxiety as to debilitate the organism. In effect, therefore, all the defense mechanisms reflect in one form or another the effort at repression, but they differ in the combination of cognitive and motor-system involvement.

Although repression is a general defense mechanism, it also is a specific style of dealing with problems. Repressers often have a poorer memory for the details of events and for potentially traumatic situations in their environ- ment (Byrne, 1964). They pay less attention to the details of events going on around them and respond more to the totality of the situation. Closely related to repression is *selective attentiveness*. Once recognizing the anxiety-arousing possibilities of a situation, an individual may systematically avoid looking or listening, and in this way greatly limit the scope of attention (Luborsky, Blinder, and Mackworth, 1965; see Chapter 9).

Repression can be understood not just as a forgetting process—a phe- nomenon extremely difficult to demonstrate experimentally (Holmes, 1974)— but also as a style of information-processing, in which an individual's approach

DENYING ANXIETY: THE REPRESSIVE STYLE

An experiment carried out by Weinberger, Schwartz, and Davidson (1979) examined in detail the way anxiety can be related to physiological coping patterns and to particular defenses. These investigators studied three groups of subjects. One group consisted of high scorers on a questionnaire testing anxiety. These subjects also showed very little evidence of defensiveness—that is, of attempting to deny problems or present themselves in socially desirable fashion. The second group was subjects who scored low on the anxiety scale and who also showed low scores on defensiveness. The third group had low anxiety scores but very *high* scores on the defensiveness scale. Presumably these were persons whose self-report of low anxiety was based not so much on genuine lack of fear in relation to stress but rather on a general pattern of avoiding exposure to others or perhaps even on a lack of self-awareness of any anxiety or other signs of "weakness." This last group was designated as *repressers*.

The subjects then engaged in two tasks. One was an association task in which they were asked to respond to a series of phrases—some that were neutral, some with sexual content, and some that were likely to evoke aggressive associations. The second task involved a biofeedback situation—learning how to modify heart rate in response to sound. The subjects' own heart rates, their skin temperatures, and the electrical activity of the frontalis muscle of the face were recorded while they engaged in these two tasks.

During the association task, the experimenters also measured the subjects' reaction times, their avoidance of particularly disturbing content, and evidence of verbal disturbance, such as stuttering or other speech blockages. Graph A in Figure 13-4 shows the repressers' reaction times. Their avoidance of disturbing content may be reflected in the long time between the presentation of the word and their own associations—much longer than the reaction time of the low-anxious, low-defensive, subjects. Indeed, the repressers' reactions generally gave more indications of stress than those of the high-anxious subjects. This trend is manifested also in the subjects' physiological responses as measured by heart rate and galvanic skin response (graphs B and C).

At the conclusion of the experiment, when the subjects were asked to rate the significance of the experience, the high-anxious, low-defensive subjects said that it had interfered with their sense of self-esteem, whereas the repressers reported that, if anything, their self-esteem had increased. The low-anxious subjects simply reported no change in their self-attitudes. Thus, the defensiveness of the repressers seems to reflect a genuine lack of awareness of the extent to which they had actually revealed considerable fear and distress both in verbal expression and in physiological response. These data are among the strongest now available suggesting that a repressive style can be identified from questionnaires, that it can be related differentially to a style of self-awareness of anxiety, and that evidence of its manifestations can be obtained through both physiological and psychological techniques.

to situations precludes the storing of information that might evoke emotional distress if thought about for any length of time. Habitual short-samplers (Chapter 9) may simply not mentally replay new material, particularly if it is threatening, and they may not match it with previous experiences so that it takes on a richer meaning and can be stored and easily retrieved.

FIGURE 13-4
Anxiety and Repression

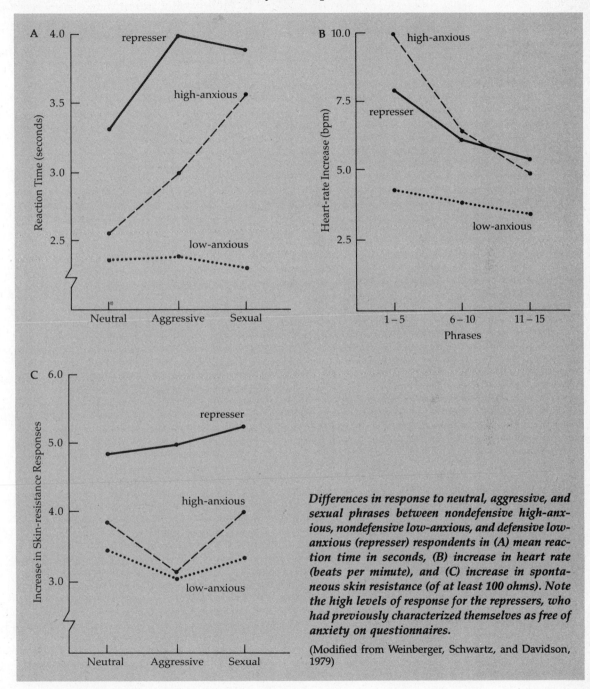

Differences in response to neutral, aggressive, and sexual phrases between nondefensive high-anxious, nondefensive low-anxious, and defensive low-anxious (represser) respondents in (A) mean reaction time in seconds, (B) increase in heart rate (beats per minute), and (C) increase in spontaneous skin resistance (of at least 100 ohms). Note the high levels of response for the repressers, who had previously characterized themselves as free of anxiety on questionnaires.

(Modified from Weinberger, Schwartz, and Davidson, 1979)

Also closely related to repression are mechanisms such as *denial*, in which a person systematically fails to recognize his or her own responses—or external circumstances that are obvious to others—that might evoke anxiety or other mixed emotions. A man who is ashamed of overt displays of emotion (Tomkins, 1962, 1963) may see a sad or sentimental movie and be so moved as to weep at the tragic ending. His companions might notice tears trickling from his eyes when the lights go on. When one of them says, "That was a tear-jerker—it had me bawling!" the denier may say, "Really? It just didn't get to me at all."

It is sometimes hard to distinguish between outright lying and unconscious mechanisms of repression or denial. Probably there is a gray area in which a person is dimly aware of the unpleasant thought or action or witnessed event but tries to interpose alternative thoughts and alternative images. Sometimes the person will engage in what is called a "flight into reality" (a form of short-sampling); this is a bustling round of activity designed to decrease the likelihood that a potentially dangerous event or thought will be stored.

As suggested, defense mechanisms have both maladaptive and adaptive implications. Clearly, we give up some realistic awareness and ability to remember events with detail and precision if we adopt the style of repression or denial. In extreme forms, repression is characteristic of the neurotic styles of hysteria or, in the most extreme cases, in forms of schizophrenia where the individual's emotions are utterly inappropriate. While repression and denial have maladaptive implications, we must also recognize that we need these processes in order to cope effectively with the complexities of daily life. We must respond selectively and retain selectively; otherwise the incredible array of material we encounter in the environment would stagger our information-processing capacity. In addition, if we think seriously about all of the potentially anxiety-provoking features of daily life, we would be incapacitated by fear.

Anxiety is an inevitable response for everyone when we recall that at almost any moment our cities can be totally destroyed by nuclear weapons. Indeed, if we allow ourselves to dwell on all the risks to life posed by over-population, severe energy-source depletion, artificial chemical additives in foods, the health hazards of smoking, smog, water pollution, and so on, it would be hard to get through a day. Obviously, we can only function to the extent that we temporarily ignore many of these risks and go about our business.

Sublimation   Freud believed that the defense mechanism he called *sublimation* is one in which we transform a threatening impulse into some socially valued artistic or creative product. It is more likely that sublimation is really a general concept that incorporates a variety of defense mechanisms put to socially useful purposes. Thus, the act of courage of a woman who risks her life to rescue others reflects a personal denial of death or an unwillingness to look at all of the frightening outcomes. The creation of artwork about the afterlife similarly reflects a denial of mortality. Dante's *Divine Comedy* is such a work, and the soaring cathedrals of Europe are human attempts to forge a link with God. Such visible works help us to avoid contemplating the possibility that there may be no life after death and, indeed, no God at all.

There is no significant research on how sublimation develops. What seems clear is that hobbies, skills, or artistic and creative expression make it more likely that some children will have access to highly valued, socially rewarded activities to which they can turn when confronted by fears and anxieties. Soon the rewards for creative or skillful activity foster further development of the activity in its own right without the incentive to use it as a defense.

Regression   A major defense mechanism particularly related to pathological behavior is *regression*. Here the individual avoids the thought or experience of threatening situations by reverting to a style of life more characteristic of childhood or of an early stage of development. Sometimes, for various reasons, an individual feels threatened by the fear of failure when having to assume a status in society that includes commitments relating to work and long-term intensive interpersonal relationships. Such an individual may simply stay more or less at the level of an adolescent or even a younger child and try to maintain only the most superficial relationships.

In its most extreme form, regression is evident in psychotic reactions in which individuals are so helpless that they must be treated as children. In somewhat less extreme forms, we see individuals who remain tied to their parents and do not move away from home or become independent adults. A dramatic instance of regression and fixation is portrayed in Dickens' *Great Expectations* where Miss Havisham, who has been deserted on her wedding day, decides to remain as she was on that day. For the rest of her life, she lives in the room where the wedding feast was set up, dressed in her wedding gown, and undertakes no responsibilities, shielded by her wealth from the outside world.

Regression can be seen therefore as closely related to escape into fantasy. Although fantasy and daydreaming may have constructive and adaptive uses, there are individuals who find themselves most comfortable when they create a make-believe world and spin out much of their lives playing the kind of "let's pretend" that is normal for children but no longer reasonable for adults. Miss Havisham is such a person, a bride to her death.

Regression and escape into fantasy do have some psychological adaptive value. Certainly there are times when otherwise responsible and mature adults feel the need to indulge in childish hijinks, such as drinking parties, fraternity bashes, and alumni get-togethers. Masquerades and party games provide adults with chances to slip back to the less responsible, more casual behavior of youth and to dwell at least temporarily in make-believe worlds. For a brief period we need not think about the many unfinished tasks or heavy responsibilities that confront us in our daily lives.

Again, we have little systematic evidence of how regressive patterns develop. It is possible that individuals who show such behavior were either extremely overprotected in childhood or received attention primarily for childish behavior, "cuteness," or tantrums.

A Halloween procession. For an evening, these Wizard of Oz masqueraders can recapture the carefree ways of childhood—free, for the time being, from adult anxiety.

Projection   With projection, an individual is especially able to reduce anxiety greatly, but at a drastic cost to recognition of reality and to effective coping. Projection is a form of thinking in which we completely avoid awareness of our own anxiety-provoking desires by either attributing these desires to others or, as is sometimes the case, actually inverting the desire to its opposite and then attributing that belief to others. In the classical instance when Freud identified this mechanism, he described the case of a German Supreme Court judge who was apparently experiencing homosexual inclinations, and who attributed to others hostility toward him, turning his love for other men into their hatred of him.

The mechanism of projection is not necessarily as complicated as it seems in psychotic patients. When we have behaved in a way that would be embarrassing if it became known, we begin to be keenly alert to the possibility that others might indeed recognize the fact. Suppose a football player in strict training has just yielded to his secret desire and gorged himself on three large slices of chocolate cream pie. As he walks into the locker room, he is acutely aware that he has done something shameful and he keeps looking at his teammates to see if they sense it. He can still taste some of the pie crumbs and his lips feel sticky—maybe some chocolate is smeared on his mouth. Someone who seems to be staring at him adds to his suspicions. If two of the players go by him and glance his way, laughing and talking in low tones, he may be even more suspicious that everyone knows about the dereliction that fills his own thoughts. We are all prone to such fleeting suspiciousness and projection of our own thoughts onto others after some potentially embarrassing act, but such feelings are usually transient.

Projection may develop in a family setting in which suspiciousness already prevails. Parents who talk of the neighbors as "unfriendly" or warn their children against playing with "one of *that* kind" may be setting a tone that allows the children to avoid inner conflict by projecting their own concerns onto others. Projection can be one of the most pathological of all defense mechanisms and is often associated with hearing of voices, with extreme suspiciousness, with outbreaks of violence toward others, and with excessive legal actions and persecutions of others. Nevertheless, there are instances when individuals who are themselves experiencing such distortions have emerged as leaders of groups, religions, or social movements that have had broader adaptive effects. The heightened vigilance of people who are concerned lest their own guilt or presumed crimes be revealed may also sensitize them to real injustices or hypocrisies in the world around them. Holt (1969) proposed that projection may be a maladaptive side of the more effective coping strategy of *empathy*, in which we experience the emotions of others by carefully noticing their gestures, facial expressions, and comments.

Displacement   A mechanism such as displacement involves avoidance of anxiety and conflict through thought and action that only somewhat distort reality. Displacement is a shifting of our own unacceptable feelings onto someone else. In James Joyce's short story "Counterparts," the protagonist, a meek and ineffective Dublin clerk, has a series of experiences in which he is made aware of his own limitations in relation to others. He has been denounced and humiliated by his boss. He comes home to find no supper and only one of his small sons around. He reacts toward the child much as his boss reacted toward him, humiliating and threatening the lad, who pleads for mercy at this undeserved outburst.

Undoubtedly, many instances of child or spouse abuse are the result of such displacement, as is the abuse of animals by children. A vivid television documentary presented a young man who described how, after having been brutalized at home by his father, he went out into the street carrying a bat and hit a passing boy over the head with it. "I enjoyed the cracking of his head," he said, and subsequently found himself doing this more and more whenever he could get away with it.

Displacement can have its constructive expressions. Some individuals cannot accept the extent to which they themselves deserve to be the objects of pity, while others are unable to deal with the frustration of not being able to produce social change in their own community. Such persons may find themselves greatly concerned about the poor or downtrodden in other communities or countries. Indeed, much missionary and charitable work can be understood as displacement in this sense. Many socially useful outcomes can emerge from missionary work, from projects like Care, from hospital ships visiting underdeveloped countries, or from the Peace Corps. In a sense, our capacity to set aside our own comfort and security for the love of another or of an ideal is one of our greatest gifts as human beings. Displacement, even if it covers up some self-awareness, may be an extension of this capacity.

Reaction-Formation   Another mechanism by which we can avoid self-awareness or awareness by others of our unacceptable thoughts or intentions is by behaving in a manner completely opposite to the way we feel. In the play within a play scene in Shakespeare's *Hamlet*, the unfaithful queen speaks lovingly to the husband she plans to murder. This prompts Hamlet's mother to remark, "The lady doth protest too much, methinks."

It is not difficult to understand why reaction-formation can be effective. If we are constantly on the lookout for situations that are the opposite of a threatening one, we are scarcely likely to notice our own real inclinations. Often people who feel guilty about their sexual desires or inclinations become prudish and obsessed with denouncing books and movies that imply sexuality. Cynical attitudes reflect a reaction-formation against anxiety about exposing our great need for affection and "tender loving care" from others.

Since reaction-formation is closely related to hypocrisy, it may, however, be one of the more conscious of the defenses. In Dickens' *David Copperfield*, the character Uriah Heep speaks in an unctuous and flattering tone, constantly referring to himself as an "umble" person, and preventing others by his humility and meekness from recognizing how desperately he seeks to win power.

Although reaction-formation often does conceal villainy, it can be a useful social trait. Young people who are ashamed of or frightened by the great rage they feel against their parents may try to become excessively good persons and take up a socially useful profession, such as medicine or the ministry. Social and political reform movements may be led by individuals who themselves have been, or continue to be, tempted toward corrupt thoughts and practices. Many worthwhile changes may result from their efforts.

Compensation   This defense mechanism, which is especially emphasized in the work of Alfred Adler, suggests that people who have obvious or noticeable weaknesses or a sense of inferiority may avoid shame and anxiety by attaining greatness in some other area. A familiar example is Napoleon Bonaparte, who was extremely short but whose energy and intellect led him to become one of the greatest generals of all time. Certainly, when he rode on horseback along the ranks of thousands of cheering troops, most of whom towered above him in height, it was easy for him to forget any worries about his small stature.

Compensation often leads to socially useful activities, but it can also have destructive outcomes. It seems likely that an important feature in the personality of Lee Harvey Oswald, the assassin of John F. Kennedy, was the fact that he was, throughout much of his childhood, an isolated social outcast; furthermore, shortly before the assassination he is said to have been tortured by feelings of sexual inferiority and rejection by his wife.

Identification   Identification bears some similarities to compensation in the sense that it may often be an attempt to avoid feelings of inferiority and shame. It is related to modeling in social-learning theory, since it involves the effort to imitate the behavior or values of another person. Indeed, this imitation forms the basis for much of what we later recognize as our personality, based as it is on identification with parents or siblings or well-known public figures. The social value of identification is well recognized by, for example, having prominent athletes urge teenagers from poor backgrounds not to drop out of school and to stay away from crime.

Sometimes this mechanism is manifested in what is called *introjection*, in which we not only imitate the style, appearance, or overt activities of another, but incorporate as our own the values and attitudes of someone who is admired or feared. A combination of these patterns is seen in *identification with the aggressor*, which is initially manifested, in the psychoanalytic view, by a child

In a scene from a TV commercial, a boy offers his Coke to his hero, ex-Pittsburgh Steeler "Mean Joe" Greene. Later, when the boy puts on the jersey Mean Joe gives him in exchange, his sense of identification with his hero will be even stronger.

DEFENSE MECHANISMS AND COPING STRATEGIES

taking on some of the manners and values of the father because of a fear of parental retaliation for Oedipal wishes. Such behavior is evident when we see servants of the rich adopting upper-class snobbish ways or when individuals who are themselves powerless and victimized adopt the political and social values of their oppressors. A leader of the American Nazi party turned out to be a young man who was himself the son of a survivor of the Dachau camp.

Rationalization   Rationalization is at the opposite pole from defense mechanisms such as regression and denial. Here there is overt expression of a thought or idea that is guarded against, but at the same time, an attempt to avoid its full emotional impact. A father who punishes his son after the boy has publicly embarrassed him may avoid confronting the intensity of his own anger and shame as well as his fears of expressing his emotion by explaining to the boy that "I am doing this only for your good. You have to learn better public behavior!"

Generally speaking, rationalization is often employed to conceal the anxiety we feel about our own self-centeredness. The legal system, which is one of the great bulwarks of human society, is to some extent a rationalization by all the powerful in the society so that they need not feel quite so much guilt or anxiety about their uses of power. Rationalization in many ways is one of the more socially adaptive of the defenses and is more easily transferred to an effective coping mechanism in societies in which there is "payoff" for intellectual activities and orderly behavior.

Intellectualization   Here, too, as in rationalization, the emotions that might be frightening are separated from the emotional experience. Thus, in a classic psychoanalytic model, a child who is curious about sounds of sexual behavior coming from the parents' bedroom might prevent anxiety by developing a curiosity about the strange events of the universe. This could lead to an interest in biology or science generally.

An extreme example would be the individual who chooses to make a career of studying sexuality itself. Alfred Kinsey, who made important advances in our understanding of the range and patterning of adult sexual behavior, took great pains to present his work in a properly scientific manner, avoiding any hints of humor or the other emotions often found in public discussions of sexuality. Physicians discussing the histology and neurochemistry of a malignant tumor may do so with a scientific precision that seems to a patient like unfeeling callousness. Yet if they were to allow themselves to feel the emotional implications of a patient's death, the genuine emotion would be too difficult to bear and would distract them from the task at hand.

Intellectualization, rationalization, and other aspects of emotional isolation are often related to the obsessive-compulsive neurosis. The housewife who is obsessed with the cleanliness of her home and engages in compulsive daily cleaning may be forestalling her anxiety about sexuality or her resentment at the boredom of her marriage. She can, however, explain the value of keeping a clean house, and since in many groups considerable value is placed on being a good housewife, in effect the woman is rewarded for her obsession. The petty bureaucrat or artisan who becomes completely caught up in small details and loses track of the purposes of the job may be avoiding some of his or her own guilt or fear. Nevertheless, our society needs people who do pay attention to details, or things would work even less well than they do. As a matter of fact, as society becomes more technologically developed and gross physical labor less necessary, obsessive and compulsive behavior will have many rewards in terms of job opportunities and careers. Forgetful or overly casual "represser types" are not going to make it in jobs such as computer programming, banking, or space technology.

The defense mechanisms we have described, while helpful in aiding us to organize information about personality characteristics we observe in others, have a good deal of overlap. We need more research to determine which situations we confront are most likely to evoke particular types of defensive operations. The origins of the defenses have not been extensively studied, although it is likely that they are socialized in part by family patterns. Clearly, they also relate to the broader patterns of cognitive style.

Madison (1961) and Sarnoff (1971) attempted theoretical and research examination of the operation of the defenses, but more remains to be done, particularly in determining at what point defense mechanisms may be inadequate and inappropriate and at what point they have genuine social value. Indeed, it is far from certain that these patterns of behavior always reflect efforts to avoid underlying fears. It is possible that Freud overemphasized the defensive side of what actually may be intrinsically useful methods for organizing and dealing with the great ambiguities of daily experience.

IMPLICATIONS

In general, the results of research point to the notion that we cannot label anxiety as a completely independent emotion. It is likely that it represents some combination of fear with distress, guilt, or shame. Also it is unlikely that anxiety can only be identified with early experiences of loss of love or rejection. It seems better to view this emotion as a reflection of the inherent ambiguity of our experiences in the environment and our need to organize experience into a reasonable structure in order to eliminate extraneous information and to match incoming information with already established schema. Since the major schema we use in relating ourselves to new situations, particularly those of an interpersonal nature, involve our own personal efficacy or value, it is likely that we will experience stress when confronted with situations that threaten our self-concept or that threaten to expose weaknesses of which we are aware, but are ashamed to have others observe. All of us are undoubtedly prey, as well, to the inherent fear of death and of the nothingness that may follow it.

The recognition that so many of the things we do are efforts to avoid confronting our fears of extreme novelty, of exposing our limitations or risking public shame, or of confronting the reality of death supports the argument that anxiety defense or attainment of security is the central human motive. Another way of looking at this, however, is to argue—as Tomkins, Izard, and other cognitive-affective psychologists do—that we are equally motivated to explore novelty; we experience positive emotions in the face of moderate uncertainty. Thus, the defense mechanisms may be general coping and information-processing styles that we develop in early childhood or perhaps bring with us into the world. Certain types of early socialization may lead some people to overemphasize the avoidance of fear, while others may be encouraged to identify and face their anxieties and to talk about them to the point of excessive sensitivity. The represser-sensitizer styles, like introversion and extraversion and the cognitive styles of locus of control or field dependence-independence, may be major poles around which we organize our experience and overt behavior. Fear and anxiety, like pain, are unpleasant emotions, but if we did not sometimes experience them we would also never be prepared for the real dangers that confront us in our journey through life.

SUMMARY

1. Anxiety is the term used to describe our emotions in situations in which we experience a high level of fear that is not appropriate or fear without a clear object. Anxiety also often reflects an intense inner conflict in which some of the elements of the conflict may not be conscious. Anxiety usually involves a mixture of fear and another emotion such as anger, sadness, or distress.

2. Anxiety is accompanied by rapid, almost audible heartbeats, dizziness, higher blood pressure, loss of breath, tightness in the chest, and sometimes nausea and diarrhea. Transmission of norepinephrine at nerve endings is especially prominent in extreme fear. The anti-anxiety drugs, as well as alcohol, interfere with the transmission of norepinephrine.

3. From the standpoint of personality, most of the research on anxiety has been concerned with identifying persons who consistently differ in their levels of anxiety and with determining the extent to which such persisting characteristics make a difference in behavior patterns.

4. Test anxiety, or the fear of taking tests or examinations, has been extensively studied. Research with school children shows that those who have high scores on a questionnaire measuring their fears about tests have poorer performance on ability tests. With college students, the high-scorers on test anxiety perform more poorly, especially when there is a threat to their sense of personal identity. The role of attention is important in test anxiety. A training program to help test-anxious subjects gives specific practice on

how to take tests by focusing on the task and ignoring other thoughts and fantasies. More extended training involves control of attention, observing how others control attention, and self-relaxation.

5. The Manifest Anxiety Scale (MAS) was designed to test the hypothesis that anxiety is a drive rather than an emotion. Janet Taylor, who constructed the scale, hypothesized that if anxiety is a drive, it should lead to increased speed in acquisition of conditioned responses by high-anxious subjects. Research confirmed this hypothesis for eyelid conditioning. With verbal learning, however, high-anxious subjects performed less well because high drive, or anxiety, leads to more interference from old habits. Despite the popularity and effectiveness of the MAS, many psychologists have reservations about its interpretation. For example, it has been argued that high scorers are susceptible to the stress of potential failure, and low scorers to the stress of physical pain. This kind of interpretation moves away from an emphasis on anxiety as a drive and toward an information-processing point of view.

6. An important direction in research on anxiety has been to examine differences between (1) anxiety under specific stress situations (A-State) and (2) anxiety as a chronic or continuing characteristic of some individuals (A-Trait). Situations of threat generate a state of anxiety in almost everyone, but some people consistently perceive potential failure or risks to self-esteem as threatening, and they would score on anxiety as a trait.

7. One of Freud's greatest contributions was his identification of the defense mechanisms and his demonstration that many personality differences in adults reflect the repeated use of certain defenses to ward off anxiety. Defenses may be viewed as ways of coping with anxiety that are part of broader adaptive strategies for organizing complex information and dealing with a variety of adverse or demanding situations.

8. The defense mechanisms include (1) repression, (2) sublimation, (3) regression, (4) projection, (5) displacement, (6) reaction-formation, (7) compensation, (8) identification, (9) rationalization, and (10) intellectualization. These defenses, which vary in both the degree to which they reduce anxiety and distort reality, may also be aspects of adaptive or coping strategies that have constructive possibilities for effective living.

CHAPTER
14

Anger and Aggression

Most Americans like to think of the United States as one of the safest and most peaceable places on earth. Yet incidents of violence in this country and from around the world come to our attention every day from the news on television and in the newspapers. Within a year's time during 1980–81, the popular Beatle John Lennon was slain and two of the world's most important leaders, President Reagan and Pope John Paul II, were wounded by assassins. Often, however, the attacker is a person who is close to the victim—a relative, friend, or acquaintance. In one year in New York City, for example:

> Seven brothers were slain by their brothers. . . . Two sisters were killed by their sisters, while 11 sons and 13 daughters were murdered by their mothers; and 5 sons and 1 daughter by their father. Forty wives were dispatched by their husbands and 17 husbands by their wives. In all, close family relationships accounted for 35 percent of all homicides in that year. Indeed in fewer than 20 percent of all homicides were the victim and perpetrator complete strangers (New York City Police Department). About 40 percent of aggravated assault and rape (constituting most of the serious crimes against the person) take place within the victim's home. . . . Cross-national studies yield similar findings throughout western society (Bard, 1971).

Why do people do violent things to one another? Are we human beings born with a basic drive to destroy others—or to destroy ourselves, as Freud came to believe? Are some people more prone to violence than others? Can we determine how aggressive patterns get started in children and what factors in the environment and social experience sustain such tendencies into later life? Are there personality styles in which a tendency toward impulsive or aggressive actions plays a major role? In exploring these issues, we shall begin by examining the way researchers define anger and aggression and then look at the emotion of anger before exploring more direct manifestations of aggression or violence.

Let us begin by making some distinctions that have grown out of theory and research. Although there is extensive psychological research on aggressive behavior, there is surprisingly little work on the emotion of anger. It is now clear that psychologists must separate the *emotion* of anger from the *behavior pattern* that can be described as aggressive. In general, therefore, it is useful to look upon aggression as an overt act that involves an attempt to harm other people or at least to damage their property (Kaufmann, 1970). It may also involve a serious effort at self-harm, such as suicide or self-mutilation. Aggression can be divided into *direct* efforts at attack (threats of violence, attempted assaults, as well as actual successful violence) and *indirect* acts of aggression. Indirect aggression includes verbal insults, expressed wishes for harm such as "Drop dead!" and, more seriously, lying, deception, and slander. These are hard to study scientifically and, as we shall see, personality research has little to say about persisting personality styles of indirect aggression.

Anger is a basic human emotion. It is experienced in a distinctive way and is expressed by a definable facial expression and by muscular and physiological body responses. Anger is aroused by extreme persisting frustration of our intentions or by the continuation of circumstances in which we cannot assimilate a mass of information or cannot match up new information with our well-established plans or programs for coping and organizing. Anger does not necessarily lead to aggressive actions. Millions of people have been furious at the policies, or lack of policies, of our political leaders but it has not occurred to them to take direct violent measures. It is well to recognize that anger is a negative emotion or affect, an unpleasant experience that can lead to hostile thoughts, but it is separable from direct or even indirect acts of aggression. There are reasons to believe that persisting anger may be physiologically harmful to us even if we do not engage in violence toward others.

ANGER

Let us begin this exploration of some of the uglier sides of the human personality with an examination of the emotion of anger. What determines the emergence of this feeling? How can someone tell that you are angry? What are the physical and social consequences of suppressing anger? How can people cope with anger?

The Determinants of Anger

In Chapters 6 and 8 we discussed the information-processing origins of anger in relation to the presentation of new material that is difficult to assimilate into established cognitive schema. A loud persisting noise that will not go away arouses our anger. The awareness of an obstacle in the attainment of a goal, which cannot be easily explained away or dealt with in any obvious manner, leads to many mental associations in an attempt to make sense of the situation. As these associations, thoughts of remedies, memories of previous similar frustrations pile up without any solution, they lead to the emergence of the affect of anger.

As Izard (1977) points out, the frustration of intentions is a major cause of anger. Other instigators of anger may include the experience of being insulted, of having emotions of interest or joy interrupted, of finding evidence that we have been deceived or manipulated into an action we did not intend to take. Many of these instigators of anger are examples of the difficulty of assimilating information into well-established expectations or previous schema.

Suppose you are watching a movie and laughing uproariously at the antics of a comedian and then suddenly find someone is blocking the screen, perhaps a person who is looking for a seat in the row ahead. Already highly aroused by joy, you may react with anger at the interruption. Zillman and Bryant (1974) found that people who are already emotionally aroused and who are then subjected to provocation are much more likely to become angry. The ongoing level of emotional arousal, even if positive, is important in whether or not a momentary frustration arouses anger. Research by Malamuth, Feshbach, and Jaffe (1977) indicated that young men exposed to an erotic film later showed more inclination toward aggressive behavior, presumably because of a combination of psychological arousal and the implicit disinhibiting signal sent by the usually taboo film.

The Facial Expression of Anger

Anger is readily apparent in facial expression as well as in menacing gestures. In anger, the muscles just above the eyes move in and somewhat downward, creating a frown. The eyes usually are fixed in a stare at the instigator of the anger. The nostrils are flared, and the teeth are usually clenched, sometimes visibly if the lips are opened. There is a rush of blood to the face so that we speak of someone "red-faced" with anger. The experience of anger is accompanied by a feeling of facial warmth and tension of the facial muscles. Angry individuals have a sense of power and also move actively or attack the instigator of anger. "In rage, the mobilization of energy is so great that one feels one will explode if one does not bite, hit, or kick something" (Izard, 1977, p. 331).

Suppressed Anger

At one time anger was probably important in human survival because it led to a rapid mobilization of energy and preparation for self-defense. But in day-to-day life in modern society, anger is not so useful except in rare instances involving self-defense. People learn, therefore, to respond to provocation by a variety of methods for *suppressing* the show of anger—averting their eyes, setting their jaws, simulating anger's opposite with an overly polite smile (reaction-formation), or by some other unconscious device such as denial or

FIGURE 14-1

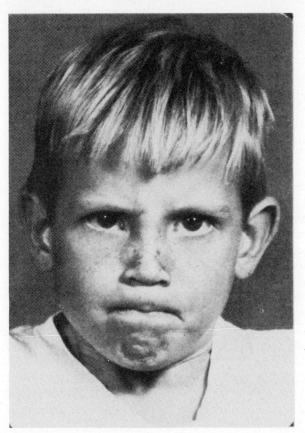

As children grow older, they are taught to try to control their anger. This boy shows an angry expression, but his compressed lips hide the bared teeth usually associated with anger.

(From Izard, 1977)

displacement, thus suppressing even their awareness of being angry. Because anger must be suppressed in so many cases, someone who is continually in an anger-producing situation may eventually suffer physiological consequences (Holt, 1976). Recent research often links hypertension to a life-style that involves a recurring suppression of anger (Glass, 1977).

If a person has been brought up in a fashion that reinforced the suppression of angry feelings, the result may ultimately be grossly self-defeating behavior. An unrealistically demanding husband continually criticized his young wife for her domestic inexperience. Because of her upbringing, she was unable to express her resentment with his impatience, but could only say repeatedly, "Yes, I know. You're right. I'm sorry." At some point, however, she became aware that she was drinking in the afternoon to relieve unexplained tension and that she was daydreaming about adultery. In fact, she might well have acted on these fantasies, without real awareness of the extent to which she had failed to deal with her husband's criticism through a direct expression of anger.

In a civilized society there are many opportunities for direct manifestations of anger without engaging in overly aggressive behavior. A forceful and clear expression that one is angry usually leads to continuing communication with the person involved and to resolution of the situation. A too-threatening display of anger beyond what is reasonably appropriate can, of course, result in a breakdown of communication and destructive or self-destructive consequences.

Research by David Glass and his colleagues revealed a personality type they called "Type A." Such persons are more likely to have heart attacks than a comparison group, called "Type B's" (Carver, Coleman, and Glass, 1976; Carver and Glass, 1977; Glass, 1977). Personality measurements and behavioral descriptions suggest that Type A's are extremely concerned with success and achievement and are constantly pushing themselves to accomplish their goals. In a study of suppressed anger, individuals classified as Type A's or Type B's were put in a situation in which they delivered electric shocks to another person as part of a learning experiment (Carver and Glass, 1977). When there was no provocation by the experimenter, no difference emerged between the Type A's and Type B's in the level of shock they administered. But when they were angered by insulting comments, both types significantly increased the intensity of the shocks, but the Type A's showed twice as great an increase in intensity. These data suggest that the Type A's are indeed carrying around with them a continuing set of expectations of being angered and a higher level of intensity so that, given a new provocation, they respond with an excessive reaction.

Coping with Anger

Responses that are incompatible with anger may help to reduce its intensity to manageable proportions. Persuading an angry person to smile may not reduce the original instigation but may lead to more constructive communication. Baron (1977) analyzed some of the ways in which humor can reduce anger and subsequent aggression. He described studies indicating that getting people to laugh or smile reduces annoyance and subsequent aggressive behavior. Of course, the humor must be appropriate to the situation. If you have just publicly insulted a person, trying to tell jokes will not necessarily do the trick and may indeed provoke even greater anger.

Anger is an emotion with important social consequences. People who are continuously angry and who express their anger eventually provoke hostility from others. This happens even if the anger is justified. Many well-intentioned reformers or consumer advocates go around angrily pointing out injustices and are surprised when people become annoyed with them. People frequently need training in identifying situations in which an overt expression of anger is appropriate; they also need to learn ways in which they can express this

MITIGATING ANGER
AND AVOIDING AGGRESSION

An experiment by Zillman and Cantor (1976) demonstrated circumstances under which appropriate explanation can modify or mitigate the persistence of anger. In one experiment, just before exposure to a rude and insulting experimenter the participants were told by a more polite assistant that the experimenter was "uptight" about an important examination (*prior mitigation*). In another condition of this study, this explanation was provided *after* the experimenter's rudeness (*subsequent mitigation*); in a third condition no explanation was provided. Blood-pressure changes were used to measure presumed anger aroused by the insult. As seen in Figure 14-2, all the subjects showed an arousal reaction immediately after insult, but the effect for the group with prior explanation was milder and it quickly wore off as time went on. The group with subsequent mitigation showed a sharp drop in blood-pressure change 30 seconds after the explanation, and their blood pressure soon fell to a baseline level, but the group with no explanation stayed at a higher rate of presumed anger. Later ratings by subjects of the experimenter also showed that the prior explanation yielded moderately favorable reactions; the subsequent explanation yielded moderately negative reactions, but the absence of mitigation left subjects strongly negative in their appraisal of the experimenter.

FIGURE 14-2

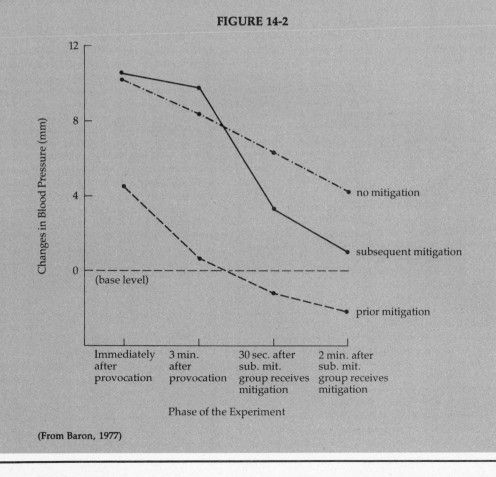

(From Baron, 1977)

anger verbally without physically attacking another person or provoking a reaction directed at themselves (Novaco, 1975). Self-assertiveness training groups are now in use, particularly by women, who are more inclined to suppress anger than men.

EXPLAINING AGGRESSION

From the earliest years of this century observers of human and animal behavior have theorized that aggression is a basic instinct, an inborn drive. Psychologists who emphasize learning have not gone that far; they view aggression as an inherent organismic response, an inevitable reaction to frustration of the kind discussed in Chapter 12 (Berkowitz, 1969; Dollard and others, 1939, Feshbach, 1970). Only in the past decade has sufficient research evidence been accumulated to allow a new point of view that emphasizes the social learning of aggression. Since the nature of human aggression is of major concern for us all, this section will review some of the contrasting theories proposed by behavioral and social-learning psychologists.

Biological Theories

Eros and Thanatos Having experienced the impact of World War I and the destructive acts that followed the Versailles "peace," Freud decided that all human behavior is motivated by two basic cyclical drives or impulses that press for discharge. One is *eros*, the life-building principle of love, of the desire for reproduction and sexual expression; the other is *thanatos*, the drive toward death and destruction.

The death instinct presses us toward our own destruction. But this aggressive drive can be redirected toward others, and this accounts for violence in behavior and for the cruel and harmful things we do and say, even to those closest to us. The aggressive drive may also be redirected toward activities that symbolically express destructiveness but do not have a conscious representation. For example, Freud might have argued that the tremendous preoccupation of millions of people with the details of the funeral of President Kennedy in November 1963 reflected the fact that their own aggressive drives had been aroused and were at least partially reduced by watching the slow, drawn-out ceremony.

Ethological Factors Ethology has emerged in the past thirty years as an exciting field of research. It involves careful observation of the spontaneous behavior of animals and birds in their natural habitats rather than in the artificial laboratory world of mazes and bar presses.

Popularly written books by Konrad Lorenz (1966) and Robert Ardrey (1966) have sustained the interest in an instinctual view of aggression. Ardrey emphasized the notion of *territoriality*, proposing that the males of many species innately establish their own "turf" for the organization of their life cycles

Bighorn rams fighting in breeding season. In the territorial view of aggression, male animals fight to protect their exclusive claim to their turf and to their females.

of mating and reproduction and that they will inevitably fight to maintain their territory. Lorenz believed that aggressive energy accumulates up to a certain point and then must be discharged; overt aggression will take place if there is in the organism a buildup of aggression and in the environment a set of appropriate cues for eliciting aggressive activity.

Lorenz called attention to the fact that all animals possess inhibitions against harming their own species; otherwise there would be endless combat. Indeed, there are signals by which a defeated animal may, in effect, surrender—as a dog does by turning over on its back—and thus avoid the final killing blow or bite. Unlike animals, humans are in particular danger, because our destructiveness does not depend only on direct physical activities, but it can be discharged far more lethally merely by the pull of a trigger or the press of a button. Although Ardrey's and Lorenz's views have not been widely accepted by other ethologists, many social scientists as well as lay persons have taken them seriously.

Neurophysiological Factors   Activation of certain parts of the nervous system by stimuli in the environment results in aggressive behavior toward such stimuli (Moyer, 1971). Most of the evidence comes from research with animals. Using implanted electrodes, researchers have been able to locate the brain areas tied to specific aggressive acts (Flynn, 1967). For example, if stimulated in the region of the lateral hypothalamus, a cat will ignore the experimenter and make a direct attack on an available rat. But if the medial hypothalamus is stimulated, the cat ignores the rat, its natural prey, and turns on the experimenter.

In experimentation that is very controversial because it involved using a human being as an experimental subject and altering her brain, King (1961) implanted electrodes in the brain of a female patient in a mental hospital. This otherwise mild-mannered woman became extremely nasty and threatened violence when she was electrically stimulated near the amygdala, an area of the brain often linked to emotional reactivity. As soon as the current was turned off, she resumed her mild behavior. Thus, hostile feelings and potentially aggressive behavior were aroused by the flick of a switch. This reaction was not attributable to pain from the electrical stimulation since none was reported, but rather by an immediate experience of anger and hostility.

It is important to note that although the amygdala region of the brain consistently seems to be linked to aggressive responses in animals, particularly in the presence of appropriate cues in the environment, careful examination of the data suggests that the effects of stimulation of this area may essentially be the arousal of anger. Only if aggressive cues are present will aggression occur. The response of attack may also depend on whether or not aggression is a regular feature of the animal's behavior and also on the social characteristics of the setting (Ellison and Flynn, 1968). An animal whose hypothalamus has been surgically removed may still engage in attacking behavior if exposed to cues for attack in the environment, a provocative bait or hostile opponent.

An important study by Delgado (1967) called attention to the fact that the social experience of an animal may determine whether or not aggressive behavior will occur, even when there is direct stimulation of the hypothalamic region through implanted electrodes. A monkey who was the dominant animal in a colony could be stimulated through electrical innervation of the hypothalamus to fight with other males below him in the hierarchy. He did not, however, attack females, with whom males rarely fight. Nor did he attack the animal who was closest to him and in a sense his "best friend." But with a monkey who was low in the hierarchy and accustomed to being dominated by others, stimulation of the hypothalamus did not produce attack behavior but rather cowardly and yielding reactions. When the same animal moved into a group where he was more dominant, the stimulation that formerly produced cowering and fearful reactions now led to overt aggression.

Analysis clearly shows, then, that while certain areas of the brain are likely, when stimulated, to yield aggressive behavior, anger and intensity of feelings must be separated from overt aggressive responses (Delgado, 1968). It is likely that aggressive behavior occurs only when there are specific circumstances evoking it—that is, cues such as a natural "enemy" or threatening person, or previous experience in the use of aggression.

Genetic Factors   Are some people born with a tendency to become violent? Before concluding our exploration of biological theories and aggression, we shall review briefly the so-called genetic basis for aggression. Observations in the 1960s by mental-health specialists led to a proposal that males with an extra Y chromosome in their gene structure—the so-called XYY chromosomal type, which occurs only once in about one thousand newborn males—were especially prone to violence. The initial scientific report implied that men born with this unusual chromosomal structure were almost helplessly victims of their own heredity and might not be able to control their aggressive behavior.

The origin of the notion that the XYY chromosome is a link to aggression was in findings reported by Jacobs, Brunton, and Melville (1965), which indicated that prison inmates were far more likely to show this XYY pattern than males in the general population—fifteen times more likely, according to Jarvik, Klodin, and Matsuyama (1973).

The truth of the matter seems finally to have been resolved by impressive research carried out by a team of investigators led by Herman Witkin (1976a). Using Denmark's excellent statistical records, the investigators focused on the city of Copenhagen. More than 4,000 men were contacted, 16 had the XYY variation and the remaining men were the normal XY chromosomal types. It turned out that almost 42 percent of the XYY men had been convicted of at least one crime, while less than 10 percent of the XY men had such a record. Thus, it looked as if there must be something to the hypothesis. Closer examination, however, showed that when the actual nature of the crimes was taken into account, XYYs had not committed more crimes of violence than the XYs.

It was also found that XYYs showed lower intellectual capacity than XYs as measured by standardized tests that are administered to all Danish men. In addition, among the XYY group, the criminals had lower intelligence levels than the noncriminals. Witkin's group concluded simply that XYY individuals are more likely to get caught at crimes because they are less intelligent. The care with which the work by the Witkin group was carried out suggests that it is time to put to rest the XYY theory of the genetic basis for aggression.

Frustration and Aggression   An important advance in understanding aggression came from the learning theorists such as Dollard and his collaborators at Yale in the late 1930s (Dollard and others, 1939). Although they adopted Freud's view of aggression as a basic drive, they argued that it was not inherently cyclical, like hunger or thirst, but rather that it was aroused by frustrated intentions or impulses.

An important point in the learning-theory perspective is the likelihood of displacement of an aggressive drive from its original target to one with some similarity to the cause of frustration. Miller's studies with animals (1948) showed that such displacements follow definite rules:

1. They depend on the degree of similarity.

2. They occur more frequently when there are fewer inhibitions against attacking a particular individual.

3. They depend on the original strength of the aggressive drive.

THE BOBO DOLL: AGGRESSION IN YOUNG CHILDREN

A technique widely used to study aggression in children is based on the Bobo doll, a large plastic or rubber toy with a solid base, which when hit, falls down and bounces back up again. Bandura and his collaborators have used these dolls extensively to demonstrate that children will imitate the aggression they observe in others by hitting the Bobo doll (Bandura, 1973). It is important to note that these experiments chiefly indicate how aggressive responses can be acquired in a laboratory-type situation through direct observation of others. They do not necessarily predict whether children will behave similarly toward live human beings. Johnston and others (1977) showed, however, that children who were reported by either their teachers or other children to be especially likely to engage in fights also were more likely to attack a Bobo doll. Thus the Bobo doll, like the shock machine, has some demonstrable external validity as a measure of aggression.

We all recognize our tendency to "kick the dog" when circumstances arise we cannot deal with directly—for example, if a ball game we were to play in is postponed by rain, or if we are forced to do chores we had tried to avoid.

The proponents of the frustration-aggression hypothesis made a useful contribution by relating aggressive behavior to a process of learning and by suggesting experimental approaches for testing their hypotheses. Their views did, however, perpetuate the biological emphasis on aggression as a fundamental, almost inevitable, human drive, arousable in everyone since all of us experience frustrations.

The Social-Learning Perspective

The social-learning approach views aggression as behavior that is acquired through early experience and through observing others. The emergence of the social-learning approach to understanding and, to some extent, modifying aggressive behavior has been one of the major developments in modern psychology. It has stimulated careful and thoughtful research and clarified issues previously shrouded in mystery or in a mystique of inborn evil and destructiveness in the human species.

Social-learning theorists have accumulated a sizable body of data from sociological studies, anthropological reports, observations of spontaneous human behavior, and laboratory experiments, all of which show how interpersonal experiences and cultural patterns give us ideas of aggressive acts, reinforce such acts, and sustain aggressive patterns in individuals. Buss (1971) called attention to the widespread social reinforcement for aggressive behavior in describing the innumerable situations in our day-to-day lives in which "aggression pays." Rather than viewing aggression as an inescapable consequence of biological-drive buildup, many psychologists now regard it as a *response that is relatively frequently reinforced in our society once it occurs.* It is a product of social learning.

THE SHOCK MACHINE: AN EXPERIMENTAL PROCEDURE FOR STUDYING AGGRESSION

Arnold Buss (1961) devised a laboratory procedure for studying aggression. This procedure calls for subjects to participate in what they believe to be an experiment in which they are teaching others a learning task. The "learner," a confederate of the experimenter, performs certain prearranged tasks. The subject is the "teacher," who is required to flash a light if the learner gets the right response or to deliver an electric shock when the response is incorrect. The shock machine usually has ten buttons for delivering mild to severe shock, and the teacher-subject is given a sample of the shocks available to make sure that he or she has some notion of the intensity of shock that the machine can deliver to the learner. The confederate, who is generally unseen by the subject, does not actually receive the shock when the button is pressed, but may simulate extreme pain by shouting or otherwise communicating discomfort to the subject.

Do persons who are known from other evidence to be aggressive act aggressively on the shock machine? Hartmann (1969) and Shemberg, Leventhal, and Allman (1968) studied teenagers who had been described by counselors as very aggressive or who had known histories of aggressive behavior. These youngsters actually did deliver higher levels of shock to learners than subjects who had no history of aggressive behavior. Wolfe and Baron (1971) were able to study a group of prisoners between the ages of 18 and 20 with a history of assaultiveness and to compare their responses to those of college students. The assaultive prisoners showed a significantly higher level of shock intensity than the college students. Both groups increased their shock levels after they had been exposed to a model who emphasized aggression, but the differences between the prisoners and the college students remained approximately the same.

The shock machine has been especially useful because it allows researchers to determine the degree of pain the subject of an experiment is willing to deliver to another person under various circumstances. Of course, it must be assumed that the subject genuinely believes that he or she is delivering a painful shock to the "learner" in the experiment. It is possible that many subjects, knowing that they are participating in an experiment, never really believe that they would be put into a position of doing real harm to another person. From more than a hundred experiments with this procedure, however, evidence suggests that it does indeed simulate what actually happens when people are instigated to harm others (Bandura, 1973). Many social scientists believe that the shock machine can be employed as an ethical method for studying the important question of human aggressive activities or intentions, provided the subjects are adequately debriefed.

Nevertheless, one of the objections to research using the shock machine is that it inevitably involves deception. Moreover, the widespread publicity this procedure has received on television and in the press may have reduced the chances that participants will take it seriously.

Experiments directed by Leonard Berkowitz (1969, 1974), for example, had groups of young-adult subjects watch aggressive or non-aggressive films, or watch other people engaging in aggressive acts. These studies consistently demonstrated that exposure to aggression by others increases the chances that an individual will subsequently act aggressively. The presence of cues that suggest violence, such as weapons, also increases the likelihood that a provoked individual will later behave aggressively without even using the available weapons. A link between the cognitive and social perspective is apparent in the finding that when people interpret a situation as one that culturally calls for aggression, they will act accordingly, depending on previous social experience in the use of aggression (Baron, 1977).

The most extensive social-learning theory of aggression has been proposed by Bandura (1973). He emphasizes the following points:

1. Aggression is learned primarily through social experience. Children early in life observe their parents, brothers, and sisters engaging in aggressive acts and they imitate them. Observational learning is not just mimicry; observing respected family members engage in aggressive responses *encourages* children, by reducing inhibitions, to do the same.

2. Aggression depends on specific factors that are likely to instigate such behavior. Again, these are in part learned by the child, who recognizes that under certain types of provocation, an older sibling or a parent will respond by shouting or hitting.

3. Certain circumstances support the likelihood of the aggressive behavior continuing in the immediate situation. This occurs when a person succeeds in obtaining things from others through fighting. Bandura also emphasizes the fact that individuals reinforce themselves through their own thoughts and private praise for the effectiveness of aggressive behavior.

SOCIAL FACTORS AND AGGRESSION

Sociocultural Differences One way of looking at sociocultural patterns of human aggression is to take advantage of the statistics on the number of violent assaults, homicides, or other aggressive acts that are recorded, generally in police records, from various countries or in various subregions of a country. Figure 14-3, drawn from the report of the National Commission on the Causes and Prevention of Violence, indicates the evidence for the rising crime rate in the United States in the period between 1960 and 1967, a general increase that has continued beyond the dates indicated. Since a greater percentage of individuals involved in robbery are under 21, and since youthful offenders tend to be more violent, then if there is a large number of young people in a society the percentage of violent crimes will rise sharply along with robbery.

An important index of the extent of extreme violence carried out by individuals in a given region is provided by what is called the suicide-homicide ratio. In this formula, it is assumed that acts of self-destruction and acts of murder represent the total amount of destructiveness by individuals. The higher the ratio of suicides, the less externally directed violence in the society.

FIGURE 14-3
The Rising U.S. Crime Rate, 1960–1967

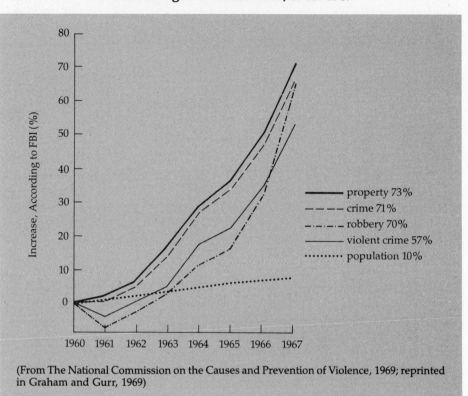

(From The National Commission on the Causes and Prevention of Violence, 1969; reprinted in Graham and Gurr, 1969)

Graham and Gurr (1969) assessed the extent to which there were relatively more suicides or relatively more homicides in a particular American state. Restricting their study to whites only, they found that there was a much greater likelihood that individuals from the Southern and Southwestern states would attack others rather than themselves and that the Southern states seemed especially to stand out in this grouping for the United States. This point is further emphasized by statistical analyses (Graham, 1969) indicating that Southern whites were more given to acting out their aggression than either urban or rural whites anywhere else in the nation. More elaborate statistical analyses indicate that the relatively high percentage of homicides among Southerners cannot be accounted for by the degree of urbanization, education, wealth, or age. These data suggest a cultural pattern among Southerners, both whites and blacks, that cannot easily be explained by the usual factors. Perhaps these statistics reflect a longstanding cultural pattern that is in part a conse-quence of the defeat of the South in the Civil War, the turmoil of the Reconstruction period, and the attempt of Southern whites to reassert their dominance in the 1880–1900 period. The much higher percentage of Southern or Southwestern families who own firearms compared to the rest of the nation undoubtedly has increased the likelihood that altercations will end in homicide. It is hard to avoid the conclusion that the sheer availability of easily used deadly weapons, such as pistols or rifles, increases the chances of extreme violence erupting during family quarrels or drunken arguments among friends.

The rate of homicide on the island of Manhattan with a population of somewhat less than 2 million is much higher than that of England with a population of about 50 million. The police in England, Scotland, and Wales do not usually carry guns. Despite the lack of firearms, they nevertheless have rarely been the victims of attacks by criminals. That this fact is often surprising to people in the United States suggests the important role of cultural differences among nations. Social and cultural factors seem, on the whole, to suggest that the emergence of aggressive behavior depends heavily on the cultural setting, expectations about violence within a culture, and the regular availability of cues in the environment for stimulating aggression.

"Obedient Aggression"   Is it possible that acts of violence can occur without either momentary or accumulated anger? Some of the most significant research in the past two decades involved the studies initiated by Stanley Milgram (1974) on the question of whether normal individuals would behave aggressively to comply with the requests of an experimenter—an authority figure—and in conformity with the "contract" the subject agreed to in accepting the terms of the experiment. Milgram was impressed by the fact that some of the most horrible acts of aggression in history—the deliberate murder of millions of Jews, Gypsies, and other Central European concentration camp inmates by the Nazis during World War II, were performed by functionaries who perceived themselves as merely "carrying out orders." Is this argument that terrible violence can come through bureaucratic obedience believable?

Milgram's experiments involved a shock-machine apparatus with which the subject was to administer higher and higher levels of shock to a "learner"—the experimenter's confederate—in order to help him make the "right" responses in a presumed research experiment. The subjects were told again and again by the experimenter in a quiet but firm manner to increase the level of shock even though they had indications from the "learner" that he was in pain. A surprising number of the participants delivered very high levels of shock, even though they were reluctant to do so and were personally upset by the pain they believed they were inflicting (see Figure 14-4).

The results of these experiments are a stunning demonstration of the extent to which ordinary individuals, free of any history of violence, will follow orders and engage in aggressive procedures directed at others. Simply accepting the terms of the contract with the experimenter accounts for the delivery of extremely high levels of shock to the confederates.

FIGURE 14-4

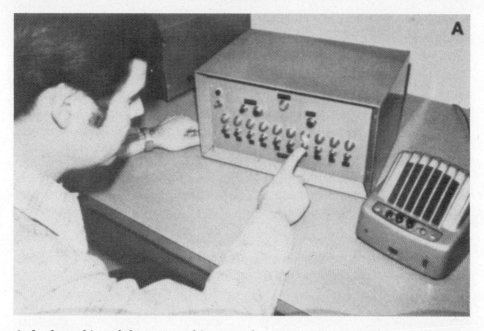

A shock machine of the type used in research on aggression. Buttons on the right represent higher levels of intensity: the "shock" the subject is delivering is therefore quite severe. (In actual experiments, the shock-delivery apparatus is disconnected without the knowledge of the subject.)

If anyone believes that these experiments do not relate sufficiently to reality and that individuals will not perform aggressive acts without personal anger at the recipients, here is an excerpt from an interview conducted by Mike Wallace of CBS News with an American soldier (discharged at the time of the interview) who had served in Vietnam:

A. *Well, there was about forty, fifty people that we gathered in the center of the village. And we placed them in there, and it was like a little island, right there in the center of the village, I'd say. . . and . . .*

Q. *What kind of people—men, women, and children?*

A. *Men, women, children.*

Q *Babies?*

A. *Babies. And we huddled them up. We made them squat down and Lieutenant Calley came over and said, "You know what to do with them, don't you," and I said yes. So, I took it for granted that he just wanted us to watch them. And he left, and came back about ten or fifteen minutes later and said, "How come you ain't killed them yet?" And I told them I didn't think you wanted us to kill them, that you just wanted us to guard them. He said, "No. I want them dead." So—*

Q. He told this to all of you, or to you particularly?

A. Well, I was facing him. So, but the other three, four guys heard it and stepped back about ten, fifteen feet, and he started shooting them. And he told me to start shooting. So I started shooting, I poured about four clips into the group" (*New York Times*, November 25, 1969).

It is possible, of course, that acts of "obedient aggression" may be committed by persons who have had years of pent-up anger or recurrent aggressive fantasies. So far we have little clear evidence that this is the case. In general, Milgram asserts that he was impressed with how few personality differences determine whether or not a person responds, suggesting that the situational demands of obedience may be remarkably powerful in determining whether or not individuals will engage in acts of presumed violence. More extensive research is needed to rule out the possibility that obedient aggression is more likely to take place when a person has a persistent pattern of resentment or social insensitivity. There is evidence that persons with dogmatic political views and a tendency to respond to irrational authorities ("authoritarian personalities") were more likely to show obedience and aggression in the Milgram experiments (Milgram, 1974).

Watching Aggression

What are the consequences of watching aggression? There is practically no support for the notion that watching aggressive acts performed by others (as in prizefight movies) reduces the likelihood that someone will engage in subsequent aggressive behavior (Bandura, 1973; Baron, 1977; Berkowitz and Geen, 1966). If anything, the vicarious experience of aggression is more likely to *increase* aggression, at least in the sense that it teaches the individual a way to act aggressively if there is provocation.

Robert Baron has shown that only when an individual is directly insulted is it likely that frustration will lead to a specific aggressive reaction. He writes:

Generations of parents urge their children to play with aggressive toys, e.g., Bobo dolls, punching bags, thousands of psychotherapists urge their patients to "release" their hostile feelings and syndicated columnists advise frustrated people to "vent" their aggressive urges through participation in vigorous sports or simulated aggression.

At first glance, a notion of catharsis seems to make good sense. Doing something when we are angry does indeed appear to be preferable to simply stifling our emotions and, in many cases, seems to lessen our annoyance. But is the catharsis hypothesis totally valid? Is it actually the case that the performance of one aggressive act—even a relatively noninjurious one— serves both to lower our level of emotional arousal and to reduce the probability that we will later engage in further aggressive actions? . . . Existing evidence seems to offer relatively strong support for the first of these suggestions, while leaving the second somewhat in doubt (Baron, 1977, p. 240).

Although there are indications that jokes and humor may reduce the continuation of angry feelings or of potential aggression, the evidence suggests that if this does happen it is not because of catharsis, the partial reduction of an aroused drive through symbolic representation, in the original sense proposed by Freud. Rather, the fantasy and humorous thoughts about hurting someone who has offended or frustrated us may temporarily distract us from the continuing high level of emotional arousal that was generated after an insult (Singer, 1975a). The laughter evoked by the humor is pleasing in its own right and turns our thoughts in a somewhat different direction. That does not mean that confronted directly with the same provoking person we would not be aggressive. On the other hand, it is also possible that creating a fantasy about a person or seeing the person in a humorous light cuts down on the threat posed by the person. We may see the individual as more human than we previously thought—less of a monster, perhaps more of a clown.

Most psychologists now regard aggression as behavior learned within the family or peer group. There may, however, be a cognitive developmental sequence involved in the process as well. Studies of monkeys show that only after a certain age has been reached (6–8 months) do they show aggression. Much of this takes the form of play-fighting (Aldis, 1975; Suomi, 1977)—rough and tumble, pushing, shoving, and chasing. Only animals reared in isolation from their mothers or the social group are likely to go beyond the bounds of playful aggression at this age (Suomi, 1977). Indeed, chimpanzees learn early an open-mouthed "play-face," a signal indicating that the aggression is not for real (see Chapter 16).

Learning Aggression

In human development, the baby first reaches an awareness that obstacles or blocks to attaining goals can be pushed aside or removed, and that, for example, a toy seized by another child can be tugged back. The baby also attains a certain level of cognitive differentiation, a separation of self from others, and a sense of possession, before it can assert itself forcefully to regain a lost toy or to pull a desirable one from another child (Maccoby, 1980).

In the period from 2 to 3 years of age, children become much more mobile. They are out of their cribs and begin exploring their surroundings. This inevitably brings them into conflict with their parents (who protect them against accidents) and, perhaps, older siblings or other children in a play group. Here the earlier omnipotence of the baby, who could get things done by reaching and crying (Ausubel, 1958), must give way to a continuing series of restrictions, peremptory warnings from parents, and often slaps or spankings.

Parental and adult attitudes are crucial for the child in the learning of aggressive responses, the establishment of limits, and the development of self-control. The child must learn to be able to move as freely in space as possible, but also to identify danger areas, to learn the "house rules" ("Don't go into the living room" "Don't walk out the door into the hallway or the street") and to learn self-assertion.

CHILDREN'S AGGRESSIVENESS AND PARENTS' RESPONSE

Parents often wonder what to do when their children are aggressive. Should they punish them? Figure 14-5 summarizes the results of research on the relation of children's aggressiveness and parental patterns of response.

The parents were classified into those who were permissive or non-permissive about aggressiveness and those who were punitive or nonpunitive. Thus, for example, a parent could be permissive—that is, accepting of aggres-

sion—but at the same time would punish a child for actually showing aggressive behavior. As can be seen from the diagram, children whose parents were permissive about aggression were, on the average, more aggressive than children of nonpermissive parents. But note that parents who were both punitive and permissive had the most aggressive children. And, at the other extreme, note that nonpunitive and nonpermissive parents had the least aggressive children.

FIGURE 14-5

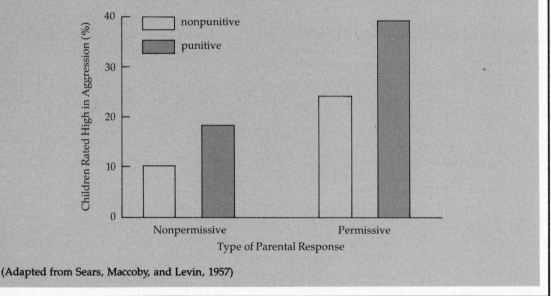

(Adapted from Sears, Maccoby, and Levin, 1957)

The observations of Patterson, Littman, and Bricker (1967) demonstrated that as children interacted in a nursery school there was an average of seventeen confrontations per hour over toys and space. Those children who behaved aggressively (kicking, biting, forcefully threatening) were often reinforced by attaining a toy or seeing the other child flee, yield a toy, or burst into tears. Such reinforcement usually led to other acts of aggression so that by the end of the year some children were consistently aggressive.

At home parents who themselves resolve a sibling conflict by aggressive acts or who show overt aggression toward each other are establishing aggression as an appropriate behavior for coping with frustration. Even without overt acts, parental remarks made about neighbors or about news on television ("Somebody who does that ought to be shot!") may be inadvertently laying the basis for their children to try aggressive actions when facing an obstacle. The research by Sears, Maccoby, and Levin (1957) made it clear that parents who responded to children's aggression at home by permissiveness or who took aggressive measures when they objected to the child's aggression were most likely to have children who behaved aggressively outside the home.

Careful work on the development of aggression has been done in the longitudinal studies of the Swedish psychologist Dan Olweus (1978). He showed that by middle childhood, boys can be delineated as (1) *bullies*, or consistent aggressors; (2) *whipping boys*, or children who seem to be the main, nonretaliatory victims of all children, especially bullies; and (3) the more sizable number of boys who are "well-adjusted," fighting if absolutely necessary but generally handling frustration with a variety of approaches and not instigating fights, as do the bullies. These patterns are consistent when measured in the sixth grade and again in the ninth. The aggressiveness of the bullies, toward adults as well as peers, cannot be explained as a consequence of school failure, peer rejection, or any special rewards of popularity, nor was the tendency linked to social class differences. Olweus proposed that bullies themselves *create* many of the aggressive situations that they react to with fighting and that they show few controls or inhibitions. Whipping boys tend, on the whole, to be anxious, overly sensitive, often physically weaker, lacking in self-assertion and self-esteem.

Olweus (1980) carried out extensive observations and interviews with hundreds of Swedish parents to tease out the origins of the aggressive personality pattern (see Figure 14-6). He found that the boys differed in temperament, that is, the amount of sheer activity and impulsivity they had shown from birth. In addition, mothers varied in the extent to which they had negative or rejecting attitudes toward their sons early in life. Permissiveness of aggression by the mothers also proved to be important. Another crucial variable turned out to be the extent to which both parents used power-assertive methods to control their children, particularly physical punishment and threats or violent outbursts.

Patterns of Aggression

Between 3 and 5 years of age, consistent patterns of aggression in children are formed. Yarrow and Waxler (1976) studied unstructured activities of children in this age group. They found that many children in the 3 to 5 year age group showed prosocial behavior (helping, sharing, comforting). There was, however, a significant minority of boys who spent a surprising amount of time in fighting or otherwise engaging in destructive behavior and who showed few prosocial acts.

Singer and Singer (1980, 1981) observed several hundred preschoolers during free play over a year's time. They, too, found that the behavior of the children fell into two major categories: (1) *playfulness*, including imaginative

PATHWAYS TO BOYHOOD AGGRESSION

Statistical analyses by Olweus (1980) based on data obtained at different times in the lives of sixth-grade boys make it possible to estimate the various possible causes of later aggression (Figure 14-6). The two independent starting points are x_1, a rejecting or negative mother (M), and x_2, an active, impulsive temperament in the boy. For the 76 boys in the study, the straight one-directional arrows indicate direct causal effects of one variable on another while all other variables are held constant. Thus, permissive mothers of active boys will directly influence later aggression. If mothers are rejecting and if they and the fathers (F) use power-assertive or physically punitive disciplinary methods, later aggression is also likely to occur.

FIGURE 14-6

Pathways to Boyhood Aggression

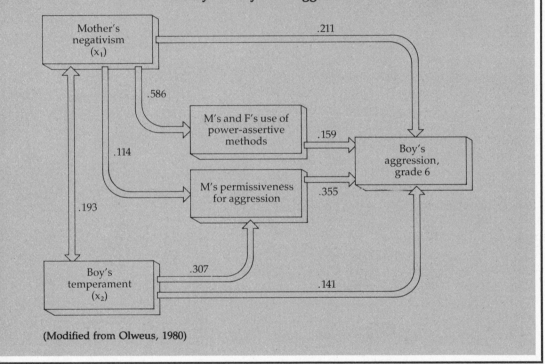

(Modified from Olweus, 1980)

and prosocial behavior, and (2) *aggression*, including random motor activity and expressions of anger as well as fighting. While some children showed both playful and aggressive behavior, a sizable minority, made up mainly of boys but including many girls as well, demonstrated consistent aggressive behavior and very little playfulness or prosocial behavior. Aggression tended to increase, especially for boys, from ages 3 to 5, but the patterns were fairly consistent as early as 3.

These aggressive patterns are surprisingly consistent. Olweus (1979) reviewed sixteen studies in which aggressive behavior in boys was measured at least twice over a span of months or years. For younger children, when aggression was measured twice within eighteen months or less, quite high correlations emerged. For older children and adolescents correlations were still sizable when the time gap was several years, but the older the boys, the greater the likelihood that substantial consistency would emerge when aggression was measured as much as 15 years later. Olweus suggests that aggression shows almost as strong a consistency over time as do measures of intelligence.

In the past thirty years a new element has entered the environment of the growing child—the television set. With preschool children watching upwards of 25 hours a week, they are exposed by midchildhood to thousands of hours of violence and aggression. If socialization and observational learning play a role in the development of an aggressive-prone personality, as Bandura (1973) suggests, then television-watching, especially of the action-detective shows or hyped-up game shows, will stimulate aggressive behavior. Of course, it is unlikely, in view of our national history of violence and gun use, that aggression among youth can be attributed solely to television, since it is a newcomer in the American home. But if heavy TV-watching does have an effect and if it influences even only ten percent of children to be a little more aggressive, the number of persons affected runs in the hundreds of thousands. In view of this figure, television is clearly more than mere harmless entertainment.

Television and Aggression

Two types of studies have examined the impact of television. The laboratory work stimulated by Bandura (1973) demonstrates that imitation by young children of violent acts shown on television is definitely possible. Field studies in which children's home-viewing patterns are related to concurrent or subsequent aggressive behavior are more convincing to many, because they reflect ordinary daily life. The surveys of research carried out by advisory committees to the National Institute of Mental Health in 1972 and in 1982 have yielded consistent evidence that there are positive correlations between watching action shows or violent cartoons and aggressive behavior at school (Comstock and others, 1978; D. Singer and J. Singer, 1980; Singer and Singer, 1981).

In a ten-year study (Lefkowitz, Eron, Walder, and Huesmann, 1977) it was found that the amount of violent television watched by a group of 9-year-olds was correlated not only with how aggressive they were at that time but also with how aggressive they were, according to their friends, ten years later. A pair of field studies directed by Singer and Singer (1980, 1981) looked at aggression in preschoolers across a year's time and the type and frequency of home TV-viewing. These studies indicate that watching violent action shows and violent cartoons is correlated for both boys and girls with aggressive behavior in school. It seems likely, therefore, that theories of the development of consistent aggression will have to take into account the child's television-viewing experience (Eron, 1980).

AGGRESSIVE PERSONALITIES

Are there persisting aggressive styles in adults? Let us look at some recent research findings.

Cognitive Styles and Aggression

Which personality styles make it more probable that individuals will engage in aggression? There is some evidence that those who score high on internal locus of control (Chapter 11) are more likely to act aggressively where it seems appropriate. They may also react to frustration with anger followed by aggression. Those who score high on external locus of control, however, show little evidence of using aggressive acts to attain their goals. In view of their generally fatalistic orientation, they conceivably might respond with aggression only when directly provoked to anger rather than using that behavior as a means of changing a situation in a calculating fashion.

A study employing shock was carried out by Dengerink, O'Leary, and Kasner (1975). While subjects classified as Internals and Externals on locus-of-control measures were using a shock machine, they were given either increasing or decreasing amounts of provocation by a partner (actually a confederate of the experimenters). As the provocation decreased, there was a sharp drop in the intensity of shock given by the Internals as well as Externals. But when provocation was increased, Internals increased the shock sharply to a high level, while the increase for Externals was much less rapid and at a much lower level. It was as if the Externals were more willing to turn the other cheek. The investigators imply that Internals may be more inclined to be generally aggressive.

Imagination and Controls for Violence in Adolescents

A whole series of studies has been done with assaultive adolescents and young adults, identified in institutions and from police records. A consistent finding about these assaultive young people is that even when general intellectual ability is taken into account, those who engage in more frequent acts of aggression or violence or other antisocial acts turn out to have less developed imaginative and fantasy patterns. When they are administered the Thematic Apperception Test, they show a pattern in which their fantasies are directly violent with no evidence of mitigating circumstances, inhibitions, or guilt reactions (Klinger, 1971; Singer 1968). Their responses to Rorschach inkblots are much less likely to show evidence of imagination as measured by Human Movement responses (Singer and Brown, 1977).

Goldberg (1973) examined the behavior patterns of a group of children, some of whom had histories of overt aggression while others did not. Those who had histories of aggression were more likely to have aggressive parents, but they also showed less well-developed fantasies as measured by projective techniques. Individuals who have an elaborate fantasy life can imagine a variety of ways for dealing with provoking situations, only some of which might be violent. Individuals who have been consistently violent seem, for whatever reason, not to have developed sufficiently varied backgrounds of options in their fantasies; instead, they focus on a direct violent outcome in any frustrating situation, and this limited range of fantasy is translated into a limited range of predominantly violent responses.

Megargee (1970) carried out studies in which he compared two groups of men who were in prison for acts of violence. One group had regularly gotten into fights and had engaged in physical assault, but had never carried out an act of terrible violence. A second group were men whose histories were free of overt acts of violence with the single exception of one act of appalling destruction, such as suddenly shooting someone not only once but emptying a full revolver into the prostrate body. A difference between these two groups of men was that the regularly assaultive group showed a less developed imaginative life than those who were assaultive with great intensity on only one occasion.

Extremely Violent Men

In effect, persons who are capable of acts of extreme violence may be regularly reflecting it in uninhibited fantasies of violence. Sirhan Sirhan, who assassinated Robert Kennedy, wrote elaborate fantasies in his diary, endlessly repeating "kill Kennedy, kill Kennedy" without any indication in his ruminations of alternative possibilities or any signs of a wider range of fantasies.

Perhaps the most extensive study of men with records of aggressive behavior was carried out by Toch (1969, 1975). He analyzed recorded interviews of prisoners in order to locate patterns of situations that led to recurring aggressive acts. Toch classified them in terms of the dominant motives they expressed for engaging in aggressive behavior. The single largest group–about forty percent—had "self-image–promoting" patterns. These men were especially insecure and seemed to need aggressive victories either to reduce their feelings of persecution by others or to convince themselves that they were something special.

Other patterns of violence included men who had a great need to defend their reputation as tough guys in their social group, men who seemed to feel a tremendous sense of pressure, and who sought regular opportunities for taking advantage of the weakness of others. Toch's results suggest that some of these aggressive patterns are so closely tied to day-to-day experiences of satisfaction or relief of tension that simply increasing the penalties for crime or strengthening the police forces may not prevent such persons from engaging in aggressive acts.

McCord, McCord, and Howard (1969) identified and studied 174 adolescent boys over a period of five years. They classified the boys as regularly (1) *aggressive*, (2) *assertive*, or (3) *nonaggressive*. The aggressive boys instigated unprovoked attacks on others, while the assertive boys sometimes fought in self-defense or under social pressure but generally dealt more peacefully with

Determinants of Persistent Violence

frustration. The results indicated that the aggressive boys came from families where the parents were rejecting, did not impose controls on the boys' behavior, and were themselves likely to be involved in conflict. Although the assertive boys' parents were likely to be inconsistent, and were also often involved in conflict, they did try to control the boys' behavior and they did not reject their children. These results are similar to the findings of Olweus, discussed above, on childhood determinants of aggression.

Sex Differences in Aggression

As you may have noticed, almost all the studies described so far have involved males. The reason is that direct aggressive acts are far less common in girls and women according to most studies (Maccoby, 1980). Certain evidence (Eron, 1980; Singer and Singer, 1981) suggests aggression in preschool or elementary school girls is on the increase, and some of these changes have been attributed to greater emphasis on female assertiveness and to the increase of female superheroes on television. There is also evidence that girls show a good deal of indirect aggression and do not differ from boys in this form of activity (Maccoby, 1980). Yet many questions remain to be answered, for we have little research on indirect forms of aggression, such as slander and backbiting.

Implications of Studies of the Aggressive Personality

There are clear indications that some persons, especially males, are consistently aggressive from an early age. While temperamental trends toward impulsivity have to be considered (Kipnis, 1971), the data argue against the notion of an inherent aggressive drive but rather suggest that we have a whole range of responses, some of which involve aggression. A great deal depends on early experiences and then on further experiences, either of reinforcement for acts of violence or impulsivity or failures to receive other experiential opportunities that suggest alternatives to aggression. In addition, the development of fantasy may be important in determining the extent to which an individual has a range of alternatives and a set of possible actions that can be tried out and practiced in imagination before they have to be implemented in action. Aggression may then become only one of a large repertory of potential reactions to frustration or aroused anger.

Aggression has been the subject of a kind of romantic or poetic mystique, as suggested by some of the psychoanalytic emphasis on the death instinct. Oscar Wilde wrote that "each man kills the thing he loves." Do people attack and murder those with whom they have been intimately involved because there is an inherent tie between love and death? Or is it rather because the very closeness of the attachment increases the chances that one has built up a whole host of wishes and desires and fantasies about the other person? Thus, when these wishes or fantasies are frustrated by the other person, as happens when a lover is unfaithful, the likelihood of the arousal of anger is much greater. For some persons the major response pattern to aroused anger is aggression. For persons who are limited in their ability to use imagery or in their range of responses, the chances of actual homicide or spouse- and child-beating are greater. We probably all carry around the potentiality of violence under extreme provocation, but for most circumstances we possess a useful repertory of more adaptive responses for coping with the inevitable frustrations of life.

SUMMARY

1. Anger, a basic human emotion, is aroused by extreme, persisting frustration of intentions or by the continuation of circumstances in which people cannot make sense of a large amount of information or cannot match new information with well-established plans. Anger is a negative unpleasant emotion that can lead to hostile thoughts, but it is separable from direct or indirect acts of aggression. Anger is apparent in facial expression as well as in menacing gestures. Angry individuals have a sense of power and move about actively, sometimes attacking the instigator. At one time anger was probably important for survival, but in modern society it is not so useful except for self-defense.

2. Because anger must often be suppressed, people who are constantly in anger-producing situations may experience physiological consequences, such as hypertension, or they may engage in behavior that disrupts their social relationships. Research has revealed individuals, called "Type A's," who are more likely to have heart attacks than other individuals. Type A's seem to expect to be angered and have a higher level of intensity, so that they overreact to provocation.

3. Learning to cope with anger is an important skill. Humor often reduces anger to manageable proportions. People need to be taught when anger is appropriate and when it is not appropriate. Assertiveness training is sometimes used, as well as other training programs.

4. Aggression is an overt act that involves an attempt to harm other people or damage their property. It also may involve self-harm, suicide or self-mutilation. Aggression may be direct, as in threats of violence and actual violence, or it may be indirect, as in verbal insults, lying, deception, and slander. In attempting to explain aggression, some observers have theorized that aggression is a basic instinct or an inborn drive. Recently a new point of view has emerged that emphasizes social learning of aggression.

5. Using implanted electrodes in animals, researchers have located brain areas tied to specific aggressive behavior. Only if aggressive cues are present will aggression occur. The social experience of an animal may determine whether or not aggressive behavior takes place.

6. Observations in the 1960s led to a proposal that men with an anomalous gene structure—the XYY chromosomal type—were especially prone to violence. In a careful study done in Denmark, it was found that XYY men had not committed any more crimes of violence than normal XY men, but

that the XYYs had lower intelligence levels. The conclusion was that XYY men are simply more likely to get caught at crimes.

7. An important advance in understanding aggression came from the learning theorists who proposed that aggression is aroused by frustrated intentions or impulses. They also showed that there is a likelihood of displacement of an aggressive drive from its original target to one that resembles it.

8. The social-learning approach views aggression as behavior that is acquired by experiences in childhood and by observation of others. The most extensive social-learning theory of aggression has been proposed by Bandura. He states that: (1) aggression is learned primarily through social experience, (2) aggression depends on specific factors that are likely to instigate aggression, and (3) certain circumstances support the likelihood of aggressive behavior continuing in the immediate situation. Aggression is related to social and cultural factors, which suggests that emergence of aggression depends on the cultural setting, expectations of violence, and availability of cues in the environment for stimulating aggression.

9. Aggression may take place without any feelings of anger, but rather in response to instructions or requests of an authority figure. Milgram's experiments showed that subjects would administer what they thought were extremely painful shocks merely because the experimenter told them to do so. Many of the horrible acts in Nazi concentration camps were done by functionaries who perceived themselves as carrying out orders. Certain incidents in the Vietnam war seemed to be based on this kind of "obedient aggression."

10. Although aggression can be viewed as behavior learned in a family or peer group, there also is a cognitive developmental sequence. When children begin to move around, they are faced with a continuing series of restrictions, warnings from parents, conflicts with siblings and playmates, and sometimes slaps and spankings. Between the ages of 3 and 5, patterns of aggression are formed that are surprisingly consistent over many years.

11. Research in the laboratory and in field settings shows that watching television, especially the violent action-detection shows, is correlated with an increase in children's aggressive behavior.

12. Aggressive behavior has been linked to certain personality styles and other variables. There is some evidence that persons who score high on the internal locus of control are more likely to make use of aggression. With assaultive young people, a consistent finding is that those who engage in more frequent acts of aggression have less developed imaginative and fantasy patterns. Similarly, a study of regularly assaultive men and men who were violent only once showed that those who were regularly assaultive had a less developed imaginative life. Direct aggression is much more common in males than in females, but there are indications that aggression in girls is increasing. Also, there is evidence that girls show a good deal of indirect aggression.

CHAPTER 15

Interest, Joy, Creativity, and Love

Here are three poetry excerpts that convey in vivid terms some of the most meaningful and uplifting impulses of the human spirit.

In the first, John Keats describes the excitement of reading a great book and compares the emotion to astronomical or geographical discoveries:

> Then felt I like some watcher of the skies
> When a new planet swims into his ken;
> Or like stout Cortez when with eagle eyes
> He star'd at the Pacific—and all his men
> Looked at each other with a wild surmise—
> Silent, upon a peak in Darien.

> —from *"On First Looking into Chapman's Homer"*

In his "Ulysses," Tennyson writes of the legendary Greek adventurer who in old age sets forth once again on a final journey:

> Come my friends,
> Tis not too late to seek a newer world
> . . . For my purpose holds
> To sail beyond the sunset and the paths
> Of all western stars, until I die;
> It may be that we shall touch the Happy Isles,
> And see the Great Achilles, whom we knew.
> Though much is taken, much abides; and though
> We are not now that strength which in the old days
> Moved earth and heaven; that which we are, we are—
> One equal temper of heroic hearts,
> Made weak by time and fate, but strong in will
> To strive, to seek, to find, and not to yield.

And here is a sonnet by Elizabeth Barrett Browning, a famous expression of quiet intimacy and personal passion:

> How do I love thee? Let me count the ways.
> I love thee to the depth and breadth and height

My soul can reach, when feeling out of sight
For the ends of Being and ideal Grace.
I love thee to the level of everyday's
Most quiet need, by sun and candle-light.
I love thee freely, as men strive for Right;
I love thee purely, as they turn from Praise.
I love thee with the passion put to use
In my old griefs, and with my childhood's faith.
I love thee with a love I seemed to lose
With my lost saints,—I love thee with the breath,
Smiles, tears, of all my life!—and, if God choose,
I shall but love thee better after death.

—from *Sonnets from the Portugese*

In tracing the theories and research that make up the field of modern personality psychology, we saw how little attention has been paid to the constructive or positive features of human experience. We dwelt upon fear and terror, conflict and anxiety, anger and aggression because most research and personality theories emphasized such actions or experiences as the keys to personality development and organization. If you think about your own daily life—your thoughts, memories, and anticipations—you will realize, however, that much of what we value in life is built around positive emotions and constructive experiences. These include curiosity and intense interest, the excitement of creativity, the warmth of shared collaboration in work and play, and the tender moments of intimacy with a relative, friend, lover, or spouse.

INTEREST AND JOY: THE POSITIVE EMOTIONS

Maslow's call for personality theorists to accept enthusiasm, excitement, exploration, and joy as inherent in the human condition is now being answered by careful studies of positive emotions. Let us take a closer look at some recent approaches to studying the affects of interest and joy and of surprise and happiness, their determinants, and the variations in individual emphasis on them.

Interest Interest is an important emotion closely tied to the cognitive system of the personality. It is related to such processes as alert attention to environmental change—the orienting reactions described by Sokolov (1958)—and to general arousal or wakefulness. But interest has a special property—it is related primarily to the way we confront situations of moderate complexity or ambiguity. If we are exposed to extreme novelty and unexpectedness, we may startle—that is, show excessive surprise, fear, or terror, negative emotions linked to paralysis of action or to flight. Interest, however, is a positive emotion that motivates us to move toward an object for exploration or that stimulates thoughts about causes or meanings (Izard, 1977; Tomkins, 1962).

In contrast with responses like the startle response or the orienting reflex, the emotion of interest is aroused not only by external signals and cues but also by our own memories and thoughts. As a matter of fact, we may first show interest in a situation by gazing intently at the object or person that confronts us and by exploring the environment with our eye movements. There may also be times when we avert our eyes from the face of another person in order to be able to explore in more detail our own thoughts about the subject under discussion. Looking away or at the ceiling, or even shutting our eyes, may reflect the necessity to clear our mental channels so that our brain's visual system can process memories and associations from the past that may relate to what we are discussing (Meskin and Singer, 1974; Singer, 1978).

Izard and various collaborators (Izard, 1972, 1977) asked subjects to imagine an event from their lives in which they had experienced interest. They were asked to visualize the situation as fully as possible and then to fill out forms describing their emotions. Along with interest, joy and surprise were the emotions most often mentioned. Interest is consistently viewed as a pleasant emotion, generally rated just slightly below joy. This is understandable, since joy can be experienced after a sharp reduction in tension or distress—as in relief when a relative survives a serious operation—while interest may still involve mild tension and higher levels of physiological arousal, part of the inclination to move toward the object, scene, or person stimulating the emotion.

The Motivational Aspects of Curiosity   A major way in which we experience interest is through the attitude of *curiosity*, of which exploratory behavior is the overt expression. The work of Berlyne (1960) demonstrated how important curiosity is as a motivating influence in animal as well as human behavior. Research by Zajonc (1968) showed that repeated familiarity with material leads to greater feelings of liking and positive affect, and Maddi (1976) suggests that moderate familiarity in an otherwise ambiguous situation is what leads to further exploration. Some of our greatest pleasures come from a combination of curiosity and exploration along with the joy of familiarity. In music a new melody arouses our interest and then once it is familiar we enjoy hearing it again. The highest forms of classical music and jazz involve the development of a theme. A melody or tune is stated, repeated so we get familiar with it, and then varied through a dozen turns and twists so that our curiosity is piqued. Beethoven was a superb master of such an approach, sustaining our interest for long periods of time by the dramatic construction of a whole symphonic movement from the development of a theme sometimes consisting of just a few notes. Jazz improvisation reflects a similar style, as a band plays around with a popular tune in a "Now you hear it, now you don't" technique.

Sometimes the excitement of exploration becomes a dominant theme in a person's life. Bertrand Russell, the English philosopher and political activist who lived well into his nineties, was constantly exploring each new intellectual current, whether in the form of educational practices, sexual attitudes, political concepts, the implications of the development of the H-bomb for future civilization, and so on. As a philosopher and mathematician he also kept on top of the latest developments in science, exploring their implications from a rigorous logical and technical standpoint.

Dimensions of Activation and Curiosity   Salvador Maddi (1976) developed a theory of personality patterns that puts special emphasis on interest, curiosity, and the desire for moderate stimulation and variety. He proposed that people vary in (1) whether they seek high or low activation—that is, the generalized intense emotion associated with novelty and variety; (2) whether they seek such activation in external (environmental) or internal (thoughtlike) experiences (a dimension akin to Jung's introversion-extraversion); and (3) whether they are active or passive in seeking to control their environments (see Figure 15-1).

Some support for Maddi's emphasis on the importance of a dimension of stimulus activation comes from the research on sensation-seeking by Zuckerman (1979) and by Segal, Huba, and Singer (1980) (Chapter 8). Using a series of scales to measure general sensation-seeking, experience sensation-seeking, thrill sensation-seeking, and disinhibitory sensation-seeking, Zuckerman found evidence that people differ systematically and consistently in their efforts to attain different levels of activation.

Segal, Huba, and Singer (1980) administered a battery of questionnaires involving motives or needs, sensation-seeking tendencies, and daydreaming to more than a thousand college students. From a statistical analysis of the way the students' responses to these scales clustered together, the researchers were able to identify several factors along which the respondents varied systematically. One factor showed links between a motive such as the need for understanding, a scale in Jackson's Personality Research Form (Chapter 7), general and experience sensation-seeking, and a variety of scales indicating sensitivity to private experiences and constructive daydreaming as well as considerable curiosity about people (Imaginal Processes Inventory) (Chapter 10). A second factor links a low achievement motivation, an external locus-of-control orientation, high disinhibitory sensation-seeking (that is, desire for experiences of an uncontrolled type), inability to sustain attention, and susceptibility to boredom. Still a third factor was defined by high scores on needs for dominance, affiliation, and external stimulation, low scores on harm avoidance, and especially high scores on thrill and adventure sensation-seeking. These factors seem to define three of Maddi's dimensions—the high activation–high internal orientation, the low activation–external orientation, and the

FIGURE 15-1
Maddi's Personality Patterns

	High Activation		Low Activation	
	Internal	External	Internal	External
Active Control	thinker, day-dreamer; subtle, complex, scholarly, philosophical, poetic, creative	"go-getter," pursuer of causes; statesman, athlete, journalist; "facts not fantasy"; energetic	self-protective, integrated, dependable, orderly in thought	conformist, conservationist, striver after simplicity; efficient; prefers the predictable
Passive Control	same interests as above but lacks ability to accomplish; dissatisfied, bored, uninvolved; at extreme, has potential for thought disorder	same interests as above but less effective; dilettante and consumer; prefers to repeat experiences that were exciting before	advocate of golden mean; simple and uncomplex; ruminates obsessively; constantly trying to repress thoughts	swamped by stimulation; unable to act on conservation interests; renunciation of world; hermit, tramp, or schizophrenic

The personality patterns Maddi proposed yield eight categories of personality types, described here through lists of personality traits. Compare these types with Galen's four temperaments in the diagram in Figure 1-1.

(Derived from Maddi, 1976)

high activation–external orientation and active control. It remains to be determined from future research whether Maddi's proposal of activation-seeking, inner versus outer orientation, and active versus passive control as major determinants of personality variation will be sustained.

Curiosity, Competence, and the State of Flow The psychology of personality has benefited greatly from the introduction of the notion of *competence* by Robert White (1959, 1960). White reexamined the psychoanalytic or drive theorists' views on development during the first five years of life. He stressed the limitations of the emphasis on the child's mastery of "body zonal" conflicts through toilet training or overcoming the Oedipus complex. Instead, White said that growth of personality reflects the child's developing control over "locomotion, language, and imagination." Our ability to master new challenges as well as our curiosity about the unknown often combine to lead us to some of our greatest moments of enthusiasm and happiness.

Investigations directed by Mihalyi Csikszentmihalyi (1975) explored in detail the experiences of people who were already talented in a particular field and who constantly sought new heights of accomplishment. He was interested in the challenge of something slightly beyond one's previous performance but not beyond one's overall capacity. Csikszentmihalyi studied rock climbers, composers, chess players, dancers, and basketball players, asking them to rate the various components that make these activities rewarding. He wanted to discover whether the hobbyists' motivation was *instrumental*—that is, whether they viewed their activity as helping them to get ahead or providing financial gain, social prestige, power, or direct emotional release—or whether their motivation was *autotelic*—that is, whether the activity was self-justifying, with an intrinsically satisfying quality. As Table 15-1 shows, for all but the basketball players, the motivation was autotelic, with the most frequently cited reasons being enjoyment, the use of skills, and the world of the activity itself. Csikszentmihalyi also asked the hobbyists how other activities compared with the thrill they obtained from their own special activity (see Table 15-2). Note that "designing or discovering something new" and "exploring a strange place" rank highest for all groups except the basketball players. How do you account for the fact that for each question the basketball players made a somewhat different set of choices?

Csikszentmihalyi developed a theoretical model to explain the "state of flow" that most of the subjects reported as occurring during their activity. The state of flow is a sense of almost pure exhilaration—a pure train of movements or thoughts when a person is functioning beautifully in an activity. This experience is shown in a graph that relates the flow state to the relationship between the challenge of the task (the mental or physical difficulties involved) and the actual skills of the person. For an experienced rock climber, a nearly sheer cliff face with some possible path up is a challenge, and as the climber moves up, mastering each intricacy and thus making it "familiar," he or she moves from interest to joy into the state of flow (see Figure 15-2).

Joy and Happiness

The smile is a form of communication that binds together all humanity on this earth. An American physician and his wife arrived at a village in the Amazon jungles of Brazil to set up an immunization program for a group of Indians who were just emerging from centuries of isolation from the rest of Brazilian society. The Americans felt great trepidation as they first encountered the crowd of spear-carrying naked men and women of the tribe. But when the villagers broke into broad smiles, the visitors were reassured at once, and could respond with their own smiles and with gestures of friendship.

The smile of joy appears in the first eight weeks of an infant's life. We know that it is more than "gas," as it used to be described, and that it occurs most often in the presence of another human being (Emde and Koenig, 1969). Joy is more than the direct experience of need gratification, taking in food when one is hungry or feeling sexual release. It can, of course, accompany

TABLE 15-1
Reasons for Enjoying Activity

Reason for enjoying activity	Rock climbers	Composers	Dancers	Mean rank scores Male chess players	Female chess players	Basketball players
N =	30	22	27	30	22	40
Enjoyment of the experience and use of skills	1	1.5	1.5	1	1	5
The activity itself: the pattern, the action, the world it provides	2	1.5	1.5	2	2	4
Friendship, companionship	3	6.5	6	4	4.5	3
Development of personal skills	4	3	3	3	3	2
Measuring self against own ideals	6	4	5	6	6.5	6
Emotional release	5	5	4	7	6.5	8
Competition, measuring self against others	7	8	8	5	4.5	1
Prestige, regard, glamour	8	6.5	7	8	8	7
Total autotelic rank	3	1	2	4	5	6

(Modified from Csikszentmihalyi, 1975, p. 17)

such experiences, but it is found in a much broader range of situations than physiological satisfaction. As Izard (1977) has written:

> *Being amused or entertained is not equivalent to the joy experience. Amusement often involves interest and sexual arousal, and it may include fear in the case of the thrill-seeker . . . , aggression in the case of the sadist, or pain in the case of the masochist. Perhaps in its purest and most meaningful form, joy is what obtains after some creative or socially beneficial act that was not done for the express purpose of obtaining joy or doing good (p. 240).*

Izard proposed that the experience of joy involves not only self-contentment but satisfaction with others and with life itself. Inevitably, therefore, the tragedies and dangers that surround us in this world make it impossible for us to experience a continuing state of joy. We find our joy in brief periods of interaction with others, in moments of esthetic appreciation, in activities in which we help others or share with others a sense of commitment and accomplishment.

Some of the supreme moments of human artistic achievement are those in which a great composer attempts to capture in music the peaks of enthusiasm and joy of which humans are capable. In Bach's *Magnificat* or Handel's *Messiah*, these peaks of excitement are connected with spiritual experiences

TABLE 15-2

Ranking of Related Experiences

Experiences	Rock climbers	Composers	Dancers	Male chess players	Female chess players	Basketball players
			Mean rank scores			
1. Friendship and relaxation						
Making love	6	6.5	4.5	16.5	17.5	14
Being with a good friend	3	9	4.5	9	14.5	8
Watching a good movie	15.5	5	9	12	17.5	6
Listening to good music	6	3	2	10	12.5	3
Reading an enjoyable book	8	8	6.5	5	12.5	15.5
2. Risk and Chance						
Swimming too far out on a dare	13	13.5	15	14	7	17
Exposing yourself to radiation to prove your theory	17	10	12	12	10	9.5
Driving too fast	10	16.5	12	12	10	6
Taking drugs	10	13.5	15	15	14.5	9.5
Playing a slot machine	18	18	15	18	16	17.5
Entering a burning house to save a child	13	11	12	16.5	10	13
3. Problem-solving						
Solving a mathematical problem	4	2	9	1.5	2	12
Assembling equipment	13	6.5	17	7.5	7	15.5
Exploring a strange place	1	4	3	4	4	12
Playing poker	15.5	13.5	18	6	5	12
4. Competition						
Running a race	6	16.5	9	7.5	7	2
Playing a competitive sport	10	13.5	6.5	1.5	3	1
5. Creative activity						
Designing or discovering something new	2	1	1	3	1	6

(Modified from Csikszentmihalyi, 1975, p. 29)

and the thrill of closeness to God. For Beethoven, the great "Ode to Joy" at the end of his Ninth Symphony glorifies the humanistic ideal of the day when "all men will be brothers!"

In Goethe's *Faust*, the aging doctor sells his soul to the devil to regain his youth. He agrees that he can be doomed to hell if ever he finds the moment of pure joy when he can say, "Let this moment stay with me, it is so beautiful." Through many dramatic adventures, Faust never does make the statement until, as a very old man again, he directs an ecological project and preserves

FIGURE 15-2
The State of Flow

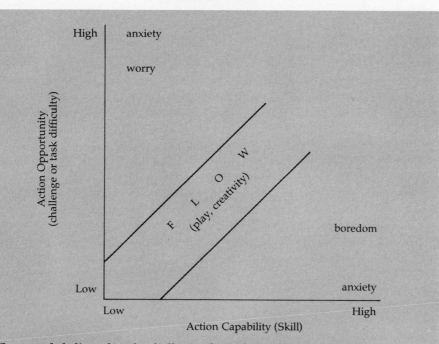

When people believe that the challenge of a task or activity is too great for their capability, they experience anxiety; when the skill is higher but the challenge still too demanding, they experience worry. When the skill is greater than the opportunity, people experience boredom; if this ratio becomes too large, the result, again, is anxiety. As the graph shows, the state of flow—an autotelic experience—is the product of a balance between skill and opportunity.

(Modified from Csikszentmihalyi, 1975)

the cottage of an elderly couple from destruction. This act of social concern and loss of self in the service of others finally evokes from him the cry of pure joy.

Joy can be linked to moments of high exhilaration such as a rock climber's attainment of the summit of a cliff, or to quieter moments, such as the memory of a wonderful moment on a recent vacation or the recall of happy times spent with grandparents on a farm. These moments may come to mind years later and bring forth a smile of joy without any external stimulation at all.

Humor and Laughter   Humor and the appreciation of jokes and comic situations are day-to-day contributors to our sense of joy. Freud made an important contribution to our understanding of jokes by calling attention to how often they provide a socially acceptable "release" for sexual or aggressive ten-

A moment of sheer joy.

sions, since so many jokes do have an erotic or sadistic twist. More recently it has been recognized that a key element in humor is also the resolution of some kind of cognitive incongruity. Zigler, Levine, and Gould (1967) demonstrated that children are most likely to laugh at jokes which are neither too obvious nor too far beyond their capacity for understanding. In other words, there is first an arousal of interest in material that seems odd or unusual and then a resolution of this incongruity once the children see the material as matching their earlier established knowledge. If the material is too incongruous, they simply do not grasp the humor at all and are put off by it.

Deficiencies in Experiencing Humor or Joy   The capacity to experience joy through appreciation of art and culture, through enjoyment of work or of service to others, or through brief moments of intimacy may be lacking in some individuals to a surprising degree. Chapman and Chapman (1973) carried out work to demonstrate that an unfortunate concomitant of schizophrenic illness is an inability to appreciate pleasure or to experience such moments of joy. Indeed, they feel that this may be a critical difficulty from which many other serious symptoms of the illness flow. Levine (1968) and various collaborators showed that emotionally disturbed individuals, such as schizophrenics, often fail to catch on to many kinds of jokes that other people find hilarious. Brown (1978) explored consistencies in experiences of joy, facial expression, and underlying psychophysiology in depressed college students

PATTERNS OF CHILDHOOD HUMOR

Studies of the way humor develops in children have identified four categories of ambiguity in jokes that are appreciated by elementary schoolers. All four types show a mixture of cognitive incongruity, arousal of interest, and resolution with a familiar phrase that evokes laughter. The lexical category involves ambiguity of meaning because of similarity in words; the phonological category involves the ambiguity of sound; surface-structure ambiguity depends on the sound, meaning and rhythm of the sentence, while deep-structure ambiguity involves a more subtle element combining meaning and grammar.

Lexical ambiguity
"Order! Order in the court!"
"Ham and cheese on rye, please, Your Honor."

Phonological ambiguity
"Waiter, what's this?"
"That's bean soup, ma'am."
"I'm not interested in what it's been, I'm asking what it is now."

Surface-structure ambiguity
"I saw a man eating shark in the aquarium."
"That's nothing. I saw a man eating herring in the restaurant."

Deep-structure ambiguity
"Call me a cab."
"You're a cab."

(From Schultz and Horibe, 1974)

and psychiatric patients. These subjects indicated that they sometimes felt good and enjoyed moments of pleasure, but their emotions were not likely to register in their facial expressions or in their psychophysiological patterns. In effect, there is a dissociation of the physiological, communicative, and experiential features in the emotional system of depressed persons that may limit their capacity for the full experience of happiness.

Happiness in College and in Marriage   The most extensive research on the relation of personality development, life status, and levels of happiness was carried out by Constantinople (1970). She found that women college students showed a decrease in their levels of happiness from the freshman through the senior years. In contrast, male students showed a general increase in happiness across the four-year period. Both sexes showed a decrease in negative emotions, such as shame and guilt, over the four years' time. Reports of happiness by students were positively correlated with feelings that they could trust others, that they had some independence, and had a clear sense of personal identity.

Constantinople's research was done in the late 1960s, and she explained the decrease in women's levels of happiness in terms that may not apply to the current generation. In those days it was still widely expected by young women that college attendance would lead to a long-term relationship with a man and probably to marriage. Men's goals were much more oriented toward careers, so that over the four years they usually could perceive steady progress. The women, with their emphasis on marriage, became less certain of their goal from freshman to senior year and therefore more doubtful about themselves. It would be intriguing to know whether similar results would be obtained today.

A study of happiness in young adults points up again the persisting sex difference, although from another vantage point. In this study (*Psychology Today*, 1979) young wives reported that they received more pleasure from reading than from sex. When asked to rate the components of daily life that brought them joy, men emphasized direct physical gratifications, while women put more value on their own private distillation of an experience. These results may reflect the reality that a good deal of joy comes from our own imagination and memory, the sort of controlled vicarious living we can get from reading and thinking about our experiences. This research demonstrates that experiences of joy are not solely dependent on drive satisfaction, or reduction of "tissue needs." Rather, much of what we feel to be our quieter, happy moments of day-to-day living comes from vicarious experiences—"travel" through fantasy, anticipations, and sharing many different lives by reading an interesting book or watching a good film or drama.

Identifying the Happy Person

Sophocles concluded his tragedy *Oedipus the King* with the words "Call no man happy until he has crossed the threshold from life to death." Despite these grim words, psychologists have found that a sizable number of individuals describe themselves as at least moderately happy in their day-to-day lives (Veroff and others, 1962; Wessman and Ricks, 1966).

Veroff and his collaborators found that for a sample of 265 men a report of moderate happiness was correlated negatively with worry, problems with children, and psychosomatic symptoms, and was correlated positively with marital happiness. For women, happiness was also negatively associated with worry, psychological anxiety, physical anxiety, and psychosomatic symptoms. While the women did not emphasize a positive association between happiness and marriage, they did indicate that unhappiness was strongly linked to marital dissatisfaction. Knupfer, Clark, and Room (1966) also found that for men a good marriage is strongly linked to a sense of happiness. For women there is no specific pattern linked to happiness, but an unsatisfactory marriage is negatively correlated with happiness. It seems as if women expect less of life and marriage and count themselves lucky if their marriage is at least not too unhappy!

A group of investigators at Harvard University carried out a study of day-to-day fluctuations in mood in a large group of Radcliffe and Harvard students. They also looked at the differences between young men who showed consistent patterns of variation in their daily moods as against those who showed stable mood levels. Gorman, Wessman, and Ricks (1975) found that a pattern of positive reactions was not simply a "response set" but reflected pleasant events and situations that occurred from day to day. Wessman and Ricks (1966) and

Gorman and Wessman (1974) were able to identify groups of "stable" men and men who could be considered as "moody":

> The moody men were more liable to inner turmoil, but were rewarded with the more intense inner life and greater responsiveness and originality. . . . Stable men were more tightly organized and controlled. They were generally objective, cautious, "rational," and little given to imagination. The variable men were more impulsive, carried along by their whims and enthusiasms with little critical control.

Wessman concluded:

> The variable people seem to be seeking self-actualization and peak experience (Gorman and Wessman, 1974; Maslow, 1954, 1962). Their goals were not stable habits and routines but initiative, drive to achieve, and desire to change themselves and the world and to be recognized for doing this. Their preferences among various metaphors for time, for instance, were images like "a soaring bird," "ceaseless effort," "unappeasable ambition," and "the thrust of forward purpose." Like Icarus, they break the bounds of ordinary experience, and if they at times fall into the sea of gloom, they also fly high into the thin air and bright sunshine of peak experiences (Wessman, 1979, p. 97).

Wessman and Ricks identified individuals who consistently rated themselves as "happier" on scales of elation-depression over a period of time. Such self-ratings were reasonably valid since a group of psychologists who observed these young men for two years also rated them as happier. The "happy" men showed a pattern of clearer personal identity, a sense of structure or organization in their lives, more self-esteem, and better social relationships. The consistently unhappy men showed a generally pessimistic orientation, greater sense of isolation, and more anxiety and guilt—and since they actually performed less well academically, their inferiority feelings were realistic.

We have cited studies by Rizley (1978) and by Alloy and Abramson (1979) that suggested that nondepressed young adults often show an illusory optimism (Chapters 7 and 12). Yet the research by Wessman and his collaborators provided indications that happy men had better childhoods and more satisfying relationships during their childhood development. Perhaps earlier successes do engender a mood of optimism and self-confidence that, even if exaggerated, helps people to continue to strive in the face of adversity. Even if their optimism or belief in a "just" world is inaccurate, their continued efforts may thereby increase their chances of dealing with the common difficulties of life.

Costa and McCrae (1980), for example, found that high scores on measures of social extraversion in adolescence predicted happiness as measured on scales administered ten years later. High scores on emotional instability predicted later unhappiness. Thus, adult happiness and positive affects are generated by early temperamental factors like vigor and sociability, while later negative affects are produced by early signs of anxiety, hostility, and impulsivity.

CREATIVITY

Two important areas of personality variation that grow from the positive emotions of interest-curiosity and joy are (1) *creativity*, an attitude toward developing new ideas, problem-solutions, or artistic products, and (2) *love and intimacy*. Let us first take a look at the research on the process of creativity and its implications for personality.

The Process of Creativity

Creativity has a positive value in society, and it has been the subject of a great deal of theorizing; in the past twenty years a sizable body of research has emerged as well (Stein, 1975; Stein and Heinze, 1960). One line of investigation focused on the creative process itself—the way in which people come up with original or novel ideas. In the classic studies of Patrick (1935, 1937) the steps necessary for creative achievement were outlined:

1. *preparation*, in which there is a rapid shifting around of associations and assembling of new ideas
2. *incubation*, in which there is a sometimes involuntary period of waiting and almost unconscious working over of the material
3. *illumination*, in which the idea that has been "incubating" suddenly emerges in startling clarity, sometimes seeming to come from outside as an inspiration of the mythical Muses
4. *revision*, in which the creative person, having come up with original and exciting material, now reshapes it into a form that is effective for communication and that meets the technical requirements of the person's field of endeavor

Patrick actually studied about 50 poets and nonpoets, each writing a poem after looking at a picture. She also studied artists drawing a picture after reading a poem. Of course, it is questionable whether any major work of art emerged from these efforts. After all, there is little reason to think that a group of minor poets and artists working together could indeed create a masterpiece. Nevertheless, she did find the sequence of preparation, incubation, illumination, and revision in the production of an original poem or painting.

Psychoanalytic theorists from Freud through Ernst Kris have emphasized the fact that creative products represent the emergence into consciousness, sometimes in symbolic form, of taboo, unconscious conflictual material. Indeed Kris (1951) has been widely quoted because of his belief in the artist's capacity to engage in "regression in the service of ego." Kris meant that the mature behavior of adults as directed by the ego (Chapter 3), especially in creative activity, often requires patterns of thought and action that draw upon childlike ways of looking at the world.

This notion—the childlike directness of the artist—has been criticized in studies of creative and imaginative people by Barron (1972) and Singer (1966,

1975a). These investigators proposed that a creative person's imaginativeness and juxtaposition of novel elements, which come from dreams and fantasies or which involve a closeness to sensory experience, are highly developed capacities that mature through the years. They are not simply "regressions" to a more infantile way of looking at things. Indeed, children rarely produce truly artistic or creative works.

Attention to the research on the creative process has, however, led to a number of methods now employed particularly in industry, science, and engineering to stimulate creative problem-solution in technologically different tasks. Stein (1975) explored at length the full array of such techniques and showed that several of them have genuine value. Some are particularly effective for groups. For example, Parnes' method of creative problem-solving is frequently employed and occasionally yields concrete results. It involves bringing together a group of people who systematically engage in the following specific steps:

1. statements and restatements of the problem
2. a good deal of free association
3. willingness to engage in fantasies of various kinds
4. development of mutual trust as the process goes on
5. tossing back and forth of various possibilities, and then
6. a kind of enthusiastic movement toward the goal of problem-solution

Still another approach, *synectics*, developed by Gordon (1961, 1971), makes extensive use of fantasy processes. In this approach the effort to break traditional sets and to move away from commonplace points of view, which often prevent problem-solution, is carried out through occasional wild flights of fantasy, psychological self-examination, and the recall of fantasies and dreams. From the standpoint of personality theory it is important to note that the process of creativity closely intertwines and melds the cognitive and affective orientations. It involves active information-seeking, which in itself is a characteristic of achievement-oriented persons (Jensen, 1978). In addition, creative individuals are especially aroused to explore areas in which they work with novel material that is just beyond their reach (Csikszentmihalyi, 1975). In general, there also seems to be a kind of creative attitude engendered by the structure of a synectics or creative problem-solving meeting in which license is given to free-ranging thought.

Some of the research approaches to the study of creativity try to identify **Creative** potentially creative individuals or to examine the lives of creative persons. **Personalities** Reports of their childhood by persons of demonstrated creativity in the arts or sciences often indicate that at some point they spent a good deal of time alone, that they often were lost in fantasies and daydreams, and that they sometimes had imaginary playmates with whom they conversed (Cobb, 1977; Helson, 1967; Roe, 1952). Accounts of the lives of other artists also point to

A SYNECTIC GROUP AT WORK

The following is an example of a synectic group that is meeting to try to resolve a problem in automobile technology. During production, car tires often develop leaks. This group of engineers was trying to solve the problem "How can we make leakers cure themselves?"

Leader: OK, let's examine speeding. What does this speeding idea bring to mind?

Ron: There is an exhilaration about speeding that is very sensual. It is, in a way, almost as exciting as sex . . .

Horace: I wonder if that is a male thing or do girls feel the same way? . . .

Leader: Let's go back to our problem: How can we make leakers cure themselves? How can we use this speeding idea—any of them—to help us?

Al: I think of a cop speeding to the scene of . . . of a leak? . . .

Ron: He pulls a gun and fills the hole with lead. . .

Leader: We could fill his gun with thumbs. . .but what is this saying?

Horace: I like the cop idea because we can do that—our dye speeds to the scene of the crime, but then it just lies there.

Ron: You know, on the side where you look for leaks with black light?

Horace: Yes.

Ron: Could you shoot lead or something wherever you see dye coming through?

Horace: You know, we have never thought of making a repair at that point. We were so obsessed with detecting we haven't thought of that. That is a good thought, but lead bothers me.

Leader: What concerns you, Horace?

Horace: These holes are really small—like pores really. Black light shows you a stain, but that only tells the general area. We would have to have a very thin, dyelike lead that would stay molten until we knew it had filled the pore.

Al: Horace, could you use two different dyes—boy-girl—type dyes? That turn thick?

Horace: Yes, I like two components . . . like an epoxy. A slow-curing one. . . . But we have to make it really penetrate somehow.

Dick: I thought Al meant boy on one side, girl on the other.

Horace: That is it! A two-component epoxy, both thin as dye. Spray one on the outside, the other on the inside. . . . They meet and react in the hole.

(Prince, 1970, pp. 149–50)

the importance of at least one key adult figure—a father or mother, or in some cases a relative or teacher—who took time with the child, told stories, shared experiences, and introduced the child to some of the mysteries of nature. Cobb's (1977) examination of autobiographies suggests that again and again there are reports of early heightened curiosity, a mix of playfulness and joy related to exploration of novelty, whether in physical nature or in make-believe games, and a continuing sense of "wonder." Creativity does indeed seem to emerge from a persistent attempt to experience the emotions of interest and joy.

Barron (1956, 1957, 1958) conducted studies of creativity, especially with respect to artistic achievement, with the use of such measures as questionnaires, Rorschach inkblots, the Thematic Apperception Test, extended interviews, and solutions to anagrams. He concluded that creative persons tend to prefer forms that are complex, ambiguous, or asymmetrical rather than simple and symmetrical. He also found that creative persons are more likely to produce associations of human movement and complicated imaginative responses, and also to show independence of judgment.

In general, the creative process is something available in one form or another to most human beings of at least reasonable intelligence. In many ways creativity is largely an attitude toward the physical and social environment. While it is certainly true that some artists in history have been unhappy and have led tortured lives, others have not had serious neurotic difficulties or problems and have functioned effectively in interpersonal relationships as well as in their creative endeavors.

LOVE AND INTIMACY

Shakespeare wrote that lunatics, lovers, and poets are much alike. It seems appropriate, therefore, to move from our discussion of creativity to a consideration of love and intimacy and their role in the human personality. Because of the influence of psychoanalysis throughout much of this century, a great deal of attention has been paid to the significance of sexuality, particularly in its more sensual and early childhood forms, and in personality development and disorder. But human intimacy—love and commitment to shared experience—has been rather neglected until recently.

From the time when St. Paul wrote, "There abideth faith, hope and love and the greatest of these is love," the word "love," at least in Western civilization, has always been laden with meaning, nuance, and emotion. It can, of course, mean merely an act of sex, as in the phrase "they made love"—a usage that may or may not imply any tenderness or lasting concern for the partner. But as the Browning poem at the beginning of the chapter says, the word conveys many other connotations—the tender feelings and concern of a mother for her baby, or a father for his family; the warmth of feeling between husband and wife throughout a marriage; the romantic passion between a man and a woman; the deep concern for fellow human beings of the nurse, physician, or social worker; and the feeling of a religious person for God.

Popular Beliefs and Myths about Love

One important contribution of social-science research is to dispel myths and misunderstandings fostered by popular literature or music about love in intimate relationships and marriage. Hunt (1959) identified four major myths about love:

1. the "one-person" theory of a "Mr. or Ms. Right"
2. the notion of love at first sight (the "thunderclap" effect)

3. the concept that "love is blind"

4. the belief that love conquers all—that a great love such as Romeo's for Juliet can surmount differences of social class, family, and religion

The evidence suggests that geography plays a bigger role in pair-ups than any mystical meeting with the fated person, a surprise encounter with a "Mr. Right." For example, in a given period, half of all the people who applied for marriage licenses in the cities of Philadelphia and New Haven lived within a mile of each other (Hunt, 1959).

With respect to the idea that "love is blind" there is contrary evidence from a study by Burgess and Wallin (1953), who obtained reports from two thousand engaged young people. Sixty-seven percent of the men and seventy-five percent of the women named shortcomings or limitations in their partners. These included hot temper, stubbornness, shortness in height, unattractive teeth, tendencies to nail-biting, excessive religiosity, and so on. Kerckhoff and Davis (1962) showed that couples who agree with each other's values are more likely to move on to increased intimacy and marriage than those who show serious discrepancies in such values. There is a fairly regular series of steps that involve the matching of educational experiences, general social class, background, and common family attitudes that occur before couples move to the more subtle aspects of personality compatibility. Along the road to intimacy partners look each other over more carefully than popular belief suggests.

The principle of "complementarity" between needs or personality characteristics may come into play in the decision of a couple to establish a longer-term relationship. Once they reach some general agreement on fundamental values, there may be a tendency for somewhat inhibited men to choose uninhibited or extraverted women, for women who themselves feel unsure of their own long-range goals in a career to be attracted to men who have strong self-defined career prospects.

Finally, in respect to the myth of the overpowering forces of love, there is considerable contrary evidence from sociological and psychological research. Differences in cultural background, in social class, in personal taste, and in attitudes, values, and intelligence all increase the chances that couples will have periods of unhappiness and maladjustment, and that divorce will become more likely. Research findings reviewed by Rubin (1973) lead to the conclusion that persisting areas of difference, such as continuing differences in religion or parental interference, are likely to create discord between lovers.

Here are some of the methods used to study love:

1. large-scale surveys through questionnaires and interviews (Burgess and Wallin, 1953; Kerckhoff and Davis, 1962; Freedman, 1978)

2. intensive questionnaire, interview, and psychological test studies of dating and engaged couples with follow-ups over time (Driscoll, Davis and Lipitz, 1972; Levinger and Raush, 1977)

3. experimental studies of mutual attraction and affiliation (Berscheid and Walster, 1978; Byrne, 1971; Kiesler and Baral, 1979; Schachter, 1959)

New approaches, including long-term studies of couples who have stayed in a close relationship over many years, are obviously needed.

Love and the Emotions

Many people use the word "love" as an emotion. While it is certainly clear that, of all words, love is most closely linked to a variety of emotional responses, it is confusing to consider the term as synonymous with an emotion. Love essentially involves a relationship between two persons under particular sets of circumstances. The nature of the social context often determines whether or not an individual will be perceived as lovable, or indeed even as attractive or likable (Helmreich, Aronson, and Le Fan, 1970; Walster, 1965).

The emotions in a love relationship are undoubtedly interest and joy (Izard, 1977). The beloved person always possesses an element of moderate novelty to the lover, "something" to be explored, some new bit of information to be found out. In the absence of the loved person, we find our thoughts dwelling on him or her, creating possibilities for seeing our beloved again, or fantasizing our lover in different situations. When indeed such anticipatory fantasies are fulfilled—that is, when the loved person comes down the street or enters our apartment and fantasy and current reality become one—the result is, of course, an experience of great joy.

The loved person becomes a subject for extensive fantasies about possible mutual activities ranging from sex to the sharing of common experiences, as is the case in strong friendships or paternal or filial love. When these fantasies become reality, in the form of a letter or a telephone call from the beloved person as well as in actual direct contact, there is again the reduction of that moderate degree of uncertainty about the beloved person and the result is the experience of joy.

Viewed from this cognitive-affective point of view, love is not greatly different from other situations of intense personal investment. As a matter of fact, people occasionally talk of love for objects or for situations and have some of the same feelings about them as they do for individuals. A baseball star may talk of loving his bat or loving the feeling of being out there on the diamond with thousands of people shouting, men on bases, and the pitcher winding up to throw the ball.

If we recognize, then, that love describes a pattern of relationships and separate it clearly from the specific emotions, many of the curious patterns of behavior people show when in love or when betrayed become clear. We all like to hear others tell us that they love us. The single most common fantasy in a survey of daydreams (Singer and McCraven, 1961) was: "I am held in the arms of a warm and loving person who satisfies all my needs." Approximately 96 percent of normal individuals responded by saying they had a fantasy like this quite frequently (Chapter 10).

Principles of Attraction   Relatively little is known from the standpoint of personality characteristics about why some people are, on the whole, more lovable or more capable of loving others. Social psychological research has made clear the bases for, at least, shorter-term attraction. These include physical attractiveness, competence, similarity in interests and attitudes, general familiarity with each other's habits, values, and beliefs, and indications of socially approved patterns of behavior (Byrne, 1969; Kerckhoff and Davis, 1962; Levinger, Senn, and Jorgensen, 1970; Walster, 1970; Walster, Aronson, Abrahams and Rottman, 1966). Zajonc (1968), for example, demonstrated that liking developed simply by having pairs of persons meet each other without any real contact on a regular basis. Young women who saw each other more often in the course of activities that involved no real interaction were much more likely to indicate positive liking than those who saw each other less frequently.

Such experiments, however, clever as they may be, clearly say little about the powerful and complex passions we know about not only from novels but also from news reports and history books. The Roman leader, Mark Antony, did indeed ruin his career and lose his life because of his helpless passion for Cleopatra, and perhaps for the style of life she represented.

More research is needed not just on the principles of short-term attraction, but on case studies of situations in which individuals with different patterns of relationship are followed over periods of time to determine how romantic love does occur and run its special course.

Sexual Fantasy and Attraction   Too little attention has been paid to the early origins of romantic feelings as they begin to shape themselves in the fantasies of puberty and early adolescence. Young children do form friendships of an intense kind with same- or opposite-sex children, and there is research underway to determine the nature of these early mutual attractions (Berndt 1979, 1981). Children are also exposed, if they are fortunate, to ample family affection from parents, siblings, uncles, aunts, and cousins, and they see numerous examples of friendships on television. Sexual attraction, however, is more difficult for children to grasp because although they are exposed to it, particularly on television, they lack the necessary physiological and emotional responses, until they are early adolescents, to appreciate the full component of that attraction. As a result, there is a kind of mystery about sexuality, which provokes, on the one hand, extreme curiosity and, on the other, a good deal of fantasy activity in an attempt to comprehend the strangeness of these activities.

In effect, then, a good deal of the shaping of the kinds of partners, the kinds of love experiences, and the notion of what is attractive may take place when the child or adolescent lacks sufficient experience to identify all of the appropriate parameters for a love relationship, parameters that as an adult he or she might consciously want to take into account. In this sense, a continuing element of irrationality may play a role in first evidences of attractiveness and this may be reinforced by actual experiences in social activity. In other words, many children have very different, even confused or distorted, notions of what sexual intimacy involves. If they play these out in fantasy, and experience some physical arousal, they may practice such fantasies over and over until they develop an "appetite" or "script" for a particular kind of sexual involvement (Gagnon, 1974).

Campagna (1975), for example, carried out a study of masturbation fantasies in male college freshmen. He found four types of fantasies: one type involved imagining relatively commonplace forms of sexual interaction with an actual person. A second type reflected a more unusual quality, such as the subject imagining he was a sultan with a harem of young women from whom he could choose. The third type reflected more sadistic, masochistic, or other deviant patterns of sexual activity. Finally, a pattern emerged in which sexual activity could only be envisaged in fantasy with faceless anonymous women, usually prostitutes, and in which the image was of only a part of the woman's body without a full sense of emotional involvement. Campagna's evidence suggests that only the fourth type was indicative of some recurrent emotional difficulties. By and large, most young men had some fantasies of all types, although the first two patterns predominated.

Sexual fantasy continues into adult life and yet may often reflect a pattern of the earliest adolescent fantasy. Hariton and Singer (1974) conducted a study combining questionnaires and interviews with married women. About 65 percent of the women had sexual fantasies while engaged in intercourse with their husbands. Most of these fantasies were reported by the women as not interfering with the enjoyment of sex. The women who had the most fantasies were often those who were, in general, given to a great deal of daydreaming outside of the sexual situation. Quite a number of women reported fantasies of being forced to submit, being raped, or being a member of a harem or a captive of some gang or of foreign troops. These fantasies had often started in later childhood or early adolescence and were apparently adopted by the women who were rather strictly brought up and who were trying, on the whole, to limit their preoccupation with sex because of religious or family moral strictures. As a result, many of these women when they were younger drifted into fantasies of being forced to enjoy sex, because they could then experience the pleasure through masturbation or simply from arousal. These fantasies then became linked to actual sexual enjoyment, and the women continued to use the fantasies as part of normal sexual intercourse once they were married.

There is little evidence that sexual fantasy in its own right is disturbing. More information is needed about the extent to which people who show striking deviations in their sexual behavior have been significantly influenced by early fantasies. Many individuals who have been in trouble because of aggressive acts related to sexuality have a background of limited sexual fantasy or a limited capacity to use their imagination. Such individuals often rely on external cues, peep shows, centerfolds in magazines, and so on. It seems likely that sexual fantasies, beliefs about sexual prowess, and beliefs that sexuality is the key to human relationships may lead to distortions. After all, sex can, for practical purposes, take up only a small part of our day-to-day activities.

More research is also needed to examine the extent to which people who develop longer and more satisfying intimate relationships do so because they have in earlier years generated not only fantasies about sexuality but a whole range of fantasies about other aspects of shared behavior with a loved person.

Models of Intimacy   It is easier for social psychologists to set up experiments to ascertain why strangers like or dislike each other after brief, experimentally controlled encounters than to determine how couples move from casual acquaintance into long-term intense relationships. Zick Rubin (1973) attempted to see what predispositions and attitudinal characteristics best predict the persistence of a relationship over time. Using two scales of "liking" and "loving," he studied about 180 couples over a six-month period. He classified his participants as "romantic" or "nonromantic," the romantic respondents showing more belief in the powers of love as well as a belief that love follows a progressive line toward increased intimacy and marriage irrespective of social or practical concerns. Rubin found that only for those men and women who scored as "romantic" was there a significant correlation between "loving" or "liking" in October and a report of progress toward increased intimacy by April.

In an attempt to look at how a relationship might develop over time, Huesmann and Levinger (1976) developed a set of eleven steps of progressive involvement, along with all the options possible for a male and female in the situation. Yale students role-played "John" or "Susan" and wrote down estimates of what the "payoff" for each partner could be from each possible interaction. These quantitative estimates then became the data employed in programming a computer to simulate the progress of a relationship based on the student judges' guesses of how couples would behave. The result is described in the box on page 373.

Such computer simulation is intriguing, but it is based on the judgments of college students, who are usually not very experienced in how relationships progress. Nevertheless, this is a promising way of approaching the problem of relationships over time. Researchers could get judgments from persons of different age groups, cultural or economic backgrounds, and degrees of experience and see how they compare as the computer produces time-course simulations.

Surprisingly, there is little satisfactory research on actual patterns of progress across time in close relationships, with almost no data on what kinds of personality characteristics or previous life experiences make for smoother or rockier passages in the life course of couples. Falbo and Peplau (1980) carried out a study of the ways in which heterosexual men and women used power in their intimate relationships. Heterosexual men showed more direct use of power and more willingness for bilateral sharing, while heterosexual women relied more on indirect uses of power. Apparently women continue to feel that a direct assertion of power will not be effective in influencing male lovers. Raush, Barry, Hertel, and Swain (1974) tracked young married couples and found that in those relationships that seemed most durable and characterized

COMPUTER SIMULATION OF A ROMANTIC RELATIONSHIP

Huesmann and Levinger (1978) describe the outcome of the computer analysis as follows:

At the beginning of the simulation shown in Figure 15-3, John and Susan are described as meeting with each other for the first time in a class (time 1). Susan initiates a friendly interaction, and asks John for a date at the same time as John is asking her. (Our computer apparently was poorly informed about dating etiquette.) On their initial dates, they each actively, though nonverbally, communicate liking for each other. However, neither is willing to be very intimate in their disclosure to the other (times 4 and 5).

After a period of time in this situation, John learns that Susan is willing to reveal intimate information in response to his disclosures, and he begins to confide in her completely (time 6). This outcome leads the pair into active striving for a deep romantic involvement. They engage in intimate sexual interaction. They next enter a pattern where Susan is willing to yield completely to John's wishes, though John is not ready to reciprocate. Subsequently, though, when John proposes future plans for the pair, Susan becomes evasive and noncommittal (times 11–13). Eventually, John stops proposing such plans and the pair remains in this situation for some time—in other words, alternating between the two states called "Establish Harmony" and "Plan for the Future" (times 15–19).

Gradually Susan adopts a more positive stance toward the future; John, when he notices this, proposes future plans again (time 20). This time Susan accepts his plans, and they both commit themselves to a long-term relationship (time 23). They move into a state of informal permanency, where each partner feels positively about a permanent relationship, but neither is ready for marriage.

FIGURE 15-3

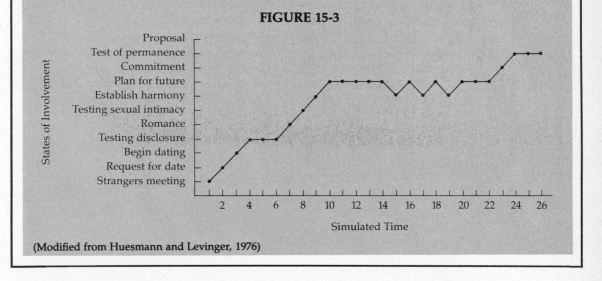

(Modified from Huesmann and Levinger, 1976)

by strong mutual affection, conflicts were dealt with not only by some immediate solution but also by practical understanding, emotional warmth, mutual agreement on sharing new activities, and even discussion about how to deal with future conflicts. These couples showed a commitment to a mutual working out of difficulties rather than an assertion of power or a desire for retaliation or responses meant simply to enchance the other's self-esteem.

Living Together   Macklin (1978) carried out an extensive review of the research on cohabitation, the term describing the relationship of couples living together but not legally married. A high percentage of college students indicated that they would, if given the opportunity, engage in cohabitation. At City College in New York it was almost 80 percent, and at Illinois State University only 23 percent of the women and 8 percent of the men said they would not live with someone if in love. At Cornell University only 7 percent of those who had not lived with someone indicated that it was because of moral reasons. Table 15-3 provides indications of the circumstances under which young college adults indicate they would live together.

What we see, therefore, is a tremendously strong interest and push toward extended intimacy on the part of young people. Has such activity created an atmosphere in which marriage is no longer necessary or valued? The evidence from a whole series of studies suggests that living together on a college campus is an added step in the courtship process—a form of trial among young people already strongly related to each other emotionally but not yet in a position, for a variety of practical reasons, to undertake a long-term commitment. Despite adult fears, the evidence is that in the case of two groups of married couples— those who had and had not cohabited prior to marriage—about the same percentage of each group had outside sexual partners during their marriage. That is, prior cohabitation did not lead to more liberal sexual behavior during marriage itself (Clatworthy and Scheid, 1977).

Loving and Sharing   In the long run, the positive side of shared intimacy between human beings will probably come not simply from opportunities for sexual gratification, but much more from the fact that both partners approach their day-to-day life with a sense of shared wonder and interest. They can tell

TABLE 15-3

Relationship Young Adults Believe Should Exist before a Person Cohabits with Someone of the Opposite Sex

	Percentage agreeing
$N = 299$	
Married	5
Officially engaged	1
Tentatively engaged	6
Strong, affectionate, monogamous relationship	45
Strong, affectionate relationship, but may be dating others	13
Good friends	10
No relationship need exist	19

(Modified from Macklin, 1978)

each other with delight and concern about the day's events, experience joy at each other's successes or accomplishments, and at the same time offer sympathy and support when problems arise. This chapter opened with a discussion of the emotions of interest and joy. It should now be clear that love and intimacy best exemplify the motivating power of attempts to experience these positive emotions.

Our survey of the emotions of interest and joy and the attitudes of curiosity, creativity, and love reveals that psychologists of personality are just beginning to look at the constructive features of the human personality. Surprisingly little is known about how interest, curiosity, and the capacity for joy or love develop. How do such emotions become crystallized into longstanding personality dispositions? A major direction for future personality research lies in identifying factors in childhood and characteristics of adult life-styles that contribute to a continuing sense of wonder, to the potentiality for excitement and challenge, and for experiencing and expressing joy.

SUMMARY

1. Until recently the field of personality psychology paid little attention to the constructive or positive features of human experience, including the emotions of interest and joy and the attitudes and actions that reflect such feelings as curiosity, creativity, and love.

2. Interest is an emotion tied to the cognitive system of the personality and related to the way that people confront situations of moderate complexity or ambiguity. It is an emotion that motivates action toward an object for exploration or that stimulates thoughts about causes or meanings.

3. Curiosity is an important motivating influence for animals and for human behavior. Some of the greatest pleasure comes from a combination of curiosity and exploration, along with the joy of familiarity. Maddi proposed a theory of personality patterns according to which people vary in whether (1) they seek high or low activation, (2) they strive to have external or internal experiences, or (3) they are active or passive in controlling their environments. This proposal is supported by Zuckerman's research on sensation-seeking. Curiosity may take at least two forms: (1) an interest in people and (2) an interest in objects. In general, women show more interpersonal curiosity and men more curiosity about objects and natural phenomena.

4. Csikszentmihalyi studied talented people who constantly seek new heights of experience. He proposed a theoretical model to explain the "state of flow" that most of these people have in their activities. This state of flow is a sense of exhilaration when a person is functioning beautifully in an activity.

5. Joy involves self-contentment and satisfaction with others and with life itself. Humor and comic situations contribute to a sense of joy. A key ele-

ment in humor is also the resolution of cognitive incongruity. Some people seem to be unable to experience joy or humor. A concomitant of schizophrenic illness is an inability to appreciate pleasure or to experience joy. With depressed individuals, also, there seems to be a dissociation of the physiological, communicative, and experiential features of the emotional system that limits their capacity for happiness.

6. Two areas of personality variation that grow from the positive emotions of interest and joy are (1) creativity and (2) love or intimacy. Patrick outlined the following steps as necessary for the creative process: preparation, incubation, illumination, and revision. Psychoanalytic theorists emphasize that creative products represent the emergence into consciousness, often in symbolic form, of taboo, unconscious conflictual material, and that creativity involves a childlike way of looking at the world. Others criticize this notion, stating that the creative person's imaginativeness and juxtaposition of novel elements are highly developed capacities that mature through the years.

7. Several methods are used to stimulate creative problem-solving. Many have genuine value and some are particularly useful for groups. The process of creativity intertwines and melds the cognitive and affective orientations, involving active information-seeking, exploring material just beyond one's reach, and an attitude encouraging free-ranging thought. Creative people, as children, often had one key figure in their lives. They seem to spend a good deal of time alone and to fantasize and daydream. In many ways, creativity is an attitude toward the physical and social environment that is available to most human beings of reasonable intelligence.

8. The meaning of love, marriage, and intimate behavior varies widely across cultures. An important contribution of social-science research has been to dispel myths and misunderstandings about intimate relationships and marriage. Although many people consider love to be an emotion, love essentially involves a relationship between one individual and another under a particular set of circumstances. The emotions in a love relationship are interest and joy. From a cognitive-affective point of view, love is not much different from other situations of intense personal investment. What distinguishes love from liking is usually the more highly aroused state of the former.

9. Research on the predispositions and attitudes that predict persistence in a relationship has found that subjects classified as "romantic" made more progress toward an enduring relationship. Another study developed a model of levels of relationships to show what different predictions and outcomes about interpersonal attraction and love follow from the level that a relationship has reached. Computer simulations of progress in a relationship have been used. Intimacy usually moves on to a more structured pattern, usually marriage.

PART FOUR

The Developing and Changing Personality

CHAPTER
16

Early and Middle Childhood

A devil, a born devil, on whose nature
Nurture can never stick; on whom my pains,
Humanely taken, all, all lost, quite lost!

—*Shakespeare, The Tempest*

Prospero's anguished outcry is over the brutishness of the witch's son, Caliban. The exiled nobleman and magician had found the infant Caliban on a desert island and reared him with love, taught him language, and sought to civilize him. The old magician's complaint echoes that of many parents. Despite their efforts in child-rearing and fostering certain interests and attitudes in their child ("nurture"), the longstanding patterns of activity, emotionality, or impulsivity that may have characterized the child from birth seem to persist ("nature").

Are children born with particular personality traits or temperamental characteristics? Do these continue through childhood to emerge as the basis for adolescent and adult interest patterns or interactive styles? What role do patterns of child-rearing or the values and attitudes of parents play in shaping personality development? Are the early experiences and fantasies of the baby truly the basis of later attitudes about interpersonal trust or of mental scenarios about human relationships, as many psychoanalysts believe? Are there inevitable stages of development through which children must pass in order to be capable of certain levels of cognitive or social functioning? Or are variations in children's reaction patterns to strangers, their attachments, their fears, their exploratory tendencies, and their skills chiefly a function of learning opportunities and imitative possibilities provided by parents or siblings? Is there any continuity at all between characteristics observable in children and their adult behavior patterns?

Until well into the 1960s, except for the work of the great Swiss child psychologist, Jean Piaget, much of the theorizing about personality development stemmed from reports made by adults to clinicians. In more recent years there has been a dramatic explosion of careful and insightful studies of infant, baby, and early childhood behavior and also of parent-child interaction patterns. A good deal of evidence now exists about how children of the same age differ, how a child differs in responses to parents or strangers at different ages or in different situations, when sex-linked patterns emerge, and whether self-oriented or emotional responses are more closely linked to a developmental stage or to social influences occurring at the time. More direct evidence is also available on the social, cognitive, and emotional characteristics of children in the early and middle childhood periods (approximately ages 2–6 and 7–12), and new studies are suggesting that personality can develop and change during adolescence, adulthood, and old age.

The best available evidence indicates that personality does reflect certain kinds of developments. Thus, a child who fails to attain the capacity to anticipate the future may not only be late to develop a normal fear of strangers but may be handicapped later in the necessity to think conceptually, to plan, or to resist immediate temptation in the interest of longer-term gain. At the same time, however, there is evidence for new learning possibilities or discontinuities (Brim and Kagan, 1980). Each new phase of experience across the life span carries with it challenges and opportunities so that life routines or personality patterns may change throughout life (Baltes, 1978; Levinson, 1977).

Psychologists are increasingly studying not just specific "critical periods" or psychosexual stages but are looking at the relative contributions of factors such as hereditary temperament, social history, cognitive capacity, and situational demands in producing a particular personality reaction. Thus, for example, studies of how adults behave with children have found that it is not only the parents who reinforce the youngsters but that a complex interaction between child and adult takes place. By smiling and cooing a young infant may reward and encourage certain kinds of parental behavior. Often the variations of temperamental characteristics in siblings may evoke different behavior toward each of the children from the parents. Reflecting on the most recent evidence, Maccoby (1980) concluded:

> It is now widely accepted that developmental change is the rule rather than the exception. . . . The characteristics a child has at a given age will not be the same characteristics the same child has later on, even though the two may be connected. Considering these developmental transformations, it now seems unlikely that the parents' primary contribution to the child's long-range development comes from teaching specific behaviors. Rather the parents' most lasting influence probably comes from teaching certain modes of adaptation to changing life circumstances. Recently, interest has revived in the parental contribution to the child's developing sense of identity or

self. The assumption is that a coherent self-concept may function as a child's gyroscope, keeping the individual to a relatively steady course and producing long-term consistencies in behavior (p. 29).

TOWARD A COMPREHENSIVE VIEW OF DEVELOPMENT

Students of human development now need a more comprehensive approach, a broader perspective on "growing up" than simply focusing on the first five or even ten years of life. Current evidence suggests that although children may possess certain temperamental characteristics from heredity and prenatal experience, there are great variations within families and within the subcultures of any society that establish sets of performance demands on the limited capacities of a child in each growth stage. Very often parents or other adults may believe that children can understand requests or commands the way adults do or that they can perform acts intentionally with the same meanings that adults attribute to them. Yet the children's cognitive capacity or control of their movements may be at a different level of development. "What's the matter? Why are you afraid? It's your grandma! Don't you love your grandmother?" an irate mother may say to her frightened 9-month-old. She may not realize that the child's fear of grandma is not a defect or naughtiness. The distinction between mother and "stranger," with a natural fear of the novel, is a critical step in the cognitive growth of a child at that age.

The "atmosphere" of a family—the parents' values, expressed in the way they talk to children and to each other, their attitudes toward the broader society shown in the way they refer to religion, education, socioeconomic opportunity—influences a child's expectations and anticipation about life. What may appear to adults as casual talk or letting off steam can lead to frightening or humiliating thoughts and fantasies in children, whose cognitive development cannot assimilate this material.

Developmental Tasks

To be useful, the study of personality development must go beyond an analysis of what an individual "possesses" at any developmental stage in terms of temperamental patterns, cognitive style, and social experience of physical skill. Havighurst (1953) proposed that growth be looked at in terms of developmental tasks that vary at different age levels. The child by age 1 must master creeping, pulling itself upright, standing alone, walking, and, by age 2, running and jumping. If by age 3 such tasks are not a regular part of the child's repertory of actions, pediatricians will suspect some serious developmental difficulty and parents will be dismayed, saddened, or even rejecting.

Tryon and Lillienthal (1950) have chosen five development periods, *infancy, early childhood, late childhood* (age 7 to pubescence), *early adolescence* (puberty), and *late adolescence* and have charted the developmental tasks for each phase based on the following ten categories of behavior:

CHARLES DICKENS: THE PERSISTENCE OF A CHILDHOOD ATTITUDE

Growing children must cope not only with their emergent new skills and cognitive capacities but with expectations about life as influenced by a particular family's private "mythology" or by the broader demands of a society. For the first nine years of his life Charles Dickens was reared in early nineteenth-century England as a young scholar and gentleman's son, educated in good schools and accustomed to long walks with his intelligent, talkative father. At ten, when his father went bankrupt and was thrown into debtors' prison, Charles was sent to work in a factory. For more than ten hours a day, he sat near a ground-floor window in full view of the passers-by and pasted labels on cans of shoe polish. This experience, a mixture of physical stress and humiliation, colored Dickens' thinking for the rest of his life. Although by his early twenties he was financially well off through his enormous skills as a writer, Dickens' thoughts turned again and again to this childhood experience.

His social philosophy, his financial dealings, as well as events depicted in his novels, reflect his shame and anxiety concerning that early drop in the family life-style. It was not so much the work itself—9- or 10-year olds from poor families routinely did factory work in England in those days—it was the contrast with his former status and expectations of education that contributed to Dickens' special feelings.

Dickens' experience highlights the necessity for a comprehensive view of development that takes account of the special, perhaps constitutional, qualities of *temperament* (in Dickens' case almost certainly great emotionality, sensitivity, and intelligence), of the stage of *cognitive maturity* (as bright as he was, the boy still felt humiliated by what a more mature person might perceive as simply bad luck beyond one's control), and of the stressful demands British society's work ethic imposed on the children of the poor.

1. achieving independence or appropriate dependency (what today might be called secure attachment)

2. giving and receiving affection (emergence of positive emotions)

3. relating to social groups

4. developing a conscience (emergence of shame and guilt)

5. learning psychobiological and social sex roles

6. accepting and adjusting to one's changing body

7. learning new motor skills

8. learning to understand and control the physical world

9. developing an appropriate symbol system and conceptual abilities

10. relating oneself to the broader world and the universe

These categories of tasks are fairly comprehensive although the capacities for play and imagination and, later, the potentiality for creativity as further expectations of the fully developed personality might be added. It is important to note that Tryon and Lillienthal stopped with late adolescence.

Developmental Crises and Life-span Expectations

Erikson (1964) expanded the notion of developmental tasks across the life span (Chapter 3). Using the term *developmental* or *life crisis* rather than developmental tasks, Erikson stressed that in adolescence a sense of identity must be developed. Erikson's scheme, originally tied to the psychoanalytic oral, anal, and phallic stages, today seems less satisfying than Havighurst's or Tryon and Lillienthal's formulations, which specify a series of demands at each age. Perhaps each new age phase calls forth different representations of the same general tasks, so that learning new symbol systems or motor or conceptual skills and confronting physical or sex-role changes recur again and again throughout the life span. A 10-year-old boy tries to master rudimentary statistics to keep up with sports talk and baseball batting averages. An adolescent learns math to get through school or because she finds it intellectually challenging. And a family man in his forties learns about interest rates, investment possibilities, or stocks in order to plan for his retirement.

Table 16-1 presents a more extended view of the life span including (but not necessarily endorsing) (1) the original psychoanalytic psychosexual stages, plus Sullivan's modifications; (2) the range of developmental tasks or crises; and (3) their implications for personality characteristics and constructive or self-defeating life patterns. This table, derived from proposals of Tryon and Lillienthal, Freud, Erikson, and Sullivan, contains terminology and life-task requirements based on more recent research on cognitive and emotional development.

An important principle emerging from recent studies of development across the life span is that many of the developmental tasks emerging first at a given age recur again and again at each new phase of the life cycle. Certain kinds of play and friendship skills are valuable in early or middle childhood, but new forms of self-entertainment and socializing may have to be generated in adulthood or in old age. As family patterns change in American society (only about one-quarter of family units in early 1980 consisted of both parents and children living together with mother at home full time), as people move about the nation and generations no longer live in close proximity, as career changes become possible even in midlife, as women no longer remain tied to the home and dependent on male support, new forms of developmental requirements are appearing. In addition, more and more people are living longer and often survive for thirty or forty years beyond the stage when child-rearing and support of a nuclear family are their major responsibilities.

HEREDITY AND TEMPERAMENT

The newborn infant comes out of the womb into a world filled with a huge array of complexities from which the prepartum environment protected it. It must breathe properly, coordinate its head and mouth movements sufficiently to grasp the nipple of a breast or bottle, and react with appropriate crying, squirming, or facial expressions to pain (as from an open diaper pin or hunger pangs). A simple test of adaptive coordination—shucking aside a piece of cloth lightly placed over the nose—has provided an important clue to neurologists and pediatricians of effective functioning in the infant. Imagine the surprise, then, of physicians who discovered from controlled studies that whereas Caucasian newborns struggle at once and try to push away the cloth, babies from Chinese-American parents seem to "accept" the cloth and just lie there, shifting their breathing to the mouth (see Figure 16-1).

The relationship of activity level shortly after birth to innate characteristics and to social or parental demands is exquisitely demonstrated in an example

Like the cloth over the nose referred to in the text, the Navaho cradle board shown here may reveal an inborn difference in adaptive behavior. The Navaho baby lies quietly and happily on the board, but the Caucasian baby immediately protests the confinement.

TABLE 16-1
Developmental Tasks and Their Personality Implications

Age (approximately when task first appears or is critical)	Psychosexual stage	Developmental tasks (or life crises)	Personality implications
Infancy (to 18 months)	Sensory/oral (Freud)	Achieving independence or appropriate dependence (secure attachment); giving and receiving affection	Trust vs. mistrust; optimism vs. malevolence (Sullivan)
Early childhood (2–5)	Muscular/anal (Freud)	Developing a conscience	Autonomy vs. shame
	Locomotor/genital (Freud)	Developing a capacity for play and imagination	Initiative vs. guilt
Middle childhood (7–12)	Latency (Freud)	Relating to social groups; forming close friendships; learning new motor skills; accepting or adjusting to one's changing body	Industry vs. inferiority
Puberty and early adolescence (12–15)	Juvenile chumship (Sullivan)	Learning psychobiological and social sex roles; developing specific sexual "appetites" (hetero- or homosexual attractions)	
Late adolescence (16–19)		Learning to understand and control the physical world and the broader social milieu; developing an appropriate symbol system and conceptual abilities; learning creative expression	Identity vs. diffusion
Young adulthood (20–30)		Relating to the world of occupations; family formation; and citizenship	Intimacy vs. isolation

TABLE 16–1 (continued)

Developmental Tasks and Their Personality Implications

Age (approximately when task first appears or is critical)	Psychosexual stage	Developmental tasks (or life crises)	Personality implications
Adulthood (30–50)		Relating to child-rearing and to economic stress and opportunity	Generativity vs. stagnation
Maturity and seniority (50 and over)		Relating to the broader world and the universe	Ego integrity vs. despair

(Modified from Erikson, 1963; Tryon and Lillienthal, 1950)

cited by Freedman (1981). Navaho children, like Chinese-Americans, tend to be much less active and less prone to crying than Caucasian infants. They are customarily carried around wrapped onto a cradleboard. Some infants are upset at this procedure and their mothers then do not use it, but the vast majority of Navaho babies accept the practice with the same passivity they show on psychological infant tests. When a group of Caucasian mothers decided to follow the Navaho method and to swaddle and use cradleboards with their infants, the Caucasian babies set up such a howl that the practice was quickly abandoned.

Variations in activity levels and in a limited number of measurable dimensions, such as emotionality and reactions to novelty, turn out to be characteristic of newborns. These differences are not unlike the kinds of variations observed in different breeds of dogs; for example, cocker spaniels are more placid and less likely to try to escape from a frightening situation than are wirehaired terriers (Scott and Fuller, 1965).

Evidence of Temperament

The term *temperament* has generally been used to describe phenomena such as susceptibility to emotional situations, strength and speed of response, and persistence and intensity of particular moods, all of which may be a part of the constitutional or hereditary makeup of an individual (Allport, 1961). Evidence from observations of babies and from studies of twins or of biological versus adoptive parent-child similarities support this view. Consider Freedman's (1981) striking findings that Chinese or Japanese babies are consistently less physically active and easier to calm when upset than Caucasian babies. Such differences are still evident in fourth-generation American-Japanese babies where, even when the "Americanized" mother vocalizes a great deal to the child in contrast with traditional Japanese practice, babies show less finger sucking or playfulness than Caucasian babies. Indications of racial differences between Caucasian, Australian Aboriginal, Mongolian (Chinese, Japanese, and Native American), and Black African babies all suggest longstanding hereditary differences in temperamental patterns (Freedman, 1981).

That such gross racial differences are not limited to newborns is apparent from a recent study of Chinese-American and Caucasian preschoolers observed in a day-care setting (Kagan, Kearsley, and Zelazo, 1978). Chinese-American children whether in day-care or in home-care were less likely to talk and make noise, less active, less likely to smile, and more likely to move fearfully in separation or social situations. Maternal reports confirmed these observations; Chinese toddlers were significantly less talkative, less disobedient, less active and less aggressive, less prone to laughter, and significantly more fearful of the dark, more cautious and shy with adults than were the Caucasian children. Physiological measurement indicated a much more stable heart rate to be characteristic of the Chinese-American preschoolers. These data also suggest that patterns of ethnic variation in inhibition or passivity evident in newborn babies are manifest three years later—more differentiated because the children's response repertoire is greater, but still consistent in pattern.

Specific Temperaments and Emergent Interest Patterns

Buss and Plomin (1975) developed a theory that four basic temperaments are identifiable very early in life and are attributable to heredity. These are emotionality, activity, sociability, and impulsivity (EASI). As Figure 16-2 indicates, *emotionality* involves quickness to weep or to show distress, fearfulness, or anger. *Activity* is evident from fidgetiness, high energy level, inability to sit still, preference for vigorous games rather than block play, coloring, or other quiet games. *Sociability* involves friendliness, avoidance of isolation or extreme independence, and a lack of shyness. *Impulsivity* refers to difficulty in self-control, inability to resist temptation, and rapid shifts from toy to toy.

With the cooperation of the National Organization of the Mothers of Twins, Buss studied 139 pairs of children who were, on the average, 55 months in age, about equally divided into monozygotic (one-egg or genetically identical) twins and dizygotic (two-egg or fraternal) twins. The findings indicate similarities in the four temperaments for the genetically identical children, and little relationship (except for impulsivity among girls) for the fraternal twins (see Table 16-2). Allowing for the possibility that the mothers of identical twins exaggerated the similarities, the results do indeed support the heredity hypothesis; one-egg twins show much greater similarities in all four temperaments.

As children get older, temperamental groupings become more differentiated and can also be organized into behavior and attitudinal variations that can be labeled as personality dimensions or interest and value patterns. Gottesman (1966) compared personality-questionnaire responses of adolescent twins whose backgrounds were Scandinavian-American, Italian, Irish, and Jewish. Despite the environmental differences between these various subcultures, identical twins were more alike than fraternal twins on a measure of *social introversion*. Further support for the hereditary basis of sociability and

FIGURE 16-2
The EASI Temperament Survey

Emotionality
   Child gets upset easily.
   Child tends to cry easily.
   Child is easily frightened.
   Child is easygoing or happy-go-lucky. (reverse)
   Child has a quick temper.

Activity
   Child is always on the go.
   Child likes to be off and running immediately on awakening.
   Child cannot sit still long.
   Child prefers quiet games such as block play or coloring to more active games. (reverse)
   Child fidgets at meals and similar occasions.

Sociability
   Child likes to be with others.
   Child makes friends easily.
   Child tends to be shy. (reverse)
   Child tends to be independent. (reverse)
   Child prefers to play by himself rather than with others. (reverse)

Impulsivity
   Child tends to be impulsive.
   Child has difficulty learning self-control.
   Child gets bored easily.
   Child learns to resist temptation easily. (reverse)
   Child goes from toy to toy quickly.
(Modified from Buss and Plomin, 1975)

indications of a hereditary basis for soberness versus enthusiasm and inhibition versus spontaneity have come from studies by Cattell and his colleagues (1957) and by Scarr (1966). The results support to some degree Buss and Plomin's claim that sociability, emotionality, activity, and impulsivity are genetically determined.

Traits may also become crystallized into longstanding interest or hobby patterns. Grotevant, Scarr, and Weinberg (1977) carried out a carefully controlled study of the similarities and differences in interest patterns for biological child-parent and sibling pairs and for adoptive child-parent and sibling pairs. Biological families share both heredity and environment, that is, both *nature* and *nurture*. Adoptive families (where children were reared from ages of less than 3 months on) share only *nurture*. The results from questionnaires clearly indicate that biologically related child-parent or child-child pairs are more similar with respect to interests, such as artistic, social, enterprising

TABLE 16-2

Correlations between Twins on the Scales of the EASI Temperament Survey

	Boys		Girls	
	Identical (38 pairs) r	Fraternal (33 pairs) r	Identical (43 pairs) r	Fraternal (24 pairs) r
Emotionality	.68	.00	.60	.05
Activity	.73	.18	.50	.00
Sociability	.65	.20	.58	.06
Impulsivity	.84	.05	.71	.59

(Modified from Buss and Plomin, 1975)

(business-oriented), conventional, realistic, and investigative. Moreover, biological brothers were more like one another than adoptive brothers, biological sisters were more like one another than adoptive sisters. These investigators conclude that introversion-extraversion and activity level, as temperamental factors from birth, lay the foundation for the later development of interest patterns by influencing the choice of attractive and congenial hobbies or occupations.

Of course, to recognize that hereditary temperamental variations exist does not preclude an important contribution to personality variation by socialization and child-parent interaction. But it does help to explain why parents may treat siblings differently; the babies themselves may have "demanded" different reactions, or social expectations in a family may not accord with a child's temperamental pattern or developmental pace. The active, vigorous baby may evoke an angry response from a parent who is struggling to control impulsivity. Such a situation could lead to subtle or even direct rejection or hostility toward a growing child. Child-rearing involves a complex interaction between the baby's temperamental characteristics, the parents' expectations about the baby, the parents' personality problems, the consequent pattern of interaction between parents and child, and the level of cognitive development of the child.

EARLY DEVELOPMENTAL STAGES

Once psychologists began studying infants in a systematic way in the 1960s, it became clear that most of the speculations from the older personality theories were largely unfounded. Within the first six months of life a baby turns

EARLY STIMULATION
AND INTELLECTUAL DEVELOPMENT

Children born with extremely low birth weights provide a good example of infants who, because of survival necessity, must be kept in isolation in a hospital setting for many months. Scarr-Salapatek and Williams (1973) provided a group of these infants with a structured sequence of stimulation and compared them with a control group that received good hospital care, were fed and diapered, but received no visual stimulation. Infants in the experimental group were exposed to a bird mobile that hung over the isolation crib and later the bassinet. Eight half-hour stimulation sessions of rocking, being talked to, fondling, and sitting upright were presented. After discharge from the hospital the infants were further exposed to visual stimuli and to play. At the end of one year the experimental group's IQ averaged 95.3, whereas that of the control group averaged 85.7, with two thirds of the control group's scores below 90. Thus, active adult stimulation, especially through initial visual stimuli and later through playful interaction, can prevent the genuine hazard to intellectual development of early enforced physical restriction and social isolation.

out to be more active, curious, motorically differentiated, and attentive than described by psychoanalytic theories, with their overemphasis on orality.

The Eyes versus the Mouth

Contrary to early psychoanalytic theory, the infant is not active and responsive simply under drive pressure. As Piaget reported, there is a constant search for stimulation and response to novelty. Indeed, much of the time the eyes seem more important than the mouth in these earliest days. Piaget (1952) suggested that the infant needs stimulation to develop its cognitive skills much as it needs milk to survive. Novel stimulation provides opportunities to practice focusing the eyes and coordinating the grasping responses; as described in Tomkins' theory (Chapter 6), it also gives positive affective feedback. Studies of infants reared in institutions where they simply lay in cribs and were fed regularly but otherwise not played with, talked with, or provided with opportunities for exploring their environment, suggest that such children may suffer severe depression and die early (Spitz, 1946) or show severe limitations in subsequent exploratory or intellectual competencies (Dennis, 1960). Fortunately, such deprivation in early stimulation and maternal care can in many cases be reversed in later childhood (Kagan, Kearsley, and Zelazo, 1978). Children's hospitals often need volunteers whose sole duty is to play with the children.

In general, it seems clear that particular experiences have different impacts at different stages of cognitive development. Once children have attained a certain level of cognitive capacity, they can rapidly acquire skills and competencies that more stimulated or more active children may have picked up earlier because of mothering or inherent temperamental tendencies for exploration (Kagan, Kearsley, and Zelazo, 1978).

Maternal Attachment   Most theories of personality derived from adult retrospective reports about childhood have placed great emphasis on the long-term consequences of early separation fears and of failures in close maternal or other adult attachment. Actual observations of children have not confirmed this emphasis. Recent careful studies of the behavior of babies and toddlers demonstrate a significant interaction between the level of cognitive development of the child and actual social experience. As Kagan, Kearsley, and Zelazo (1978) have shown, children must attain a sufficient capacity for sustained attention, retrieval of recent information, and expectancy before they will show distress at separation from the mother or other regular caregiver. Past experience and the extent of attachment—socialization factors—also play a role.

If a mother actively socializes with her child and fosters interchanges, she may also be encouraging earlier development of those cognitive capacities for producing fear of strangers and separation distress. Children with advanced cognitive capacities show earlier separation distress or stranger anxiety and, by age 2 or so, are also least likely to show distress and anxiety because by this time they have developed capacities for resolving the discrepancy between "mother here-mother not here." For less cognitively advanced children or for children who have had less experience of active adult-child play and interaction, separation anxiety emerges later and also disappears later (Kagan, Kearsley, and Zelazo, 1976).

Emergence of Early Attachment   A major dimension of adult personality involves the extent to which a person may be overly dependent on parents or authority figures or, at the other extreme, incapable of close relationships. Freud and other psychodynamic theorists believed that the origin of the capacity for close attachments to particular persons is closely linked to early feeding experiences, usually at the mother's breast. While feeding is no doubt important, visual and other sensory cues may also be critical. Even baby lambs can become attached to a television set that provides appropriate "sheeplike" auditory and visual cues that they hear while they are being fed or that they see in their first hours of visual exploration outside the womb (Cairns, 1966). The well-known research of the Harlows (1969) indicates that infant monkeys become more attached to cloth dummies whose softness they can cling to than to the wire dummies from whom they obtain milk. Attachment thus involves much more than gratification of the hunger drive; it relates to cues for softness, for cuddling, for vocal response, for familiarity through regularity, and for smell in some animal species.

For the human infant a mutual signaling or communication system develops between caregiver and child at a very early age. Investigators working with deaf children found that although the mothers provided direct nurturing, the children became attached to professional trainers who were using sign

The child psychiatrist Donald Winnicott proposed that children cling to soft blankets, dolls, and teddy bears as "transitional objects" that help them move from close attachment to mother toward a sense of personal possessions and independence. Consoling a stuffed animal may help ease the child's own sadness and provide a sense of power.

language with them. It thus became necessary right from the start to train the mothers themselves to use sign language so that their children would relate more closely to them (Schlesinger, 1980).

An experiment with normal 5-month-olds provided evidence that babies were drawn more to a stranger who regularly maintained eye contact, who smiled and talked but never touched them, than to an uncommunicative adult who cuddled and held them without speaking or laughing (Roedell and Slaby, 1977). The study suggests that attraction in young children requires adult facial cues, positive affect, and vocalization. Maccoby (1980) suggested that the infant may need to experience some control by noticing the pattern of interaction or at least to be aware that the adult is verbally or visually responsive.

In keeping with a cognitive-affective orientation, it seems increasingly clear that children move between the poles of (1) seeking for familiarity and matching up moderate novelty with established schema and (2) modest exploration and efforts at control. In addition to nurturance, the affect of joy at matchups and reduction of novelty through the reappearance of a familiar figure or through an expected response produced on demand is a critical feature in the formation of attachments (Kagan, Kearsley, and Zelazo, 1978; Sroufe and Waters, 1977). The important early role of perceived control is also evident (Gunnar, 1978).

As the infant progresses cognitively and motorically, the importance of attachment is not necessarily lessened but it takes different forms. The adult must help by establishing conditions that allow the baby to explore more and more of the environment, and to test its growing motor skills by trying to crawl across a room and pull itself to its feet. The smothering, overly fearful caretaker may inhibit some of this necessary development and lay the basis for a more pathological attachment and an inhibited or delayed development.

The conditions for conceptualizing the mother as separate and for taking the perspective of the other person must also be established. In the slow and subtle processes of differentiating self from mother and learning to inhibit or delay reactions in the interest of taking turns can be seen the origins of the ego, in the psychoanalytic sense of a system of adaptive self-control and delaying capacity (Singer, 1955), and the first manifestations of an experience of self (Maccoby, 1980).

Secure Attachment   During the 1940s and 1950s a great deal of attention was focused upon the importance for personality of early experiences of love or rejection. But a loving parent may still expect too much or too little from a child at a certain age. Love alone does not lead parents to show certain reactions that are necessary for the formation of what Ainsworth and Bell (1969) have labeled *secure attachment* of infant to parent, as distinguished from nonattachment (obliviousness) or malattachment (resistance). These investigators studied babies who could be classified as securely attached during a series of experiments. Securely attached babies had mothers who were rated more highly for sensitivity, acceptance, cooperation, and accessibility. Mothers of children who showed malattachment were more likely to be rated as relatively insensitive to cues, less accepting or more prone to show anger and irritation, more likely to interfere with the child's ongoing activity or moves toward exploration and autonomy, and more self-preoccupied so that they often ignored children's signals or communications.

Careful studies by Clarke-Stewart (1973) support these findings (see Figure 16-3). She visited babies and their mothers at home over a period from age 6 weeks to 18 months, tested the children for levels of attachment, and observed the pattern of the mother's responses. Children who showed an optimal level of attachment were also those whose mothers were the most

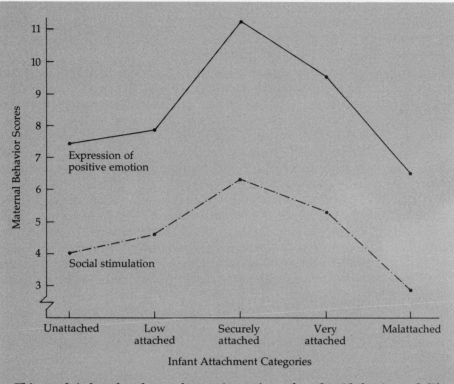

FIGURE 16-3

Infant Attachment and Maternal Behavior

This graph is based on home-observation ratings of mothers' behavior and different types of infant attachment. Note that the highest degree of secure attachment is consistently linked to mothers' displays of positive emotion and social relatedness to their babies.

(From Clarke-Stewart, 1973)

likely to show positive affects, who were most responsive in picking up children's signals or distress calls, and who provided the most social stimulation for the child by talking, playing, and imitating.

Other studies have shown that children who are securely attached, according to measures made between 12 and 18 months of age, turned out several years later to be functioning better in a variety of situations (Yarrow and others, 1973). They showed more enthusiasm, coping responses, and curiosity and also played more imaginatively; the less securely attached children continued later on to show either clinging or avoidant responses to their mothers (Matas, Arend, and Sroufe, 1978) and were also less curious and persistent (Waters, Wippman, and Sroufe, 1979). This continuity into the third year of life suggests that early patterns of attachment have some important personality consequences in the earliest phases of childhood.

Emergence of Differentiated Emotions

Although infants' smiling and other responses can be imitations of adult expressions (Sherrod, 1979), smiling also emerges quite naturally without imitation. Oster's research on early smiling links it to an initial tightening of the brows associated with an effort at mastery of novelty. Once a familiar feature is presented or recognition occurs the brows relax and a smile occurs (Oster, 1978). The early smile seems to conform to Tomkins' (1962) proposal that the affect of joy is tied to matching of novel stimuli.

Izard (1978) has been able to show that within the first year specific stimuli (for example, a sudden change of balance), especially designed to evoke different emotions such as fear, anger, disgust, interest, surprise, or joy, can indeed provoke differing facial expressions in children below one year of age. These facial expressions were described by adult raters as reflections of the specific affects the experimenter intended to provoke, even though the raters themselves were unaware of the specific stimuli that occasioned these facial or body reactions in the babies.

The child's repertory of emotions depends on the level of cognitive development. Shyness can emerge only after children have made a strong attachment to a parent, have delineated themselves to some degree from the parent, and can identify a stranger. From experience with many interactions they can predict dependable sequences: "If I do this, Mommy does that." With a stranger, a child cannot predict what will happen. As the child's sense of self emerges, shyness may be transformed into shame, a feeling that one's performance with a stranger may be not only unpredictable but inept or foolish. Izard has proposed that the anticipation of shame has motivational value for the development of skills and competencies and reduces the chances that one will experience shame. Shame heightens self-awareness, whereas anger, which is first evident at 4 to 6 months, involves the self as a causal agent: anger occasions moves to eliminate a frustrating or disgust-arousing stimulus. Fear emerges by about 8 or 9 months, once the child can cognitively anticipate physical danger or separation.

Hoffman (1978) examined the origin of *empathic responses*, the ability to feel what someone else is experiencing. Altruism, behavior intended to help others, is related to such experiences. When a child's efforts to help others fail or when assertion of rights over a toy provokes distress in another child, empathy may lead to the beginnings of a guilt response. By the ages of 2 to 3, guilt responses are fairly frequent (Izard, 1978). In addition to the emergence of the cognitive capacity for empathy and the occurrence of altruistic or self-assertive responses, it seems likely that guilt depends on the specific contribution of parents who label certain behavior as "naughty" or "sinful." Studies of patterns of parental orientation also indicate that guilt and the acceptance of personal responsibility for misbehavior are fostered when there is (1) minimal physical punishment but (2) a strong positive relationship with parents who praise the child for "correct" behavior (Mussen and others, 1979).

There are many ways in which parents' behavior at particular stages of a child's cognitive development can lead to over- and underemphasis on certain emotions or even failure to develop certain emotional reactions. It should be obvious, for example, that humiliating a child for his or her curiosity or joyful elation can create a persisting conflict about expressing wonder and joy. English children—both boys and girls—have a much higher threshold for weeping than American boys and girls, and men in general weep much less frequently than women. These differences are indications of how cultural values, usually transmitted through parents, lead to socialization of innate emotions (Tomkins, 1963).

We have stressed the importance of the private personality—the awareness of our thoughts, wishes, fantasies, and expectations. How early can we find evidence of some sort of reflective awareness of ongoing thought in children?

The Beginnings of the Private Personality

Spontaneous Play and Language As Kagan (1978) suggested, fear of strangers and separation anxiety, which emerge around age 1, may well reflect the first signs of retrievable schema and anticipatory imagery. Within the next six months, imagery capacity increases and, of course, language begins. The nature of language is inherently symbolic, and children who practice talking with adults and also with themselves may be creating sets of new symbolic schema because they hear themselves speaking. Observers of early childhood like Vygotsky (1934), Luria (1932), and Piaget (1926) have noted that thought and speech seem indistinguishable in toddlers. Children talk out loud to themselves about their ongoing activities much as adults carry on their own private interior monologues. Piaget called attention to the "collective monologue" of several preschool children at play, each describing his or her own activities or taking different "roles" within a self-generated game and only occasionally addressing a direct remark to another child.

Luria (1932) demonstrated that gradually a child begins to internalize speech. A very young child (3 or 4) asked to simulate a parade will make loud noises, movements, and terse verbal descriptions. A year or two later the child may draw the scene, but still accompany the drawing with talk and sound effects; finally, when the child is about 6, the drawing, though still primitive, may be accompanied only by *private* speech, internally elaborated. Thus, speaking becomes increasingly social communication and not just an expression of egocentric thought, to use Piaget's phrase. Somewhere in the period between ages 3 and 5 there is a flowering of overt speech closely associated with play (Singer, 1973; Singer and Singer, 1981). There follows a gradual recognition that only direct communicative speech is acceptable, and the child is then eased into a recognition of a private self of thought and inner communication.

Relatively little is known about how this internalization process occurs although a clue seems to lie in the child's development of skills at pretending and make-believe (Singer, 1973) and, perhaps, even at deception (Bannister and Agnew, 1976; Jaynes, 1976). Once the child starts to pretend that a pencil is an airplane or that he or she is putting a fuzzy animal or doll to sleep there is an ongoing practice of *me* and *not me, real* and *not real, possible* and *not possible*. Play and imagination in early childhood appears to be a process of building a sense of self that controls huge events and situations by bringing them down to manageable size—for example, turning a gigantic airplane into a miniature stick.

What factors foster the development of play and speech, and the internalization of such behavior into a private self? In the first two years of life, the beginning of the private self seems dependent on the basic cognitive capacities of the child. In view of the extensive psychoanalytic speculation about the crucial role of the first two years and about the persistence into adult life of fantasies of omnipotence or paranoia developed then, the recent cognitive research can provide a useful balance. The self can emerge only as the cognitive capacities for a memory storage, retrieval, anticipation, language-processing, and recognizing the permanency of objects also develop. This seems to be an extremely gradual process in the first six years; it may be abetted or slowed somewhat by inborn temperament and by social experience, especially helped by optimum or secure attachment to a responsive, stimulating adult, but it is a natural developmental process.

Adaptive Features of Imaginative Play   Although all children in our society engage in some forms of play as part of their natural development, recent studies suggest that there are wide individual differences. Analysis of the consequences of imaginative play ("pretending" or "make-believe," for example) suggests that children who engage in more of such play show advantages in general positive emotionality (happiness, liveliness, and interest), fluency of speech, persistence at tasks, ability to distinguish reality from fantasy, empathy and cooperation with other children, leadership, and the ability to resist temptation and tolerate delays (Shmukler, 1982a, 1982b; J. Singer and D. Singer, 1976b, 1981; Smilansky, 1968). When children play at make-believe, they practice new combinations of imagery and of verbal expression, they learn to take turns (Garvey, 1976), and they are forced by the necessity of keeping a make-believe story going to try out different roles, to persist at the task because of the inherent logic (beginning, middle, and end) of the plot, and to anticipate consequences (Singer, 1973).

Children who have not developed the ability to engage in much imaginative play often seem restless. They cannot amuse themselves in waiting rooms or during periods of necessary delay before receiving food or some other reward. Singer (1955, 1961) showed that imaginativeness can be a useful method for children to learn to tolerate delays. Mischel and Moore (1980) demonstrated that children can resist temptation most effectively when encouraged to engage in playful distracting imagery, for example, thinking of desired marshmallows as "fluffy white clouds" rather than focusing their thoughts directly on the food.

Playfulness as a Personality Trait   By ages 3 and 4, children show fairly consistent differences in play patterns. Several factor-analytic studies of spon-

The reenactment, through pretend play, of a familiar sequence—in this case, "going to the doctor"—gives children an opportunity to practice roles and behavior that they have not previously fully understood and mastered.

taneous play patterns over a year's time have identified distinct styles of naturally occurring behavior. Some children consistently show a tendency to play at games of pretending and they are, as suggested above, also more likely to be lively and smiling, cooperative and interactive with other children, and to be leaders in play groups. They talk more and use more complex language. These differences are not necessarily related to intelligence (Shmukler, 1982a, 1982b; Singer, Singer and Sherrod, 1980; D. Singer and J. Singer, 1980).

Lieberman (1977) in an extensive study of kindergarten children examined differences in physical spontaneity, social spontaneity, cognitive spontaneity, manifest joy, and sense of humor. She found factor-analytic evidence of a playful behavioral style—children who were regularly more joyful, who made up jokes and stories and showed more make-believe play. These children also showed more capacity for divergent or creative responses to special tests. A study of high school adolescents who were rated for their behavior by their teachers revealed a similar playfulness dimension; some students were consistently more humorous, cheerful and laughing, enthusiastic and imaginative. Lieberman suggested that "bubbling effervescence" in adolescents reflects the continuation of the kindergartener's playfulness.

Studies of adult personality make it clear that playfulness can be identified as a style of relatedness. In a factor analysis of personality descriptions emerging from the case records of psychotherapists, Meehl and others (1971) found a strong factor called surgency/pleasure/play. Items and descriptions such as *jocular, cheerful, enthusiastic, smiles often, colorful personality*, and *stimulating* were linked together. The recent studies of children suggest that this enthusiastic and colorful personality pattern is evident by the third or fourth year of life.

Learning to Delay Gratification

An early body of theory and some research supported the general outlines of Freud's views of the delaying function of imagination and its relation to a benign, supportive parent figure (Singer, 1955). Studies of adult and child fantasy, however, show that thinking directly about a goal increases desire or impulsive-action tendencies; imagination is most useful as a form of delay when it reshapes the goal into a symbol or metaphor or when it completely shifts attention to an alternative set of scenes that are interesting or entertaining (Mischel and Mischel, 1976; Singer, 1966, 1975).

Walter Mischel has been the major investigator studying the nature of delaying behavior and of resistance to temptation in children. His experiments have shown that children can learn to delay impulsive efforts to gratification by observing a model who shows such behavior, by talking to themselves, and by using distracting imagery when confronted with a choice between an immediate smaller reward and a later larger one (Bandura and Mischel, 1965; Mischel and Moore, 1980; Mischel, Zeiss, and Zeiss, 1974).

Mischel's work demonstrates the kinds of conditions that theoretically can help a child delay gratification: parent models, resources for self-entertainment and imagery, clear understanding of the distinction between immediate and delayed response. There is as yet no solid evidence that delaying capacity is a general trait. Studies of adults have found support for a general factor of delaying or motor-inhibition tendencies linked to great imaginativeness, but research in this area is scarce (Singer, Wilensky, and McCraven, 1956).

Children who are less impulsive and who can wait longer often have specific resources at their command. They can distract themselves with imagery or fantasy or slow themselves down with self-talking (Meichenbaum and Goodman, 1971). They may also have a whole set of positive reactions—curiosity, feelings for others, and a desire to help—that makes it less likely that all of their concentration will be on one specific goal, gratification of a desire for candy or a plaything. They have more kinds of interests and more kinds of reactions, so that no one source of gratification dominates their thoughts. For the playful and imaginative child every new room and every new social setting can be reduced in "size" to a series of exploratory encounters or pretend-games, and self-entertainment or sharing-games with others can quickly become engrossing.

We have placed considerable emphasis on the emergence of particular personality patterns in the preschool age period because there is more substantial research data available for these ages and also because it is more feasible to disentangle constitutional temperamental factors, emergent cognitive stages, and parental influences in this period. As the quotation from Maccoby (1980) near the beginning of this chapter states, parental influences may not be specific for particular responses but may establish an atmosphere that helps the child develop a guiding set of beliefs. Actually, there is evidence that the parents' own values rather than their actions may be subtly influential.

Parental Values and Early Personality Formation

Tower (1980a, 1980b) studied the value patterns of fathers and mothers of a group of 5-year-olds whose behavior at school was rated by teachers. It turned out that the parents' own values were surprisingly good predictors of the children's prosocial behaviors, play styles, and emotional patterns at school. The children's responses were also scored for optimal activity, for example, socially responsive but also capable of playing alone if necessary or cooperative with other children but not overly dependent. In general, when parents shared a common set of values, their children showed optimal levels of social maturity, assertiveness, focused attention, sociability, and imaginativeness in play. Parental differences in values were predictive of negative affect, withdrawal, and signs of guilt in the child's school behavior.

Parental values are probably transmitted not only through modeling but also through dozens of specific reinforcing statements or actions. Often, simply tolerating spontaneous acts of sociability, assertiveness, or imaginativeness conveys to children the sense that these behaviors are approved of, while others evoke a quick negative affective reaction or punishment. Parental comments about the behavior of other children or of other families expressed with approval or disapproval undoubtedly also convey a specific parental value.

Comments about television characters' actions, overheard conversations between parents or grandparents, observation of what actions of siblings evoke parental approval or anger—all of these undoubtedly influence the child's sense of what parents think is important. If the father's and mother's values differ, children may reflect some of these mixed messages by showing maladaptive behavior patterns. It seems likely that even with the importance of heritability and early constitutional influences, parents' general value systems, as well as their specific actions, can still influence the personality characteristics of the child in the preschool period. There is good evidence that as children grow older the likelihood of showing socially adaptive, constructive, altruistic, and helpful behaviors depends not only on parents' actions or "teaching" but on their creation of an atmosphere that evokes positive emotions (Maccoby, 1980; Shmukler, 1982b).

MIDDLE CHILDHOOD

The emphasis in this chapter on the early years should not be understood to imply that personality patterns become crystallized within the first five years of life. While temperament and early secure or maladaptive attachments undoubtedly limit some of the potentialities for later change, the evidence suggests that many aspects of preschool personality are drastically modifiable through experiences in middle childhood (Kagan, Kearsley, and Zelazo, 1978).

Researchers in the newly emerging field of life-span studies also call attention to changes in the total environmental experience available for one generation of children compared to another generation. In Charles Dickens' day in the 1820s or 1830s most children of 9 or 10, except those from aristocratic families, worked regularly in shops, factories, or even mines. By the age of 15 Dickens had taught himself shorthand and was working full time as a newspaper reporter in courtrooms and in Parliament. But in our century children and adolescents spend much more time in school and are dependent on parents for a much longer period. And in the last sixty years, many changes in the environment such as radio, the movies, and especially television have provided school-aged children with examples of many other styles of life. What will happen, then, in the 1990s, when preteens will be exposed constantly not only to the usual peer or teacher influences but also to daily visual experience through videodiscs or cable TV music channels of their favorite music idols and to other influences that cannot now be envisioned?

The Task Demands of Middle Childhood   If we consider some of the demands made on children aged 7 to 12, we see at once how tremendously important this phase of development is in shaping personality.

School Learning and Adjustments   The first major demand on the 6-year-old is to adjust to school routine and to acquire the basic conceptual or symbolic skills needed to continue effectively in school. The child who is restless, inexperienced with sitting quietly and looking at picture books or at using pencils, soon falls behind the others and cannot master reading as well as other classmates. Difficulties in learning to read, to write, or to perform simple arithmetic soon lead children to perceive themselves as different, perhaps even as fools or dummies. Defensively, slow learners may turn against school and join forces with those peers having similar difficulties. Thus, when even moderate school difficulties are confronted—and especially when parents are unaware or unconcerned about these or, perhaps, too disorganized to help the children to catch up—some children begin to develop personality patterns or life-styles more associated with anti-intellectual or peer-oriented values. The availability in the past two decades of drugs at the elementary school level may provide an outlet and source of gratification with drastic effects on later development of competencies. Studies of school dropouts make it clear that only a small proportion of these youngsters are significantly disadvantaged economically or even mildly intellectually retarded. Once having started off on the wrong foot in school, they become increasingly hostile to the educational system, perceiving teachers as cold and unfeeling; they resent authority generally and view the world as an unpredictable, violent, and exploitative place (Mussen and others, 1979).

Friendship, Skills, and Early Fantasy   Middle childhood is also a period when children learn to form friendships and to develop the capacity for mutual caring and reciprocity in close relationships with peers. Sullivan recognized the significance of this phase, and recent careful experimental research by Berndt (1981) appears to demonstrate that middle childhood is characterized by a sequential growth in the capacity for mutuality in peer relations and friendship formation (see Table 16-3).

Reviewing Table 16-1 on page 384, we see that middle childhood involves considerable self-definition in terms of physical or mental skills. During this period, children find that they can coordinate their athletic abilities; drawing or other artistic capacities; musical talents; expressive potential in games or in writing; and their arithmetic, scientific, and mechanical capacities. As they succeed or fail in some of these activities, they begin to form a coalesced set

TABLE 16-3
Friendship Patterns in Early and Middle Childhood

Measure	Fall		Spring	
	First grade	Fourth grade	First grade	Fourth grade
Helping	21.17	38.21	28.68	51.04
Refusals to help	.62	.75	3.49	1.33
Sharing	99.71	98.24	83.3	109.04
Refusals to share	7.35	3.66	8.23	4.20

Age changes in evidence of friendship patterns in middle childhood. Pairs of children who designated each other as friends were observed during specially designed situations providing opportunities for helping and sharing. As the data show, older children helped their friends longer and refused to share with them less frequently than did the younger children. The older children were also more consistent over the year than younger ones.

(From Berndt, 1981)

of beliefs about themselves. Their internalization of earlier make-believe patterns may also lead to different degrees of expectation about the future. Daydreams of athletic fame, of careers in dance or drama, of adventure and romance are all common and are a kind of trial balloon in the formation of a sense of identity that becomes a major task in adolescence. Projections into the future through fantasy increase from middle childhood to adolescence. By ages 13 to 16, as a study by Klineberg (1967) showed, fantasies are more realistic and reflective of social experience and also capable of more "extension" across time spans. Poorly adjusted adolescents' fantasies are much less future-oriented. The extensive observations of Spivack and Levine (1964), carried out with groups of middle-class teenagers who were impulsive and involved in antisocial acts, suggested that they lacked a fully developed pattern of future fantasy by comparison with their better-adjusted peers. Their imaginative world was barren, as these investigators suggest, and they often sought to satisfy immediate needs—a fast car ride, a drug high—with little projection into future consequences or into interesting or lively experiences later in life.

Origins of Group Loyalties   Middle childhood is also the first major exposure of children (except through television) to significant adults, groups of peers, and broader social groups at the community or national levels. The tendency of boys to play with boys and girls with girls probably does not reflect sexual latency but more likely a positive effort to clarify biological identity as male or female and to learn the presumed rituals that the broader society defines as "maleness" and "femaleness." This is certainly a key feature of the origin of self-belief systems, in which self-beliefs about religion and ethnic background or race may be highlighted, and school experiences or club memberships further clarify social status. Teachers, Little League coaches, dancing, music, or gymnastic instructors all become focal points for imitation of adults outside the family. Many anecdotes document important changes in a child's sense of direction and identity through exposure to an attractive and supportive teacher or coach.

Middle childhood also exposes boys and girls to *reference groups*—groups they can identify with beyond their family and relatives. Through reading, movies, television, and popular music, they begin to find attractive role-models and social circles well beyond their own direct daily experience. Boys may begin with athletic teams and heroes—a fascination many men never lose—but they also move on to pop singers or to adventurers, scientists, and artists. Girls share these same reference groups and also, depending on the conventionality of their surroundings, develop a sense of communion with nurturant activities such as teaching and nursing.

Middle childhood has been seriously underestimated by personality theorists in its role in personality development. It is a period when physical skills and imaginative capacities burst into full flower—when public- and private-personality characteristics can be experimented with without the constraints of social reality, social injustice, and the restrictions imposed by older authorities, cultural sexual taboos, and religious or economic limitations.

If you reminisce for a moment about your own thoughts, fantasies, and behavior in junior high school, for example, you may recognize how many of your current beliefs about your psychological maleness or femaleness; your athletic, intellectual, or artistic skills; your attraction to outside groups or individual heroines and heroes were then being crystallized. You may even be able to recall specific friendships or recurring daydreams that allowed you to explore your aspirations and the reaches of your mind, on the one hand, and your social skills, popularity, or enjoyment of intimacy, on the other. Think too of the books, movies, TV shows, and music or sports events you were excited about and see if you can identify continuities with your present beliefs and skills or aspirations.

As we shall see shortly in Chapter 17 in reviewing the literature on personality consistency, measures of personality traits and fantasy patterns made in middle childhood are more highly correlated with later scores on such variables than those obtained in early childhood (Olweus, 1979). It may well be that middle childhood is even more critical a phase than early childhood in the formation of adult personality patterns.

SUMMARY

1. Observation of infants and children shows that personality reflects certain kinds of developmental continuities. In addition, evidence suggests that discontinuities or new learning possibilities can cause personality patterns to change throughout the life span. Students of human development now recognize that a comprehensive approach is needed rather than one that focuses on the first five years of life. The importance of social settings in addition to developmental stages is now apparent. Growth of a child, or of an adolescent or adult, can be looked at in terms of developmental tasks that must be accomplished at different ages.

2. Personality differences in development involve the ease or difficulty with which individuals confront tasks or social expectations at each phase of life. An important principle is that many developmental tasks recur again and again at each new phase of the life cycle.

3. The term *temperament* describes such phenomena as susceptability to emotional situations, strength and speed of response, and persistence and intensity of moods. All these characteristics may be part of an individual's constitutional or hereditary makeup. Observations of babies and studies of twins and children of different racial and ethnic backgrounds support this view. Buss and Plomin theorize that there are four hereditary temperaments: emotionality, activity, sociability, and impulsivity. Hereditary temperamental differences help explain why parents may treat their children differently.

4. In the first six months of life babies are active, curious, motorically differentiated, and attentive. They show a constant search for stimulation and response to novelty. If infants are subjected to sensory deprivation, even though their physical needs are met, they may suffer depression and some of them die.

5. Research on separation fear, stranger anxiety, and maternal attachment has shown that children must reach a certain level of cognitive capacity, information-retrieval ability, and expectancies before they will be distressed at separation from the mother and show anxiety with strangers. Children whose cognitive capacities develop earlier show earlier signs of separation fear and stranger anxiety, and they also lose these fears and anxieties earlier.

6. An important aspect of adult personality is the extent to which an individual may be overly dependent on authority figures or be incapable of close relationships. Psychoanalysts linked this capacity to early feeding experiences and other oral gratifications. Recent research indicates that visual and other sensory cues and especially communication are also critical.

7. Only recently have psychologists examined the origins of the specific emotions. Smiling emerges naturally, and seems to be related to the effect of joy when novel stimuli are matched to familiar schema. In the first year of life, specific stimuli will evoke fear, anger, disgust, interest, and joy, and also provoke characteristic facial expressions.

8. How the private personality emerges and develops is of particular interest. Spontaneous imaginative play and use of language are important to the private personality. When children first learn to talk, speech and thought seem to be indistinguishable. Children talk about their ongoing activities to themselves much as adults carry on an internal monologue. Gradually children begin to internalize speech, and speaking becomes social communication. Between ages 3 and 5 overt speech flourishes and is closely associated with play. Then comes a recognition that only communicative speech is acceptable, and the child begins to be aware of a private self of thought and inner communication.

9. Children who engage in imaginative play show positive emotionality, fluency of speech, persistence, ability to distinguish reality from fantasy, empathy, cooperation, leadership, and ability to resist temptation and tolerate delays. Although play emerges as a part of cognitive development, adult influences are important in sustaining a child's play. Teachers and some TV shows also can help children learn to play spontaneously. Children differ in their styles of play, with some of them consistently playing at games of pretending or make-believe.

10. The ability to delay gratification is important in the development of maturity. Mischel's studies show that children can learn to delay gratification through observation of a model, talking to themselves, and using distracting imagery.

11. As children grow older, the likelihood of their showing socially adaptive, constructive, altruistic, and helpful behavior depends not only on parents' specific actions and teachings but on their creating an atmosphere that evokes positive emotions.

12. Many aspects of preschool personality are modifiable through experience in the years of middle childhood. The first major development-task demand at this age is adjusting to school routines and acquiring the conceptual and symbolic skills needed to stay in school. Middle childhood also is a time when children learn to form friendships and close relationships with peers. Considerable self-definition in terms of physical and mental skills occurs in middle childhood; children begin to learn about their athletic abilities and their artistic and musical talents.

13. Middle childhood is also the first major exposure of children to significant adults, peers, and broader social groups at the community and national level. The fact that boys play with boys and girls with girls is probably an effort to clarify biological identity as male or female and to learn how society defines maleness and femaleness. Beliefs about religion, ethnic background, and race may be highlighted, and school experiences and club membership may clarify social status. It may well be that middle childhood is just as critical a phase as early childhood in the development of personality.

CHAPTER 17

Adolescence and the Adult Years

PERSONALITY CONSISTENCY, CONTINUITY, AND CHANGE

In attempting to develop a scientific conception of personality that reflects the tremendous range of possible variations of experiences across a typical seventy-year life span, psychologists have had to confront difficult questions related to consistency of personality, continuity of patterns, and potentiality for personality change. Consistency refers to the question of whether a certain personality trait, such as introversion, locus of control, or field dependence-independence, remains evident (1) if behavior is sampled through different measuring methods, for example, a questionnaire and an interview, or (2) if the person is studied in different situations. Continuity refers to evidence that patterns discernible in early or middle childhood persist into adolescence or even into adult life and old age, a position implicit in most psychodynamic theories.

Recently psychologists who study personality across the life span have questioned this view. Some have proposed that different age periods in adult life evoke genuinely new patterns of behavior. Others suggest that the nature of personality across time involves continuous conflict between opposing tendencies—for instance, the inherent need for autonomy versus the need for intimacy or affiliation, making change rather than continuity inevitable and typical.

Consistency across Situations

Most people do not need to be convinced by scientific evidence that private personality is consistent across different situations. After all, they remember their specific experiences, their fantasies, their nightdreams, and their wishes. Yet in communicating their experiences, or in self-descriptions, people show considerable variability in the consistency of their reports or even in their views of the regularities in their public-personality characteristics. A clever demonstration of such variation emerged from research by Bem and Allen

(1974). They asked people to rate themselves on how consistent they would be in various traits from one situation to the next. They assessed traits such as dependency and friendliness both through self-reports and through ratings of the subjects made by friends or both parents. They also obtained data on the actual behavior of the subjects while they sat in waiting rooms with other people or while they engaged in group discussions. There was clear evidence that those persons who rated themselves as, for example, consistently friendly actually did show such a pattern across the various situations. Indeed, they found evidence for a trait of personality consistency, a style of self-description that reflected a tendency to show similar characteristics—for example, friendliness, dependency, or dominance—in many settings. Other persons who were less likely to stress consistency across situations in self-descriptions turned out to "look" different to others in the different settings.

Findings such as Bem and Allen's are important because during the late 1960s personality researchers were undergoing a kind of crisis of faith concerning the reality of personality traits. Walter Mischel, the social-learning and personality theorist, called attention to the fact that many studies involving measurements of personality characteristics failed to show adequate correlations between such measures and the way people behaved in specific experimental situations (Mischel, 1968, 1969, 1972). He and other critics (Fiske, 1974) pointed out that personality traits measured by self-report questionnaires often did not correlate appreciably with the traits measured by other kinds of procedures, such as interviews or observations. The criticisms of Mischel and Fiske, among others, spurred personality psychologists to reexamine their data-collection procedures and their assumptions about the nature of personality consistency across situations and time.

One reason that earlier studies did not find evidence for trait consistency might have been that researchers typically gathered data on only one day in a person's life. If all the extraneous factors that might affect a person's behavior on a given day are considered—a bad night's sleep, an argument with a roommate, unpleasant news on the radio, a mild viral attack—it is understandable that a questionnaire filled out in the morning might not correlate with the person's performance in an experiment the next day. If traits are to be assessed properly, many measurements of a person are needed.

The advantages of studying an individual on a number of occasions are evident from an investigation by Seymour Epstein (1977). He asked 14 undergraduate men and 14 undergraduate women to keep daily records of their experiences for up to 34 days. These records were classified under two categories, the most positive emotional experience and the most negative emotional experience. The subjects described actual incidents and checked off their feeling states from a list of 90 adjectives. These descriptions were scored by trained raters in keeping with Henry A. Murray's emphasis on *press*—a measure that reveals the extent to which situational factors or others' actions play a role in the occurrence of particular emotions. Scales for negative presses, including *loss of love, negative evaluation by others, lack of consideration, failure,* and *moral transgression,* were developed to estimate the influence of situations.

Positive presses were rated as *love and affection*, *positive evaluations*, *affiliation*, *success*, and *esthetic stimulation*.

Since the subjects had been observed on so many days, odd-day scores on the adjective checklist could be correlated with the even-day scores. Table 17-1 shows the pattern of correlations over time for each of the four kinds of measurements, grouped by "unpleasant" and "pleasant." As can be seen from Epstein's table, as the number of days in the sample is increased, the reliability coefficients of the various measures—the emotions, the impulses, the behavior, and the situations—increase steadily. The average reliability for *pleasant emotions* is .88, and a variable like *happiness* yields an extremely high reliability of .92 within that category.

What contexts or situations yielded the most consistent ratings? It appears that situations involving loss of love are particularly highly correlated. These results indicate not only that self-described emotions, impulsive tendencies, or behavioral tendencies turn out to be remarkably consistent when measured over time, but that even the perception of the nature of external circumstances provided by the subjects turns out to be reasonably reliable. This is especially important, because many theorists of personality-situation interactions have called attention to the fact that how the individual views a given situation is especially significant for personality (Alker, 1976).

It might be argued that Epstein's findings merely reflect the fact that people can be consistent in describing themselves and that this is certainly a kind of personality trait (Bem and Allen, 1974). It is also possible that reliability of this kind is found mainly in self-reports. What would have happened if Epstein's subjects had been observed by other people over a period of time, who recorded their behavior daily? Would there have been the same degree of consistency? A study by Leon (1977) followed thirty people over four weeks with raters

TABLE 17-1
Personality Consistency Reflected in Frequent Measurements

| | Number of daily observations included in calculating reliability coefficients | | | |
	1	4	6	12
Unpleasant experiences				
Emotions	.22	.49	.68	.75
Impulses	.15	.34	.60	.68
Behavior	.14	.25	.50	.52
Situations	.02	.13	.32	.43
Pleasant experiences				
Emotions	.34	.63	.79	.83
Impulses	.10	.48	.65	.70
Behavior	.08	.38	.57	.68
Situations	.00	.29	.36	.52

(Derived from Epstein, 1977)

observing them on measures related either to sociability or impulsiveness. Compared with the relatively low correlations for any two days, the average correlation for 14 days was quite high (.81). In other words, it does indeed appear that given enough time and repeated measurements, a reasonably sizable amount of consistency in personality traits can be demonstrated.

A useful breakdown of the different methods of measuring personality characteristics has been proposed by Jack Block (1977). He distinguished three types of personality data: *R data*, *S data*, and *T data*.

Consistency across Specific Methods

R data represent observations by outsiders of the ongoing behavior of persons in normal settings of their daily lives. Measurements carried out by Leon's observers in the study described above are an example. Similarly, in research carried out by Singer and Singer (1981), children in nursery schools were observed for 10-minute periods on eight different occasions over a year's time.

S data represent information based on the self-reports of individuals. These self-reports can relate to private experiences—daydreams, fantasies, prejudices, expectations, beliefs—or they can be self-descriptions of behavior in specific situations or of more general behavioral characteristics. Such self-reports can be obtained from questionnaires, personality inventories, checklists, or actual self-descriptions such as those in the study by Epstein described above.

T data represent information based on relatively structured, carefully controlled laboratory situations in which the subject is, in effect, maneuvered into behaving in a particular way according to the demands of the experimental situation. Examples are experiments in which observations are made of the reactions of an individual to frustration or to failure or the helping behavior of an individual when confronted with someone in distress.

On the basis of a review of a great range of personality research, Block proposed the following conclusions about the evidence for personality consistency:

1. Well-done R-data studies demonstrate undeniable and impressive personality consistency and continuity residing within the persons being studied.

2. S-data studies using carefully constructed personality inventories also show indisputable and appreciable personality coherence and stability within the persons studied.

3. Strong relationships exist between the dispositional qualities of persons as studied via R data and as evaluated using S data.

4. The evidence for personality consistency as derived from studies using T data is extremely erratic, sometimes positive but often not.

5. As a corollary of the inconsistency manifested by T data, it follows that the relationship between T data, on the one hand, and either R data or S data, on the other hand, must also be uneven (Block, 1977, p. 45).

Consistency and Continuity over Time

Block supported his arguments with examples drawn from some of his own research. As described in his book *Lives Through Time* (1971), a large group of children were followed over the years and evaluated fairly regularly by two or three clinical psychologists, each carrying out observations separately from the others (R data).

Children were observed during a three-year transitional period from junior high to senior high school. For the boys, ratings such as "is a genuinely dependable and responsible person" correlated .58 across the three-year span from junior high (middle childhood and puberty) to senior high (adolescence), while ratings like "tends towards undercontrol of needs and impulses, unable to delay gratification" correlated .57 in that same time span. When the comparison is made between senior high school (adolescence) and data obtained when the participants reached their thirties, the correlations on these variables were .53 and .59. These results suggest, therefore, that there is rather good consistency of R data on personality characteristics and also rather substantial evidence for continuity of adolescent personality traits into adult life.

Block also assembled evidence to show that self-ratings by individuals (S data), such as responses to questionnaires like the California Psychological Inventory (CPI), show impressive consistency with comparable measures as well as continuity over a ten-year period. An interesting example is found in a questionnaire used in Block's research called "What I Like To Do" (WILTD); this questionnaire consists of 50 questions about attitudes and behavioral tendencies in a variety of situations. One factor that emerged from the pattern of answers to these questions was labeled by Block as "overcontrol." It was possible to make up a score based on the overcontrol items and then correlate this score with the score obtained by the same subjects who filled out the California Psychological Inventory about 25 years later. The overcontrol scores on the WILTD were correlated with the CPI ego-control scores. Considering how different the inventories are in terms of format and phraseology and the fact that more than twenty years intervened between administrations, Block's finding of correlations of .52 for males and .53 for females across time is indeed impressive.

Behavior observed by others (R data) can also be shown to correlate with self-reports on questionnaires across time. A series of descriptions of the subjects in their junior or senior high school years had been prepared by the psychologists who interviewed them. These were correlated with self-rated scores on the CPI scales of *dominance* and *socialization* administered about 20 years later to the same persons. All in all, a very high number of individual descriptive comments made by the psychologists about the adolescent subjects correlated positively with the CPI self-ratings about twenty years later.

Implications

Because life situations are also important in measuring personality, psychologists also sample the kinds of circumstances that people confront at different age periods. By combining trait measurements with a consideration of the

SITUATIONS AND THEIR MEANINGS

Psychologists are becoming increasingly alert to the need to sample the different kinds of situations people confront as adolescents or adults. They must take into account the special meaning a given situation has for an individual and also find out whether particular kinds of situations share common meanings for a particular subculture or age group (Alker, 1976; Moos, 1973).

Price and Bouffard (1974) carried out studies that open the way for psychologists to learn more about the meaning of situations and how such meanings can themselves be used to classify environments or situations. They asked young adults to read descriptions of fifteen situations such as *family dinners* or *dates*, and fifteen actions, such as *writing* or *belching*, that might occur in each of the situations. A rating of zero to ten was used, with zero representing behavior that would be regarded as utterly unacceptable or inappropriate in a given situation, while the maximum score represented clearly appropriate behavior. Thus, belching on a date or at a family dinner might be less acceptable and appropriate than in the privacy of a bathroom. Writing would be perceived as appropriate in a classroom but far less appropriate at a family dinner. Certain actions, such as eating or talking, are appropriate in a fairly wide variety of situations, while belching or running have a much smaller range of appropriate situations. Thus, a particular type of behavior such as belching can be classified as being of very limited appropriateness in a great variety of situations in American society (although it would be more appropriate in Bali, where belching at dinner is regarded as a sign of appreciation of the food). This procedure can be used to classify both behaviors and situations, because some situations may be very restricted in terms of the range of behaviors possible or appropriate within them.

Price and Bouffard were able to show that situations that are greatly limited in the range of appropriate behavior evoke particular kinds of emotional reactions. For example, an audience with the Pope would probably allow only a few socially and religiously restricted behaviors, since people are much more watchful and self-attentive in such situations than in others. The possibilities of this technique are impressive, because psychologists can ultimately obtain ratings for a large number of behaviors in relation to settings and then examine the average ratings, the variability, and also the clusterings or major groupings of situations. This technique has the advantage of representing not only an externally defined setting but one that includes an appraisal, or at least an average of appraisals, by a group of persons. Sampling settings and observing the range of appropriateness of actions for different age groups may become an important method for studying variations of personality over the life cycle.

range of situations that confront a person, psychologists can better evaluate the degree of consistency a person shows across settings and also whether an individual or an age group shows continuity across several years in traits and in different situations.

A combination of trait and situation measurement is advocated by psychologists who adopt an interactionist or transactional approach (Magnusson and Endler, 1977; Pervin, 1977). They propose that there is a continuous feedback between the traits, styles, and expectations a person brings to a specific situation, such as being stuck in an elevator, and the demands for reaction the situation evokes.

ADOLESCENCE

Although the period from ages 12 to 16 has always been characterized by dramatic changes in physical development, the concept of adolescence as a special stage in the life cycle is a twentieth-century creation. In previous centuries (and in many cultures today) children of this age were already at work on farms or in factories and, by 16, many were married and starting families. But in the United States, the twentieth century brought universal public education at the primary and secondary levels. Young people between 12 and 18 no longer entered the work force but were identifiable as students in a special age period called *adolescence*, a term introduced formally into psychology by G. Stanley Hall in 1904. Nowadays, this period is extended from the early teens through age 18 or 20.

The objective markers of adolescence are (1) sex changes such as the beginning of the menstrual cycle in girls and nocturnal emissions and the change of voice in boys; (2) the spurts of physical growth that peak around ages 11–13 for girls and 13–15 for boys; and (3) the attainment by age 16 of high levels of abstract thinking capacity as measured by intelligence tests and of cognitive capacity as evaluated in the extensive work of Kohlberg (1976). These changes in physical characteristics and in cognitive capacity sharply delineate adolescence from middle childhood.

Elaboration and Extension of the Private Personality

One of the major characteristics of adolescence is the flowering of the imaginative capacity. By age 13 teenagers have a past of many memories to recall and, perhaps, to regret as well to delight in. They also have a broader range of future possibilities that are not yet foreclosed by circumstance. The inner world is now expanded by romantic fantasies, as studies of thematic apperception responses of teenagers have shown (Gottlieb, 1973). At 13 or 14 a boy can still daydream about becoming a professional athlete or a military hero, a girl about a gymnastic victory in the Olympics, a ballet career, or a starring role in a movie. And at these ages both boys and girls also begin to fantasize about intimate personal relationships and erotic satisfaction with, usually, persons of the opposite sex. Although children in middle childhood still play fantasy games, by adolescence most make-believe is completely internalized and takes the form of extended and elaborate daydreams, often influenced by popular music, television and movies, or reading (Singer 1973, 1975a).

Adolescence is thus the time of possibility. This hopeful stance is crushed soon enough in the period between 16 and 21 when the majority of young people realize that they are not tall enough, strong enough, fast enough, or skilled enough to make high school or college athletic teams, let alone to attain national or world-class standards, or gifted enough in drama, dance, or music to contemplate them as a career. Fantasies may persist for a time, and a few may become a lifetime habit as in the case of a chubby woman of 40 who

© 1968 Jules Feiffer. Dist. Publishers-Hall Syndicate

imagines herself as a willowy ballerina each night as she drifts off to sleep (Singer and Switzer, 1980).

The close tie between fantasy patterns, wishes, and self-awareness in adolescence is hinged to the accelerated physical development of this period. Studies of the fantasies of boys and girls who show relatively precocious secondary sexual development (breast development, pubic hair, voice and genital changes) suggest that, at first, early maturers feel awkward and uncomfortable and worry more about acne and related concomitants of bodily changes. Soon, however, they are characterized by more forcefulness, social leadership, popularity, and higher social status, whereas relatively later-maturing youngsters experience awkwardness and some self-doubts (Mussen, Conger, and Kagan, 1969). Fortunately, most physical changes occur for most young people in a short span of time between ages 12 and 15. Before the changes occur, many youths spend a great deal of time on elaborate fantasies about the consequences of remaining sexually undeveloped or of proving to be thoroughly unattractive to their acquaintances.

As the early adolescent tries out a wide range of fantasies, the formation of what may be called sexual appetite or object-choice begins to be formed. Gender identity—that is, the awareness of being a boy or a girl and recognition of biological sexual structures—occurs in early childhood. On the other hand, sex-role identity—how one behaves as a male or a female in terms of society's expectations—is formed somewhat separately and more gradually (Chapters 11 and 16). Recent evidence also suggests that there is a clear distinction between sexual object-choice and sex role. Contrary to popular beliefs, homosexual men are not necessarily more feminine in their sex-role identification, nor are homosexual women necessarily more masculine in theirs (Rosenberg,

Sex-Role Identity, Erotic Fantasy, and Sexual Appetite

Early adolescent girls and boys. Note how much taller and gawkier the girls are than the boys. In late adolescence, boys are taller than girls, on the average, and more muscular.

1981; Storms, 1980). Male and female homosexuals tend to adopt many of the traditional sex-role patterns of their biological sex group despite the fact that their fantasies about sex, intimacy, and love are oriented toward persons of their own gender. The crucial role of erotic fantasy for establishing sexual orientation and behavior is evident from recent research (Kelly and Byrne, 1978; Storms, 1980).

A new theory (Storms, 1981) links the formation of heterosexual or homosexual object-choice to erotic fantasy and biological maturation in early adolescence. The theory proposes that the particular form of sexual object-choice depends on the early adolescent's existing social relationships—that is, the timing of sexual excitement and arousal tendencies is crucial. If the relationships are almost exclusively with same-sex companions when the child becomes strongly aware of sexual stirrings and arousal, then homosexual fantasies and, at least to some degree, a homosexual erotic orientation and, ultimately, overt sexual practice may develop. If the child's sexual maturation occurs when heterosexual social groups are already being formed, then the more typical heterosexual erotic orientation will develop (see Figure 17-1).

Storms admits that retrospective reports by homosexuals of early sexual maturation may not be accurate. He does provide evidence from a longitudinal study showing that sexually early-maturing boys reported much less hetero-

FIGURE 17-1
Sex-Drive Development in Males and Females

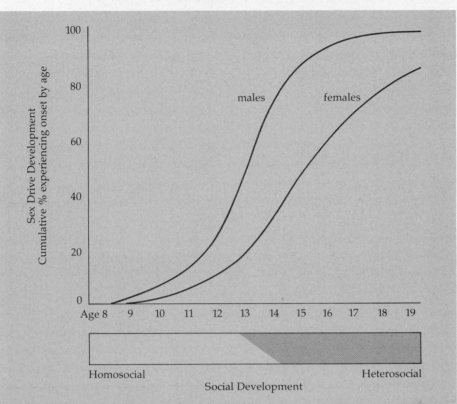

The two curves in this graph were derived from the data of Kinsey and others (1948, 1953) on the two principal overt signs of sex-drive onset—first masturbation and first orgasm—occurring, on the average, at about age 13 for males and about 15 for females. Storm's research also suggests that these curves represent the periods of maximum erotic development in males and females.

(From Storms, 1981)

sexual fantasy later on at 18 years of age than late-maturing boys. Athletes, who spend more time later in life in same-sex groups show a much greater incidence of homosexual behavior or even exclusive homosexuality than do otherwise comparable college males. Finally, many homosexuals come from families in which there is a higher than average incidence of same-sex siblings. They grow up, therefore, not only with homosocial groups but also with same-sex siblings. An important implication of this theory, if it is supported by further evidence, is that "homoeroticism develops out of normal, common-place experiences that occur to nearly everyone during the period of homo-

HOMOEROTIC ORIENTATION AND CHUMSHIP: A CASE STUDY

In his emphasis on "chumship," Harry Stack Sullivan was perhaps the first personality theorist to identify the juvenile period as a critical phase of personality development that went beyond classic psychoanalytic theorizing (Chapters 3 and 16). He also suggested that if a youngster was emotionally involved with a good friend of the same sex at the time of sexual maturation, this relationship might form the basis for a long-standing homosexual orientation, in fantasy if not in overt actions.

The recent publication of a biography of Sullivan (Perry, 1982) provides new information that sheds light on how Sullivan might have developed this insight out of his own personal experience. Sullivan grew up as an introverted only child on a farm in a rural New York county. His only friend through elementary and high school was an older boy, Clarence Bellinger, comparably shy and also an only child from a farm family. The two boys, the best students in the school, were inseparable until Sullivan's

friend went off to college. After this they had no further real contact although, curiously, both went on to medical school and became psychiatrists, a rare choice of profession in pre–World War I days. Neither ever married.

Sullivan was decidedly homoerotic in his sexual fantasies and behavior. As social isolates, the two boys had clung together, and when Sullivan moved into the phase of his biological sexual maturity, his attachment to Clarence may have taken on an erotic tinge that became a lifelong style. Certainly Sullivan never became a regular member of a heterosexual social group in his rural community once the older boy went off to college. Nothing is known of Bellinger's own erotic development, but his rather hostile attitude toward Sullivan as a grown man and his later references to Sullivan's homosexuality may have reflected an attempt to deny early childhood feelings or even a reaction-formation defensiveness.

social bonding. . . . Some individuals simply have stronger sex drives during this period and thus eroticize these homosocial experiences to a greater extent. . . ." (Storms, 1981, p. 351).

Not only does the hetero- or homosexual focus of sexuality develop in the adolescent's fantasies, but also the particular preferred types of sexual activity and physical types. The kinds of sexual foreplay or physical positions favored in direct sexual activity or in fantasy may emerge from the talk, action, and availability of same- or opposite-sex social groups and from movies or TV shows seen when an adolescent begins to experience sexual desires. Such erotic fantasies may be elaborated and practiced extensively during masturbation (Chapter 15).

Identity-Formation As Erikson has emphasized, a crucial task demand or life crisis of adolescence involves the formation of an integrated sense of identity (Erikson, 1959; see also Chapters 3 and 16). Adolescents by ages 16–18 possess the physical and intellectual powers of an adult and a capacity for moral reasoning of the highest order (Kohlberg, 1964). Yet in terms of social power they are still in transition;

most live at home, subject to their parents' financial control as well as, to some degree, their discipline. Adolescents' actions are strictly regulated by society, which denies them activities, such as driving, that are open to young adults a year or two older. Thus, even as they experience some successes and sense of autonomy through athletic or academic achievement and increasing sexual experience and opportunities for intimacy, adolescents also realize that they lack any inherent power in society, that their future careers and opportunities for influence on the broader group are still uncertain.

Through reading, records, television, movies, and peer associations, the adolescent is exposed to a wider variety of potential paths into the future than is available from parents or extended family. Between the ages of 16 and 22 most young people in our society must define themselves sexually and vocationally; they must accept or reject a deep commitment to their own private ideals; they must decide on a style of life; and they must decide whether they will undertake services required by the broader community, such as military enlistment. The establishment of a strong sense of identity and of a group of clear goals and values (whether altruistic or simply oriented toward solid middle-class virtues of a home, family, and good job) becomes a critical determinant of the continuing sense of well-being of the young adult.

The problem for the adolescent in the United States is made especially difficult because the American tradition emphasizes self-made identities, as Erikson suggests. In earlier times or in other cultures a young person moved directly into the family occupation, whether it was farming, seafaring, medicine, shipbuilding, weaving, or selling groceries. The choice of a vocation remains a major feature of identify formation, a key aspect of clarity of direction in life. Because young people today are exposed to such a wide variety of seeming alternatives, however, the move into the family line of work no longer is as automatic or as desirable for many adolescents. The result is often an almost desperate thrashing about for a sense of vocation, an identification of one's own skills, a search for a heroic model—athletic, artistic, religious, or professional—on whose example a life can be built. If clear models are not available, if skills fall short of what is required, if the possibilities seen on television seem out of reach for someone from an ethnic minority group or a poverty-stricken background, then identity diffusion, a sense of confusion and powerlessness, overtakes the adolescent.

Research on adolescent identity formation shows that parental and peer influences work together in establishing career choices. When boys from middle-class backgrounds become primarily linked in social groups to boys from less affluent or less educated backgrounds, they show more downward mobility in career aspirations or more confusion about choices. The reverse is true for boys from poorer backgrounds who form bonds with peers from more affluent families. Yet parental influences remain crucial. Parents' vocations and careers are the single most powerful determinant in the aspirations of adolescents (Simpson, 1962).

Parental attitudes, family conflicts, and the constructive or coercive nature of parental orientations continue to be a major determinant of the young person's thought stream even into the college years (Klos and Singer, 1981). The availability of positive relationships with at least one parent, usually the parent of the same sex, turns out to be a crucial determinant for the development of a strong sense of ego identity. Role consistency and a sense of direction, both indices of ego identity, usually are evident in the behavior of boys whose fathers are masculine in personal orientation but nurturant in their behavior toward sons (Mussen, Conger, and Kagen, 1969). The research of Jack Block (1971) has provided evidence that girls who showed a clear pattern of identification with their mothers reflected a similar sense of identity, whereas girls who reported much less maternal identification described themselves as "impulsive," "restless," and "touchy," patterns suggestive of ego diffusion. For many adolescents, problems of ego diffusion make them vulnerable to reference groups that offer some sense of identity. Drug-use cliques in high school (Jessor and Jessor, 1977) or memberships in religious cults may often seem espccially attractive.

Idealism and the Search for Meaningfulness

A special feature of the elaboration of the inner world of the adolescent that often spills over into public action is the emergence of idealism. Research on the development of the capacity for ethical thought and of the ability to engage in abstract thinking suggests that such powers reach their maturity by the late high school or early college years (Mussen, Conger, and Kagan, 1969). The adolescent is intellectually capable of recognizing the prevalence of injustice or poverty in the world, but has not yet had the discouraging experience that comes with age of finding how difficult it is to bring about change. The mind of the young adult can penetrate the emptiness of many of society's rituals and traditions. A 16-year-old who learned about the interplay of economics and politics and their influence, through advertising, in the press, realized that his father, an espoused liberal, subscribed to a daily newspaper with a very conservative editorial stance. After being challenged by his son, the father admitted that he enjoyed the paper because of the fine sports coverage, and the youth became so enraged that he tore up the paper in front of the family and guests!

A crucial feature of adolescence is the discrepancy between the intellectual or moral reasoning skills pointing to what might be or what is possible and desirable and the actual mixture of direct experiences and heavy daily responsibilities that characterize the adult's life. While not every adolescent deals with these issues, the search for a sense of meaningfulness and value, for a way of making sense of the world, characterizes many young people. If a young person fails to master the crisis of resolving the discrepancy between ideals and the injustices of society—a factor dramatically evident during the 1960s when millions of youth participated in the Peace Corps, Vista Volunteers, marches for racial equality and, finally, the widespread demonstrations against the Vietnam war—there may result a deep sense of alienation or loss of contact with family, community, religion, or national group (Keniston, 1968). A consequence of such alienation may be, for some young people, a persistent sense of *anomie*—social disorganization and isolation from the productive and enjoyable facets of the society (Reimanis, 1974). Heavy drug use and alcohol abuse have been related to patterns of extreme sense of need for new sensations or self-reported needs for autonomy or disconnection from the broader culture (Jessor and Jessor, 1977; Segal, Huba, and Singer, 1980).

How can those young people who are confronting the discrepancy between their ideals and the complexity, dangers, and sheer evil in their own environments or in the whole world move through this critical phase? Research suggests that this is often accomplished through finding some narrower, crystallized role that leads to ego identity and avoids diffusion. After a period of imprisonment, the famous activist of the 1960s, Tom Hayden, married the idealistic but commercially successful movie actress Jane Fonda. Together they formed an organization, financed by public solicitation plus the proceeds of her best-selling exercise book, that is designed to serve as a public advocate of liberal causes. Thus, Hayden has continued his idealism, but it has become a career style; he now appears in business suits and seeks public office in traditional ways. Probably the large majority of adolescents resolve discrepancies by finding a sense of identity in a commitment to a vocation and to the devotion of family life. Social responsibility becomes transformed to family responsibilities or adherence to a work ethic, and the young adult moves into what Erikson called the phase of generativity, family organization, and work productivity.

A major problem facing personality researchers involves *cohort* differences, that is, changes in social or world circumstances that may be reflected in widespread attitudinal variations from one chronological period to another (Schaie and Parham, 1974). For example, the idealism and yearning for national and international social change and a break with tradition so characteristic of youth of the period from about 1960 to 1972 was replaced by a remarkable shift in the direction of well-defined vocational and career choices, and the law, medicine, and business career orientations evident in college students from the mid-1970s to the present. The youth of the later 1970s and early 1980s have not eschewed social responsibility, but they seem to have focused much more on attempting to develop a more private family-focused life-style as an expression of that adolescent idealism.

THE ADULT YEARS: CONCEPTIONS OF THE LIFE SPAN

Except for Hall's labeling of adolescence and Sullivan's largely ignored identification of the juvenile period, most personality theorists in the first half of this century accepted some form of the psychoanalytic idea that personality was largely formed by age 6. In the next two decades, spurred by the emphasis of Erikson, more attention was paid to adolescence and to the beginnings of young adulthood. The 1970s have been characterized by greater research and theoretical scrutiny to the middle years and the aging process. In the United States people are living to quite advanced ages and the number of resort communities, such as those in Florida and Arizona, and the numerous senior citizens' communities springing up in suburban areas attest to a recognition of the extension and complexities of life situations. The extreme mobility of American society has led to elderly citizens living at great distances from their children; the old tradition of grandparents, parents, and children sharing a common home is largely past. Many people are living a quarter of a century beyond "retirement," forming new life-styles and confronting the necessity of continued employment as a means of making ends meet in the face of inflation; the elderly are also becoming an active political force.

Life Scripts   How can psychologists get a handle on the complexities of an ongoing life that spreads across decades? An approach growing out of the psychoanalytic orientation is to look for recurrences in themes that were evident in early childhood and persist into the later years. One form of such an orientation has been termed the life-script approach (Wrightsman, 1981). As suggested in Berne's "games people play" approach (1964, 1972), organized ways of relating to others developed in childhood crystallize into recurrent "games" or role enactments. People continue to play the role of "alcoholic," "martyr," or "loser" all their lives. While clinical evidence supports some forms of this approach, most empirical evidence suggests that such complex consistency beginning in the earliest childhood years cannot be identified. Studies of special groups, such as comedians and clowns (Fisher and Fisher, 1981), do indicate that experiences in middle childhood are important in forming self-schema. In the case of comedians the experiences led them to seek laughter and group approval by pratfalls and humor; such patterns, once crystallized into a career, can be extremely long-lasting.

The notion of scripts proposed by cognitive scientists (Schank and Abelson, 1971; Chapter 6) has not yet been widely applied as a means of gathering data about persisting patterns across the life-span. The more specific proposals of Tomkins (1979) and Carlson (1980), which emphasize that scripts involving positive emotions lead to one style of orientation whereas scripts linked to negative affect lead to a different one, seem a promising lead for further research. The researcher might accumulate a series of spontaneous memories reflecting "critical life incidents" from adults and then classify them according to the predominance of positive or negative affect. Then these adults might be asked to respond with expectancies about a whole array of future situations. Presumably persons characterized by positive memory scripts should seek opportunities to extend and maximize opportunities for enjoyment or excitement. Persons whose predominant memories reflect negative affects should reflect an acute sensitivity to unpleasant or dangerous events in each new future script. Such research remains to be done. The potential for studying the life scripts that people bring from earlier years to a range of new situations is a promising area for investigating personality variation across the life span.

An approach such as Erikson's suggests that at each phase of life people confront critical stages that they must cope with. If they fail to cope effectively, they may not move to a more advanced stage. Thus once past adolescence, even young adults with a clear sense of identity—for example, as a heterosexual and committed teacher or accountant—may still fail to confront the key problem of how to establish a continuing relationship of intimacy with a member of the opposite sex. According to a stage theory like Erikson's, failure to establish truly intimate, continuing relationships in the decade from 20 to 30 may lead to lifelong acceptance of isolation even when a person has success in a career. Unfortunately, we have relatively little systematic data to test the implications of Erikson's theory, although studies of "happy" people continually suggest that married persons, especially men, report more positive experiences than do the unmarried (Chapter 15). **Stage Theories**

For a large percentage of adults the over quarter of a century between ages 20 to 50 is usually caught up in the problems and joys of establishing and maintaining a family as well as in the sustained hard work of a job or career. Erikson's term "generativity" implies that the adult is not only creating a family but is also gaining pleasures in the quality of work and the presumably constructive interactions with relatives, friends, and work associates. The depression of the 1930s and the recession of the early 1980s have poignantly emphasized the tremendous importance of regular employment. The despair and despondency, loss of self-confidence, and apathy that follow unemployment, even when starvation is not imminent, attest to the significance for our well-being of a continuing constructive work experience. From the standpoint of Erikson's stage theory, then, without opportunities for productive labor or professional or artistic work and for the development of families, men and women confront a sense of loneliness, despair, apathy, and detachment. Extreme examples are the skid-row bums, lonely, isolated, shabby men sipping cheap wine from bottles in paper bags, or the "bag ladies" who scrounge in trashcans for articles to put in their shopping bags.

For the fortunate millions who form families and have regular jobs, the period of generativity is still not one of continual happiness. By its very nature, this phase of life involves many responsibilities, such as care of children, attention to the details of a job, physical maintenance of home and automobile, and countless other chores. The commitment to family and to work involves the risk that something, often many things, can go wrong. The car breaks down; a child becomes ill, another does poorly in school; a wife or husband is unfaithful; the roof leaks; a parent dies leaving another aged parent to be cared for; and a desired job promotion is lost. Surviving the stage of generativity unscathed is no easy task!

WHAT MAKES A HAPPY (HARVARD) MAN?

Love and marriage and money and work. George Vaillant of Harvard University tested and interviewed some 268 men from the Harvard classes of 1939 through 1944 when they were undergraduates. He then sent them a follow-up questionnaire every year until 1955 and every two years after that. In 1967 he did extensive interviews with some of the men who had been chosen as representative of the group. And in his book *Adaptation to Life* (1977), he described what had happened to these men.

In general, the successful man did well at just about everything he attempted. If he was successful in business, the chances were good that he had a stable, happy marriage; played well at sports; and had many friends. Also it appeared that the men who were rather conventional had fuller and more interesting lives than those who were described as eccentric or unconventional.

No variable was as good a predictor of a mentally healthy man as a satisfactory marriage. Vaillant also reported that there was a high correlation between the amount of money a man earned and his degree of happiness as rated by the psychologists and by the man himself. Such factors as the willingness and capacity to work in childhood and isolated early traumatic events had some effects on health and happiness, but how the man coped with day-to-day life and his relationships with other people were more significant.

Vaillant looked at the defense mechanisms—he calls them adaptive mechanisms—of these men. Those most common for the mentally healthy men were the inhibition of desires until more appropriate occasions, suppression, and sublimation. Humor and altruism were especially important and were often noted in the men who seemed to have made the best adaptations to life. And the positive emotions and attitudes of joy, interest, love, and affection were characteristic of the men who had retained their physical and mental health throughout the thirty or more years.

Vaillant's report is mainly in the form of anecdotal case studies. More long-term research on the determinants of physical and mental health are needed to confirm these findings.

Health and Daily Hassles

Considerable recent research has been oriented to examining the close ties between the practical concerns of life, the stressful events that occur, and the capacities to cope with daily difficulties and physical as well as mental health. While some earlier work pointed to the importance for physical or mental stability of major life changes such as bereavements, divorces, and relocations (Holmes and Rahe, 1967), more recent evidence suggests that such occurrences are not really good predictors of the probability of later physical breakdown (Rabkin and Struening, 1976). In Kurt Lewin's terms, the only really stressful events are likely to be *proximal* (close to the person) rather than *distal* (distant from the person). In other words, an immediately urgent and personally meaningful event, such as locking oneself out of the car, may be more stressful than a less personally urgent or meaningful event, such as family relocation. Therefore, the concept of "daily hassles" has been introduced to get more direct evidence of proximal experiences that really are distressing.

A study was carried out with a carefully selected group of fairly representative middle-aged adults from the San Francisco Bay area. Results indicated that the frequency of specific daily annoyances, such as dissatisfactions at work, feelings of not enough time to spend with family, unexpected guests, losing keys, inability to collect debts, showed a consistent relation to physical health. More general or distal life events did not have any predictive power compared with daily hassles (De Longis and others, 1982). One might expect that the joys and daily satisfactions of the middle years would prove to have a positive effect on the course of physical health; although some evidence was found to support this in one study (Kanner, Coyne, Schaefer, and Lazarus, 1981), it did not emerge in the study by De Longis and others.

The research on daily hassles or satisfactions holds considerable promise for examining the busy years of early or middle adult life. Repeated measurement of hassles or daily joys may give a better sense of an ongoing life than the broad generalizations of a life-cycle crisis implied by Erikson or Tryon and Lillienthal's graphs (Chapter 16). After all, for some parents the busy days of having babies and toddlers around the house may be the most stressful; for others, these years may be exciting and fulfilling, and the boredom of an "empty nest" when the children are grown may actually prove more stressful on a day-to-day basis.

Recently researchers have identified variations in personality development that can occur in the adult years. Daniel Levinson and others (1978) formulated a series of adult life periods that occur roughly within the Erikson generativity stage. Levinson's approach entailed many hours of intensive interviewing of forty adult males in an effort to gain the in-depth information that might be comparable to a clinician's but with a larger sample of subjects. He has proposed a sequence of (1) separation from primary family in the age period 16–24, (2) beginning to establish oneself in the adult world during the later twenties, (3) settling down by the end of the thirties decade or the early forties. During the forties men begin to face periods of doubt and indecision—have they made the right choices in work, in marriage, in commitment to a family, in an urban or suburban life-style? This concept of a "midlife transition" has been picked up by Gail Sheehy in her best-selling *Passages*, the widespread response to which suggests that the book touches a chord in many middle-aged adults.

As Wrightsman (1981) suggested, Levinson's approach is intriguing not only because it elaborates on the generative or middle years, but because it adds what may be called a dialectical element to the conception of the life course. The concept of *dialectics* has been introduced into studies of the life span to suggest that development is not simply a continuous upward sequence or even a natural unfolding process or a passing through stages by meeting the task demands of each period (Chapter 16). Rather, there are inherent tensions or conflicting needs that characterize all human experience so that even as people progress by temporary resolution of one crisis, they confront a new conflict just by that very resolution. Thus, getting married deals with the need to resolve the dilemma of loneliness and permits the development

Midlife Crisis and Passages

of interdependence. Once married, however, adults must deal with the need for autonomy, for independent self-assertion, and for sheer privacy, needs threatened by marriage. Levinson's approach suggests that in early adult life people express autonomy by moving out of the family, but then face loneliness that can be assuaged at home by marriage and sexual intimacy and at work by a mentor, a teacher, or a boss to whom they can become attached. Ultimately, however, people must free themselves from this mentor, and at this point occurs the period of independent self-assertion in the early forties. The midlife crisis may represent a further tension as people question their marriage or commitment to a particular career or life-style. Even if such a conflict is resolved by a new integration—a divorce and remarriage, a change of job or career, a reformulation of relationships within a marriage or at work—new tensions will emerge in later life.

The concept of midlife crises has been useful chiefly in forcing psychologists to look more closely at the continuing ups and downs in the balance of pressures between dependence and self-assertion—the continuing dialectical nature of life. "Happily ever after" is not a good way to characterize personality across the life span once people reach stages of marriage, child-rearing, and established careers. Personality researchers will have to rely more and more on combinations of data, interviews, daily-hassle questionnaires, analyses of biographies, and perhaps accumulations of correspondence when they are available (Wrightsman, 1981). With larger and more representative samples and with alertness to fundamental cognitive styles or personality variables like autonomy-homonomy or introversion-extraversion, psychologists can look at interactions between personality styles and specific situations to ascertain the personality variations that lead to more or less continuing crises and shifts of patterns in adult life.

THE OLDER YEARS

> For age is opportunity no less
> Than youth itself, though in another dress,
> And as the evening twilight fades away
> The sky is filled with stars, invisible by day.

As Longfellow's lines suggest, the notion that old age is a period of withdrawal or disengagement from life and a decline into physical decay and uselessness does not capture the opportunity aging presents to many adults. Old age reduces physical vigor and increases the chance of serious illness and painful bereavement through the death of relatives and friends. Yet the shift of emphasis from direct care of children or from primary economic responsibility for a family does not preclude continuing involvement in generative activities. Even in the most poverty-stricken or underdeveloped societies elderly people are often accorded a reduction in heavy physical labor, treated with respect, and provided with opportunities to advise or lead. In middle- and upper-class India the patriarch of an extended family, which usually resides in a common compound, will withdraw from major daily responsibilities to engage in more contemplative, scholarly, and religious devotional activities. In the relatively affluent industrial countries of the West, people above the mid-sixties usually can get by on pensions, social security, and savings, so many retire or work only part time if at all. In a mobile society like the United States or Canada, where the nuclear family is often widely scattered because of job opportunities, elderly people are increasingly gathering in special communities and creating new life-styles that may last for decades.

In view of the complexity and variety of life-styles that now characterize adults in their sixties and over, Erikson's emphasis on ego integrity versus despair (Chapters 3 and 16) as the major crisis of old age seems limited indeed. It is true that many old people do confront the question of whether their years of hard work and of devotion to children have been worthwhile (as Shakespeare's old, abandoned King Lear cries out, "How sharper than a serpent's tooth it is to have a thankless child!") and many seek solace in religion. A sizable number of the followers of the Reverend James Jones who committed suicide at Jonestown in Guyana were old people who seemed briefly to have found in his church some sense of community and meaningfulness for their lives.

There is a question, however, as to whether most elderly people do actually confront in thought or through social involvement a specific crisis of meaningfulness. If anything, studies of the elderly suggest a continuous process involving continuing fantasies and daydreams, a continuing need for personal control and autonomy, service and a sense of usefulness, physical and social intimacy, and, with some reduction of the busy responsibilities of midlife, pleasure and recreation (Butler, 1975; Langer and Rodin, 1976; Maddox, 1968; Neugarten, Havighurst, and Tobin, 1968).

Studies of the private experiences of older people continue to demonstrate that they have many daydreams and fantasies. Leonard Giambra (1974, 1977) at the National Institute on Aging has shown that there is no decline in frequency of daydreaming or related imaginal processes well into the eighties. His studies, using questionnaires like the Imaginal Processes Inventory, indicate that old people continue to show the pattern of positive-constructive daydreaming that characterizes adolescents and young adults and, if anything, show a reduction in guilty or hostile daydreaming. The elderly have wishful fantasies and playful daydreams, although they also drift into long reminiscences about past experiences.

Considerable attention has been paid to the needs of old people to review their lives in repetitive fantasies and, where possible, in conversations with others (Butler, 1975). Some of these life-review activities may reflect a struggle to find a meaning or a value in life, perhaps to justify choices, or to understand why early fantasies never were fulfilled. Such reminiscence may also reflect

Life Review and Reminiscence

the fact that contemplation of the future in fantasy only leads to thoughts of potential illness and suffering, death, or doubts about an afterlife. In addition, for many old people whose mobility is limited, daily routines are so well set and boring that variety and excitement can only be obtained through replays of past adventures. The endless "novelty" of television soap operas, game shows, and news affords a means, never before so widely available to the old, of external stimulation for vicarious events and adventure. A consequence of heavy TV viewing by the elderly, however, is that the huge amount of violence depicted in news and dramatic programs has led to fears of the dangers of the outside world and perhaps to increased tendencies to stay at home (Gerbner, Gross, Signorelli, and Morgan, 1980).

The life-review and reminiscence patterns of the aged have important adaptive and constructive potentialities. Young children enjoy the stories of grandparents and elderly relatives; the opportunity to share their lives through reminiscence with children is an exciting experience to the elderly. Some specialists in gerontology have recognized the psychotherapeutic value of encouraging life reviews (Butler, 1975). A creative project developed by a high school teacher who encouraged students to interview local old folks about their experiences and crafts has led to the *Foxfire* books, a widely read series. Similarly, the concept of oral history used by Studs Terkel in his *Hard Times* (1978) has yielded invaluable information about the past.

Personal Control: Autonomy versus Dependency

A major hazard of extreme age is the loss of control over one's life situation and daily activities. Increasing physical disability plays a role in this reduced autonomy, and by the eighties most old people can no longer drive or care for themselves by shopping and attending to daily physical needs. Thus, a preoccupation of the elderly involves the tension between the desire to be well cared for when ill or disabled and the opposite need for a sense of personal control and autonomy. The same dialectic that characterizes adolescence—the antithetical desires for dependency and autonomy—resurfaces in a new form in old people. Much of the bitterness and despondency or even the high rate of mental illness in the aged (Butler, 1975) is traceable to unfulfilled yearnings to be cared for, as another quote from King Lear exemplifies, "Ingratitude, thou marble-hearted fiend! More hideous, when thou show'st thee in a child, than the sea-monster." In earlier centuries, parents quite consciously anticipated that their reward for taking good care of their children was that they could reduce their chores when their offspring matured and could count on the younger generation for care when disabilities of age struck. A dilemma of modern American society is posed by the widespread ethic of independence or autonomy and self-control. Yet as old people experience aches and pains and reduced vigor, the yearning that everyone has from childhood for some dependency presents itself, only to be frustrated by the changed patterns of modern life with scattered families or by the independence ethic.

Remarkable studies carried out by Ellen Langer now at Harvard and Judith Rodin of Yale examined the important role of personal control in old people

The young are an important source of stimulation for old people, and the reminiscences of the elderly are an enjoyable learning experience for the young.

who already had reached the stage of dependency that required them to be in nursing homes. Rodin and Langer gave these relatively disabled and dependent old people a chance to have a potted plant in their rooms. A control group simply enjoyed the plant without any responsibility for its care; it was taken care of by the attendants. Another group, comparable in age and infirmity, were given hints on the value of responsibility and were assigned the task of personal care for their plants. Subsequently, there was clear evidence that the old people who had responsibility for their plants showed more day-to-day social activities, participation in nursing-home projects, and better health over the next year and a half. Indeed, the percentage of the control group who had died by the end of this time was twice as large as the percentage of the noncontrol participants who had died. Personal responsibility and at least some degree of autonomy was thus shown to have a remarkable positive effect even on dependent people of extreme age (Langer and Rodin, 1976; Rodin and Langer, 1977).

Disengagement and Service to Others

Another major dialectical tension that characterizes the aging process deals with the inevitable conflict between the opportunity that old age provides to disengage from responsibilities, such as child care and community service, and the continuing desire to feel needed, wanted, useful, and influential in family, community or nation. The concept of retirement with pensions for citizens over 65 represents a broad social recognition of the desirability of allowing the elderly to disengage themselves from the economic pressures of the nation. Yet the very statesman who pioneered in instituting this national policy in the 1890s, Prince Otto von Bismarck of Germany, had to be unceremoniously dismissed as Chancellor by the new Emperor when he was in his late seventies. Retirement was all right for others, but Bismarck was not ready to disengage himself even so late in life from the fortunes of the empire he had founded!

Some gerontologists have viewed the concept of disengagement as an inevitable and welcome opportunity in old age (Cumming and Henry, 1961). Yet evidence suggests that nearly half the men who retired at age 65, especially those with fewer financial resources for hobbies and continuing social or athletic activities, reported that they felt forced to retire. More often, of course, retirement affords those persons whose work is physically hard or dangerous or who have little power in their job, a welcome change indeed. By contrast, business and government executives and professionals may resent retirement because it reduces their sense of importance and power. A study of adjustment to retirement indicated that those persons who seemed to have made poor adjustments to this enforced disengagement were also persons characterized by feelings of unfulfilled efforts or resentments at failures or externally imposed frustrations. Better-adjusted men were those who, in general, had showed maturity and stability and who could continue in new jobs or hobbies or those whose life-styles had already reflected an avoidance of responsibility; in other words, they had been more or less disengaged to start with (Mussen and others, 1979).

Disengagement is largely a natural consequence of change in status: the mother's "empty nest" with no children around; the reductions of power that occur with shifts in administration of a business, factory, or government agency; the aches and pains or life-threatening ailments that force more attention to one's own body. Despite such largely uncontrollable environmental factors, psychological disengagement does not seem inevitable or even common, according to research (Maddox, 1970). A sense of personal competence or an intense investment in a specific interest, hobby, or work activity characterizes many people who continue to function well and to be well-liked or respected even if they have reduced, through illness or choice, some of their social involvements. Others—often characterized by "armored" or well-defended personality structures and well-controlled emotions—continue to maintain an active, socially engaged life-style. For such persons the conscious thought of growing old can be avoided by the sheer busyness of their lives and by the evidence of commitment and engagement (Neugarten, Havighurst, and Tobin, 1968).

One of the features often held to divide youth from the elderly is the "boring" nature of old folks' recitals of their ailments, visits to physicians, stays in the hospital. Yet this behavior seems essentially the same as the adolescents' preoccupation with acne, weight, breast development, hairdos. For old people, not actually in physical pain, much probably depends on the availability of other interests, hobbies, and skills so that attention can be drawn away from a gradually decaying body.

Bodily Preoccupation and Pleasure-Seeking

The sensual needs of the elderly—their desires for physical intimacy—are often overlooked by the young. There is little reason to assume that the enjoyment of sexuality disappears or that the sheer pleasures of physical contact fade. Often through deaths of spouse and friends the elderly are forced into solitary lives to which most adjust well, but this does not mean that with appropriate opportunities even 80-year-olds will not seek the opportunity for social and sexual intimacies. In the past, widowed parents stayed on in the nuclear family, and social contacts with a broad group of same-age peers were less common. Now, thousands of old people live in communities in which they share social and recreational activities, and new attachments and marriages are more common. Elderly people no longer adopt dress styles that specifically define old age; they attend dances, continue athletics, and many learn new skills such as painting or sculpture.

To sum up, the past quarter century has witnessed a major change in the life-style of persons over 60. Many of the same issues—the dialectical conflicts between intimacy and selfishness, sharing and autonomy, bodily preoccupation and involvement in society, intellectual elaboration and direct social interchange, the search for moderate novelty as well as the enjoyment of familiarity—these issues emerge again and again. Certain longstanding preoccupations, cognitive styles, or personal scripts about the nature of aging or confrontation with illness or death may determine whether old age is enjoyed or suffered through. Yet new opportunities for self-development, for the emergence of new interests, skills, or activities, even for new kinds of interpersonal relationships, still present themselves. The challenge for personality researchers is no longer to identify those basic task demands or life crises that determine maturity but to move beyond such limited concepts to an identification of the continuing opportunities for personality change across the entire life span.

SUMMARY

1. In order to develop a conception of personality that reflects the many differences in experiences during an entire lifetime, psychologists have faced the issues of the consistency of personality, continuity of personality patterns, and the potentialities for personality change. In reporting their experiences, people show considerable variation in the consistency of their reports. Consistency is increased if several measures are taken at different times, and some contexts or situations yield more consistent ratings than others. Self-described emotions, impulse tendencies, and behavioral tendencies all are remarkably consistent when measured over time.

2. Another problem is that when personality characteristics are measured with different methods, the results are often different. Block described three types of personality measures: R data are observations by others of normal ongoing behavior of an individual; S data are self-reports obtained with questionnaires, checklists and other self-descriptions; T data are based on information from experimental laboratory-type situations. Block concluded that R data and S data both demonstrate personality consistency and continuity, but that T data do not yield evidence for consistency.

3. The concept of adolescence as a special stage of life began in the twentieth century. A major characteristic of adolescence is an increase in imaginative capacities. Fantasy, wishes, and self-awareness are related to the rapid physical development, especially sexual maturation, of adolescence.

4. In early adolescence sexual object-choice begins to be formed. Gender identity appears earlier in childhood, but sex-role identity develops more gradually. Erotic fantasies are crucial in establishing sexual orientation.

5. A critical task demand of adolescence is the formation of an integrated sense of identity. Young people must define themselves sexually, vocationally, and in terms of their life-style and commitments to private ideals. The choice of a career is a major feature of identity formation. A positive relationship and identification with a parent, usually of the same sex, is especially important for the development of a strong ego identity.

6. Adolescence is a period when the capacity for ethical thought and ability to think abstractly reach maturity. Adolescents often experience a crisis between their idealism and the many injustices they see in the world. The result can be feelings of alienation and loss of contact with family and other groups. Many adolescents resolve discrepancies between their idealism and the difficulties of changing the world by finding their identity in commitment to a vocation and to family life.

7. For most adults the period from age 20 to about 50 involves work and the family. Erikson's term "generativity" implies that adults gain pleasure from work and constructive interactions with family, friends, and work associates. But the adult age period is also one of constant problems, large and

small. Some research points to the impact of major life changes, such as death, divorce, and change of jobs, on physical and mental health, but it appears that the impact depends on how personally meaningful and urgent the change is. Constant daily problems have more effect on health; repeated measures of daily hassles or joys may give more information about an ongoing life than generalizations about life crises.

8. Levinson proposed a sequence of (1) separation from family at ages 16 to 24, (2) establishing oneself in the adult world in the late twenties, (3) settling down in the thirties, and (4) a sense of being "one's own person" by the late thirties. Levinson's work adds a dialectical element to the conception of the life course; there are inherent tensions and conflicting needs in all human experience, so that as people resolve one conflict, another emerges. Midlife crises may add further tension as adults question their marriages, careers, or life-styles.

9. Although old age reduces physical vigor and increases the chances of bereavement and loneliness, it does not seem to preclude continuing involvement in generative activities. Studies of the elderly show a continuous process involving (1) an elaboration of inner personality activities, (2) a continuing need for personal control and autonomy, (3) a need for physical and social intimacy, (4) a search for pleasure and recreation.

10. Older people continue to have wishful fantasies and playful daydreams, and their life reviews and reminiscences have many adaptive and constructive possibilities. Television offers a way for older people to continue to receive stimulation from the outside world.

11. A major hazard of old age is loss of control over one's life and daily activities. This leads to internal conflict between a desire for dependency and a desire for autonomy. Another dialectical tension deals with the desire to disengage oneself from the duties and responsibilities of adulthood and the desire to remain active and wanted. Disengagement resulting from physical and social changes characterizes the lives of many elderly persons, but loss of interest in life and in social causes seems to depend more on longstanding personality patterns.

CHAPTER
18

Psychotherapy and Social Change

Marilyn, a sophomore at a midwestern university, seemed to have reached a dead end at school. Unable to concentrate on reading and course assignments, she began skipping lectures and soon was in real danger of failing all her courses. Her roommates, who had always respected her as intelligent, quietly witty, and deeply moral without being prudish, began to be terribly worried. Marilyn was obviously nervous, increasingly disorganized, and had begun to refuse to participate in social activities. Persuaded by her roommates, Marilyn finally paid a few visits to a college counselor, and was then referred to a psychotherapist whom she saw twice a week for a year.

The experience was at first awkward and painful. Marilyn had never confided much in others, and she had trouble talking. But the therapist was patient and seemed genuinely concerned. Gradually, as Marilyn talked of her childhood memories and of her relations with her parents— both successful, hard-working high-school teachers—she began to realize the connection between her current problems and some of the conflicts she had felt while growing up. She had always felt a tremendous pressure to follow in her parents' footsteps by becoming a teacher. Yet despite her obvious general intelligence, she did poorly in education courses. Her lack of interest, she saw, might stem from unconscious resistance to simply becoming a "clone" of her parents.

As she related her nightdreams and daydreams and tried some guided imagery exercise (imagining herself in various settings, then allowing a series of mental pictures to unfold), Marilyn began to identify a part of her personality she had been suppressing. Although she had always been an avid reader of novels, history, biographies, and travel books, only gradually did she recognize her yearning to travel and deal with people in foreign settings. Timidly at first but with increasing confidence, Marilyn switched her major and studied languages, foreign affairs, and world history. She joined a campus foreign-policy club. Suddenly college was no longer a drag; she met foreign students, she found that some of her professors in the international areas thought her a promising student, and she won an overseas travel fellowship. In her therapy she worked hard, using role-playing methods to improve her assertiveness; in the past she had approached authority figures with a mousy, self-deprecating manner. Although Marilyn never became a dominating or extraverted figure on campus, by her senior year she was clearly heading toward a career in international business or government and could speak effectively if quietly to authorities or small groups.

Although Marilyn still preserved some of her quiet dignity and soft-spoken style, her clear-sighted, lively, and direct manner was recognized by her friends as a positive personality change. She was pleased to find that her altered career plans were not as distressing to her parents as she had feared, and she recognized that much of the pressure she had previously felt stemmed from her own exaggeration and incorporation of her parents' attitudes. In fact, she felt closer to her family now that she was not unconsciously fighting them.

The quest for ways to change personality and to overcome limitations in public and private behavior and beliefs is a major concern of many young adults. In previous chapters we have identified the consistencies in cognitive styles, personality traits, and interest or career patterns across the life span. Yet—at least in North America and Western Europe—the tremendous popularity of a wide variety of forms of psychotherapy and of religious or secular movements purporting to reshape personality suggests that many young people believe that their personality characteristics are not immutable. As the example of Marilyn suggests, a good psychotherapeutic experience—that is, the combination of a skilled and concerned therapist and a cooperative and committed client—can lead to shifts in public and private personality. Nonetheless, psychotherapy has clear limitations; it cannot produce significant changes in all beliefs, attitudes, mannerisms, and overt behavior.

DRASTIC PERSONALITY CHANGE

Before examining the role of psychotherapy in personality change, we shall discuss briefly two other phenomena—religious conversion and brainwashing—both of which can bring about drastic personality change. Following religious conversion and brainwashing, the total personality and life-style are often pointed in radically new directions. In many instances, converts move away from their families and reject old friends. Their behavior, attitudes, values, and beliefs are sometimes completely altered.

Religious Conversion　History provides striking examples of people who made profound changes in their personalities. Most of these instances occurred in connection with religious conversion. In the waning days of the Roman Empire, a sophisticated and urbane professor of rhetoric found himself troubled about his sexual and other sensual desires. He underwent years of self-examination and intellectual torment before converting to Christianity, adopting a celibate life, and emerging as a bishop and great intellectual leader of the church. He is known as Saint Augustine.

A little over a thousand years later, a young German monk with many physical ailments, self-doubts, and erotic inhibitions became determined to oppose the corrupt practices of the Catholic church. Within a few years this awkward, uncomfortable man had confronted the awesome power of the Catholic hierarchy and had converted numerous German priests and bishops to a new form of Christianity. He married a former nun and was established as one of the most influential figures in Europe. This remarkable personality change in Martin Luther, the father of Protestant Christianity, has been extensively documented in a psychohistorical study by Erik Erikson (1958).

These instances suggest really remarkable shifts of personality and changes in attitudes, belief systems, and public self-presentation. However, certain key features of the earlier personality persist—Augustine's intellectuality, Luther's stubborn determination, for example.

Brainwashing　Recently much attention has been directed to personality changes in people who have been subjected to intensive mixtures of deprivation and propaganda. This technique, which began to be called "brainwashing" when it was applied to American prisoners of war by their Chinese Communist captors during the Korean War, became the subject of scientific attention because of its apparently dramatic effect in some cases. Brainwashing usually involves periods of extreme isolation and sensory deprivation, repetitive "hounding" with single-minded propaganda messages, and various conditioning procedures, such as use of electric shock. Although its effectiveness has been documented, it affected only a tiny minority of American P.O.W.'s (Sargent, 1957).

In the 1970s a spectacular brainwashing occurred when Patty Hearst, member of a wealthy and prominent California family, was kidnapped by a small group of radicals calling themselves the Symbionese Liberation Army. Prior to her kidnapping, Hearst apparently had not been interested at all in political issues, but shortly afterward she made several tape recordings denouncing her family and capitalist society, and was actually photographed holding a machine gun during a bank robbery. After a period as a fugitive, she was captured (or "rescued"); at the time she still seemed to have a revolutionary attitude, raising her fist in the traditional sign of revolution.

At her trial for bank robbery, it was revealed that after being kidnapped she had been confined in a small closet for weeks at a time and subjected to the sexual attentions of her captors, who often presented themselves as very affectionate and loving. The simultaneous mixture of fear and the affection she began to experience for her captors was undoubtedly tremendously confusing to her, and eventually led, at least temporarily, to a seeming personality change in which she adopted the toughness and political militancy of her captors. During her trial and two-year imprisonment, she seems to have gradually given up these ideologies and has since married and returned to an apparently conventional way of life. This example clearly shows that personality change is not necessarily permanent or irreversible.

Instances of milder, but still intensive, forms of brainwashing have been reported, usually involving adolescents or young adults who were converted from traditional religions to new sects such as the Unification Church (the "Moonies") or to forms of Hinduism (the Hare Krishnas). Some of these conversions involve the use of sensory deprivation, physical deprivation, repetitive propaganda, and periods of seeming love or affection by leaders or group members—techniques that are similar to brainwashing procedures.

In contrast to religious conversion and brainwashing, psychotherapies that stem from a scientific orientation are subject to systematic evaluation and to research appraisal of their component procedures, objectives, and specific effects. To understand the various theories about what produces personality change, let us now examine how some of these methods are used and evaluated.

PSYCHOANALYSIS

The most influential and carefully applied method of modifying personality in the twentieth century has been psychoanalysis. When Breuer and Freud began working with hysterical patients in the late 1880s, their goal as typical physicians was relief of a specific symptom. Freud himself wrote that the goal of psychoanalysis was to transform neurotic misery into common everyday unhappiness. He meant that his treatment had the limited goal of sufficiently reducing the persisting early childhood conflicts that—when added to the naturally occurring difficulties of life, family illnesses, school and job pressures, ethnic prejudices, social inequities, and war—make life intolerable. Freed of childhood-based "hangups," a patient could make more rational choices about how to confront the inevitable disappointments and problems that are a part of normal life.

This symptom-oriented approach was gradually modified as psychoanalysis began to deal with a broader clientele and when therapists discovered that the relief of symptoms did not always improve patients' psychological maturity and capacity for coping with interpersonal difficulties. In the 1920s psychoanalysts began talking more of character analysis (the German word for "character," *Persönlichkeit*, is roughly equivalent to the English term "personality").

Thus the modifications of psychoanalysis in the 1920s were oriented toward personality analysis and a shift in the balance of relationships between id, ego, and superego. With this change in goals, psychoanalysis took much longer and became more complex. Toward the end of his life, in a paper called *Analyses Terminable and Interminable*, Freud noted that even extensive psychoanalysis often could not come to grips with the complex personality distortions developed over years of growing up and that re-emerging transference reactions could lead to interpersonal problems years after a presumably thorough psychoanalysis had been completed. To this day psychoanalysis—particularly as practiced by adherents of the American Psychoanalytic Association and the most direct lineal descendants of Freud—emphasizes the lofty and difficult goal of extensive intrapsychic personality reorganization.

How Psychoanalysis Works

Between 1895 and 1910 Freud crystallized the basic method of psychoanalysis. It consists of establishing a unique opportunity for personality change through the cooperative activities of a well-motivated patient and an alert, empathic, but relatively unobtrusive therapist. The treatment usually takes the following form:

1. Free association, saying everything that comes to mind.
2. A neutral or "blank screen" therapist, who does not give advice and shows almost no emotion.
3. Interpretation of resistances and defenses.
4. Revival, with appropriate accompanying emotions, of significant childhood experiences.
5. Identification and analysis of the transference phenomena.
6. Insights about childhood fantasies and misunderstandings and early patterns of parent-child or sibling relationships.
7. "Working through" of recurrent defenses and maladaptive reactions.
8. Termination when the patient can identify the uniqueness of the therapist as an individual rather than an authority figure, and can undertake further analysis and "working through" independently.

Eventually the patient not only gains a greater sense of personal awareness of life, but may begin to try out in daily life new patterns of interpersonal response. In trying these new responses, the patient may occasionally regress to earlier defensiveness. The therapist continuously supports the patient by pointing out again and again the resistances to change and the reversions to neurotic patterns. This difficult working-through phase calls for forbearance on the part of both participants if the treatment process is to be effective.

Finally the patient may define new personal goals, new ways of relating to others, and new forms of sensual experience. Ideally, removal of neurotic complexes leads to greater effectiveness in both love and work—the two great goals of human life, according to Freud.

This couch, used by Freud in his office in Vienna, remains a symbol of the psychoanalytic method.

Weiner (1976) identified five kinds of psychoanalytic interventions that may help to promote an atmosphere conducive to personality change:

Therapist's Interventions

1. *Questions.* With these, the therapist focuses the patient's attention on particular issues and continues the flow of important free associations and new information. Questions are, however, of little significance in themselves.

2. *Clarifications.* These are attempts to highlight specific problem areas or to "place a mirror" before the patient, pointing up ways in which the patient's remarks are ambiguous or evasive. Sometimes one of the best tactics for a therapist, one that reflects a genuine respect for the patient, is not to accept clichés and not to permit unspoken assumptions to prevail. Clarifications usually call for concrete and detailed accounts of events so the therapist can experience them fully without interpolating his or her own prejudices or fantasies (countertransferences).

3. *Exclamations.* These are little comments such as "aha" or "yes, go on" or "I see." They are intended simply to maintain the flow of associations but, as research has revealed, they may also reinforce particular types of comment by the patient.

4. *Confrontations.* These occur when the therapist challenges the patient and identifies specific defenses, or calls attention to movement or verbalizations that reflect important material.

5. *Interpretations.* Here the therapist advances a guess or hypothesis about a connection between the patient's behavior or thoughts and some important conflict or difficulty not currently in awareness. For example, a young woman patient remarks in a rather annoyed fashion that she is getting fed up with the smoke in the room and with the therapist's use of cigarettes during her sessions. The therapist quietly points out that he is a nonsmoker and indeed no one has smoked in the room today. Perhaps, he interprets, she has linked him to her uncle whose cigar smoking she found so offensive when he dangled her on his knee when she was a little girl. This interpretation leads to the patient's willingness to delve further into her early ambivalent feelings about the uncle, who had made some seemingly sexual overtures to her when she was about 8 or 9. He had also been one of the few members of the family to show any real interest in her, thereby generating her ambivalent feelings of repulsion and attraction. The interpretation also reveals the beginnings of a transference reaction to the therapist and permits exploration of some significant factors in this young woman's early development and in her attitudes toward men.

What Produces Personality Change in Psychoanalysis?

1. The psychoanalytic "fifty-minute hour" offers a novel situation in the lives of patients, a kind of safe haven in a pleasant, different atmosphere with a neutral but concerned therapist who will listen without complaint to all of the carping, whining, and "crazy" ideas that they may bring up in the course of free association.

2. The encouragement of free association circumvents some of the well-established habits of defensiveness and avoidance of private thoughts and conflict that patients have been practicing for many years.

3. The analysis of dreams and fantasies provides patients with new information about many relatively unconscious wishes or conflict. It also provides a healthy respect for the complexity of the private personality and for the usefulness of exploring images, daydreams, and nightdreams.

4. In examining the relationship between earlier childhood experiences and their recurrences in fantasies or interpersonal difficulties, patients begin to gain a sense of organization and meaningfulness that they may not have had before.

5. The awareness of a transference of feelings to the therapist, both positive and negative, helps patients to appreciate, with considerable emotional conviction, the power of the distortions they have retained from childhood.

6. In the so-called working-through phase, patients are actively practicing to identify such recurrent mechanisms as defensive or evasive maneuvers and regressive behavior.

There are, of course, a number of additional possibilities for understanding how classical psychoanalysis produces personality change. In general, however, the theoretical basis of the treatment hinges on the acquisition of *insight* and the strengthening of the conscious awareness of the patient. As Freud said, "Where Id was, there shall Ego be." In other words, what was once unconscious becomes subject to conscious control and adaptation to the realities of social life. A key element in a successful analysis may also be the patient's continued acceptance of the working alliance between patient and analyst.

MORE ACTIVE FORMS OF PSYCHOTHERAPY

A classical or even neo-Freudian psychoanalysis tends to be a somewhat "passive" experience, developing gradually and with considerable deliberation. The analyst may say very little during a given session, waiting for opportune moments for transference or defense interpretations. Many psychoanalysts began to be concerned that the procedure was too lengthy and that some patients dropped out because they could not produce associations and confront their problems. Certainly, the neo-Freudian therapies, as practiced in the training institutes, did not shorten psychoanalyses. Consequently, these classical and neo-Freudian methods of psychoanalysis did not accomplish all that had been hoped.

In the 1940s group psychotherapies were developed in an attempt to provide opportunities for personality change to large numbers of patients— for example, veterans of World War II—or to use the interactions among group members to speed up the "corrective emotional experience" and "insight" objectives of dynamic therapy (Powdermaker and Frank, 1953). Because it is more psychologically taxing for the therapist, group therapy often involves cotherapist teams. Despite its widespread use in the 1950s and 1960s, there is no evidence that group therapy has greatly reduced the amount of time required for producing change or that it has any significant advantages over individual dynamic psychotherapy.

Other forms of psychotherapy with a dynamic focus but with a greater emphasis on action and livelier interchanges between patient and therapist appeared in the 1960s. Eric Berne's *transactional analysis* can be employed in individual treatment, but it is often used in groups or in weekend workshops. It represents a drastic simplification of the concepts of psychoanalysis. According to Berne, everyone is assumed to behave at times as a *child* (the id), an *adult* (the ego), or a *parent* (the superego); the problem is to ascertain when each role is appropriate and adaptive. People also crystallize their personalities around particular "games," roles that have been rewarded or effective in earlier times, but which no longer have any "payoff." By identifying these games and linking them to earlier experience and encouraging patients to try new patterns, transactional therapy, in effect, has some of the psychodynamic treatment goals, but is closer to behavior therapies in providing active practice for new types of movement and speech.

Gestalt therapy and the various "humanistic" approaches also involve more active methods, role-playing, interchanges between patient and therapist, and trying out forms of behavior that have been avoided in the past. These methods are similar to behavior-modification techniques such as *flooding*, *assertiveness training*, and *role rehearsal* in that they emphasize active practice with the therapist. They also rely heavily on *corrective emotional experience* and, to some degree, on *insight*, thus demonstrating their relationship to psychodynamic theories of personality change. They involve frequent examinations of early childhood reactions persisting into adult life and often attempt, by reenacting scenes from earlier days (such as simulated arguments between patients and their parents) to provide *catharsis* and various new ways of handling comparable situations.

European Imagery Methods

A group of psychotherapeutic procedures developed in Europe use imagery associations to treat neuroses and psychosomatic reactions, to resolve intrapsychic conflicts, and to modify personality traits. These methods can be traced to the work of Oskar Vogt and Johannes Schultz, German physicians, who early in the twentieth century began studying the connections between bodily processes, body images, and physiological responses. Indeed, Schultz developed an elaborate treatment procedure called *autogenics* in which the patient attempts to reduce symptoms as different as skin conditions or anxiety attacks by deep relaxation, and by intense imagery of scenes such as cool water running over one's arm or the heat of a fire warming one's fingertips (Luthe and Schultz, 1969).

Eventually a method called the "waking dream" in France, or "guided affective imagery" in Germany, evolved. A patient, after an appropriate diagnostic interview, relaxes by using a form of Jacobsen's progressive relaxation technique. Then he or she is encouraged to imagine as vividly as possible being in some natural setting, for example, a forest. The patient then allows a series of images to develop naturally from that scene so that there follows an "imagery trip." For example, a male patient describes himself walking through a forest, feeling lonely and uncertain. He imagines hearing a lovely bird call, and he cuts through the underbrush to reach the bird. Suddenly, a menacing wildcat bars the patient's way. Despite efforts to get around the wildcat, the patient reports that he is frozen in place. Here the therapist, sometimes actually called a "guide," may suggest some magical method of circumventing the block, for example, finding a sleeping pill that the patient can trick the cat into eating. The images continue as the patient continues his journey, encountering other animals, perhaps mythological or fairy-tale creatures or figures from his own childhood.

Each therapy session involves such an imagery trip. There is minimal interpretation by the therapist and no emphasis on transference. The imagery trips—in a forest, along a stream, climbing a mountain, exploring a steamer trunk, looking at a family album—all provide a symbolic method for working out key conflicts.

While the mental-imagery therapies seem somewhat exotic and almost mythical to many American mental-health workers, a sizable body of clinical reports and some fairly well-controlled studies summarized by Luthe and Schultz (1969) and by Leuner (1978) attest to the usefulness of these approaches with a wide variety of patients. An examination of the characteristics these methods have in common with psychodynamic and behavior therapies has been carried out by Singer (1974, 1978), who found that while the imagery techniques draw on psychoanalytic notions of conflict and on Jung's approach to symbolism, they also employ behavior-modification procedures such as relaxation, positive imagery, desensitization, and symbolic modeling.

So far we have reviewed methods of treatment that focus primarily on the *private personality*. They are based, to a large extent, on an assumption that intervention—which modifies self-awareness and patterns of memory or which leads to cognitive and emotional restructuring of private experience—will also lead to changes in how we relate to other people and in how we express anger or engage in sex. In contrast, behavior therapy and the earlier versions of social-learning theory (before Bandura's interest in self-efficacy or Mischel's interest in cognitive structure; see Chapter 4) paid little attention to the private personality. Most behavior therapists felt that psychodynamic therapies were indirect, vague, and often irrelevant in confronting symptomatology; instead, their goal of treatment was to modify specific response patterns and to remove symptoms. **Behavior Therapies**

Behavior therapy addresses itself to direct modification of unwanted behavior and makes no assumptions about underlying personality structure. Unlike the European imagery therapies, the images used in behavior treatments are focused directly on the patient's complaints, fears, or distresses. A person who is afraid of going out and walking in crowds is given systematic practice, under relaxed conditions, in imagining scenes with open spaces and crowds, with the scenes imagined in order from least to most frightening. Once the person can envision the most fearful scene without experiencing panic in the therapist's office, he or she is encouraged to go out in crowds under controlled conditions, such as with a good friend, and if that is successful, to try even more difficult life situations. Thus, a case of *agoraphobia* (fear of open spaces) or *ochlophobia* (fear of crowds) might be cured without any effort to probe into the patient's early childhood or any examination of dreams, fantasies, or transference reactions. This treatment, now called *systematic desensitization*, is essentially a form of systematic practice—that is, the unlearning of a fear reaction.

The behavior therapies generated tremendous excitement because they were demonstrably effective and much less time-consuming than any previously known psychotherapies. They also attracted American and British psychologists interested in social-learning theories because they were amenable to carefully controlled research.

Systematic Desensitization The single most widely used form of behavior therapy, *systematic desensitization*, is applied to help people overcome phobias (irrational fears) and other kinds of anxiety, such as difficulties in public speaking or socializing. As previously described, the method calls for the use of relaxation (sometimes accompanied by positive imagery involving nature or effective actions) to counteract the anxiety associated with images of fearful scenes, which are produced by the patient in hierarchical sequences, from least to most frightening. The method was developed by Joseph Wolpe, a South African psychiatrist, who was largely responsible for the spread of behavior therapy throughout the United States in the mid-1950s.

Aversive Conditioning   This procedure derives from so-called aversive-conditioning techniques designed to extinguish an undesirable response. Sometimes mild electric shock was administered to persons who wanted to get rid of an undesirable and annoying mannerism, such as constantly clearing the throat or biting fingernails. The use of *aversive imagery* was developed by Cautela and McCullough (1978) as a substitute for electric shocks or chemicals. For example, a patient who wanted to "unlearn" habitual voyeuristic behavior (being a "peeping Tom") practiced imagining loathsome skin diseases in conjunction with all the steps that were part of his peeping routine. Before long he stopped having voyeuristic fantasies and the behavior—which could have led to his arrest—disappeared (Singer, 1974).

Modeling   Fears or social inhibitions can be eliminated by having patients carefully observe someone they respect engaging in the behavior they would like to carry out themselves. A boy who is afraid of snakes may be more willing to approach or touch a reptile if he sees a teacher or good friend doing so (*direct modeling*). *Symbolic modeling* relies on imagining others engaging in these actions and then mentally substituting oneself in the scene. This procedure, derived from Bandura's observational-learning theory (Chapter 4), has been extensively researched especially in laboratory studies (Rosenthal and Bandura, 1981).

Flooding   *Flooding* is similar to systematic desensitization but it requires more exaggerated emotion and involves extensive and intensive practice, often in imagery, of the unwanted or fearful scenes or actions. While there are risks of increasing fear through this procedure (Bandura, 1969a; Singer, 1974), some evidence suggests that imagining the worst possibilities while in the safety of the therapist's office does reduce the fear and permits the patient to engage in appropriate action (Smith, Glass, and Miller, 1980).

Assertiveness Training   Behavior-therapy procedures are being applied to teaching people socially effective responses. Assertiveness training involves first having people identify areas in which they believe they have suffered or lost out on opportunities because they are too inhibited to speak out or take some direct action on their own behalf. Many women have been raised to defer to men by underplaying their own intelligence. Assertiveness training is widely used to give women systematic practice in speaking more forcefully, in making clear their needs to others, in organizing and presenting their positions, sometimes even in resisting physical force. Rehearsals and psychodrama-like situations are employed. Sometimes rehearsing procedures involve imagined encounters, as well as acted-out situations with the therapist or other members of an assertiveness-training group (Kazdin, 1980).

Stress Control   Many behavior therapists now recognize that behavior change comes about not only through the practice of specific responses but through a shift in information-gathering orientation or appraisal of situations (Arnkoff and Mahoney, 1981; Murray and Jacobson, 1978). Donald Meichenbaum (1977), for example, pioneered in training individuals to cope more effectively with potential stress situations or to gain control over impulsive behavior. His methods include training people to talk to themselves, using calming phrases that can lead them to approach a situation more productively. Instead of at once saying, "Uh-oh, this is it again. I'd better scram!" a person is encouraged to try an interior monologue like "Uh-oh, this is it again. I'd better slow myself down and not run away. Let me take a better look around. What's really going on? Is there something here worth giving a try?" Procedures for using imagery as distraction during pain and to explore alternative possibilities in difficult situations are also included. In effect, an effort is made to provide a whole series of coping strategies that can help a person deal more effectively with stress situations as they arise. The term *stress inoculation* implies that having available a host of coping strategies will have the same preventive effect on maladjusted reactions to new stress as a vaccine has on catching a disease.

There are, of course, other behavior therapies and numerous variations on the ones presented here. The operant-conditioning techniques developed from the animal research of B. F. Skinner have been successfully employed—chiefly in simple habit change in retarded persons, chronic schizophrenics, and hyperactive children—but they have, on the whole, had little impact on personality change.

But even a straightforward method like systematic desensitization can lead to personality change. Kamil (1970), for example, showed that young adults who had overcome a specific anxiety also show more signs of self-acceptance or competence as measured by projective tests. Behavior therapists have pointed out that learning to overcome a fear or to change a bad habit not only helps us feel better, but may also allow us to enter into rewarding social situations that may feed back more positive self-attitudes (Bandura, 1978).

Problem-Focused Approaches to Personality Change

The most general forms of treatment designed to deal with broad categories of personality description, such as obsessive-compulsive neurosis or hysterical personality, are not as useful as originally had been thought. Much of the research on the evaluation of psychotherapy suggests that the best results are obtained when a clear-cut problem is identified and treated with reasonable specificity (Meltzoff and Kornreich, 1970; Smith, Glass and Miller, 1980). A problem-focused approach does not, of course, preclude use of techniques from either the psychodynamic or the behavioral orientations. We shall consider two examples, one concerned with the problem of anger and the other with the problem of shyness.

Expressing and Controlling Anger   An example of a problem-focused orientation was described by Novaco (1977) in an analysis of anger and the consequences when it is inappropriately expressed or inhibited. Although everyone is likely to experience and express anger under certain severe provocations, many individuals do not learn to discriminate which social situations are appropriate for the expression of this emotion and which are not. Others have experienced such extensive efforts to shame them or punish them when they expressed anger as children that they inhibit their annoyance or resentment even under appropriate circumstances.

In Novaco's work a series of exercises designed to identify circumstances in which anger is either useful or inappropriate are provided. Patients are then given specific training in expressions of anger that will enable them to communicate effectively with others but, at the same time, will not lead to overt aggression or violence. This problem-focused approach is useful not only for people who are unable to express or control anger, but for those who can express it but cannot recognize the appropriate situation in which to do so.

Understanding and Overcoming Shyness   A similar problem-focused orientation grew out of the research of Pilkonis and Zimbardo (1979). Using a variety of psychological instruments, they explored shyness in relation to its potential hazards for both normal and seriously maladjusted individuals. They distinguished public from private shyness: public shyness is primarily demonstrated in group situations, public places, and formal settings, while private shyness occurs in intimate, interpersonal, or sexual situations.

According to Pilkonis and Zimbardo, shyness is best dealt with in a small group setting including members of both sexes with comparable difficulties. It is probably advisable to have cotherapists who can themselves play the part of models for various appropriate interpersonal behaviors. They recommend the occasional use of videotapes to provide feedback that will allow clients to observe themselves and practice different methods of self-expression in public and in more intimate situations. The clients are expected to keep records of their actual experiences, from which they can begin to identify their typical behavior patterns. The records become a basis for evaluating change as improvement takes place.

Practice exercises are outlined for shy persons—greeting strangers, asking people for information or advice, calling up for dates, asking questions in class, and so on. Many shy people lack certain social skills. Because of the very nature of their shyness, they avoid sufficient day-to-day practice in smiling, nodding, taking the little "digs" that others offer, making various kinds of eye contact, and knowing how to begin or end conversations. Twentyman and McFall (1975) developed a whole series of behavioral rehearsal techniques to help shy young college men improve their ability to ask for dates and to behave appropriately during an actual date.

It should be apparent, then, that even these focused problem-solving approaches have broader implications for personality change. Some of the loftier objectives of psychoanalytic psychotherapy may be attainable not only through the extended and somewhat vague approach of a classical analysis, but also through more direct and problem-focused procedures in psychotherapy.

Implications of Psychotherapeutic Approaches

We have reviewed briefly quite a range of approaches to modifying personality through psychotherapy. A surprising number of these approaches are linked by the use of the individual's imaginative capacities as a tool in reorienting self-attitudes and in anticipating potential social or intimate personal situations.

To a greater degree than the psychodynamic forms of psychotherapy, behavior therapies rely heavily on practice of specific behavior and, wherever possible, on direct actions by clients. But practical considerations usually do not permit the clients or patients to move out into the world and engage in direct practice. Rather, the clients must come into the therapist's office or some other appropriate setting to describe the events or experiences that have been troubling them. Therefore, the imagery processes of both clients and therapists are critical. Effective therapy inevitably calls for therapists to elicit sufficiently explicit content from the client so that the private images of both of them about the events in question come closer together. This then permits further examination and practice in the therapist's office of critical life situations. Ultimately, of course, the client must independently try out new action patterns in the outside world. In a way, however, both dynamic psychotherapy and behavior modification, as they have evolved since the 1970s, are merging the public and private personalities. The key to improvement or change is self-regulation, not dependence on the therapist. As the client tries new ways of thinking and interacting with others, he or she will develop an increased sense of personal control, self-efficacy, and competence. Thus, even modest symptomatic treatment may lead to some degree of personality change.

Psychologists studying psychotherapeutic outcomes are also becoming increasingly concerned about measuring changes in various ways. For example, a patient who *feels* better may still engage in behavior that the therapist or the relatives feel is unsatisfactory. Ultimately we must view personality changes in terms of (1) how patients feel about themselves, (2) how professionals evaluate these changes (based on interviews or tests), and (3) how society evaluates these changes—that is, is the patient still an obnoxious spouse, a danger to others, a potential risk for hospitalization? (Strupp and Hadley, 1977)

Does Psychotherapy Work?

One of the most important tasks of a scientific psychology is to move beyond the class of individual practitioners to a systematic examination of whether or not the methods purporting to ameliorate emotional or interpersonal difficulties through personality change are actually effective. A statistically sophisticated review of the literature on the outcomes of psychotherapy was carried

FIGURE 18-1
Is Psychotherapy Effective?

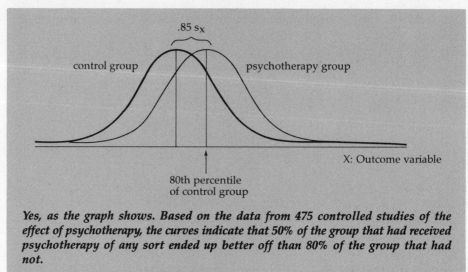

Yes, as the graph shows. Based on the data from 475 controlled studies of the effect of psychotherapy, the curves indicate that 50% of the group that had received psychotherapy of any sort ended up better off than 80% of the group that had not.

(Based on Smith, Glass, and Miller, 1980)

out by Smith, Glass, and Miller (1980). They identified 475 controlled studies and classified them in terms of the differences in outcome between psychotherapy or some form of behavior modification and the control or untreated condition. They were then able to calculate the extent to which psychotherapy or behavior modification could be shown systematically to be more effective than some alternative approach to amelioration of symptoms—such as use of a placebo (pseudotherapy) or drugs—or no treatment at all. Figure 18-1 provides the statistical frequency of the amounts of improvement for the clients in those studies. Looking at this figure, we see that a person who has been treated by psychotherapy shows a greater likelihood of improvement than someone who has not been treated. In fact, as Smith, Glass, and Miller note, because the average person showed an advantage for treatment over no treatment of .85, more than two-thirds of a standard deviation (a measure of variability), we may conclude that 50 percent of the clients who underwent psychotherapy ended up better off than 80 percent of those who obtained no help.

Smith, Glass, and Miller also compared the different kinds of psychotherapy. As Table 18-1 shows, the strongest effects are obtained from the behavior-modification techniques, hypnosis, and the cognitively oriented therapies. But most of the other treatment procedures also yield rather strong results and are not widely apart from one another.

Some controlled studies comparing humanistic and behavioral approaches to other forms of psychotherapy show on the whole relatively few differences

TABLE 18-1

Which Psychotherapy Is Most Effective?

Type of therapy (arbitrary order)	Average effect size	Number of effects*
1. Psychodynamic therapy	0.69	108
2. Dynamic-eclectic therapy	0.89	103
3. Adlerian therapy	0.62	15
4. Hypnotherapy	1.82	19
5. Client-centered therapy	0.62	150
6. Gestalt therapy	0.64	68
7. Rational-emotive therapy	0.68	50
8. Other cognitive therapies	2.38	57
9. Transactional analysis	0.67	28
10. Reality therapy	0.14	9
11. Systematic desensitization	1.05	373
12. Implosion	0.68	60
13. Behavior modification	0.73	201
14. Cognitive-behavioral therapy	1.13	127
15. Eclectic-behavioral therapy	0.89	37
16. Vocational-personal development	0.65	59
17. Undifferentiated counseling	0.28	97
18. Placebo treatment	0.56	200
Total	0.85	1,761

*The number of effects, not the number of studies; 475 studies produced 1,761 effects, or about 3.7 effects per study.

(Modified from Smith, Glass, and Miller, 1980, p. 89)

between the various methods, but all of the forms of psychotherapy were more effective than no treatment at all (Luborsky, Singer, and Luborsky, 1975). Analyzing the studies from another vantage point, Beutler (1976) concluded that the behavior therapies are particularly effective in changing specific habit patterns, whereas the more cognitively oriented therapies (which include the psychodynamic approaches) may actually have advantages for patients showing adjustment difficulties.

Researchers who are evaluating psychotherapy are beginning to ask more and more sophisticated questions. They consider not just whether or not therapy works, but *which* therapy using *which* method with *which* particular client and with *which* particular therapist under *which* special life circumstances.

SOCIAL CHANGE AND PERSONALITY MODIFICATION

We have devoted most of this chapter to examining psychotherapy, the major systematic scientific procedure for modifying personality. We have seen that psychotherapy does have potential value in changing personality to make people happier, more effective, and more socially valued (Strupp and Hadley, 1977). Nevertheless, for most people in our society, opportunities to obtain short-term psychotherapy are rare. If there are to be changes in personality for large numbers of people, they must come from other methods.

Social Change at the National Level

At various times it has been hoped that massive social change would lead to more effective personality integration. In his early writings, Karl Marx, for example, was concerned not only with the economic welfare of the peasantry and industrial workers of Europe, but also with what he felt was the increasing alienation of workers from their own productive efforts. To some extent Marx hoped to produce through economic revolution a massive personality change. Similar hopes of genuine economic and personality reconstruction were held out for the Chinese Revolution. In the 1960s many young people, disappointed in the Russian experiment, turned their hopes toward the communal orientation advocated by Mao Zedong, the Chinese leader. Visitors to China were impressed by the atmosphere of good feeling, obvious cooperativeness, and mental health. Changes in the Chinese government since Mao's death have made it clear that the situation was far more complex than it appeared and more conflicting opinions have emerged. Nevertheless, it does seem that certain aspects of the Chinese personality have been drastically modified. The traditional family hierarchy has been deemphasized, and extra-familial group cooperativeness seems to play a more critical role in China and in the Soviet Union than it does elsewhere.

Religious Groups and Cults

At a more personal level, group structures can also be extremely important in influencing personality. One way for many otherwise shy and inhibited young people to avoid extreme withdrawal into psychotic behavior is to find groups who provide mutual stimulation. In the United States, the extended family unit of grandparents, uncles, aunts, parents, and children all living in close proximity is no longer the rule because of the great mobility of the society. Many adults live isolated from what are called *reference groups*—family units and ethnic, social, and religious groups that once formed part of the identity of a growing child.

It is not surprising, therefore, that many of us find ourselves constantly on the lookout for some form of reference group—some way of breaking out of the isolation and loneliness that can easily overwhelm us in large urban centers or even in rural areas if we are essentially "strangers." We all seem to need to belong to some larger group with which we can share beliefs, traditions, and regular social contact.

A current American concern is the many young people who are attracted to so-called "fringe" religious groups—the Jesus People, "Moonies," Hare Krishnas, among others. Of course, we need to view such movements in perspective. A young Roman who became a Christian in A.D. 60 would certainly have seemed odd to his family by linking himself to this small and peculiar Jewish sect. At that time he probably would have been burned to death in the public gardens by the Emperor Nero, but three hundred years later Christians were the dominant group not only in Rome but throughout the Western Empire. A more recent example are the members of the Church of the Latter Day Saints, or Mormons. In mid–nineteenth-century America, Mormons were considered to be a fringe group, but today they are respected and prominent members of government and industry.

The Cult Personality   Levine and Salter (1976) carried out a study of 106 young men and women who were confirmed adherents of nine cults or fringe religions: Hare Krishna, Jesus People, Scientology, Unification Church, Foundation, Process, 3HO, Divine Light, and Children of God. These young subjects (median age 21.5) had volunteered for the study with the knowledge of their cult leaders. Those of Catholic and Jewish background gravitated toward the so-called Oriental religions, such as the Hindu Hare Krishna or the Korean Christian Unification Church, while Protestant youths moved toward Western Christian groups such as the Jesus People. The adherents of the Oriental religions were more likely to have used drugs prior to conversion and to have

A group of Hare Krishnas in New York City. Note the shaved heads, a symbol of their membership in the cult.

been sexually active, while adherents of the Western religions usually were involved with drinking rather than drugs and had little sexual experience.

The adherents interviewed seemed to be of average intelligence and few showed any signs of serious emotional disturbance or pathology. The most common reasons given for joining the religious groups were "feeling lonely, rejected, not belonging anywhere" or "life had no meaning . . . drifting." All reported positive experiences and a sense of real change once they had stayed in the organization for a while.

These subjects were volunteers, so firm conclusions cannot be drawn, but these young people did not appear to be brainwashed. They were white and predominantly middle class, and they were not generally antagonistic to their families. The investigators were impressed that symptoms of anxiety and depression such as insomnia, headaches, weeping, and nervousness were markedly reduced, that the respondents were no longer on drugs, and that they seemed happier, more self-accepting, and in better physical health. The suddenness of the changes did evoke some skepticism from the interviewers, however.

We do not yet know the long-term consequences of fringe-group adherence for personality structure. It is clear, however, that two major ingredients are necessary for young people to join groups like these: the need to believe and the need to belong. Levine and Salter propose that the highly organized, hierarchical belief systems of the sects filled a cognitive void that existed for these young people before they joined. The tightly organized group itself— its communal structure and its constant interpersonal relations—reinforced a sense of group affiliation that was missing earlier. Rituals, mystical experiences, and opportunities for service to others all seemed to be a part of the process.

Reference Groups Fortunately, for most people feelings of alienation or meaninglessness are not so pervasive or profound as to necessitate joining groups that involve a lifetime commitment. Yet many of us benefit from membership in some reference group. Besides the larger organized religions or the political and social clubs that attract most persons in our society, there are all sorts of clubs or affinity groups such as stamp and coin societies, ethnic groups, the Sierra Club, and the Gay Rights movement. Many adults are attracted to quasi-fantasy groups like the Society for Creative Anachronism in which members take weekend jaunts and assume a Medieval or Renaissance identity like Reynaud of Anjou or Mistress Marianne de Poitiers. They dress in period costumes and engage in jousts or antic dancing to the sounds of recorders or viole da gamba. Other groups re-enact battles of the Revolutionary or Civil War and spend many weeks practicing their roles. In a sense, such groups provide, at least temporarily, additional opportunities for self-actualization or for trying out alternative life-styles and behavior patterns without the risks of complete commitment. As yet, however, we have little systematic research evidence on the consequences for personality of affiliation with such secular reference groups.

On the one hand, we have seen that personality can indeed be changed—by strenuous voluntary efforts, as in the case of Augustine or Luther; by systematic influences by others, as in brainwashing; by psychotherapy of many kinds; and by social and political forces. But on the other hand, the evidence for personality change is not all that compelling. If you think about your own personality, you will proably find considerable continuity—at least in your thought processes and, to some extent, in your manner of relating to others. And if you think back to your earliest childhood recollections of your classmates, it is likely that those who were very bright and who set the pace in elementary school are probably still setting the pace in college. Those who were troublemakers or in difficulties because of poor attendance or inattention to studies may be in other academic difficulties today—or may not have made it to college at all.

A good deal also depends on how personality is defined. In terms of dimensions such as ego strength, introversion-extraversion, field dependence-independence, or other facets of the private personality, change is likely to be very small indeed. But if personality is defined in terms of observable behavior, then it is obvious that change is easier and more susceptible to influence by situational demands and rewards or punishments.

Despite the dramatic instances of brainwashing or other forms of conversion, most of the systematic efforts at changing personality, especially psychotherapy, show rather disappointing results. Psychological treatment has not altered the incidence of emotional disorders in the way that medical science has reduced or eliminated smallpox, cholera, and typhus. Although psychological approaches to modifying addictions and maladaptive habit patterns such as smoking and excessive drinking or eating are successful in milder cases, they have not proved effective with the many severe instances of these disorders.

In the United States today there are hundreds of thousands of well-trained psychiatrists, psychologists, social workers, psychiatric nurses, and marital and pastoral counselors. If personality change could be accomplished relatively quickly and efficiently, there would be little public interest in the many additional newer therapies and techniques such as EST, Esalen, and the various types of humanistic therapy; nor would there be a market for the dozens of self-help books such as *Be Your Own Best Friend* and *Your Erroneous Zones*. From this proliferation of schools of psychotherapy and treatment methods, it seems reasonable to conclude the following:

1. No specific therapy has yet found the true key to personality change.
2. It is difficult to change strong personal habits, patterns of emotional expression, and attitudes or beliefs about the self.

3. Scientifically based approaches to personality change through systematic psychotherapy can lead to a measurable degree of personality change or symptom relief.

What is less certain is how long-lasting such changes are and how processes directed to producing change become incorporated into the personality over longer periods of time. Surprisingly little research has been carried out involving long-term follow-up of persons who have undergone psychotherapy or who have been altered in personality through religious conversion or participation in a sect or social group designed to influence personality. A promising possibility is to be found in recent work by Geller, Cooley, and Hartley (1982). These investigators located professionals who had undergone psychoanalysis and administered a battery of questionnaires designed to elicit their memories of treatment and their current experiences. They found that those who seemed to have benefited most from psychoanalysis and felt they had changed their personality significantly were likely to have continuing memories of an active dialogue or interchange with their therapist, a kind of ongoing therapeutic alliance. Those persons who had not benefited so much were more likely to recall only extreme dependency or attachment to the therapist but not a sense of active, shared participation. Further studies of this type might help us ultimately to identify what features in therapy may lead to longer-term benefits. Long after the conclusion of formal treatment, people can use memories of their earlier therapeutic interaction to help them in facing new dilemmas in their lives.

SUMMARY

1. Personality can be changed by religious conversion, brainwashing, psychotherapy, and other social, cultural, and political forces. History provides striking examples of people who made profound changes in their personalities, usually in connection with religious conversion.

2. Brainwashing usually consists of periods of extreme isolation and sensory deprivation, repetitive sessions with single-minded propaganda messages, and conditioning procedures, such as electric shock. Milder, but still intensive, brainwashing has been reported by people who were converted to some of the new religious sects.

3. Psychotherapy is one of the most important procedures for changing personality. The psychodynamic therapies focus on the private personality and are based largely on the assumption that an intervention that modifies self-awareness and leads to cognitive and emotional restructuring will also lead to changes in the public personality. Behavior therapies focus on the public personality, specific response patterns, and removal of symptoms.

4. The most influential and carefully applied form of psychotherapy has been psychoanalysis, the basic components of which are: (1) free association; (2) a neutral therapist who does not give advice or show emotion; (3) interpretation of resistances and defenses; (4) revival of significant childhood experiences; (5) identification and analysis of transference phenomena; (6) insights about childhood fantasies, misunderstandings, and family relationships; (7) "working through" of defenses and maladaptive reactions; and (8) termination, with freedom from transference distortions and skill in continuing the analytic work on one's own.

5. The standard psychoanalytic interventions are: (1) questions, (2) clarifications, (3) exclamations or comments, (4) confrontations, and (5) interpretations. In general, the treatment hinges on the acquisition of insight and the strengthening of the conscious awareness of the patient.

6. Group psychotherapies treat larger numbers of patients and use the interactions of the group members to achieve and speed up the objectives of dynamic therapy. There is little evidence that they have any great advantage over individual therapy. Other forms of dynamic psychotherapy are transactional analysis and gestalt therapy.

7. Other psychotherapeutic procedures attempt to modify personality through imagery associations. These include the "waking dream" procedure in France and the "guided affective imagery" procedure in Germany.

8. Behavior therapy addresses itself to direct modification of unwanted behavior and makes no assumptions about underlying personality structure. Although behavior therapy has the primary goal of symptom relief, it does open the way for people to try new experiences and thus produces personality change. Among the forms of behavior therapies are: (1) systematic desensitization, (2) aversive conditioning and aversive imagery, (3) modeling and symbolic modeling, (4) flooding, (5) assertiveness training, and (6) cognitive-behavior modification and stress inoculation.

9. The best results in therapy are often obtained when a clear-cut problem is identified and treated with reasonable specificity. Two areas in which research and treatment have been carried out are the problems of (1) expressing and controlling anger and (2) understanding and overcoming shyness.

10. Evaluation of psychotherapy has many problems, including what criteria to use as a measure of success. Three criteria have been used: (1) how the patients feel and describe themselves, (2) how the therapist or other professionals evaluate the changes, and (3) how society in general evaluates the changes. A review of controlled studies of the effects of therapy concluded that a person who has been treated with some form of psychotherapy shows a greater likelihood of improvement than someone who has not been treated. Researchers are beginning to ask not merely whether psychotherapy works, but also (1) by what method of therapy, (2) with

what client, (3) with what kind of therapist, and (4) under what circumstances.

11. At various times it has been hoped that social change would result in personality changes of a whole population. Two Communist revolutions—in the Soviet Union and in China—had this goal. Group structures can be important in influencing personality. With the change in the extended family that formerly lived in close proximity, many people are finding other reference groups.

12. Many people are attracted to religious groups and cults. A study of such groups found that their members were of average intelligence, had few signs of emotional disturbance, came from white middle-class families, and joined the group because of loneliness, drifting, and a lack of meaning of life. All reported positive experiences and real change in themselves.

13. For most people, feelings of alienation and ineffectuality are not so serious as to require joining groups that necessitate a change in life-style and long-term commitment. However, many people benefit from membership in reference groups, such as organized religions, political and social clubs, and hobby and sports clubs.

14. Personality can indeed be changed by strenuous voluntary efforts, by brainwashing, by psychotherapies of many kinds, and by social and political forces. At the same time, however, evidence for personality change is not compelling. In general, personality is remarkably consistent and continuous. Much depends on how personality is defined. If it is defined in terms of the private personality, then change is likely to be small; but if it is defined in terms of the public personality, then more change seems possible. What is needed is long-term follow-ups of persons who have undergone psychotherapy or whose personalities have been changed by religious conversion or membership in sects or social groups.

Glossary

active imagination A method used by Carl G. Jung in which dreams are a starting point for exploring imagery sequences.

activity affect In Ernst Schachtel's theory, a type of affect experience related to joy and excitement and to expressiveness and action.

adolescence The age period from the early teens through ages 18–20; a transitional phase of development from the beginnings of puberty through early adulthood.

affect An emotion, or feeling. Sometimes specifically employed for direct expressions of emotion reflected in speech, facial expression, or body movement. (See also *emotion*.)

affective polarity In Silvan Tomkins' theory, socialization in the family or cultural group that may lead to a lifelong emphasis on either positive or negative emotions.

aggression An overt act that involves an attempt to harm other people or to damage their property. It may also involve an effort at self-harm.

allocentric senses The distance senses of sight and hearing in contrast to the autocentric (close-to-the-body) senses of smell, touch, and taste.

analytic psychology Carl G. Jung's theory of personality, in which human beings are considered to be purposive and seeking self-fulfillment. Jung emphasized the importance of unconscious experience and of cultural symbols.

androgyny The characteristic of being neither stereotypically feminine nor masculine.

anger A basic negative human emotion involving hostile thoughts aroused by extreme persisting frustration of intentions or by continuing unexpected circumstances.

anomie A persistent feeling of isolation from society or one's family and culture.

anxiety A feeling of fear and dread without an obvious reason, generally the result of extreme, usually unconscious, inner conflict.

archetypes In Jung's theory, inherited symbols shared by all human beings that make up the content of the collective unconscious, e.g., earth as mother and nurturer.

arousal An excited state of the organism; also used to contrast with states of inactivity or sleep.

artificial intelligence The study of how to program computers to "think" and to solve problems. The field, also known as cognitive science, in which the rules for programming computers for thought and character-recognition may be able to help shed light on the psychology of thinking and perceiving.

assertiveness training Training and systematic practice in speaking forcefully, making one's wants known to others, and presenting one's opinions.

attachment A sense of closeness between a child and an adult, usually the closeness between mother and child.

attitudes Organized and evaluative groups of opinions or beliefs.

attribution theory Theory that people may attribute success or failure either to external forces or to internal or private events. More generally, human efforts to explain observations or experiences by attributing causes to sequences of events.

autocentric senses The "primitive" senses of smell, taste, and touch. (See also *allocentric senses.*)

autogenics A form of psychotherapy involving deep relaxation and intense imagery.

autonomy In Andreas Angyal's theory, a tendency of human beings to strive toward individuality and independence.

aversive-conditioning therapy Procedure designed to extinguish an unwanted response by mentally pairing the response with a noxious or extremely unpleasant image.

basic anxiety In Karen Horney's theory, the anxiety experienced by a young child in a family that does not attend to its needs.

basic drives (primary drives) Innate bodily signals that life-endangering deficits are present (e.g., hunger or thirst) or that important needs are unfilled (e.g., sexuality). In psychoanalysis, sex and aggression have been viewed as the psychologically significant motivating drives for most human thought and behavior.

behaviorism A psychological approach that studies only observable behavior, such as actions, movements, and the adaptive responses of animals and humans.

behavior modification Therapeutic procedures based on objective learning theory, designed to use repetitive behavior to develop new habits or to extinguish unwanted habits.

belief system A person's organized group of beliefs about causality in the world or how experiences are combined into meaningful units.

biofeedback A method of identifying and attending to recurrent physiological responses to gradually learn to use them as signs of inner distress or to self-regulate often unnoticed basic bodily processes.

b-love (being-love) In Maslow's theory, a term used to describe deep feelings for a person because of that person's inherently attractive self-fulfilling qualities.

body image Mental representation of one's own body.

brainwashing A technique for changing personality and behaviors that involves periods of extreme isolation and sensory deprivation, repetitive questioning, and various conditioning procedures.

cardinal traits or dispositions In Allport's theory, the dominant themes of a person's life (e.g., Napoleon's power-striving).

case study (case history) The detailed examination of an individual, social unit, or event.

castration anxiety In psychoanalytic theory, a boy's fear that his penis will be cut off or lost and a girl's that this loss has already occurred. A fantasy that presumably occurs to most children, male and female, at ages 3–5, the Oedipal period, when they become aware of sexual anatomy and of the sexual relations in the family unit.

catecholamine A type of neurotransmitter, an electrochemical substance transmitted at the junction of two nerve cells in the central nervous system and brain.

catharsis Aristotle's term for the "draining off" of the viewer's intense emotions at the climax of a tragic drama. Used in psychoanalysis to represent the view that the expression of impulses in action, observation, or fantasy will lead to their reduction and to less likelihood of their spontaneous later manifestation.

cathexis An investment of instinctual energy in objects or people. A term used in psychoanalysis to represent intense and specialized attachments.

central traits (central dispositions) In Allport's theory, general or stabilizing factors in people's lives.

chlorpromazine One of the psychoactive drugs widely used in the treatment of schizophrenia.

chumship In Sullivan's theory, same-sex friendships that develop in the juvenile and early adolescent period.

client-centered psychotherapy A form of psychotherapy, developed by Carl Rogers, that is nonevaluative and accepting, and that concentrates on present feelings and relationships.

cognition The processes by which we know the world through sensation, perception, learning, memory, imagery, recall, thinking, and problem-solving.

cognitive-behavior modification Behavior modification using imagery, self-communication and appraisal of situations to develop effective coping strategies.

cognitive map In Tolman's theory, the "picture" of the environment a person uses to attain a goal. More generally, an organized group of images that can help us make sense of a complex physical or social setting and plan effective action.

cognitive orientation Attitudes around which beliefs cluster and which can lead to specific action.

cognitive self Identification of one's own thoughts and images and recognition that others have different thoughts and feelings.

cognitive style A person's own consistent way of processing information.

collective unconscious Jung's term for the part of the human mind that contains a set of capacities and images representative of the experiences of earlier generations. (See also *archetypes*.)

compensation A defense mechanism in which a person avoids a sense of inferiority, shame, or anxiety for various weaknesses by attaining strengths in other areas.

conditioned reflex A response produced by pairing a new stimulus with a stimulus that already produces a well-established response. This reflex is the basis for classical conditioning theories of learning and for certain forms of behavior modification.

conflict A psychological experience or state in which two or more alternative desires, fears, or powerful impulses to thought and action are present simultaneously.

consciousness The state of mental awareness or self-knowledge of personal experience.

construct In Kelly's theory, an organized system of beliefs and expectations about human relations.

correlation A measure of the statistical relation—whether positive, negative, or nonexistent—between two variables.

critical test A specific experiment or other form of data collection designed to disprove a theory or to indicate the relative power of two or more competing theories.

cue A signal that directs a response.

daydream A waking revery, elaboration of memory, or creation of possible future events. Daydreams usually involve thoughts that occur in shifts of attention away from an immediate physical or mental task.

death instinct (thanatos) In Freud's theory, the drive toward death and destruction or aggression that, in Freud's view, is one of the major motives of all human behavior.

debriefing In psychological research, informing a subject of the true nature and purpose of the experiment after an experiment is completed.

defense mechanism In psychoanalytic theory, a mental operation designed to prevent emergence of anxiety-provoking unacceptable or embarrassing drive demands into consciousness.

denial   A basic defense mechanism by which a person denies the existence of a threatening or unacceptable impulse or event.

dependent variable   In research, the response that is expected to change as a result of changes in the independent variables; the measured response in an experiment.

depression   A persisting mood or emotional state involving sadness, reduced physical or mental activity, and often thoughts of regret and self-recrimination.

depth psychology   A field of psychology that examines the private personality and unconscious thoughts; often considered synonymous with psychoanalysis or its offshoots.

desensitization   Procedure for reducing or eliminating anxiety or fear in which a person learns to make an incompatible response to a series of images or experiences of increasingly anxiety- or fear-provoking situations.

dichotic listening   A procedure in which one sound or message is conveyed to one ear and a different sound to the other ear simultaneously.

differential-emotions theory   The theory that there are a limited number of clearly differentiated basic emotions, e.g., joy, interest, anger, and sadness. These are reflected in thought and feeling, facial expression and body posture, and in physiological patterns.

diffuse anxiety   A free-floating and uncontrollable fear produced by the discharge of unacceptable drives or the coming to consciousness of desires that conflict with other desires.

discrimination   Identification of different responses to the same stimuli or of differences in stimuli which yield a common response.

displacement   A defense mechanism that involves a shifting of one's unacceptable feelings on to someone else or to another situation.

dissociation   In Sullivan's theory, one of the security operations in which a person denies or is unaware of the relationship between actually related events.

d-love (deficiency-love)   In Maslow's theory, the attraction for a person occasioned because that person satisfies a state of deprivation—e.g., loving a person chiefly for providing economic security or social status.

dopamine   A neurotransmitter.

dream   An imagery sequence or series of thoughts occurring during sleep. (See *daydream* and *nightdream*.)

drive   A strong inner stimulus that leads to action; usually considered to be biological needs such as hunger or thirst but extended by psychoanalysis to organismic impulses of sexuality and aggression or, in learning theory, to anxiety.

drive-reduction theory   The theory that new responses are acquired when they occur at almost the same time as there is satisfaction or reduction in the intensity of a basic drive.

D-sleep   Sleep accompanied by desynchronous brain-wave activity and associated rapid eye movements; a stage of sleep (also known as REM-sleep) often linked to recall of dreams.

dyad   A two-person group.

dynamic   A term describing the causes of change or, more specifically, the motives or drives that lead people to engage in particular actions or to experience particular kinds of thoughts.

effectance   In White's theory, the need to develop physical and cognitive capacities to their fullest as part of normal growth. Effectance is linked to the concept of competence as a major factor in human motivation.

ego In Freudian theory, the part of the mind responsible for delay of impulse-gratification and self-control, which permit an effective adaptation to reality.

ego ideal In psychoanalytic theory, the idealistic and noble aspirations of the superego (in contrast to its punitive or restrictive aspects).

ego psychology Psychoanalytic theories that emphasize ego functions rather than instinctual drives.

eidetic imagery Ability to experience images with an apparent photographic clarity.

Electra complex See *Oedipus complex*.

embeddedness affect In Schachtel's theory, the emotion experienced by people when wanting to be part of a larger whole, to be satisfied, to withdraw to states of quiescence.

emotion A person's reaction to the rate and complexity or the appraisal of threat of new information manifested through facial expression and bodily gestures, physiological responses, and awareness of feelings or thoughts. (See also *affect*.)

emotional inoculation See *stress inoculation*.

empathy The ability to feel what someone else is experiencing, to assume another's point of view.

encoding Translating complex sensory patterns into cognitive or neutral structures susceptible to brain storage and later retrieval.

enzyme A substance in the body that produces other substances by catalytic action.

epinephrine (adrenalin) A hormone produced by the adrenal gland and also secreted at nerve endings.

episodic memory Storage in long-term memory of events, faces, nature scenes, etc. In Tulving's cognitive theory, used to provide a contrast with verbal or semantic memory.

eros In psychoanalytic theory, the sexual desires or instincts, the life-building principle of love, desire for reproduction, and sexual expression.

ethology A field of research involving observation of the behavior of animals in their natural habitats.

existentialism A philosophy emphasizing freedom of choice and responsibility for one's actions.

expectancy An attitude that determines behavior by anticipating that certain goals will be achieved and that certain events have a greater probability of occurrence in a particular set of circumstances than in others.

exploitative personality In Fromm's theory, a personality style that seeks to possess what others own and is willing to use force and guile to obtain possessions and power.

expressive behavior The movements, gestures, and speaking mannerisms that define the public personality. In Maslow's theory, behavior motivated by existing, growing, and self-actualization rather than by conflict and biological or psychological deficiency.

extinction Disappearance of a conditioned response after repeated presentation of a conditioned stimulus without the unconditioned stimulus or of a learned response that has not been appropriately rewarded (reinforced) on a continuing basis.

extravert Jung's term for people who are oriented toward the external environment and the reactions of other people rather than towards their own feelings and thoughts; can refer either to thinking or to social orientation.

extrinsic motivation Directed activity brought about by desire or expectation of a reward from external sources rather than from one's bodily impulses or private thoughts (intrinsic motivation).

factor analysis A statistical method used to derive common clusters or factors presumed to underlie a larger number of measures.

fantasy The process of imagining objects or future events, especially those that are unlikely to occur.

fear A strong negative emotion experienced in the presence of danger or possible pain.

feeling In Jung's theory, the experience of positive or negative emotions about an object or person. One of the four basic styles of experiencing the world, with thinking, sensing, and intuiting.

fictive goals In Adler's theory, the mental images that people use to guide their lives.

field dependence Habitual reliance on the visual environment or the external world for information on which to base judgment or action.

field independence Habitual reliance on bodily cues or inner experience rather than environmental cues for information on which to base judgment or action.

fixation In psychoanalysis, a state in which a person remains attached to persons, objects, or activities more suitable to an earlier stage of psychological development.

flight into reality An increase in random motor or perceptual activity used as a defense to interfere with awareness of threatening events or thoughts.

flooding A form of therapy similar to *systematic desensitization* but with more extreme emotion and intensive practice.

forgetting In Dollard and Miller's theory, the loss of a previously learned response because it was not practiced.

free association A technique used primarily in psychoanalysis in which a patient says everything that comes to mind during the therapy session without any restrictions whatsoever.

frustration Prevention of an individual's efforts to satisfy a bodily need or the blocking of attainment of a psychological goal.

functional autonomy Allport's term to describe the tendency of a developed motive to become independent of the original underlying childhood drive that may have occasioned it.

galvanic skin response (GSR) Electrical reactions on the skin that are measured by a galvanometer to estimate general emotional arousal or reactivity.

gender identity Awareness of being male or female; often used to reflect a more general awareness in contrast to the emphasis on specific sexual activities of males or females.

generalization In learning theory, the transfer of learning from one situation to another, usually along a gradient of relative similarity of the situations.

Gestalt psychology A school of psychology based on the principle that psychological phenomena are organized wholes or "Gestalts."

Gestalt therapy A form of therapy developed by Frederick Perls intended to expand the patient's awareness of self, feelings, and potential through attention to broader experiences in contrast to the "analytic" tendencies of psychoanalysis or learning theories.

goal gradient Gradient changes in response strength dependent on distance from a goal and positive or negative reinforcement.

gradient The amount of slope in a learning curve.

guided affective imagery A method of therapy in which the person imagines being in some natural setting and then develops a series of mental pictures so that an "imagery trip" makes up the treatment periods (Hanscarl Leuner).

hoarding personality A personality style described by Erich Fromm in which a person's life-style is characterized by saving and owning possessions.

homonomy In Angyal's theory, the human tendency to strive toward becoming part of a large whole, such as the family, nation, or world order.

homophobia Fear of homosexuality.

humanistic psychology A group of schools of thought that emphasize the experience of self, the direct consciousness of the human being, and the growth or actualization of potentialities in contrast with the drive-reduction or conflict-resolution emphasis of the psychodynamic or learning theories.

hypnosis A state of sharply restricted consciousness in which the individual is highly responsive to suggestions of the hypnotist.

hypnotic susceptibility The ease and depth with which individuals enter into hypnosis as measured by special test procedures.

id In psychoanalytic theory, the part of the psychic structure that is closely tied to the biological drives and is the source of mental energy. It operates on the pleasure principle.

ideal self The part of the self that represents what a person would most like to be or hope to become.

identification A defense mechanism often used to avoid feelings of inferiority and shame by imitating, or identifying with, the behavior or values of another person.

identity crisis In Erikson's theory, a major crisis of psychosocial development in which an adolescent or young adult tries to establish a sense of personal identity and meaningful goals.

idiographic approach A method of personality research that studies the uniqueness of each individual or particular event.

image A mental reproduction of external events, objects, or persons.

imagery The capacity for mentally duplicating, in a roughly analogous form, what is experienced through the sense organs.

importers persons who tend to introduce additional material when recalling a story (I. H. Paul).

incentive Something that arouses an individual to action; a goal.

independent variable The variable in an experiment that is systematically changed to determine what influence it has on a dependent variable.

individual psychology Alfred Adler's theory of personality, so called to emphasize the unique development of each person.

instinct A built-in or innate tendency to engage in specific actions.

intellectualization A defense mechanism in which anxiety is avoided by dealing with conflictual material in a detached, extremely rational way.

interest A pleasant emotion that motivates action toward an object for exploration or that stimulates thoughts about causes or meanings.

introvert Jung's term for people who are oriented toward their own feelings and thoughts rather than the external environment; also used for person preferring solitary to social activities.

intuition In Jung's theory, the subliminal and unconscious perception of the meaning or intent of information. One of the four basic functions of the mind, with thinking, sensing, feeling.

joy A positive emotion that involves self-contentment and satisfaction with others and with life itself.

latency period In psychoanalytic theory, the period after the Oedipal phase at about age 5 or 6 when children repress all sexual impulses and ally themselves with same-sex groups.

law of effect A generalization that an animal or human learns more quickly if responses made in association with other actions are satisfying.

learned helplessness A state of acquired apathy or sadness that follows repeated frustrating or painful circumstances beyond one's control.

learning dilemma   A situation in which learned response is not reinforced and several other trial responses are evoked.

level of aspiration   Lewin's term for the standard by which people judge their performance; an experimental approach to studying changes in motivation for achievement.

life crises   In Erikson's theory, the series of problems everyone faces while passing through the eight psychosocial stages.

life-styles   In Adler's theory, a person's consistent pattern of relating to others or to society.

life support   Themes present in childhood that persist into later years.

locus of control   In Rotter's theory, a style of belief in which people attribute causality (a) to their own actions (Internals) or (b) to action over which they have no control (Externals).

long sampler   A person who waits until information is complete within a context or who matches information against previous information before making an overt response (Donald Broadbent).

long-term memory   A hypothesized stage in the memory sequence in which material, after passing through short-term memory, is stored relatively permanently for later retrieval.

marketing personality   A personality style described by Erich Fromm in which a person's orientation is toward selling a product or service or one's personality regardless of the quality.

masculine protest   In Adler's theory, a term used to describe people who overcompensate in their struggle to attain power.

modeling   A procedure to eliminate unwanted behavior by observing others engaging in the desired behavior or by imagining such activity (vicarious modeling).

moderator variable   A variable in an experiment that has an effect on the dependent variable while varying itself in relation to an independent variable.

motive   Bodily responses and thoughts that give a specific direction and intensity to general actions; goals or needs.

neo-Freudians   Psychoanalysts who came after Freud and who, in general, placed more emphasis on sociocultural influences and ego functions in the development of personality.

neurotransmitter   Chemical substances secreted by nerve endings that are increasingly being related to emotional behavior.

nomothetic approach   A method of personality study that is designed to find general principles applicable to many people rather than just to specific individuals.

nondirective psychotherapy   See *client-centered psychotherapy*.

norepinephrine (noradrenalin)   A hormone produced by the adrenal gland and also secreted at nerve endings.

norms   Quantified values of responses that are representative of a group, often broken down by age, education, social status, and other characteristics.

nuclear scene   An especially significant event with strong emotional components, usually experienced in childhood, that may be a key unit in the formation of personality (Silvan S. Tomkins).

object-relations school   An offshoot of Freudian psychoanalysis that emphasizes childhood motivation as based on attachment to objects, especially to parents and the degree of differentiation or emphasis on mental representation of parental figures.

objects   In psychoanalysis, a term referring to all the people, bodily parts, or psychological situations that growing children relate to gratification of their impulses or in which they invest (cathect) mental energy.

observational learning Learning based on the observation of the actions of a real (live) or symbolic model.

obsessional substitution In Sullivan's theory, a security operation involving use of irrelevant concerns to avoid anxiety and insecurity.

Oedipus complex In psychoanalytic theory, a quasi-sexual attraction to the parent of the opposite sex, specifically the boy's attraction to his mother during the fourth and fifth years of life. A desire to displace the father-figure is a feature of this psychosexual stage of development. (The female form is termed the Electra complex.)

organismic psychology An approach to psychology that emphasizes the whole and undivided individual and the person's striving toward self-actualization.

paradigm Style of experimental design.

parataxic distortion In Sullivan's theory, a mode of thinking characteristic of early childhood development before the child knows about causality, logical sequences of events, and the differences between accident and determinism.

peak experience Maslow's term to describe a temporary experience of fulfillment, joy, wonder, and self-actualization.

penis envy In psychoanalytic theory, the envy Freud believed all little girls and grown women feel for the penis, and their sense of loss because they do not have one.

persona In Jung's theory, the side of the personality that people present to others.

personal constructs In Kelly's theory, the tendency for people to organize what they perceive into their own individual constructs.

personality The patterns of public actions, gestures and statements or nonverbal expressions, as well as the private motives, wishes, beliefs, attitudes, day and night dreams, and styles of organizing information or experiencing emotions that delineate the unique individuality of each person in a given society.

personal unconscious In Jung's theory, the middle level of the mind made up of unconscious content based on experience and desire. (See also *collective unconscious*.)

personifications In Sullivan's theory, internalized mental pictures of acceptable attitudes or behaviors based on experiences with adults in early childhood.

personology The study of people, usually through tests and interviews, by following them in their different life situations so as to focus on lives through time.

phenomenology The theory that emphasizes the immediacy and uniqueness of human experience.

pleasure center An area of the brain which if stimulated electrically leads an animal to act as if it has been rewarded.

pleasure principle The immediate satisfaction of drives and wishes; in Freudian theory, the principle on which the id operates.

primary drives See *basic drives*.

primary-process thinking A concept proposed by Freud to describe primitive childlike thinking that is concrete, pictorial in quality, and oriented toward direct satisfaction of basic drives such as hunger, thirst, sex, and aggression.

principle of opposites In Jung's theory, the concept that for every conscious wish and attitude, an alternative wish and attitude is present in unconscious thought.

private personality The private thoughts, feelings, and images that are part of each individual's experience.

private self-consciousness Self-awareness of one's own body, thoughts, and dreams (Arnold Buss).

projection In psychoanalytic theory, a defense mechanism by which an unacceptable desire or thought is attributed to someone else.

projective method A psychological test using a subject's reactions to ambiguous stimuli to reveal the subject's private personality, inner feelings, wishes, and underlying motives.

proprium Allport's term for the self, the aspects of the personality that are peculiarly one's own and that make for individuality.

prosocial behavior Behavior characterized by an interest in, and concern for other, e.g., helpfulness sharing, cooperation.

prototaxic Sullivan's term to describe a mode of thinking characteristic of an infant's preverbal experiences.

psychoanalysis A theory and a form of therapy originally developed by Sigmund Freud, which emphasizes the important role of unconscious wishes and motives in the early development and later expression of the human personality.

psychohistory Biography written from the psychoanalytic point of view.

psychometrics Study of psychological testing or mental measurement.

psychosexual stages In psychoanalytic theory, the stages of development—oral, anal, phallic, and genital—through which every child must pass and which remain at the core of personality variation.

psychosocial stages In Erikson's theory, a series of eight life stages, each with different problems and crises, through which persons must pass as they go through life.

public personality A person's external and overt appearance and behavior, which are visible to others and which are used to characterize personal styles.

public self-consciousness A personality predisposition based on an attitude of self-awareness in public situations (Arnold Buss).

punishment center An area of the brain which if stimulated electrically leads an animal to act as if it had been punished.

rationalization In psychoanalytic theory, a defense mechanism by which unacceptable desires or actions are disguised or are made acceptable by being assigned plausible or rational explanations which may not actually explain the underlying motives involved.

R data Personality data based on observations by outsiders of the ongoing behavior in normal settings of people's daily lives.

reaction formation A defense mechanism involving avoidance of unacceptable thoughts or intentions by thinking or behaving in a way opposite to one's underlying or unconscious intention.

reality principle In Freudian theory, the principle on which the ego operates; it provides an awareness of the constraints on expression of drives from conflicting wishes or from dangers of the outside world.

receptive character A personality style described by Erich Fromm in which persons need support from others and depend on what is given to them.

reductionism An approach to science that analyzes complex phenomena into simple, elementary components; in psychology, it refers to attempts to describe behaviors in stimulus-response or physiological terms.

reference group A group with which a person identifies and assumes some of the characteristics as part of a sense of self, e.g., a patriotic or religious group.

regression A defense mechanism by which an individual avoids the thought or experience of threatening situations by reverting to a style of life or thought more characteristic of childhood or an earlier stage of development.

reinforcement In learning theory, a consequence that leads an act to be repeated; often synonymous with reward.

reinforcement schedule A plan or program indicating how and when a subject will be reinforced or rewarded.

reliability In psychological testing, the stability of a test on repeated administrations or its internal consistency as established statistically.

REM-sleep Rapid-eye-movement stage of deep sleep usually associated with a particular type of brain-wave activity (EEG-Stage 1). Also known as D-sleep or paradoxical sleep it is associated with more frequent reports of vivid dreaming than other sleep stages.

repression In psychoanalytic theory, a basic defense mechanism by which the memory or images of a desired object or of a conflictual situation are forgotten or expelled from consciousness. Repression forms the basis of the unconscious.

reserpine A psychoactive drug or tranquilizer used to treat mental illness.

resistance In psychoanalysis, problems in producing free associations or other blockages that prevent progress in psychotherapy. Usually attributed to unconscious defenses.

response set A tendency or attitude to follow a certain pattern in responding to test items, such as answering every question "yes."

reticular system A group of structures in the brain that are linked to wakefulness and activation.

role-playing A technique used in research and therapy in which people assume the role of another person and act out how the other person would behave or anticipate their own actions in future situations by enactments.

satisfaction In Sullivan's theory, the gratification of basic bodily drives.

schizophrenia A severe form of mental illness characterized by distortions of thinking, social isolation, and sometimes by hallucinations.

script theory A theory that people deal with situations on the basis of preconceived anticipations with which they can fill in the details when they are presented with limited information. An alternative to stimulus-response association theories of memory by emphasizing that all thought involves more complex storylike structures.

S data Personality data based on self-reports such as questionnaire responses.

secondary-process thinking Freud's term for mature thought involving the capacity for abstract thinking, the precise use of language, and the ability to anticipate consequences of one's actions.

secondary traits In Gordon Allport's theory, factors in personality that emerge in specific situations.

security operations In Sullivan's theory, the ways a child develops to avoid anxiety provoked by insecurity and uncertainty; similar to defense mechanisms.

selective inattention A process by which a person apparently forgets an unpleasant situation either by not noticing it in the first place or by not attending to the appropriate information in memory that might recall it.

self The image of oneself or a set of beliefs one has about one's personal goals, capacities, or values.

self-actualization Maslow's term to describe behavior characterized by a complete immersion in experiences, development of a sense of self, directness and honesty, peak experiences, and awareness of one's own failings.

self-concept A person's view or belief system of herself or himself.

self-consciousness Awareness of ongoing inner experience.

self-efficacy An individual's beliefs about his or her own effectiveness or capacity to reach a particular goal (Albert Bandura).

self-esteem A feeling or attitude of self-worth.

semantic memory Storage of meanings, such as verbal labels or abstracts concepts (Endel Tulving).

sensation In Jung's theory, the direct realistic perception of the environment. One of the four basic functions of the mind, with thinking, feeling, and intuiting.

sensory register A first stage in the cognitive process in which sensations from the environment enter the cognitive system.

sensory self The direct concrete self that the senses perceive, e.g., one's body seen directly or in a mirror.

separation anxiety A child's fear or anxiety of being separated from its mother or caregiver.

serotonin A neurotransmitter.

sex-role stereotypes Rigid, often inaccurate beliefs about the behavior and attitudes characteristic of males and females and the differences between them.

sex-typed behavior Behavior considered appropriate for one sex but not for the other.

sexual identity A person's sense of being male or female and of the social and sexual functions believed to be associated with his or her sex.

shadow In Jung's theory, the suppressed opposite side of the personality which may emerge in dreams or fantasies.

shaping Systematic control of learning and the recurrent responses by controlling the schedule of reinforcement.

short sampler A person who reacts immediately to each new stimulus by choosing the most immediate match from long-term memory (Donald Broadbent).

short-term memory A hypothesized stage in the memory sequence in which material from the environment is held briefly before either decaying or being processed into long-term memory.

situational approach An approach to learning and personality through analysis of social settings and their characteristics.

sleep cycle A consistent and cyclical pattern of brain-wave activity and rapid eye movements during sleep.

social anxiety Distress or discomfort about a series of situations in which one is being scrutinized by others (Arnold Buss).

socialization The process whereby a child learns to get along with, and to behave like, others in the family group, neighborhood, culture, or society.

social-learning theory Theory that most human learning takes place in social situations and that observational learning and reinforcement through interaction with other people are crucial to the way behavior is organized.

source trait Cattell's term for basic private tendencies for thought and action.

S sleep Sleep accompanied by synchronous brain-wave activity; also known as EEG-Stages 2–4 or non-REM sleep (Ernest Hartmann).

stage theory Erikson's theory that at each phase of life people confront critical stages they must cope with.

state anxiety (A-state) Anxiety evoked by specific situations.

stream of thought (stream of consciousness) The ongoing flow of our thoughts, images, and interior monologues during the waking state (William James).

stress A physiological and psychological state resulting from present or imminent dangerous or unpleasant events or from our estimate of the serious threat or risk of specific interpersonal or environmental circumstances.

stress inoculation   A procedure in which coping strategies are learned and thus have a preventive effect on possible maladjustment to new stress.

sublimation   In psychoanalytic theory, a defense mechanism by which primitive impulses and unacceptable thoughts or behavior are displaced or transmitted into socially valued forms, such as art, creativity or altruism.

superego   In psychoanalytic theory, the component of the mind that focuses on the moral commands, ideals, values, and prohibitions incorporated from parents or from representatives of society or religion.

surface trait   Cattell's term for observable traits or public manifestations of personality.

symbolic modeling   A procedure to eliminate fears and other unwanted behavior by imagining others engaging in the desired behavior, then substituting oneself in the imagined scene.

synapse   The region at which a nerve impulse passes from one nerve ending to another.

syntaxic mode   In Sullivan's theory, a mode of thought involving logical thought, awareness of causality, and ability to communicate in a way that is consensually valid for a given society.

systematic desensitization   A behavior therapy using relaxation and sequenced positive imagery to reduce anxiety associated with specific actions or settings.

T data   Personality data based on information in structured laboratory situations, e.g., reactions to a specific experiment involving delayed gratification, expression of aggression, and so on.

temperament   Susceptibility to emotional situations, strength of response, persistence, and intensity of moods, all of which may be part of the constitutional or hereditary makeup of an individual.

territoriality   An innate tendency for animals, especially males, to establish and maintain an area for the organization of their life cycle of mating and reproduction.

test anxiety   Extreme anxiety when taking or faced with the prospect of taking a test.

thanatos   See *death instinct*.

thinking   In Jung's theory, the orderly, rational sequence of appraisal of information. One of the four basic functions of the mind, with feeling, sensing, and intuiting.

Third Force   A term often used to describe the approach to psychology that emphasizes the self, personal experiences, and wholeness in presumed contrast with the reductionism of psychoanalysis, on the one hand, and learning theory on the other.

trait anxiety (A-trait)   A person's characteristic level of anxiety across a variety of situations.

trait theory   The theory that the human personality can be described in terms of a person's specific enduring characteristics.

transactional analysis   A form of therapy developed by Eric Berne based on the concept that everyone behaves sometimes like a child, sometimes like an adult, and sometimes like a parent, and that people crystallize their behavior around "games" that formerly were rewarding to them.

transference   In psychoanalysis, the tendency for patients to develop strong feelings of affection (positive transference) or of anger and hostility (negative transference) toward the psychoanalyst.

type-A personality   A highly competitive and aggressive person; a characteristic style observed in persons at risk for coronary disease or other physical ailments associated with stress.

unconscious   The part of the personality that is not open to conscious awareness and of which the ego is unaware.

validity The accuracy with which a psychological test measures what it is intended to measure.

variable Whatever is measured or systematically changed in an experiment.

verbalizers Persons who prefer to encode information in verbal form, and who emphasize verbal formulations and abstract terms when retrieving memories of specific events.

vicarious modeling See *symbolic modeling*.

visualizers Persons who prefer to encode material in visual form and who describe memories in concrete, visual terms.

waking-dream procedure See *guided affective imagery*.

wish-fulfillment In psychoanalytic theory, presumed reduction in tension by imagining a satisfying situation.

Copyrights and Acknowledgments

CHAPTER 1   Box: "The Unsociable Man": Reprinted by permission of Warren Anderson.   Figure 1-1   Reprinted by permission of H. J. Eysenck and Springer Verlag.

CHAPTER 2   Figure 2-1   Reprinted by permission of *American Scientist*.

CHAPTER 4   Figure 4-1   Reprinted by permission of McGraw-Hill, Inc.   Figure 4-2   Reprinted by permission of Aldine/Atherton and A. Bandura.

CHAPTER 6   Figure 6-1   Reprinted by permission of Clark University Press.   Figure 6-2   Reprinted by permission of W. W. Norton & Company, Inc. Copyright © 1955 by George A. Kelly.   Figure 6-3   Reprinted by permission of G. A. Miller, E. Galanter, and K. H. Pribram.   Figure 6-4   Copyright © 1962 by Springer Publishing Company, Inc., New York. Used by permission.

CHAPTER 7   Table 7-1   Copyright © 1982 by St. Martin's Press, Inc. Adapted from J. N. Butcher, *Objective Personality Measurement* (Morristown, NJ: General Learning Press, 1971).   Table 7-2   Copyright 1967 by Duke University Press, Durham, NC. Reprinted by permission. All rights reserved.   Table 7-3   Copyright © 1982 by St. Martin's Press, Inc.   Figure 7-1   Reprinted by permission of Research Psychologists Press, Inc.   Figure 7-2   A modification of the original Rorschach card. Reproduced by permission of Hans Huber Publishers.   Figure 7-3   Reprinted by permission of Harvard University Press. Copyright © 1943 by the President and Fellows of Harvard College. Copyright © 1971 by Henry A. Murray.

CHAPTER 8   Figure 8-1   Photos © Martin Eiger.   Figure 8-2   Reprinted by permission of Yale University Press. Figure 8-3   Reprinted by permission of S. S. Tomkins and P. Ekman. Photos 1 and 3 by Edward Gallob.   Table 8-1   Data included by permission of C. E. Izard and P. Ekman.   Figure 8-4   Reprinted by permission of P. Ekman. Table 8-2   Data included by permission of N. Livson and Random House, Inc.

CHAPTER 9   Figure 9-2   © Ron Doty.   Figure 9-3   Reprinted by permission of International Universities Press, Inc. Figure 9-4   Copyright 1977, American Educational Research Association, Washington, D.C. Reprinted by permission. Figure 9-5   Reprinted by permission of International Universities Press, Inc.

CHAPTER 10   Excerpt from *Ulysses* Copyright 1914, 1918 by Margaret Caroline Anderson and renewed 1942, 1946 by Nora Joseph Joyce. Reprinted by permission of Random House, Inc. Reprinted also by permission of The Bodley Head.   Figure 10-1   Copyright © 1971 by Scientific American, Inc. All rights reserved.   Figure 10-2   (*Guernica*) © Spadem, Paris/Vaga, New York 1984.   Figure 10-3   Reprinted by permission of Academic Press.   Figure 10-4 Copyright 1981 by the American Psychological Association. Reprinted by permission of the authors.   Table 10-1 Reprinted by permission of J. R. Hilgard.

CHAPTER 11   Figure 11-1   Copyright © 1976 by Springer Publishing Company, Inc., New York. Used by permission. Figure 11-2   Copyright 1975 by the American Psychological Association. Reprinted by permission of the authors. Figures 11-3 and 11-4   Copyright © 1980 by W. H. Freeman and Company. All rights reserved.   Figure 11-5 Copyright 1981 by the American Psychological Association. Reprinted by permission of A. Bandura and D. H. Schunk.

CHAPTER 12   Table 12-1   Reprinted by permission of T. H. Holmes. Copyright 1967 by Pergamon Press, Ltd.   Figure 12-1   Reprinted by permission of Academic Press.   Box: "A Hostage Remembers"   Copyright 1980 by Newsweek, Inc. All rights reserved. Excerpt reprinted by permission.   Tables 12-2, 12-3, 12-4   Reprinted by permission of M. J. Horowitz.

CHAPTER 13   Figure 13-1   Reprinted by permission of C. E. Izard and Academic Press.   Figure 13-2   Reprinted by permission of Plenum Publishing Corporation.   Figure 13-3   Reproduced by permission of C. E. Izard.   Figure

13-4 Copyright 1979 by the American Psychological Association. Adapted by permission of the publisher and D. A. Weinberger.

CHAPTER 14 Figure 14-1 Reproduced by permission of C. E. Izard. Figure 14-2 Reprinted by permission of Plenum Publishing Corporation and R. A. Baron. Figure 14-4 Reprinted by permission of Plenum Publishing Corporation and R. A. Baron. Figure 14-5 Reprinted by permission of Stanford University Press. Figure 14-6 Copyright 1979 by the American Psychological Corporation. Adapted by permission of D. Olweus.

CHAPTER 15 Figure 15-1 Reprinted by permission of Dorsey Press. Tables 15-1 and 15-2 Reprinted by permission of M. Csikszentmihalyi and Jossey-Bass. Figure 15-2 Reprinted by permission of M. Csikszentmihalyi and Jossey-Bass. Box: "A Synectic Group at Work" Copyright © 1970 by George M. Prince. Reprinted by permission of Harper & Row, Publishers, Inc. Figure 15-3 Reprinted by permission of L. R. Huesmann, G. Levinger, and Academic Press. Table 15-3 Reprinted by permission of E. D. Macklin.

CHAPTER 16 Figure 16-2 Reprinted by permission of John Wiley & Sons. Table 16-2 Reprinted by permission of John Wiley & Sons. Figure 16-3 © The Society for Research in Child Development, Inc. Table 16-3 Copyright 1981 by the American Psychological Association. Reprinted by permission of T. J. Berndt.

CHAPTER 17 Table 17-1 Reprinted by permission of Lawrence Erlbaum Associates, Inc. Figure 17-1 Copyright 1980 by the American Psychological Association. Reprinted by permission of D. Storms.

CHAPTER 18 Table 18-1 Reprinted by permission of M. L. Smith, G. V. Glass, T. I. Miller, and The Johns Hopkins University Press.

UNNUMBERED PHOTO ACKNOWLEDGMENTS

Page 2 From the MGM release *The Brothers Karamazov*, © 1957 Loew's Incorporated and Avon Productions, Inc.; **5** Robin Risque; **26** Mary Evans Picture Library/Sigmund Freud Copyrights/Basic Books; **34** Copyright © by Universal Pictures, a Division of Universal City Studios, Inc., courtesy MCA Publishing, a Division of MCA Communications, Inc.; **41** a Selznick International Picture (released through United Artists), © 1945; **51** Culver Pictures; **54** United Artists Corporation © 1936/Museum of Modern Art Film Archives; **63, 65** courtesy William A. White Institute; **92, 93** courtesy the Film Study Center, Harvard University; **104** from the United Artists release *The Miracle Worker*, © 1962 Playfilm Productions, Inc.; **112** Copyright Oslo Kommunes Kunstsamlinger Munich-Museet; **119** Abigail Heyman/Archive Pictures; **128** courtesy Sheldon J. Korchin; **132** Movietone News, Inc.; **134** Sylvia Plachy/Archive; **216** Jean-Claude Lejeune/Stock, Boston; **234** © 1977 United Feature Syndicate, Inc.; **237** George Gardner; **256** Peter Menzel/Stock, Boston; **262** Earl Dotter/Archive; **288** Gary Wolinsky/Stock, Boston; **290** Melanie Kaestner/Zephyr; **316** Stock, Boston; **319** courtesy The Archives, The Coca-Cola Company; **331** Len Rue, Jr./Photo Researchers; **360** Don Bartletti/Focus West; **383** Doris Pinney; **391** Ulrike Welsch/Stock, Boston; **397** David S. Strickler/The Picture Cube; **413** Jules Feiffer. Dist. Publishers Hall Syndicate; **414** Donald Dietz/Stock, Boston; **427** Hildegard Adler; **437** Mary Evans Picture Library/Sigmund Freud Copyrights/Edmund Engelman; **449** Charles Gatewood/Stock, Boston

References and Index to Authors of Works Cited

The numbers in boldface following each reference give the text page where the work is cited by author and date of publication.

Abramson, L. Y., Seligman, M. E. P., & Teasdale, J. D. (1978). Learned helplessness in humans: Critique and reformulation. *Journal of Abnormal Psychology, 87*, 49–74. **284**

Ahern, G. L. (1981). Differential lateralization for positive and negative emotion in the human brain: EEG spectral analysis. Unpublished doctoral dissertation, Yale University. **184, 206**

Aldis, O. (1975). *Play fighting.* New York: Academic Press. **341**

Alker, H. A. (1976). Is personality situationally specific or intrapsychically consistent? In N. S. Endler & D. Magnusson (Eds.), *Interactional psychology and personality.* Washington, DC: Hemisphere. **408, 411**

Allen, G. J. (1971). Effectiveness of study counseling and desensitization in alleviating test anxiety in college students. *Journal of Abnormal Psychology, 77*, 282–89. **307**

Alloy, L., & Abramson, L. (1979). Judgment of contingency in depressed and nondepressed students: Sadder but wiser? *Journal of Experimental Psychology: General, 108*, 441–85. **261, 284, 363**

Allport, G. (1937). *Personality: A psychological interpretation.* New York: Holt, Rinehart & Winston. **13**

Allport, G. (1961). *Pattern and growth in personality.* New York: Holt, Rinehart & Winston. **385**

Amsterdam, B. (1972). Mirror self-image reactions before age two. *Developmental Psychology, 5*, 297. **254**

Anderson, W. (Trans.) (1970). *Theophrastus: The character sketches.* Kent, OH: Kent State University Press. **7**

Angyal, A. (1965). *Neurosis and treatment: A holistic theory.* New York: Wiley. **101, 102**

Antrobus, J. S., Coleman, R., & Singer, J. L. (1967). Signal detection performance by subjects differing in predisposition to daydreaming. *Journal of Consulting Psychology, 31*, 487–91. **230**

Antrobus, J. S., Singer, J. L., Goldstein, S., & Fortang, W. (1970). Mindwandering and cognitive strucure. *Transactions of the New York Academy of Science, Series II, 32*, 242–52. **230**

Antrobus, J. S., Singer, J. L., & Greenberg, S. (1966). Studies in the stream of consciousness: Experimental enhancement and suppression of spontaneous cognitive processes. *Perceptual and Motor Skills, 23*, 399–417. **230**

Archibald, H. C., & Tuddenham, R. D. (1965). Persistent stress reaction after combat. *Archives of General Psychiatry, 12*, 475–81. **288**

Ardrey, R. (1966). *The territorial imperative: A personal inquiry into the animal origins of property and nations.* New York: Atheneum Publishers. **330**

Arkin, A. M., Antrobus, J. S., & Ellman, S. J. (Eds.). (1978). *The mind in sleep: Psychology and psychophysiology.* Hillsdale, NJ: Erlbaum. **240**

Arnkoff, D. B., & Mahoney, M. J. (1981). The role of perceived control in psychopathology. In L. C. Perlmuter & R. A. Monty (Eds.), *Choice and perceived control.* Hillsdale, NJ: Erlbaum. **443**

Atkinson, J. W. (1981). Studying personality in the context of an advanced motivational psychology. *American Psychologist, 36,* 117–28. **164**

Ausubel, D. P. (1958). *Theory and problems of child development.* New York: Grune & Stratton. **341**

Bakan, P. (1969). Hypnotizability, laterality of eye movement and functional brain asymmetry. *Perceptual and Motor Skills, 28,* 927–32. **238**

Bakan, P. (1971). The eyes have it. *Psychology Today, 4,* 64–67, 96. **206**

Bakan, P. (1978). Two streams of consciousness: A typological approach. In K. S. Pope & J. L. Singer (Eds.), *The stream of consciousness.* New York: Plenum Press. **206, 207**

Baltes, P. B. (1979). Life span developmental psychology: Observations on history and theory. In P. B. Baltes & C. Brim, Jr. (Eds.), *Life span development and behavior* (Vol. 2). New York: Holt, Rinehart & Winston. **379**

Bandura, A. (1969). *Principles of behavior modification.* New York: Holt, Rinehart & Winston. **442**

Bandura, A. (1971). *Psychological modeling: Conflicting theories.* Chicago: Aldine/Atherton. **90**

Bandura, A. (1973). *Aggression: A social learning analysis.* Englewood Cliffs, NJ: Prentice-Hall. **334, 335, 336, 340, 345**

Bandura, A. (1977). Self-efficacy: Toward a unifying theory of behavioral change. *Psychological Review, 84,* 191–215. **267, 287**

Bandura, A. (1978). The self system in reciprocal determinism. *American Psychologist, 33,* 344–58. **95, 443**

Bandura, A., & Mischel, W. (1965). Modification of self-imposed delay of reward through exposure to live and symbolic models. *Journal of Personality and Social Psychology, 2,* 698–705. **398**

Bandura, A., & Schunk, D. H. (1981). Cultivating competence, self-efficacy, and intrinsic interest through proximal self-motivation. *Journal of Personality and Social Psychology, 41,* 586–98. **267, 268**

Bandura, A., & Walters, R. H. (1959). *Adolescent aggression: A study of the influence of child-training practices and family interrelationships.* New York: Ronald Press. **91**

Bandura, A., & Walters, R. H. (1963). *Social learning and personality development.* New York: Holt, Rinehart & Winston. **91**

Bannister, D., & Agnew, J. (1976). The child's construing of self. In J. K. Cole & A. W. Landfield (Eds.), *Nebraska Symposium on Motivation* (Vol. 24). Lincoln: University of Nebraska Press. **395**

Barber, T. X. (1979). Suggested ("hypnotic") behavior: The trance paradigm versus an alternative paradigm. In E. Fromm & R. E. Shor (Eds.), *Hypnosis: Developments in research and new perspectives.* New York: Aldine Press. **236, 239**

Barber, T. X., & Glass, L. B. (1962). Significant factors in hypnotic behavior. *Journal of Abnormal and Social Psychology, 64,* 222–28. **237**

Barber, T. X., & Wilson, S. C. (1979). Guided imagining and hypnosis: Theoretical and empirical overlap and convergence in a new creative imagination scale. In A. Sheikh & J. Schaffer (Eds.), *The potential of fantasy and imagination.* New York: Bradon House. **239**

Bard, M. (1971). The study and modification of intra-familial violence. In J. L. Singer (Ed.), *The control of aggression and violence.* New York: Academic Press. **324**

Barker, R. G., Dembo, T., & Lewin, K. (1943). Frustration and regression. In R. G. Barker, J. S. Krounin & H. F. Wright (Eds.), *Child behavior and development.* New York: McGraw-Hill. **278**

Baron, R. A. (1977). *Human aggression.* New York: Plenum Press. **277, 328, 336, 340.**

Barrios, M., & Singer, J. L. (1981). The treatment of creative blocks: A comparison of waking imagery, hypnotic dream and rational discussion techniques. *Imagination, Cognition and Personality, 1,* 89–116. **258**

Barron, F. (1956). The disposition toward originality. In *First research conference on the identification of creative scientific talent.* Salt Lake City: University of Utah Press. **366**

Barron, F. (1957). Originality in relation to personality and intellect. *Journal of Personality, 25,* 730–42. **366**

Barron, F. (1958). The psychology of imagination. *Scientific American, 199,* 150–56, 159–60, 162–64, 166. **366**

Barron, F. (1972). *Artists in the making.* New York: Seminar Press. **364**

Bartlett, E. S., & Izard, C. E. (1972). A dimensional and discrete emotions investigation of the subjective experience of emotion. In C. E. Izard (Ed.), *Patterns of emotions: A new analysis of anxiety and depression*. New York: Academic Press. **302**

Bauer, S. R., & Achenbach, T. M. (1976). Self-image disparity, repression-sensitization, and extra-version-introversion: A unitary dimension? *Journal of Personality Assessment, 40*, 46–51. **267**

Beck, A. T. (1967). *Depression: Clinical, experimental and theoretical aspects*. New York: Hoeber. **283, 284**

Belz, M., Parker, E. Z., Sank, L. I., Shaffer, C., Shapiro, J., & Shriber, L. (1977). Is there a treatment for terror? *Psychology Today*, October, *11*, 54–56, 108, 111–12. **275, 291**

Bem, D. J., & Allen, A. (1974). On predicting some of the people some of the time: The search for cross-situational consistencies in behavior. *Psychological Review, 81*, 506–20. **406, 408**

Bem, S. L. (1975). Sex role adaptability: One consequence of psychological androgyny. *Journal of Personality and Social Psychology, 31*, 634–43. **265**

Berkowitz, L. (1969). The frustration-aggression hypothesis revisited. In L. Berkowitz (Ed.), *Roots of aggression*. New York: Atherton Press. **330, 335**

Berkowitz, L. (1974). Some determinants of impulsive aggression: The role of mediated associations with reinforcements for aggression. *Psychological Review, 81*, 165–76. **335**

Berkowitz, L., & Geen, R. G. (1966). Film violence and the cue properties of available targets. *Journal of Personality and Social Psychology, 3*, 525–30. **340**

Berlyne, D. E. (1960). *Conflict, arousal, and curiosity*. New York: McGraw-Hill. **353**

Berndt, T. (1979). Developmental changes in conformity to peers or parents. *Developmental Psychology, 15*, 608–16. **370**

Berndt, T. (1981). Age changes and changes over time in prosocial intentions and behavior between friends. *Developmental Psychology, 17*, 408–16. **167, 370, 401**

Berne, E. (1964). *Games people play*. New York: Grove Press. **420**

Berne, E. (1972). *What do you say after hello?* New York: Grove Press. **420**

Berry, J. L., & Martin, B. (1957). GSR reactivity as a function of anxiety, instructions, and sex. *Journal of Abnormal and Social Psychology, 54*, 9–12. **307**

Berscheid, E., & Walster, E. H. (1978). *Interpersonal attraction* (2nd ed.). Reading, MA: Addison-Wesley. **369**

Beutler, L. E. (1976). Psychotherapy: When what works with whom. Unpublished manuscript, Baylor College of Medicine, Houston, TX. **447**

Blatt, S. J., & Wild, C. M. (1976). *Schizophrenia: A developmental analysis*. New York: Academic Press. **203**

Block, J. (1971). *Lives through time*. Berkeley, CA: Bancroft Books. **158, 410, 418**

Block, J. (1975). Recognizing the coherence of personality. Unpublished draft, University of California, Berkeley. **158**

Block, J. (1977). Advancing the psychology of personality. Paradigmatic shift or improving the quality of research? In D. Magnusson & H. S. Endler (Eds.), *Personality at the crossroads. Current issues in interactional psychology*. Hillsdale, NJ: Erlbaum. **409**

Bolles, R. C. (1967). *Theory of motivation*. New York: Harper and Row. **278**

Bower, G. H. (1981). Mood and memory. *American Psychologist, 36*, 129–48. **201**

Bowers, P. (1979). Hypnosis and creativity: The search for the missing link. *Journal of Abnormal Psychology, 88*, 564–72. **238**

Breger, L., Hunter, I., & Lane, R. W. (1971). *The effect of stress on dreams*. New York: International Universities Press. **242**

Brim, O. G., Jr., and Kagan, J. (Eds.) (1980). *Constancy and change in human development*. Cambridge, MA: Harvard University Press. **379**

Broadbent, D. (1958). *Perception and communication*. London: Pergamon Press. **202, 203**

Brown, S. L. (1978). Relationships between facial expression and subjective experience of emotion in depressed and normal subjects. Unpublished dissertation, Yale University. **360**

Burgess, E. W., & Wallin, P. (1953). *Engagement and marriage*. Philadelphia: Lippincott. **368**

Buss, A. H. (1961). *The psychology of aggression*. New York: Wiley. **335**

Buss, A. H. (1971). Aggression pays. In J. L. Singer (Ed.), *The control of aggression and violence*.

New York: Academic Press. **334**

Buss, A. H. (1980). *Self-consciousness and social anxiety.* San Francisco: Freeman. **254, 255, 259, 260**

Buss, A., and Plomin, R. (1975). *A temperament theory of personality development.* New York: Wiley. **386, 388**

Butler, R. N. (1975). *Why survive?* New York: Harper & Row. **425, 426**

Byrne, D. (1964). Repression-sensitization as a dimension of personality. In B. A. Maher (Ed.), *Progress in experimental personality research* (Vol. 1). New York: Academic Press. **311**

Byrne, D. (1969). Attitudes and attraction. In L. Berkowitz (Ed.), *Advances in experimental social psychology* (Vol. 4). New York: Academic Press. **370**

Byrne, D. (1971). *The attraction paradigm.* New York: Academic Press. **369**

Cairns, R. B. (1966). Development, maintenance and extinction of social attachment behavior in sheep. *Journal of Comparative and Physiological Psychology, 62,* 298–306. **390**

Campagna, A. F. (1975). The function of men's erotic fantasies during masturbation. Unpublished doctoral dissertation, Yale University. **371**

Carlson, R. (1971). Where is the person in personality research? *Psychological Bulletin, 75,* 203–19. **146**

Carlson, R. (1980). Studies of Jungian typology: II. Representations of the personal world. *Journal of Personality and Social Psychology, 38,* 801–10. **56**

Carrigan, P. M. (1960). Extraversion-introversion as a dimension of personality: A reappraisal. *Psychological Bulletin, 57,* 329–60. **144**

Cartwright, R. D. (1977). *Night life.* Englewood Cliffs, NJ: Prentice-Hall. **243**

Carver, C. S., Coleman, A. E., & Glass, D. C. (1976). The coronary-prone behavior pattern and the suppression of fatigue on a treadmill test. *Journal of Personality and Social Psychology, 33,* 460–66. **328**

Carver, C. S., & Glass, D. C. (1977). The coronary prone behavior pattern and interpersonal aggression. Unpublished manuscript, University of Texas. **328**

Cattell, R. B. (1956). A shortened 'basic English' (Form C) version of the 16 P. F. Questionnaire. *Journal of Social Psychology, 44,* 257–78. **156**

Cattell, R. B. (1969). Is field independence an expression of the general personality source trait of independence, U. I. 19? *Perceptual and Motor Skills, 28,* 865–66. **217**

Cattell, R. B., & Stice, G. F. (1957). *Handbook for the Sixteen Personality Factor Questionnaire.* Champaign, IL: Institute for Personality and Ability Testing. **156**

Cautela, J. R., & McCullough, L. (1978). Covert conditioning: A learning-theory perspective on imagery. In J. L. Singer & K. S. Pope (Eds.), *The power of human imagination.* New York: Plenum Press. **442**

Chance, J. E. (1952). Generalization of expectancies as a function of need relatedness. Unpublished doctoral dissertation, Ohio State University. **89**

Chapman, J. P., & McGhie, A. (1962). A comparative study of disordered attention in schizophrenia. *Journal of Mental Science, 108,* 487–500. **360**

Chapman, L. J., & Chapman, J. P. (1973). *Disordered thought in schizophrenia.* Englewood Cliffs, NJ: Prentice-Hall. **360**

Clarke-Stewart, A. K. (1973). Interactions between mothers and their young children: Characteristics and consequences. *Monographs of the Society for Research in Child Development, 38* (6 and 7). **392**

Clatworthy, N. M., & Scheid, L. (1977). *A comparison of married couples: Premarital cohabitants with non-premarital cohabitants.* Unpublished manuscript, Ohio State University. **374**

Coates, S., Lord, M., & Jakabovics, E. (1975). Field dependence-independence, social-nonsocial play and sex differences in preschool children. *Perceptual and Motor Skills, 40,* 195–202. **215**

Cobb, E. (1977). *The ecology of imagination in childhood.* New York: Columbia University Press. **365, 366**

Collins, B. E. (1974). Four components of the Rotter I-E scale. *Journal of Personality and Social Psychology, 29,* 381–91. **249**

Constantinople, A. (1970). Some correlates of average level of happiness among college students. *Developmental Psychology, 2,* 447. **361**

Cooper, L. W. (1979). Hypnotic amnesia. In E. Fromm & R. E. Shor (Eds.), *Hypnosis: Developments in research and new perspectives.* New York: Aldine Press. **236**

Coopersmith, S. (1967). *The antecedents of self-esteem.* San Francisco: Freeman. **267**

Costa, P. T., & McCrae, R. R. (1980). Influence of extraversion and neuroticism on subjective well-being: Happy and unhappy people. *Journal of Personality and Social Psychology, 38,,* 668–78. **363**

Craik, F. I. M. (1977). Depth of processing in recall and recognition. In S. Dornic (Ed.), *Attention and performance* (Vol. 6). Hillsdale, NJ: Erlbaum. **205**

Crawford, H. J. (1982). Hypnotizability, daydreaming styles, imagery vividness, and absorption: A multidimensional study. *Journal of Personality and Social Psychology, 42,* 915–26. **237**

Csikszentmihalyi, M. (1974). *Flow: Studies of enjoyment.* PHS grant report N. R01 HM 22883–02. **166**

Csikszentmihalyi, M. (1975). *Beyond boredom and anxiety.* San Francisco: Jossey-Bass. **231, 357, 358, 359, 365**

Cumming, E., & Henry, W. H. (1961). *Growing old.* New York: Basic Books. **428**

Darwin, C. R. (1872). *The expression of emotions in man and animals.* London: John Murray. **183**

Davis, W. L., & Phares, E. J. (1967). Internal-external control as a determinant of information seeking in a social influence situation. *Journal of Personality, 35,* 547–61. **248**

Deglin, V. L. (1973). Clinical-experimental studies of unilateral electroconvulsive block. *Journal of Neuropathology and Psychiatry, 11,* 1609–21. **184**

Delgado, J. M. R. (1967). Social rank and radio-stimulated aggressiveness in monkeys. *Journal of Nervous and Mental Disease, 144,* 383–90. **332**

Delgado, J. M. R. (1968). Electrical stimulation of the limbic system. *Proceedings of the XXIV International Congress of Physiological Sciences, 6,* 222–23. **332**

Delgado, J. M. R., Roberts, W. W., & Miller, N. E. (1954). Learning motivated by electrical stimulation of the brain. *American Journal of Physiology, 178,* 587–93. **175, 184**

DeLongis, A., Coyne, J. C., Dakof, G., Folkman, S., & Lazarus, R. S. (1982). Relationship of daily hassles, uplifts and major life events to health status. *Health Psychology, 1,* 119–36. **423**

Dengerink, H. A., O'Leary, M. R., & Kasner, K. H. (1975). Individual differences in aggressive responses to attack: Internal-external locus of control and field dependence-independence. *Journal of Research in Personality, 9,* 191–99. **346**

Dennis, W. (1960). Causes of retardation among institutional children. *Journal of Genetic Psychology 96,* 47–59. **389**

Dickey, E. C., & Knower, F. H. (1941). A note on some ethnological differences in recognition of simulated expressions of the emotions. *American Journal of Sociology, 47,* 190–93. **185**

DiStefano, J. J. (1970). Interpersonal perceptions of field independent and field dependent teachers and students. (Doctoral dissertation, Cornell University, 1969). *Dissertation Abstracts International, 31,* 463A–464A. (University Microfilms No. 70–11, 225). **214**

Dobbs, D., & Wilson, W. P. (1960). Observations on the persistence of war neurosis. *Diseases of the Nervous System, 21,* 686–91. **289**

Dollard, J., Doob, L. W., Miller, N. E., Mowrer, O. H., & Sears, R. R. (1939). *Frustration and aggression.* New Haven, CT: Yale University Press. **330, 333**

Dollard, J., & Miller, N. (1950). *Personality and psychotherapy: An analysis in terms of learning, thinking and culture.* New York: McGraw-Hill. **80, 81**

Dor-Shav, N. K. (1978). On the long-range effects of concentration camp internment on Nazi victims: 25 years later. *Journal of Consulting and Clinical Psychology, 46,* 1–11. **289**

Driscoll, R., Davis, K., & Lipitz, M. (1972). Parental interference and romantic love: The Romeo and Juliet effect. *Journal of Personality and Social Psychology, 24,* 1–10. **368**

Duffy, E. (1962). *Activation and behavior.* New York: Wiley. **183**

Dweck, C. S., & Reppucci, N. D. (1973). Learned helplessness and reinforcement responsibility in children. *Journal of Personality and Social Psychology, 25,* 109–16. **282**

Edmunson, E. D., & Nelson, D. L. (1976). Anxiety, imagery, and sensory interference. *Bulletin of the Psychonomic Society, 8*, 319-22. **309**

Eiduson, B. (1974). Ten-year longitudinal Rorschachs on research scientists. *Journal of Personality Assessment, 38*, 405–11. **165**

Ekman, P., Friesen, W. V., & Ellsworth, P. C. (1972). *Emotion in the human face: Guidelines for research and an integration of findings.* New York: Pergamon Press. Revised edition, Cambridge, Eng.: Cambridge University Press, 1982. **183**

Ekman, P., & Friesen, W. V. (1975). *Unmasking the face.* Englewood Cliffs, NJ: Prentice-Hall. **189, 190, 304**

Ellison, G. D., & Flynn, J. P. (1968). Organized aggressive behavior in cats after surgical isolation of the hypothalamus. *Archives Italiennes de Biologie, 106*, 1–20. **332**

Emde, R. N., & Koenig, K. L. (1969). Neonatal smiling, frowning, and rapid eye-movement states. *Journal of the American Academy of Child Psychology, 8*, 57. **356**

Endler, N. S., & Magnusson, D. (Eds.) (1976). *Interactional psychology and personality.* Washington, DC: Hemisphere. **309**

Epstein, S. (1977). Traits are alive and well. In D. Magnusson & N. S. Endler (Eds.), *Personality at the crossroads: Current issues in interactional psychology.* Hillsdale, NJ: Erlbaum. **407**

Epstein, S. (1983). The stability of confusion: A reply to Mischel and Peake. *Psychological Review, 90*, 179–84. **407**

Erikson, E. H. (1958). *Young man Luther.* New York: Norton. **434**

Erikson, E. H. (1959). *Identity and the life cycle.* New York: International Universities Press. **416**

Erikson, E. H. (1963). *Childhood and society* (2nd ed.). New York: Norton. **71, 385**

Erikson, E. H. (1964). *Insight and responsibility.* New York: Norton. **382**

Erikson, K. T. (1976). *Everything in its path: Destruction of a community in the Buffalo Creek flood.* New York: Simon & Schuster. **276**

Eron, L. D. (1980). Prescription for reduction of aggression. *American Psychologist, 35*, 244–52. **345, 348**

Exline, R., Gray, D., & Schuette, D. (1965). Visual behavior in a dyad as affected by interview content and sex of respondent. *Journal of Personality and Social Psychology, 1*, 201–09. **187**

Eysenck, H. J. (1953). *The structure of human personality.* New York: Wiley. **144**

Eysenck, H. J. (1965). The effects of psychotherapy. *International Journal of Psychiatry, 1*, 97–178. **157**

Eysenck, H. J. (1981) (Ed.). *A model for personality.* New York: Springer. **11, 157**

Eysenck, M. W. (1979). Anxiety, learning, and memory: A reconceptualization. *Journal of Research in Personality, 13*, 363–85. **267**

Eysenck, M. W. (1976). Extraversion, verbal learning, and memory. *Psychological Bulletin, 83*, 75–90. **207**

Falbo, T., & Peplau, L. A. (1980). Power strategies in intimate relationships. *Journal of Personality and Social Psychology, 38*, 618–28. **372**

Fein, G., Johnson, D., Kossan, N., Stark, L., & Wasserman, L. (1975). Sex stereotypes and preferences in the toy choices of 20-month-old boys and girls. *Developmental Psychology, 11*, 527–28. **263**

Fenigstein, A. (1974). *Self-consciousness, self-awareness, and rejection.* Unpublished doctoral dissertation, University of Texas at Austin. **259**

Fenigstein, A., Scheier, M., & Buss, A. H. (1975). Public and private self-consciousness: Assessment and theory. *Journal of Consulting and Clinical Psychology, 43*, 522–24. **256, 257**

Feshbach, S. (1970). Aggression. In P. H. Mussen (Ed.), *Carmichael's manual of child psychology.* New York: Wiley. **330**

Fishbein, M., & Ajzen, I. (1975). *Belief attitude, intention, and behavior: An introduction to theory and research.* Reading, MA: Addison-Wesley. **250, 251**

Fisher, A. E. (1962). Effects of stimulus variation on sexual satiation in the male rat. *Journal of Comparative and Physiological Psychology, 55*, 614–20. **278**

Fisher, S., & Fisher, R. L. (1981). *Pretend the world is funny and forever: A psychological analysis of comedians, clowns, and actors*. Hillsdale, NJ: Erlbaum. **420**

Fisher, S., & Greenberg, R. P. (1977). *The scientific credibility of Freud's theories and therapy*. New York: Basic Books. **44,45**

Fiske, D. W. (1973). Can a personality construct be validated empirically? *Psychological Bulletin, 80,* 89–92. **158**

Fiske, D. W. (1974). The limits of the conventional science of personality. *Journal of Personality, 42,* 1–11.

Flaherty, J. E., & Dusek, J. B. (1980). An investigation of the relationship between psychological androgyny and components of self-concept. *Journal of Personality and Social Psychology, 38,* 984–92. **265**

Flynn, J. P. (1967). The neural basis of aggression in cats. In Glass, D. C. (Ed.), *Neurophysiology and emotion*. New York: Rockefeller University Press. **331**

Foulkes, D., & Fleisher, S. (1975). Mental activity in relaxed wakefulness. *Journal of Abnormal Psychology, 84,* 66–75. **239**

Foulkes, D., Spear, P. S., & Symonds, J. D. (1966). Individual differences in mental activity at sleep onset. *Journal of Abnormal Psychology, 71,* 280–86. **241**

Frank, S. J. (1978). Just imagine how I feel: How to improve empathy through training in imagination. In J. L. Singer & K. S. Pope (Eds.), *The power of human imagination*. New York: Plenum Press. **190, 234**

Freedman, D. G. (1981). Ethnic differences in babies. In M. Heatherington & R. Parke (Eds.), *Contemporary readings in child psychology* (2nd ed.). New York: McGraw Hill. **385, 386**

Freedman, J. L. (1978). *Happy people*. New York: Harcourt Brace Jovanovich. **368**

Freud, S. (1900). *The interpretation of dreams*. In J. Strachey (Ed. and trans.), *The standard edition of the complete psychological works of Sigmund Freud* (Vols. 4, 5). London: Hogarth, 1962. **27**

Freud, S. (1913). The claims of psychoanalysis to scientific interest. In J. Strachey (Ed. and trans.), *The standard edition of the complete psychological works of Sigmund Freud* (Vol. 13). London: Hogarth, 1962. **36**

Freud, S. (1926). *Inhibitions, symptoms, and anxiety* (J. Strachey, trans.). New York: Norton, 1959. **300**

Fromm, E. (1947). *Man for himself, an inquiry into the psychology of ethics*. New York: Rinehart. **62**

Fusella, V. (1972). Blocking of an external signal through self-projected imagery: The role of inner acceptance, personality style, and categories of imagery. Unpublished doctoral dissertation, City University of New York. **226**

Gagnon, J. H. (1974). Scripts and the coordination of sexual conduct. In J. K. Cole & R. Dienstbier (Eds.), *Nebraska symposium on motivation, 1973*. Lincoln, NB: University of Nebraska Press. **371**

Gallup, G. (1977). Self-recognition in primates. A comparative approach to the bidirectional properties of consciousness. *American Psychologist, 32,* 329–38. **254**

Garvey, C. (1976). Some properties of social play. In J. S. Bruner, D. Jolly, & K. Sylva (Eds.), *Play—its role in development and evaluation*. Middlesex: Penguin Books. **396**

Gates, D. W. (1971). Verbal conditioning, transfer and operant level "speech style" as functions of cognitive style. (Doctoral dissertation, City University of New York, 1971). *Dissertation Abstracts International, 32,* 3634 B. (University Microfilms No. 71–30, 719). **214**

Gazzaniga, M. S., & Ledoux, J. E. (1978). *The integrated mind*. New York: Plenum Press. **205**

Gellhorn, E. (1967). *Principles of autonomic-somatic integrations: Physiological basis and psychological and clinical implications*. Minneapolis: University of Minnesota Press. **305**

Gerbner, G., Gross, L., Morgan, M., & Signorielli, N. (1980). Some additional comments on cultivation analysis. *Public Opinion Quarterly, 44,* 408–11. **426**

Gerbner, G., Gross, L., Morgan, M., & Signorielli, N. (1982). Charting the mainstream: Television's contribution to political orientations. *Journal of Communications, 32,* 100–27. **426**

Giambra, L. M. (1974). Daydreaming across the life span: Late adolescent to senior citizen. *International Journal of Aging and Human Development, 5,* 115–40. **229, 425**

Giambra, L. M. (1977). A factor analytic study of daydreaming, imaginal process and temperament: A replication on an adult male life-span sample. *Journal of Gerontology, 17,* 35–38. **425**

Gill, M., & Holzman, P. (1976). (Eds.), *Psychology versus Metapsychology.* New York: International Universities Press. **44**

Glass, D. C. (1977). *Behavior patterns, stress and coronary disease.* Hillsdale, NJ: Erlbaum. **327, 328**

Glass, D. C., & Singer, J. E. (1972). *Urban stress: Experiments on noise and social stressors.* New York: Academic Press. **281, 282, 283**

Glover, C. B., & Cravens, R. W. (1974). Trait anxiety, stress, and learning—a test of Saltz's hypothesis. *Journal of Research in Personality, 8,* 243–53. **308**

Glucksberg, S., & King, L. J. (1967). Motivated forgetting mediated by implicit verbal chaining: A laboratory analog of repression. *Science, 158,* 517–19. **31**

Goldberg, L. (1973). Aggression in boys in a clinic population. Unpublished doctoral dissertation, City University of New York. **346**

Golding, J., & Singer, J. L. (1983). Patterns of inner experience: Daydreaming styles, depressive moods and sex roles. *Journal of Personality and Social Psychology, 45,* 663–75. **265**

Goodenough, D. R. (1976). The role of individual differences in field dependence as a factor in learning and memory. *Psychological Bulletin, 83,* 675–94. **210, 240**

Gordon, W. J. (1961). *Synectics: The development of creative capacity.* New York: Harper and Row. **365**

Gordon, W. J. (1971). *The metaphorical way.* Cambridge, MA: Porpoise Books. **365**

Gorman, B. S., & Wessman, A. E. (1974). The relationships of cognitive styles and moods. *Journal of Clinical Psychology, 30,* 18–25. **363**

Gorman, B. S., Wessman, A. E., & Ricks, D. F (1975). Social desirability and self-report of moods: A rejoinder. *Perceptual and Motor Skills, 40,* 272–74. **362**

Gottesman, I. I. (1966). Genetic variance in adaptive personality traits. *Journal of Child Psychology and Psychiatry, 7,* 199–208. **386**

Gottlieb, S. (1973). Modeling effects upon fantasy. In J. L. Singer (Ed.), *The child's world of make-believe.* New York: Academic Press. **412**

Graham, H. D. (1969). A contemporary history of American crime. In H. D. Graham & T. R. Gurr (Eds.), *The history of violence in America: Historical and comparative perspectives.* New York: New American Library. **337**

Graham, H. D., & Gurr, T. R. (Eds.) (1969). *The history of violence in America: Historical and comparative perspectives.* New York: New American Library. **337**

Gray, J. A. (1976). Biological dimensions of stress and anxiety. In I. G. Sarason & C. D. Spielberger (Eds.), *Stress and anxiety* (Vol. 3). New York: Wiley. **305, 337**

Gray, J. A. (1978). Anxiety. *Human Nature, 1,* 38–45. **305**

Greene, L. R. (1973). Effects of field independence, physical proximity and evaluative feedback on affective reactions and compliance in a dyadic interaction. (Doctoral dissertation, Yale University, 1973.) *Dissertation Abstracts International, 34,* 2284B–2285B. University Microfilms No. 73–26, 285. **214**

Grotevant, H. D., Scarr, S., & Weinberg, R. A. (1977). Patterns of interest similarity in adoptive and biological families. *Journal of Personality and Social Psychology, 35,* 667–76. **387**

Gunnar, M. (1978). Changing a frightening toy into a pleasant toy by allowing the infant to control its actions. *Developmental Psychology, 14,* 157–62. **392**

Gur, R. E., & Reyher, J. (1973). The relationship between style of hypnotic induction and direction of lateral eye movement. *Journal of Abnormal Psychology, 82,* 499–505. **207**

Haan, N. (1969). A tripartite model of ego functioning, values, and clinical and research applications. *Journal of Nervous and Mental Disease, 148,* 14–30. **311**

Hall, C. S. (1956). Current trends in research on dreams. In D. Brower & L. Abt (Eds.), *Progress in Clinical Psychology* (Vol. 2). New York: Grune & Stratton. **239**

Hall, C. S., & Nordby, V. J. (1972). *The individual and his dreams.* New York: New American Library. **239**

Hamilton, D. L. (1971). A comparative study of five methods of assessing self-esteem, dominance, and dogmatism. *Education and Psychological Measurement, 31,* 441–52. **266**

Hariton, E. B., & Singer, J. L. (1974). Women's fantasies during sexual intercourse: Normative and theoretical implications. *Journal of Consulting and Clinical Psychology, 42,* 313–22. **371**

Harlow, H. F., & Harlow, M. K. (1965). The affectional system. In A. M. Scjroer, H. F. Harlow, & F. Stollnitz (Eds.), *Behavior of non-human primates* (Vol. 2). New York: Academic Press. **390**

Harlow, H. F., & Harlow, M. K. (1969). Effects of various mother-infant relationships on rhesus monkey behaviors. In B. M. Foss (Ed.), *Determinants of infant behavior* (Vol. 4). London: Methuen. **390**

Hartmann, D. P. (1969). Influence of symbolically modeled instrumental aggression and pain cues on aggressive behavior. *Journal of Personality and Social Psychology, 11,* 280–88. **335**

Hartmann, E. (1973). *The functions of sleep.* New Haven, CT: Yale University Press. **179, 180, 181**

Harvey, C. J., Hunt, D. E., & Schroder, H. M. (1961). *Conceptual systems and personality organization.* New York: Wiley. **136**

Havighurst, R. J. (1953). *Human development and education.* New York: Longmans & Green. **380**

Helmreich, R., Aronson, E., & Le Fan, J. (1970). To err is humanizing—sometimes: Effects of self-esteem, competence, and a pratfall on interpersonal attraction. *Journal of Personality and Social Psychology, 16,* 259–64. **369**

Helson, R. (1967). Personality characteristics and developmental history of creative college women. *Genetic Psychology Monographs, 76,* 205–26. **365**

Hilgard, E. R. (1965). *Hypnotic suggestibility.* New York: Harcourt Brace Jovanovich. **236**

Hilgard, J. R. (1979). Imaginative and sensory-affective involvements in everyday life and in hypnosis. In E. Fromm & R. E. Schor (Eds.), *Hypnosis: Developments in research and new perspectives.* New York: Aldine Press. **236, 237, 238**

Hiroto, D. S. (1974). Locus of control and learned helplessness. *Journal of Experimental Psychology, 102,* 187–93. **249**

Hiscock, M. (1978). Imagery assessment through self-report: What do imagery questionnaires measure? *Journal of Consulting and Clinical Psychology, 46,* 223–30. **205**

Hoelscher, T. J., Klinger, E., & Barta, S. G. (1981). Incorporation of concern- and nonconcern-related stimuli into dream content. *Journal of Abnormal Psychology, 90,* 88–91. **202**

Hoffman, M. L. (1978). Toward a theory of empathic arousal and development. In M. Lewis and L. A. Rosenblum (Eds.), *The development of affect.* New York: Plenum Press. **394**

Holmes, D. S. (1974). Investigations of repression: Differential recall of material experimentally or naturally associated with ego threat. *Psychological Bulletin, 81,* 632–53. **311**

Holmes, T. H., & Rahe, R. H. (1967). The social readjustment rating scale. *Journal of Psychosomatic Research, 11,* 213–18. **277, 278, 422**

Holt, R. R. (1969). Assessing personality. In I. Janis, G. Mahl, J. Kagan, & R. R. Holt (Eds.), *Personality.* New York: Harcourt Brace Jovanovich. **317**

Holt, R. R. (1976). Drive or wish? A reconsideration of the psychoanalytic theory of motivation. In *Psychology versus metapsychology: Psychoanalytic essays in memory of George S. Klein. Psychological issues,* Monograph 36. New York: International Universities Press. **327**

Holtzman, W. H., Thorpe, J. S., Swartz, J. D., & Herron, E. W. (1961). *Inkblot perception and personality: Holtzman Inkblot Technique.* Austin: University of Texas Press. **161**

Holzman, P. S., Levy, D. L., & Proctor, L. R. (1976). Smooth pursuit eye-movements, attention and schizophrenics. *Archives of General Psychiatry, 33,* 1415–20. **203**

Horney, K. (1945). *Our inner conflicts: A constructive theory of neurosis.* New York: Norton. **310**

Horowitz, M. J. (1976). *Stress response syndromes.* New York: Aronson. **294, 295, 296**

Horowitz, M., & Wilner, N. (1976). Stress films, emotions, and cognitive responses. *Archives of General Psychiatry, 33,* 1339–44. **230, 232**

Huba, G. J., Aneshensel, C. S., & Singer, J. L. (1981). Development of scales for three second-order factors of inner experience. *Multivariate Behavioral Research, 16,* 181–206. **229**

Huba, G. J., & Hamilton, D. L. (1976). On the generality of trait relationships: Some analyses based on Fiske's paper. *Psychological Bulletin, 5,* 868–76. **158**

Huesmann, L. R., & Levinger, G. (1976). Incremental exchange theory: A formal model for progression in dyadic social interaction. In L. Berkowitz & E. Walster (Eds.), *Advances in experimental social psychology* (Vol. 9). New York: Academic Press. **372, 373**

Hunt, J. McV. (1965). Intrinsic motivation and its role in psychological development. In D. Levine (Ed.), *Nebraska Symposium on Motivation* (Vol. 13). Lincoln: University of Nebraska Press. **175**

Hunt, M. M. (1959). *The natural history of love.* New York: Knopf. **367, 368**

Hurlburt, R. (1976). Self-observation and self-control. Unpublished doctoral dissertation, University of South Dakota. **231**

Hymbagh, K., & Garrett, J. (1974). Sensation seeking among skydivers. *Perceptual and Motor Skills, 38,* 118. **290.**

Irey, P. A. (1974). Personality dimensions of crisis interveners vs. academic psychologists, traditional clinicians and paraprofessionals. Unpublished doctoral dissertation, Southern Illinois University. **290**

Izard, C. E. (1971). *The face of emotion.* New York: Appleton-Century-Crofts. **183**

Izard, C. E. (1972). *Patterns of emotion: A new analysis of anxiety and depression.* New York: Academic Press. **183, 186, 301, 302, 353**

Izard, C. E. (Ed.) (1977). *Human emotions.* New York: Plenum Press. **183, 186, 300, 303, 304, 325, 353, 357, 369**

Izard, C. E. (1978). On the ontogenesis of emotion and emotion-cognition relationships in infancy. In M. Lewis & L. A. Rosenblum (Eds.), *The development of affect.* New York: Plenum Press. **394**

Izard, C. E. (1979). *Emotions in personality and psychopathology.* New York: Plenum Press. **183**

Jackson, D. N. (1967). *Personality research form manual.* Port Huron, MI: Research Psychologists Press, Inc. **158**

Jackson, J. H. (1878). On affectations of speech from disease of the brain. *Brain, 1,* 304. **242**

Jacobs, P. A., Brunton, M., & Melville, M. M. (1965). Aggressive behavior, mental subnormality, and the XYY male. *Nature, 208,* 1351–52. **333**

James, W. (1890). *The principles of psychology* (2 vols.). New York: Dover Publications, 1950. **198**

Janis, I. (1971). *Stress and frustration.* New York: Harcourt Brace Jovanovich. **286, 287**

Jarvik, L. F., Klodin, V., & Matsuyama, S. S. (1973). Human aggression and the extra Y chromosome: Fact or fantasy? *American Psychologist, 28,* 674–682. **333**

Jaynes, J. (1976). *The origins of consciousness in the breakdown of the bicameral mind.* Boston: Houghton Mifflin. **395**

Jensen, M. J. (1978). Information seeking and the achievement motive. Unpublished masters thesis, Hebrew University of Jerusalem. **365**

Jessor, R., & Jessor, S. L. (1977). *Problem behavior and psychosocial development.* New York: Academic Press. **418, 419**

Johnston, A., DeLuca, D., Murtaugh, K., & Diener, E. (1977). Validation of a laboratory play measure of child aggression. *Child Development, 48,* 324–27. **334**

Jung, C. G. (1959). *The archetypes and the collective unconscious.* In *Collected works of C. G. Jung* (Vol. 9). Princeton, NJ: Princeton University Press, 1976. **53**

Jung, C. G. (1963). *Memories, dreams, reflections.* New York: Pantheon. **48**

Jung, C. G. (with von Franz, M. L., Henderson, J. L., Jacobi, L., & Jaffe, A.) (1964). *Man and his symbols.* New York: Doubleday. **49**

Kagan, J. (1978). *The growth of the child: Reflections on human development.* New York: Norton. **395**

Kagan, J., Kearsley, R., & Zelazo, P. (1978). *Infancy.* Cambridge, MA: Harvard University Press. **386, 389, 390, 392, 400**

Kagan, J., & Lewis, M. (1965). Studies of attention in the human infant. *Merrill-Palmer Quarterly, 11,* 95–127. **187**

Kamil, L. J. (1970). Psychodynamic changes through systematic densensitization. *Journal of Abnormal Psychology, 76,* 199–205. **443**

Kanner, A. D., Coyne, J. C., Schaefer, C., & Lazarus, R. S. (1981). Comparison of two modes of stress measurement: Daily hassles and uplifts vs. major life events. *Journal of Behavioral Medicine, 4,* 1–39. **423**

Kaplan, N., & Singer, E. (1963). Dogmatism and sensory alienation: An empirical investigation. *Journal of Consulting Psychology, 27,* 486–91. **127**

Karabenick, S. A. (1972). Valence of success and failure as a function of achievement motives and locus of control. *Journal of Personality and Social Psychology, 21,* 101–110. **247**

Katz, P. A., Zigler, E., & Zalk, S. R. (1975). Children's self-image disparity: The effects of age, maladjustment, and action-thought orientation. *Developmental Psychology, 11,* 546–50. **267**

Kaufmann, H. (1970). *Aggression and altruism.* New York: Holt, Rinehart & Winston. **325**

Kazdin, A. E. (1980). *Research design in clinical psychology.* New York: Harper & Row. **443**

Kelly, G. A. (1955). *The psychology of personal constructs* (Vol. 1). *A theory of personality.* New York: Norton. **120, 123**

Kelly, K., & Byrne, D. (1978). The function of imaginative fantasy in sexual behavior. *Journal of Mental Imagery, 2,* 239–46. **414**

Keniston, K. (1968). *Young radicals: Notes on committed youth.* New York: Harcourt Brace Jovanovich. **418**

Kerckhoff, A. C., & Davis, K. E. (1962). Value consensus and need complementarity in mate selection. *American Sociological Review, 27,* 295–303. **368, 370**

Kiesler, S. G., & Baral, R. L. (1970). The search for a romantic partner: The effects of self-esteem and physical attractiveness on romantic behavior. In K. J. Gergen and D. Marlowe (Eds.), *Personality and Social Behavior.* Reading, MA: Addison-Wesley. **369**

Kipnis, D. (1971). *Character structure and impulsiveness.* New York: Academic Press. **348**

Kistiakovskaia, M. I. (1965). Stimuli evoking positive emotions in infants in the first months of life (In Russian). *Soviet Journal of Psychiatry, 3,* 39–48. **187**

Kleinmuntz, B. (1982). *Personality and psychological assessment.* New York: St. Martin's Press. **149**

Klineberg, S. L. (1967). Changes in outlook on the future between childhood and adolescence. *Journal of Personality and Social Psychology, 7,* 185–93. **402**

Klinger, E. (1971). *Structure and functions of fantasy.* New York: Wiley. **227, 239, 346**

Klinger, E. (1977). The nature of fantasy and its clinical uses. *Psychotherapy: Theory, research and practice, 14,* 223–31. **240**

Klinger, E. (1978). Modes of normal conscious flow. In K. S. Pope & J. L. Singer (Eds.), *The stream of consciousness.* New York: Plenum Press. **231, 232**

Klos, D. S., & Singer, J. L. (1981). Determinants of the adolescent's ongoing thought following simulated parental confrontations. *Journal of Personality and Social Psychology, 41,* 975–87. **232, 233, 418**

Knupfer, G., Clark, W., & Room, R. (1966). The mental health of the unmarried. *American Journal of Psychiatry, 122,* 841–51. **362**

Kohlberg, L. (1964). Development of moral character and moral ideology. In M. L. Hoffman & L. W. Hoffman (Eds.), *Review of child development* (Vol. 1). New York: Russell Sage Foundation. **416**

Kohlberg, L. (1976). Moral stages and moralization: The cognitive-developmental approach to socialization. In T. Lickona (Ed.), *Moral development and behavior.* New York: Holt, Rinehart & Winston. **412**

Korchin, S. J. (1976). *Modern clinical psychology.* New York: Basic Books. **150, 307**

Krech, D., Crutchfield, R., & Livson, N. (1974). *Elements of psychology.* New York: Knopf. **194**

Krech, D., Crutchfield, R., Livson, N., Wilson, W., & Parducci, A. (1982). *Elements of psychology,* 4th ed. New York: Knopf. **194**

Kreitler, H., & Kreitler, S. (1976). *Cognitive orientation and behavior.* New York: Springer. **250, 251**

Kreitler, H., & Kreitler, S. (1982). The theory of cognitive orientation: Widening the scope of behavior prediction. In B. Maher (Ed.), *Experimental personality research.* New York: Springer. **251**

Kren, G. M., & Rappoport, L. (1980). *The holocaust and the crisis of human behavior.* New York: Holmes & Meier. **285**

Kris, E. (1951). On preconscious mental processes. In D. Rapaport (Ed.), *Organization and pathology of thought.* New York: Columbia University Press. **364**

Kroeber, T. C. (1963). The coping functions of the ego mechanisms. In R. W. White (Ed.), *The study of lives.* New York: Atherton Press. **311**

Lamb, D. H. (1973). The effects of two stressors on state anxiety for students who differ in trait anxiety. *Journal of Research in Personality, 7*, 116–26. **310**

Langer, E. J., & Rodin, J. (1976). The effects of choice and enhanced personal responsibility for the aged: A field experiment in an institutional setting. *Journal of Personality and Social Psychology, 34*, 191–98. **425, 428**

Lanzetta, J. T., & Kleck, R. E. (1970). Encoding and decoding of nonverbal affect in humans. *Journal of Personality and Social Psychology, 16*, 12–19. **188**

Lazarus, R. S. (1966). *Psychological stress and the coping process.* New York: McGraw-Hill. **187**

Lazarus, R. S., Erickson, C. W., & Fonda, C. P (1951). Personality dynamics and auditory perceptual recognition. *Journal of Personality, 19*, 471–82. **207**

Leeper, R. W. (1965). Some needed developments in the motivational theory of emotions. In D. Levine (Ed.), *Nebraska Symposium on Motivation* (Vol. 13). Lincoln: University of Nebraska Press. **183**

Lefcourt, H. M. (1976). *Locus of control: Current trends in theory and research.* Hillsdale, NJ: Erlbaum. **249**

Lefkowitz, M. M., Eron, L. D., Walder, L. O., & Huesmann, L. R. (1977). *Growing up to be violent.* New York: Pergamon Press. **345**

Leon, B. (1976). Evidence for behavioral constancy. Paper presented at the annual meeting of the Eastern Psychological Association, New York, 1976. **408**

Lesser, G. S., and Abelson, R. P. (1959). Personality correlates of persuasibility in children. In C. I. Hovland & I. L. Janis (Eds.), *Personality and persuasibility.* New Haven, CT: Yale University Press. **267**

Leuner, H. (1978). Basic principles and therapeutic efficacy of guided affective imagery (GAI). In J. L. Singer and K. S. Pope (Eds.), *The power of human imagination.* New York: Plenum Press. **441**

Levine, J. (1968). *Motivation in humor.* New York: Atherton. **360**

Levine, S. V., & Salter, N. E. (1976). Youth and contemporary religious movements: Psychological findings. *Canadian Psychiatric Association Journal, 21*, 411–20. **449**

Levinger, G. K., & Raush, H. L. (1977). *Close relationships: Perspectives on the meaning of intimacy.* Amherst, MA: University of Massachusetts Press. **368**

Levinger, G. K., Senn, D. J., & Jorgenson, B. (1970). Progress toward permanence in courtship. A test of the Kerckhoff-Davis hypothesis. *Sociometry, 33*, 427–43. **370**

Levinson, D. J. (1978). *The seasons of a man's life.* New York: Knopf. **379**

Levinson, D. J., Darrow, C. N., Klein, E. B., Levinson, M. H., & McKee, E. (1977). Periods in the adult development of men: Ages 18 to 48. In H. K. Schlossberg & A. D. Entine (Eds.), *Counseling adults.* Monterey, CA: Brooks/Cole, 47–59. **379**

Levitt, E. E., & Chapman, R. H. (1979). Hypnosis as a research method. In E. Fromm & R. E. Shor (Eds.), *Hypnosis: Developments in research and new perspectives.* New York: Aldine Press. **236**

Lewin, K. (1935). *A dynamic theory of personality.* New York: McGraw-Hill. **118, 276**

Lewin, K. (1936). *Principles of topological psychology.* New York: McGraw-Hill. **276**

Lewinsohn, P. M., Mischel, W., Chaplin, W., & Barton, R. (1980). Social competence and depression: The role of illusory self-perceptions. *Journal of Abnormal Psychology, 89*, 203–13. **284**

Lewis, H. B. (1971). *Shame and guilt in neurosis.* New York: International Universities Press. **212, 213, 217**

Lewis, H. B. (1976). *Psychic war in women and men.* New York: New York University Press. **217**

Lewis, M., & Brooks-Gunn, J. (1979). *Social cognition and the acquisition of self.* New York: Plenum Press. **254**

Lidz, T., Fleck, S., & Cornelison, A. (1965). *Schizophrenia and the family.* New York: International Universities Press. **165**

Lieberman, J. N. (1977). *Playfulness.* New York: Academic Press. **397**

Lindsley, D. (1957). Psychophysiology and motivation. In M. R. Jones (Ed.), *Nebraska Symposium on Motivation* (Vol. 5). Lincoln: University of Nebraska Press. **187**

Lindzey, G., & Kalnins, D. (1958). Thematic Apperception Test: Some evidence bearing on the "hero assumption." *Journal of Abnormal and Social Psychology, 57*, 76–83. **164**

Linville, P. W. (1982). Affective consequence of complexity regarding the self and others. In M. S. Clark & S. T. Fiske (Eds.), *Affect and cognition: 17th Annual Carnegie Symposium on Cognition.* Hillsdale, NJ: Erlbaum. **166**

Lorenz, K. (1966). *On aggression.* New York: Harcourt Brace Jovanovich. **330**

Luborsky, L. (1977). New directions in research on neurotic and psychosomatic symptoms. In I. L. Janis (Ed.), *Current trends in psychology. Readings from the American Scientist.* Los Altos, CA: Kaufmann. **32**

Luborsky, L., Blinder, B., & Mackworth, N. (1963). Eye fixation and recall of pictures as a function of GSR responsivity. *Perceptual and Motor Skills, 16,* 469–83. **204**

Luborsky, L., Blinder, B., & Mackworth, N. (1965). Recalling and GSR as a function of defense. *Journal of Abnormal Psychology, 70,* 270–80. **311**

Luborsky, L., Singer, B., & Luborsky, L. (1975). Comparative studies of psychotherapies. Is it true "Everyone has won and all must have prizes"? *Archives of General Psychiatry, 32,* 995–1007. **447**

Luria, A. R. (1932). *The nature of human conflicts: An objective study of disorganisation and control of human behavior.* (W. H. Gantt, Ed. and trans.). New York: Liveright. **395**

Luthe, W., & Schultz, J. (1969). *Autogenic methods* (Vols. 1–6). New York: Grune & Stratton. **440, 441**

MacLean, P. D. (1970). The limbic brain in relation to the psychoses. In P. Black (Ed.), *Physiological correlates of emotion.* New York: Academic Press. **184**

McAdams, D. P., & Vaillant, G. E. (1982). Intimacy motivation and psychosocial adjustment: A longitudinal study. *Journal of Personality Assessment, 46,* 586–93. **164**

McCall, R. B., & Kagan, J. (1967). Attention in the infant: Effects of complexity, contours, perimeters, and familiarity. *Child Development, 38,* 939–52. **187**

McClelland, D. C. (1961). *The achieving society.* Princeton, NJ: Van Nostrand. **164, 227**

McClelland, D. C. (1975). *Power: The inner experience.* New York: Irvington. **164, 193**

McClelland, D. C., Davis, W. N., Kalin, R., & Wanner, E. (1972). *The drinking man.* New York: Free Press. **227**

McCord, W., McCord, J., & Howard, A. (1969). Familial correlates of aggression in nondelinquent male children. *Journal of Abnormal and Social Psychology, 62,* 79–83. **347**

McFarlin, D. B., & Blascovich, J. (1981). Effects of self-esteem and performance feedback on future affective preferences and cognitive expectations. *Journal of Personality and Social Psychology, 40,* 521–31. **284**

McGuire, W. (1984). Search for the self: Going beyond self-esteem and the reactive self. In R. A. Zucker, J. Arnoff, & A. I. Rabin (Eds.), *Personality and the prediction of behavior.* New York: Academic Press. **254**

Maccoby, E. E. (1980). *Social development.* New York: Harcourt Brace Jovanovich. **262, 263, 264, 341, 342, 379, 391, 392, 399, 400**

Macklin, E. D. (1978). Review of research on nonmarital cohabitation in the United States. In B. I. Murstein (Ed.), *Exploring intimate lifestyles.* New York: Springer. **374**

Maddi, S. R. (1976). *Personality theories: A comparative analysis* (3rd ed.). Homewood, IL: Dorsey Press. **114, 353, 354, 355**

Maddox, G. L. (1968). Fact and artifact: Evidence bearing on disengagement theory. In E. Palmore (Ed.), *Middle age and aging.* Chicago: University of Chicago Press. **425**

Madison, P. (1961). *Freud's concept of repression and defense: Its theoretical and observational language.* Minneapolis: University of Minnesota Press. **321**

Magnussen, D., & Endler, N. S. (Eds.) (1977). *Personality at the crossroads: Current issues in interactional psychology.* Hillsdale, NJ: Erlbaum. **411**

Malamuth, N. M., Feshbach, S., & Jaffe, Y. (1977). Sexual arousal and aggression: Recent experiments and theoretical issues. *Journal of Social Issues, 32,* 110–33. **326**

Maslow, A. H. (1954). *Motivation and personality.* New York: Harper & Row. **363**

Maslow, A. H. (1962). *Toward a new psychology of being.* Princeton, NJ: Van Nostrand. **363**

Matarazzo, J. D., & Wiens, A. W. (1972). *The interview: Research on its anatomy and structure.* Chicago: Aldine-Atherton Press. **150**

Matas, L., Arend, R. A., & Sroufe, L. A. (1978). Continuity of adaptation in the second year: The relationship between quality of attachment and later competence. *Child Development, 49,* 547–56. **393**

Maw, W. H., & Maw, E. W. (1970). Nature of creativity in high- and low-curiosity boys. *Developmental Psychology, 2,* 325–29. **267**

May, R. (1967). *Psychology and the human dilemma.* Princeton, NJ: Van Nostrand. **113**

Meehl, P. E., Lykken, D. T., Schofield, W., & Tellegan, A. (1971). Recaptured-Item Technique (RIT): A method for reducing somewhat the subjective element in factor naming. *Journal of Experimental Research in Personality, 5,* 171–90. **398**

Meer, S. (1952). A study of the dynamic relationship between ideology and dreams. Unpublished doctoral dissertation, Western Reserve University. **239**

Megargee, E. I. (1970). Undercontrolled and over controlled personality types in extreme antisocial aggression. In E. I. Megargee & J. E. Hokanson (Eds.), *The dynamics of aggression: Individual, group, and international analyses.* New York: Harper & Row. **347**

Meichenbaum, D. H. (1977). *Cognitive behavior modification: An integrative approach.* New York: Plenum Press. **398, 443**

Meichenbaum, D. H., & Goodman, J. (1971). Training impulsive children to talk to themselves: A means of developing self-control. *Journal of Abnormal Psychology, 77,* 115–26. **398**

Meltzoff, J., & Kornreich, M. (1970). *Research in psychotherapy.* Chicago: Atherton Aldine Press. **443**

Meltzoff, J., & Litwin, D. (1956). Affective control and Rorschach human movement responses. *Journal of Consulting Psychology, 20,* 463–65. **228**

Meskin, B., & Singer, J. L. (1974). Daydreaming, reflective thought, and laterality of eye movements. *Journal of Personality and Social Psychology, 30,* 64–71. **187, 207, 353**

Messer, S. B. (1972). The relation of internal-external control to academic performance. *Child Development, 43,* 1456–62. **247**

Milgram, S. (1974). *Obedience to authority.* New York: Harper & Row. **338, 340**

Miller, G. A., Galanter, E., & Pribram, K. H. (1960). *Plans and the structure of behavior.* New York: Holt, Rinehart & Winston. **333**

Miller, N. E. (1944). Experimental studies of conflict. In J. McV. Hunt (Ed.), *Personality and the behavior disorders.* New York: Ronald. **82**

Miller, N. E. (1948). Theory and experiment relating psychoanalytic displacement to stimulus-response generalization. *Journal of Abnormal and Social Psychology, 43,* 155–78. **333**

Miller, R. E., and Caul, W. F. (1974). Sex, personality, and physiological variables in the communication of affect via facial expression. *Journal of Personality and Social Psychology, 30,* 587–96. **188.**

Mischel, W. (1968). *Personality and assessment.* New York: Wiley. **95, 158, 407**

Mischel, W. (1969). Continuity and change in personality. *American Psychologist, 24,* 1012–18. **407**

Mischel, W. (1972). Direct versus indirect personality assessment: Evidence and implications. *Journal of Consulting and Clinical Psychology, 38,* 319–24. **407**

Mischel, W. (1973). Toward a cognitive social learning reconceptualization of personality. *Psychological Review, 80,* 252–83. **95**

Mischel, W., & Mischel, H. (1976). A cognitive social-learning approach to morality and self-regulation. In T. Lickona (Ed.), *Moral development and behavior.* New York: Holt, Rinehart, & Winston. **95, 398**

Mischel, W., & Moore, B. (1980). The role of ideation in voluntary delay for symbolically presented rewards. *Cognitive Therapy and Research, 4,* 211–21. **396, 398**

Mischel, W., Zeiss, R., & Zeiss, A. (1974). Internal-external control and persistence: Validation and implications of the Stanford preschool internal-external scale. *Journal of Personality and Social Psychology, 29,* 265–78. **398**

Mones, A. G. (1975). Humor and its relation to field dependence-independence and open mindedness-closed mindedness. (Doctoral dissertation, Long Island University, 1974.) *Dissertation Abstracts International, 35,* 4657B–4658B. (University Microfilms No. 75–1782). **214**

Money, J., Hampson, J. G., & Hampson, J. L. (1957). Imprinting and the establishment of gender role. *AMA Archives of Neurology, 77,* 333–36. **264**

Moos, R. (1973). Conceptualization of human environments. *American Psychologist, 28,* 652–65. **411**

Moray, N. (1970). *Attention: Selective processes in vision and hearing.* New York: Academic Press. **202**

Morgan, A. H., Johnson, D. L., & Hilgard, E. R. (1974). The stability of hypnotic susceptibility: A longitudinal study. *International Journal of Clinical and Experimental Hypnosis, 22,* 249–57 **236, 238**

Mowrer, O. H. (1961). *Learning theory and behavior.* New York: Wiley. **183**

Moyer, K. E. (1971). *The physiology of hostility.* Chicago: Markham. **331**

Murray, E. J., & Jacobson, L. I. (1978). Cognition and learning in traditional and behavioral therapy. In S. L. Garfield & A. E. Bergin (Eds.), *Handbook of psychotherapy and behavior change: An empirical analysis* (2nd ed.). New York: Wiley. **443**

Murray, H. A. (1938). *Explorations in personality.* New York: Oxford University Press. **162**

Murray, H. A. (1943). *Thematic Apperception Test: Manual.* Cambridge, MA: Harvard University Press. **163**

Mussen, P. H., Conger, J. J., & Kagan, J. (1969). *Child development and personality* (3rd ed.). New York: Harper & Row. **413**

Mussen, P. H., Conger, J. J., Kagan, J., & Geiwitz, J. (1979). *Psychological development: A life-span approach.* New York: Harper & Row. **413, 418**

Myers, I. B. (1962). *Manual for the Myers-Briggs Type Indicator.* Princeton: Educational Testing Service. **56**

Nebelkopf, E. B., & Dreyer, A. S. (1973). Continuous-discontinuous concept attainment as a function of individual differences in cognitive style. *Perceptual and Motor Skills, 36,* 655–62. **212**

Neisser, U. (1967). *Cognitive psychology.* New York: Appleton-Century-Crofts. **197**

Neisser, U. (1976). *Cognition and reality.* San Francisco, CA: Freeman. **202**

Neugarten, B. L., Havighurst, R. J., & Tobin, S. S. (1968). Personality and patterns of aging. In B. L. Neugarten (Ed.), *Middle age and aging.* Chicago: University of Chicago Press. **425, 429**

Noton, D., & Stark, L. (1971). Eye movements and visual perception. *Scientific American, 224,* 34–43. **222**

Novaco, R. W. (1975). *Anger control: The development and evaluation of an experimental treatment.* Lexington, MA: Lexington Books. **330**

Novaco, R. W. (1977). Stress inoculation: A cognitive therapy for anger and its application to a case of depression. *Journal of Consulting and Clinical Psychology, 45,* 600–08. **494**

Olds, J. A., & Milner, P. (1954). Positive reinforcement produced by electrical stimulation of the septal area and other regions of the rat brain. *Journal of Comparative and Physiological Psychology, 47,* 419–27. **175, 184**

Olweus, D. (1978). *Aggression in the schools: Bullies and whipping boys.* New York: Halsted. **343, 344**

Olweus, D. (1979). The stability of aggressive reaction pattern in human males: A review. *Psychological Bulletin, 86,* 852–75. **345, 403**

Olweus, D. (1980). Familial and temperamental determinants of aggressive behavior in adolescent boys: A causal analysis. *Developmental Psychology, 16,* 644–60. **343, 344**

Ornstein, R. E. (1977). *The psychology of consciousness* (2nd ed.). New York: Harcourt Brace Jovanovich. **205**

Oster, H. (1978). Facial expression and affect development. In M. Lewis & L. A. Rosenblum (Eds.), *The development of affect.* New York: Plenum Press. **394**

Oswald, I., Taylor, A. M., & Treisman, M. (1960). Discrimination responses to stimulation during human sleep. *Brain, 83,* 440–53. **202**

Paivio, A. (1971). *Imagery and verbal processes*. New York: Holt, Rinehart & Winston. **242**

Papez, J. W. (1951). Correlation of the Papez mechanism of emotion with the attitude theory of Nina Bull. In N. Bull (Ed.), *The attitude theory of emotion. Nervous and mental disease monographs.* New York: Coolidge Foundation. **184**

Parsons, T. (1963). *Social structure and personality*. New York: Free Press of Glencoe. **258**

Patrick, C. (1935). Creative thought in poets. *Archives of Psychology, 26*, 1–74. **364**

Patrick, C. (1937). Creative thought in artists. *Journal of Psychology, 4*, 35–73. **364**

Patterson, G. R., Littman, R. A., & Bricker, W. (1967). Assertive behavior in children: A step toward a theory of aggression. *Monographs of the Society for Research in Child Development, 32* (Serial No. 113). **342**

Paul, I. H. (1959). *Studies in remembering: The reproduction of connected and extended verbal material.* New York: International Universities Press. **207**

Perry, H. S. (1982). *Psychiatrist of America: The life of Harry Stack Sullivan*. Cambridge, MA: Harvard University Press. **416**

Pervin, L. A. (1977). The representative design of person-situation research. In D. Magnusson & N. S. Endler (Eds.), *Personality at the crossroads: Current issues in interactional psychology.* Hillsdale, NJ: Erlbaum. **411**

Phares, E. J. (1976). *Locus of control in personality*. Morristown, NJ: General Learning Press. **307**

Piaget, J. (1926). *The language and thought of the child*. New York: Harcourt Brace Jovanovich. **395**

Piaget, J. (1952). *The origins of intelligence in children*. New York: International Universities Press. **389**

Pilkonis, P. A., & Zimbardo, P. G. (1979). The personal and social dynamics of shyness. In C. E. Izard (Ed.), *Emotions in personality and psychopathology*. New York: Plenum Press. **444**

Pope, K. S. (1978). How gender, solitude, and posture influence the stream of consciousness. In K. S. Pope & J. L. Singer (Eds.), *The stream of consciousness: Scientific investigations into the flow of human experience.* New York: Plenum Press. **231**

Pope, K. S. & Singer, J. L. (Eds.) (1978). *The stream of consciousness*. New York: Plenum Press. **227**

Powdermaker, F. B., & Frank, J. B. (1953). *Group psychotherapy: Studies in methodology of research and therapy.* Cambridge, MA: Harvard University Press. **439**

Pribram, K. H. (1963). Reinforcement revisited: A structural view. In M. R. Jones (Ed.), *Nebraska Symposium on Motivation* (Vol. 11). Lincoln: University of Nebraska Press. **175, 192**

Pribram, K. H. (1970). Feelings as monitors. In M. E. Arnold (Ed.), *Feelings and emotions*. New York: Academic Press. **184**

Pribram, K. H., Spinelli, D. N., & Kamback, M. C. (1967). Electrocortical correlates of stimulus response and reinforcement. *Science, 157*, 94–96. **175, 192**

Price, R. H., & Bouffard, D. L. (1974). Behavioral appropriateness and situational constraint as dimensions of social behavior. *Journal of Personality and Social Psychology, 30*, 579–86. **411**

Prince, G. M. (1970). *The practice of creativity*. New York: Harper & Row. **366**

Rabkin, J. G., & Struening, E. L. (1976). Life events, stress, and illness. *Science, 194*, 1013–20. **422**

Rana, S., Ballentine, R., & Ajaya, S. (1976). *Yoga and psychotherapy*. Glenview, IL: Himalayan Institute. **206**

Rapaport, D. (1960a). The structure of psychoanalytic theory: A systematizing attempt. *Psychological Issues, 6*. New York: International Universities Press. **28**

Rapaport, D. (1960b). On the psychoanalytic theory of motivation. In M. R. Jones (Ed.), *Nebraska Symposium on Motivation* (Vol. 8). Lincoln: University of Nebraska Press. **28**

Raush, H. L., Barry, W. A., Hertel, R. K., & Swain, M. A. (1974). *Communication conflict and marriage.* San Francisco: Jossey Bass. **372**

Read, P. P. (1975). *Alive: The story of the Andes survivors*. New York: Avon. **279**

Reich, W. (1945). *Character-analysis: Principles and technique for psychoanalysts in practice and in training.* (2nd ed.) (T. P. Wolfe, trans.). New York: Orgone Institute Press. **310**

Reimanis, G. (1974). Psychosocial development, anomie, and mood. *Journal of Personality and Social Psychology, 29*, 355–57. **419**

Repetti, R. (1980). Determinants of children's sex stereotyping: Parental attitudes, television viewing, and imaginary play. Unpublished manuscript, Yale University. **264**

Rescorla, R. A., & Solomon, R. L. (1967). Two-process learning theory: Relationships between Pavlovian conditioning and instrumental learning. *Psychological Review, 74*, 151–82. **301**

Richardson, A. (1977). Meaning and measurement in mental imagery. *British Journal of Psychology, 68*, 29–43. **205**

Rickers-Ovsiankina, M. C. (Ed.) (1977). *Rorschach psychology.* Huntington, NY: Krieger. **162**

Ricks, D., & Berry, J. (1970). Family and symptom patterns that precede schizophrenia. In Ricks, D., & Roff, M. (Eds.), *Life history research in psychotherapy.* Minneapolis: University of Minnesota Press. **166**

Rizley, R. (1978). Depression and distortion in the attribution of causality. *Journal of Abnormal Psychology, 87*, 32–48. **168, 261, 284, 363**

Rodin, J., & Langer, E. J. (1977). Long-term effects of a control-relevant intervention with the institutionalized aged. *Journal of Personality and Social Psychology 35*, 897–902. **428**

Rodin, J., & Singer, J. L. (1977). Eyeshift, thought, and obesity. *Journal of Personality, 44*, 594–610. **187, 207, 229**

Roe, A. (1952). Crucial life experiences in the development of scientists. In E. P. Torrance (Ed.), *Talent and education: Present status and future directions.* Minneapolis: University of Minnesota Press. **365**

Roedell, W. C., & Slaby, R. G. (1977). The role of distal and proximal interaction in infant social preference formation. *Developmental Psychology, 13*, 266–73. **391**

Rogers, C. R. (1959). Theory of therapy, personality and interpersonal relationships, as developed in the client-centered framework. In S. Koch (Ed.), *Psychology: A study of the science* (Vol. 3). New York: McGraw Hill. **110**

Rorschach, H. (1942). *Psychodiagnostics.* New York: Grune & Stratton. **159**

Rosenberg, B. A. (1980). Mental-task instructions and optokinetic nystagmus to the left and right. *Journal of Experimental Psychology: Human Perception and Performance, 6*, 459–72. **206**

Rosenberg, L. (1981). Sex-roles, erotic fantasy, and sexual orientation. Unpublished pre-dissertation, Yale University. **266**

Rosenberg, M. (1965). *Society and the adolescent self-image.* Princeton, NJ: Princeton University Press. **266**

Rosenthal, T., & Bandura, A. (1981). Psychological modeling: Theory and practice. In S. L. Garfield & A. E. Bergin (Eds.), *Handbook of psychotherapy and behavior change: An empirical analysis* (2nd. ed.). New York: Wiley. **442**

Roth, S., & Bootzin, R. R. (1974). Effects of experimentally induced expectancies of external control: An investigation of learned helplessness. *Journal of Personality and Social Psychology, 29*, 253–64. **281**

Rotter, J. B. (1954). *Social learning and clinical psychology.* Englewood Cliffs, NJ: Prentice-Hall. **87, 88**

Rotter, J. B. (1966). Generalized expectancies for internal versus external control of reinforcement. *Psychological Monographs, 80 (Whole No. 609).* **247**

Rotter, J. B. (1967). A new scale for the measurement of interpersonal trust. *Journal of Personality, 35*, 651–65. **152,153**

Rotter, J. B. (1971). External control and internal control. *Psychology Today, June*, 36–42, 58–59. **152**

Rotter, J. B. (1975). Some problems and misconceptions related to the structure of internal-external control of reinforcement. *Journal of Consulting and Clinical Psychology, 43*, 56–67. **249**

Rubin, Z. (1973). *Liking and loving: An introduction to social psychology.* New York: Holt, Rinehart & Winston. **368, 372**

Rychlak, J. F. (1977). *The psychology of rigorous humanism.* New York: Wiley. **201**

Sackeim, H. A., & Gur, R. C. (1978). Self-deception, self-confrontation and consciousness. In G. E. Schwartz & D. Shapiro (Eds.), *Consciousness and self-regulation: Advances in research* (Vol. 2). New York: Plenum Press. **238, 253**

Sackeim, H. A., & Gur, R. C. (1979). Self-deception, other-deception, and self-reported psycho-pathology. *Journal of Consulting and Clinical Psychology, 47*, 213–15. **261**

Saltz, E. (1970). Manifest anxiety: Have we misread the data? *Psychological Review, 77*, 568–73. **308**

Sarason, I. G. (1971). Experimental approaches to test anxiety: Attention and the uses of information. In C. D. Spielberger (Ed.), *Anxiety and behavior*, (Vol. 2). New York: Academic Press. **306, 307, 308**

Sarason, S. B., Davison, K. S., Lighthall, F. S., Waite, R. R., & Ruebush, B. K. (1960). *Anxiety in elementary school children*. New York: Wiley. **306**

Sarbin, T. R. (1972). Imagination as muted role-taking: A historical-linguistic analysis. In P. W. Sheehan (Ed.), *The function and nature of imagery*. New York: Academic Press. **236**

Sarbin, T. R., & Coe, W. C. (1972). *Hypnosis: A social psychological analysis of influence communication*. New York: Holt, Rinehart & Winston. **237**

Sargent, W. W. (1957). *Battle for the mind: A physiology of conversion and brainwashing*. Garden City, N.Y.: Doubleday. **434**

Sarnoff, I. (1971). *Testing Freudian concepts: An experimental social approach*. New York: Springer. **321**

Scarr, S. (1981). *Race, social class, and individual differences in I.Q.* Hillsdale, NJ: Erlbaum. **387**

Scarr-Salapatek, S., & Williams, M. L. (1973). The effects of early stimulation on low-birth-weight infants. *Child Development, 44*, 94–101. **389**

Schachtel, E. G. (1959). *Metamorphosis: On the development of affect, perception, attention, and memory*. New York: Basic Books. **125, 137**

Schachter, S. (1959). *The psychology of affiliation: Experimental studies of the sources of gregariousness*. Stanford, CA: Stanford University Press. **369**

Schaie, K. W., & Parham, I. A. (1974). Social responsibility in adulthood: Ontogenetic and socio-cultural change. *Journal of Personality and Social Psychology, 30*, 483–92. **419**

Schank, R. R., & Abelson, R. P. (1977). *Scripts, plans, goals, and understanding*. New York: Halsted. **133**

Schaya, L. (1971). *The universal meaning of the Kabbalah*. Baltimore, MD: Penguin. **206**

Schlesinger, H. (1980). The impact of deafness on the life style. In J. M. Stack (Ed.), *The special child*. New York: Human Sciences Press. **391**

Schreiber, L. B. (1972). *Field dependence-independence and athletic team choice*. Unpublished master's thesis, Boston University. **215**

Schultz, T. R., & Horibe, F. (1974). Development of the appreciation of verbal jokes. *Developmental Psychology, 10*, 13–20. **361**

Schwartz, G. E., Fair, P. L., Greenberg, P. S., Freedman, M., & Klerman, J. L. (1974). Facial electromyography in the assessment of emotion. *Psychophysiology, 11*, 237. **184, 186, 190**

Schwartz, G. E., Weinberger, D., & Singer, J. A. (1981). Cardiovascular differentiation of happiness, sadness, anger, and fear following imagery and exercise. *Psychosomatic Medicine, 43*, 343–64. **183, 186**

Scott, J. P., & Fuller, J. L. (1965). *Genetics and the social behavior of the dog*. Chicago: University of Chicago Press. **385**

Seamon, J. G. (1973). Retrieval processes for organized long-term storage. *Journal of Experimental Psychology, 97*, 170–76. **204**

Sears, R. R. (1970). Relation of early socialization experiences to self-concepts and gender role in middle childhood. *Child Development, 41*, 267–89. **268**

Sears, R. R., Maccoby, E. E., & Levin, H. (1957). *Patterns of child rearing*. Evanston, IL: Row Peterson. **343**

Seeman, M., & Evans, J. W. (1962). Alienation and learning in a hospital setting. *American Sociological Review, 27*, 772–83. **248**

Segal, B., Huba, G. J., & Singer, J. L. (1980). *Drugs, daydreaming and personality: A study of college youth*. Hillsdale, NJ: Erlbaum. **158, 193, 229, 265, 384, 419**

Segal, S. J. (1971). Processing of the stimulus in imagery and perception. In S. J. Segal (Ed.), *Imagery*. New York: Academic Press. **224, 225, 226**

Seligman, M. E. P. (1975). *Helplessness: On depression, development, and death*. San Francisco: Freeman. **278, 280, 281, 282**

Selman, R. L. (1974). The development of conceptions of interpersonal relations. Harvard University, Judge Baker Social Reasoning Project. **190**

Shaffer, H. R., & Emerson, P. E. (1964). Patterns of response to physical contact in early human development. *Journal of Child Psychology and Psychiatry, 5,* 1–13. **187**

Shakow, D. (1963). Psychological deficit in schizophrenia. *Behavioral Science, 8,* 275–305. **203**

Shapiro, D. (1965). *Neurotic styles.* New York: Basic Books. **311**

Shapiro, K. J., & Alexander, I. E. (1969). Extraversion-introversion, affiliation, and anxiety. *Journal of Personality, 37,* 387–406. **168**

Shedletsky, R., & Endler, N. S. (1974). Anxiety: The state-trait model and the interaction model. *Journal of Personality, 42,* 511–27. **310**

Sheehan, P. W. (1972). A functional analysis of the role of visual imagery in unexpected recall. In P. W. Sheehan (Ed.), *The function and nature of imagery.* New York: Academic Press. **224**

Sheehan, P. W. (1979). Hypnosis and the processes of imagination. In E. Fromm & R. E. Shor (Eds.), *Hypnosis: Developments in research and new perspectives.* New York: Aldine Press. **236, 237**

Sheldon, W. H. (1942). *The varieties of temperament.* New York: Harper. **144**

Shemberg, K. M., Leventhal, D. B., & Allman, L. (1968). Aggression machine performance and rated aggression. *Journal of Experimental Research in Personality, 3,* 117–19. **335**

Sherrod, L. (1979). Social cognition in infants: Attention to the human face. *Infant Behavior and Development, 2,* 219–94. **394**

Shmukler, D. (1982a). A factor analytic model of elements of creativity in preschool children. *Genetic Psychology Monographs, 105,* 25–39. **396, 397**

Shmukler, D. (1982b). Early home background features in relation to imaginative and creative expression in third grade. *Imagination, Cognition and Personality, 2,* 311–22. **396, 400**

Simonov, P. V. (1975). Higher nervous activity of man: Motivational-emotional aspects (In Russian). Moscow: Izdatelstro Nauka. **184**

Simpson, R. L. (1962). Parental influence, anticipatory socialization, and social mobility. *American Sociological Review, 27,* 517–22. **417**

Sims, J. H., & Baumann, D. D. (1972). The tornado threat: Coping styles of the north and south. *Science, 176,* 1386–92. **248**

Singer, D. G., & Singer, J. L. (1980). Television viewing and aggressive behavior in preschool children: A field study. In F. Wright, C. Bahn, & R. Rieber (Eds.), *Annals of the New York Academy of Sciences* (Vol. 347). New York: New York Academy of Sciences. **343, 397**

Singer, J. L. (1955). Delayed gratification and ego-development: Implications for clinical and experimental research. *Journal of Consulting Psychology, 19,* 259–66. **392, 396, 398**

Singer, J. L. (1961). Imagination and waiting behavior in young children. *Journal of Personality, 29,* 396–413. **396**

Singer, J. L. (1966). *Daydreaming.* New York: Random House. **227, 239, 241, 255, 365, 398**

Singer, J. L. (1968). Research applications of the projective techniques. In A. Rabin (Ed.), *Projective techniques in personality assessment.* New York: Springer. **346**

Singer, J. L. (Ed.) (1973). *The child's world of make-believe.* New York: Academic Press. **395, 396, 412**

Singer, J. L. (1974). *Imagery and daydreaming methods in psychotherapy and behavior modification.* New York: Academic Press. **52, 135, 224, 441, 442**

Singer, J. L. (1975a). *The inner world of daydreaming.* New York: Harper & Row. **227, 239, 340, 364, 398, 412**

Singer, J. L. (1975b). Navigating the stream of consciousness: Research in daydreaming and related inner experience. *American Psychologist, 30,* 727–38. **227, 339**

Singer, J. L. (1978). The constructive potential of imagery and fantasy processes: Implications for child development, psychotherapy and personal growth. In E. Witenberg (Ed.), *Interpersonal psychoanalysis: New directions.* New York: Gardner Press. **353, 441**

Singer, J. L. (1979). Affect and imagination in play and fantasy. In C. Izard (Ed.), *Emotions in personality and psychopathology.* New York: Plenum Press. **162, 164**

Singer, J. L. (1981). Research implications of projective methods. In A. I. Rabin (Ed.), *Assessment with projective techniques.* New York: Springer. **162, 164**

Singer, J. L., & Antrobus, J. S. (1963). A factor-analytic study of daydreaming and conceptually-related cognitive and personality variables. *Perceptual and Motor Skills Monograph Supplement,* *3–V17,* 187–209. **229**

Singer, J. L., & Antrobus, J. S. (1972). Daydreaming, imaginal processes, and personality: A normative study. In P. W. Sheehan (Ed.), *The function and nature of imagery.* New York: Academic Press. **229, 231**

Singer, J. L., & Brown, S. L. (1977). The experience type: Some behavioral correlates and theoretical implications. In M. M. Rickers-Ovsiankana (Ed.), *Rorschach psychology.* Huntington, NY: Krieger. **144, 162, 228, 346**

Singer, J. L., & McCraven, V. G. (1961). Some characteristics of adult daydreaming. *Journal of Psychology, 51,* 151–64. **367**

Singer, J. L., & Schonbar, R. (1961). Correlates of daydreaming: A dimension of self-awareness. *Journal of Consulting Psychology, 25,* 1–6. **258**

Singer, J. L., & Singer, D. G. (1976). Imaginative play and pretending in early childhood: Some experimental approaches. In A. Davids (Ed.), *Child personality and psychopathology.* New York: Wiley. **398**

Singer, J. L., & Singer, D. G. (1981). *Television, imagination and aggression: A study of preschoolers.* Hillsdale, NJ: Erlbaum. **263, 343, 348, 395, 396, 409**

Singer, J. L., Singer, D. G., & Sherrod, L. (1980). A factor analytic study of preschooler's play behavior. *Academic Psychology Bulletin,* **2,** 143–56. **392**

Singer, J. L., & Switzer, E. (1980). *Mind-play: The creative uses of fantasy.* Englewood Cliffs, NJ: Prentice-Hall. **234, 413**

Singer, J. L., Wilensky, H., & McCraven, V. (1956). Delaying capacity, fantasy, and planning ability: A factorial study of some basic ego functions. *Journal of Consulting Psychology, 20,* 375–83. **398**

Smilansky, S. (1968). *The effects of sociodramatic play on disadvantaged preschool children.* New York: Wiley. **396**

Smith, C. P., & Winterbottom, M. T. (1970). Personality characteristics of college students on academic probation. *Journal of Personality, 38,* 379–91. **254**

Smith, M. B. (1950). The phenomenological approach to personality theory: Some critical remarks. *Journal of Abnormal and Social Psychology, 45,* 516–22. **254**

Smith, M. L., Glass, G. V., & Miller, T. I. (1980). *The benefits of psychotherapy.* Baltimore, MD: Johns Hopkins University Press. **442, 443, 446, 447**

Sokolov, E. N. (1958). *Perception and the conditioned reflex* (In Russian). Moscow: University of Moscow Press. **352**

Solomon, S., Holmes, D. S., & McCaul, K. D. (1980). Behavioral control over aversive events: Does control that requires effort reduce anxiety and physiological arousal? *Journal of Personality and Social Psychology, 39,* 729–36. **309**

Spielberger, C. D. (1971). Anxiety as an emotional state. In C. D. Spielberger (Ed.), *Anxiety: Current trends in theory and research.* New York: Academic Press. **309**

Spielberger, C. D., Gorsuch, R. L., & Lushene, R. E. (1970). *The state-trait anxiety inventory manual.* Palo Alto, CA: Consulting Psychologists Press. **302**

Spitz, R. A. (1946). Hospitalism: An inquiry into the genesis of psychiatric conditions in early childhood. In R. S. Eissler and others (Eds.), *The psychoanalytic study of the child* (Vol. 1). New York: International Universities Press. **389**

Spivack, G., & Levine, M. (1964). Self regulation in acting out and normal adolescents. *Report of the Devereux Foundation.* **402**

Sroufe, L. A., & Waters, E. (1977). Attachment as an organization construct. *Child Development, 48,* 1184–99. **392**

Stagner, R. (1937). *Psychology of personality.* New York: McGraw-Hill. **13**

Starker, S. (1974). Daydreaming styles and nocturnal dreaming. *Journal of Abnormal Psychology, 83,* 52–55. **239**

Stein, M. I. (1975). *Stimulating creativity: Group procedures* (Vol. 2). New York: Academic Press. **364, 365**

Stein, M. I., & Heinze, S. J. (1960). *Creativity and the individual.* Glencoe, IL: Free Press. **364**

Steinberg, E. (Ed.) (1979). *Stream of consciousness technique in the modern novel.* Port Washington, NY: Kennikat Press, National University Publications. **244**

Storms, M. D. (1980). Theories of sexual orientation. *Journal of Personality and Social Psychology, 38*, 783–92. **414**

Storms, M. D. (1981). A theory of erotic orientation development. *Psychological Review, 88*, 340–53. **414, 415, 416**

Stotland, E. (1969). *The psychology of hope.* San Francisco: Jossey-Bass. **281**

Strupp, H. H., & Hadley, S. W. (1977). A tripartite model of mental health and therapeutic outcomes: With special reference to negative effects in psychotherapy. *American Psychologist, 32*, 187–96. **445, 448**

Sullivan, H. S. (1956). *Clinical studies in psychiatry.* New York: Norton. **311**

Suomi, S. J. (1977). Adult male-infant interaction among monkeys living in nuclear families. *Child Development, 48*, 1255–71. **341**

Sutton-Smith, B. (1971). A syntax for play and games. In R. E. Herron & B. Sutton-Smith (Eds.), *Child's play.* New York: Wiley. **60**

Sutton-Smith, B., & Rosenberg, B. G. (1965). Age changes in the effects of ordinal position on sex role identification. *Journal of Genetic Psychology, 107*, 61–73. **263**

Taylor, J. A. (1951). The relationship of anxiety to the conditioned eyelid response. *Journal of Experimental Psychology, 41*, 81–92. **308**

Taylor, J., & Spence, K. W. (1952). The relationship of anxiety level to performance in serial learning. *Journal of Experimental Psychology, 44*, 61–64. **308**

Terkel, S. (1978). *Hard times.* New York: Washington Square Press. **426**

Tesser, A., & Conlee, M. C. (1975). Some effects of time and thought on attitude polarization. *Journal of Personality and Social Psychology, 31*, 262–70. **258**

Thompson, C. (1942). Cultural pressures in the psychology of women. *Psychiatry, 5*, 331–39. **63**

Thompson, C. (1964). *Interpersonal psychoanalysis: The collected papers of Clara Thompson.* (M. Green, Ed.). New York: Basic Books. **63**

Thorndike, R. L. (1959). Review of the California Psychological Inventory. In O. K. Buros (Ed.), *Fifth mental measurements yearbook.* Highland Park, NJ: Gryphon Press. **156**

Toch, H. (1969). *Violent men.* Chicago: Aldine Press. **347**

Toch, H. (1975). *Men in crisis: Human breakdowns in prison.* Chicago: Aldine Press. **347**

Tomkins, S. S. (1947). *The Thematic Apperception Test: The theory and technique of interpretation.* New York: Grune & Stratton. **164**

Tomkins, S. S. (1962, 1963). *Affect, imagery, consciousness* (2 vols.). New York: Springer. **130, 183, 186, 192, 201, 281, 314, 353, 394, 395**

Tomkins, S. S. (1965). Affect and the psychology of knowledge. In S. S. Tomkins & C. E. Izard (Eds.), *Affect, cognition and personality: Empirical studies.* New York: Springer. **193**

Tomkins, S. S. (1979). Script theory: Differential magnification of affects. In H. E. Howe, Jr., & R. A. Dienstbier (Eds.), *Nebraska Symposium on Motivation, 1978* (Vol. 26). Lincoln: University of Nebraska Press. **133, 420**

Tomkins, S. S. (1981). The quest for primary motives: Biography and autobiography of an idea. *Journal of Personality and Social Psychology, 41*, 306–29. **183**

Tower, R. B. (1980a). Parents' self-concepts and preschool children's behaviors. *Journal of Personality and Social Psychology, 39*, 710–18. **399**

Tower, R. B. (1980b). The influence of parents' values on preschool children's behaviors. Unpublished doctoral dissertation, Yale University. **399**

Trego, R. E. (1972). An investigation of the rod and frame test in relation to emotional dependence and social cue attentiveness. (Doctoral dissertation, Texas Christian University, 1971.) *Dissertation Abstracts International, 32*, 4910E (University Microfilms No. 72–7617). **214**

Treisman, A. M. (1969). Strategies and models of selective attention. *Psychological Review, 76* 282–99. **202**

Tryon, C., & Lillienthal, J. (1950). *Fostering mental health in our schools.* Washington, DC: National Education Association. **380, 385**

Tucker, D. M. (1981). Lateral brain function, emotion, and conceptualization. *Psychological Bulletin, 89,* 19–46. **206**

Tulving, E. (1972). Episodic and semantic memory. In B. Tulving & W. Donaldson (Eds.), *Organization and memory.* New York: Academic Press. **201, 204**

Twentyman, C. T., & McFall, R. M. (1975). Behavioral training of social skills in shy males. *Journal of Consulting and Clinical Psychology, 43,* 384–95. **444**

Veroff, J., Feld, S., & Gurin, G. (1962). Dimensions of subjective adjustment. *Journal of Abnormal and Social Psychology, 64,* 192–205. **362**

Vygotsky, L. S. (1934). *Thought and language.* Cambridge, MA: MIT Press. **395**

Walster, E. (1965). The effect of self-esteem on romantic liking. *Journal of Experimental Social Psychology 1,* 184–97. **369**

Walster, E. (1970). The effect of self-esteem on liking for dates of various social desirabilities. *Journal of Experimental Social Psychology, 6,* 240–52. **370**

Walster, E., Aronson, V., Abrahams, D., & Rottman, L. (1966). Importance of physical attractiveness in dating behavior. *Journal of Personality and Social Psychology, 4,* 508–16. **370**

Walters, R. H., & Parke, R. D. (1965). The role of the distance receptors in the development of social responsiveness. In L. P. Lipsitt & C. C. Spikes (Eds.), *Advances in child development and behavior* (Vol. 2). New York: Academic Press. **187**

Waterbor, R. (1972). Experimental bases of the sense of self. *Journal of Personality, 40,* 162–79. **255**

Waters, E., Wippman, J., & Sroufe, L. A. (1979). Attachment positive affect, and competence in the peer group: Two studies in construct validation. *Child Development, 50,* 821–29. **393**

Webb, W. B. (1971). Twenty-four hour sleep-cycling. In A. Kales (Ed.), *Sleep: Physiology and pathology.* Philadelphia: Lippincott. **179**

Weinberger, D., Schwartz, G., & Davidson, R. (1979). Low-anxious, high-anxious and repressive coping styles: Psychometric patterns and behavioral and physiological responses to stress. *Journal of Abnormal Psychology, 88,* 369–80. **312, 313**

Weiner, B. (1972). *Theories of motivation: From mechanism to cognition.* Chicago: Markham. **138, 248**

Weiner, B., Nierenberg, R., & Goldstein, M. (1976). Social learning (locus of control) versus attributional (causal stability) interpretations of expectancy of success. *Journal of Personality, 44,* 52–68. **248**

Weiner, I. B. (1976). Individual psychotherapy. In I. B. Weiner (Ed.), *Clinical methods in psychology.* New York: Wiley. **437**

Werner, H. (1957). The concept of development from a comparative and organismic point of view. In D. B. Harris (Ed.), *The concept of development: An issue in the study of human behavior.* Minneapolis: University of Minnesota Press. **137**

Wessman, A. E. (1979). Moods: Their personal dynamics and significance. In C. E. Izard (Ed.), *Emotions in personality and psychopathology.* New York: Plenum Press. **362**

Wessman, A. E., & Ricks, D. F. (1966). *Mood and personality.* New York: Holt, Rinehart & Winston. **166, 363**

White, R. W. (1959). Motivation reconsidered: The concept of competence. *Psychological Review, 66,* 297–333. **126, 355**

White, R. W. (1960). Competence and the psychosexual stages of development. In M. R. Jones (Ed.), *Nebraska Symposium on Motivation* (Vol. 8). Lincoln: University of Nebraska Press. **126, 355**

White, R. W. (1966). *Lives in progress: A study of the natural growth of personality* (2nd. ed.). New York: Dryden. **165**

White, R. W. (1972). *The enterprise of living: Growth and organization of personality.* New York: Holt, Rinehart & Winston. **310**

Wine, J. (1971a). *Investigations of attentional interpretation of test anxiety.* Unpublished doctoral dissertation, University of Waterloo, Ontario. **307**

Wine, J. (1971b). Test anxiety and direction of attention. *Psychological Bulletin, 76,* 92–104. **307**

Witelson, S. F. (1976). Sex and the single hemisphere: Right hemisphere specialization for spatial processing. *Science, 183*, 425–427. **262**

Witkin, H. A. (1976). Theory in cross-cultural research: Its uses and risks. Selected papers from the Third International Congress of the International Association for Cross-Cultural Psychology held at Tilburg University, Tilburg, The Netherlands. **333**

Witkin, H. A., & Berry, J. (1975). Psychological differentiation in cross-cultural perspective. *Journal of Cross-Cultural Psychology, 6*, 4–87. **216**

Witkin, H. A., & Goodenough, D. (1977a). Field dependence and interpersonal behavior. *Psychological Bulletin, 84*, 661–689. **210, 213, 214**

Witkin, H. A., & Goodenough, D. (1977b). *Field dependence revisited.* Research Bulletin, ETS. **211, 214**

Witkin, H. A., Goodenough, D. R., Oltman, P. K., Friedman, F., Owen, D., & Raskin, E. (1977). The role of field dependent and field independent cognitive styles in academic evolution: A longitudinal study. *Journal of Educational Psychology, 69*, 197–211. **210, 213, 214**

Witkin, H. A., & Goodenough, D. R. (1981). *Cognitive styles, essence and origins: Field dependence and field independence.* New York: International Universities Press. **136, 209, 216, 311**

Witkin, H. A., Mednick, S. A., Schalsinger, F., Bajjestrom, E., Christiansen, K. O., Goodenough, D. R., Hirschorn, K., Lundsteen, C., Owen, D. W., Phillip, J., Rubin, D. B., & Stocking, M. (1976). Criminality in XYY and XXY men. *Science, 196*, 547–55. **333**

Wolfe, B. M., & Baron, R. A. (1971). Laboratory aggression related to aggression in naturalistic social situations: Effects of an aggressive model on the behavior of college students and prisoner observers. *Psychonomic Science, 24*, 193–94. **335**

Wolff, P. H. (1963). Observations on the early development of smiling. In B. M. Foss (Ed.), *Determinants of infant behavior, II.* New York: Wiley. **186**

Wrightsman, L. S. (1981). Personal documents as data in conceptualizing adult personality development. *Personality and Social Psychology Bulletin, 7*, 367–85. **420, 423, 424**

Yarrow, M. R., & Waxler, C. Z., with Barrett, D., Darby, J., King, R., Pickett, M., & Smith, J. (1976). Dimensions and correlates of prosocial behavior in young children. *Child Development, 47*, 118–25. **343**

Zachary, R. (1978). Cognitive and affective determinants of ongoing thought. Unpublished doctoral dissertation, Yale University. **232**

Zajonc, R. B. (1968). Cognitive theories in social psychology. In G. Lindzey & E. Aronson (Eds.), *The handbook of social psychology* (2nd ed.). New York: Addison-Wesley. **60, 353, 370**

Zajonc, R. B. (1976). Family configuration and intelligence. *Science, 192*, 227–36. **60, 353**

Zajonc, R. B. (1980). Feeling and thinking: Preferences need no inferences. *American Psychologist, 35*, 151–75. **201**

Zigler, E. F., & Child, I. L. (1973). *Socialization and personality development.* Reading, MA: Addison-Wesley. **137**

Zigler, E., Levine, J., & Gould, L. (1967). Cognitive challenge as a factor in children's humor appreciation. *Journal of Personality and Social Psychology, 6*, 332–36. **360**

Zillmann, D., & Bryant, J. (1974). Effect of residual excitation on emotional response to provocation and delayed aggressive behavior. *Journal of Personality and Social Psychology, 30*, 787–91. **326**

Zillmann, D., & Cantor, J. R. (1976). Effect of timing of information about mitigating circumstances on emotional responses to provocation and retaliatory behavior. *Journal of Experimental Social Psychology, 12*, 38–55. **329**

Zuckerman, M. (1978). Sensation seeking. In H. London & J. Exner (Eds.), *Dimensions of personality.* New York: Wiley. **193, 290**

Zuckerman, M. (1979). *Sensation seeking: Beyond the optimal level of arousal.* Hillsdale, NJ: Erlbaum. **217, 229, 290, 354**

Index

Behavior therapies, 441–43
Behaviorism, 18, 77–95; emergence of, 78–79
Belief systems. *See* Attitudes
Birth order, 59–60
Bobo doll, 334
Body-Adjustment Test (BAT), 210
Brain: emotions and, 182–83, 184; left–right hemispheres, 205–07; motivation and, 175–76; norepinephrine and, 178; sleep and, 179–81
Brain injury, 99–100
Brainwashing, 434–35

C

CLEM. *See* Conjugate lateral eye movement
CO. *See* Cognitive-orientation cluster
CPC cycle, of behavior, 120–21
CPI. *See* California Psychological Inventory
California Psychological Inventory (CPI), 156
Case studies, 165–66
Castration fear, 38
Child development: cognitive-affective theory and, 136–37; social experience and, 137; spiral, 136, 137
Childhood, 378, 403; as a psychosocial state, 71–72
Chumship (Sullivan), 416
Circumspection, 120
Client-centered therapy, 109
Clinical case studies method, 147–48
Cloud pictures test, 159
Cognition, 125. *See also* Cognitive system
Cognitive-affective theory, 77, 117–39; of anxiety, 300; current approaches, 124–28; forerunners of, 117–24; love and, 369; overview of, 133–39; Tomkins' theory, 128–33
Cognitive appraisal: experiments in, 168
Cognitive map, 79
Cognitive-orientation cluster (CO), 251–53
Cognitive processes, 118
Cognitive style: personality variation and, 136
Cognitive system, 198–217
Cohabitation, 374
Collective unconscious, 52–53; archetypes and, 53
College: happiness in, 361–62
Color: inkblot test and, 161
Communication, 68
Compensation (Adler), 318
Competence, 126, 355–56

Conditioned reflex, 77–78
Conditioning, aversive, 442
Conflict, 82–85
Conjugate lateral eye movement (CLEM), 206
Conscience, 114
Consciousness, altered state of. *See* Dreams (night); Hypnosis
Consciousness, stream of. *See* Stream of Consciousness
Consistency: of personality, 408–10
Constructs, 88, 120–24; characteristics of, 120–24; and emotions, 121–22; hierarchy of, 120; individual differences, 122
Control, 120
Conversion, religious, 434
Correlation: definition of, 150–51
Counseling and Psychotherapy (1942), 109
Creativity, 364–67; process of, 364–65
Critical test, 144
Cue, 80
Cults, 448–50
Culture: facial expressions and, 185, 187; field dependence and, 216–17; self-concept, 264–65
Curiosity, 353–56
Current concerns: in dreams, 231–32, 233, 240–41
Cybernetic phenomena, 124

D

D-love (Deficit-love), 105
D sleep, 179; functions of, 180
DES. *See* Differential Emotions Scale
Danger, 285–91; consequences of, 288–90; physical, 285–87; seekers of, 290–91
Daydreams, 221, 226–34; advantages of, 234; aggression and, 231; drugs and, 229; nightdreams and, 239; sex differences and, 229; sex drive and, 231; study methods, 227–31; weight and, 229. *See also* Fantasy
Defense mechanisms, 31–33, 204, 310–21; aspects of, 311; types of, 207–08, 311–21
Denial, 31, 314
Dependency: in old age, 426–27
Depression: learned helplessness and, 282–84; MMPI and, 154; theories of, 168
Deprivation, physiological: frustration and, 278–81
Development, 380–82; human, 380–82; language, 395–96; periods of, 380–81; personality, 380–82; psychosocial stages

of, 70–74; stages of, 36–40; of values, 399–400

Dialectics, 423

Differential Emotions Scale (DES), 301–02

Differential-emotions theory, 183, 186

Differentiation, 102

Discrimination, 91

Disengagement, 428–29

Displacement, 29, 317–18

Disposition. *See* Personal disposition.

Dissociation, 66, 67

Dopamine, 178–79

Double approach-avoidance conflict, 85

Dreams (night), 239–44; archetypes and, 53; current concerns and, 240–41; daydreams and, 239; Jung's approach to, 50–52; meaning of, 40–42; recall, 240–42; stress and, 242–44. *See also* Daydreams

Drive, 29, 80, 81, 125, 126, 181–82; conflict in, 82–85; secondary, 80

Drive-reduction: model, of behavior (Hull), 78, 80–82; theories of motivation and, 62, 175–76

Drugs: daydreaming and, 229

Duality, 101–02

E

EASI temperament survey, 386–88

EFT. *See* Embedded Figures Test

Effect, law of, 77

Effectance, 126

Ego, 30–31, 35; Jung's theory of, 52–55; psychology, 49

Eidetic imagery, 221

Elderly, 424–49

Electra complex, 38

Embedded Figures Test (EFT), 210–11

Embeddedness effect, 126

Emotionality, 386–87

Emotions, 174–95: affective systems, 182–83; basic, 190–91; control of, 188–89; differentiated, 394–95; facial expressions and, 182–92; field dependence and, 212–14; internalizers and externalizers, 189; motivation and, 190–95; personal constructs and, 121–22; as primary motivation, 125, 126; psychology of, 188–89; role, 129–30; socialization and, 137–38, 192–93

Encoding, 204–05

Epinephrine, 178

Eros, 330

Ethology: aggression and, 330–31

Existence, levels of, 101

Existentialism: anxiety and, 300; as theory of personality, 111–14

Expectancy theory, of social learning (Rotter's), 87–90

Expectations, 91

Experience, 109, 110–11. *See also* Peak experiences

Experiments: characteristics of in personality psychology, 167; methods of, 12–13

Expressive behavior, 103, 107

Externals: and Locus of Control Scale, 247–49

Extinction, 78–83

Extraversion, 55, 56, 203; experiments with, 168–69; 16PF and, 157

Eyes: facial expressions and, 187; movements of, 222

F

Facial expressions: anger and, 326; anxiety and, 304; as communicator, 129–30; culture and, 185, 187; emotions and, 182–92; and interpersonal relations, 186–87; psychology of, 188–89

Fantasy, 226; early, 401–03; erotic, 414–16; regression and, 315; sexual, 370–72; studying, 227–31; TAT and, 164. *See also* Daydreams

Fear, 285–86

Fictive goal, 88

Field dependence-independence, 208–17; as cognitive style, 136

Figure and ground, 99

Fixation, 37

Flooding, 442

Forgetting, 82

Free association, 147, 227

Free will, 113

Friendship, 401–03

Frustration, 275–84; aggression and, 333–34; coping with, 282; physiological deprivation and, 278–81

Functional autonomy, 108

Functionalism, 77

G

General self-concept, 255

Generalization, 82, 91

Genital stage, 40

Gestalt psychology, 98–106

Goal-setting, 267–68

Gratification, 29, 398

Guilt, 122

N

Nature-nurture, 387–88
Neo-Freudians, 61–69
Nervous system: aggression and, 331–32
Neurosis, 157; stress and, 291–97
Neurotransmitters, 178–79
Nightdreams. *See* Dreams
Nomothetic method, 107
Norepinephrine, 178; anxiety and, 305

O

Obedient aggression, 338–40
Object-relations school, 49
Objective behaviorism, 79
Observational learning, 90–94
Obsessional substitution, 67
Obsessive-compulsive, 102, 103, 320–21
Oedipus complex, 38
Oral stage, 37
Organismic psychology, 98–106
Orienting reflex, 353
Overt response, 201

P

PRF. *See* Personality Research Form
Paradigms, 78
Paranoia: and MMPI, 154
Parataxic mode, 68
Parental confrontation: daydreams and, 232–34
Peak experiences, 103, 105–06, 363
Penis envy, 38
Perky phenomenon, 224–26
Persona, Jung's theory of, 53–55
Personal construct. *See* Construct
Personal disposition: cardinal, 107; central, 107; secondary, 107
Personality: in adolescence, 406–19; assessment of, 142–71; birth order and, 59–60; changes in, 122, 146–47; 433–39; 443–45; cognitive sequence and, 201–08; definition of, 6–7; development of, 85–86, 102; dreams and, 241–42; exploitive, 62; field dependence and, 212–17; hoarding, 62; humanistic theories of, 98–114; life scripts and, 420–21; marketing, 64; motivation and, 174–77; normal, 62; patterns of, 354–55; psychoanalytic theory and, 24–45; private, 3–6, 395–98; public, 3–6, 57–61; receptive, 62; scientific approach to, 3–10, 107; stages of development of, 36–40; structural characteristics of, 52–55;

temperaments, 11; theory of, 14–19; traits of, 396–97; typology, 7, 11, 55–57; use of tests and, 142–64. *See also* Personality psychology
Personality and Psychotherapy (1950), 80
Personality measurement, 145–46
Personality psychology, 7–10; history of, 10–13
Personality questionnaires, 150–59; construction of, 150–52; evaluation of, 158
Personality research, 142–71; experimental method, 166–69; objective of, 145
Personality Research Form (PRF), 157–58
Personality Scale (Rotter's), 152
Personality typology (Jung), 55–57
Personifications, 67
Phallic stage, 38
Phenomenology, 18–19, 99, 107
Phi phenomenon, 99
Physical self-concept, 255, 262–63
Plans and the Structure of Behavior (1960), 124
Plans of action, 124
Play, 395–97
Power: TAT and, 164
Prägnanz, principle of, 99
Preemption, 120
Principle of opposites, 52
Probability of occurrence, 81
Processing strategies, 203
Projection, 31, 316–17
Projective methods, 12–13, 159–64; study of dreams and, 227–28
Proprium, 107–08
Prototaxic mode, 68, 128
Psychasthenia: and MMPI, 154
Psychoanalysis. *See* Psychoanalytic theory
Psychoanalytic theory, 12, 24–45, 435–49; changes within classical, 149–51; data collection and, 147–48; drive theory and, 62; evolution of, 42–45, 48–74; forms of treatment, 436; interventions of, 437; limitations of, 44–45; personality change and, 438–39
Psychodiagnostics, 159
Psychodynamic theories, 17–18, 73–74
Psychological field, 117, 118
Psychology, analytic, 50; clinical, 13; individual, 58–59; projective methods of, 159–64; theory of, 13–15
Psychopathic deviation: and MMPI, 154
Psychosocial stages (Erikson), 70–74
Psychotherapy: active forms of, 439–47; effectiveness of, 445–47; self-deception and, 260–61
Puberty, 380
Purposive–behavior orientation (Tolman), 79

A 4
B 5
C 6
D 7
E 8
F 9
G 0
H 1
I 2
J 3